# English Prose

## 1600–1660

# English Prose
## 1600–1660

Edited by

VICTOR HARRIS
Brandeis University

ITRAT HUSAIN
Late of University of Windsor, Ontario

HOLT, RINEHART AND WINSTON
New York   Chicago   San Francisco   Toronto   London

SELECTIONS FROM THE FOLLOWING WORKS HAVE BEEN REPRINTED WITH THE
KIND PERMISSION OF THE COPYRIGHT HOLDERS:

*Religio Medici* by Sir Thomas Browne, edited by Jean-Jacques Denonain. Reprinted by permission of Cambridge University Press, New York, 1955; *The
Works of Sir Thomas Browne,* edited by Geoffrey Keynes. Reprinted by permission of Faber and Faber Limited, London, 1928; *The Anatomy of Melancholy* by Robert Burton, edited by Floyd Dell and Paul Jordan-Smith. Reprinted by permission of Tudor Publishing Co., 1927; "The Synopsis of the
Second Partition" from *Anatomy of Melancholy* by Robert Burton is repro-
duced from The Nonesuch Press edition, 1927, with their permission; *Devotions upon Emergent Occasions* by John Donne, edited by John Sparrow. By
permission of Cambridge University Press, New York, 1923; *Essays in Divinity*
by John Donne, edited by E. M. Simpson. By permission of the Clarendon
Press, Oxford, 1952; *The Sermons of John Donne,* Vol. VII, edited by
Evelyn M. Simpson and George R. Potter. By permission of the University of
California Press, Berkeley, 1953-1962; *Complete Poetry and Selected Prose* by
John Donne, edited by John Hayward. By permission of The Nonesuch Press,
Ltd., 1929; *Leviathan* by Thomas Hobbes, edited by M. Oakeshott. Oxford:
Basil Blackwell, 1946; *Ben Jonson: The Man and His Work,* edited by C. H.
Harford, Percy Simpson, and Evelyn Simpson. By permission of the Clarendon
Press, Oxford, 1925-1952.

# Preface

This anthology is designed to offer a substantial introduction to the prose of nine major writers of the seventeenth century. The selections are made in part to show how prose, in the hands of these master stylists, became a supple instrument, suited to the many uses it had to serve. Even more, however, we wish to document in some depth the principal intellectual currents in this time of dislocation, change, and discovery.

Bacon and Hobbes explore the implications of the new philosophy, and reshape many of the traditional formulations in matters of science, faith, the state, private and public morality, the passions, the imagination, and the uses and methods of poetry. The 85 pages from Bacon's works, for example, are chosen and arranged to show all this as part of the *Magna Instauratio,* his grand scheme for revolutionizing the empire of learning. Donne, Andrewes, Parsons, and Taylor illustrate the extraordinary vitality of religious writing in a period of doctrinal controversy, introspection, terrifying doubts, and subtle accommodations. Jonson's *Timber* and the *Conversations with Drummond* are given in detail to show the range of interests and the combination of independent and conventional judgments of England's first great critic and professional man of letters. Burton and Browne appear as unclassifiable geniuses, one rough and the other burnished with art, whose peculiar mixtures of popular science, confession, penetrating observations, and credulities belong uniquely to this century. The temptation to sample the work of other attractive and important writers has been resisted in order to represent these with greater fullness and fidelity.

We have restricted our own comments to a few essential historical and critical remarks about each author, and offer instead a selective but comprehensive bibliography to guide the reader to a more detailed examination of particular issues. A number of general studies, arranged according to several major subjects, are listed here at the beginning.

Separate lists for the several authors appear in place throughout the volume.

Itrat Husain (Zuberi) died in December 1964, after a brief illness. He was Professor of English at the University of Windsor, Ontario, and the University of Iowa. This edition was already at the press, as was his edition of Donne's *Pseudo-Martyr*. His death removes an active scholar of wide learning: "The *Chappell* wants an eare, *Councell* a tongue." Those of us who knew him will miss also a colleague's courtesy and wit, and the warmth of a generous friend.

Waltham, Mass.
August 1965                                                      V.H.

# Contents

PREFACE                                                    v

TEXTUAL NOTE                                               xv

GENERAL BIBLIOGRAPHY                                       xvii
  Bibliography and Reference                     xvii
  History and Biography                           xviii
  General Intellectual History                    xviii
  Scientific Background                            xxi
  Religious Thought                                xxii
  Literary Currents                                xxiv
  Prose Style                                      xxvi

## FRANCIS BACON                                           1

ESSAYS                                                     8
  Of Studies (1597)                               8
  Of Marriage and Single Life (1612)              8
  Of Parents and Children (1612)                  9
  Wisdome for a Mans Selfe (1612)                 10
  Of Truth (1625)                                 11
  Of Love (1625)                                  13

THE GREAT INSTAURATION                                     14
  The Plan of the Work                            14
    *1. The Divisions of the Sciences*   15
    *2. The New Organon*                 16
    *3. The Phenomena of the Universe*   16
    *4. The Ladder of the Intellect*     17
    *5. Anticipations of the New Philosophy*   17
    *6. The New Philosophy*              18

OF THE ADVANCEMENT OF LEARNING                                    19
  *To the King*                                          19
  *The Distempers of Learning*                           19
  *The Peccant Humours*                                  23
  *On Poesy and the Imagination*                         27
  *Conclusion*                                           30

DE DIGNITATE ET AUGMENTIS SCIENTIARUM                            32
  *Book II, Chap. XIII*                                  32
    ON THE SECOND PRINCIPAL PART OF LEARNING, NAMELY,
    POESY                                       32
    THE THIRD EXAMPLE OF PHILOSOPHY . . . OF DESIRE ACCORD-
    ING TO THE FABLE OF DIONYSUS                35
  *Book III, Chap. I*                                    38
    DIVISION OF SCIENCE INTO THEOLOGY AND PHILOSOPHY   38

NOVUM ORGANUM                                                    42
  Preface                                                42
  Book I—Aphorisms Concerning the Interpretation of Nature
  and the Kingdom of Man                                 43
  *Human Knowledge and Human Power*                      43
  *Idols*                                                47
    IDOLS OF THE TRIBE                          47
    IDOLS OF THE CAVE                           51
    IDOLS OF THE MARKET-PLACE                   53
    IDOLS OF THE THEATRE                        55
  *Application of the Method*                            62
  Book II                                                63
  *Tables of Instances*                                  63
  *Tables of Deviation*                                  65
  *Tables of Degrees*                                    66
  *Forms*                                                66
  *Process of Exclusion*                                 68
  *First Vintage*                                        70
  *Prerogative Instances*                                70

NATURAL AND EXPERIMENTAL HISTORY                                 72
  Phenomena of the Universe                              72
  *To Prince Charles*                                    72

SYLVA SYLVARUM OR A NATURAL HISTORY     73
    EXPERIMENT SOLITARY TOUCHING CURE BY EXCESS     73
    EXPERIMENT SOLITARY TOUCHING CURE BY MOTION OF CONSENT     73
    EXPERIMENTS CONCERNING MUSIC     74
    EXPERIMENTS IN CONSORT TOUCHING VENUS     74
    EXPERIMENT SOLITARY TOUCHING MEDICINES THAT CONDENSE
        AND RELIEVE THE SPIRITS     76
    EXPERIMENT SOLITARY TOUCHING PAINTINGS OF THE BODY     76
    EXPERIMENT SOLITARY TOUCHING THE USE OF BATHING AND
        ANOINTING     77
    EXPERIMENTS TOUCHING TEETH     77
    EXPERIMENT SOLITARY TOUCHING MALEFICIATING     78

DE SAPIENTIA VETERUM (THE WISDOM OF THE
ANCIENTS)     78
  Preface     78
  Narcissus; or Self-Love     81
  Styx; or Treatises     83

NEW ATLANTIS     84
  Salomon's House     84

ROBERT PARSONS     93

THE JUDGMENT OF A CATHOLICKE ENGLISH-MAN
LIVING IN BANISHMENT FOR HIS RELIGION     96
  Concerning the Popes Two Breves, against the Receaving of the
  Oath     96

LANCELOT ANDREWES     115

SERMONS     119
  A Sermon Preached before the King's Majesty, 1606     119
  A Sermon Preached before the King's Majesty, 1620     136

THE PRIVATE DEVOTIONS     153

# ROBERT BURTON 163

THE ANATOMY OF MELANCHOLY 166
  Democritus to the Reader 166
    *To Ease My Mind by Writing* 166
    *I Call a Spade a Spade* 166
    *Our Religious Madness* 168
    *An Utopia of My Own* 170
    *My Purpose and Endeavour* 180
    *Pardon These My Witticisms* 181
  The First Partition 182
    *Man's Excellency, Fall, Miseries, Infirmities; the Causes of Them* 182
    *A Chronick or Continuate Disease* 189
    *Digression of Anatomy* 191
    *The Four Humours* 192
    *Definition of Melancholy, Name, Difference* 193
    *Love of Learning or Over-much Study* 195
    *From Natural and Inward Causes* 204
  The Synopsis of the Second Partition 213
  The Third Partition 218
    *Heroical Love Causing Melancholy* 218
    *How Love Tyrannizeth over Men* 218
    *Other Causes of Love-Melancholy* 221
    *Dancing* 226
    *Remedies of Love* 228
    *A Corollary and Conclusion* 230

# JOHN DONNE 233

JUVENILIA: OR CERTAINE PARADOXES AND PROBLEMS 241
  Paradoxes 241
    *I. A Defence of Womens Inconstancy.* 241
    *II. That Women Ought to Paint.* 242
    *III. That by Discord Things Increase.* 243
    *IV. That Good Is More Common than Evill.* 244
    *V. That All Things Kill Themselves.* 245
    *VI. That It Is Possible To Find Some Vertue in Some Women.* 246

*VII. That Old Men Are More Fantastique than Young.*     247

*VIII. That Nature Is Our Worst Guide.*     248

*IX. That Only Cowards Dare Dye.*     249

*X. That a Wise Man Is Knowne by Much Laughing.*     250

*XI. That the Gifts of the Body Are Better than Those of the Minde.*     251

The Problemes     253

*I. Why Have Bastards Best Fortune?*     253

*II. Why Puritanes Make Long Sermons?*     253

*III. Why Did the Divell Reserve Jesuites till These Latter Dayes?*     254

*IV. Why Is There More Variety of Greene, than of Other Colours?*     254

*V. Why Doe Young Lay-men So Much Studie Divinity?*     254

*VI. Why Hath the Common Opinion Afforded Women Soules?*     255

*VII. Why Are the Fairest, Falsest?*     255

*VIII. Why Venus-Starre Onely Doth Cast a Shadow?*     256

*IX. Why Is Venus-Starre Multi-nominous, Called Both Hesperus and Vesper?*     257

*X. Why Are New Officers Least Oppressing?*     258

IGNATIUS HIS CONCLAVE     259

ESSAYES IN DIVINITY     264

DEVOTIONS UPON EMERGENT OCCASIONS     267

Devotion No. 9     267

*Meditation*     267

*Expostulation*     269

*Prayer*     271

Devotion No. 10     272

*Meditation*     272

Devotion No. 17     273

*Meditation*     273

LETTERS     275

To My Honoured Friend Sʳ T. Lucey     275

To the Right Honourable the Countess of Montgomery     278

To Sir H. R.     279

To Sir H. G.                                                                            281
To Sir G. F.                                                                            283
To the Best Knight Sir H. Wootton                                                       285
To His Mother: Comforting Her after the Death of Her
    Daughter                                                                            286
To Sir Robert Carre Now Earle of Ankerum, with My Book
    *Biathanatos* at My Going into Germany                                              288

SERMON PREACHED AT THE FUNERALS OF SIR WIL-
LIAM COKAYNE KNIGHT, ALDERMAN OF LONDON,
DECEMBER 12, 1626                                                                       289

# BEN JONSON                                                                            309

BEN JONSON'S CONVERSATIONS WITH WILLIAM
DRUMMOND OF HAWTHORNDEN                                                                  312

TIMBER, OR DISCOVERIES                                                                  329
    *Winter-Love in a Dark Corner*                                                      329
    *Ancients and Moderns*                                                              329
    *The Trimming of a Scholar*                                                         330
    *Artificers as Liars*                                                               331
    *Eloquence*                                                                         332
    *Wits, Poets, and Playwrights*                                                      332
    *Masters of Wit and Language*                                                       337
    *Francis Bacon*                                                                     338
    *Poets and the Good Life*                                                           339
    *I Durst Not Leave Myself Undefended*                                               339
    *Poetry and Picture*                                                                340
    *Flatterers and Gossips*                                                            342
    *Think, Excogitate, Repeat, Imitate*                                                343
    *Sydney before Donne*                                                               345
    *Pure and Neat Language*                                                            346
    *Language Plain and Juicy*                                                          350
    *Awake Antiquity*                                                                   351
    *The Writing of Letters*                                                            352
    *Of Poets and Poetry*                                                               356
    *Poets and Critics*                                                                 361
    *Comedy*                                                                            363
    *Of the Magnitude, and Compasse of Any Fable, Epicke, or
        Dramatick*                                                                      365

# THOMAS HOBBES    369

THE ANSWER TO THE PREFACE TO GONDIBERT    376

LEVIATHAN    381
  The Introduction    381
  The First Part: of Man    383
    *Chapter II, of Imagination*    383
    *Chapter VIII, of the Virtues Commonly Called Intellectual;*
      *and Their Contrary Defects*    384
    *Chapter XII, of Religion*    387
    *Chapter XIII, of the Natural Condition of Mankind as Con-*
      *cerning Their Felicity, and Misery*    391
    *Chapter XIV, of the First and Second Natural Laws, and of*
      *Contracts*    395
  The Second Part: of Commonwealth    398
    *Chapter XVII, of the Causes, Generation, and Definition of a*
      *Commonwealth*    398
  The Fourth Part: of the Kingdom of Darkness    402
    *Chapter XLVI, of Darkness from Vain Philosophy, and Fabu-*
      *lous Traditions*    402
  A Review and Conclusion    413

# SIR THOMAS BROWNE    413

RELIGIO MEDICI    418
  Part I    418
  Part II    429

PSEUDODOXIA EPIDEMICA    435
  *Of the Causes of Common Errors*    435
  *Of the Second Cause of Popular Errors, the Erroneous Dispo-*
    *sition of the People*    435
  *Of Credulity and Supinity*    436
  *Of Adherence unto Antiquity*    438
  *Of Sex in Hares*    438
  *Concerning Weight*    444
  *Of the Picture of Adam and Eve with Navels*    446

HYDRIOTAPHIA, URNE-BURIALL    448
  Chapter III    448
  Chapter IV    458
  Chapter V    464

## JEREMY TAYLOR     473

THE RULE AND EXERCISES OF HOLY LIVING     477

*Sect. I. The First General Instrument of Holy Living, Care of Our Time*     477

*Sect. II. The General Instrument of Holy Living, Purity of Intention*     485

THE RULE AND EXERCISES OF HOLY DYING     488

*Sect. I. Consideration of the Vanity and Shortness of Man's Life*     488

*Sect. II. The Consideration Reduced to Practice*     493

*Sect. III. Rules and Spiritual Arts of Lengthening Our Days*     499

*Sect. IV. Consideration of the Miseries of Man's Life*     507

*The Wealth of My Hope*     512

# Textual Note

The texts used in this edition are listed below. The spelling and punctuation of the source have been followed in almost all instances except that modern usage prevails in the handling of u and v, i and j, the old long s, and in contractions such as conditiō and thē. In some instances headings have been supplied for greater clarity.

LANCELOT ANDREWES, *Ninety-six Sermons,* ed. by J. P. Wilson. Oxford: John Henry Parker, 5 vols., 1841–1843.

———, *The Private Devotions of Lancelot Andrewes,* trans. by John Henry Newman. Nashville, Tenn.: Abingdon Press, 1950.

FRANCIS BACON, *The Works of Francis Bacon,* ed. by J. Spedding, R. L. Ellis, and D. D. Heath. Boston, 1860–1864.

SIR THOMAS BROWNE, *Religio Medici,* ed. by Jean-Jacques Denonain. New York: Cambridge University Press, 1955.

———, *The Works of Sir Thomas Browne,* ed. by Geoffrey Keynes. London: Faber and Faber Limited, 6 vols., 1928. (A new edition, issued by Faber and Faber Limited and the University of Chicago Press, appeared in 1963.)

ROBERT BURTON, *The Anatomy of Melancholy,* ed. by Floyd Dell and Paul Jordan-Smith. New York: Tudor Publishing Co., 1927.

JOHN DONNE, *Devotions upon Emergent Occasions,* ed. by John Sparrow. New York: Cambridge University Press, 1923.

———, *Essays in Divinity,* ed. by E. M. Simpson. Oxford: Clarendon Press, 1952.

———, *Ignatius His Conclave.* Facsimile Text Society and Columbia University Press, 1941.

———, *Juvenilia: or, Certain Paradoxes and Problems.* Facsimile Text Society and Columbia University Press, 1936.

———, *The Sermons,* ed. by Evelyn M. Simpson and George R. Potter. Berkeley, Calif.: University of California Press, 10 vols., 1953–1962.

———, *Complete Poetry and Selected Prose,* ed. by John Hayward. London: The Nonesuch Press, 1929. (Two letters.)

THOMAS HOBBES, *The English Works of Thomas Hobbes,* ed. by Sir William Molesworth. London: John Bohn, 16 vols., 1839–1845.

——, *Leviathan,* ed. by M. Oakeshott. Oxford: Basil Blackwell, 1946.

BEN JONSON, *Ben Jonson: The Man and His Work,* ed. by C. H. Herford, Percy Simpson, and Evelyn Simpson. Oxford: Clarendon Press, 11 vols., 1925–1952.

ROBERT PARSONS, *The Judgment of a Catholicke English-man Living in Banishment for His Religion.* London, 1608. Facsimile edition ed. by William T. Costello, S. J., 1957.

JEREMY TAYLOR, *The Rule and Exercises of Holy Living; The Rule and Exercises of Holy Dying.* Bohn's Standard Library, 1850.

# General Bibliography[*]

## BIBLIOGRAPHY AND REFERENCE

*The Year's Work in English Studies,* Eng. Assoc., 1919 to date.

*Annual Bibliography of English Language and Literature,* Modern Humanities Research Assoc., 1920 to date.

"Annual Bibliography," *PMLA,* 1922 to date.

"Recent Literature of the English Renaissance," *SP,* 1922 to date.

A. W. POLLARD, G. R. REDGRAVE, *et al., Short Title Catalogue of Books Printed in England, Scotland, and Ireland . . . 1475–1640,* 1926. Donald Wing, ed., *Short Title Catalogue . . . 1641–1700,* 1945–1951; supplements 1953, 1956, 1958.

F. W. BATESON, ed., *The Cambridge Bibliography of English Literature,* 1941. Supplement, ed. by George Watson, 1957. *The Concise CBEL,* ed. by George Watson, 1958.

*Seventeenth-Century News,* 1950 to date.

V. DE S. PINTO, *The English Renaissance, 1510–1688,* 2d ed., 1951.

*Abstracts of English Studies,* 1958 to date.

DOUGLAS BUSH, *English Literature in the Earlier Seventeenth Century, 1600–1660,* 2d ed., 1962. (Includes extensive bibliographies.)

JOHN BUXTON, *Elizabethan Taste,* 1963.

MAURICE ASHLEY, *Life in Stuart England,* 1964.

SEARS JAYNE, "Scholarship in the Renaissance: English Nondramatic Literature," *Ren. News,* XVII (1964).

WALTER J. ONG, "Recent Studies in the English Renaissance," *Studies in Eng. Lit.,* IV (1964).

* The following abbreviations are used for the indicated reference works and magazines in the bibliographical entries and those under each author in the text:

*DNB (Dictionary of National Biography)*

*ELH (English Literary History)*

*HLQ (Huntington Library Quarterly)*

*JEGP (Journal of English and Germanic Philology)*

*JHI (Journal of the History of Ideas)*

*MLN (Modern Language Notes)*

*MLQ (Modern Language Quarterly)*

*MLR (Modern Language Review)*

*MP (Modern Philology)*

*N&Q (Notes and Queries)*

*PMLA (Publications of the Modern Language Association)*

*PQ (Philological Quarterly)*

*RES (Review of English Studies)*

*SP (Studies in Philology)*

*TLS (London Times Literary Supplement)*

## HISTORY AND BIOGRAPHY

THOMAS FULLER, *The History of the Worthies of England,* 1662; ed. by J. Freeman, 1952.

ANTHONY WOOD, *Athenae Oxonienses,* 1691–1692, 1721; ed. by. P. Bliss, 1813–1820.

DONALD STAUFFER, *English Biography before 1700,* 1930.

NORMAN E. MCCLURE, ed., *The Letters of John Chamberlain* (1554–1628), *Memoirs of the Am. Phil. Soc.,* XII (1939).

GEORGE M. TREVELYAN, *English Social History,* 1940, 2d ed., 1946.

GEORGE N. CLARK, *The Seventeenth Century,* 1929; rev., 1947, 1961.

JOHN AUBREY, *Brief Lives,* ed. by A. Clark, 1898; ed. by O. L. Dick, 1949, 1957.

GEORGE H. SABINE, *A History of Political Theory,* 1937; rev., 1950.

MAURICE ASHLEY, *England in the Seventeenth Century,* 1952.

C. J. FRIEDRICH, *The Age of the Baroque, 1610–1660,* 1952.

J. G. A. POCOCK, *The Ancient Constitution and the Feudal Law: A Study of English Historical Thought in the Seventeenth Century,* 1957.

MARGARET BOTTRALL, *Every Man a Phoenix: Studies in Seventeenth-century Autobiography,* 1958.

GODFREY DAVIES, *The Early Stuarts, 1603–1660,* 1937; 2d ed., 1959.

LOUIS B. WRIGHT AND VIRGINIA A. LAMAR, eds., *Life and Letters in Tudor and Stuart England,* 1962.

HENRY PEACHAM, *The Complete Gentleman, The Truth of Our Times, and the Art of Living in London,* ed. by Virgil B. Heltzel ("Folger Documents of Tudor and Stuart Civilization"), 1962.

## GENERAL INTELLECTUAL HISTORY

FOSTER WATSON, *The Beginnings of the Teaching of Modern Subjects in England,* 1909.

THOMAS M. FORSYTH, *English Philosophy,* 1910.

GEORGE S. BRETT, *A History of Psychology,* Vol. II, 1921; abridged by R. S. Peters, 1953.

WILLIAM R. SORLEY, *A History of English Philosophy,* 1921, 1937.

R. SENCOURT, *Outflying Philosophy,* 1924.

MURRAY W. BUNDY, *The Theory of Imagination in Classical and Mediaeval Thought, Ill. Studies in Lang. and Lit.,* XII (1927).

PRESERVED SMITH, *A History of Modern Culture.* Vol. I, *The Great Renewal, 1543–1687,* 1930.

LOUIS I. BREDVOLD, *The Intellectual Milieu of John Dryden: Studies in Some Aspects of Seventeenth-Century Thought,* 1934.

BASIL WILLEY, *The Seventeenth Century Background,* 1934, 1953.

ARTHUR O. LOVEJOY, *The Great Chain of Being,* 1936, 1960.

PERRY MILLER, *The New England Mind: The Seventeenth Century*, 1939, 1954.

THEODORE SPENCER, *Shakespeare and the Nature of Man*, 1942.

JACOB BURCKHARDT, *The Civilization of the Renaissance in Italy*, trans. by S. G. C. Middlemore, 1944.

LEO SPITZER, "Classical and Christian Ideas of World Harmony," *Traditio*, II–III (1944–1945).

BERTRAND RUSSELL, *A History of Western Philosophy*, 1945.

HERSCHEL BAKER, *The Dignity of Man*, 1947.

E. CASSIRER, P. O. KRISTELLER, and J. H. RANDALL, JR., *The Renaissance Philosophy of Man*, 1948.

DON CAMERON ALLEN, *The Legend of Noah: Renaissance Rationalism in Art, Science, and Letters, Ill. Studies in Lang. and Lit.*, XXXIII (1949).

MEYRICK H. CARRÉ, *Phases of Thought in England*, 1949.

VICTOR HARRIS, *All Coherence Gone*, 1949.

HIRAM C. HAYDN, *The Counter-Renaissance*, 1950.

MOLLY M. MAHOOD, *Poetry and Humanism*, 1950.

E. M. W. TILLYARD, *The Elizabethan World Picture*, 1950.

LAWRENCE BABB, *The Elizabethan Malady: A Study of Melancholia in Elizabethan Literature from 1580 to 1642*, 1951.

SAMUEL L. BETHELL, *The Cultural Revolution of the Seventeenth Century*, 1951.

ERNST CASSIRER, *The Philosophy of the Enlightenment*, trans. by F. Koelln and J. P. Pettegrove, 1951.

BASIL WILLEY, "The Touch of Cold Philosophy," *The Seventeenth Century*, 1951.

HERSCHEL BAKER, *The Wars of Truth: Studies in the Decay of Christian Humanism in the Earlier Seventeenth Century*, 1952.

JOHN B. BAMBOROUGH, *The Little World of Man*, 1952.

ERNST CASSIRER, *The Platonic Renaissance in England*, trans. by J. P. Pettegrove, 1953.

LESLIE A. PAUL, *The English Philosophers*, 1953.

EMERSON R. MARKS, *Relativist and Absolutist: The Early Neoclassical Debate in England*, 1955.

WYLIE SYPHER, *Four Stages of Renaissance Style: Transformations in Art and Literature, 1400–1700*, 1955.

WILBUR S. HOWELL, *Logic and Rhetoric in England, 1500–1700*, 1956.

ALEXANDRE KOYRÉ, *From the Closed World to the Infinite Universe*, 1957.

STEPHEN MERTON, "Microcosm, Epitome, and Seed: Some Seventeenth-Century Analogies," *Hist. of Ideas News Letter*, III (1957).

FRANK THILLY and LEDGER WOOD, *A History of Philosophy*, 3d ed., 1957.

JASON WINNY, ed., *The Frame of Order: An Outline of Elizabethan Belief Taken from Treatises of the Late Sixteenth Century*, 1957.

WILLIAM T. COSTELLO, *The Scholastic Curriculum at Early Seventeenth-Century Cambridge,* 1958.

MICHAEL MACKLEM, *The Anatomy of the World: Relations between Natural and Moral Law from Donne to Pope,* 1958.

FREDERICK C. COPLESTON, *A History of Philosophy,* Vols. III–V, 1953–1959.

MARJORIE H. NICOLSON, *Mountain Gloom and Mountain Glory: The Development of the Aesthetics of the Infinite,* 1959.

JACOB BRONOWSKI and BRUCE MAZLISH, *The Western Intellectual Tradition from Leonardo to Hegel,* 1960.

NEAL W. GILBERT, *Renaissance Concepts of Method,* 1960.

GEORGE WILLIAMSON, "Mutability, Decay, and Jacobean Melancholy," (*ELH,* 1935), *Seventeenth Century Contexts,* 1960.

T. HELTON, ed., *The Renaissance,* 1961.

JOHN HOLLANDER, *The Untuning of the Sky: Ideas of Music in English Poetry 1500–1700,* 1961.

PAUL E. CORNELIUS, "Languages in Seventeenth- and Early Eighteenth-Century Imaginary Voyages," Dissertation, Columbia University, 1962; *Dissertation Abstr.,* XXIII (1963).

R. HOOPES, *Right Reason in the English Renaissance,* 1962.

PAUL OSKAR KRISTELLER, "Studies on Renaissance Humanism during the Last Twenty Years," *Studies in the Renaissance,* IX (1962).

J. A. MAZZEO, ed., *Reason and the Imagination: Studies in the History of Ideas 1600–1800,* 1962.

GLENN NEGLEY and J. MAX PATRICK, *The Quest for Utopia: An Anthology of Imaginary Societies,* 1962.

ERNEST WILLIAM TALBERT, *The Problem of Order: Elizabethan Political Commonplaces and an Example of Shakespeare's Art,* 1962.

ERNST CASSIRER, *The Individual and the Cosmos in Renaissance Philosophy,* trans. with an intr. by Mario Domandi, 1963, 1964.

C. A. PATRIDES, "The Microcosm of Man: Further References to a Commonplace," *N&Q,* X (1963).

HENRY G. VAN LEEUWEN, *The Problem of Certainty in English Thought, 1630–1690,* 1963.

DON CAMERON ALLEN, *Doubt's Boundless Sea: Skepticism and Faith in the Renaissance,* 1964.

R. L. COLIE, "Rhetoric of Transcendence," *PQ,* XLIII (1964).

HUGH SYKES DAVIES and GEORGE WATSON, eds., *The English Mind: Studies in the English Moralists Presented to Basil Willey,* 1964.

HAROLD FISCH, *Jerusalem and Albion: The Hebraic Factor in Seventeenth-Century Literature,* 1964. (Treats Bacon, Browne, Hobbes, Taylor, and others.)

C. S. LEWIS, *The Discarded Image: An Introduction to Medieval and Renaissance Literature,* 1964.

JOSEPH A. MAZZEO, *Renaissance and Seventeenth-Century Studies,* 1964.

MARIO PRAZ, "Baroque in England," *MP,* LXI (1964).

## SCIENTIFIC BACKGROUND

ALFRED NORTH WHITEHEAD, *Science and the Modern World,* 1925.

E. A. BURTT, *Metaphysical Foundations of Modern Physical Science,* 1924; rev. 1932; 1954.

KATHARINE B. COLLIER, *Cosmogonies of Our Fathers: Some Theories of the Seventeenth and the Eighteenth Centuries,* 1934.

RICHARD FOSTER JONES, *Ancients and Moderns: A Study of the Rise of the Scientific Movement in Seventeenth-Century England,* 1936, 1961.

EDWARD W. STRONG, *Procedures and Metaphysics: A Study in the Philosophy of Mathematical-Physical Science in the Sixteenth and Seventeenth Centuries,* 1936.

FRANCIS R. JOHNSON, *Astronomical Thought in Renaissance England,* 1937.

ROBERT K. MERTON, "Science, Technology and Society in Seventeenth Century England," *Osiris,* IV (1938).

FRANCIS R. JOHNSON, "Gresham College: Precursor of the Royal Society," *JHI,* I (1940).

JAMES B. CONANT, "The Advancement of Learning during the Puritan Commonwealth," *Proc. Mass. Hist. Soc.,* LXVI (1942).

WALTER E. HOUGHTON, JR., "The English Virtuoso in the Seventeenth Century," *JHI,* III (1942).

R. G. COLLINGWOOD, *The Idea of Nature,* 1945.

A. H. DODD, "The Influence of Early Science on English Thought," *Hibbert Jour.,* XLIII (1945)

CHARLES E. RAVEN, *English Naturalists from Neckham to Ray,* 1947.

HERBERT BUTTERFIELD, *The Origins of Modern Science, 1300–1800,* 1949; rev., 1957.

DOUGLAS BUSH, *Science and English Poetry: A Historical Sketch, 1590–1950,* 1950.

ABRAHAM WOLF, *A History of Science, Technology, and Philosophy in the Sixteenth and Seventeenth Centuries,* 2d ed., 1950.

RICHARD FOSTER JONES, "Science and Criticism in the Neo-Classical Age of English Literature" (*JHI,* 1940), and "Science and Language in England of the Mid-Seventeenth Century" (*JEGP,* 1932), *The Seventeenth Century,* 1951.

ALFRED R. HALL, *The Scientific Revolution, 1500–1800: The Formation of the Modern Scientific Attitude,* 1954.

MEYRICK H. CARRÉ, "The Old Order and the New: The Intellectual Revolution of the Seventeenth Century," *Hist. Today,* V (1955).

MARJORIE H. NICOLSON, *Science and Imagination,* 1956.

T. S. KUHN, *The Copernican Revolution,* 1957.

ROBERT K. MERTON, "Puritanism, Pietism, and Science," and "Science and Economy of Seventeenth-century England," *Social Theory and Social Structure*, rev., 1957.

P. P. WIENER and A. NOLAND, eds., *Roots of Scientific Thought*, 1957.

RICHARD S. WESTFALL, *Science and Religion in Seventeenth-Century England*, 1958.

L. W. HULL, *The History and Philosophy of Science*, 1959.

EDWARD H. MADDEN, RALPH M. BLAKE, and CURT J. DUCASSE, *Theories of Scientific Method: The Renaissance through the Nineteenth Century*, 1960.

MARJORIE H. NICOLSON, *The Breaking of the Circle: Studies in the Effect of the "New Science" Upon Seventeenth-century Poetry*, 1950; 2d ed., 1960.

WILLIAM C. DAMPIER, *A History of Science and Its Relations with Philosophy and Religion*, 4th ed., with postscript, 1961.

HAROLD BRODBAR, "Late Renaissance Astronomy and the 'New Philosophy,'" *Forum* (Houston), III (1963).

RICHARD FOSTER JONES, "The Rhetoric of Science in England of the Mid-Seventeenth Century," *Restoration and Eighteenth-Century Literature*, 1963.

ROBERT ELLRODT, "Scientific Curiosity and Metaphysical Poetry in the Seventeenth Century," *MP*, LXI (1964).

RENÉ TATON, ed., *The Beginnings of Modern Science, from 1450 to 1800*, trans. by A. J. Pomerans, 1964.

## RELIGIOUS THOUGHT

THOMAS FULLER, *The Church-History of Britain, from the Birth of Jesus Christ until the Year 1648*, 1655; ed. by James Nichols, 1837; ed. by J. S. Brewer, 1845.

JOHN TULLOCH, *Rational Theology and Christian Philosophy in England in the Seventeenth Century*, 1872.

EDWARD DOWDEN, *Puritan and Anglican*, 1900.

EDWARD A. GEORGE, *Seventeenth Century Men of Latitude: Forerunners of the New Theology*, 1908.

CHARLES S. CARTER, *The Anglican Via Media: Being Studies in the Elizabethan Religious Settlement and in the Teaching of the Caroline Divines*, 1927.

CAROLINE F. RICHARDSON, *English Preachers and Preaching, 1640–1670*, 1928.

HELEN C. WHITE, *English Devotional Literature (Prose), 1600–1640*, 1931.

W. K. JORDAN, *The Development of Religious Toleration in England*, 1932–1940.

W. FRASER MITCHELL, *English Pulpit Oratory from Andrewes to Tillotson*, 1932.

P. E. MORE and F. L. CROSS, *Anglicanism: The Thought and Practice of the Church of England, Illustrated from the Religious Literature of the Seventeenth Century*, 1935, 1957.

DOROTHY STIMSON, "Puritanism and the New Philosophy in Seventeenth Century England," *Bull. of the Institute of the Hist. of Med.*, III (1935).

WILLIAM HALLER, *The Rise of Puritanism*, 1938.

PERRY MILLER and THOMAS H. JOHNSON, eds., *The Puritans*, 1938.

M. M. KNAPPEN, *Tudor Puritanism*, 1939.

DOUGLAS BUSH, "Two Roads to Truth: Science and Religion in the Early Seventeenth Century," *ELH*, VIII (1941).

ARTHUR BARKER, *Milton and the Puritan Dilemma*, 1942, 1955.

K. KOLLER, "The Puritan Preacher's Contribution to Fiction," *HLQ*, XI (1947–1948).

HELEN C. WHITE, "Sixteenth-Century English Devotional Literature," *Joseph Quincy Adams Memorial Studies*, ed. by James G. McManaway, 1948.

ARNOLD WILLIAMS, *The Common Expositor: An Account of the Commentaries on Genesis, 1527–1633,* 1948.

H. R. McADOO, *The Structure of Caroline Moral Theology*, 1949.

ERNEST LEE TUVESON, *Millennium and Utopia*, 1949.

BASIL WILLEY, *Christianity Past and Present*, 1952.

PAUL H. KOCHER, *Science and Religion in Elizabethan England*, 1953.

CHARLES RAVEN, *Natural Religion and Christian Theology. First Series: Science and Religion*, 1953.

H. CAPLAN and H. H. KING, "Pulpit Eloquence: A List of Doctrinal and Historical Studies in English," *Speech Monographs*, XXII (1955).

M. MACLURE, *The Paul's Cross Sermons 1534–1642*, 1958.

C. A. PATRIDES, "Renaissance and Modern Thought on the Last Things," *Harvard Theological Rev.*, LI (1958).

FRANK P. WILSON, "The Sermon," *Seventeenth Century Prose*, 1960.

JAROSLAV PELIKAN, "Cosmos and Creation: Science and Theology in Reformation Thought," *Proc. Amer. Philos. Soc.*, CV (1961).

L. A. SASEK, *The Literary Temper of the English Puritans*, 1961.

M. J. HAVRAN, *Catholicism in Caroline England 1625–1640*, 1962.

JOHN RICHARD ROBERTS, "A Critical Anthology of English Recusant Devotional Prose, 1558–1603," Dissertation, University of Illinois, 1962; *Dissertation Abstr.*, XXIII (1963).

ARTHUR POLLARD, *English Sermons*, 1963.

HELEN C. WHITE, *Tudor Books of Saints and Martyrs*, 1963.

J. W. BLENCH, *Preaching in England in the Late Fifteenth and Sixteenth Centuries: A Study of English Sermons 1450–c. 1600*, 1964.

CHRISTOPHER HILL, *Society and Puritanism in Pre-Revolutionary England*, 1964.

JOHN F. H. NEW, *Anglican and Puritan*, 1964.

C. A. PATRIDES, *The Phoenix and the Ladder*, 1964. (On the Christian view of history.)

D. P. WALKER, *The Decline of Hell: Seventeenth-Century Discussions of Eternal Torment,* 1964.

## LITERARY CURRENTS

WILLIAM HAZLITT, *Lectures on the Dramatic Literature of the Age of Elizabeth,* 1820 (Lecture VII deals with Bacon, Browne, Taylor, and others).

SAMUEL T. COLERIDGE, *The Complete Works of Samuel Taylor Coleridge,* ed. by W. G. Shedd, 1854 (extensive comments on Donne, Taylor, Browne, and others).

GEORGE E. SAINTSBURY, *History of Criticism and Literary Taste in Europe,* 1900–1904.

G. C. SMITH, *Elizabethan Critical Essays,* 1904.

BARRETT WENDELL, *The Temper of the Seventeenth Century in English Literature,* 1904.

JOEL E. SPINGARN, ed., *Critical Essays of the Seventeenth Century,* 1908–1909, 1957.

A. W. WARD and A. R. WALLER, eds., *The Cambridge History of English Literature,* Vols. IV–VIII, 1909–1912.

GEORGE E. SAINTSBURY, *A History of English Criticism,* 1911.

DONALD L. CLARK, *Rhetoric and Poetry in the Renaissance,* 1922.

ELBERT N. S. THOMPSON, *The Seventeenth-Century English Essay,* 1926.

HERBERT J. C. GRIERSON, *Cross-Currents in English Literature of the Seventeenth Century,* 1929.

FREDERICK W. BATESON, *English Poetry and the English Language: An Experiment in Literary History,* 1934.

HARDIN CRAIG, *The Enchanted Glass,* 1936.

CHARLES S. BALDWIN, *Renaissance Literary Theory and Practice,* 1939, 1959.

GEORGE SAMPSON, *Concise Cambridge History of English Literature,* 1941; 2d ed., 1961.

VERNON HALL, *Renaissance Literary Criticism: A Study of Its Social Content,* 1945, 1959.

FRANK P. WILSON, *Elizabethan and Jacobean,* 1945.

WALTER JACKSON BATE, *From Classic to Romantic,* 1946.

B. BOYCE, *The Theophrastan Character in England to 1642,* 1947.

TUCKER BROOKE, *The Renaissance (1500–1660),* 1948.

HARDIN CRAIG, *et al., A History of English Literature,* 1950.

RUTH WALLERSTEIN, *Studies in Seventeenth-Century Poetic,* 1950.

C. V. WEDGWOOD, *Seventeenth-century English Literature,* 1950, 1961.

JOHN W. ATKINS, *English Literary Criticism: The Renascence,* 1947; 2d ed., 1951.

JOHN W. ATKINS, *English Literary Criticism: Seventeenth and Eighteenth Centuries*, 1951.

OWEN BARFIELD, *Poetic Diction: A Study in Meaning*, 1928; 2d ed., 1952.

MEYER H. ABRAMS, *The Mirror and the Lamp: Romantic Theory and the Critical Tradition*, 1953, 1958.

RICHARD FOSTER JONES, *The Triumph of the English Language: A Survey of Opinions Concerning the Vernacular from the Introduction of Printing to the Restoration*, 1953.

B. BOYCE, *The Polemic Character 1640–1661*, 1955.

BORIS FORD, ed., *Guide to English Literature*. Vol. II: *The Age of Shakespeare*, 1955. Vol. III: *From Donne to Marvell*, 1956.

PAUL HARVEY, *Oxford Companion to English Literature*, 3d ed., 1955.

WILLIAM K. WIMSATT and CLEANTH BROOKS, *Literary Criticism: A Short History*, 1957.

WILLIAM ROSSKY, "Imagination in the English Renaissance: Psychology and Poetic," *Studies in the Ren.*, V (1958).

DON CAMERON ALLEN, *Image and Meaning: Metaphoric Traditions in Renaissance Poetry*, 1960.

DAVID DAICHES, *A Critical History of English Literature*, 1960.

ERNEST LEE TUVESON, *The Imagination as a Means of Grace: Locke and the Aesthetics of Romanticism*, 1960.

GEORGE WILLIAMSON, "Strong Lines" (*Eng. Studies*, 1936), *Seventeenth Century Contexts*, 1960.

———, *The Proper Wit of Poetry*, 1961.

FREDERICK B. ARTZ, *From the Renaissance to Romanticism: Trends in Style in Art, Literature, and Music, 1300–1830*, 1962.

DOUGLAS BUSH, *English Literature in the Earlier Seventeenth Century*, 1945; 2d ed., 1962.

O. B. HARDISON, JR., *The Enduring Monument: A Study of the Idea of Praise in Renaissance Literary Theory and Practice*, 1962.

K. G. HAMILTON, *The Two Harmonies: Poetry and Prose in the Seventeenth Century*, 1963.

O. B. HARDISON, JR., ed., *English Literary Criticism: The Renaissance*, 1963.

DAVID KLEIN, *The Elizabethan Dramatists as Critics*, 1963.

CARROLL CAMDEN, ed., *Literary Views*, 1964.

NATALIE G. LAWRENCE and J. A. REYNOLDS, *Sweet Smoke of Rhetoric: A Collection of Renaissance Essays*, 1964.

E. W. TAYLER, *Nature and Art in Renaissance Literature*, 1964.

HARRY BERGER, JR., "The Renaissance Imagination: Second World and Green World," *Centennial Rev.*, IX (1965).

## PROSE STYLE

George Saintsbury, *A History of English Prose Rhythm*, 1912.

George P. Krapp, *The Rise of English Literary Prose*, 1915.

Morris W. Croll, "The Cadence of English Oratorical Prose," *SP*, XVI (1919).

——, " 'Attic Prose' in the Seventeenth Century," *SP*, XVIII (1921).

——, "Attic Prose: Lipsius, Montaigne, Bacon," *Schelling Anniversary Papers*, 1923.

——, "Muret and the History of 'Attic' Prose," *PMLA*, XXXIX (1924).

——, "The Baroque Style in Prose," *Studies in English Philology in Honor of Frederick Klaeber*, 1929.

Norton R. Tempest, *The Rhythm of English Prose*, 1930.

William G. Crane, *Wit and Rhetoric in the Renaissance, The Formal Basis of Elizabethan Prose Style*, 1937.

Joan Bennett, "An Aspect of the Evolution of Seventeenth-Century Prose," *RES*, XVII (1941).

Hugh MacDonald, "Another Aspect of Seventeenth-Century Prose," *RES*, XIX (1943).

A. C. Howell, " 'Res et Verba': Words and Things," *ELH*, XIII (1946).

Don Cameron Allen, "Style and Certitude," *ELH*, XV (1948).

Richard Foster Jones, "Science and English Prose Style in the Third Quarter of the Seventeenth Century" (*PMLA*, 1930), *The Seventeenth Century: Studies in the History of English Thought and Literature from Bacon to Pope*, 1951.

George Williamson, *The Senecan Amble: A Study in Prose Form from Bacon to Collier*, 1951.

Harold Fisch, "The Puritans and the Reforms of Prose Style," *ELH*, XIX (1952).

Samuel E. Sprott, "Cicero's Theory of Prose Style," *PQ*, XXXIV (1955).

Jackson I. Cope, "Seventeenth-Century Quaker Style," *PMLA*, LXXI (1956).

James R. Sutherland, *On English Prose*, 1957.

Frank P. Wilson, *Seventeenth Century Prose*, 1960.

Robert Beum, "The Scientific Affinities of English Baroque Prose," *Eng. Miscellany*, XIII (1962).

# Francis Bacon

## 1561–1626

In the essay "On Nature in Man" Bacon warns that a man not set himself "too great nor too small tasks, for the first will make him dejected by often failings, and the second will make him a small proceeder, though by often prevailings." He is himself no small proceeder: "I have taken all knowledge to be my province," he writes in a letter to Lord Burleigh, and the task he sets himself is the remaking of all philosophy. But he also guards against often failings: the work is to be accomplished methodically—that is, in well-marked stages, and by a new method that would assure success.

This method is the Novum Organum, the new logic with which he would replace the old Organon of Aristotle. He begins with the raw data of experience, sorting, eliminating, and regrouping as he moves steadily up the ladder of generalizations. The method is not actually new, however: Aristotle, though granting it only a minor place in his scheme, had described the essential features of induction clearly enough. Nor is it adequate to Bacon's ambitions. He does not know how vast are the data to be gathered and ordered, or how cumbersome is any process of system-building that does not fully use the abstracting powers of reason and mathematics.

On the other hand, neither does he have a wholly naive approach to the problem of knowledge. He understands that he is dealing with probabilities and not with certainties. He provides for a series of hypotheses, starting with a "first vintage." He sees that there are often "prerogative instances" which permit the quick leap of insight into the forms and relationships in nature. And the method itself is to be refined with use; the art of discovery will improve as it leads to discoveries. Like Descartes, Bacon makes method the key to his entire philosophy.

He is, then, both a collector of minutiae and the architect of a grand design, both analytic and synthetic, a man of wide-ranging curiosity who also hopes to incorporate all knowledge into one unified whole. The division of the sciences that he proposes is as intricately worked out as is a medieval *Summa,* yet it is in no sense medieval. Theology is no longer queen of the sciences. He accepts the microcosm as only a figure of speech, and one that tricks us into seeking truths in the little world of man instead of in the "great and common world" of nature. He seeks only those parallels and harmonies that exist completely in nature, available to reason and the senses.

He is explicit about the twin ends that learning should serve: knowledge (or truth) and power. The kind of power to be sought is power over nature and not over men; it must work for the good of all, and not for private or even national profit or prestige. Even so, where truth and power are in conflict, truth is the loftier and must prevail. When all is said, however, he finds truth and power to be the same. The test of truth is not its fidelity to some prior principle, or its self-sufficiency or inner coherence, but its ability to withstand examination and verification in experience; "truth, therefore, and utility, are here perfectly identical, and the effects are of more value as pledges of truth than from the benefit they confer on men" (*Novum,* I, cxxiv).

His high hopes for learning are set forth in *The Great Instauration,* the renewal of learning that he blueprints and expects to see significantly advanced in his own time. Though he recognizes the achievements of the past, he respects no argument for its antiquity and no man for the weight of his authority.

Even if his techniques proved in the end to have been of limited value to the scientist in the laboratory, Bacon brought a new dignity and independence to the pursuit of learning, and particularly to the study of nature, and he is rightly remembered as prophet and groundbreaker of the Enlightenment. Diderot and d'Alembert, in dedicating the French Encyclopedia to Bacon, Descartes, Newton, and Locke, honor the "prodigious" Bacon as "the greatest, the most universal, and most eloquent of all philosophers" (Vol. I, 1751).

Bacon provides for an independent and revitalized science, furthermore, without crowding out religious faith. He makes a place both for natural religion, which he includes as a branch of philosophy and which thus exists in the domain of reason, and for sacred theology, which is drawn only from the oracles of God, and not from nature or reason. The mysteries of faith are therefore not to be sought in nature, nor the laws of nature in the Scriptures. In the realm of faith, "more worthy it is to believe than to know as we now know" (*Advancement,* II).

Bacon gives poetry an important role also, indeed makes it equal and parallel to that of philosophy itself. Sometimes, to be sure, he regards poetry as only the "dream of learning," or even a mere play of wit. And since poetry is not one of the deficient arts, he has relatively little to say about it. But if a dream, it is also a vision. The poet has a genius for discovering hidden harmonies. Parables and figures are like hieroglyphics: they incorporate and hint at the forms of nature. Myths enfold layers of truth and let us glimpse the underlying order. Tropes of rhetoric, like tropes in music, or the intricate correspondences between natural and civil matters, are not merely similitudes, but "the same footsteps of nature, treading and printing upon several subjects or matters" (*De Augmentis,* III, i). Poetry, in its way, is knowledge.

But poetry is also, according to Bacon, a *way* of knowing, an act or process. Imagination is the faculty and poetry the art that invents, joins, separates, recombines the elements of experience. Poetry thus links reason and the passions, engages the affections, and moves us to action. On the one hand, it expresses our natural delight in the variety and vicissitudes of things. On the other, it accommodates "the shows of things to the desires of the mind" (*De Augmentis,* II, xiii), and cultivates our appetite for a more perfect order. Thus it gives us the experience of "a more ample greatness, a more exact goodness, and a more absolute variety" (*Advancement,* II), and moves us to magnanimity and morality.

Both as critic and as writer Bacon is sensitive to problems of style. He attacks the prevailing if already old-fashioned Ciceronianism for affecting words rather than matter, and calls it "luxuriant" and the first vanity of learning. But he disapproves of the newer Senecan vogue also, and speaks of the pointed and chiming symmetries that make it seem more weighty and witty than it is. His own prose moves from a Senecan tightness and balance in the early *Essays* to the handsomely relaxed ease of the *New Atlantis.* Figures, examples and allusions enliven his pages throughout, but he rarely becomes mannered. His sentences are well knit, and not heavily loaded with modifiers. There are few inversions, and verbs are close to their subjects. It is a style varied enough to serve his many needs, and one that appeals to widely divergent tastes: Bishop Sprat, in the *History of the Royal Society,* praised it for being "short, allusive, and abounding with metaphors," and Shelley, in *A Defence of Poetry*, found in it "a sweet and majestic rhythm which satisfies the sense."

In this volume we have placed first some representative essays from each of the three original editions. Then, in order to trace the comprehensive design of the *Magna Instauratio*, we offer substantial selections from each of the following works: *The Advancement of Learning*, written before his project took shape; its later expansion, *De Dignitate et Augmentis Scientiarum;* the *Novum Organum;* and the *Sylva Sylvarum*. In these sections Bacon's exposition of method is given in detail, as are major statements about poetry, style, and the imagination. The handling of myth is illustrated from the *De Sapientia Veterum*. Finally, his description of the House of Salomon, the utopian scientific society of the *New Atlantis*, is included in its entirety.

## EDITIONS

*Essayes,* 1597, 1612, 1625; facs. 1903, 1904; ed. G. Grigson, 1937.
*Of the Proficience and Advancement of Learning,* 1605; ed. by W. A. Wright, 1868, 1900, 1920; ed. by F. G. Selby, 1892–1895.
*De Sapientia Veterum,* 1609. *The Wisedome of the Ancients,* trans. by Sir Arthur Gorges, 1619.
*Novum Organum,* 1620 (in *Instauratio Magna*); trans. by Gilbert Wats, 1640; ed. by Joseph Devey, 1902; ed. by Fulton H. Anderson, 1960.
*The Historie of the Raigne of King Henry the Seventh,* 1622; ed. by J. R. Lumby, 1876.
*De Dignitate et Augmentis Scientiarum,* 1623. *Of the Advancement and Proficience of Learning,* trans. by Gilbert Wats, 1640; ed. by Joseph Devey, 1901.
*New Atlantis,* 1626 (with *Sylva Sylvarum*); ed. by G. C. Moore Smith, 1900; ed. by A. B. Gough, 1915.
*Sylva Sylvarum: or a Naturall History,* 1626.
*The Works,* ed. by J. Spedding, R. L. Ellis, and D. D. Heath, 1857–1874.
*Essays, Advancement of Learning, New Atlantis and Other Pieces,* ed. by R. F. Jones, 1937.

## HISTORICAL AND CRITICAL STUDIES

T. B. MACAULAY, "Francis Bacon," *Edin. Rev.,* LXV (1837).
G. W. STEEVES, *Francis Bacon,* 1910.

R. S. CRANE, "The Relation of Bacon's Essays to His Program for the Advancement of Learning"; and MORRIS CROLL, "Attic Prose: Lipsius, Montaigne, and Bacon," *Schelling Anniversary Papers*, 1923.

ADOLFO LEVI, *Il Pensiero di Francesco Bacone*, 1925.

C. D. BROAD, *The Philosophy of Francis Bacon*, 1926.

A. E. TAYLOR, *Francis Bacon*, 1926.

MURRAY W. BUNDY, "Bacon's True Opinion of Poetry," *SP*, XXVII (1930).

MARY STURT, *Francis Bacon*, 1932.

CHARLES W. LEMMI, *The Classic Deities in Bacon*, 1933.

TADEUSZ KOTARBINSKI, "The Development of the Main Problem in the Methodology of Francis Bacon," *Studia Philosophica*, 1935.

GEOFFREY BULLOUGH, "Bacon and the Defense of Learning"; and RUDOLPH METZ, "Bacon's Part in the Intellectual Movement of His Time," *Seventeenth-Century Studies Presented to Sir Herbert Grierson*, 1938.

LEONARD F. DEAN, "Sir Francis Bacon's Theory of Civil History-Writing," *ELH*, VIII (1941).

GEOFFREY TILLOTSON, "Words for Princes: Bacon's Essays," *Essays in Criticism and Research*, 1942.

KARL WALLACE, *Francis Bacon on Communication and Rhetoric*, 1943.

L. C. KNIGHTS, "Bacon and the Seventeenth-Century Dissociation of Sensibility," *Explorations*, 1946.

FULTON H. ANDERSON, *The Philosophy of Francis Bacon*, 1948.

R. P. ADAMS, "The Social Responsibilities of Science in *Utopia, New Atlantis and After*," *JHI*, X (1949).

BENJAMIN FARRINGTON, *Francis Bacon: Philosopher of Industrial Science*, 1949.

R. W. GIBSON, *Francis Bacon: A Bibliography . . . to the Year 1750*, 1950; supplement, 1959.

M. BOAS, "Bacon and Gilbert," *JHI*, XII (1951).

C. J. DUCASSE, "Francis Bacon's Philosophy of Science," *Structure, Method, and Meaning*, ed. by Paul Henle, 1951.

D. G. JAMES, *The Dream of Learning*, 1951.

ADWIN W. GREEN, *Sir Francis Bacon: His Life and Works*, 1952.

BENJAMIN FARRINGTON, "On Misunderstanding the Philosophy of Francis Bacon," *Science, Medicine and History*, ed. by Edgar A. Underwood, 1953.

JEANNE ANDREWS, "Bacon and the 'Dissociation of Sensibility,' " *N & Q*, n.s., I (1954).

THOMAS H. JAMESON, *Francis Bacon: Criticism and the Modern World*, 1954.

MOODY E. PRIOR, "Bacon's Man of Science," *JHI*, XV (1954).

SISTER MARY FAITH SCHUSTER, "Philosophy of Life and Prose Style in Thomas More's *Richard III* and Francis Bacon's *Henry VII*," *PMLA*, LXX (1955).

THOMAS WHEELER, "Bacon's Henry VII as a Machiavellian Prince," *Renaissance Papers*, ed. by Allan H. Gilbert, 1957.

JOHN L. HARRISON, "Bacon's View of Rhetoric, Poetry, and the Imagination," *HLQ*, XX (1957).

Paul Kocher, "Francis Bacon on the Science of Jurisprudence," *JHI*, XVIII (1957).

Robert McRae, "The Unity of the Sciences: Bacon, Descartes, and Leibnitz," *JHI*, XVIII (1957).

Thomas Wheeler, "The Purpose of Bacon's *History of Henry the Seventh*," *SP*, LIV (1957).

Rexmond Cochrane, "Francis Bacon in Early Eighteenth-Century English Literature," *PQ*, XXXVII (1958);

————, "Francis Bacon and the Architect of Fortune," *Studies in the Renaissance*, V (1958).

Paul Kocher, "Francis Bacon and His Father," *HLQ*, XXI (1958).

Sidney Warhaft, "The Anomaly of Bacon's Allegorizing," *Papers of the Michigan Acad. of Sci., Arts and Letters*, XLIII (1958).

L. Anceschi, *L'estetica dell' empiricismo inglese, i: Da Bacone a Shaftesbury*, 1959.

W. O. Scott, "Shelley's Admiration for Bacon," *PMLA*, LXXIII (1958).

Bryan Bevan, *The Real Francis Bacon*, 1960.

John Crossett, "Bacon and Donne," *N & Q*, n.s., VII (1960).

James G. Crowther, *Francis Bacon: The First Statesman of Science*, 1960.

Elizabeth Sewell, "Bacon and Shakespeare: Postlogical Thinking," *The Orphic Voice*, 1960.

Vernon F. Snow, "Francis Bacon's Advice to Fulke Greville on Research Techniques," *HLQ*, XXIII (1960).

Meyrick H. Carré, "Francis Bacon: 1561–1626," *Quar. Rev.*, CCXCIX (1961).

Sister Scholastica Mandeville, "The Rhetorical Tradition of the *Sententia;* with a Study of Its Influence on the Prose of Sir Francis Bacon and of Sir Thomas Browne," Dissertation, St. Louis University, 1960, *Dissertation Abst.*, XXI (1961).

Henry Margenau, "Bacon and Modern Physics: A Confrontation," *Proc. Am. Phil. Soc.*, CV (1961).

John Max Patrick, *Francis Bacon*, 1961.

Fulton H. Anderson, *Francis Bacon, His Career and His Thought*, 1962.

Edmund H. Creeth, "Bacon's Humanism," *Papers of the Michigan Acad. of Sci., Arts and Letters*, XLVII (1962).

Loren Eiseley, *Francis Bacon and the Modern Dilemma*, 1962.

Paul H. Kocher, "Francis Bacon on the Drama," *Essays on Shakespeare and Elizabethan Drama in Honor of Hardin Craig*, ed. by Richard Hosley, 1962.

Robert E. Larsen, "The Aristotelianism of Bacon's *Novum Organum*," *JHI*, XXIII (1962).

Hugh Trevor-Roper, "Francis Bacon," *Encounter*, XVIII (1962).

Virgil Whitaker, *Francis Bacon's Intellectual Milieu*, 1962.

Judah Bierman, "Science and Society in the *New Atlantis* and Other Renaissance Utopias," *PMLA*, LXXVIII (1963).

Catherine Drinker Bowen, *Francis Bacon: The Temper of a Man*, 1963.

Marie Boas Hall, "In Defense of Bacon's Views on the Reform of Science," *Person.*, XLIV (1963).

Sidney Warhaft, "Bacon and the Renaissance Ideal of Self-Knowledge," *Person.*, XLIV (1963).

Benjamin Farrington, *The Philosophy of Francis Bacon*, 1964.

Anne Righter, "Francis Bacon," *The English Mind: Studies in the English Moralists*, ed. by Hugh S. Davies and George Watson, 1964.

Thomas Wheeler, "Sir Francis Bacon in the Laboratory," *Tenn. Studies in Lit.*, IX (1964).

# ESSAYS

## OF STUDIES (1597)

Studies serve for pastimes, for ornaments and for abilities. Their chiefe use for pastime is in privatenes and retiring; for ornamente is in discourse, and for abilitie is in judgement. For expert men can execute, but learned men are fittest to judge or censure.

¶ To spend too much time in them is slouth, to use them too much for ornament is affectation: to make judgement wholly by their rules, is the humour of a Scholler. ¶ They perfect *Nature,* and are perfected by experience. ¶ Craftie men continue them, simple men admire them, wise men use them: For they teach not their owne use, but that is a wisedome without them: and above them wonne by observation. ¶ Reade not to contradict, nor to believe, but to waigh and consider. ¶ Some bookes are to bee tasted, others to bee swallowed, and some few to bee chewed and disgested: That is, some bookes are to be read only in partes; others to be read, but cursorily, and some few to be read wholly and with diligence and attention. ¶ Reading maketh a full man, conference a readye man, and writing an exacte man. And therefore if a man write little, he had neede have a great memorie, if he conferre little, he had neede have a present wit, and if he reade little, hee had neede have much cunning, to seeme to know that he doth not. ¶ Histories make men wise, Poets wittie: the Mathematickes subtle, naturall Phylosophie deepe: Morall grave, Logicke and Rhetoricke able to contend.

## OF MARRIAGE AND SINGLE LIFE (1612)

Hee that hath wife and children, hath given hostages to fortune. For they are impediments to great enterprises, either of vertue or mischief. Certainly the best works, and of greatest merit for the publike have proceeded from the unmarried, or childlesse men; which have sought eternity in memory, and not in posterity; and which both in affection and means, have married and endowed the publike. Yet some there are, that lead a single life whose thoughts doe ende with themselves, and doe account future times, impertinences. Nay there are some others, that esteeme wife & children, but as bils of charges. But the most ordinarie cause of a single life, is liberty; specially in certain self-pleasing & humorous minds, which are so sensible of every restriction, as they wil go neere to thinke their girdles and garters to be bonds and shakles. Unmarried men are best friends; best masters; best servants; not alwaies best subjects; for they are light to run away; and almost all fugitives are of that condition. A single life is proper for Churchmen. For charity wil hardly water the ground, where it must first fill a poole. It is indifferent for Judges and Magistrates. For if they be facile & corrupt, you shall have a servant five times worse than a wife. For Souldiers, I find the Generals commonly in their hortatives, put men in minde of their wives, and children: and I thinke the despising of marriage, amongst the Turkes, maketh the vulgar Souldier more base. Certainely, wife and children are a kinde of discipline of humanity: and single men are more cruell and hard-hearted: good to make severe inquisitors. Grave natures led by custome, and therefore constant, are commonly loving husbands: as was said of *Ulisses; Vetulam prætulit immortalitati.* Chaste women are often proud and froward, as presuming upon the merit of their chastity. It is one of the best bonds both of chastity & obedience in the wife; if shee thinke her husband wise; which shee will never doe, if shee finde him jelous. Wives are young mens mistresses; companions for middle age; and old mens nurses. So as a man may have a quarrel to marry when hee will; but yet hee was reputed one of the wise men, that made answere to the question; *When a man should marrie?* A young man not yet, an elder man not at all.

## OF PARENTS AND CHILDREN (1612)

The joyes of *Parents* are secret, and so are their griefs and feares: they cannot utter the one, nor they will not utter the other. Children sweeten labors, but they make misfortunes more bitter: they increase the cares of life, but they mitigate the remembrance of death. The perpetuitie by generation, is common to beasts; but memorie, merit, & noble works are proper to men. They that are the first raisers of their house, are most indulgent towards their children; beholding them, as the continuance, not only of their kind, but of their worke; and so both children and creatures. The difference of affection in parents towards their severall children, is many times unequall; and sometimes un-worthy; specially in the mother; as *Salomon* saith; *A wise sonne rejoiceth the Father, but an ungracious son shames the mother.* A man shall see where there is a house full of children, one, or two of the eldest respected, and the youngest made wantons; but in the middle, some that are as it were forgotten; who neverthelesse proove the best. The illiberality of Parents in allowance towards their children is an harmefull error: makes them base; acquaints them with shifts, makes them sort with meane companie; and makes them surfet more, when they come to plenty. And therefore the proofe is best, when men keepe their authority towards their children, but not their purse. Men have a foolish manner, both Parents, Schoolemasters, and servants, in creating and breeding an emulation betweene brothers during childhood, which many times sorteth to discord when they are men, and disturbeth families. The *Italians* make little difference betweene children and nephewes, or neere kinsfolke: But so they be of the lumpe, they care not, though they passe not through their owne body: and to say truth, in nature it is much a like matter, in so much that wee see a nephewe sometimes resembleth an uncle, or a kinsman, more than his owne Parent, as the blood happens.

## WISDOME FOR A MANS SELFE (1612)

An *Ante* is a wise creature for it selfe: But it is a shrewd thing in an Orchard or garden. And certainly men that are great lovers of them-selves, waste the publike. Divide with reason betweene selfe love, and society: and bee so true to thy selfe, as thou be not false to others. It is a poore Centre of a mans actions, *himselfe*. It is right earth. For that only stands fast upon his owne centre: whereas all things that have affinity with the heavens, move upon the centre of an other, which they benefit. The referring of all to a mans selfe, is more tollerable in a soveraigne Prince; because themselves are not themselves; but their good and evill is at the perill of the publike fortune. But it is a desperate evill in a servant to a *Prince,* or a Citizen in a *Republike.* For whatsoever affaires passe such a mans hand, hee crooketh them to his owne ends: which must needs bee often *Eccentrike* to the ends of his master or state. Therefore let Princes or States, chuse such servants, as have not this marke; except they meane their service should bee made but the

accessary. And that which maketh the effect more pernitious, is, that al
proportion is lost. It were disproportion enough for the servants good
to be preferred before the masters: But yet it is a greater extreme,
when a little good of the servants, shall carrie things against a great
good of the masters. And yet that is the case; for the good such servants
receive; is after the modell of their owne fortune: but the hurt they
sell for that good, is after the modell of their Masters *Fortune*. And
certainely it is the nature of extreme selfe-lovers, as they will set an
house on fire, and it were but to rost their egges; and yet these men
many times hold credit with their masters; because their study is but to
please them, and profit themselves; and for either respect they will
abandon the good of their affaires.


## OF TRUTH (1625)

*What is Truth?* said jesting Pilate ; and would not stay for an answer.
Certainly there be that delight in giddiness, and count it a bondage to
fix a belief ; affecting free-will in thinking, as well as in acting. And
though the sects of philosophers of that kind be gone, yet there remain
certain discoursing wits which are of the same veins, though there be
not so much blood in them as was in those of the ancients. But it is not
only the difficulty and labour which men take in finding out of truth ;
nor again that when it is found it imposeth upon men's thoughts ; that
doth bring lies in favour; but a natural though corrupt love of the lie
itself. One of the later school of the Grecians examineth the matter,
and is at a stand to think what should be in it, that men should love
lies, where neither they make for pleasure, as with poets, nor for advantage, as with the merchant; but for the lie's sake. But I cannot tell: this
same truth is a naked and open day-light, that doth not shew the masks
and mummeries and triumphs of the world, half so stately and daintily
as candle-lights. Truth may perhaps come to the price of a pearl, that
sheweth best by day; but it will not rise to the price of a diamond or
carbuncle, that sheweth best in varied lights. A mixture of a lie doth
ever add pleasure. Doth any man doubt, that if there were taken out of
men's minds vain opinions, flattering hopes, false valuations, imaginations as one would, and the like, but it would leave the minds of a
number of men poor shrunken things, full of melancholy and indisposition, and unpleasing to themselves? One of the Fathers, in great

severity, called poesy *vinum dæmonum* [devil's-wine], because it filleth the imagination; and yet it is but with the shadow of a lie. But it is not the lie that passeth through the mind, but the lie that sinketh in and settleth in it, that doth the hurt; such as we spake of before. But howsoever these things are thus in men's depraved judgments and affections, yet truth, which only doth judge itself, teacheth that the inquiry of truth, which is the love-making or wooing of it, the knowledge of truth, which is the presence of it, and the belief of truth, which is the enjoying of it, is the sovereign good of human nature. The first creature of God, in the works of the days, was the light of the sense; the last was the light of reason; and his sabbath work ever since, is the illumination of his Spirit. First he breathed light upon the face of the matter or chaos; then he breathed light into the face of man; and still he breatheth and inspireth light into the face of his chosen. The poet that beautified the sect that was otherwise inferior to the rest,[1] saith yet excellently well: *It is a pleasure to stand upon the shore, and to see ships tossed upon the sea; a pleasure to stand in the window of a castle, and to see a battle and the adventures thereof below: but no pleasure is comparable to the standing upon the vantage ground of Truth,* (a hill not to be commanded, and where the air is always clear and serene,) *and to see the errors, and wanderings, and mists, and tempests, in the vale below;* so always that this prospect be with pity, and not with swelling or pride. Certainly, it is heaven upon earth, to have a man's mind move in charity, rest in providence, and turn upon the poles of truth.

To pass from theological and philosophical truth, to the truth of civil business; it will be acknowledged even by those that practise it not, that clear and round dealing is the honour of man's nature; and that mixture of falsehood is like allay in coin of gold and silver, which may make the metal work the better, but it embaseth it. For these winding and crooked courses are the goings of the serpent; which goeth basely upon the belly, and not upon the feet. There is no vice that doth so cover a man with shame as to be found false and perfidious. And therefore Montaigne saith prettily, when he inquired the reason, why the word of the lie should be such a disgrace and such an odious charge? Saith he, *If it be well weighed, to say that a man lieth, is as much to say, as that he is brave towards God and a coward towards men.*[2] For a lie faces God,

---

[1] Lucretius. See the beginning of the second book.
[2] *Essais,* II, 18.

and shrinks from man. Surely the wickedness of falsehood and breach of
faith cannot possibly be so highly expressed, as in that it shall be the last
peal to call the judgments of God upon the generations of men; it being
foretold, that when Christ cometh, *he shall not find faith upon the
earth.*

# OF LOVE (1625)

The stage is more beholding to Love, than the life of man. For as to
the stage, love is ever matter of comedies, and now and then of tragedies;
but in life it doth much mischief; sometimes like a syren, sometimes
like a fury. You may observe, that amongst all the great and worthy
persons (whereof the memory remaineth, either ancient or recent,) there
is not one that hath been transported to the mad degree of love: which
shews that great spirits and great business do keep out this weak passion.
You must except nevertheless Marcus Antonius, the half partner of the
empire of Rome, and Appius Claudius, the decemvir and lawgiver;
whereof the former was indeed a voluptuous man, and inordinate; but
the latter was an austere and wise man: and therefore it seems (though
rarely) that love can find entrance not only into an open heart, but also
into a heart well fortified, if watch be not well kept. It is a poor saying
of Epicurus, *Satis magnum alter alteri theatrum sumus:* [Each is to
other a theatre large enough]; as if man, made for the contemplation of
heaven and all noble objects, should do nothing but kneel before a little
idol, and make himself a subject, though not of the mouth (as beasts
are), yet of the eye; which was given him for higher purposes. It is a
strange thing to note the excess of this passion, and how it braves the
nature and value of things, by this; that the speaking in a perpetual
hyperbole is comely in nothing but in love. Neither is it merely in the
phrase; for whereas it hath been well said that the arch-flatterer, with
whom all the petty flatterers have intelligence, is a man's self; certainly
the lover is more. For there was never proud man thought so absurdly
well of himself as the lover doth of the person loved; and therefore it was
well said, *That it is impossible to love and to be wise.* Neither doth this
weakness appear to others only, and not to the party loved; but to the
loved most of all, except the love be reciproque. For it is a true rule, that
love is ever rewarded either with the reciproque or with an inward and
secret contempt. By how much the more men ought to beware of this

passion, which loseth not only other things, but itself. As for the other losses, the poet's relation doth well figure them; That he that preferred Helena, quitteth the gifts of Juno and Pallas. For whosoever esteemeth too much of amorous affection quitteth both riches and wisdom. This passion hath his floods in the very times of weakness; which are great prosperity and great adversity; though this latter hath been less observed: both which times kindle love, and make it more fervent, and therefore shew it to be the child of folly. They do best, who if they cannot but admit love, yet make it keep quarter; and sever it wholly from their serious affairs and actions of life; for if it check once with business, it troubleth men's fortunes, and maketh men that they can no ways be true to their own ends. I know not how, but martial men are given to love: I think it is but as they are given to wine; for perils commonly ask to be paid in pleasures. There is in man's nature a secret inclination and motion towards love of others, which if it be not spent upon some one or a few, doth naturally spread itself towards many, and maketh men become humane and charitable; as it is seen sometime in friars. Nuptial love maketh mankind; friendly love perfecteth it; but wanton love corrupteth and embaseth it.

# THE GREAT INSTAURATION

## THE PLAN OF THE WORK

### THE WORK IS IN SIX PARTS:

1. The Divisions of the Sciences.
2. The New Organon; or Directions concerning the Interpretation of Nature.
3. The Phenomena of the Universe; or a Natural and Experimental History for the foundation of Philosophy.
4. The Ladder of the Intellect.
5. The Forerunners; or Anticipations of the New Philosophy.
6. The New Philosophy; or Active Science.

### The Arguments of the Several Parts.

It being part of my design to set everything forth, as far as may be, plainly and perspicuously (for nakedness of the mind is still, as nakedness of the body once was, the companion of innocence and simplicity), let me first explain the order and plan of the work. I distribute it into six parts.

## I. The Divisions of the Sciences

The first part exhibits a summary or general description of the knowledge which the human race at present possesses. For I thought it good to make some pause upon that which is received; that thereby the old may be more easily made perfect and the new more easily approached. And I hold the improvement of that which we have to be as much an object as the acquisition of more. Besides which it will make me the better listened to; for "He that is ignorant (says the proverb) receives not the words of knowledge, unless thou first tell him that which is in his own heart." We will therefore make a coasting voyage along the shores of the arts and sciences received; not without importing into them some useful things by the way.

In laying out the divisions of the sciences however, I take into account not only things already invented and known, but likewise things omitted which ought to be there. For there are found in the intellectual as in the terrestrial globe waste regions as well as cultivated ones. It is no wonder therefore if I am sometimes obliged to depart from the ordinary divisions. For in adding to the total you necessarily alter the parts and sections; and the received divisions of the sciences are fitted only to the received sum of them as it stands now.

With regard to those things which I shall mark as omitted, I intend not merely to set down a simple title or a concise argument of that which is wanted. For as often as I have occasion to report anything as deficient, the nature of which is at all obscure, so that men may not perhaps easily understand what I mean or what the work is which I have in my head, I shall always (provided it be a matter of any worth) take care to subjoin either directions for the execution of such work, or else a portion of the work itself executed by myself as a sample of the whole: thus giving assistance in every case either by work or by counsel. For if it were for the sake of my own reputation only and other men's interests were not concerned in it, I would not have any man think that in such cases merely some light and vague notion has crossed my mind, and that the things which I desire and offer at are no better than wishes; when they are in fact things which men may certainly command if they will, and of which I have formed in my own mind a clear and detailed conception. For I do not propose merely to survey these regions in my mind, like an augur taking auspices, but to enter them like a general who means to take possession.—So much for the first part of the work.

## 2. The New Organon

Having thus coasted past the ancient arts, the next point is to equip the intellect for passing beyond. To the second part therefore belongs the doctrine concerning the better and more perfect use of human reason in the inquisition of things, and the true helps of the understanding: that thereby (as far as the condition of mortality and humanity allows) the intellect may be raised and exalted, and made capable of overcoming the difficulties and obscurities of nature. The art which I introduce with this view (which I call *Interpretation of Nature*) is a kind of logic; though the difference between it and the ordinary logic is great; indeed immense. For the ordinary logic professes to contrive and prepare helps and guards for the understanding, as mine does; and in this one point they agree. But mine differs from it in three points especially; viz. in the end aimed at; in the order of demonstration; and in the starting point of the inquiry. . . .

## 3. The Phenomena of the Universe

But I design not only to indicate and mark out the ways, but also to enter them. And therefore the third part of the work embraces the Phenomena of the Universe; that is to say, experience of every kind, and such a natural history as may serve for a foundation to build philosophy upon. For a good method of demonstration or form of interpreting nature may keep the mind from going astray or stumbling, but it is not any excellence of method that can supply it with the material of knowledge. Those however who aspire not to guess and divine, but to discover and know; who propose not to devise mimic and fabulous worlds of their own, but to examine and dissect the nature of this very world itself; must go to facts themselves for everything. Nor can the place of this labour and search and worldwide perambulation be supplied by any genius or meditation or argumentation; no, not if all men's wits could meet in one. This therefore we must have, or the business must be for ever abandoned. . . .

## 4. The Ladder of the Intellect

And now that we have surrounded the intellect with faithful helps and guards, and got together with most careful selection a regular army of divine works, it may seem that we have no more to do but to proceed to philosophy itself. And yet in a matter so difficult and doubtful there are still some things which it seems necessary to premise, partly for convenience of explanation, partly for present use.

Of these the first is to set forth examples of inquiry and invention according to my method, exhibited by anticipation in some particular subjects; choosing such subjects as are at once the most noble in themselves among those under inquiry, and most different one from another; that there may be an example in every kind. I do not speak of those examples which are joined to the several precepts and rules by way of illustration (for of these I have given plenty in the second part of the work); but I mean actual types and models, by which the entire process of the mind and the whole fabric and order of invention from the beginning to the end, in certain subjects, and those various and remarkable, should be set as it were before the eyes. For I remember that in the mathematics it is easy to follow the demonstration when you have a machine beside you; whereas without that help all appears involved and more subtle than it really is. To examples of this kind,—being in fact nothing more than an application of the second part in detail and at large,—the fourth part of the work is devoted.

## 5. Anticipations of the New Philosophy

The fifth part is for temporary use only, pending the completion of the rest; like interest payable from time to time until the principal be forthcoming. For I do not make so blindly for the end of my journey, as to neglect anything useful that may turn up by the way. And therefore I include in this fifth part such things as I have myself discovered, proved, or added,—not however according to the true rules and methods of interpretation, but by the ordinary use of the understanding in inquiring and discovering. For besides that I hope my speculations may in virtue of my continual conversancy with nature have a value beyond the pretensions of my wit, they will serve in the meantime for wayside inns, in which the mind may rest and refresh itself on its journey to more certain conclusions. Nevertheless I wish it to be understood in the meantime that they are conclusions by which (as not being discovered and proved by the true form of interpretation) I do not at all mean to bind myself. Nor need any one be alarmed at such suspension of judgment, in one who maintains not simply that nothing can be known, but only that nothing can be known except in a certain course and way; and yet establishes provisionally certain degrees of assurance, for use and relief until the mind shall arrive at a knowledge of causes in which it can rest. For even those schools of philosophy which held the absolute impossibility of knowing anything were not inferior to those which took upon them to pronounce. But then they did not provide helps for the sense and understanding, as I have done, but simply took away all their authority: which is quite a different thing—almost the reverse.

## 6. The New Philosophy

The sixth part of my work (to which the rest is subservient and ministrant) discloses and sets forth that philosophy which by the legitimate, chaste, and severe course of inquiry which I have explained and provided is at length developed and established. The completion however of this last part is a thing both above my strength and beyond my hopes. I have made a beginning of the work—a beginning, as I hope, not unimportant:—the fortune of the human race will give the issue;—such an issue, it may be, as in the present condition of things and men's minds cannot easily be conceived or imagined. For the matter in hand is no mere felicity of speculation, but the real business and fortunes of the human race, and all power of operation. For man is but the servant and interpreter of nature: what he does and what he knows is only what he has observed of nature's order in fact or in thought; beyond this he knows nothing and can do nothing. For the chain of causes cannot by any force be loosed or broken, nor can nature be commanded except by being obeyed. And so those twin objects, human Knowledge and human Power, do really meet in one; and it is from ignorance of causes that operation fails.

And all depends on keeping the eye steadily fixed upon the facts of nature and so receiving their images simply as they are. For God forbid that we should give out a dream of our own imagination for a pattern of the world; rather may he graciously grant to us to write an apocalypse or true vision of the footsteps of the Creator imprinted on his creatures.

# OF THE ADVANCEMENT OF LEARNING

## To the King

. . . Therefore I did conclude with myself, that I could not make unto your Majesty a better oblation than of some treatise tending to that end; whereof the sum will consist of these two parts: the former concerning the excellency of learning and knowledge, and the excellency of the merit and true glory in the augmentation and propagation thereof; the later, what the particular acts and works are which have been embraced and undertaken for the advancement of learning, and again what defects and undervalues I find in such particular acts; to the end that though I cannot positively or affirmatively advise your Majesty, or propound unto you framed particulars, yet I may excite your princely cogitations to visit the excellent treasure of your own mind, and thence to extract particulars for this purpose agreeable to your magnanimity and wisdom.

In the entrance to the former of these,—to clear the way, and as it were to make silence to have the true testimonies concerning the dignity of learning to be better heard without the interruption of tacit objections,—I think good to deliver it from the discredits and disgraces which it hath received; all from ignorance; but ignorance severally disguised; appearing sometimes in the zeal and jealousy of divines, sometimes in the severity and arrogancy of politiques, and sometimes in the errors and imperfections of learned men themselves. . . .

## The Distempers of Learning

Now I proceed to those errors and vanities which have intervened amongst the studies themselves of the learned; which is that which is principal and proper to the present argument; wherein my purpose is not to make a justification of the errors, but, by a censure and separation of the errors, to make a justification of that which is good and sound, and to deliver that from the aspersion of the other. For we see that it is the manner of men to scandalize and deprave that which retaineth the state and virtue, by taking advantage upon that which is corrupt and degenerate: as the Heathens in the primitive church used to blemish and taint the Christians with the faults and corruptions of heretics. But nevertheless I have no meaning at this time to make any exact animadversion of the errors and impediments in matters of learning which are more secret and remote from vulgar opinion; but only to speak unto such as do fall under, or near unto, a popular observation.

## 1. Fantastical Learning

There be therefore chiefly three vanities in studies, whereby learning hath been most traduced. For those things we do esteem vain, which are either false or frivolous, those which either have no truth or no use: and those persons we esteem vain, which are either credulous or curious; and curiosity is either in matter or words: so that in reason as well as in experience, there fall out to be these three distempers (as I may term them) of learning; the first, fantastical learning; the second, contentious learning; and the last, delicate learning; vain imaginations, vain altercations, and vain affectations; and with the last I will begin. Martin Luther, conducted (no doubt) by an higher Providence, but in discourse of reason finding what a province he had undertaken against the Bishop of Rome and the degenerate traditions of the church, and finding his own solitude, being no ways aided by the opinions of his own time, was enforced to awake all antiquity, and to call former times to his succors to make a party against the present time; so that the ancient authors, both in divinity and in humanity, which had long time slept in libraries, began generally to be read and revolved. This by consequence did draw on a necessity of a more exquisite travail in the languages original wherein those authors did write, for the better understanding of those authors and the better advantage of pressing and applying their words. And thereof grew again a delight in their manner of style and phrase, and an admiration of that kind of writing; which was much furthered and precipitated by the enmity and opposition that the propounders of those (primitive but seeming new) opinions had against the schoolmen; who were generally of the contrary part, and whose writings were altogether in a differing style and form; taking liberty to coin and frame new terms of art to express their own sense and to avoid circuit of speech, without regard to the pureness, pleasantness, and (as I may call it) lawfulness of the phrase or word. And again, because the great labour then was with the people, (of whom the Pharisees were wont to say, *Execrabilis ista turba, quæ non novit legem,*) [the wretched crowd that has not known the law,] for the winning and persuading of them, there grew of necessity in chief price and request eloquence and variety of discourse, as the fittest and forciblest access into the capacity of the vulgar sort. So that these four causes concurring, the admiration of ancient authors, the hate of the schoolmen, the exact study of languages, and the efficacy of preaching, did bring in an affectionate study of eloquence and copie of speech, which then began to flourish. This grew speedily to an excess; for men began to hunt more after words than matter; and more after the choiceness of the phrase, and the round and clean composition of the sentence, and the sweet falling of the clauses, and the varying and illustration of their works with tropes and figures, than after the weight of matter, worth of subject, soundness of argument, life of invention, or depth of judgment. Then grew the flowing and watery vein of Osorius, the Portugal bishop, to be in price. Then did Sturmius spend such infinite and curious pains upon Cicero the orator and Hermogenes the rhetorician, besides his own books of periods and imitation and the like. Then did Car of Cambridge, and Ascham, with their lectures and writings, almost deify Cicero and Demosthenes, and allure all young men that were studious unto that delicate and polished kind of learning. Then did Erasmus take occasion to make the scoffing echo; *Decem annos consumpsi in legendo Cicerone,* [I have spent ten years in reading Cicero:] and the echo answered in Greek, *one, Asine.* Then grew the learning of the schoolmen to be utterly despised as barbarous. In sum, the whole inclination and bent of those times was rather towards copie than weight.

Here therefore [is] the first distemper of learning, when men study words and not matter: whereof though I have represented an example of late times, yet it hath been and will be *secundum majus et minus* in all time. And how is it possible but this should have an operation to discredit learning, even with vulgar capacities, when they see learned men's works like the first letter of a patent or limned book; which though it hath large flourishes, yet it is but a letter? It seems to me that Pygmalion's frenzy is a good emblem or portraiture of this vanity: for words are but the images of matter; and except they have life of reason and invention, to fall in love with them is all one as to fall in love with a picture. . . .

## 2. Contentious Learning

The second, which followeth, is in nature worse than the former; for as substance of matter is better than beauty of words, so contrariwise vain matter is worse than vain words: wherein it seemeth the reprehension of St. Paul was not only proper for those times, but prophetical for the times following; and not only respective to divinity, but extensive to all knowledge: *Devita profanas vocum novitates, et oppositiones falsi nominis scientiæ:* [shun profane novelties of terms and oppositions of science falsely so called]. For he assigneth two marks and badges of suspected and falsified science; the one, the novelty and strangeness of terms; the other, the strictness of positions, which of necessity doth induce oppositions, and so questions and altercations. Surely, like as many substances in nature which are solid do putrefy and corrupt into worms, so it is the property of good and sound knowledge to putrefy and dissolve into a number of subtile, idle, unwholesome, and (as I may term them) vermiculate questions, which have indeed a kind of quickness and life of spirit, but no soundness of matter or goodness of quality. This kind of degenerate learning did chiefly reign amongst the schoolmen; who having sharp and strong wits, and abundance of leisure, and small variety of reading; but their wits being shut up in the cells of a few authors (chiefly Aristotle their dictator) as their persons were shut up in the cells of monasteries and colleges; and knowing little history, either of nature or time; did out of no great quantity of matter, and infinite agitation of wit, spin out unto us those laborious webs of learning which are extant in their books. For the wit and mind of man, if it work upon matter, which is the contemplation of the creatures of God, worketh according to the stuff, and is limited thereby; but if it work upon itself, as the spider worketh his web, then it is endless, and brings forth indeed cobwebs of learning, admirable for the fineness of thread and work, but of no substance or profit. . . .

## 3. Delicate Learning

For the third vice or disease of learning, which concerneth deceit or untruth, it is of all the rest the foulest; as that which doth destroy the essential form of knowledge, which is nothing but a representation of truth: for the truth of being and the truth of knowing are one, differing no more than the direct beam and the beam reflected. This vice therefore brancheth itself into two sorts; delight in deceiving, and aptness to be deceived; imposture and credulity; which, although they appear to be of a diverse nature, the one seeming to proceed of cunning, and the other of simplicity, yet certainly they do for the most part concur: for as the verse noteth,

*Percontatorem fugito, nam garrulus idem est,*

an inquisitive man is a prattler, so upon the like reason a credulous man is a deceiver: as we see it in fame, that he that will easily believe rumours will as easily augment rumours and add somewhat to them of his own; which Tacitus wisely noteth, when he saith, *Fingunt simul creduntque,* [as fast as they believe one tale they make another:] so great an affinity hath fiction and belief. . . .

### The Peccant Humours

Thus have I gone over these three diseases of learning; besides the which, there are some other rather peccant humours than formed diseases, which nevertheless are not so secret and intrinsic but that they fall under a popular observation and traducement, and therefore are not to be passed over.

The first of these is the extreme affecting of two extremities; the one Antiquity, the other Novelty: wherein it seemeth the children of time do take after the nature and malice of the father. For as he devoureth his children, so one of them seeketh to devour and suppress the other; while antiquity envieth there should be new additions, and novelty cannot be content to add but it must deface. Surely the advice of the prophet is the true direction in this matter, *State super vias antiquas, et videte quænam sit via recta et bona, et ambulate in ea:* [stand ye in the old ways, and see which is the good way, and walk therein]. Antiquity deserveth that reverence, that men should make a stand thereupon, and discover what is the best way; but when the discovery is well taken, then to make progression. And to speak truly, *Antiquitas sæculi juventus mundi.* These times are the ancient times, when the world is ancient, and not those which we account ancient *ordine retrogrado,* by a computation backward from ourselves.

Another error, induced by the former, is a distrust that any thing should be now to be found out, which the world should have missed and passed over so long time; as if the same objection were to be made to time that Lucian maketh to Jupiter and other the heathen gods, of which he wondereth that they begot so many children in old time and begot none in his time, and asketh whether they were become septuagenary, or whether the law *Pappia,* made against old men's marriages, had restrained them. So it seemeth men doubt lest time is become past children and generation; wherein contrariwise we see commonly the levity and unconstancy of men's judgments, which, till a matter be done, wonder that it can be done; and as soon as it is done, wonder again that it was no sooner done; as we see in the expedition of Alexander into Asia, which at first was prejudged as a vast and impossible enterprise; and yet afterwards it pleaseth Livy to make no more of it than this, *Nil aliud quàm bene ausus vana contemnere:* [it was but taking courage to despise vain apprehensions]. And the same happened to Columbus in the western navigation. But in intellectual matters it is much more common; as may be seen in most of the propositions of Euclid, which till they be demonstrate, they seem strange to our assent; but being demonstrate, our mind accepteth of them by a kind of relation (as the lawyers speak) as if we had known them before.

Another error, that hath also some affinity with the former, is a conceit that of former opinions or sects, after variety and examination, the best hath still prevailed and suppressed the rest; so as if a man should begin the labour of a new search, he were but like to light upon somewhat formerly rejected, and by rejection brought into oblivion: as if the multitude, or the wisest for the multitude's sake, were not ready to give passage rather to that which is popular and superficial than to that which is substantial and profound; for the truth is, that time seemeth to be of the nature of a river or stream, which carrieth down to us that which is light and blown up, and sinketh and drowneth that which is weighty and solid.

Another error, of a diverse nature from all the former, is the over-early and peremptory reduction of knowledge into arts and methods; from which time commonly sciences receive small or no augmentation. But as young men, when they knit and shape perfectly, do seldom grow to a further stature; so knowledge, while it is in aphorisms and observations, it is in growth; but when it once is comprehended in exact methods, it may perchance be further polished and illustrated, and accommo-

dated for use and practice; but it increaseth no more in bulk and substance.

Another error, which doth succeed that which we last mentioned, is
that after the distribution of particular arts and sciences, men have abandoned universality, or *philosophia prima;* which cannot but cease and
stop all progression. For no perfect discovery can be made upon a flat
or a level: neither is it possible to discover the more remote and deeper
parts of any science, if you stand but upon the level of the same science,
and ascend not to a higher science.

Another error hath proceeded from too great a reverence, and a kind
of adoration of the mind and understanding of man; by means whereof
men have withdrawn themselves too much from the contemplation of
nature and the observations of experience, and have tumbled up and
down in their own reason and conceits. Upon these intellectualists, which
are notwithstanding commonly taken for the most sublime and divine
philosophers, Heraclitus gave a just censure, saying, *Men sought truth
in their own little worlds, and not in the great and common world;* for
they disdain to spell and so by degrees to read in the volume of God's
works; and contrariwise by continual meditation and agitation of wit do
urge and as it were invocate their own spirits to divine and give oracles
unto them, whereby they are deservedly deluded.

Another error that hath some connection with this later is, that men
have used to infect their meditations, opinions, and doctrines, with some
conceits which they have most admired, or some sciences which they
have most applied; and given all things else a tincture according to them,
utterly untrue and unproper. So hath Plato intermingled his philosophy
with theology, and Aristotle with logic, and the second school of Plato,
Proclus and the rest, with the mathematics. For these were the arts
which had a kind of primogeniture with them severally. So have the alchemists made a philosophy out of a few experiments of the furnace;
and Gilbertus, our countryman, hath made a philosophy out of the observations of a loadstone. . . .

Another error is an impatience of doubt, and haste to assertion without due and mature suspension of judgment. For the two ways of contemplation are not unlike the two ways of action commonly spoken of
by the ancients; the one plain and smooth in the beginning, and in the
end impassable; the other rough and troublesome in the entrance, but
after a while fair and even. So it is in contemplation; if a man will begin

with certainties, he shall end in doubts; but if he will be content to begin with doubts, he shall end in certainties.

Another error is in the manner of the tradition and delivery of knowledge, which is for the most part magistral and peremptory, and not ingenuous and faithful; in a sort as may be soonest believed, and not easiliest examined. It is true that in compendious treatises for practice that form is not to be disallowed. But in the true handling of knowledge, men ought not to fall either on the one side into the vein of Velleius the Epicurean, *Nil tam metuens, quàm ne dubitare aliqua de re videretur,* [who feared nothing so much as the seeming to be in doubt about anything,] nor on the other side into Socrates his ironical doubting of all things; but to propound things sincerely, with more or less asseveration, as they stand in a man's own judgment proved more or less.

Other errors there are in the scope that men propound to themselves, whereunto they bend their endeavours; for whereas the more constant and devote[1] kind of professors of any science ought to propound to themselves to make some additions to their science, they convert their labours to aspire to certain second prizes; as to be a profound interpreter or commenter, to be a sharp champion or defender, to be a methodical compounder or abridger; and so the patrimony of knowledge cometh to be sometimes improved, but seldom augmented.

But the greatest error of all the rest is the mistaking or misplacing of the last or furthest end of knowledge. For men have entered into a desire of learning and knowledge, sometimes upon a natural curiosity and inquisitive appetite; sometimes to entertain their minds with variety and delight; sometimes for ornament and reputation; and sometimes to enable them to victory of wit and contradiction; and most times for lucre and profession; and seldom sincerely to give a true account of their gift of reason, to the benefit and use of men: as if there were sought in knowledge a couch, whereupon to rest a searching and restless spirit; or a terrace, for a wandering and variable mind to walk up and down with a fair prospect; or a tower of state, for a proud mind to raise itself upon; or a fort or commanding ground, for strife and contention; or a shop, for profit or sale; and not a rich storehouse, for the glory of the Creator and the relief of man's estate. But this is that which will indeed dignify and exalt knowledge, if contemplation and action may be more nearly and straitly conjoined and united together than they have been;

[1] So the original. Ed. 1633 has *devoute.*

a conjunction like unto that of the two highest planets, Saturn the planet of rest and contemplation, and Jupiter the planet of civil society and action. Howbeit, I do not mean, when I speak of use and action, that end before-mentioned of the applying of knowledge to lucre and profession: for I am not ignorant how much that diverteth and interrupteth the prosecution and advancement of knowledge; like unto the golden ball thrown before Atalanta, which while she goeth aside and stoopeth to take up, the race is hindered,

*Declinat cursus, aurumque volubile tollit.*

Neither is my meaning, as was spoken of Socrates, to call philosophy down from heaven to converse upon the earth; that is, to leave natural philosophy aside, and to apply knowledge only to manners and policy. But as both heaven and earth do conspire and contribute to the use and benefit of man, so the end ought to be, from both philosophies to separate and reject vain speculations and whatsoever is empty and void, and to preserve and augment whatsoever is solid and fruitful; that knowledge may not be as a curtesan, for pleasure and vanity only, or as a bond-woman, to acquire and gain to her master's use; but as a spouse, for generation, fruit, and comfort.

Thus have I described and opened, as by a kind of dissection, those peccant humours (the principal of them) which have not only given impediment to the proficience of learning, but have given also occasion to the traducement thereof. . . .

## On Poesy and the Imagination

The parts of human learning have reference to the three parts of Man's Understanding, which is the seat of learning: History to his Memory, Poesy to his Imagination, and Philosophy to his Reason. Divine learning receiveth the same distribution; for the spirit of man is the same, though the revelation of oracle and sense be diverse: so as theology consisteth also of History of the Church; of Parables, which is divine poesy; and of holy Doctrine or precept. For as for that part which seemeth supernumerary, which is Prophecy, it is but divine history; which hath that prerogative over human, as the narration may be before the fact as well as after. . . .

Poesy is a part of learning in measure of words for the most part restrained, but in all other points extremely licensed, and doth truly refer to the Imagination; which, being not tied to the laws of matter, may at pleasure join that which nature hath severed, and sever that which nature hath joined, and so make unlawful matches and divorces of things: *Pictoribus atque poetis,* &c. [Painters and Poets have always been allowed to take what liberties they would.] It is taken in two senses, in respect of words or matter. In the first sense it is but a character of style, and belongeth to arts of speech, and is not pertinent for the present. In the later, it is (as hath been said) one of the principal portions of learning, and is nothing else but Feigned History, which may be styled as well in prose as in verse.

The use of this Feigned History hath been to give some shadow of satisfaction to the mind of man in those points wherein the nature of things doth deny it; the world being in proportion inferior to the soul; by reason whereof there is agreeable to the spirit of man a more ample greatness, a more exact goodness, and a more absolute variety, than can be found in the nature of things. Therefore, because the acts or events of true history have not that magnitude which satisfieth the mind of man, poesy feigneth acts and events greater and more heroical; because true history propoundeth the successes and issues of actions not so agreeable to the merits of virtue and vice, therefore poesy feigns them more just in retribution, and more according to revealed providence; because true history representeth actions and events more ordinary and less interchanged, therefore poesy endueth them with more rareness, and more unexpected and alternative variations. So as it appeareth that poesy serveth and conferreth to magnanimity, morality, and to delectation. And therefore it was ever thought to have some participation of divineness, because it doth raise and erect the mind, by submitting the shews of things to the desires of the mind; whereas reason doth buckle and bow the mind unto the nature of things. And we see that by these insinuations and congruities with man's nature and pleasure, joined also with the agreement and consort it hath with music, it hath had access and estimation in rude times and barbarous regions, where other learning stood excluded.

The division of poesy which is aptest in the propriety thereof, (besides those divisions which are common unto it with history, as feigned chronicles, feigned lives; and the appendices of history, as feigned epistles, feigned orations, and the rest;) is into Poesy Narrative, Representative, and Allusive. The Narrative is a mere imitation of history, with the excesses before remembered; choosing for subject commonly wars and love, rarely state, and sometimes pleasure or mirth. Representative is as a visible history, and is an image of actions as if they were present, as history is of actions in nature as they are, (that is) past. Allusive or Parabolical is a narration applied only to express some special purpose or conceit.[3] Which later kind of parabolical wisdom was much more in use in the ancient times, as by the fables of Æsop and the brief sentences of the Seven and the use of hieroglyphics may appear. And the cause was, for that it was then of necessity to express any point of reason which was more sharp or subtile than the vulgar in that manner; because men in those times wanted both variety of examples and subtilty of conceit: and as hieroglyphics were before letters, so parables were before arguments: and nevertheless now and at all times they do retain much life and vigour, because reason cannot be so sensible, nor examples so fit.

But there remaineth yet another use of Poesy Parabolical, opposite to that which we last mentioned: for that tendeth to demonstrate and illustrate that which is taught or delivered, and this other to retire and obscure it: that is when the secrets and mysteries of religion, policy, or philosophy are involved in fables or parables. Of this in divine poesy we see the use is authorized. In heathen poesy we see the exposition of fables doth fall out sometimes with great felicity; as in the fable that the giants being overthrown in their war against the gods, the Earth their mother in revenge thereof brought forth Fame:

> *Illam Terra parens, irâ irritata deorum,*
> *Extremam, ut perhibent, Cœo Enceladoque sororem*
> *Progenuit:*

expounded that when princes and monarchs have suppressed actual and open rebels, then the malignity of people (which is the mother of rebellion) doth bring forth libels and slanders and taxations of the state, which is of the same kind with rebellion, but more feminine. So in the fable that the rest of the gods having conspired to bind Jupiter, Pallas called Briareus with his hundred hands to his aid: expounded that

---

[3] This obscure sentence is explained in the translation to mean that Parabolic Poesy is *historia cum typo, quæ intellectualia deducit ad sensum,*—typical history, by which ideas that are objects of the Intellect are represented in forms that are objects of the Sense.

monarchies need not fear any curbing of their absoluteness by mighty subjects, as long as by wisdom they keep the hearts of the people, who will be sure to come in on their side. So in the fable that Achilles was brought up under Chiron the Centaur, who was part a man and part a beast: expounded ingeniously but corruptly by Machiavel, that it belongeth to the education and discipline of princes to know as well how to play the part of the lion in violence and the fox in guile, as of the man in virtue and justice.[4] Nevertheless in many the like encounters, I do rather think that the fable was first, and the exposition devised, than that the moral was first, and thereupon the fable framed. For I find it was an ancient vanity in Chrysippus, that troubled himself with great contention to fasten the assertions of the Stoics upon the fictions of the ancient poets. But yet that all the fables and fictions of the poets were but pleasure and not figure, I interpose no opinion. Surely of those poets which are now extant, even Homer himself, (notwithstanding he was made a kind of Scripture by the later schools of the Grecians,) yet I should without any difficulty pronounce that his fables had no such inwardness in his own meaning; but what they might have upon a more original tradition, is not easy to affirm; for he was not the inventor of many of them.

In this third part of learning, which is poesy, I can report no deficience. For being as a plant that cometh of the lust of the earth, without a formal seed, it hath sprung up and spread abroad more than any other kind. But to ascribe unto it that which is due; for the expressing of affections, passions, corruptions, and customs, we are beholding to poets more than to the philosophers' works; and for wit and eloquence not much less than to orators' harangues. But it is not good to stay too long in the theatre. Let us now pass on to the judicial place or palace of the mind, which we are to approach and view with more reverence and attention.

## Conclusion

Thus have I concluded this portion of learning touching Civil Knowledge; and with civil knowledge have concluded Human Philosophy; and with human philosophy, Philosophy in General. And being now at

---

[4] The Prince, c. 18. As two of the animals are the same it is possible that Macchiavelli was thinking of what was said of Boniface VIII. by the predecessor whom he forced to abdicate,—that he came in like a fox, would reign like a lion, and die like a dog.—*R. L. Ellis.*

some pause, looking back into that I have passed through, this writing seemeth to me, (*si nunquam fallit imago*) as far as a man can judge of his own work, not much better than that noise or sound which musicians make while they are tuning their instruments; which is nothing pleasant to hear, but yet is a cause why the music is sweeter afterwards. So have I been content to tune the instruments of the muses, that they may play that have better hands. And surely, when I set before me the condition of these times, in which learning hath made her third visitation or circuit, in all the qualities thereof; as the excellency and vivacity of the wits of this age; the noble helps and lights which we have by the travails of ancient writers; the art of printing, which communicateth books to men of all fortunes; the openness of the world by navigation, which hath disclosed multitudes of experiments, and a mass of natural history; the leisure wherewith these times abound, not employing men so generally in civil business, as the states of Græcia did in respect of their popularity, and the state of Rome in respect of the greatness of their monarchy; the present disposition of these times at this instant to peace; the consumption of all that ever can be said in controversies of religion, which have so much diverted men from other sciences; the perfection of your Majesty's learning, which as a phœnix may call whole vollies of wits to follow you; and the inseparable propriety of time, which is ever more and more to disclose truth; I cannot but be raised to this persuasion, that this third period of time will far surpass that of the Græcian and Roman learning: only if men will know their own strength and their own weakness both; and take one from the other light of invention, and not fire of contradiction; and esteem of the inquisition of truth as of an enterprise, and not as of a quality or ornament; and employ wit and magnificence to things of worth and excellency, and not to things vulgar and of popular estimation. As for my labours, if any man shall please himself or others in the reprehension of them, they shall make that ancient and patient request, *Verbera sed audi,* [strike me if you will, only hear me;] let men reprehend them, so they observe and weigh them. For the appeal is (lawful though it may be it shall not be needful) from the first cogitations of men to their second, and from the nearer times to the times further off. . . .

# DE DIGNITATE ET AUGMENTIS SCIENTIARUM

## Book II, Chap. XIII

On the Second Principal Part of Learning, Namely, Poesy. The Division of
Poesy into *Narrative, Dramatic,* and *Parabolical.* Three
Examples of Parabolical Poesy Are Propounded.

I now come to Poesy, which is a part of learning in measure of words
for the most part restrained, but in all other points extremely free and
licensed; and therefore (as I said at first) it is referred to the Imagination, which may at pleasure make unlawful matches and divorces of
things. Now Poesy (as I have already observed) is taken in two senses;
in respect of words or matter. In the first sense it is but a character of
speech; for verse is only a kind of style and a certain form of elocution,
and has nothing to do with the matter; for both true history may be
written in verse and feigned history in prose. But in the latter sense, I
have set it down from the first as one of the principal branches of learning, and placed it by the side of history; being indeed nothing else but
an imitation of history at pleasure. And therefore, endeavouring as I do
in these divisions to trace out and pursue the true veins of learning, without (in many points) following custom and the divisions which are
received, I dismiss from the present discourse Satires, Elegies, Epigrams,
Odes, and the like; and refer them to philosophy and arts of speech.
And under the name of Poesy, I treat only of feigned history.

The division of Poesy which is aptest and most according to the propriety thereof, besides those divisions which it has in common with History (for there are feigned Chronicles, feigned Lives, and feigned Relations), is into Poesy *Narrative, Dramatic,* and *Parabolical.* Narrative
Poesy is a mere imitation of History, such as might pass for real, only
that it commonly exaggerates things beyond probability. Dramatic Poesy
is as History made visible; for it represents actions as if they were present, whereas History represents them as past. Parabolical Poesy is typical
History, by which ideas that are objects of the intellect are represented
in forms that are objects of the sense.

As for Narrative Poesy,—or Heroical, if you like so to call it (understanding it of the matter, not of the verse)—the foundation of it is truly
noble, and has a special relation to the dignity of human nature. For as
the sensible world is inferior in dignity to the rational soul, Poesy seems

to bestow upon human nature those things which history denies to it; and to satisfy the mind with the shadows of things when the substance cannot be obtained. For if the matter be attentively considered, a sound argument may be drawn from Poesy, to show that there is agreeable to the spirit of man a more ample greatness, a more perfect order, and a more beautiful variety than it can anywhere (since the Fall) find in nature. And therefore, since the acts and events which are the subjects of real history are not of sufficient grandeur to satisfy the human mind, Poesy is at hand to feign acts more heroical; since the successes and issues of actions as related in true history are far from being agreeable to the merits of virtue and vice, Poesy corrects it, exhibiting events and fortunes as according to merit and the law of providence; since true history wearies the mind with satiety of ordinary events, one like another, Poesy refreshes it, by reciting things unexpected and various and full of vicissitudes. So that this Poesy conduces not only to delight but also to magnanimity and morality. Whence it may be fairly thought to partake somewhat of a divine nature; because it raises the mind and carries it aloft, accommodating the shows of things to the desires of the mind, not (like reason and history) buckling and bowing down the mind to the nature of things. And by these charms, and that agreeable congruity which it has with man's nature, accompanied also with music, to gain more sweet access, it has so won its way as to have been held in honour even in the rudest ages and among barbarous peoples, when other kinds of learning were utterly excluded.

Dramatic Poesy, which has the theatre for its world, would be of excellent use if well directed. For the stage is capable of no small influence both of discipline and of corruption. Now of corruptions in this kind we have enough; but the discipline has in our times been plainly neglected. And though in modern states play-acting is esteemed but as a toy, except when it is too satirical and biting; yet among the ancients it was used as a means of educating men's minds to virtue. Nay, it has been regarded by learned men and great philosophers as a kind of musician's bow by which men's minds may be played upon. And certainly it is most true, and one of the great secrets of nature, that the minds of men are more open to impressions and affections when many are gathered together than when they are alone.

But Parabolical Poesy is of a higher character than the others, and appears to be something sacred and venerable; especially as religion itself commonly uses its aid as a means of communication between divinity and humanity. But this too is corrupted by the levity and idleness of wits in dealing with allegory. It is of double use and serves for contrary purposes; for it serves for an infoldment; and it likewise serves for illustration. In the latter case the object is a certain method of teaching, in the former an artifice for concealment. Now this method of teaching, used for illustration, was very much in use in the ancient times. For the inventions and conclusions of human reason (even those that are now common and trite) being then new and strange, the minds of men were hardly subtle enough to conceive them, unless they were brought nearer to the sense by this kind of resemblances and examples. And hence the ancient times are full of all kinds of fables, parables, enigmas, and similitudes; as may appear by the numbers of Pythagoras, the enigmas of the Sphinx, the fables of Æsop, and the like. The Apophthegms too of the ancient sages commonly explained the matter by similitudes. Thus Menenius Agrippa among the Romans (a nation at that time by no means learned) quelled a sedition by a fable. In a word, as hieroglyphics were before letters, so parables were before arguments. And even now, and at all times, the force of parables is and has been excellent; because arguments cannot be made so perspicuous nor true examples so apt.

But there remains yet another use of Poesy Parabolical, opposite to the former; wherein it serves (as I said) for an infoldment; for such things, I mean, the dignity whereof requires that they should be seen as it were through a veil; that is when the secrets and mysteries of religion, policy, and philosophy are involved in fables or parables. Now whether any mystic meaning be concealed beneath the fables of the ancient poets is a matter of some doubt. For my own part I must confess that I am inclined to think that a mystery is involved in no small number of them. Nor does the fact that they are left commonly to boys and grammarians, and held in slight repute, make me despise them; but rather, since it is evident that the writings in which these fables are related are, next to sacred story, the most ancient of human writings, and the fables themselves still more ancient (for they are related not as being invented by the writers, but as things believed and received from of old), I take them to be a kind of breath from the traditions of more ancient nations, which fell into the pipes of the Greeks. But since that which has hitherto been done in the interpretation of these parables, being the work of unskilful men, not learned beyond common places, does not by any means satisfy me, I think fit to set down Philosophy according to the Ancient Parables among the *desiderata*. Of which work I will subjoin one or two examples; not so much perhaps for the value of the thing as for the sake of carrying out my principle; which is this; whenever I set down a work among the desiderata (if there be anything obscure about it), I intend always to set forth either instructions for the execution of it, or an example of the thing; else it might be thought that it was merely some light notion that had glanced through my mind; or that I am like an augur measuring countries in thought, without knowing the way to enter them. I can report no other deficiency in Poesy; for being as a plant which comes from the lust of the earth without a formal seed, it has sprung up and spread abroad more than any other kind of learning. But I will now propound the examples, only three in number; one taken from things Natural, one from things Political, and one from things Moral. . . .

The Third Example of Philosophy according to the Ancient Fables, *in Moral Philosophy*. Of Desire, according to the Fable of *Dionysus*.

They say that Semele, the mistress of Jupiter, having bound him by an inviolable oath to grant her a request whatever it might be, desired of him to come to her arms in the same form as he would to Juno; and so she was scorched to death in his embrace. The child which she bore in her womb was taken by his father and sewn up in his thigh, till the time of gestation was accomplished. And because the child, when in the thigh of Jupiter, pinched and galled him so as to make him limp, he received the name of Dionysus. After he was brought forth he was nursed for some years by Proserpine; and when he grew up his face was so like a woman's that it seemed doubtful of which sex he was. He was likewise once dead and buried for a time, but came to life again not long after. In his early youth he was the first to invent and explain the culture of the vine, and the making of wine, and its use; whereby becoming renowned and illustrious, he subdued the whole world and advanced to the furthest parts of India. He rode in a chariot drawn by tigers, round which danced certain deformed demons called Cobali; Acratus and others. The Muses also attended in his train. He took to wife Ariadne, whom Theseus had deserted and abandoned. His sacred tree was the ivy. He was regarded likewise as the inventor and institutor of sacred rites and orgies; but such as were fanatical and full of corruption, and moreover cruel. He had also the power of exciting phrensy. At least it was by women excited to phrensy in his orgies that two renowned men, Pentheus and Orpheus, are said to have been torn to pieces; the one having climbed into a tree out of curiosity to see what they were doing; the other while playing sweetly and skilfully on the lyre. Moreover the actions of this god are often confounded with those of Jupiter.

The fable appears to relate to morals; and indeed there is scarcely anything better to be found in moral philosophy. Under the person of Bacchus is depicted the nature of Desire, or the passions and perturbations of the mind. First therefore, with regard to the origin of Desire. The mother of all desire (though ever so hurtful) is nothing else than apparent good. For as the mother of virtue is real good, so the mother of desire is apparent good. One the lawful wife of Jupiter (in whose person the human soul is represented), the other his mistress; who nevertheless aspires, like Semele, to the honours of Juno. Now the conception of Desire is always in some unlawful wish, rashly granted before it has been understood and weighed; and as the passion warms, its mother (which is the nature and species of good), not able to endure the heat of it, is destroyed and perishes in the flame. Then the progress of Desire from its first conception is of this kind. It is both nursed and concealed in the human mind (which is its father); especially in the lower part of it, as in the thigh; where it causes such prickings, pains, and depressions, that the actions and resolutions of the mind labour and limp with it. And even when it has grown strong with indulgence and custom, and breaks forth into acts (as if it had now accomplished its time and were fairly born and delivered), yet at first it is brought up for a time by Proserpine; that is, it seeks hiding-places and keeps itself secret, and as it were underground; until throwing off all restraints of shame and fear, and growing bolder and bolder, it either assumes the mask of some virtue, or sets infamy itself at defiance. And it is most true that every passion of the more violent kind is as it were of doubtful sex; for it has at once the force of a man and the weakness of a woman. It is well said likewise that Bacchus died and came to life again; for the passions seem sometimes lulled to sleep, and as it were dead; yet can they never be trusted, no not though they be buried. For give them matter and opportunity and they will rise again.

It is a wise allegory too, that of the invention of the vine. For every passion is very ingenious and sagacious in discovering the things which nourish and foster itself. Now of all things known to man wine is the most powerful and efficacious in stimulating and inflaming every kind of excitement; serving as a common fuel to desires in general. Very elegantly too is passion or desire described as the subduer of provinces and the undertaker of an endless course of conquests. For it is never content with what it has got, but with infinite and insatiable appetite tries for something more, and ever craves for new triumphs. Tigers likewise are kept in the stables of the passions, and at times yoked to their chariot; for when passion ceases to go on foot and comes to ride in its chariot, as in celebration of its victory and triumph over reason, then is it cruel, savage, and pitiless towards all that withstand or oppose it. Again there is humour in making those ridiculous demons dance about the chariot of Bacchus. For every passion of the more vehement kind produces motions in the eyes, and indeed in the whole countenance and gesture, which are uncomely, unsettled, skipping, and deformed; insomuch that when a man under the influence of any passion (as anger, scorn, love, or the like) seems most grand and imposing in his own eyes, to the lookers on he appears unseemly and ridiculous. It is true also that the Muses are seen in the train of passion; there being scarce any passion which has not some branch of learning to flatter it. For herein the majesty of the Muses suffers immensely from the license and wantonness of men's wits, turning those that should be the guides and standard-bearers of man's life into mere followers in the train and ministers to the pleasures of the passions.

Especially noble again is that part of the allegory which represents Bacchus as lavishing his love upon one whom another man had cast off. For most certain it is that passion ever seeks and aspires after that which experience has long since repudiated. And let all men who in pursuit and indulgence of their passions care not what price they pay for the enjoyment of them, know this: that whatever be the object of their pursuit—be it honour or fortune or love or glory or knowledge, or what it may—they are paying court to things cast off,—things which many men in all times have tried, and upon trial rejected with disgust.

Nor is the consecration of Ivy to Bacchus without its mystery. For this has a double propriety. First, because ivy flourishes in the winter; next because it has the property of creeping and spreading about so many things, as trees, walls, buildings, &c. For as to the first, every passion flourishes and acquires vigour by being resisted and forbidden, as by reaction or *antiperistasis;* like the ivy by the cold of winter. As to the second, any predominant passion in the human spirit spreads itself like ivy round all its actions and resolves, so that you cannot find anything free from the embrace of its tendrils Neither is it to be wondered at if superstitious rites are attributed to Bacchus; for almost every insane passion grows rank in depraved religions, insomuch that the pollutions of heretics are worse than the Bacchanalian orgies of the heathen; whose superstitions likewise have been no less bloody than foul. Neither again is it wonderful that phrensies are thought to be inspired by Bacchus; since every passion, in the excess thereof, is like a short madness, and if it continue vehement and obstinate, commonly ends in insanity. And that circumstance of the tearing to pieces of Pentheus and Orpheus amid the orgies of Bacchus, has an evident allegorical meaning; for every ruling passion is extremely hostile and inveterate against two things; whereof the one is curious inquisition; the other, free and wholesome advice. Nor does it make any difference if that inquisition be merely for the sake of looking on, as from a tree, without any ill-feeling; nor again if the advice be tendered ever so sweetly and skilfully; for the orgies cannot upon any conditions endure either Pentheus or Orpheus. Lastly, the confusion of the persons of Jupiter and Bacchus may well be taken in an allegorical sense. For noble and illustrious actions and glorious and distinguished services proceed sometimes from virtue, right reason, and magnanimity; and sometimes (however they are extolled and applauded without distinction) only from lurking passion and hidden desire; and thus the deeds of Bacchus are not easily distinguished from the deeds of Jupiter.

But we stay too long in the theatre; let us now pass to the palace of the mind, which we are to approach and enter with more reverence and attention.

## Book III, Chap. I

Division of Science into *Theology* and *Philosophy*. Division of Philosophy into Three Doctrines; Concerning the *Deity,* Concerning *Nature,* and Concerning *Man*. Constitution of *Primary Philosophy,* as the Common Mother of All.

All History, excellent King, walks upon the earth, and performs the office rather of a guide than of a light; whereas Poesy is as a dream of learning; a thing sweet and varied, and that would be thought to have in it something divine; a character which dreams likewise affect. But now it is time for me to awake, and rising above the earth, to wing my way through the clear air of Philosophy and the Sciences.

The knowledge of man is as the waters. Some waters descend from above, and some spring from beneath; and in like manner the primary division of sciences is to be drawn from their sources; of which some are above in the heavens, and some here below. For all knowledge admits of two kinds of information; the one inspired by divine revelation, the other arising from the senses. For as to that knowledge which man receives by teaching, it is cumulative and not original; as it is likewise in waters, which beside their own springheads, are fed with other springs and streams. I will therefore divide knowledge into Divinity and Philosophy; meaning by Divinity Sacred or Inspired, not Natural Divinity; of which I will speak hereafter. But this (namely, Inspired Divinity) I will reserve to the end, that with it I may conclude my discourse; being as it is the haven and sabbath of all human contemplations.

The object of philosophy is threefold—God, Nature, and Man; as there are likewise three kinds of ray—direct, refracted, and reflected. For nature strikes the understanding with a ray direct; God, by reason of the unequal medium (viz. his creatures), with a ray refracted; man, as shown and exhibited to himself, with a ray reflected. Philosophy may therefore be conveniently divided into three branches of knowledge: knowledge of God, knowledge of Nature, and knowledge of Man, or Humanity. But since the divisions of knowledge are not like several lines that meet in one angle; but are rather like branches of a tree that meet in one stem (which stem grows for some distance entire and continuous, before it divide itself into arms and boughs); therefore it is necessary before we enter into the branches of the former division, to erect and constitute one universal science, to be as the mother of the rest, and to be regarded in the progress of knowledge as portion of the main and common way, before we come where the ways part and divide themselves. This science I distinguish by the name of *Philosophia Prima,* primitive or summary philosophy; or *Sapience,* which was formerly defined as the knowledge of things divine and human. To this no other is opposed; for it differs from the rest rather in the limits within which it ranges than in the subject matter; treating only of the highest stages of things. Which science whether I should report as deficient or not, I stand doubtful, though I rather incline to do so. For I find a certain rhapsody and incongruous mass of Natural Theology, of Logic, and of some parts of Natural Philosophy (as those concerning First Principles and the Soul), all mixed up and confused, and in the lofty language of men who take delight in admiring themselves advanced as it were to the pinnacle of the sciences. But setting all high conceits aside, my meaning is simply this: that a science be constituted, which may be a receptacle for all such axioms as are not peculiar to any of the particular sciences, but belong to several of them in common.

Now that there are very many axioms of that kind need not be doubted. For example, "if equals be added to unequals the wholes will be unequal," is a rule of mathematics. The same holds in ethics, as regards distributive justice; for in commutative justice the rule of equity requires that equals be given to unequals; whereas in distributive, if unequals be not given to unequals there is the greatest injustice. Again "things that are equal to the same are equal to one another," is likewise a rule of mathematics; but it is at the same time so potent in logic as to be the basis of the syllogism. "The nature of everything is best seen in its smallest portions," is a rule in Physics of such force that it produced the atoms of Democritus; and yet Aristotle made good use of it in his Politics, where he commences his inquiry of the nature of a commonwealth with a family. "All things are changed and nothing is lost," is in like manner a rule in Physics, exhibited thus, "The Quantum of nature is neither diminished nor increased." The same holds in Natural Theology, with this variation, "It is the work of omnipotence to make somewhat nothing, and to make nothing somewhat;" which likewise the Scripture testifies; "I know that whatsoever God doeth, it shall be for ever; nothing can be put to it, nor anything taken from it." "Things are preserved from destruction by bringing them back to their first principles," is a rule in Physics; the same holds good in Politics (as Macchiavelli rightly observed), for there is scarcely anything which preserves states from destruction more than the reformation and reduction of them to their ancient manners. "Putrefaction is more contagious before than after maturity," is a rule in Physics; the same is eminently true in Morals, for the men who are most wicked and profligate produce less corruption in the public manners than those who appear to have some soundness and virtue in them, and are only partly evil. "Whatever is preservative of a greater Form is more powerful in action," is a rule in Physics; for that the connexion of things should not be severed, nor a vacuum (as they call it) admitted, tends to preserve the fabric of the universe; whereas the collection of heavy bodies towards the mass of the earth tends to preserve only the region of dense bodies; and therefor the first motion overcomes the last. The same holds in Politics; for whatsoever contributes to preserve the whole state in its own nature, has greater power than that which only benefits the particular members of that state. It holds likewise in Theology; for of the theological virtues, charity, which is the virtue most communicative of good, excels all the rest. "The force of an agent is increased by the reaction of a contrary," is a rule in Physics. The same has wonderful efficacy in Politics, since every faction is violently irritated by the encroachment of a contrary faction. "A discord ending immediately in a concord sets off the harmony," is a rule in Music. The same holds in Ethics and in the affections. The trope of Music, to glide gently from the close or cadence (as they call it) when you seem to be on the point of it, resembles the trope of Rhetoric, of deceiving expectation. The quavering upon a stop in music gives the same pleasure to the ear as the playing of light on water or a diamond gives to the eye;

——*splendet tremulo sub lumine pontus.*[1]

"The organs of the senses resemble the organs of reflexions," is a rule in Perspective; for the eye is like to a glass, or to water; and it is the same in Acoustics, for the instrument of hearing is like an obstruction in a cavern. These few cases are enough by way of examples. But indeed the chief business of the Persian magic (so much celebrated) was to note the correspondences between the architectures and fabrics of things natural and things civil. Neither are all these which I have mentioned, and others of this kind, only similitudes (as men of narrow observation may perhaps conceive them to be), but plainly the same footsteps of nature treading or printing upon different subjects and matters. And it is a thing which has not as yet been carefully handled. You may perhaps find in the writings of the profounder sort of wits such axioms here and there sparingly inserted for the use of the argument they have in hand; but for any body of such axioms, which should tend primitively and summarily to the advancement of the sciences, no one has as yet collected one; though it is a thing of excellent use for displaying the unity of nature; which is supposed to be the true office of Primitive Philosophy.

There is also another part of this philosophy, which, if you look to the terms, is ancient, if to the thing which I mean, is new. It is an inquiry with regard to the Adventitious Conditions of Essences (which we may call Transcendentals), as Much, Little; Like, Unlike; Possible, Impossible; likewise Being and Not-Being, and the like. For since these do not properly come under Physic, and the logical discussion concern-

[1] Virg. Æn. vii. 9.:—Beneath the trembling light glitters the sea.

ing them belongs rather to the laws of reasoning than to the existence
of things, it is very proper that the consideration of them (wherein there
is no little dignity and profit) should not be altogether neglected, but
should find at least some place in the divisions of the sciences. Nevertheless I mean that it should be handled in a way very different from
the common. For example; no one who has treated of Much and Little
has endeavoured to assign a reason why some things in nature are and
can be so numerous and plentiful, others so few and scanty; for it
certainly cannot be that in the nature of things there should be as much
gold as iron; that roses should be as abundant as grass; and that there
should be as great variety of the specific as of the non-specific. In like
manner no one in handling Similitude and Diversity has sufficiently
explained why betwixt different species there almost always lie certain
individuals which partake of the nature of both; as moss between corruption and a plant; fishes that stick to rocks and cannot move away,
between a plant and an animal; rats and mice, and some other things,
between animals generated of putrefaction and of seed; bats, between
birds and beasts; flying-fish (which are now well known), between birds
and fishes; seals, between fishes and quadrupeds; and the like. Nor has
any one inquired the reason why, seeing that likes delight in likes,
iron does not attract iron, which the magnet does; nor why gold does not
attract gold, though it does attract quicksilver. With regard to these
and similar things in the discussion of Transcendentals there is a deep
silence; for men have aimed rather at height of speech than at the
subtleties of things. Wherefore I wish the real and solid inquiry, according to the laws of nature and not of language, concerning these Transcendentals or Adventitious Conditions of Essences, to have a place in
Primitive or Summary Philosophy. And so much for *Philosophia Prima*
(or Sapience), which I have with reason set down as deficient.

# NOVUM ORGANUM

## PREFACE

Now my method, though hard to practise, is easy to explain; and it
is this. I propose to establish progressive stages of certainty. The evi-

dence of the sense, helped and guarded by a certain process of correction, I retain. But the mental operation which follows the act of sense I for the most part reject; and instead of it I open and lay out a new and certain path for the mind to proceed in, starting directly from the simple sensuous perception. The necessity of this was felt no doubt by those who attributed so much importance to Logic; showing thereby that they were in search of helps for the understanding, and had no confidence in the native and spontaneous process of the mind. But this remedy comes too late to do any good, when the mind is already, through the daily intercourse and conversation of life, occupied with unsound doctrines and beset on all sides by vain imaginations. And therefore the art of Logic, coming (as I said) too late to the rescue, and no way able to set matters right again, has had the effect of fixing errors rather than disclosing truth. There remains but one course for the recovery of a sound and healthy condition,—namely, that the entire work of the understanding be commenced afresh, and the mind itself be from the very outset not left to take its own course, but guided at every step; and the business be done as if by machinery. Certainly if in things mechanical men had set to work with their naked hands, without help or force of instruments, just as in things intellectual they have set to work with little else than the naked forces of the understanding, very small would the matters have been which, even with their best efforts applied in conjunction, they could have attempted or accomplished. Now (to pause awhile upon this example and look in it as in a glass) let us suppose that some vast obelisk were (for the decoration of a triumph or some such magnificence) to be removed from its place, and that men should set to work upon it with their naked hands; would not any sober spectator think them mad?

## BOOK I—APHORISMS CONCERNING THE INTERPRETATION OF NATURE AND THE KINGDOM OF MAN

### Human Knowlege and Human Power

1. Man, being the servant and interpreter of Nature, can do and understand so much and so much only as he has observed in fact or in thought of the course of nature: beyond this he neither knows anything nor can do anything.

II.  Neither the naked hand nor the understanding left to itself can effect much. It is by instruments and helps that the work is done, which are as much wanted for the understanding as for the hand. And as the instruments of the hand either give motion or guide it, so the instruments of the mind supply either suggestions for the understanding or cautions.

III.  Human knowledge and human power meet in one; for where the cause is not known the effect cannot be produced. Nature to be commanded must be obeyed; and that which in contemplation is as the cause is in operation as the rule.

IV.  Towards the effecting of works, all that man can do is to put together or put asunder natural bodies. The rest is done by nature working within.

V.  The study of nature with a view to works is engaged in by the mechanic, the mathematician, the physician, the alchemist, and the magician; but by all (as things now are) with slight endeavour and scanty success.

VI.  It would be an unsound fancy and self-contradictory to expect that things which have never yet been done can be done except by means which have never yet been tried.

VII.  The productions of the mind and hand seem very numerous in books and manufactures. But all this variety lies in an exquisite subtlety and derivations from a few things already known; not in the number of axioms.

VIII.  Moreover the works already known are due to chance and experiment rather than to sciences; for the sciences we now possess are merely systems for the nice ordering and setting forth of things already invented; not methods of invention or directions for new works.

IX.  The cause and root of nearly all evils in the sciences is this—that while we falsely admire and extol the powers of the human mind we neglect to seek for its true helps.

x. The subtlety of nature is greater many times over than the subtlety of the senses and understanding; so that all those specious meditations, speculations, and glosses in which men indulge are quite from the purpose,[1] only there is no one by to observe it.

xi. As the sciences which we now have do not help us in finding out new works, so neither does the logic which we now have help us in finding out new sciences.

xii. The logic now in use serves rather to fix and give stability to the errors which have their foundation in commonly received notions than to help the search after truth. So it does more harm than good.

xiii. The syllogism is not applied to the first principles of sciences, and is applied in vain to intermediate axioms; being no match for the subtlety of nature. It commands assent therefore to the proposition, but does not take hold of the thing.

xiv. The syllogism consists of propositions, propositions consist of words, words are symbols of notions. Therefore if the notions themselves (which is the root of the matter) are confused and over-hastily abstracted from the facts, there can be no firmness in the superstructure. Our only hope therefore lies in a true induction.

xv. There is no soundness in our notions whether logical or physical. Substance, Quality, Action, Passion, Essence itself, are not sound notions: much less are Heavy, Light, Dense, Rare, Moist, Dry, Generation, Corruption, Attraction, Repulsion, Element, Matter, Form, and the like; but all are fantastical and ill defined.

xvi. Our notions of less general species, as Man, Dog, Dove, and of the immediate perceptions of the sense, as Hot, Cold, Black, White, do not materially mislead us; yet even these are sometimes confused by the flux

[1] Literally, "are a thing insane." The meaning appears to be, that these speculations, being founded upon such an inadequate conception of the case, must necessarily be so wide of the truth that they would seem like mere madness if we could only compare them with it: like the aim of a man blindfolded to bystanders looking on.—*J. Spedding*

and alteration of matter and the mixing of one thing with another. All the others which men have hitherto adopted are but wanderings, not being abstracted and formed from things by proper methods.

xvii.    Nor is there less of wilfulness and wandering in the construction of axioms than in the formations of notions; not excepting even those very principles which are obtained by common induction; but much more in the axioms and lower propositions educed by the syllogism.

xviii.    The discoveries which have hitherto been made in the sciences are such as lie close to vulgar notions, scarcely beneath the surface. In order to penetrate into the inner and further recesses of nature, it is necessary that both notions and axioms be derived from things by a more sure and guarded way; and that a method of intellectual operation be introduced altogether better and more certain.

xix.    There are and can be only two ways of searching into and discovering truth. The one flies from the senses and particulars to the most general axioms, and from these principles, the truth of which it takes for settled and immoveable, proceeds to judgment and to the discovery of middle axioms. And this way is now in fashion. The other derives axioms from the senses and particulars, rising by a gradual and unbroken ascent, so that it arrives at the most general axioms last of all. This is the true way, but as yet untried.

xx.    The understanding left to itself takes the same course (namely, the former) which it takes in accordance with logical order. For the mind longs to spring up to positions of higher generality, that it may find rest there; and so after a little while wearies of experiment. But this evil is increased by logic, because of the order and solemnity of its disputations.

xxi.    The understanding left to itself, in a sober, patient, and grave mind, especially if it be not hindered by received doctrines, tries a little that other way, which is the right one, but with little progress; since the understanding, unless directed and assisted, is a thing unequal, and quite unfit to contend with the obscurity of things.

xxii.    Both ways set out from the senses and particulars, and rest in the highest generalities; but the difference between them is infinite. For the

one just glances at experiment and particulars in passing, the other
dwells duly and orderly among them. The one, again, begins at once
by establishing certain abstract and useless generalities, the other rises by
gradual steps to that which is prior and better known in the order of
nature.

## Idols

xxiii.   There is a great difference between the Idols of the human mind
and the Ideas of the divine. That is to say, between certain empty dogmas, and the true signatures and marks set upon the works of creation
as they are found in nature. . . .

xxxviii.   The idols and false notions which are now in possession of
the human understanding, and have taken deep root therein, not only
so beset men's minds that truth can hardly find entrance, but even after
entrance obtained, they will again in the very instauration of the sciences
meet and trouble us, unless men being forewarned of the danger fortify
themselves as far as may be against their assaults.

xxxix.   There are four classes of Idols which beset men's minds. To
these for distinction's sake I have assigned names,—calling the first class
*Idols of the Tribe;* the second, *Idols of the Cave;* the third, *Idols of the
Market-place;* the fourth, *Idols of the Theatre.*

xl.   The formation of ideas and axioms by true induction is no doubt
the proper remedy to be applied for the keeping off and clearing away of
idols. To point them out, however, is of great use; for the doctrine of
Idols is to the Interpretation of Nature what the doctrine of the refuta-
tion of Sophisms is to common Logic.

### Idols of the Tribe

xli.   The Idols of the Tribe have their foundation in human nature
itself, and in the tribe or race of men. For it is a false assertion that the
sense of man is the measure of things. On the contrary, all perceptions
as well of the sense as of the mind are according to the measure of the
individual and not according to the measure of the universe. And the
human understanding is like a false mirror, which, receiving rays irregu-

larly, distorts and discolours the nature of things by mingling its own nature with it.

XLV. The human understanding is of its own nature prone to suppose the existence of more order and regularity in the world than it finds. And though there be many things in nature which are singular and unmatched, yet it devises for them parallels and conjugates and relatives which do not exist. Hence the fiction that all celestial bodies move in perfect circles; spirals and dragons being (except in name) utterly rejected. Hence too the element of Fire with its orb is brought in, to make up the square with the other three which the sense perceives. Hence also the ratio of density of the so-called elements is arbitrarily fixed at ten to one. And so on of other dreams. And these fancies affect not dogmas only, but simple notions also.

XLVI. The human understanding when it has once adopted an opinion (either as being the received opinion or as being agreeable to itself) draws all things else to support and agree with it. And though there be a greater number and weight of instances to be found on the other side, yet these it either neglects and despises, or else by some distinction sets aside and rejects; in order that by this great and pernicious predetermination the authority of its former conclusions may remain inviolate. And therefore it was a good answer that was made by one who when they showed him hanging in a temple a picture of those who had paid their vows as having escaped shipwreck, and would have him say whether he did not now acknowledge the power of the gods,—"Aye," asked he again, "but where are they painted that were drowned after their vows?" And such is the way of all superstition, whether in astrology, dreams, omens, divine judgments, or the like; wherein men, having a delight in such vanities, mark the events where they are fulfilled, but where they fail, though this happen much oftener, neglect and pass them by. But with far more subtlety does this mischief insinuate itself into philosophy and the sciences; in which the first conclusion colours and brings into conformity with itself all that come after, though far sounder and better. Besides, independently of that delight and vanity which I have described, it is the peculiar and perpetual error of the human intellect to be more moved and excited by affirmatives than by negatives; whereas it ought properly to hold itself indifferently disposed towards both alike. Indeed in the establishment of any true axiom, the negative instance is the more forcible of the two.

XLVII.   The human understanding is moved by those things most which strike and enter the mind simultaneously and suddenly, and so fill the imagination; and then it feigns and supposes all other things to be somehow, though it cannot see how, similar to those few things by which it is surrounded. But for that going to and fro to remote and heterogeneous instances, by which axioms are tried as in the fire, the intellect is altogether slow and unfit, unless it be forced thereto by severe laws and overruling authority.

XLVIII.   The human understanding is unquiet; it cannot stop or rest, and still presses onward, but in vain. Therefore it is that we cannot conceive of any end or limit to the world; but always as of necessity it occurs to us that there is something beyond. Neither again can it be conceived how eternity has flowed down to the present day; for that distinction which is commonly received of infinity in time past and in time to come can by no means hold; for it would thence follow that one infinity is greater than another, and that infinity is wasting away and tending to become finite. The like subtlety arises touching the infinite divisibility of lines, from the same inability of thought to stop. But this inability interferes more mischievously in the discovery of causes: for although the most general principles in nature ought to be held merely positive, as they are discovered, and cannot with truth be referred to a cause; nevertheless the human understanding being unable to rest still seeks something prior in the order of nature. And then it is that in struggling towards that which is further off it falls back upon that which is more nigh at hand; namely, on final causes: which have relation clearly to the nature of man rather than to the nature of the universe; and from this source have strangely defiled philosophy. But he is no less an unskilled and shallow philosopher who seeks causes of that which is most general, than he who in things subordinate and subaltern omits to do so.

XLIX.   The human understanding is no dry light, but receives an infusion from the will and affections; whence proceed sciences which may be called "sciences as one would." For what a man had rather were true he more readily believes. Therefore he rejects difficult things from impatience of research; sober things, because they narrow hope; the deeper things of nature, from superstition; the light of experience, from arrogance and pride, lest his mind should seem to be occupied with things mean and transitory; things not commonly believed, out of deference to the opinion of the vulgar. Numberless in short are the ways, and sometimes imperceptible, in which the affections colour and infect the understanding.

L. But by far the greatest hindrance and aberration of the human understanding proceeds from the dulness, incompetency, and deceptions of the senses; in that things which strike the sense outweigh things which do not immediately strike it, though they be more important. Hence it is that speculation commonly ceases where sight ceases; insomuch that of things invisible there is little or no observation. Hence all the working of the spirits inclosed in tangible bodies lies hid and unobserved of men. So also all the more subtle changes of form in the parts of coarser substances (which they commonly call alteration, though it is in truth local motion through exceedingly small spaces) is in like manner unobserved. And yet unless these two things just mentioned be searched out and brought to light, nothing great can be achieved in nature, as far as the production of works is concerned. So again the essential nature of our common air, and of all bodies less dense than air (which are very many), is almost unknown. For the sense by itself is a thing infirm and erring; neither can instruments for enlarging or sharpening the senses do much; but all the truer kind of interpretation of nature is effected by instances and experiments fit and apposite; wherein the sense decides touching the experiment only, and the experiment touching the point in nature and the thing itself.

LI. The human understanding is of its own nature prone to abstractions and gives a substance and reality to things which are fleeting. But to resolve nature into abstractions is less to our purpose than to dissect her into parts; as did the school of Democritus, which went further into nature than the rest. Matter rather than forms should be the object of our attention, its configurations and changes of configuration, and simple action, and law of action or motion; for forms are figments of the human mind, unless you will call those laws of action forms.

LII. Such then are the idols which I call *Idols of the Tribe;* and which take their rise either from the homogeneity of the substance of the human spirit, or from its preoccupation, or from its narrowness, or from its restless motion, or from an infusion of the affections, or from the incompetency of the senses, or from the mode of impression.

## Idols of the Cave

XLII. The Idols of the Cave are the idols of the individual man. For every one (besides the errors common to human nature in general) has a cave or den of his own, which refracts and discolours the light of nature; owing either to his own proper and peculiar nature; or to his education and conversation with others; or to the reading of books, and the authority of those whom he esteems and admires; or to the differences of impressions, accordingly as they take place in a mind preoccupied and predisposed or in a mind indifferent and settled; or the like. So that the spirit of man (according as it is meted out to different individuals) is in fact a thing variable and full of perturbation, and governed as it were by chance. Whence it was well observed by Heraclitus that men look for sciences in their own lesser worlds, and not in the greater or common world.

LIII. The *Idols of the Cave* take their rise in the peculiar constitution, mental or bodily, of each individual; and also in education, habit, and accident. Of this kind there is a great number and variety; but I will instance those the pointing out of which contains the most important caution, and which have most effect in disturbing the clearness of the understanding.

LIV. Men become attached to certain particular sciences and speculations, either because they fancy themselves the authors and inventors thereof, or because they have bestowed the greatest pains upon them and become most habituated to them. But men of this kind, if they betake themselves to philosophy and contemplations of a general character, distort and colour them in obedience to their former fancies; a thing especially to be noticed in Aristotle, who made his natural philosophy a mere bond-servant to his logic, thereby rendering it contentious and well nigh useless. The race of chemists again out of a few experiments of the furnace have built up a fantastic philosophy, framed with reference to a few things; and Gilbert also, after he had employed himself most laboriously in the study and observation of the loadstone, proceeded at once to construct an entire system in accordance with his favourite subject.

LV. There is one principal and as it were radical distinction between different minds, in respect of philosophy and the sciences; which is this: that some minds are stronger and apter to mark the differences of things, others to mark their resemblances. The steady and acute mind can fix its contemplations and dwell and fasten on the subtlest distinctions: the lofty and discursive mind recognises and puts together the finest and most general resemblances. Both kinds however easily err in excess, by catching the one at gradations the other at shadows.

LVI. There are found some minds given to an extreme admiration of antiquity, others to an extreme love and appetite for novelty; but few so duly tempered that they can hold the mean, neither carping at what has been well laid down by the ancients, nor despising what is well introduced by the moderns. This however turns to the great injury of the sciences and philosophy; since these affectations of antiquity and novelty are the humours of partisans rather than judgments; and truth is to be sought for not in the felicity of any age, which is an unstable thing, but in the light of nature and experience, which is eternal. These factions therefore must be abjured, and care must be taken that the intellect be not hurried by them into assent.

LVII. Contemplations of nature and of bodies in their simple form break up and distract the understanding, while contemplations of nature and bodies in their composition and configuration overpower and dissolve the understanding: a distinction well seen in the school of Leucippus and Democritus as compared with the other philosophies. For that school is so busied with the particles that it hardly attends to the structure; while the others are so lost in admiration of the structure that they do not penetrate to the simplicity of nature. These kinds of contemplation should therefore be alternated and taken by turns; that so the understanding may be rendered at once penetrating and comprehensive, and the inconveniences above mentioned, with the idols which proceed from them, may be avoided.

LVIII. Let such then be our provision and contemplative prudence for keeping off and dislodging the *Idols of the Cave,* which grow for the most part either out of the predominance of a favourite subject, or out of an excessive tendency to compare or to distinguish, or out of partiality for particular ages, or out of the largeness or minuteness of the objects contemplated. And generally let every student of nature take this as a rule,—that whatever his mind seizes and dwells upon with peculiar satisfaction is to be held in suspicion, and that so much the more care is to be taken in dealing with such questions to keep the understanding even and clear.

### Idols of the Market-place

XLIII. There are also Idols formed by the intercourse and association of men with each other, which I call Idols of the Market-place, on account of the commerce and consort of men there. For it is by discourse that men associate; and words are imposed according to the apprehension of the vulgar. And therefore the ill and unfit choice of words wonderfully obstructs the understanding. Nor do the definitions or explanations wherewith in some things learned men are wont to guard and defend themselves, by any means set the matter right. But words plainly force and overrule the understanding, and throw all into confusion, and lead men away into numberless empty controversies and idle fancies.

LIX. But the *Idols of the Market-place* are the most troublesome of all: idols which have crept into the understanding through the alliances of words and names. For men believe that their reason governs words; but it is also true that words react on the understanding; and this it is that has rendered philosophy and the sciences sophistical and inactive. Now words, being commonly framed and applied according to the capacity of the vulgar, follow those lines of division which are most obvious to the vulgar understanding. And whenever an understanding of greater acuteness or a more diligent observation would alter those lines to suit the true divisions of nature, words stand in the way and resist the change. Whence it comes to pass that the high and formal discussions of learned men end oftentimes in disputes about words and names; with which (according to the use and wisdom of the mathematicians) it would be more prudent to begin, and so by means of definitions reduce them to order. Yet even definitions cannot cure this evil in dealing with natural and material things; since the definitions themselves consist of words, and those words beget others: so that it is necessary to recur to individual instances, and those in due series and order; as I shall say presently when I come to the method and scheme for the formation of notions and axioms.

LX.  The idols imposed by words on the understanding are of two kinds. They are either names of things which do not exist (for as there are things left unnamed through lack of observation, so likewise are there names which result from fantastic suppositions and to which nothing in reality corresponds), or they are names of things which exist, but yet confused and ill-defined, and hastily and irregularly derived from realities. Of the former kind are Fortune, the Prime Mover, Planetary Orbits, Element of Fire, and like fictions which owe their origin to false and idle theories. And this class of idols is more easily expelled, because to get rid of them it is only necessary that all theories should be steadily rejected and dismissed as obsolete

But the other class, which springs out of a faulty and unskilful abstraction, is intricate and deeply rooted. Let us take for example such a word as *humid;* and see how far the several things which the word is used to signify agree with each other; and we shall find the word *humid* to be nothing else than a mark loosely and confusedly applied to denote a variety of actions which will not bear to be reduced to any constant meaning. For it both signifies that which easily spreads itself round any other body; and that which in itself is indeterminate and cannot solidise; and that which readily yields in every direction; and that which easily divides and scatters itself; and that which easily unites and collects itself; and that which readily flows and is put in motion; and that which readily clings to another body and wets it; and that which is easily reduced to a liquid, or being solid easily melts. Accordingly when you come to apply the word,—if you take it in one sense, flame is humid; if in another, air is not humid; if in another, fine dust is humid; if in another, glass is humid. So that it is easy to see that the notion is taken by abstraction only from water and common and ordinary liquids, without any due verification.

There are however in words certain degrees of distortion and error. One of the least faulty kinds is that of names of substances, especially of lowest species and well-deduced (for the notion of *chalk* and of *mud* is good, of *earth* bad); a more faulty kind is that of actions, as *to gen-*

*erate, to corrupt, to alter;* the most faulty is of qualities (except such as are the immediate objects of the sense) as *heavy, light, rare, dense,* and the like. Yet in all these cases some notions are of necessity a little better than others, in proportion to the greater variety of subjects that fall within the range of the human sense.

### Idols of the Theatre

XLIV.   Lastly, there are Idols which have immigrated into men's minds from the various dogmas of philosophies, and also from wrong laws of demonstration. These I call Idols of the Theatre; because in my judgment all the received systems are but so many stage-plays, representing worlds of their own creation after an unreal and scenic fashion. Nor is it only of the systems now in vogue, or only of the ancient sects and philosophies, that I speak; for many more plays of the same kind may yet be composed and in like artificial manner set forth; seeing that errors the most widely different have nevertheless causes for the most part alike. Neither again do I mean this only of entire systems, but also of many principles and axioms in science, which by tradition, credulity, and negligence have come to be received.

LXI.   But the *Idols of the Theatre* are not innate, nor do they steal into the understanding secretly, but are plainly impressed and received into the mind from the play-books of philosophical systems and the perverted rules of demonstration. To attempt refutations in this case would be merely inconsistent with what I have already said: for since we agree neither upon principles nor upon demonstrations there is no place for argument. And this is so far well, inasmuch as it leaves the honour of the ancients untouched. For they are no wise disparaged—the question between them and me being only as to the way. For as the saying is, the lame man who keeps the right road outstrips the runner who takes a wrong one. Nay it is obvious that when a man runs the wrong way, the more active and swift he is the further he will go astray.

But the course I propose for the discovery of sciences is such as leaves but little to the acuteness and strength of wits, but places all wits and understandings nearly on a level. For as in the drawing of a straight line or a perfect circle, much depends on the steadiness and practice of the hand, if it be done by aim of hand only, but if with the aid of rule or compass, little or nothing; so is it exactly with my plan. But though particular confutations would be of no avail, yet touching the sects and general divisions of such systems I must say something; something also touching the external signs which show that they are unsound; and finally something touching the causes of such great infelicity and of such lasting and general agreement in error; that so the access to truth may be made less difficult, and the human understanding may the more willingly submit to its purgation and dismiss its idols.

LXII. Idols of the Theatre, or of Systems, are many, and there can be and perhaps will be yet many more. For were it not that now for many ages men's minds have been busied with religion and theology; and were it not that civil governments, especially monarchies, have been averse to such novelties, even in matters speculative; so that men labour therein to the peril and harming of their fortunes,—not only unrewarded, but exposed also to contempt and envy; doubtless there would have arisen many other philosophical sects like to those which in great variety flourished once among the Greeks. For as on the phenomena of the heavens many hypotheses may be constructed, so likewise (and more also) many various dogmas may be set up and established on the phenomena of philosophy. And in the plays of this philosophical theatre you may observe the same thing which is found in the theatre of the poets, that stories invented for the stage are more compact and elegant, and more as one would wish them to be, than true stories out of history.

In general however there is taken for the material of philosophy either a great deal out of a few things, or a very little out of many things; so that on both sides philosophy is based on too narrow a foundation of experiment and natural history, and decides on the authority of too few cases. For the Rational School of philosophers snatches from experience a variety of common instances, neither duly ascertained nor diligently examined and weighed, and leaves all the rest to meditation and agitation of wit.

There is also another class of philosophers, who having bestowed much diligent and careful labour on a few experiments, have thence made bold to educe and construct systems; wresting all other facts in a strange fashion to conformity therewith.

And there is yet a third class, consisting of those who out of faith and veneration mix their philosophy with theology and traditions; among whom the vanity of some has gone so far aside as to seek the origin of sciences among spirits and genii. So that this parent stock of errors—

this false philosophy—is of three kinds; the Sophistical, the Empirical, and the Superstitious.

LXIII. The most conspicuous example of the first class was Aristotle, who corrupted natural philosophy by his logic: fashioning the world out of categories; assigning to the human soul, the noblest of substances, a genus from words of the second intention; doing the business of density and rarity (which is to make bodies of greater or less dimensions, that is, occupy greater or less spaces), by the frigid distinction of act and power; asserting that single bodies have each a single and proper motion, and that if they participate in any other, then this results from an external cause; and imposing countless other arbitrary restrictions on the nature of things; being always more solicitous to provide an answer to the question and affirm something positive in words, than about the inner truth of things; a failing best shown when his philosophy is compared with other systems of note among the Greeks. For the Homœmera of Anaxagoras; the Atoms of Leucippus and Democritus; the Heaven and Earth of Parmenides; the Strife and Friendship of Empedocles; Heraclitus's doctrine how bodies are resolved into the indifferent nature of fire, and remoulded into solids; have all of them some taste of the natural philosopher,—some savour of the nature of things, and experience, and bodies; whereas in the physics of Aristotle you hear hardly anything but the words of logic; which in his metaphysics also, under a more imposing name, and more forsooth as a realist than a nominalist, he has handled over again. Nor let any weight be given to the fact, that in his books on animals and his problems, and other of his treatises, there is frequent dealing with experiments. For he had come to his conclusion before; he did not consult experience, as he should have done, in order to the framing of his decisions and axioms; but having first determined the question according to his will, he then resorts to experience, and bending her into conformity with his placets leads her about like a captive in a procession; so that even on this count he is more guilty than his modern followers, the schoolmen, who have abandoned experience altogether.

LXIV. But the Empirical school of philosophy gives birth to dogmas more deformed and monstrous than the Sophistical or Rational school. For it has its foundations not in the light of common notions, (which though it be a faint and superficial light, is yet in a manner universal, and has reference to many things, but in the narrowness and darkness of a few experiments. To those therefore who are daily busied with these experiments, and have infected their imagination with them, such a philosophy seems probable and all but certain; to all men else incredible and vain. Of this there is a notable instance in the alchemists and their dogmas; though it is hardly to be found elsewhere in these times, except perhaps in the philosophy of Gilbert. Nevertheless with regard to philosophies of this kind there is one caution not to be omitted; for I foresee that if ever men are roused by my admonitions to betake themselves seriously to experiment and bid farewell to sophistical doctrines, then indeed through the premature hurry of the understanding to leap or fly to universals and principles of things, great danger may be apprehended from philosophies of this kind; against which evil we ought even now to prepare.

LXV.  But the corruption of philosophy by superstition and an admixture of theology is far more widely spread, and does the greatest harm, whether to entire systems or to their parts. For the human understanding is obnoxious to the influence of the imagination no less than to the influence of common notions. For the contentious and sophistical kind of philosophy ensnares the understanding; but this kind, being fanciful and tumid and half poetical, misleads it more by flattery. For there is in man an ambition of the understanding, no less than of the will, especially in high and lofty spirits.

Of this kind we have among the Greeks a striking example in Pythagoras, though he united with it a coarser and more cumbrous superstition; another in Plato and his school, more dangerous and subtle. It shows itself likewise in parts of other philosophies, in the introduction of abstract forms and final causes and first causes, with the omission in most cases of causes intermediate, and the like. Upon this point the greatest caution should be used. For nothing is so mischievous as the apotheosis of error; and it is a very plague of the understanding for vanity to become the object of veneration. Yet in this vanity some of the moderns have with extreme levity indulged so far as to attempt to found a system of natural philosophy on the first chapter of Genesis, on the book of Job, and other parts of the sacred writings; seeking for the dead among the living: which also makes the inhibition and repression of it the more important, because from this unwholesome mixture of things human and divine there arises not only a fantastic philosophy but also an heretical religion. Very meet it is therefore that we be sober-minded, and give to faith that only which is faith's.

LXVI. So much then for the mischievous authorities of systems, which are founded either on common notions, or on a few experiments, or on superstition. It remains to speak of the faulty subject-matter of contemplations, especially in natural philosophy. Now the human understanding is infected by the sight of what takes place in the mechanical arts, in which the alteration of bodies proceeds chiefly by composition or separation, and so imagines that something similar goes on in the universal nature of things. From this source has flowed the fiction of elements, and of their concourse for the formation of natural bodies. Again, when man contemplates nature working freely, he meets with different species of things, of animals, of plants, of minerals; whence he readily passes into the opinion that there are in nature certain primary forms which nature intends to educe, and that the remaining variety proceeds from hindrances and aberrations of nature in the fulfilment of her work, or from the collision of different species and the transplanting of one into another. To the first of these speculations we owe our primary qualities of the elements; to the other our occult properties and specific virtues; and both of them belong to those empty *compendia* of thought wherein the mind rests, and whereby it is diverted from more solid pursuits. It is to better purpose that the physicians bestow their labour on the secondary qualities of matter, and the operations of attraction, repulsion, attenuation, conspissation, dilatation, astriction, dissipation, maturation, and the like; and were it not that by those two compendia which I have mentioned (elementary qualities, to wit, and specific virtues) they corrupted their correct observations in these other matters,—either reducing them to first qualities and their subtle and incommensurable mixtures, or not following them out with greater and more diligent observation to third and fourth qualities, but breaking off the scrutiny prematurely,—they had made much greater progress. Nor are powers of this kind (I do not say the same, but similar) to be sought for only in the medicines of the human body, but also in the changes of all other bodies.

But it is a far greater evil that they make the quiescent principles, *wherefrom,* and not the moving principles, *whereby,* things are produced, the object of their contemplation and inquiry. For the former tend to discourse, the latter to works. Nor is there any value in those vulgar distinctions of motion which are observed in the received system of natural philosophy, as generation, corruption, augmentation, diminution, alteration, and local motion. What they mean no doubt is this:—If a body in other respects not changed, be moved from its place, *this is local motion;* if without change of place or essence, it be changed in quality, this is *alteration;* if by reason of the change the mass and quantity of the body do not remain the same, this is *augmentation* or *diminution;* if they be changed to such a degree that they change their very essence and substance and turn to something else, this is *generation* and *corruption.* But all this is merely popular, and does not at all go deep into nature; for these are only measures and limits, not kinds of motion. What they intimate is *how far,* not *by what means,* or *from what source.* For they do not suggest anything with regard either to the desires of bodies or to the development of their parts: it is only when that motion presents the thing grossly and palpably to the sense as different from what it was, that they begin to mark the division. Even when they wish to suggest something with regard to the causes of motion, and to establish a division with reference to them, they introduce with the greatest negligence a distinction between motion natural and violent; a distinction which is itself drawn entirely from a vulgar notion, since all violent motion is also in fact natural; the external efficient simply setting nature working otherwise than it was before. But if, leaving all this, any one shall observe (for instance) that there is in bodies a desire of mutual contact, so as not to suffer the unity of nature to be quite separated or broken and a vacuum thus made; or if any one say that there is in bodies a desire of resuming their natural dimensions or tension, so that if compressed within or extended beyond them, they immediately strive to recover themselves, and fall back to their old volume and extent; or if any one say that there is in bodies a desire of congregating towards masses of kindred nature,—of dense bodies, for instance, towards the globe of the earth, of thin and rare bodies towards the compass of the sky; all these and the like are truly physical kinds of motion;—but those others are entirely logical and scholastic, as is abundantly manifest from this comparison.

Nor again is it a less evil, that in their philosophies and contemplations their labour is spent in investigating and handling the first principles of things and the highest generalities of nature; whereas utility and the means of working result entirely from things intermediate. Hence it is that men cease not from abstracting nature till they come to potential and uninformed matter, nor on the other hand from dissecting nature till they reach the atom; things which, even if true, can do but little for the welfare of mankind.

LXVII.  A caution must also be given to the understanding against the intemperance which systems of philosophy manifest in giving or with-holding assent; because intemperance of this kind seems to establish Idols and in some sort to perpetuate them, leaving no way open to reach and dislodge them.

This excess is of two kinds: the first being manifest in those who are ready in deciding, and render sciences dogmatic and magisterial; the other in those who deny that we can know anything, and so introduce a wan-dering kind of inquiry that leads to nothing; of which kinds the former subdues, the latter weakens the understanding. For the philosophy of Aristotle, after having by hostile confutations destroyed all the rest (as the Ottomans serve their brothers), has laid down the law on all points; which done, he proceeds himself to raise new questions of his own sug-gestion, and dispose of them likewise; so that nothing may remain that is not certain and decided: a practice which holds and is in use among his successors.

The school of Plato, on the other hand, introduced *Acatalepsia,* at first in jest and irony, and in disdain of the older sophists, Protagoras, Hippias, and the rest, who were of nothing else so much ashamed as of seeming to doubt about anything. But the New Academy made a dogma of it, and held it as a tenet. And though theirs is a fairer seeming way than arbitrary decisions; since they say that they by no means destroy all investigation, like Pyrrho and his Refrainers, but allow of some things to be followed as probable, though of none to be maintained as true; yet still when the human mind has once despaired of finding truth, its in-terest in all things grows fainter; and the result is that men turn aside to pleasant disputations and discourses and roam as it were from object to object, rather than keep on a course of severe inquisition. But, as I said at the beginning and am ever urging, the human senses and under-standing, weak as they are, are not to be deprived of their authority, but to be supplied with helps.

LXVIII.  So much concerning the several classes of Idols, and their equipage: all of which must be renounced and put away with a fixed and solemn determination, and the understanding thoroughly freed and cleansed; the entrance into the kingdom of man, founded on the sciences, being not much other than the entrance into the kingdom of heaven, whereinto none may enter except as a little child. . . .

## Application of the Method

cxxiv.  Again, it will be thought, no doubt, that the goal and mark of knowledge which I myself set up (the very point which I object to in others) is not the true or the best; for that the contemplation of truth is a thing worthier and loftier than all utility and magnitude of works; and that this long and anxious dwelling with experience and matter and the fluctuations of individual things, drags down the mind to earth, or rather sinks it to a very Tartarus of turmoil and confusion; removing and withdrawing it from the serene tranquillity of abstract wisdom, a condition far more heavenly. Now to this I readily assent; and indeed this which they point at as so much to be preferred, is the very thing of all others which I am about. For I am building in the human understanding a true model of the world, such as it is in fact, not such as a man's own reason would have it to be; a thing which cannot be done without a very diligent dissection and anatomy of the world. But I say that those foolish and apish images of worlds which the fancies of men have created in philosophical systems, must be utterly scattered to the winds. Be it known then how vast a difference there is (as I said above) between the Idols of the human mind and the Ideas of the divine. The former are nothing more than arbitrary abstractions; the latter are the creator's own stamp upon creation, impressed and defined in matter by true and exquisite lines. Truth therefore and utility are here the very same things: and works themselves are of greater value as pledges of truth than as contributing to the comforts of life.

cxxvii.  It may also be asked (in the way of doubt rather than objection) whether I speak of natural philosophy only, or whether I mean that the other sciences, logic, ethics, and politics, should be carried on by this method. Now I certainly mean what I have said to be understood of them all; and as the common logic, which governs by the syllogism, extends not only to natural but to all sciences; so does mine also, which proceeds by induction, embrace everything. For I form a history and tables of discovery for anger, fear, shame, and the like; for matters political; and again for the mental operations of memory, composition and division, judgment and the rest; not less than for heat and cold, or light, or vegetation, or the like. But nevertheless since my method of interpretation, after the history has been prepared and duly arranged, regards not the working and discourse of the mind only (as the common logic does) but the nature of things also, I supply the mind with such rules and guidance that it may in every case apply itself aptly to the nature of things. And therefore I deliver many and diverse precepts in the doctrine of Interpretation, which in some measure modify the method of invention according to the quality and condition of the subject of the inquiry.

# BOOK II

## *Tables of Instances*

x. . . . . Now my directions for the interpretation of nature embrace two generic divisions; the one how to educe and form axioms from experience; the other how to deduce and derive new experiments from axioms. The former again is divided into three ministrations; a ministration to the sense, a ministration to the memory, and a ministration to the mind or reason.

For first of all we must prepare a *Natural and Experimental History,* sufficient and good; and this is the foundation of all; for we are not to imagine or suppose, but to discover, what nature does or may be made to do.

But natural and experimental history is so various and diffuse, that it confounds and distracts the understanding, unless it be ranged and presented to view in a suitable order. We must therefore form *Tables and Arrangements of Instances,* in such a method and order that the understanding may be able to deal with them.

And even when this is done, still the understanding, if left to itself and its own spontaneous movements, is incompetent and unfit to form axioms, unless it be directed and guarded. Therefore in the third place we must use *Induction,* true and legitimate induction, which is the very key of interpretation. But of this, which is the last, I must speak first, and then go back to the other ministrations.

xi. The investigation of Forms proceeds thus: a nature being given, we must first of all have a muster or presentation before the understanding of all known instances which agree in the same nature, though in substances the most unlike. And such collection must be made in the manner of a history, without premature speculation, or any great amount of subtlety. For example, let the investigation be into the Form of Heat.

## Instances Agreeing in the Nature of Heat.

1. The rays of the sun, especially in summer and at noon.

2. The rays of the sun reflected and condensed, as between mountains, or on walls, and most of all in burning-glasses and mirrors.

3. Fiery meteors.

4. Burning thunderbolts.

5. Eruptions of flame from the cavities of mountains.

6. All flame.

7. Ignited solids.

8. Natural warm-baths.

9. Liquids boiling or heated.

10. Hot vapours and fumes, and the air itself, which conceives the most powerful and glowing heat, if confined; as in reverbatory furnaces.

11. Certain seasons that are fine and cloudless by the constitution of the air itself, without regard to the time of year.

12. Air confined and underground in some caverns, especially in winter.

13. All villous substances, as wool, skins of animals, and down of birds, have heat.

14. All bodies, whether solid or liquid, whether dense or rare (as the air itself is), held for a time near the fire.

15. Sparks struck from flint and steel by strong percussion.

16. All bodies rubbed violently, as stone, wood, cloth, &c., insomuch that poles and axles of wheels sometimes catch fire; and the way they kindled fire in the West Indies was by attrition.

17. Green and moist vegetables confined and bruised together, as roses packed in baskets; insomuch that hay, if damp when stacked, often catches fire.

18. Quick lime sprinkled with water.

19. Iron, when first dissolved by strong waters in glass, and that without being put near the fire. And in like manner tin, &c., but not with equal intensity.

20. Animals, especially and at all times internally; though in insects the heat is not perceptible to the touch by reason of the smallness of their size.

21. Horse-dung and like excrements of animals when fresh.

22. Strong oil of sulphur and of vitriol has the effect of heat in burning linen.

23. Oil of marjoram and similar oils have the effect of heat in burning the bones of the teeth.

24. Strong and well rectified spirit of wine has the effect of heat; insomuch that the white of an egg being put into it hardens and whitens almost as if it were boiled; and bread thrown in becomes dry and crusted like toast.

25. Aromatic and hot herbs, as *dracunculus, nasturtium vetus,* &c., although not warm to the hand (either whole or in powder), yet to the tongue and palate, being a little masticated, they feel hot and burning.

26. Strong vinegar, and all acids, on all parts of the body where there is no epidermis, as the eye, tongue; or on any part when wounded and laid bare of the skin; produce a pain but little differing from that which is created by heat.

27. Even keen and intense cold produces a kind of sensation of burning;

*Nec Boreæ penetrabile frigus adurit.*[3]

28. Other instances.

This table I call the *Table of Essence and Presence.*

## Tables of Deviation

XII.  Secondly, we must make a presentation to the understanding of instances in which the given nature is wanting; because the Form, as stated above, ought no less to be absent when the given nature is absent, than present when it is present. But to note all these would be endless.

The negatives should therefore be subjoined to the affirmatives, and the absence of the given nature inquired of in those subjects only that are most akin to the others in which it is present and forthcoming. This I call the *Table of Deviation,* or of *Absence in Proximity.* . . .

[3] Nor burns the sharp cold of the northern blast.

## Tables of Degrees

XIII.  Thirdly, we must make a presentation to the understanding of instances in which the nature under inquiry is found in different degrees, more or less; which must be done by making a comparison either of its increase and decrease in the same subject, or of its amount in different subjects, as compared one with another. For since the Form of a thing is the very thing itself, and the thing differs from the form no otherwise than as the apparent differs from the real, or the external from the internal, or the thing in reference to man from the thing in reference to the universe; it necessarily follows that no nature can be taken as the true form, unless it always decrease when the nature in question decreases, and in like manner always increase when the nature in question increases. This Table therefore I call the *Table of Degrees* or the *Table of Comparison.* . . .

## Forms

XV.  The work and office of these three tables I call the Presentation of Instances to the Understanding. Which presentation having been made, Induction itself must be set at work; for the problem is, upon a review of the instances, all and each, to find such a nature as is always present or absent with the given nature, and always increases and decreases with it; and which is, as I have said, a particular case of a more general nature. Now if the mind attempt this affirmatively from the first, as when left to itself it is always wont to do, the result will be fancies and guesses and notions ill defined, and axioms that must be mended every day; unless like the schoolmen we have a mind to fight for what is false; though doubtless these will be better or worse according to the faculties and strength of the understanding which is at work. To God, truly, the Giver and Architect of Forms, and it may be to the angels and higher intelligences, it belongs to have an affirmative knowledge of forms immediately, and from the first contemplation. But this assuredly is more than man can do, to whom it is granted only to proceed at first by negatives, and at last to end in affirmatives, after exclusion has been exhausted.

XVI.  We must make therefore a complete solution and separation of nature, not indeed by fire, but by the mind, which is a kind of divine fire. The first work therefore of true induction (as far as regards the discovery of Forms) is the rejection or exclusion of the several natures which are not found in some instance where the given nature is present, or are found in some instance where the given nature is absent, or are found to increase in some instance when the given nature decreases, or to decrease when the given nature increases. Then indeed after the rejection and exclusion has been duly made, there will remain at the bottom, all light opinions vanishing into smoke, a Form affirmative, solid and true and well defined. This is quickly said; but the way to come at it is winding and intricate. I will endeavour however not to overlook any of the points which may help us towards it.

xvii.  But when I assign so prominent a part to Forms, I cannot too often warn and admonish men against applying what I say to those forms to which their thoughts and contemplations have hitherto been accustomed.

For in the first place I do not at present speak of Compound Forms, which are, as I have remarked, combinations of simple natures according to the common course of the universe; as of the lion, eagle, rose, gold, and the like. It will be time to treat of these when we come to the Latent Processes and Latent Configurations, and the discovery of them, as they are found in what are called substances or natures concrete.

And even in the case of simple natures I would not be understood to speak of abstract forms and ideas, either not defined in matter at all, or ill defined. For when I speak of Forms, I mean nothing more than those laws and determinations of absolute actuality, which govern and constitute any simple nature, as heat, light, weight, in every kind of matter and subject that is susceptible of them. Thus the Form of Heat or the Form of Light is the same thing as the Law of Heat or the Law of Light. Nor indeed do I ever allow myself to be drawn away from things themselves and the operative part. And therefore when I say (for instance) in the investigation of the form of heat, "reject rarity," or "rarity does not belong to the form of heat," it is the same as if I said, "It is possible to superinduce heat on a dense body;" or, "It is possible to take away or keep out heat from a rare body."

But if any one conceive that my Forms too are of a somewhat abstract nature, because they mix and combine things heterogeneous (for the heat of heavenly bodies and the heat of fire seem to be very heterogeneous; so do the fixed red of the rose or the like, and the apparent red in the rainbow, the opal, or the diamond; so again do the different kinds of death; death by drowning, by hanging, by stabbing, by apoplexy, by atrophy; and yet they agree severally in the nature of heat, redness, death); if any one, I say, be of this opinion, he may be assured that his mind is held in captivity by custom, by the gross appearance of things, and by men's opinions. For it is most certain that these things, however heterogeneous and alien from each other, agree in the Form or Law which governs heat, redness and death; and that the power of man cannot possibly be emancipated and freed from the common course of nature, and expanded and exalted to new efficients and new modes of operation, except by the revelation and discovery of Forms of this kind. And yet, when I have spoken of this union of nature, which is the point of most importance, I shall proceed to the divisions and veins of nature, as well the ordinary as those that are more inward and exact, and speak of them in their place.

## Process of Exclusion

xviii. I must now give an example of the Exclusion or Rejection of natures which by the Tables of Presentation are found not to belong to the Form of Heat; observing in the meantime that not only each table suffices for the rejection of any nature, but even any one of the particular instances contained in any of the tables. For it is manifest from what has been said that any one contradictory instance overthrows a conjecture as to the Form. But nevertheless for clearness' sake and that the use of the tables may be more plainly shown, I sometimes double or multiply an exclusion.

An Example of Exclusion, or Rejection of Natures from the Form of Heat.

1. On account of the rays of the sun, reject the nature of the elements.

2. On account of common fire, and chiefly subterraneous fires (which are the most remote and most completely separate from the rays of heavenly bodies), reject the nature of heavenly bodies.

3. On account of the warmth acquired by all kinds of bodies (minerals, vegetables, skin of animals, water, oil, air, and the rest) by mere approach to a fire, or other hot body, reject the distinctive or more subtle texture of bodies.

4. On account of ignited iron and other metals, which communicate heat to other bodies and yet lose none of their weight or substance, reject the communication or admixture of the substance of another hot body.

5. On account of boiling water and air, and also on account of metals and other solids that receive heat but not to ignition or red heat, reject light or brightness.

6. On account of the rays of the moon and other heavenly bodies, with the exception of the sun, also reject light and brightness.

7. By a comparison of ignited iron and the flame of spirit of wine (of which ignited iron has more heat and less brightness, while the flame of spirit of wine has more brightness and less heat), also reject light and brightness.

8. On account of ignited gold and other metals, which are of the greatest density as a whole, reject rarity.

9. On account of air, which is found for the most part cold and yet remains rare, also reject rarity.

10. On account of ignited iron, which does not swell in bulk, but keeps within the same visible dimensions, reject local or expansive motion of the body as a whole.

11. On account of the dilation of air in calendar glasses and the like, wherein the air evidently moves locally and expansively and yet acquires no manifest increase of heat, also reject local or expansive motion of the body as a whole.

12. On account of the ease with which all bodies are heated, without any destruction or observable alteration, reject a destructive nature, or the violent communication of any new nature.

13. On account of the agreement and conformity of the similar effects which are wrought by heat and cold, reject motion of the body as a whole, whether expansive or contractive.

14. On account of heat being kindled by the attrition of bodies, reject a principial nature. By principial nature I mean that which exists in the nature of things positively, and not as the effect of any antecedent nature.

There are other natures beside these; for these tables are not perfect, but meant only for examples.

All and each of the above-mentioned natures do *not* belong to the Form of Heat. And from all of them man is freed in his operations on Heat.

xix.  In the process of Exclusion are laid the foundations of true Induction, which however is not completed till it arrives at an Affirmative. Nor is the Exclusive part itself at all complete, nor indeed can it possibly be so at first. For Exclusion is evidently the rejection of simple natures; and if we do not yet possess sound and true notions of simple natures, how can the process of Exclusion be made accurate? Now some of the above-mentioned notions (as that of the nature of the elements, of the nature of heavenly bodies, of rarity) are vague and ill-defined. I therefore, well knowing and nowise forgetting how great a work I am about (viz. that of rendering the human understanding a match for things and nature), do not rest satisfied with the precepts I have laid down; but proceed further to devise and supply more powerful aids for the use of the understanding; which I shall now subjoin. And assuredly in the Interpretation of Nature the mind should by all means be so prepared and disposed, that while it rests and finds footing in due stages and degrees of certainty, it may remember withal (especially at the beginning) that what it has before it depends in great measure upon what remains behind.

## First Vintage

xx.  And yet since truth will sooner come out from error than from confusion, I think it expedient that the understanding should have permission, after the three Tables of First Presentation (such as I have exhibited) have been made and weighed, to make an essay of the Interpretation of Nature in the affirmative way; on the strength both of the instances given in the tables, and of any others it may meet with elsewhere. Which kind of essay I call the *Indulgence of the Understanding,* or the *Commencement of Interpretation,* or the *First Vintage.* . . .

## Prerogative Instances

xxi.  The Tables of First Presentation and the Rejection or process of Exclusion being completed, and also the First Vintage being made thereupon, we are to proceed to the other helps of the understanding in the Interpretation of Nature and true and perfect Induction. In propounding which, I mean, when Tables are necessary, to proceed upon the Instances of Heat and Cold; but when a smaller number of examples will suffice,

I shall proceed at large; so that the inquiry may be kept clear, and yet more room be left for the exposition of the system.

I propose to treat them in the first place of *Prerogative Instances;* secondly, of the *Supports of Induction;* thirdly, of the *Rectification of Induction;* fourthly, of *Varying the Investigation according to the nature of the Subject;* fifthly, of *Prerogative Natures* with respect to Investigation, or of what should be inquired first and what last; sixthly, of the *Limits of Investigation,* or a Synopsis of all Natures in the Universe; seventhly, of the *Application to Practice,* or of things in their relation to Man; eighthly, of *Preparations for Investigation;* and lastly, of the *Ascending and Descending Scale of Axioms.*

xxii. Among Prerogative Instances I will place first *Solitary Instances.* Those are Solitary Instances which exhibit the nature under investigation in subjects which have nothing in common with other subjects except that nature; or, again, which do not exhibit the nature under investigation in subjects which resemble other subjects in every respect except in not having that nature. For it is clear that such instances make the way short, and accelerate and strengthen the process of exclusion; so that a few of them are as good as many. . . .

lii. So much then for the Dignities or Prerogatives of Instances. It must be remembered however that in this Organum of mine I am handling logic, not philosophy. But since my logic aims to teach and instruct the understanding, not that it may with the slender tendrils of the mind snatch at and lay hold of abstract notions (as the common logic does), but that it may in very truth dissect nature, and discover the virtues and actions of bodies, with their laws as determined in matter; so that this science flows not merely from the nature of the mind, but also from the nature of things; no wonder that it is everywhere sprinkled and illustrated with speculations and experiments in nature, as examples of the art I teach. It appears then from what has been said that there are twenty-seven Prerogative Instances; namely, Solitary Instances; Migratory Instances; Striking Instances; Clandestine Instances; Constitutive Instances; Conformable Instances; Singular Instances; Deviating Instances; Bordering Instances; Instances of Power; Instances of Companionship and of Enmity; Subjunctive Instances; Instances of Alliance; Instances of the Fingerpost; Instances of Divorce; Instances of the Door;

Summoning Instances; Instances of the Road; Instances Supplementary; Dissecting Instances; Instances of the Rod; Instances of the Course; Doses of Nature; Instances of Strife; Intimating Instances; Polychrest Instances; Magical Instances. . . .

# NATURAL AND EXPERIMENTAL HISTORY

## FOR THE FOUNDATION OF PHILOSOPHY: OR PHENOMENA OF THE UNIVERSE: BEING THE THIRD PART OF THE INSTAURATIO MAGNA.

To the Most Illustrious and Excellent
PRINCE CHARLES
Son and Heir of His Most Serene Majesty, King James.

*Most Illustrious and Excellent Prince,*

The first fruits of my Natural History I most humbly offer to your Highness; a thing like a grain of mustard-seed, very small in itself, yet a pledge of those things which by the grace of God will come hereafter. For I have bound myself as by a vow every month that the goodness of God (whose glory is sung as in a new song) shall add to my life, to complete and set forth one or more parts of it, according as they be more or less difficult or extensive. It may be also that others will be stirred by my example to a like industry; especially when they shall fully understand what it is that we are about. For a sound and well-ordered Natural History is the key of all knowledge and operation. That God may long preserve your Highness in His keeping is the prayer of

*Your Majesty's humble and devoted Servant,*

FR. ST. ALBAN.

TITLES OF THE HISTORIES AND INQUIRIES
DESIGNED FOR THE FIRST SIX MONTHS

History of the Winds.
History of Dense and Rare, and of the Contraction and Expansion of Matter in Space.
History of Heavy and Light.
History of the Sympathy and Antipathy of Things.
History of Sulphur, Mercury, and Salt.
History of Life and Death.

# SYLVA SYLVARUM
# OR
# A NATURAL HISTORY

Experiment Solitary Touching Cure by Excess.

Divers diseases, especially chronical (such as quartan agues), are some-times cured by surfeit and excesses: as excess of meat, excess of drink, extraordinary fasting, extraordinary stirring, or lassitude, and the like. The cause is, for that diseases of continuance get an adventitious strength from custom, besides their material cause from the humours; so that the breaking of the custom doth leave them only to their first cause; which if it be anything weak will fall off. Besides such excesses do excite and spur nature, which thereupon rises more forcibly against the disease.

Experiment Solitary Touching Cure by Motion of Consent.

There is in the body of man a great consent in the motion of the sev-eral parts. We see it is children's sport to prove whether they can rub upon their breast with one hand, and pat upon their forehead with an-other; and straightways they shall sometimes rub with both hands, or pat with both hands. We see that when the spirits that come to the nos-trils expel a bad scent, the stomach is ready to expel by vomit. We find that in consumptions of the lungs, when nature cannot expel by cough, men fall into fluxes of the belly, and tthen they die. So in pestilent dis-eases, if they cannot be expelled by sweat, they fall likewise into loose-ness; and that is commonly mortal. Therefore physicians should ingeni-ously contrive, how by motions that are in their power, they may excite inward motions that are not in their power, by consent: as by the stench of feathers, or the like, they cure the rising of the mother. . . .

Experiments Concerning Music.

. . . There be in music certain figures or tropes; almost agreeing with the figures of rhetoric, and with the affections of the mind, and other senses. First, the division and quavering, which please so much in music, have an agreement with the glittering of light; as the moon-beams playing upon a wave. Again, the falling from a discord to a concord, which maketh great sweetness in music, hath an agreement with the affections, which are reintegrated to the better after some dislikes; it agreeth also with the taste, which is soon glutted with that which is sweet alone. The sliding from the close or cadence, hath an agreement with the figure in rhetoric which they call *præter expectatum;* for there is a pleasure even in being deceived. The reports and fuges have an agreement with the figures in rhetoric of repetition and traduction. The tripla's, and changing of times, have an agreement with the changes of motions; as when galliard time and measure time are in the medley of one dance.

It hath been anciently held and observed, that the sense of hearing and the kinds of music have most operation upon manners; as to encourage men and make them warlike; to make them soft and effeminate; to make them grave; to make them light; to make them gentle and inclined to pity, &c. The cause is, for that the sense of hearing striketh the spirits more immediately than the other senses, and more incorporeally than the smelling. For the sight, taste, and feeling, have their organs not of so present and immediate access to the spirits, as the hearing hath. And as for the smelling, (which indeed worketh also immediately upon the spirits, and is forcible while the object remaineth,) it is with a communication of the breath or vapour of the object odorate; but harmony, entering easily, and mingling not at all, and coming with a manifest motion, doth by custom of often affecting the spirits and putting them into one kind of posture, alter not a little the nature of the spirits, even when the object is removed. And therefore we see that tunes and airs, even in their own nature, have in themselves some affinity with the affections: as there be merry tunes, doleful tunes, solemn tunes; tunes inclining men's minds to pity; warlike tunes, &c. . . .

Experiments in Consort Touching Venus.

It hath been observed by the ancients, that much use of Venus doth dim the sight; and yet eunuchs, which are unable to generate, are nevertheless also dim-sighted. The cause of dimness of sight in the former, is the expence of spirits; in the latter, the over-moisture of the brain; for the over-moisture of the brain doth thicken the spirits visual, and obstructeth their passages; as we see by the decay in the sight in age; where also the diminution of the spirits concurreth as another cause: we see also that blindness cometh by rheums and cataracts. Now in eunuchs there are all the notes of moisture; as the swelling of their thighs, the looseness of their belly, the smoothness of their skin, &c.

The pleasure in the act of Venus is the greatest of the pleasures of the senses: the matching of it with itch is unproper; though that also be pleasing to the touch. But the causes are profound. First, all the organs of the senses qualify the motions of the spirits; and make so many several species of motions, and pleasures or displeasures thereupon, as there be diversities of organs. The instruments of sight, hearing, taste, and smell, are of several frame, and so are the parts for generation. Therefore Scaliger doth well to make the pleasure of generation a sixth sense; and if there were any other differing organs, and qualified perforations for the spirits to pass, there would be more than the five senses: neither do we well know whether some beasts and birds have not senses that we know not: and the very scent of dogs is almost a sense by itself. Secondly, the pleasures of the touch are greater and deeper than those of the other senses; as we see in warming upon cold, or refrigeration upon heat; for as the pains of the touch are greater than the offences of other senses, so likewise are the pleasures. It is true, that the affecting of the spirits immediately, and (as it were) without an organ, is of the greatest pleasure; which is but in two things; sweet smells, and wine and the like sweet vapours. For smells, we see their great and sudden effect in fetching men again when they swoon: for drink, it is certain that the pleasure of drunkenness is next the pleasure of Venus; and great joys likewise make the spirits move and touch themselves: and the pleasure of Venus is somewhat of the same kind.

It hath been always observed that men are more inclined to Venus in the winter, and women in the summer. The cause is, for that the spirits, in a body more hot and dry (as the spirits of men are), by the summer are more exhaled and dissipated; and in the winter more condensed, and kept entire: but in bodies that are cold and moist (as women's are), the summer doth cherish the spirits, and calleth them forth; the winter doth dull them. Furthermore, the abstinence or intermission of the use of Venus in moist and well habituate bodies, breedeth a number of diseases: and especially dangerous imposthumations. The reason is evident; for that it is a principal evacuation, especially of the spirits; for of the spirits there is scarce any evacuation, but in Venus and exercise. And therefore the omission of either of them breedeth all diseases of repletion.

### Experiment Solitary Touching Medicines That Condense and Relieve the Spirits.

They have in Turkey a drink called *coffa,* made of a berry of the same name, as black as soot, and of a strong scent, but not aromatical; which they take, beaten into powder, in water, as hot as they can drink it: and they take it, and sit at it in their coffa-houses, which are like our taverns. This drink comforteth the brain and heart, and helpeth digestion. Certainly this berry coffa, the root and leaf betel, the leaf tobacco, and the tear of poppy (opium), of which the Turks are great takers (supposing it expelleth all fear), do all condense the spirits, and make them strong and aleger. But it seemeth they were taken after several manners; for coffa and opium are taken down, tobacco but in smoke, and betel is but champed in the mouth with a little lime. It is like there are more of them, if they were well found out, and well corrected. *Quære* of hen-bane-seed; of mandrake; of saffron, root and flower; of folium indum; of ambergrise; of the Assyrian amomum, if it may be had; and of the scarlet powder which they call *kermez;* and (generally) of all such things as do inebriate and provoke sleep. Note that tobacco is not taken in root or seed, which are more forcible ever than leaves.

### Experiment Solitary Touching Paintings of the Body.

The Turks have a black powder, made of a mineral called *alcohole,* which with a fine long pencil they lay under their eye-lids; which doth colour them black; whereby the white of the eye is set off more white. With the same powder they colour also the hairs of their eye-lids, and of their eye-brows, which they draw into embowed arches. You shall find that Xenophon maketh mention, that the Medes used to paint their eyes. The Turks use with the same tincture to colour the hair of their heads and beards black. And divers with us that are grown grey, and yet would appear young, find means to make their hair black, by combing it (as they say) with a leaden comb, or the like. As for the Chineses, who are of an ill complexion (being olivaster), they paint their cheeks scarlet, especially their king and grandes. Generally, barbarous people, that go naked, do not only paint themselves, but they pounce and raze their skin, that the painting may not be taken forth; and make it into works. So do the West Indians; and so did the ancient Picts and Britons; so that it seemeth men would have the colours of birds' feathers, if they could tell how; or at least they will have gay skins instead of gay clothes.

### Experiment Solitary Touching the Use of Bathing and Anointing.

It is strange that the use of bathing, as a part of diet, is left. With the Romans and Grecians it was as usual as eating or sleeping; and so is it amongst the Turks at this day: whereas with us it remaineth but as a part of physic. I am of opinion, that the use of it, as it was with the Romans, was hurtful to health; for that it made the body soft, and easy to waste. For the Turks it is more proper, because that their drinking water, and feeding upon rice, and other food of small nourishment, maketh their bodies so solid and hard, as you need not fear that bathing should make them frothy. Besides the Turks are great sitters, and seldom walk, whereby they sweat less and need bathing more. But yet certain it is that bathing, and especially anointing, may be so used as it may be a great help to health and prolongation of life. But hereof we shall speak in due place, when we come to handle experiments medicinal.

### Experiments Touching Teeth.

No beast that hath horns hath upper teeth; and no beast that hath teeth above wanteth them below: but yet if they be of the same kind, it followeth not that if the hard matter goeth not into upper teeth, it will go into horns; nor yet *è converso;* for does, that have no horns, have no upper teeth.

Horses have, at three years old, a tooth put forth, which they call the colt's tooth; and at four years' old there cometh the mark-tooth, which hath a hole as big as you may lay a pea within it; and that weareth shorter and shorter every year; till that at eight years' old the tooth is smooth, and the hole gone: and then they say, that *the mark is out of the horse's mouth.*

The teeth of men breed first, when the child is about a year and a half old: and then they cast them, and new come about seven years' old. But divers have backward teeth come forth at twenty, yea, some at thirty and forty. *Quære* of the manner of the coming of them forth. They tell a tale of the old Countess of Desmond, who lived till she was seven score years old, that she did *dentire* twice or thrice; casting her old teeth, and others coming in their place.

Teeth are much hurt by sweetmeats; and by painting with mercury; and by things over-hot; and by things over-cold; and by rheums. And the pain of the teeth is one of the sharpest of pains.

Concerning teeth, these things are to be considered. 1. The preserving of them. 2. The keeping of them white. 3. The drawing of them with least pain. 4. The staying and easing of the toothache. 5. The binding in of artificial teeth, where teeth have been strucken out. 6. And last of all, that great one of restoring teeth in age. The instances that give any likelihood of restoring teeth in age are, the late coming of teeth in some; and the renewing of the beaks in birds, which are commaterial with teeth. *Quære* therefore more particularly how that cometh. . . .

### Experiment Solitary Touching Maleficiating.

In Zant it is very ordinary to make men impotent to accompany with their wives. The like is practised in Gascony; where it is called *nouër l'eguillette*. It is practised always upon the wedding-day. And in Zant the mothers themselves do it, by way of prevention; because thereby they hinder other charms, and can undo their own. It is a thing the civil law taketh knowledge of; and therefore is of no light regard. . . .

# DE SAPIENTIA VETERUM
# (THE WISEDOME OF THE ANCIENTS)

## PREFACE

. . . I do certainly for my own part (I freely and candidly confess) incline to this opinion,—that beneath no small number of the fables of the ancient poets there lay from the very beginning a mystery and an allegory. It may be that my reverence for the primitive time carries me too far, but the truth is that in some of these fables, as well in the very frame and texture of the story as in the propriety of the names by which the persons that figure in it are distinguished, I find a conformity and connexion with the thing signified, so close and so evident, that one cannot help believing such a signification to have been designed and meditated from the first, and purposely shadowed out. For who is there so impenetrable and that can so shut his eyes to a plain thing, but when he is told that after the *Giants* were put down, *Fame* sprang up as their posthumous sister, he will at once see that it is meant of those murmurs of parties and seditious rumours which always circulate for a time after the suppression of a rebellion? Or again who can hear that the *Giant Typhon* cut off and carried away *Jupiter's* sinews, and that *Mercury* stole them from Typhon and gave them back to Jupiter; without at once perceiving that it relates to successful rebellions, by which kings have their sinews both of money and authority cut off; yet not so but that by fair words and wise edicts the minds of the subjects may be presently reconciled, and as it were stolen back, and so kings recover their strength? Or who can hear that in that memorable expedition of the gods against the giants the braying of *Silenus's ass* had a principal stroke in putting the giants to flight, and not be sure that the incident was invented in allusion to the vast attempts of rebels, dissipated as they commonly are by empty rumours and vain terrors? Then again there is a conformity and significancy in the very names, which must be clear to everybody. Metis, Jupiter's wife, plainly means counsel; Typhon, swelling; Pan, the universe; Nemesis, revenge; and the like. And what if we find here and there a bit of real history underneath, or some things added only for ornament, or times confounded, or part of one fable transferred to another and a new allegory introduced? Such things could not but occur in stories invented (as these were) by men who both lived in different ages and had different ends, some being more modern, some more ancient, some having in their thoughts natural philosophy, others civil affairs; and therefore they need not trouble us.

But there is yet another sign, and one of no small value, that these fables contain a hidden and involved meaning; which is, that some of them are so absurd and stupid upon the face of the narrative taken by itself, that they may be said to give notice from afar and cry out that there is a parable below. For a fable that is probable may be thought to have been composed merely for pleasure, in imitation of history. But when a story is told which could never have entered any man's head either to conceive or relate on its own account, we must presume that it had some further reach. What a fiction (for instance) is that of Jupiter and Metis! Jupiter took Metis to wife: as soon as he saw that she was with child, he ate her up; whereupon he grew to be with child himself;

and so brought forth out of his head Pallas in armour! Surely I think no man had ever a dream so monstrous and extravagant, and out of all natural ways of thinking.

But the consideration which has most weight with me is this, that few of these fables were invented, as I take it, by those who recited and made them famous,—Homer, Hesiod, and the rest. For had they been certainly the production of that age and of those authors by whose report they have come down to us, I should not have thought of looking for anything great or lofty from such a source. But it will appear upon an attentive examination that they are delivered not as new inventions then first published, but as stories already received and believed. And since they are told in different ways by writers nearly contemporaneous, it is easy to see that what all the versions have in common came from ancient tradition, while the parts in which they vary are the additions introduced by the several writers for embellishment—a circumstance which gives them in my eyes a much higher value: for so they must be regarded as neither being the inventions nor belonging to the age of the poets themselves, but as sacred relics and light airs breathing out of better times, that were caught from the traditions of more ancient nations and so received into the flutes and trumpets of the Greeks.

Nevertheless, if any one be determined to believe that the allegorical meaning of the fable was in no case original and genuine, but that always the fable was first and the allegory put in after, I will not press that point; but allowing him to enjoy that gravity of judgment (of the dull and leaden order though it be) which he affects, I will attack him, if indeed he be worth the pains, in another manner upon a fresh ground. Parables have been used in two ways, and (which is strange) for contrary purposes. For they serve to disguise and veil the meaning, and they serve also to clear and throw light upon it. To avoid dispute then, let us give up the former of these uses. Let us suppose that these fables were things without any definite purpose, made only for pleasure. Still there remains the latter use. No force of wit can deprive us of that. Nor is there any man of ordinary learning that will object to the reception of it as a thing grave and sober, and free from all vanity; of prime use to the sciences, and sometimes indispensable: I mean the employment of parables as a method of teaching, whereby inventions that are new and abstruse and remote from vulgar opinions may find an easier passage to the understanding. On this account it was that in the old times, when the inventions and conclusions of human reason (even those that are now trite and vulgar) were as yet new and strange, the world was full of all kinds of fables, and enigmas, and parables, and similitudes: and these were used not as a device for shadowing and concealing the meaning, but as a method of making it understood; the understandings of men being then rude and impatient of all subtleties that did not address themselves to the sense,—indeed scarcely capable of them. For as hieroglyphics came before letters, so parables came before arguments. And even now if any one wish to let new light on any subject into men's minds, and that without offence or harshness, he must still go the same way and call in the aid of similitudes.

Upon the whole I conclude with this: the wisdom of the primitive ages was either great or lucky; great, if they knew what they were doing and invented the figure to shadow the meaning; lucky, if without meaning or intending it they fell upon matter which gives occasion to such worthy contemplations. My own pains, if there be any help in them, I shall think well bestowed either way: I shall be throwing light either upon antiquity or upon nature itself.

That the thing has been attempted by others I am of course aware, but if I may speak what I think freely without mincing it, I must say that the pains which have been hitherto taken that way, though great and laborious, have gone near to deprive the inquiry of all its beauty and worth; while men of no experience in affairs, nor any learning beyond a few commonplaces, have applied the sense of the parables to some generalities and vulgar observations, without attaining their true force, their genuine propriety, or their deeper reach. Here, on the other hand, it will be found (if I mistake not) that though the subjects be old, yet the matter is new; while leaving behind us the open and level parts we bend our way towards the nobler heights that rise beyond.

## NARCISSUS; OR SELF-LOVE.

Narcissus is said to have been a young man of wonderful beauty, but intolerably proud, fastidious, and disdainful. Pleased with himself and despising all others, he led a solitary life in the woods and hunting-grounds; with a few companions to whom he was all in all; followed also wherever he went by a nymph called Echo. Living thus, he came by chance one day to a clear fountain, and (being in the heat of noon) lay down by it; when beholding in the water his own image, he fell into such a study and then into such a rapturous admiration of himself, that he could not be drawn away from gazing at the shadowy picture, but remained rooted to the spot till sense left him; and at last he was changed into the flower that bears his name; a flower which appears in the early spring; and is sacred to the infernal deities,—Pluto, Proserpine, and the Furies.

In this fable are represented the dispositions, and the fortunes too, of those persons who from consciousness either of beauty or some other gift with which nature unaided by any industry of their own has graced them, fall in love as it were with themselves. For with this state of mind there is commonly joined an indisposition to appear much in public or engage in business; because business would expose them to many neglects and scorns, by which their minds would be dejected and troubled. Therefore they commonly live a solitary, private, and shadowed life; with a small circle of chosen companions, all devoted admirers, who assent like an echo to everything they say, and entertain them with mouth-homage; till being by such habits gradually depraved and puffed up, and besotted at last with self-admiration, they fall into such a sloth and listlessness that they grow utterly stupid, and lose all vigour and alacrity. And it was a beautiful thought to choose the flower of spring as an emblem of characters like this: characters which in the opening of their career flourish and are talked of, but disappoint in maturity the promise of their youth. The fact too that this flower is sacred to the infernal deities contains an allusion to the same thing. For men of this disposition turn out utterly useless and good for nothing whatever; and anything that yields no fruit, but like the way of a ship in the sea passes and leaves no trace, was by the ancients held sacred to the shades and infernal gods.

## STYX; OR TREATIES.

It is a very common tradition that of the one oath by which the gods bound themselves when they meant to leave no room for repentance; and finds a place in a great many fables. In that case they invoked in witness, not any majesty of heaven or any divine attribute, but Styx; a river in the infernal regions which with many windings encircled the palace of Dis. This form of oath alone, and no other, was held to be sure and inviolable: the penalty of breaking it being one which the deities most dreaded,

—namely that the breaker should for a certain period of years be excluded from the banquets of the gods.

The fable seems to have been invented in allusion to treaties and compacts of princes: in respect of which it is but too true that whatever be the solemnity and sanctity of the oath they are confirmed with, yet they are little to be depended on; insomuch that they are used in fact rather with an eye to reputation and fame and ceremony, than for confidence and security and effect. And even when the ties of relationship (which are as the sacraments of nature) or of mutual good services come in to aid, yet in most cases all are too weak for ambition and interest and the licence of power: the rather because princes can always find plenty of plausible pretexts (not being accountable to any arbiter) wherewith to justify and veil their cupidity and bad faith. There is adopted therefore but one true and proper pledge of faith; and it is not any celestial divinity. This is Necessity (the great god of the powerful), and peril of state, and communion of interest. Now Necessity is elegantly represented under the figure of Styx; the fatal river across which no man can return. This is the deity which Iphicrates the Athenian invoked to witness treaties; and since he was one that spoke out plainly what most men think and keep to themselves, his words are worth quoting. Finding that the Lacedæmonians were devising and propounding various cautions and sanctions and securities and bonds to hold the treaty fast, *There is only one bond and security* (said he, interrupting them) *that can hold between you and us:—you must prove that you have yielded so much into our hands that you cannot hurt us if you would.* And so it is that if the means of hurting be taken away, or if a breach of the treaty would endanger the existence or the integrity of the state and revenue,—then the treaty may be considered to be ratified and sanctioned and confirmed as by the oath of Styx: for then it is upon peril of being interdicted from the banquets of the gods; which was the ancient expression for the rights and prerogatives of empire, and wealth, and felicity.

# NEW ATLANTIS

## SALOMON'S HOUSE

"God bless thee, my son; I will give thee the greatest jewel I have. For I will impart unto thee, for the love of God and men, a relation of the true state of Salomon's House. Son, to make you know the true state of Salomon's House, I will keep this order. First, I will set forth unto you the end of our foundation. Secondly, the preparations and instruments we have for our works. Thirdly, the several employments and functions whereto our fellows are assigned. And fourthly, the ordinances and rites which we observe.

"The End of our Foundation is the knowledge of Causes, and secret motions of things; and the enlarging of the bounds of Human Empire, to the effecting of all things possible.

"The Preparations and Instruments are these. We have large and deep caves of several depths: the deepest are sunk six hundred fathom; and some of them are digged and made under great hills and mountains: so that if you reckon together the depth of the hill and the depth of the cave, they are (some of them) above three miles deep. For we find that the depth of a hill, and the depth of a cave from the flat, is the same thing; both remote alike from the sun and heaven's beams, and from the open air. These caves we call the Lower Region. And we use them for all coagulations, indurations, refrigerations, and conservations of bodies. We use them likewise for the imitation of natural mines; and the producing also of new artificial metals, by compositions and materials which we use, and lay there for many years. We use them also sometimes, (which may seem strange,) for curing of some diseases, and for prolongation of life in some hermits that choose to live there, well accommodated of all things necessary; and indeed live very long; by whom also we learn many things.

"We have burials in several earths, where we put divers cements, as the Chineses do their porcellain. But we have them in greater variety, and some of them more fine. We have also great variety of composts, and soils, for the making of the earth fruitful.

"We have high towers; the highest about half a mile in height; and some of them likewise set upon high mountains; so that the vantage of the hill with the tower is in the highest of them three miles at least. And these places we call the Upper Region: accounting the air between the high places and the low, as a Middle Region. We use these towers, according to their several heights and situations, for insolation, refrigeration, conservation; and for the view of divers meteors; as winds, rain, snow, hail; and some of the fiery meteors also. And upon them, in some places, are dwellings of hermits, whom we visit sometimes, and instruct what to observe.

"We have great lakes both salt and fresh, whereof we have use for the fish and fowl. We use them also for burials of some natural bodies: for we find a difference in things buried in earth or in air below the earth, and things buried in water. We have also pools, of which some do strain fresh water out of salt; and others by art do turn fresh water into salt. We have also some rocks in the midst of the sea, and some bays upon the shore, for some works wherein is required the air and vapour of the sea. We have likewise violent streams and cataracts, which serve us for many motions: and likewise engines for multiplying and enforcing of winds, to set also on going divers motions.

"We have also a number of artificial wells and fountains, made in imitation of the natural sources and baths; as tincted upon vitriol, sulphur, steel, brass, lead, nitre, and other minerals. And again we have little wells for infusions of many things, where the waters take the virtue quicker and better than in vessels or basons. And amongst them we have a water which we call Water of Paradise, being, by that we do to it, made very sovereign for health, and prolongation of life.

"We have also great and spacious houses, where we imitate and demonstrate meteors; as snow, hail, rain, some artificial rains of bodies and not of water, thunders, lightnings; also generations of bodies in air; as frogs, flies, and divers others.

"We have also certain chambers, which we call Chambers of Health, where we qualify the air as we think good and proper for the cure of divers diseases, and preservation of health.

"We have also fair and large baths, of several mixtures, for the cure of diseases, and the restoring of man's body from arefaction: and others for the confirming of it in strength of sinews, vital parts, and the very juice and substance of the body.

"We have also large and various orchards and gardens, wherein we do not so much respect beauty, as variety of ground and soil, proper for divers trees and herbs: and some very spacious, where trees and berries are set whereof we make divers kinds of drinks, besides the vineyards. In these we practise likewise all conclusions of grafting and inoculating, as well of wild-trees as fruit-trees, which produceth many effects. And we make (by art) in the same orchards and gardens, trees and flowers to come earlier or later than their seasons; and to come up and bear more speedily than by their natural course they do. We make them also by art greater much than their nature; and their fruit greater and sweeter and of differing taste, smell, colour, and figure, from their nature. And many of them we so order, as they become of medicinal use.

"We have also means to make divers plants rise by mixtures of earths without seeds; and likewise to make divers new plants, differing from the vulgar; and to make one tree or plant turn into another.

"We have also parks and inclosures of all sorts of beasts and birds, which we use not only for view or rareness, but likewise for dissections and trials; that thereby we may take light what may be wrought upon the body of man. Wherein we find many strange effects; as continuing life in them, though divers parts, which you account vital, be perished and taken forth; resuscitating of some that seem dead in appearance; and the like. We try also all poisons and other medicines upon them, as well of chirurgery as physic. By art likewise, we make them greater or taller than their kind is; and contrariwise dwarf them, and stay their growth: we make them more fruitful and bearing than their kind is; and contrariwise barren and not generative. Also we make them differ in colour, shape, activity, many ways. We find means to make commixtures and copulations of different kinds; which have produced many new kinds, and them not barren, as the general opinion is. We make a number of kinds of serpents, worms, flies, fishes, of putrefaction; whereof some are advanced (in effect) to be perfect creatures, like beasts or birds; and have sexes, and do propagate. Neither do we this by chance, but we know beforehand of what matter and commixture what kind of those creatures will arise.

"We have also particular pools, where we make trials upon fishes, as we have said before of beasts and birds.

"We have also places for breed and generation of those kinds of worms and flies which are of special use; such as are with you your silkworms and bees.

"I will not hold you long with recounting of our brew-houses, bakehouses, and kitchens, where are made divers drinks, breads, and meats, rare and of special effects. Wines we have of grapes; and drinks of other juice of fruits, of grains, and of roots: and of mixtures with honey, sugar, manna, and fruits dried and decocted. Also of the tears or woundings of trees, and of the pulp of canes. And these drinks are of several ages, some to the age or last of forty years. We have drinks also brewed with several herbs, and roots, and spices; yea with several fleshes, and white meats; whereof some of the drinks are such, as they are in effect meat and drink both: so that divers, especially in age, do desire to live with them, with little or no meat or bread. And above all, we strive to have drinks of extreme thin parts, to insinuate into the body, and yet without all biting, sharpness, or fretting; insomuch as some of them put upon the back of your hand will, with a little stay, pass through to the palm, and yet taste mild to the mouth. We have also waters which we ripen in that fashion, as they become nourishing; so that they are indeed excellent drink; and many will use no other. Breads we have of several grains, roots, and kernels: yea and some of flesh and fish dried; with divers kinds of leavenings and seasonings: so that some do extremely move appetites; some do nourish so, as divers do live of them, without any other meat; who live very long. So for meats, we have some of them so beaten and made tender and mortified, yet without all corrupting, as a weak heat of the stomach will turn them into good chylus, as well as a strong heat would meat otherwise prepared. We have some meats also and breads and drinks, which taken by men enable them to fast long after; and some other, that used make the very flesh of men's bodies sensibly more hard and tough, and their strength far greater than otherwise it would be.

"We have dispensatories, or shops of medicines. Wherein you may easily think, if we have such variety of plants and living creatures more than you have in Europe, (for we know what you have,) the simples, drugs, and ingredients of medicines, must likewise be in so much the greater variety. We have them likewise of divers ages, and long fermentations. And for their preparations, we have not only all manner of exquisite distillations and separations, and especially by gentle heats and percolations through divers strainers, yea and substances; but also exact forms of composition, whereby they incorporate almost, as they were natural simples.

"We have also divers mechanical arts, which you have not; and stuffs made by them; as papers, linen, silks, tissues; dainty works of feathers of wonderful lustre; excellent dyes, and many others; and shops likewise, as well for such as are not brought into vulgar use amongst us as for those that are. For you must know that of the things before recited, many of them are grown into use throughout the kingdom; but yet if they did flow from our invention, we have of them also for patterns and principals.

"We have also furnaces of great diversities, and that keep great diversity of heats; fierce and quick; strong and constant; soft and mild; blown, quiet; dry, moist; and the like. But above all, we have heats in imitation of the sun's and heavenly bodies' heats, that pass divers inequalities and (as it were) orbs, progresses, and returns, whereby we produce admirable effects. Besides, we have heats of dungs, and of bellies and maws of living creatures, and of their bloods and bodies; and of hays and herbs laid up moist; of lime unquenched; and such like. Instruments also which generate heat only by motion. And farther, places for strong insolations; and again, places under the earth, which by nature or art yield heat. These divers heats we use, as the nature of the operation which we intend requireth.

"We have also perspective-houses, where we make demonstrations of all lights and radiations; and of all colours; and out of things uncoloured and transparent, we can represent unto you all several colours; not in rain-bows, as it is in gems and prisms, but of themselves single. We represent also all multiplications of light, which we carry to great distance, and make so sharp as to discern small points and lines; also all colorations of light: all delusions and deceits of the sight, in figures, magnitudes, motions, colours: all demonstrations of shadows. We find also divers means, yet unknown to you, of producing of light originally from divers bodies. We procure means of seeing objects afar off; as in the heaven and remote places; and represent things near as afar off, and things afar off as near; making feigned distances. We have also helps for the sight, far above spectacles and glasses in use. We have also glasses and means to see small and minute bodies perfectly and distinctly; as the shapes and colours of small flies and worms, grains and flaws in gems, which cannot otherwise be seen; observations in urine and blood, not otherwise to be seen. We make artificial rain-bows, halos, and circles about light. We represent also all manner of reflexions, refractions, and multiplications of visual beams of objects.

"We have also precious stones of all kinds, many of them of great beauty, and to you unknown; crystals likewise; and glasses of divers kinds; and amongst them some of metals vitrificated, and other materials besides those of which you make glass. Also a number of fossils, and imperfect minerals, which you have not. Likewise loadstones of prodigious virtue; and other rare stones, both natural and artificial.

"We have also sound-houses, where we practise and demonstrate all sounds, and their generation. We have harmonies which you have not, of quarter-sounds, and lesser slides of sounds. Divers instruments of music likewise to you unknown, some sweeter than any you have; together with bells and rings that are dainty and sweet. We represent small sounds as great and deep; likewise great sounds extenuate and sharp; we make divers tremblings and warblings of sounds, which in their original are entire. We represent and imitate all articulate sounds and letters, and the voices and notes of beasts and birds. We have certain helps which set to the ear do further the hearing greatly. We have also divers strange and artificial echoes, reflecting the voice many times, and as it were tossing it: and some that give back the voice louder than it came; some shriller, and some deeper; yea, some rendering the voice differing in the letters or articulate sound from that they receive. We have also means to convey sounds in trunks and pipes, in strange lines and distances.

"We have also perfume-houses; wherewith we join also practices of taste. We multiply smells, which may seem strange. We imitate smells, making all smells to breathe out of other mixtures than those that give them. We make divers imitations of taste likewise, so that they will deceive any man's taste. And in this house we contain also a confiture-house; where we make all sweet-meats, dry and moist, and divers pleasant wines, milks, broths, and sallets, in far greater variety than you have.

"We have also engine-houses, where are prepared engines and instruments for all sorts of motions. There we imitate and practise to make swifter motions than any you have, either out of your muskets or any engine that you have; and to make them and multiply them more easily, and with small force, by wheels and other means: and to make them stronger, and more violent than yours are; exceeding your greatest cannons and basilisks. We represent also ordnance and instruments of war, and engines of all kinds: and likewise new mixtures and compositions of gun-powder, wildfires burning in water, and unquenchable. Also fire-works of all variety both for pleasure and use. We imitate also flights of birds; we have some degrees of flying in the air; we have ships and boats for going under water, and brooking of seas; also swimming-girdles and supporters. We have divers curious clocks, and other like motions of return, and some perpetual motions. We imitate also motions of living creatures, by images of men, beasts, birds, fishes, and serpents. We have also a great number of other various motions, strange for equality, fineness, and subtilty.

"We have also a mathematical house, where are represented all instruments, as well of geometry as astronomy, exquisitely made.

"We have also houses of deceits of the senses; where we represent all manner of feats of juggling, false apparitions, impostures, and illusions; and their fallacies. And surely you will easily believe that we that have so many things truly natural which induce admiration, could in a world of particulars deceive the senses, if we would disguise those things and labour to make them seem more miraculous. But we do hate all impostures and lies: insomuch as we have severely forbidden it to all our fellows, under pain of ignominy and fines, that they do not shew any natural work or thing, adorned or swelling; but only pure as it is, and without all affectation of strangeness.

"These are (my son) the riches of Salomon's House.

"For the several employments and offices of our fellows; we have twelve that sail into foreign countries, under the names of other nations, (for our own we conceal;) who bring us the books, and abstracts, and patterns of experiments of all other parts. These we call Merchants of Light.

"We have three that collect the experiments which are in all books. These we call Depredators.

"We have three that collect the experiments of all mechanical arts; and also of liberal sciences; and also of practices which are not brought into arts. These we call Mystery-men.

"We have three that try new experiments, such as themselves think good. These we call Pione[e]rs or Miners.

"We have three that draw the experiments of the former four into titles and tables, to give the better light for the drawing of observations and axioms out of them. These we call Compilers.

"We have three that bend themselves, looking into the experiments of their fellows, and cast about how to draw out of them things of use and practice for man's life, and knowledge as well for works as for plain demonstration of causes, means of natural divinations, and the easy and clear discovery of the virtues and parts of bodies. These we call Dowry-men or Benefactors.

"Then after divers meetings and consults of our whole number, to consider of the former labours and collections, we have three that take care, out of them, to direct new experiments, of a higher light, more penetrating into nature than the former. These we call Lamps.

"We have three others that do execute the experiments so directed, and report them. These we call Inoculators.

"Lastly, we have three that raise the former discoveries by experiments into greater observations, axioms, and aphorisms. These we call Interpreters of Nature.

"We have also, as you must think, novices and apprentices, that the succession of the former employed men do not fail; besides a great number of servants and attendants, men and women. And this we do also: we have consultations, which of the inventions and experiences which we have discovered shall be published, and which not: and take all an oath of secrecy, for the concealing of those which we think fit to keep secret: though some of those we do reveal sometimes to the state, and some not.

"For our ordinances and rites: we have two very long and fair galleries: in one of these we place patterns and samples of all manner of the more rare and excellent inventions: in the other we place the statua's of all principal inventors. There we have the statua of your Columbus, that discovered the West Indies: also the inventor of ships: your monk that was the inventor of ordnance and of gunpowder: the inventor of music: the inventor of letters: the inventor of printing: the inventor of observations of astronomy: the inventor of works in metal: the inventor of glass: the inventor of silk of the worm: the inventor of wine: the inventor of corn and bread: the inventor of sugars: and all these by more certain tradition than you have. Then have we divers inventors of our own, of excellent works; which since you have not seen, it were too long to make descriptions of them; and besides, in the right understanding of those descriptions you might easily err. For upon every invention of value, we erect a statua to the inventor, and give him a liberal and honourable reward. These statua's are some of brass; some of marble and touch-stone; some of cedar and other special woods gilt and adorned: some of iron; some of silver; some of gold.

"We have certain hymns and services, which we say daily, of laud and thanks to God for his marvellous works: and forms of prayers, imploring his aid and blessing for the illumination of our labours, and the turning of them into good and holy uses.

"Lastly, we have circuits or visits of divers principal cities of the kingdom; where, as it cometh to pass, we do publish such new profitable inventions as we think good. And we do also declare natural divinations of diseases, plagues, swarms of hurtful creatures, scarcity, tempests, earthquakes, great inundations, comets, temperature of the year, and divers other things; and we give counsel thereupon what the people shall do for the prevention and remedy of them."

And when he had said this, he stood up; and I, as I had been taught, kneeled down; and he laid his right hand upon my head, and said; "God bless thee, my son, and God bless this relation which I have made. I give thee leave to publish it for the good of other nations; for we here are in God's bosom, a land unknown." And so he left me; having assigned a value of about two thousand ducats, for a bounty to me and my fellows. For they give great largesses where they come upon all occasions.

**[The rest was not perfected.]**

# Robert Parsons
## 1546–1610

Robert Parsons, or Persons, was educated at Oxford where he held a fellowship from 1568 to 1574, left England to embrace the Roman Catholic Church, joined the Jesuit order in 1575, and returned with Edmund Campion in 1580 to organize the Marian clergy. After he set up a secret press and issued Campion's *Decem Rationes,* the government intervened: Campion was executed in 1581; Parsons fled to the continent. He then served the Jesuit cause in various capacities in Italy and Spain, principally as Rector of the English College at Rome from 1597 until his death. When he lay dying, his last act was to affirm his friendship with Campion. He had kept a piece of the rope with which Campion was hanged at Tyburn, and after kissing it he put it around his neck as the priest began reciting the prayer *Proficiscere, Anima Christiana*—"Go forward, Christian soul."

His writings include *The Christian Exercise,* which, appearing first in 1582 and then in some thirty-five subsequent editions or reprints in the next half century, became one of the great devotional books of the times, loved by Catholics and Protestants alike. But it was to the work of the Counter-Reformation that he applied most of his talents, and he never relaxed his efforts to restore the old faith in England. His provocative pages, reminding us that it was a three-cornered fight, deserve to be read with those of Hooker and Donne, Baxter and Milton.

Parsons has for the most part known only a limited audience in later centuries, but those who are not put off by his partisan commitment can find much to enjoy. Swift, for example, in *Tatler* 230, recognizes him as a master of prose of high seriousness, and Isaac Disraeli in his *Amenities of Literature* (1880, II, 85) offers a Victorian tribute to Parsons' "vernacular diction, in its purity and pristine vigour, without ornament, or polish . . . unblemished by an exotic phrase."

In controversial tracts such as *The Judgment of a Catholic English-man,* which we give in part in the following pages, his prose combines colloquial liveliness, precision of language, and a quiet formality. It is spare of ornament or figure, and given to understatement. At one extreme, in order to oppose the Protestant claim that Elizabeth had been the "happy Queene, the Blessed Queene, whose unmatched wisedome, and unconquered prowesse . . . crowned her the peerless wonder of her sexe," he can make his point by observing drily that Catholics are censured "for having had so happy & peerles a persecutour." He can rise also to a sustained and moving statement. In an appeal to James for greater tolerance, he cries:

> Nothing can be more pitifull, then to see a Noble House divided in it selfe, & the one to beate, hunt, & pursue the other, & this to be their continuall exercise, especially of Children, under the sight of their owne Father, loving them all, and desyring to be beloved. Ah! what sollicitude must there needs be in that Fathers hart! And were it not a great synne to increase the same, by casting in oyle to augment the flame?

## EDITIONS

*A Brief Discours Contayning Certayne Reasons Why Catholiques Refuse to Goe to Church,* 1580.

*A Brief Censure uppon Two Bookes Written in Answere to E. Campions Offer of Disputation,* 1581.

*The First Booke of the Christian Exercise, Appertayning to Resolution,* 1582; *A Christian Directorie Guiding Men to Their Salvation,* 1585 and after.

*The Second Parte of the Booke of Christian Exercise, Appertayning to Resolution,* 1590.

*A Conference about the Next Succession to the Crowne of Ingland,* 1594.

*A Treatise Tending to Mitigation towardes Catholicke-subjectes in England,* 1607.

*The Judgment of a Catholicke English-man,* 1608; ed. by W. T. Costello, 1957.

*A Quiet and Sober Reckoning with M. Thomas Morton,* 1609.

*A Discussion of the Answere of M. William Barlow,* 1612.

"The Memoirs of Father Robert Persons," ed. by J. H. Pollen, *Publs of the Catholic Record Society,* II, IV (1906–1907).

*Letters and Memorials of Father Robert Persons, S.J.,* ed. by Leo Hicks, *Publs of the Catholic Record Society,* XXXIX (1942).

## HISTORICAL AND CRITICAL STUDIES

THOMAS JAMES, *The Iesuits Downefall Threatned against Them by the Secular Priests for Their Wicked Lives, Accursed Manners, Hereticall Doctrine and More Than Matchiavillian Poliçie. Together with the Life of Father Parsons, an English Iesuite,* 1612.

HERBERT THURSTON, "Catholic writers and Elizabethan Readers. I. Father Parsons' Christian Directory," *The Month,* LXXXII (1894).

RICHARD SIMPSON, *Edmund Campion,* 1896.

J. H. CREHAN, "The Prose of Robert Parsons," *The Month,* CLXXV (1940).

ERNEST A. STRATHMANN, "Robert Parsons' Essay on Atheism," *Joseph Quincy Adams Memorial Studies,* ed. by James G. McManaway, 1948.

THOMAS G. LAW, "Robert Parsons," *DNB,* 1949–1950.

A. C. SOUTHERN, *Elizabethan Recusant Prose 1559–1582,* 1950.

EDWIN H. MILLER, "Robert Parsons' 'Resolution' and 'The Repentance of Robert Greene,'" *N & Q,* n.s., I (1954).

ROBERT MCNULTY, "Robert Parsons' *The First Booke of the Christian Exercise* (1582): An Edition and a Study," Dissertation, Columbia University, 1955; *Dissertation Abstr.,* XVI (1956).

DENIS MEADOWS, *Elizabethan Quintet,* 1956.

JOHN E. PARISH, "An Englishman Who Collaborated with the Spanish Armada," *Rice Institute Pamphlet,* XLIV, 1 (1957).

ROBERT MCNULTY, "The Protestant Version of Robert Parsons' *The First Booke of the Christian Exercise,*" *HLQ,* XXII (1959).

M. D. R. LEYS, *Catholics in England, 1559–1829,* 1961.

JOHN P. DRISCOLL, "*The Seconde Parte:* Another Protestant Version of Robert Persons' *Christian Directorie,*" *HLQ,* XXV (1962).

JOHN R. ROBERTS, "A Critical Anthology of English Recusant Devotional Prose," Dissertation, University of Illinois, 1962; *Dissertation Abstr.,* XXIII (1963).

# THE JUDGMENT
## OF A CATHOLICKE ENGLISH-MAN, LIVING IN BANISHMENT FOR HIS RELIGION

## CONCERNING THE POPES TWO *BREVES,* AGAINST THE RECEAVING OF THE *OATH.*

### The Summe of the Two Breves

1.   The summe of the Popes two *Breves* the first of the 21. of September, Anno 1606. the second of the 21. of August the next yeare following, is this: That wheras he had heard, that the Catholicks of *England,* were very sorely pressed with a new devised *Oath,* against their Consciences, concerning certayne poyntes, appertayning to the Authority of the Sea Apostolicke, in some cases; he wrote the first *Breve,* to admonish, comfort, and direct them; signifying his harty sorie for their long continued afflictions, and exhorting them to patience, and constancy in defence of the integrity of Catholicke faith, and the purity of their owne consciences. And after this setting downe *verbatim* the whole *Oath,* as it lyeth in the Statute, he condemneth the taking therof, as unlawfull unto a Catholicke man, in regard of divers clauses therin conteyned, contrary to the said integrity of Catholicke faith, and health of soules; though in particuler, he descendeth not to dispute, or discusse the reasons, or poynts therof, as became not a Judge: especially seeing (as he saith) the matters themselves be evident by the wordes of the *Breve.* And wheras this first *Breve* was soone after called into question by some, as not proceeding from the Popes owne motion, and intention: his second *Breve* was set forth to approve, ratify, and confirme the former; assuring all Catholicks, that both the one, and the other came from him directly, sincerely, & upon due deliberation, and consequently, that they were to be acknowledged, and obeyed by all true Catholicke people. This is the summe of what the Pope wrote: now lett us see, what advantage is taken by the Apologer against the same.

11. First of all he jesteth at the Popes sorrow for Catholicks afflictions, making them to be none at all: and wheras the late *Q. Elizabeth* is not so much as named in eyther of these *Breves,* this man will needes bring her in perforce, and justifie her actions against Catholicke people, therby the more to animate his Ma.<sup>tie</sup> to follow her example, setting downe this notorious false position concerning her, and her doings, *That according to his owne knowledge, her Ma.<sup>tie</sup> never punished any Papist for Religion.* Which how he can justify, or by what Equivocation mantayne, I know not. But being not content with this, he passeth further, and rageth exceedingly against those innocent Priests, Students, and others, that only for the profession of their Religion, gave up their lyves under her, as by their inditements, and arraignments in publike record doth appeare, and concludeth finally both of her, and them, thus: *This Gracious Princesse was as free from persecution, as these hellish Instruments from the honour of Martyrdome.* And yet further, very profanely: *Having now sacrificed, as I may say* (quoth he) *to the* Manes *of my defunct Soveraigne, as well for the discharge of my particuler duty, as love of verity; I must next performe my duty also to his Ma.<sup>tie</sup> present, &c.*

111. Wherunto a man might answere, that if he performe it with no more verity to his *present Soveraigne,* then he hath done to his *defunct Soveraigne past;* he will gayne little grace (I suppose) with his Ma.<sup>tie</sup> whom I hold to be of that noble nature, and magnanimity, as that he taketh such grosse-lying-flattery, rather for injury, then obsequie. But as for his heathen, prophane sacrificing to the *Manes* or Hob-gob-lins of his late Lady; I confesse, that it is an office fitter for a Protestant-Minister, that thinketh it unlawfull to pray for her soule, to deale with her *Manes* or Infernal spirits, then with Celestiall, by praying for her to Saints. But would God these *Manes* might now have licence to appeare, and talke with him, and relate what passeth with her after all this joylity, and ruffe in this world; I doubt not but they would coole his excessive veyne of flattering vanity. For if all the old platforme of Saints lyves, prescribed in Scriptures and practised by servants of God, were not erroneous & vayne, as much fasting, continuall prayer, dayly mortification, frequent recollection, diligent chasticement of their bodyes, humble and fervent devotion, labouring and working salvation in feare and trembling, aboundant almes-deedes, haire-cloth and ashes, contrition, sorrow and sobbing for synnes: If these things (I say) were the ancient wayes to lyfe, and to everlasting salvation: then must the pathes of *Q. Elizabeth,* which are

knowne by most men, to have byn, eyther wholy different, or most opposite to these, lead to an other opposite end, *Quia unusquisque recipiet,*
*secundum opera sua.*

IV.  But not to enter into these melancholicke matters of her *Manes,* or
of the other world, to make any certayne judgement therof, before we
arryve thither: I will only speake a word or two of the world present,
and this with protestation, that it is wholy against my will, and against
the generall inclination (as I take it) of all Catholicke people, who
would in charity be content, that the memory of her actions, & injuryes
against them, being never so many, & injurious, were buried with her
body; as may well appeare by their long silence therin since her death.
But the continuall egging of the adversary is such, as forceth us to say
somwhat, for our owne defence, and for cleering the cause, and men,
by her so eagerly and injuriously pursued.

V.  This Minister then, as in part you have heard, maketh her, *The*
*most myld, dolce, patient, and clement Princesse in the world,* even
unto Catholicks, whose bloud she shed so aboundantly, both at home, &
abroad, during all the time of her raigne: nay, *That her Ma.*<sup>tie</sup> *never*
*punished any Papist for religion:* And, That she was *most free from all*
*persecution: That she never medled with hard punishment of any Catho-*
*licke, nor made any rigorous lawes against them before the excommuni-*
*cation of Pope Pius Quintus,* that was in the eleventh yeare of her raigne:
And yet is it knowne, and cannot be denyed, but that the most grievous
law, & *Oath* of *Supremacie,* & rigorous penall Statute against saying, or
hearing Masse, were made long before that tyme: And that all the Bishops, Prelates, Religious, & chiefe Ecclesiasticall men were depryved,
spoyled, imprisoned, or forced into banishment: and this before the
Pope used any Censure against her at all: so exact, & punctuall is the
truth of this Ministers narration. And not content with this, he doth
prosecute odious comparisons, betweene the Pope, & her, laying all the
origen of hurts and wickednes to him, and merit of vertue, and inno-
cency to her, which is the very same, that is mentioned by the Prophet,
*to call evill good, & good evill.*

VI.  Nor is he alone in this devise, but that all Ministers commonly,
and Ministers mates of later dayes have taken up this Common place, to
celebrate her high prayses, for disgrace of Catholicks. And one among
the rest, that for his place, should have more equity and discretion, hath

declaymed upon this matter in publicke Audience more then once, especially upon the occasion of certayn words in *Pope* Clements *Breve,* where
she is named *Misera Fæmina,* a miserable woman (in respect no doubt
of the myseries of her soule, little respected by her:) upon which words
the *Orator* triumpheth thus, *What miserable? It is said, That,* Miseria
constat ex duobus contrariis, copia & inopia, copia tribulationis, & inopia
consolationis, *Misery consisteth of two contraries, of aboundance, and
penury, aboundance of tribulation, & penury of consolation.* And then he
sheweth in what aboundance of consolations *Q. Elizabeth* lyved in all
her life, & without want of all tribulations: which if it were true; yet is it
but the argument which the worldlings used in the Psalme, to prove
their felicity, that their cellars are full, their sheepe fertile, theyr kyne
fatt, they suffer no losse: and then, *Beatum dixerunt populum cui hæc
sunt;* Happy did they call the people that had these things. But the Holy
Ghost scorneth them, and so may all men do our Orator, that useth and
urgeth so base an argument, in so high a matter.

VII.   And as for his definition of *Miserie,* by *Copia* and *Inopia,* store
and want, it is a miserable one indeed, and never heard of before, I
thinke, to come from any mans mouth, but his owne: it being ridiculous
in Philosophy, and fitt to be applyed to any thing that hath either store
or want: As a wise man in this sort may be defined to be him, that hath
store of witt, and want of folly; and a foole to be him, that hath store
of follie, and want of witt; and so a rich man is he that hath store of
riches and want of beggary; and a poore man is he, that hath store of
beggary, and penury of riches. And are not these goodly definitions
(thinke you) for so great and grave a man to produce?

VIII.   But to returne to the matter it selfe of Q. *Elizabeth* her store of
consolations, and penury of desolations in this life, *Who* (saith this our
Orator) *was so myraculously protected by God, so strengthencd and
fortified, as she did beate her most potent enemy, did sett up a King in
his kingdome, defended nations, harboured distressed people,* and the
like. Supposing all this were true, that she had such temporall felicity in
this lyfe, and were so miraculously protected, strengthened, and fortifyed
by God as heere is said: yea and that it were evident, that God had
chosen her for his elected servant (which yet doth not appeare) and
gyven her that tytle and power, to afflict the Catholicks: yet had that
byn no more, then we read in the Scriptures to have byn gyven to dyvers

Pagan Princes, and namely to *Nabuchodonosor,* of whom *Jeremy* the prophet testifyeth in sundry places of his Prophesy, That God chose him, called him his servant, and gave him speciall power, favour, & protection to afflict his people. *Ego dedi omnes terras istas in manu Nabuchodonosor Regis Babylonis servi mei,* saith God: I have gyven all these Countryes into the hands of *Nabuchodonosor* King of Babylon my servant, and all nations shall serve him, & yield obedience to him, and to his Sonne, and Sonnes sonne: And what soever nation shall not serve him, & bow his necke under his yoke, I will visite that nation with the sword, with famyne, and with plague, till I have consumed them by his hand. *And agayne in an other place:* I will choose unto me my servant *Nabuchodonosor* king of *Babylon,* & will bring him upon this Land, and upon all the inhabitants therof, and upon all nations round about &c. And yet further God said unto *Jeremy:* Thus saith the Lord of *Hostes,* I shall take unto me my servant *Nabuchodonosor,* and shall place his throne upon these stones &c.

ıx.   By all which is evident that *Syr Edward Cookes* argument is worth nothing: that for so much as God *so miraculously* protected *Q. Elizabeth,* (if it were myraculous,) so strengthened, and fortifyed her, as she did beate her most potent enemy, & did set up an other King in his Kingdome (if any such thing were:) yet this did not make her happie. As neyther it did *Nabuchodonosor,* of whome God said in the same place, that when he had served his turne of him, and wrought his will by his hand, and people, for the purging of his owne elect; he would visit upon him also, and his Countrey, and that in a farre more grievous sort: *Ponam illam in solitudines sempiternas, & reddam eis secundum opera eorum, & secundum facta manuum suarum:* I shall make that Countrey, an everlasting wildernes, and shall restore to them (that afflicted my people) according to their workes, and to the deeds of their owne handes against my people. This then was his felicity to be a scourge to others, and fynally also to himselfe most of all.

x.   And the like, I doubt not, may be said of *Q. Elizabeths* felicity against Catholicks, if we knew all, that in the last day of judgment will appeare, and wherof her lamentable end may gyve great presage to them that are wise. For that for a woman of so long and large a lyfe, as hers was, to passe hence to eternity with so small sense or feeling of God, as never so much, as to name him, nor to suffer others to bring in any speech therof, as they attempted to do, is so pittifull an end, as can lightly fall to a Christian soule: The story of which upshot of hers, I have read written by a person of much credit that was present at all her last sicknes, combats, and death, and relateth all that passed as an eye witnesse, which I passe over for brevity and modestyes sake; but it will remayne to posterity, as a dreadfull patterne of a miserable end, after a lyfe of so much joylitie.

### Queene Elizabeth Her Felicityes Mingled with Infelicities.

xi. And thus much for spirituall infelicityes, reaching to the next world, and lyfe or death to come. But if we would rest our selves only upon vayne & brickle felicityes of this world, they were not (alas) so great in Queene *Elizabeth,* but that they were mingled and interlaced with many, and great infelicityes in like manner, and these such, as did even in the eyes of worldly men, overpoise the other, especially with them that repute honour and dishonour among humane felicityes, & infelicityes.

### Queene Elizabeth Her Dishonourable Birth.

For what more dishonorable infelicity can there be, then that which standeth *in Capite Libri* of Q. *Elizabeths* lyfe? To witt, the publike solemne Statute, and Act of *Parliament,* made within few dayes after she was borne, upon the 28. yeare of King Henryes raigne, and yet extant in Print, wherin it is declared, not only by the judgment of the King, and of all that Parliament, but by the judiciall sentence also of Archbishop *Cranmer,* she was pronounced, *to be unlawfully borne, and that her mother was never King Henryes lawfull wyfe:* wherupon the said statute useth these wordes: *That it was against all honour, equity, and good conscience, that the said Elizabeth should succeed in the Imperiall Crowne of* England. And could there be any greater worldly infelicity then this.

xii. I let passe many other infelicities, which happened by her occasion to sundry, as well under the raigne of King *Edward,* as the ruyne of the *Seymers* upon the Admiralls falling in love with her, and making away his former wife *Queene Catherine Parre* to enjoy her; as also under Queene *Marie,* when so many rebellions of *Wiat, Courtney, Carewes,*

*Stafford,* & others, were made for her. But her owne raigne had most infelicities for her, if they were well considered: and I could touch many, but modestie forbiddeth.

## The Infelicity of Cruelty.

And least I should seeme to speak out of revenge, let this one consideration serve for all; That after all her afflicting Catholicks, and by that exercise, upon the egging of others, more then of her owne propension, she was drawne into continuall suspitions, feares, and frights of her mynd and spirit, even in the midst of all these sensuall delights, & contentments (admired so much by her Attorney) which drove her to a point, wherunto by nature she was not thought much inclyned, and by profession and protestations, the most condemned in others, to wit, Cruelty, which in effect was such, out of the foresaid feares, towards Catholicke Religion, as never perhaps (yea without perhaps) were so many severall lawes, & punishments devised by any one persecutour, nor many putt togeather, as are extant of hers in Print, against the professours of that Religion, wherof herselfe had byn one, and in secret or private speaches also would not deny, to be in sundry poyntes, even to her dying day.

## Queene Elizabeth Her Cruell Persecutions.

And was not this a great infelicity? When stra[n]gers do read & behold her Edicts & Statutes, wherin not only the whole use of Catholicke Religion is condemned, and under greivous punishment prohibited: but men are forced also, by rigorous penall lawes to go to the Churches of a contrary Religion, to communicate with them, to do acts, and sweare against their owne Religion, faith and Consciences: that there are severe punishments, of losse of goods and lands, for receyving an *Agnus Dei,* or a *Medall,* or *Crucifix:* greivous punishments, for keeping of a Catholicke servant, or Schoolemaister to teach and bring up their children, or to send them over seas to Catholicke Schooles: yea, that it is the payne of death it selfe to be reconciled, by confessing his synnes to the Roman Church, or to the union of faith, with the Head therof, or to perswade another to be a Catholicke, or do the same: When they read these things (I say) and many others, which for brevity I pretermitt, and that all this notwithstanding, she would not have it said, *That she persecuted any for Religion* (which in manner this Apologer sticketh not to avouch) *nor put any Priest to death for that cause indeed,* wheras notwithstanding she shed the bloud of above one hundred and thirty, that might have had their lyves even at the last cast, if in this one point of Religion they would have yielded never so little. All this (I say) being read and considered, seemeth unto forreiners a strange infelicity both of body and soule.

XIII. Especially when it is considered to what perpetuall jealosy at length she was brought unto, of all sorts of people, *Puritans, Papists,* yea of her owne dearest, as the death of the Earle of *Essex,* and his followers, doth easily declare. Neyther was there any weeke lightly, but that she had some new feares, of some Priest or Jesuite, or Catholicke soldiours sent from *Flanders, France,* or *Italy* to kill her by violence, others from *Spayne,* and other Countryes to poyson her, or at least, her Chaire. And upon such fancyes, men must be made away for greater terrour; yea Jewes must be brought in also in this kynd of pretended poysoning, as the case of Doctor *Lopez* well declareth.

#### Queene Elizabeth Her Dealing toward Her Cosen of Scotland.

Nay further this gryping passion of feare and jealosy did so vexe & consume her inwardly, as she was never well, untill she had made away, against all law of Nature and Nations, the nearest unto her in Royall bloud, that lyved upon earth, and coequall with her in dignity, if in sundry respects not Superiour, I meane his Ma.^ties noble renowned *Mother,* Queene of *France* & *Scotland,* that by force of the former Statute, which declared this other for illegitimate and incapable of the Crowne (as now yow have heard) should have enjoyed the Crowne of *England* presently after the death of *Q. Marie,* & consequently his Ma.^tie had enjoyed the same 38. yeares at least, before he came unto it after her death, who of all other lyving Creatures, is knowne most hartily to have hated that yssue & succession. And as she went about to disinable the same in the very roote & fountayne it selfe, by seeking the disgrace of the offspring, by dishonour of the origen: so never ceased she afterward to continue practises against them both, untill she had wracked the one, and brought the other also to great probability therof, if she might have lyved to her will, or have dyed with such use of senses and judgment, as might have made way to her bad affections in that behalfe.

xiv.  Well then, all this I have beene inforced to speake upon this occasion: first to represse somwhat therby the insuitation of our foresaid
Orator, in calling her, *The happy Queene, the blessed Queene, whose
unmatched wisedome, and unconquered prowesse* (to use his words)
*crowned her the peerlesse wonder of her sexe.* All which tendeth to
the exprobration of Catholicks, for having had so happy & peerles a
persecutour; and to the insuitation also over the Pope, for calling her in
his *Breve,* as he saith, *Miseram Fæminam,* a miserable woman: which
how true or waise it is, I leave to the prudent Reader out of the former
discourse, about her byrth, youth, age and end, to censure.

### What Manner of Persecutour Queene Elizabeth Was.

xv.  Secondly I do heerin but imitate the first ancient Fathers, that
wrote for defence of those holy Martyrs, that dyed for Christian Religion
in the Primitive Church, as namely, *Justinus Martyr, Irenæus, Tertullian,* and others, who to comfort the afflicted, and to honour more their
cause, did put them in mynd what manner of people their first persecu-
tours were; as namely *Nero* and *Domitian,* what lyfe they led, what end
they made, and the like; And that indeed they were fit instruments, to
be the first, in such a worke. And the like we may say to Catholicks of
*Q. Elizabeth,* that she being the strangest woman that ever was borne
for divers circumstances, now partly touched, and the first absolutly of
that sexe, eyther Christian or created, that tooke upon her Supreme
power in Spirituall and Ecclesiasticall matters; it must needes be some
comfort to Catholicke people, that God chose such an instrument to be
their first scourge, out of all woman kynd.

xvi.  And lastly, for that this Apologer will needs take upon him, *to
sacrifice to her* Manes: I thought my selfe obliged to offer some incense
in like manner to the same, for mitigating the evill sent, which that notorious untrue assertion must needs import, to the senses of all understanding Readers: That, *Queene Elizabeth never punished any Papist
for Religion, Nor made any rigorous law against them, before* Pius
Quintus *his Excommunication, nor since that tyme, but upon private
plots, machinations, &c.* For cleare confutation wherof, I remit those
of the elder sort, that lyve in *England,* to their owne eyes, eares, and
other externall senses, and those of yonger age, to the books of Statutes,

of *Q. Elizabeths* tyme, *John Stowes* Chronicle, and other such publicke Records. And so much of this poynt.

XXVI. ... For that, not only all the most cruell Statutes and penall Lawes made by *Q. Elizabeth* were renewed and confirmed before this, with addition of others, tending to no lesse rigour & acerbitie: but also the exaction of the same was put in practice with great severitie; & namely the payment of the twenty poundes a moneth, or two partes of their goods and landes for Recusants (once remitted by his Ma.^tie as heere is confessed) were not only recalled againe: but the arrearages therof in like manner exacted; and for levying wherof, throughout sundry shyres of the Realme (especially in the North) there was such ransacking of mens houses, such dryving away of their Cattell from their groundes, such strayning of their Rents, such vexing of their tennants (not knowne perhaps to his Ma.^tie) as if the whole Countrey had byn gyven over to spoyle & desolation.

### Clemency No Cause of Desperate Attempts.

XXVII. Nor were mens goods and persons only afflicted, but the lyves also of sundry taken away for cause of their Religion before this powder-treason fell out: which desperate treason, to ascribe as an effect and fruite of too much clemency in his Ma.^tie (as this Minister doth) is a strange assertion, no doubt: for so much, as such effects do not proceed, but of exasperated myndes; which clemency worketh not, eyther in men or beasts. Neyther did ever any learned Philosopher, that wrote of the good institution of any Common wealth, or of the security of any Prince in his Government, put such effects for fruits of clemency, but rather of the contrary manner of proceeding. And if all the disasterous ends of the most unfortunate Princes, that ever have byn destroyed, should be layd togeather, and the causes therof exactly inquired, it would be found so: and consequently that this Minister is no good Counsellour to his Ma.^tie in this so great & weighty affayre. And we hope that Almighty God, by the mercy of his dearest Sonne our Saviour, and through the prayers of his Ma.^ties good Mother, and other holy Princes of his Royall bloud now in heaven, will never suffer him, at the egging of such exas-perating people, to follow so violent, troublesome, and dangerous a course, and so contrary to theirs, whiles they lyved upon earth, and so alienate from his owne sweete nature and Princely disposition.

The Cruelty of Searches.

xxviii.  But to proceed a litle further in the narration of some poyntes
of heavy persecution, that insued soone after his Ma.^ties being in *England,* much before the powder-treason was attempted: Who doth not
know what afflictions were layd upon Catholicks; even in the very first
yeare of his Ma.^ties raigne, especially towards the end therof, & much
more throughout all the second yeare, before the said powder-treason
fell out. For then not only in the Shires and Provinces abroad: but even
in *London* it selfe, and in the eyes of the Court, the violence, and insolency, of continuall searches grew to be such, as was intollerable; no
night passing commonly, but that Souldiours, & Catch-poles brake into
quiet mens houses, when they were asleepe, and not only carryed away
their persons unto prisons at their pleasure, except they would brybe
them excessively, but whatsoever liked them best besydes in the house,
eyther of Bookes, Cuppes, Chalices, or other furniture, that might any
wayes seeme, or be pretended to belong to Religion, was taken for a
prey, and seazed on. And among others, I remember, that one frend of
myne, had a drinking Cuppe of sylver taken from him, for that it had
the name of JESUS engraven upon it, though otherwise the forme therof
did well show, that it was but a Cuppe, & no Chalice. And these
searches were made with such violence, and insolency, as divers gentle-
women were drawne or forced out of their beds, to see whether they
had any sacred thing, or matter belonging to the use of Catholick Religion, either about them, or under their bedds.

xxix.  What shall I speake of the casting into prisons, & condemnation
to death of many Catholicks for the same cause, in every corner lightly
of the Countrey, as namely in *London* of *M. Hill* the Priest, and this
only for his function, and for comming into *England* against the Statutes of Queene *Elizabeth* to the contrary? Of *M. Sugar* also an other
Priest in *Warwicke,* that was not only condemned, but executed withall
rigour in that Cittie for the same cause, and a lay man with him named
*Robert Grysold,* for receyving him into his house? At *Oxford* also foure
Priests being taken at that tyme whose names were *M. Greene, Tich-
borne, Smith,* and *Brisco,* all had sentence of death passed upon them;
though after many afflictions suffered in the pryson there, which made
them desyre much the speedy execution of the sentence gyven against
them, they had instead of this one death, many deathes layd upon them,

by sending them prisoners to the Castle of *Wisbich,* where they receyved such cruell usage both in their diet, lodging & other treatie, as made even dyvers Protestants to take compassion of them. And why was all this, but for their Religion?

### Divers Examples of Severe Persecution.

xxx. I let passe the condemnation to death of a poore man in Oxford named *Shitell,* for that the Priest M. *Greene* had fledde into his house, when he was pursued by the searchers, through which condemnation, & perpetuall imprisonment therupon ensuing, were brought to extreme misery & calamity, his poore wyfe and children, most lamentable to behold, or heare recounted. And upon like occasion was apprehended, imprisoned, condemned, & executed in *Yorke,* about the same tyme, an other Lay-man named *Thomas Wylborne,* only for that he had used some words of perswasion to a certayne woman to be a Catholicke, notwithstanding the prohibition of her husband, who followed so hoatly the matter against him, as he caused him to be put to death. I pretermit M.$^{ris}$ *Shelley* a Gentlewoman of good Worshipp, cast into the common Jayle at *Worcester* for that the Priest M. *Hassells,* was found in her house. The apprehension in like manner, & condemning to death of M. *Edward Tempest* Priest and Gentleman in London at the same tyme. I passe over the cruell sentence of cutting of the ears, of so ancient & venerable a Gentleman, as is M. *Tho. Pound,* that had lyved above thirty yeares in sundry prisons only for being a Catholicke, and now last in his old age, had that honour from God, as to be sentenced to leese his eares and stand on the Pillorie in dyvers markets, for complayning of hard measure, & injust execution, used against Catholicks, contrary (as he presumed) to his Ma.$^{ties}$ intention.

xxxi. And fynally I passe over what was practised in *Herefordshire, Lancashire,* & other places in this kynd of persecution, and particulerly concerning the new angariation and pressure, then first brought up, that men should be bound to pay for their wyves, that were Recusants, a thing never before exacted in the former Queenes tyme. I pretermit it also to mention, how his M.$^{tie}$ before this, had rejected the common, & humble supplication of Catholicks, exhibited in writing for some toleration, & mitigation of the calamityes: the which supplication was answered with contempt & insultation by a Minister, and put in print.

His Ma.<sup>tie</sup> in like manner had gyven publike audience both to *Prot-estants* & *Puritanes* for three dayes togeather, concerning the differences of their Religion: but to Catholicks he never yealded to gyve any at all. . . .

### How Princes Authority Is Mediatly or Immediatly from God.

LXXXI.  . . . at the beginning God did not immediatly appoynt these particuler and different formes of Temporall government, which now the world hath, some of Kinges, some of Dukes, some of Common-wealthes, but appoynted only, that there should be Government, leaving to ech nation to take or choose what they would. But the Ecclesiasticall Government by Bishops was ordayned immediatly by Christ himselfe, for which cause *Bellarmine* faith in the second place heere alledged: *That Kingdomes are not immediatly instituted from God,* but mediatly only by meanes of the people; which people therfore may change their formes of government, as in many Countryes we see that they have: but yet when any forme of Government is established, and Governours placed therin, their authority and power is from God, and to be obeyed out of Conscience, under payne of damnation, as before I have shewed out of *Bellarmyne.* And he that will read but from his third Chapter *de Laicis* unto the 13. shall fynd store of assertions & proofes to that effect, to omitt many other places throughout his workes. So as the former proposition, *That Kings have not their Authority nor office from God nor his law,* is very fraudulently sett downe. For if he understand, that their forme of Principality and Office therin, is not immediatly from Gods institution, but by meanes of humane lawes, of succession, election, or the like; it is true. But if he meane, that their Authority is not from God, eyther mediate, or immediate, or induceth not obligation of Con-science in obeying them, as it seemeth he would have his Reader to thinke; it is most false. And the Apologer ought not to have walked in these obscurityes, if he had meant uprightly.

LXXXII.  I am weary to wade any further in these objections, and yet will I not let passe to note three more, though most briefly, and almost in three words, leaving the rest to be examined by the Reader himselfe. The first is, *That Church-men are as farre above Kings, as the soule is above the body.* The other: *That Obedience due to the Pope, is for Con-science sake.* The third: *That Obedience due to Kings, is only for certayne respects of order and policy;* The first and last being meere calumniations and the other not denyed by us. For as for the first, though the words heere mentioned be not in *Bellarmyne:* yet the comparison it self of Ecclesiasticall and Temporall powers in the Church, unto the soule, and body, is the comparison of *S. Gregorie Nazianzen* related only by *Bellarmyne,* and consequently it must needs follow, as the same Father also inferreth, that so much more eminent, as the soule is above the body, so much more excellent is the power Ecclesiasticall above Temporall, which *S. Chrisostome* in like manner proveth at large in his books *de Sacerdotio:* So as this is not Bellarmynes comparison, but of the said two auncient Fathers, and consequently *Bellarmyne* is not here reprehended, but they.

LXXXIII.   The other two places, if they be two, and not one, but made two for multiplying of odious matter against us, have byn so fully answered by us before, as we shall need to say no more heere therof. For as Obedience is due out of Conscience unto the Pope, & other Bishops, & Spirituall Governours, in spirituall Governments, by the Apostles precept, *Obedite Præpositis vestris, &c.* Obey your Prelates, & be subject unto them; for they watch, as being to render accompt for your soules: So the same Apostle hath commanded also, due Obedience to Temporall Magistrates, in temporall affayres, by the same obligation of Conscience, as Cardinall *Bellarmyne* doth shew at large, in the places by me alledged. And I marvaile with what Conscience the Apologer heere can deny it, cyting a place for the same in his margent, which hath no such matter, as he would inferre, *That not for Conscience, but only for certayne respects &c.* For that treating of the obligation of Obedience to temporall lawes, in temporall affayres, his second proposition is; *Non sunt exempti Clerici ab obedientia legum Civilium:* Clergie-men are not exempted from the obedience of temporall lawes. And in another place before cyted; *Lex Civilis non minus obligat in conscientia quam lex divina:* The Temporall law byndeth no lesse in conscience, then the Divine. So as all those odious matters are but fraudulently layd togeather to make Catholicks, & their cause hatefull, especially unto him, whom unto they desyre most of all men under God, to yield most satisfaction for their temporall dutyes, and would hope also to effectuate it, if these make-bate Ministers did not by their continuall incitations, clamours, and false suggestions disturbe the same, and renew daylie jealosyes and distrustes in his Ma.^ties mynd against us.

### The Conclusion

LXXXIV.  Wherfore to draw to an end this distastfull argument, it cannot but grieve, & afflict much the hartes of all that love eyther Prince or Countrey, & looke into the naturall sequels of like proceedings, to see matters runne dayly unto such extremityes as they do, & that by such instigators, as are both lesse carefull to foresee the hurts both private & publick that may ensue, & lesse able to remedy them when they fall out. The principall of whom (being the first & chiefe motors) besydes the generall hatred wherin they are with both extremes of opposite in Religion, are so interessed in like manner by the spoyles, & rapines which their ravenous Pursevants daylie bring home, out of their continuall searches, and ransacks of innocent mens houses, goodes and persons, as little moderation may be expected from them.

LXXXV.  Would God it might please his dyvine Ma.^tie so to inlighten and illustrate that excellent understanding of our Prince and Soveraigne, as he may see the many & great inconveniences, that do & must follow upon so violent courses as these men for their owne utilitie do suggest, & prosecute. Nothing can be more pittifull, then to see a Noble House divided in it selfe, & the one to beate, hunt, & pursue the other, & this to be their continuall exercise, especially of Children, under the sight of their owne Father, loving them all, and desyring to be beloved. Ah! what sollicitude must there needs be in that Fathers hart! And were it not a great synne to increase the same, by casting in oyle to augment the flame?

LXXXVI.  Would God his Ma.^ties eares, and those of his wise Counsell could reach into these partes beyond the seas, and to all forrayne nations of Christendome besydes, to heare what is said, what is written, what is discoursed by men of best judgment in this behalfe, not only in regard of justice and piety, but in reason also of State and Policie; no man being of so simple understanding, but that he must see, that so notorious differences, of Subjects for Religion, pursued with such hostility among themselves, must weaken greatly their forces, and make them lesse esteemed both of friends and adversaryes. So as, besydes internall dangers, which are ever consequent upon such inward divisions, if forrayne occasions should be offred us agayne (as in former tymes they have beene) by forrayne warres; we should not know how to trust the one the other.

LXXXVII. The cryes & complayntes of these afflictions running throughout Christendome, do give strange admiration unto men, and do worke strong effectes both in judgments and affections: Admiration, for that no such thing was ever expected under his Majesties government, for many causes: strong effectes, for that they worke great alterations both in the one, and the other: In judgment, for that wise men fynd not any reason, eyther of Religion or State, why such extremityes should be pursued, with such rigour at the instigation of partyes interessed, to the evident danger of so great and honorable Kingdomes, who if in wills they were united, as they are in one Prince and Governour; their forces were both admirable and dreadfull: In affections, for that the compassion which naturally doth accompany our brethrens afflictions, especially for a cause that we most esteeme and love, to wit, our Religion; must needes worke the contrary effect of inward aversion, both in Princes & people abroad, notwithstanding they hold externall amity, and friendship for the tyme.

LXXXVIII. I let passe the generall obloquies, and murmurations that are to be heard every where, almost in Christendome, upon this manner of proceeding, and much more the publicke and private complaints, outcryes, and praiers that are made and offered daylie to heaven, throughout all Catholicke Kingdomes lightly, in all particuler Congregations, Oratoryes, Chappels, & meetings of zealous men, that pray instantly to Almighty God for some remedy of these oppressions, and persecutions of English Catholicks, sufficiently (as they thinke) declared unto them & to the whole world by the very printed Catalogues of English Statutes extant in Print against them, for profession of their Religion: for that by the view of those Statutes, they do easily conceave, what enormous effectes, do, and must follow in the execution therof; albeit they did not both heare & see daily so many lamentable presidents & spectacles therin.

LXXXIX. As for example, there have not passed many moneths, since there were seene some threescore Priests more or lesse (to omit others) cast into banishment about one tyme, & wandring up and downe, throughout Christendome, according as every man had occasion, or necessity for their mayntenance, gave a lamentable spectacle to all nations, to see men of so good partes, amiable aspects, sweet behaviour, naturall borne subjects of the Land, the most of them of very worshipfull parentage, all of learned education, cleere and devoyed of any suspition of crymes that could be objected unto them (for otherwise they should not have bene dismissed) in the flower of their age, to be cast out of their native soyle, for professing that Religion only, wherby their said Countrey was first made Christian, & so continued under all their noble Princes, Kings, Queenes, and Soveraignes, Nobility, and Communatly, from the beginning of their Conversion, unto this our age.

xc. This spectacle (I say) presented to the eyes of most Nations of *Europe,* moved men not a litle, especially hearing them protest their duetifull affections to his Ma.<sup>tie</sup> and Realme in all Cyvill & Temporall respects, without seeking of any preferments, dignityes, riches, or other emoluments by staying at home; but only the rest & use of their owne Consciences in matters of Religion, which Protestants in many other Catholicke Countryes are suffered to injoy, though with farre lesser reason, in regard of the ancient right & possession, which ech part pretendeth for the use of their said Religion.

xci. And since this tyme agayne there hath beene seene very lately another spectacle, not much unlike to the former (though much more markable) to wit, a like number of Noble and Gentlemen, with their followers and trayne, passing in very good sort through sundry Countryes, being lately retyred out of his Ma.<sup>ties</sup> Kingdome of *Ireland,* for the selfe same cause of their Conscience, and Religion; which when men do behold, and heare them otherwise to speake honourably of his Ma.<sup>tie</sup> & the State, ascribing rather their afflictions to some under Magistrates in *Ireland,* and Ministers that set them on; it moveth more compassion, and maketh men thinke and muse, what may be the end of all this, and whereunto fynally it may grow? Whether the like may not be expected in tyme or doubted, out of other partes also of his Ma.<sup>ties</sup> dominions, upon like angariation of Consciences: which points seeme to be of no small consideration, and consequence to wise men; though those that be the immediate causes therof, will and must make light of all: but the naturall yssue of such eventes, are not unknowne. And if the occasioners therof were guylty of no greater fault, but only to cast his Ma.<sup>tie</sup> & the State into perpetuall cares about the same (his Royall nature being in-

clined otherwise to sweetnes, peace, and tranquillity) it were a great
synne in them, and scarce sufferable.

xcii. Nor is the remedy heere attempted by our Minister-Apologer (of
denying all, and saying that there is no persecution, nor hard dealing
with any, for matters of Religion, no not in the late Queenes dayes,
when so many were so rackt and rented for the same) any remedy at
all; but rather a doubling of the injury to the afflicted, with encrease of
exasperation & aversion of myndes; as also a leesing of all credit with
others that heare it, eyther at home or abroad: for that facts contrary to
wordes, do preponderate with all sober men, and prevaile against the
same.

xciii. And truely, I cannot but wonder, why this late Apology hath
beene so greedily published by the Apologer, both in English and
Latyn to the world, for that the Popes *Breves,* being but written privatly
to the Catholicks of *England,* for informing their Consciences in a matter of necessary doctrine about the lawfulnes, or unlawfulnes of taking
the *Oath,* and the Letter of *Cardinall Bellarmyne* being directed only to
a private friend; both of them might have remayned also private, if this
attempt had not byn made of publishing the same. But now being
drawne by the Apologer into the Universall Theatre of the world,
besydes, that divers will hold themselves obliged, or at leastwyse pro-
voked to answere the same; it will follow also, that the unlawfulnes of
the said *Oath* to Catholicke Consciences will more be seene, disputed, &
condemned by all Universityes, Schooles, Bookes & Treatises of particuler learned men, throughout all Countryes of Christendome that
professe Catholicke Religion. Wherupon also the unjust violence, in-
forcing men to sweare the same *Oath,* under so rigorous paynes, as are
the losse both of goods & libertie, and therwithall to sweare in like manner, that they do it *willingly, freely, and without coaction:* will be censured (no doubt) for one of the greatest contradictions in it selfe, and
the most injurious manner of proceeding with Christian men, that ever,
perhaps was heard of in the Christian world.

xciv. And this now occurred to me (deare Syr) to write to you concerning my judgment upon this matter. What more may be said to this
Apologie, when it shall come into the handes of learned men; you will

easily ghesse by these few notes, that I have heere laid togeather, which conteyne but little in respect of that which may be written of the matters heere handled. God of his endles mercy inclyne the hart of his Majesty, to take the best way in this his course of Royall Government: & for so much, as he hath byn pleased to joyne so many Great Kingdomes under his only Scepter, and permitted them to have so great differences of judgements in matters of Religion, that their union of wills, at least, in dutifull affections, may be so combined and conserved by sweet and temperate proceeding towards all, as despayre, the mother of headlong precipitation, enter not. The Proverbe is knowne, *Qui nimium emungit, elicit sanguine: & patientia læsa vertitur in furorem.* I never heard or read, that too much violence towards free Subjects ever ended well, especially for supposed faultes that are not acknowledged for such, by the punished: & consequently no hope of amendment by way of compulsion. Some may dissemble for feare, but they are more lost in their affections then the other. Some reasonable toleration, and friendly treatie would bynd up woundes from bleeding on all sydes: Exulceration maketh them fester more greivously, and dangerously. To Gods holy Providence the whole is to be committed, who will dispose of all to his greater glorie, *siuè in vitam, siue in mortem.* And to him also I committ yow, with my hartiest Commendations, &c. This 10. of *June.* 1608.

**Finis.**

# Lancelot Andrewes
## 1555–1626

Lancelot Andrewes was a devout and saintly man, a famous preacher, an able administrator. He was also a writer with a unique and distinguished prose style. He went from the Merchant Tailor's School in London to Pembroke Hall, Cambridge, in 1571. There he received his B.A. (1575), M.A. (1576), and B.D. (1585); he was a Fellow of his college from 1576, and its Master from 1589 to 1605. He was one of the forty-seven scholars appointed by King James in 1604 to translate the Bible, presiding over a committee of ten members responsible for the books from Genesis through Second Kings. He became Bishop of Chichester in 1605, of Ely in 1609, and of Winchester in 1618. He was also Dean of the King's Chapel and a member of the Privy Council.

Much of his career was thus spent in the service of the Church of England. Against Rome he defends the Anglican as the true Catholic church, and against Geneva he justifies its traditions and forms. He sees the church as sum and symbol of God's design on earth, the very microcosm or "*abridgement* of the world." He combines the Christian humanism of the Renaissance with the traditions and authority of the early Church fathers, to form an amalgam which, as T. S. Eliot points out, is peculiarly Anglican:

> Compare a sermon of Andrewes with a sermon by another earlier master, Latimer. It is not merely that Andrewes knew Greek, or that Latimer was addressing a far less cultivated public, or that the sermons of Andrewes are peppered with allusion and quotation. It is rather that Latimer, the preacher of Henry VIII and Edward VI, is merely a Protestant; but the voice of Andrewes is the voice of a man who has a formed visible Church behind him, who speaks with the old

authority and the new culture. It is the difference of negative and positive: Andrewes is the first great preacher of the English Catholic Church (*Selected Essays,* 301–302).

In 1605 he began his long career as court preacher, bearing the responsibility, through most of his remaining years, for the sermons preached at court on Easter, Christmas, and Whitsunday. His concern is always with substance, and he insists that a sermon is a testament, the Law itself, not merely a song or sonnet to be listened to. His sermons are learned, analytical, and closely argued. The scriptural text is minutely examined for all its implications, in the manner which caused William Chappell (*The Art and Method of Preaching,* 1656) to list Andrewes, Donne, and Jeremy Taylor as writers of "Elaborate Sermons."

Yet this reputation as a great preacher was not made by his learning and subtlety alone. His analyses are often pointed with wit. The resurrected Christ, for example, mistaken by Mary Magdalene for a gardener, was indeed a gardener, for he "made such an herb grow out of the ground this day as the like was never seen before, a dead body to shoot forth alive out of the grave"; furthermore, He worked a "kind of resurrection" in her as well: "The gardener had done His part, made her green on the sudden" (*Ninety-six Sermons,* III, 16, 21). His sentences range from those that are short, Senecan, and scholastic, to others that have a sustained, eloquent rhythm. His prose is marked by memorable figures, often realistic and even earthy, such as "true Religion is no way a *gargalisme* onely, to wash the tongue and mouth, to speake good words" (*XCVI Sermons,* 1641, 7); and by descriptions as dramatic as the passage which Eliot incorporates, almost without changing, into "The Coming of the Magi":

> It was no summer progress. A cold coming they had of it at this time of the year, just the worst time of the year to take a journey, and specially a long journey in. The ways deep, the weather sharp, the days short, the sun farthest off, *in solstitio brumali,* "The very dead of winter." (*Selected Essays,* 307)

His aim is not to display his learning or to unfold the great range of his religious sensibility, but to awaken men to a new religious life. "And sure it is," he says, "on whom a sermon works aright, it leaves him not leisure to say much, to use many words, but makes him rather full of thoughts" (*Ninety-six Sermons,* I, 423). His sermons are ultimately addressed to the inner meaning of the spiritual life: "Goe we then to the kernell, and let the huske lye: let goe the dead letter, and take we to us the spirituall meaning that hath some life in it" (*XCVI Sermons,* 568). Throughout the sermons, as in his *Devotions,* there runs the strain of contrition and tenderness, of intensely personal yet selfless piety. It is no wonder that Archbishop Laud records this in his Diary: "September 25th, Monday, about four o'clock in the morning died Lancelot Andrewes, the most worthy Bishop of Winchester, the great light of the Christian world" (*Works,* ed. by W. Scott and J. Bliss, 1847–1860, III, 126).

## EDITIONS

*The Wonderfull Combate betweene Christ and Satan,* 1592.
*Tortura Torti, sive ad Matthaei Torti Librum Responsio,* 1609; ed by J. H. Parker, 1851.
*XCVI. Sermons,* ed. by William Laud and John Buckeridge, 1629; *Ninety-Six Sermons,* ed. by J. P. Wilson, 1841–1843.
*A Manual of Directions for the Sick,* trans. by Richard Drake, 1648; *The Manual for the Sick,* ed. by F. E. Brightman, 1909.
*Preces Privatae,* 1647, 1675; ed. by H. Veale, 1895; translated as *The Private Devotions,* 1647, 1648; ed. by F. E. Brightman, 1903; ed. by J. H. Newman, 1840, 1950; ed. by T. S. Kepler, 1956.
*The Works,* ed by J. P. Wilson and J. Bliss, 1841–1854.
*Two Sermons of the Resurrection,* 1932.
*Seventeen Sermons on the Nativity,* 1898, 1955.

## HISTORICAL AND CRITICAL STUDIES

HENRY ISAACSON, *An Exact Narration of the Life and Death of . . . Lancelot Andrewes,* 1650; ed. by Stephen Isaacson, 1829.
ROBERT L. OTTLEY, *Lancelot Andrewes,* 1894.
W. H. NES, "Lancelot Andrewes and the English Church," *Theology,* XIII (1926).
T. S. ELIOT, *For Lancelot Andrewes,* 1928.
W. FRASER MITCHELL, *English Pulpit Oratory from Andrewes to Tillotson,* 1932.
M. M. KNAPPEN, "The Early Puritanism of Lancelot Andrewes," *Church History,* II (1933).
FELIX R. ARNOTT, "Anglicanism in the Seventeenth Century," *Anglicanism,* ed. by P. E. More and Frank L. Cross, 1935.

Hugh Ross Williamson, "Lancelot Andrewes," *Four Stuart Portraits*, 1949.

B. Blackstone, "Some Notes on Lancelot Andrewes," *Theology*, LIII (1950).

Charles P. Wiles, "A Historical Analysis and Appraisal of Bishop Lancelot Andrewes' Ecclesiology," Dissertation, Duke University, 1951.

Florence Higham, *Lancelot Andrewes*, 1952.

H. F. Woodhouse, *The Doctrine of the Church of England in Anglican Theology, 1547–1603*, 1954.

Maurice F. Reidy, *Bishop Lancelot Andrewes, Jacobean Court Preacher*, 1955.

Hugh Trevor-Roper, "King James and His Bishops," *History Today*, V (1955).

P. A. Welsby, *Lancelot Andrewes*, 1958. See also *Church Q. Rev.*, CLVI (1955), and *Theology*, LV (1952).

Samuel McCray Garrett, "Lancelot Andrewes' Doctrine of the Church," Dissertation, Harvard University, 1958.

Elizabeth Douglas North. McCutcheon, "Lancelot Andrewes and the Theme of Time in the Early Seventeenth Century," Dissertation, University of Wisconsin, 1961, *Dissertation Abstr.*, XXII (1961).

# SERMONS

## A SERMON PREACHED BEFORE THE KING'S MAJESTY AT WHITEHALL, ON THE FIFTH OF NOVEMBER, A.D. MDCVI.

### Of the Gunpowder Treason

Psalm cxviii. 23, 24.

*This is the Lord's doing, and it is marvellous in our eyes.*
*This is the day which the Lord hath made; let us rejoice and be glad in it.*

To entitle this time to this text, or to shew it pertinent to the present occasion, will ask no long process. This day of ours, this fifth of November, a day of God's making; that which was done upon it was "the Lord's doing." Christ's own application, which is the best, may well be applied here: "This day is this Scripture fulfilled in our ears." For if ever there were a deed done, or a day made, by God in our days, this day, and the deed of this day, was it. If ever He gave cause of marvelling, as in the first, of rejoicing, as in the second verse, to any land, to us this day He gave both. If ever saved, prospered, blessed any, this day He saved, prospered, and, as we say, fairly blessed us.

The day, we all know, was meant to be the day of all our deaths; and we, and many were appointed, as sheep to the slaughter, nay worse than so. There was a thing doing on it, if it had been done, we all had been undone. And the very same day, we all know, the day wherein that appointment was disappointed by God and we all saved, that we might "not die but live, and declare the praise of the Lord," the Lord of Whose doing that marvellous deed was, of Whose making this joyful day is that we celebrate.

This "merciful and gracious Lord," saith David, Psalm the one hundred and eleventh, verse the fourth, "hath so done His marvellous works, that they ought to be had," and kept "in remembrance." Of keeping in remembrance, many ways there be: among the rest this is one, of making days, set solemn days, to preserve memorable acts, that they be not eaten out by them, but ever revived with the return of the year, and kept still fresh in continual memory. God Himself taught us this way. In remembrance of the great delivery from the destroying Angel, He Himself ordained the day of the Passover yearly to be kept. The Church by Him taught, took the same way. In remembrance of the dis- appointing of Haman's bloody lots, they likewise appointed the days of "Purim," yearly to be kept. The like memorable mercy did He vouch- safe us; "the Destroyer" passed over our dwellings this day, it is our passover. Haman and his fellows had set the dice on us, and we by this time had been all in pieces: it is our "Purim" day.

We have therefore well done and upon good warrant, to tread in the same steps, and by law to provide that this day should not die, nor the memorial thereof perish, from ourselves or from our seed; but be con- secrated to a perpetual memory, by a yearly acknowledgment to be made of it throughout all generations. In accomplishment of which order, we are all now here in the presence of God, on this day that He first, by His act of doing, hath made; and we secondly, by our act of decreeing have made before Him, His holy Angels and men, to confess this His good- ness, and ourselves eternally bound to Him for it. And being to confess it, with what words of Scripture can we better or fitter do it than those we have read out of this Psalm? Sure I could think of none fitter, but even thus to say, *A Domino factum, &c.*

The treaty whereof may well be comprised in three points: I. The deed or "doing;" II. "The day;" and III. The duty. The deed, in these: "This is the Lord's, &c. "The day," in these: "This is the day," &c. The duty in the rest: "Let us," &c. The other two reduced to "the day," which is the centre of both. The "doing" is the cause, the duty is the consequent: from "the day" groweth the duty.

To proceed orderly, we are to begin with "the day." For though in place it stand after the deed, yet to us it is first; our knowledge is *a posteriori.* The effect ever first, where it is the ground of the rest. Of "the day" then first.

1. That such days there be, and how they come to be such. 2. Then of the "doing" that maketh them: wherein 1. that this of David's was, and 2. that ours is no less, rather more. 3. Then of the duty, how to do it? by rejoicing and being glad, for so *gaudium erit plenum,* these two

make it full. How to take order, that we may long and often do it? by saying our Hosanna, and *Benedictus;* for *gaudium nostrum nemo tollet a nobis,* those will make that "our joy no man shall take from us."

"This is the day:" "This?" Why, are not all days made by Him? Are there any days not made by Him? Why then say we, "This is the day the Lord hath made"? Divide the days into natural and civil: the natural, some are clear and some are cloudy; the civil, some are lucky days, and some dismal. Be they fair or foul, glad or sad, as the poet calleth Him, the great *Diespiter,* 'the Father of days' hath made them both. How say we then of some one day above his fellow, "This is the day," &c.?

No difference at all in the days, or in the months themselves; by nature they are all one. No more in November, than another month; nor in the fifth, than in the fifteenth. All is in God's making. For as in the creation we see all are the works, and yet a plain difference between them for all that, in the manner of making: some made with יהי, *Sit,* "Let there be light," "a firmament," "dry land;" some with *Faciamus,* with more ado, greater forecast and framing, as man, that masterpiece of His Works, of whom therefore, in a different sense, it may be said, This is the creature which God hath made—suppose, after a more excellent manner. In the very same manner it is with days: all are His making, all equal in that; but that letteth not but He may bestow a special *Faciamus* upon some one day more than another and so that day, by special prerogative, said to be indeed a "day that God hath made."

Now for God's making, it fareth with days as it doth with years. Some year, saith the Psalm, "God crowneth with His goodness," maketh it more seasonable, healthful, fruitful, than other. And so for days: God leaveth a more sensible impression of His favour upon some one, more than many besides, by doing upon it some marvellous work. And such a day on which God vouchsafeth some special *factum est,* some great and public benefit, notable for the time present, memorable for the time to come, in that case, of that day, as if God had said *Faciamus diem hunc,* shewed some workmanship, done some special cost on it, it may with an accent, with an emphasis be said, This verily is a day which God hath made, in comparison of which the rest are as if they were not, or at least were not of His making.

As for black and dismal days, days of sorrow and sad accidents, they are and may be counted, saith Job, for no days—nights rather, as having "the shadow of death" upon them; or if days, such as his were, which Satan had marred, than "which God had made." And for common and ordinary days, wherein as there is no harm, so not any notable good, we rather say, they are gone forth from God, in the course of nature, as it were, with a *fiat,* than "made" by Him; specially with a *faciamus.* So evil days no days or days marred, and common days, days, but no "made" days; only those "made," that crowned with some extraordinary great favour, and thereby get a dignity and exaltation above the rest; exempted out of the ordinary course of the calendar with a *Hic est.* Such, in the Law, was the day of the Passover made by God, the head of the year. Such, in the Gospel, of Christ's resurrection, "made" by God, *Dies Dominicus;* and to it, do all the Fathers apply this verse. And we had this day our Passover, and we had a resurrection or παραβολή, as Isaac had. But I forbear to go further in the general. By this that hath been said, we may see there be days of which it may be safely said, "This is the day," &c. and in what sense it may be said. Such there be then; that this of ours, one of them; that if it be we may so hold it, and do the duties that pertain to it.

David's "day" here, was one certainly, *dictante Spiritu;* and they that are like it to be holden for such; so that if ours be as it was, it is certainly *dies a Deo factus.* Now then, to take our rule from the former verse, *Factum Domini facit diem Domini,* 'It is God's deed that maketh it God's day;' and the greater the deed, the more God's day. There must be first, *factum est,* some "doing;" and secondly, it must be *a Domino,* He the doer; and thirdly, that somewhat must be somewhat "marvellous;" and fourthly, not in itself so, but "in our eyes." These four go to it, these four make any day a day of God's making. Let us see then these four: first, in David's here, and then in our own; and if we find them all, boldly pronounce, "This is the day," &c.

First, the *factum est,* in David's, what "was done," set down at large in the fore-part of the Psalm. It was a deliverance; all the Psalm runneth on nothing else. Every deliverance is from a danger, and by the danger we take measure of the deliverance. The greater that, the greater the delivery from it; and the greater the delivery, the greater the day, and the more likely to be of God's own manufacture. His danger first; what should have been done. He was in a great distress. Three several times, with great passion he repeats it, that his enemies 1. "came about" him; 2. "compassed" him round; 3. "compassed" and "kept" him "in on every side;" were, no swarm of "bees" so thick; that they gave a terrible lift or thrust at him, to overthrow him; and very near it they were. And at last, as if he were newly crept out of his grave, out of the very jaws of death and despair, he breaks forth and saith, I was very near my death; near it I was, but *non moriar,* "die I will not" now, for this time, but live a little longer to "declare the works of the Lord." This was his danger; and a shrewd one it seemeth it was. From this danger he was delivered. This, the *factum est.*

But man might do all this; and so it be man's day, for any thing is said yet. Though it were great, it maketh it not God's, unless God— God I say and not man, but God Himself—were the doer of it; and if He the doer, He denominates the day. This then was not any man's, not any Prince's doing, but God's alone—His might, His mercy, that brought it to pass; not any arm of flesh, but God's might, not of any merit of his, but of His own mere mercy. This was done by His might, thrice he tells of it; it was "the right hand of the Lord" that brought "this mighty thing to pass." This was done by His mercy, His ever-enduring "mercy;" four times he tells us, it was that did it. With that he begins, and makes it the key of the song. Then, as we have *factum est,* so we have *a Domino;* the deed, and the doer both.

God's doings are many, and not all of one size. The Prophet Zechariah speaketh of "a day of small things;" and even in those "small" must we learn to see God, or we shall never see Him in greater. Yet so dim is our sight, that unless they be great, commonly we see Him not; nay, unless it be great *usque ad miraculum,* so great that "marvellous" withal, we count it not worth a day, nor worthy God; unless it be such. But if it be such, then it is God's, *Qui facit mirabilia solus,* "Who only works great marvels;" then man is shut out, and then God's must the day be. *A Domino factum et mirabile.*

And yet this is not enough. The truth is, all that God doth, all His works are wonderful; *magna, sed ideo parva quia usitata,* 'great wonders all, but not wonderful, seem small to us, because they be usual.' His miracles are no more "marvellous" than His ordinary works, but that we see the one daily, and the other not. Therefore he addeth, "in our eyes," for a full period. His doings all "marvellous" in themselves, but not "marvellous in our eyes," unless they be rare, and the like not seen before; but then they be, and then we say *Digitus Dei est,* "It is the finger of God," nay "the right hand of God" that brough this "mighty thing to pass." Then we give the day for God's, without more ado. Now then, we have all that goeth to it: 1. a deliverance wrought; 2. wrought by God; 3. a wonderful deliverance; 4. and that even "in our eyes." These make David's "day," a "day" of God's making.

Will these be found in ours, and then ours shall be so too? They will, all of them certainly, and that in a higher degree, in a greater measure; match David's day, and overmatch it in all. 1. We were delivered, and from a danger, that is clear. How great? for that makes the odds. Boldly I dare say, from a greater than David's. Thus I shew it, and go no further than the Psalm itself.

1. David called upon God in his danger; he knew of it therefore. We did not; we imagined no such thing, but that all had been safe, and we might have gone to the Parliament as secure as ever. The danger never dreamt of, that is the danger.

2. His was by compassing and hemming in that is above ground, and may be descried from a watch-tower. Ours was by undermining, digging deep under ground, that none could discern.

3. One cannot be beset, but he may have hope to break through at some part. But here from this, no way, no means, no possibility of escaping. The danger not to be descried, not to be escaped, that is the danger.

4. His were a swarm of "bees"—he calleth them so; they buzz and make a noise when they come. Ours a brood of vipers, *mordentes in silentio,* still, not so much as a hiss, till the deadly blow had been given.

5. His was but of himself alone; so he saith, I was in trouble, "They came about me," "kept me in," "thrust sore at me;" but one person, David's alone. Ours of a far greater extent; David, and his three estates with him. Now though David himself were valued by them at "ten thousand" of themselves, and not overvalued neither, for he is worth more, and all Kings like him no less worth, yet he and they too must needs be more than he alone. Not only King David had gone, but Queen Esther too; and not only they, but Solomon the young Prince, and Nathan his brother. Nor these were not all. The Scriptures recount, David had Jehoshaphat for his Chancellor, Adoram his Treasurer, Seraiah his Secretary, Zadok and Abiathar, and twenty-two more, the chief of the Priests, Admo his Judge, Joab his General—all had gone; his forty-eight worthies or nobles, all they too. The principal of all the tribes in the kingdom, all they too, and many more than these, no man knoweth how many. It is out of question it had exceeded this of David's here.

6. One more. His danger, he confesseth, was from man; he goeth no further, "I will not fear what man doeth unto me." This of ours was not; merely man's, I deny it, it was the devil himself. The instruments, not

as his a swarm of "bees," but a swarm of "locusts" out of the infernal pit. Not men, no not heathen men; their stories, nay their tragedies, can shew none near it. Their poets could never feign any so prodigiously impious. Not men, no not savage wild men, the Huns, the Heruli, the Turcilingi, noted for inhumanity, never so inhuman; even among those barbarous people this fact would be accounted barbarous. How then? "Beasts" there were at Ephesus, "beasts" in shape of men; and θηριότης, 'brutishness' is the worst, philosophy could imagine of our nature. This is more than brutish; what tiger, though never so enraged, would have made the like havoc? Then, if the like, neither in the nature of men nor beasts to be found, (it is so unnatural) we must not look to pattern it upon earth, we must to hell; thence it was certainly, even from the devil. "He was a murderer from the beginning," and will be so to the ending. In every sin of blood he hath a claw, but all his claws in such an one as this; wherein so much blood as would have made it rain blood, so many baskets of heads, so many pieces of rent bodies cast up and down, and scattered all over the face of the earth. Never such a day; all Joel's signs of a fearful day, "blood, and fire, and the vapour of smoke." As he is a murderer, so we see in Mark, by his renting and tearing the poor possessed child, he is cruel; and in this, all his cruelties should have met together. Pharaoh's and Herod's, killing innocent and harmless children —yet they spared the mother; Esau's cruelty, smiting mother, children, and all; Nebuzaradan's, not sparing the King nor his lords; Haman's, not sparing Esther nor her ladies; Edom's cruelty, not sparing the sanctuary nor the walls—"Down" with them "to the ground;" his own smiting "the four corners," and bringing down the house upon the heads of Job's children. Put to all the cruelties in Jeremiah's Lamentations, the not honouring the faces of nobles, priests, judges; the making so many widows and orphans; the "voice in Ramah," of Rachael comfortless; cruelty, more cruel to them it spared and left behind, than to those it took away. It irketh me to stand repeating these; that ever age or land, but that our age and this land should foster or breed such monsters!

That you may know it for that perfectly, consider but the wickedness of it, as it were in full opposition to God, and you must needs say it could not be His doing. God forbid, saith Abraham, "Thou shouldest destroy the righteous with the wicked." Kill not dam and young ones both, saith Moses in the Law. You shall "not touch Mine anointed," saith God in the Psalms. You shall not pull up the good corn; rather let the tares stand, saith Christ in the Gospel. You shall not do evil that good may come of it, saith Paul in his Epistles. But here is Satan flat contrary, in despite of Law, Prophets, Psalm, Epistle and Gospel; *Hoc est Christum cum Paulo conculcare,* to throw down Abraham, and Moses, and David, and Paul, and Christ, and God and all, and trample upon them all.

One more yet; that this "abomination of desolation" (so calleth Daniel, so calleth our Saviour, the uttermost extremity of all that bad is; so may we this truly) that this "abomination of desolation" took up his standing "in the holy place."

1. An "abomination;" so it is, abhorred of all flesh, hated and detested of all that but hear it named; yea they themselves say they should have abhorred it, if it had taken effect. It is an "abomination."

2. Every "abomination" doth not forthwith make desolate. This had. If ever a desolate kingdom upon earth, such had this been after that terrible blow. Neither root nor branch left, all swept away; strangers called in, murderers exalted, the very dissolution and desolation of all ensued.

3. But this, that this so abominable and desolatory a plot stood "in the holy place," this is the pitch of all. For there it stood, and thence it came abroad. Undertaken with a holy oath, bound with the holy Sacrament—that must needs be in "a holy place," warranted for a holy act tending to the advancement of a holy religion, and by holy persons called by a most holy name, the name of Jesus. That these holy religious persons, even the chief of all religious persons, the Jesuits, gave not only absolution but resolution, that all this was well done; that it was by them justified as lawful, sanctified as meritorious, and should have been glorified—but it wants glorifying, because the event failed, that is the grief; if it had not, glorified—long ere this, and canonized as a very good and holy act, and we had had orations out of the conclave in commendation of it. Now I think we shall hear no more of it. These good fathers they were David's "bees" here, came hither only to bring us honey, right honey they; not to sting any body; or, as in the twenty-second verse, they as "builders" came into the land only for edification, not to pull down or to destroy any thing. We see their practice, they begun with rejecting this stone, as one that favoured heretics at least, and therefore excommunicate, and therefore deposed, and therefore exposed to any that could handle a spade well to make a mine to blow him up—him, and all his estates with him to attend him: the corner

stone being gone, the walls must needs follow. But then this shrining it —such an abomination—setting it "in the holy place," so ugly and odious, making such a treason as this, a religious, missal, sacramental treason, hallowing it with orison, oath, and eucharist, this passeth all the rest. I say no more but as our Saviour concludeth, when you see such an "abomination" so standing, *qui legit intelligat,* nay *qui videt.* God send them, that not read of it but see it, and had like to have smelt, to learn that they should by it; and so I leave it.

Tell me now if this were not his doing, and if it should not have been a day of his making, the devil's own making.

This should have been done, this the danger: what was done? This the *factum fuisset;* what the *factum est?* All these were undone and blown over, all the undermining disappointed, all this murder and cruelty and desolation defeated. The mine is discovered, the snare is broken, and we are delivered. All these, the King, Queen, Prince, Nobles, Bishops, Judges, both houses, alive all; not a hair of any of their heads perished, not so much as "the smell of fire" on any their garments. "Give thanks, O Israel, unto the Lord thy God in the congregation from the bottom of the heart. Here is little Benjamin thy Ruler, the Princes of Judah" &c. that they are here, and we see them here, and that the stone these builders refused is still the head-stone of the corner. That should have been done—this was done; and we all that are here this day are witnesses of it, witnesses above all exception of this *factum est.*

But by whom, whose "doing?" Truly not man's "doing" this, it was "the Lord's." *A dæmone factum est illud,* or *fictum est illud.* It was the devil's doing or devising, the plot; *A Domino factum est hoc,* this was "God's doing," the deliverance. The blow was the devil's, the ward was God's. Not man, but the devil, devised it; not man, but God, defeated it. He That sat in Heaven all this while, and from thence looked down and saw all this doing of the devil and his limbs, in that mercy of His which is over all His works, to save the effusion of so much blood, to preserve the souls of so many innocents, to keep this land from so foul a confusion, to shew still some token, some sensible "token upon us for good, that they which hate us may see it, and be ashamed;" but especially, that that was so lately united might not so soon be dissolved, He took the matter into His own hand. And if ever God shewed that He had a hook in the Leviathan's nose, that the devil can go no farther than his chain; if ever that there is in Him more power to help than in

Satan to hurt, in this He did it. And as the devil's claws to be seen in the former, so God's right hand in this mighty thing He brought to pass, and all the fingers of it.

1. To shew it was He. He held His peace and kept silence, sat still, and let it go on, till it came near, even to the very period, to the day of the lot; so near that we may truly say with King David, "As the Lord liveth," *uno tantum gradu nos morsque dividimur,* "there was but a step between death and us." We were upon the point of going to the hill, all was prepared, the train, the match, "the fire," "wood" and all, and we ready to be the sacrifice, and even then and there, *in monte providebat Dominus,* God provided for our safety even in that very place where we should have been the "burnt offering," from Heaven stayed the blow. It was "the Lord's doing."

2. When treachery hath his course like water, and creeps along like a "snail,"—it is the fifty-eighth Psalm—then to make it "like the untimely birth of a woman," never to "see the sun;" not as in this, *arserunt sicut ignis in spinis,* was but a blaze, as in a bush of thorns, (nay if it come so far, it had gone wrong with us) but as in that, *priusquam intelligerent spinæ,* or ever the thorns gat heat or the powder fire; then, saith he there, *dicet homo, Utique est Deus,* men shall say, "Verily there is a God," and this was His "doing."

3. And not only that it was betrayed, but that He made them the betrayers of it themselves; and even according to the place, Ecclesiastes, chapter the tenth, made things with feathers to disclose it; when, as in Psalm sixty-four, "their own tongues," or, which is all one, their own pens, "make them to fall," all that consider it shall be amazed, and then "all men shall say, This hath God done, for they shall perceive" it plain, "it is His work." They shall be charged in confession, they shall swear, they shall take the Sacrament not to do it; and yet, contrary to all this, it shall come out by themselves. Was not this "God's doing?"

4. Yet further, to shew it was so; this which was written was so written, as divers of profound wisdom knew not what to make of it. But then cometh God again, God most certainly, and as in the Proverbs, the sixteenth chapter, and tenth verse, puts קֶסֶם, a very "divination," a very oracle in "the King's lips," and his mouth missed not the matter; made him, as Joseph, "the revealer of secrets," to read the riddle, giving him wisdom to make both explication what they would do, and application where it was they would do it. This was God certainly. This,

Pharaoh would say none could, unless he were filled with "the Spirit of" the holy "God." It was *a Domino factum*.

5. Lastly, as that when it was come forth they were not reclaimed— not then, when they saw the hand of God was gone out against them, and that it was even God they strave withal; no, but even then from hidden treachery fell to open rebellion, and even perished in it, if God shewed not a miracle of His mercy on them, perished there and perished eternally; as this I say did, that it was *factum a dæmone,* who never left them till he had brought them thither, so that before they came thither God cast their own powder in their faces, powdered them and disfigured them with it, and that their quarters stand now in pieces, as they meant ours should; it is the case of the hundred and ninth Psalm, "And hereby shall they know, that it is Thy hand, and that Thou Lord hast done it." How? in that they are thus "clothed with their own shame," and even "covered with their own confusion;" that they fall as fast as they rise, are still confounded, and still Thy servants rejoice. These five, as prints, shew it was God's hand; it was "the Lord" That "made" the "day," it was "the day that the Lord made." "Be thou exalted Lord in Thine own strength;" it was Thy right hand that brought this mighty thing to pass.

This will not serve the turn. His "doing" makes it not "the day;" His doing a miracle, that makes it; and that it is too. I take no thought to prove this point; by the Law, the Prophets, the Gospel. To put them to it: Moses—"Enquire now of the days that are past, that were before us, since the day that God created man upon earth, and ask from one end of Heaven to the other, if there came to pass such a thing as this, whether any such like thing hath been heard;" and if we cannot suit it, or set such another by it, we must needs yield it for one. By the Prophets: "Go to the Isles and behold, send to Kedar and take diligent heed, and see, if you can possibly find the like;" if not, confess it for "marvellous." "Come hither," saith David, and "behold, how marvellous God is!" and what is that? that such as are rebellious are not able to exalt themselves. We need not go so far, we have it here to see; we may say to him, "Come hither." By the Gospel; for so do they there acknowledge our Saviour's for miracles: "Sure, we have seen strange things to-day;" "We never saw it on this fashion;" "The like was never seen in Israel"—therefore "marvellous" certainly. It is now no miracle, no strange thing, to have a King delivered; every other year we see it, and therefore wonder not at it. But to see King, Queen, their seed, all their estates delivered, that is *mirabile,* that is "a new thing created on the earth." I conclude, as that was the devil's doing, and was monstrous in our eyes, so "this is God's doing," and it is "marvellous in our eyes." And again, upon all these marks, that as this was a day the devil would have marred, so "this is a day that the Lord made."

"Marvellous" then it is; yet hath it not, as we say, his full Christendom, unless it be so "in our eyes." For the time it was, and that of the Psalm fits us well: "When God," saith he, "turned away the captivity, (say we, the destruction) of His people, then were we like to them that dream." No man but stood in a maze, as if he knew not well whether he saw it waking, or dreamt of it, it was so strange.

And let me go further. Not in ours only, for sure I am that which followeth there is true: "Then said they," *inter gentes,* "of other nations, The Lord hath done great things for them;" and we are to blame if we answer them not with the echo there following, "Yea, indeed, the Lord hath done great things for us, for which we have cause to rejoice." If strangers think it strange, and say and write, *A sæculo inauditum,* 'The like was never heard before;' if it were "marvellous" in their eyes, it were very "marvellous" it should not be so "in our eyes" too.

I add, they that were the actors of it, in their eyes it is so; and that of the Apostle may fitly be applied to them: "Behold, ye despisers, and wonder and vanish, for God hath wrought a work in your days, a work which you yourselves that were the doers, shall scarce believe when it shall be told;" that even astonished themselves, to see it go forward so long, and so suddenly cast down. Nay, I go further, to make it a miracle consummate. I doubt not but it was strange news, even in hell itself, insomuch as even that place had never hatched the like monster before. You see the welcome they in hell gave him of Asshur, What, art thou come, "that makest the earth to tremble, and dost shake whole kingdoms?" And yet it is well known, all his shaking was but a metaphor, he never made it shake actually, as these would have done; and therefore this of greater admiration, and I doubt not but more wonderful in their eyes; and ours are very dim, if in all other it be, and be not so in ours.

Then if such days there be, if this of ours be one of them, if the forepart of the verse do, then must the latter also belong to us; if "this the day the Lord hath made," then this the day wherein we to "rejoice."

When He makes, we to make; and our rejoicing in it, is our making of it.

To "rejoice," no hard request nor heavy yoke, let it not be grievous to us. We love to do it, we seek all means to do it in all cases else; then to essay to do it here. This sure the Prophet would not require, nor make it the office of the day, but that upon such days God Himself calls us to joy.

And even as, when God calleth us to mourning by black days of famine or war, or the like, then to fall to feasting or revelling is that that highly displeaseth God; so when God by good days calleth us to joy, then to droop and not to accommodate ourselves to seasons of His sending, is that which pleases Him never a whit.

What, saith Nehemiah upon such a blessed day as this, "Droop you to-day?" *Nolite,* at no hand to do it, *dies enim festus est,* "it is a festival day." What then? why it is essential, it is of the very nature of every feast, saith God in His law, *omnino gaudere,* by any means, in any wise, therein to "rejoice." And Nehemiah's promise is to encourage us, that if the strength of the Lord be our joy, the very "joy of the Lord" shall be our "strength."

To conclude. Sure I am that if the plot had prevailed, it would have been a high feast in Gath, and a day of jubilee in Askelon, "The daughters of the uncircumcised" would have made it a day in triumph. Let us not be behind them then, but shew as much joy for our saving as they would certainly have done for our perishing.

*Exultemus et lætemur.* God loveth our joy should be full: it is not full except we have both these, the body, as it were, and the soul of joy; the joy outward of the body, and gladness inward of the soul. So much do the two words signify in all the three tongues. Both He will have; for if one be wanting, it is but *semiplenum,* 'half full.'

And he beginneth with *exultemus,* the outward; not to ourselves within, which we call *gaudere in sinu,* 'joy of the bosom,' but such, so exuberant, as the streams of it may overflow, and the beams of it shine and shew forth in an outward sensible exultation. It is a "day;" so would he have us rejoice, that as by day-light it might be seen in our face, habit, and gesture, seen and heard both. Therefore he saith, at the fifteenth verse, "The voice of joy is in the dwellings of the righteous." And "in the dwelling" it doeth well; but yet that would not serve his turn, but "Open me," saith he at the nineteenth verse, "the gates of righteousness," that is, the church door—his house would not hold him —thither will "I go in," and there in the congregation, in the great congregation, "give thanks to the Lord." And that so great a congregation, that it may *constituere diem solennem in condensis usque ad cornua altaris,* 'that they may stand so thick in the church, as fill it from the entry of the door to the very edge of the altar.' This same joy, that is neither seen nor heard, there is some leaven of malignity in it, He cannot skill of it. He will have it seen in the countenance, heard in the voice; not only preaching, but singing forth His praise. And that not with voices alone but with instruments, and not instruments of the choir alone but instruments of the steeple too, bells and all, that so it may be *Hosanna in altissimis,* in the very "highest" key we have. This for *exultemus.*

But many a close hypocrite may do all this, and many a counterfeit Shimei and Sheba did all this to David, got them a fleering forced countenance, taken-on joy; and therefore the other, that God will have His joy not be the joy of the countenance alone, a clear face and a cloudy overcast heart, He will have the gladness of the heart too, of the inner man; *cor meum et caro mea,* "the heart" as well as the "flesh," to be joyful. The joy of the soul is the soul of joy; not a body without a soul, which is but a carcass. "Strange children" may, and "will, dissemble with me," saith the Psalm; "dissemble" a gladness, for fear of being noted; and yet within, in heart, you wot what. But God calleth for His *de fontibus Israel,* which we read, "from the ground of the heart." That is, indeed, the true fountain of joy, that "our lips may be fain when we sing unto Him, and so may our soul which He hath delivered." Nay, He delivered both; and therefore, both the body to rejoice, and the soul to be glad. This doth *lætemur* add to *exultemus.*

If then we be agreed that we will do both, I come to the last, how to order our joy, that it may please Him for Whom it is undertaken. It is not every joy that He liketh. Merry they were, and joyful they thought, that kept their "King's day," by taking in bowl after bowl, till they were "sick" again. So they that Malachi speaks of, there came nothing of their feasts but "dung"—bear with it, it is the Holy Ghost's own term—that is, all in the belly and belly-cheer. So they that "sat down to eat and drink, and rose up to play," and there was all; that is the calf's feast, a calf can do as much. "But with none of these was God pleased;" and as good no joy as not to the purpose, as not to please Him.

That it may be to the purpose, that God may take pleasure in it, it must begin at Hosanna, at *Aperite mihi portas justitiæ,* at the temple-door; there must it go in, it must bless and be blessed in the house of the Lord. I will first "make joyful in my house of prayer"—it is God by Esay; the stream of our joy must come from the spring-head of religion.

Well then, to the Church we are come; so far onward. When we are there, what is to be done? Somewhat we must say, we must not stand mute. There to stand still, that the Prophet cannot skill of. That then we may there say something, he here frames, he here indites us a versicle, which after grew into such request, as no feast ever without it, without an Hosanna; it grew so familiar as the very children were perfect in it. The sum and substance whereof briefly is no more, but, which we all desire, that God would still "save," still prosper, still bless him, that in His name is come unto us, that is King David himself, whom all the house and all of the house of the Lord, bless in His name.

And to very good purpose doth he this; for joy hath no fault, but that it is too short, it will not last, it will be taken from us too soon. It is ever a bar in all joy, *tolletur a vobis,* subject to the worm that Jonah's gourd was. It standeth us therefore in hand, to begin with Hosanna, so to joy as that we may long joy to pray for the continuance, that it be not taken from us; ever remembering, the true temper of joy is (*exultate in tremore*) not without the mixture of some fear. For this day, we see what it is, a joyful day; "we know not," saith Solomon, "what the next day will be;" and if not what the next day, what the next year much less. What will come we know not; what our sins call for to come, that we know, even that God should call to judgment, if not by fire, by somewhat else. If it be but for this, it concerns us nearly to say our Hosanna, that the next year be as this. It is our wisdom therefore to make the means for the continuance of it, that God would still establish the good work He this day wrought in us, still bless us with the continuance of the same blessings.

And this that we may do, not faintly but cheerfully with the lifting up of our souls therefore, as far as art or spirit can do it, he hath quickened his Hosanna, that he may put spirit and life in us to follow him in it, with all fervour of affection: four times, twice with *Anna,* and twice with *Na;* either of them before, and after; but eight words, and four of them interjections; all to make it passionate, and that so as in the original nothing can be devised more forcible; and so as it is hard in any other tongue to express it; which made the Evangelists let it alone, and retain the Hebrew word still. But this, as near as I can, it soundeth: "Now, good Lord, save us yet still; now, good Lord, prosper us yet still." Be to us, as last year, so this, and all the years to come, "Jesus" a Saviour, "yesterday and to-day and the same for ever."

And three things doth he thus earnestly pray for, and teacheth us to do the like. 1. To save, 2. prosper, 3. and bless.

1. To save: that should be first with us, it is commonly last, we have least sense of our souls. To save us with the true saving health—it is a word whereof our Saviour Jesus hath His name—it importeth the salvation of the soul; properly to that it belongeth, and hath joined to it Hosanna in the Gospel, *Hosanna in excelsis,* to shew it as a high and heavenly salvation.

2. Then to prosper. If He but grant us the former alone, to have our souls saved, though without prosperity, though with the days of adversity, it is *sors sanctorum,* 'the lot of many a saint of His,' of far more worth than we; even so we are bound to thank Him, if even so we may be but saved. But if He add also prosperity of the outward to the saving of the inward man, that not so much as a "leaf" of us shall "wither," but look what we do shall "prosper," and that whatsoever men of evil counsels do, shall not prosper against us; if He not only vouchsafe us *Hosanna in excelsis,* but *Hosanna de profundis* too, from deep cellars, deep vaults, those that dig deep to undermine our posperity; if He add the shadow of His wings to shelter us from perils, to the light of His countenance to save us from our sins, then have we great cause to rejoice yet more; and, both with *exultemus* from without, and *lætemur* from within, to magnify His mercy, and to say with the Prophet, "Praised be the Lord, That" not only taketh care for the safety, but "taketh pleasure in the prosperity of His servants."

3. Lastly, because both these, the one and the other, our future salvation by the continuance of His religion and truth among us, and our present prosperity, like two walls, meet upon "the Head-stone of the corner;" depend both, first, upon "the Name of the Lord," and next upon him that in His Name, and with His Name, is come unto us, that is, "the King," (so do both the Evangelists, St. Luke and St. John supply; and where we read, "Blessed be He," there they read "Blessed be the King that cometh") so that neither of them sure, unless he be safe; that He would bless him, and make him blest, that in His blessed name is come amongst us. The building will be "as mount Sion," so the corner-stone be fast; so the two walls that meet, never fall asunder. If

otherwise—but I will not so much as put the case; but as we pray, so trust, it "shall never be removed, but stand fast for ever."

This then we all wish that are now in the "House of the Lord," and we that are of "the House of the Lord," do now and ever, in the temple and out of it, morning and evening, night and day, wish and pray both, that He would continue forth His goodness, and bless with length of days, with strength of health, with increase of all honour and happiness, with terror in the eyes of his enemies, with grace in the eyes of his subjects, with whatsoever David or Solomon, or any King that ever was happy, was blessed with, him that in the Name of the Lord is come to us, and hath now these four years stayed with us, that he may be blessed, in that Name wherein he is come, and by the Lord in Whose Name he is come, many and many years yet to come.

And, when we have put this incense in our phials, and bound this "sacrifice with cords, to the altar" fast, we bless you and dismiss you, to eat your bread with joy, and to drink your wine with a cheerful heart; for God accepteth your work, your joy shall please Him, this Hosanna shall sanctify all the joy shall follow it.

To end then. "This day, which the Lord hath" thus "made" so marvellously, so marvellously and mercifully, let us rejoice in the Maker, for the making of it, by His doing on it that deed that is so "marvellous in our eyes," in all eyes; returning to the beginning of the Psalm, and saying with the Prophet, "O give thanks to the Lord, for He is gracious," &c. "Let Israel, let the house of Aaron, yea let all that fear the Lord, confess that His mercy endureth for ever."

"Who only doeth great wonders." "Who remembered us when we were in danger." "And hath delivered us from our enemies," "with a mighty hand and stretched-out arm." And, as for them, hath turned their device upon their own head. And hath made this day, to us, a day of joy and gladness. To this God of Gods, the Lord of Heaven, "glorious in holiness, fearful in power, doing wonders," be &c.

# SERMON PREACHED BEFORE THE KING'S MAJESTY, AT WHITEHALL, ON THE SIXTEENTH OF APRIL, A.D. MDCXX. BEING EASTER-DAY.

### John xx. 11—17

*But Mary stood by the sepulchre weeping; and as she wept, she stooped, and looked into the sepulchre,*

*And saw two Angels in white, sitting, the one at the head, the other at the feet, where the body of Jesus had lain.*

*And they said to her, Woman, why weepest thou? She said to them, They have taken away my Lord, and I know not where they have laid Him.*

*When she had thus said, she turned herself about, and saw Jesus standing, and knew not that it was Jesus.*

*Jesus saith to her, Woman, why weepest thou? Whom seekest thou? She, supposing He had been the gardener, said to Him, Sir, if thou have borne Him hence, tell me where thou hast laid Him, and I will take Him thence.*

*Jesus saith to her, Mary. She turned herself, and said to Him, Rabboni, that is to say, Master.*

*Jesus said to her, Touch Me not; for I am not yet ascended to My Father: but go to My brethren, and say to them, I ascend to My Father and to your Father, and to My God and your God.*

It is Easter-day abroad, and it is so in the text. We keep Solomon's rule, *Verbum diei in die suo.* For all this I have read, is nothing else but a report of Christ's rising, and of His appearing this Easter-day morning, His very first appearing of all. St. Mark is express for it, that Christ was no sooner risen this day but "He appeared first of all to Mary Magdalene;" which first appearing of His is here by St. John extended, and set down at large.

The sum of it is, 1. The seeking Christ dead; 2. The finding Him alive.

The manner of it is, That Mary Magdalene staying still by the sepulchre, first she saw a vision of Angels; and after, she saw Christ Himself. Saw Him, and was herself made an Angel by Him, a good

Angel to carry the Evangel, the first good and joyful tidings of his rising again from the dead. And this was a great honour, all considered, to serve in an Angel's place. To do that at His resurrection, His second birth, that at His first birth an Angel did. An Angel first published that, Mary Magdalene brought first notice of this. As he to the shepherds, so she to the Apostles, the Pastors of Christ's flock, by them to be spread abroad to the ends of the world.

To look a little into it. 1. Mary is the name of a woman; 2. Mary Magdalene of a sinful woman.

That to a woman first—it agreeth well to make even with Eve; that as by a woman came the first news of death, so by a woman also might come the first notice of the Resurrection from the dead. And the place fits well, for in a garden they came both.

That to a sinful woman first—that also agrees well. To her first that most needed it; most needed it, and so first sought it. And it agrees well, He be first found of her that first sought Him; even in that respect she was to be respected.

In which two there is opened unto us "a gate of hope," two great leaves, as it were; one, that no infirmity of sex—for a woman we see; the other, that no enormity of sin—for a sinful woman, one that had the blemish that she went under the common name of *peccatrix,* as notorious and famous in that kind; that neither of these shall debar any to have their part in Christ and in His resurrection; any, that shall seek Him in such sort as she did. For either of these *non obstante,* nay notwithstanding both these, she had the happiness to see His Angels—and that was no small favour; to see Christ Himself, and that first of all, before all others to see and salute Him; and to receive a commission from Him of *vade et dic,* to "go and tell," that is as it were to be an Apostle, and that to the Apostles themselves, to bring them the first good news of Christ's rising again.

There are three parties that take up the whole text, and if I should divide it, I would make those three parties the three parts; I. Mary Magdalene, II. the Angels, II. and Christ our Saviour.

Mary Magdalene begins her part in the first verse, but she goes along through them all.

Then the Angels' part in the two verses next. 1. Their appearing, 2. and their speech to her; appearing in the twelfth, speech in the thirteenth.

And last, Christ's part in all the rest. 1. His appearing, 2. and speech likewise. Appearing first, unknown, in the fourteenth, and His speech then in the fifteenth.

After, His appearing and speech again, being known, in the sixteenth and seventeenth. 1. Forbidding her, *mane et tange,* to stay and to touch; 2. and bidding her, *vade et dic,* to get her quickly to His brethren, and tell them His resurrection was past, for *ascendo,* He was taking thought for His Ascension, and preparing for that. Thus lieth the order and the parts.

The use will be, that we in our seeking carry ourselves as she did;— and so may we have the happiness that she had to find Christ, as He is now to be found in the virtue of His resurrection!

Ver. 11. "But Mary stood by the Sepulchre weeping, and as she wept she stooped, and looked into the Sepulchre."

Of the favours vouchsafed this same *felix peccatrix,* as the Fathers term her, this day; 1. To see but Christ's Angels, 2. To see Christ at all, 3. To see Him first of all, 4. But more than all these, to be employed by Him in so heavenly an errand, reason we can render none that helped her to these, but that which in a place Christ himself renders, *Quia dilexit multum,* "because she loved much."

"She loved much;" we cannot say, She believed much; for by her *sustulerunt* thrice repeated, the second, thirteenth, fifteenth verses, it seems she believed no more than just as much as the High Priests would have had the world believe, that "He was taken away by night."

*Defectus fidei non est negandus, affectus amoris non est vituperandus:* —it is Origen; 'We cannot commend her faith, her love we cannot but commend,' and so do—commend it in her, commend it to you. Much it was, and much good proof gave she of it. Before, to Him living; now, to Him dead. To Him dead, there are divers; 1. She was last at His cross, and first at His grave; 2. Stayed longest there, was soonest here; 3. Could not rest till she were up to seek Him; 4. Sought Him while it was yet dark, before she had light to seek Him by.

But to take her as we find her in the text, and to look no whither else. There are in the text no less than ten, all arguments of her great love; all as it were a commentary upon *dilexit multum.* And even in this first verse there are five of them.

The first in these words, *stabat juxta monumentum,* that "she stood by the grave," a place where faint love loves not to stand. Bring Him to the grave, and lay Him in the grave, and there leave Him; but come no more at it, nor stand not long by it. Stand by Him while He is alive—so did many; stand, and go, and sit by Him. But *stans juxta monumentum,* stand by Him dead; Mary Magdalene, she did it, and she only did it, and none but she. *Amor stans juxta monumentum.*

The next in these, *Maria autem stabat,* "But Mary stood." In the *autem,* the "but"—that helps us to another. "But Mary stood," that is as much to say as, Others did not, "but" she did. Peter and John were there but even now. Thither they came, but not finding Him, away they went. They went, but Mary went not, she stood still. Their going away commends her staying behind. To the grave she came before them, from the grave she went to tell them, to the grave she returns with them, at the grave she stays behind them. *Fortior eam figebat affectus,* saith Augustine, 'a stronger affection fixed her;' so fixed her that she had not the power to remove thence. Go who would, she would not, but stay still. To stay, while others do so, while company stays, that is the world's love; but Peter is gone, and John too; all are gone, and we left alone; then to stay is love, and constant love. *Amor manens aliis recedentibus,* 'love that when others shrink and give over, holds out still.'

The third in these, "she stood, and she wept;" and not a tear or two, but she wept a good as we say, that the Angels, that Christ Himself pity her, and both of them the first thing they do, they ask her why she wept so. Both of them begin with that question. And in this is love. For if, when Christ stood at Lazarus' grave's side and wept, the Jews said, "See, how He loved him!" may not we say the very same, when Mary stood at Christ's grave and wept, See, how she loved Him! Whose presence she wished for, His miss she wept for; Whom she dearly loved while she had Him, she bitterly bewailed when she lost Him. *Amor amare flens,* 'love running down the cheeks.'

The fourth in these, "And as she wept, she stooped, and looked in" ever and anon. That is, she did so weep as she did seek withal. Weeping without seeking, is but to small purpose. But her weeping hindered not her seeking, her sorrow dulled not her diligence. And diligence is a character of love, comes from the same root, *dilectio* and *diligentia* from *diligo,* both. *Amor diligentiam diligens.*

To seek, is one thing; not to give over seeking, is another. For I ask, why should she now look in? Peter and John had looked there before, nay, had been in the grave, they. It makes no matter; she will not trust Peter's eyes, nor John's neither. But she herself had before this, looked in too. No force, she will not trust herself, she will not suspect her own eyes, she will rather think she looked not well before, than leave off her looking. It is not enough for love to look in once. Thus we use, this is our manner when we seek a thing seriously; where we have sought already, there to seek again, thinking we did it not well, but if we now look again better, we shall surely find it then. *Amor quærens ubi quæsivit,* love that never thinks it hath looked enough. These five.

And, by these five we may take measure of our love, and of the true *multum* of it. *Ut prosit nobis ejus stare, ejus plorare et quærere,* saith Origen 'that her standing, her weeping, and seeking, we may take some good by them.'

I doubt ours will fall short. Stay by Him alive, that we can, *juxta mensam;* but *juxta monumentum,* who takes up His standing there? And our love it is dry-eyed, it cannot weep; it is stiff-jointed, it cannot stoop to seek. If it do, and we hit not on Him at first, away we go with Peter and John; we stay it not out with Mary Magdalene. A sign our love is little and light, and our seeking suitable, and so it is without success. We find not Christ—no marvel; but seek Him as she sought Him, and we shall speed as she sped.

Ver. 16. "And saw two Angels in white, sitting, the one at the head, the other at the feet, where the body of Jesus had lain."

For what came of this? Thus staying by it, and thus looking in, again and again, though she saw not Christ at first, she sees His Angels. For so it pleased Christ to come by degrees, His Angels before Him. And it is no vulgar honour this, to see but an Angel; what would one of us give to see but the like sight?

We are now at the Angels' part, their appearing in this verse. There are four points in it: 1. Their place; 2. Their habit; 3. Their site; 4. and their order. 1. Place, in the grave; 2. Habit, in white; 3. site—they were sitting; 4. and their order in sitting, one at the head, the other at the feet.

The place. In the grave she saw them; and Angels in a grave, is a strange sight, a sight never seen before; not till Christ's body had been there, never till this day; this the first news of Angels in that place. For a grave is no place for Angels, one would think; for worms rather: blessed Angels, not but in a blessed place. But since Christ lay there, that place is blessed. There was a voice heard from Heaven, "Blessed be the dead:" "Precious the death," "Glorious the memory" now, "of them that die in the Lord." And even this, that the Angels disdained not now to come thither, and to sit there, is an *auspicium* of a great change to ensue in the state of that place. *Quid gloriosius Angelo? quid vilius vermiculo?* saith Augustine. *Quid fuit vermiculorum locus, est et Angelorum.* 'That which was the place for worms, is become a place for Angels.'

Their habit. "In white." So were there divers of them, divers times this day, seen, "in white" all; in that colour. It seems to be their Easter-day colour, for at this feast they all do their service in it. Their Easter-day colour, for it is the colour of the Resurrection. The state whereof when Christ would represent upon the Mount, "His raiment was all white, no fuller in the earth could come near it." And our colour it shall be, when rising again we "shall walk in white robes," and "follow the Lamb whithersoever He goeth."

Heaven mourned on Good-Friday, the eclipse made all then in black. Easter-day it rejoiceth, Heaven and Angels, all in white. Solomon tells us, it is the colour of joy. And that is the state of joy, and this the day of the first joyful tidings of it, with joy ever celebrated, even *in albis,* eight days together, by them that found Christ.

"In white," and "sitting." As the colour of joy, so the situation of rest. So we say, Sit down, and rest. And so is the grave made, by this morning's work, a place of rest. Rest, not from our labours only—so do the beasts rest when they die; but as it is in the sixteenth Psalm, a Psalm of the Resurrection, a "rest in hope"—"hope" of rising again, the members in the virtue of their Head Who this day is risen. So to enter into the "rest," which yet "remaineth for the people of God," even the Sabbath eternal.

"Sitting," and in this order "sitting;" "at the head one, at the feet another, where His body had lain."

1. Which order may well refer to Christ Himself, Whose body was the true ark indeed, "in which it pleased the Godhead to dwell bodily;" and is therefore here between two Angels, as was the ark, the type of it, "between the two cherubims."

2. May also refer to Mary Magdalene. She had anointed His head, she had anointed His feet: at these two places sit the two angels, as it were to acknowledge so much for her sake.

3. In mystery, they refer it thus. Because *caput Christi Deus,* "the Godhead is the head of Christ," and His feet which the serpent did bruise, His manhood; that either of these hath his Angel. That to Christ man no less than to Christ God, the Angels do now their service. *In principio erat Verbum,* His Godhead; there, an Angel. *Verbum caro factum,* his manhood; there, another. "And let all the Angels of God

worship Him" in both. Even in His manhood, at His cradle, the head of it, a choir of Angels; at His grave, the feet of it, Angels likewise.

4. And lastly, for our comfort thus. That henceforth even such shall our graves be, if we be so happy as to "have our parts in the first resurrection," which is of the soul from sin. We shall go to our graves in white, in the comfort and colour of hope, lie between two Angels there; they guard our bodies dead, and present them alive again at the Resurrection.

1. Yet before we leave them, to learn somewhat of the Angels; specially, of "the Angel that sat at the feet." That between them there was no striving for places. He that "sat at the feet," as well content with his place as he that "at the head." We to be so by their example. For with us, both the Angels would have been "at the head," never an one "at the feet;" with us none would be at the feet by his good will, head-Angels all.

2. Again, from them both. That inasmuch as the head ever stands for the beginning, and the feet for the end, that we be careful that our beginnings only be not glorious—O an Angel at the head in any wise—but that we look to the feet, there be another there too. *Ne turpiter atrum desinat,* 'that it end not in a black Angel,' that began in a white. And this for the Angels' appearing.

Ver. 13. "And they said to her, Woman, why weepest thou? She said to them, They have taken away my Lord, and I know not where they have laid Him."

Now to their speech. It was not a dumb show this, a bare apparition, and so vanished away. It was *visio et vox,* 'a vocal vision.' Here is a dialogue too, the Angels speak to her.

And they ask her, *Quid ploras?* Why she wept, what cause she had to weep. They mean she had none, as indeed no more she had. All was in error, *piæ lachrymæ sed cæcæ,* 'tears of grief but false grief,' imagining that to be that was not, Him to be dead that was alive. She weeps, because she found the grave empty, which God forbid she should have found full, for then Christ must have been dead still, and so no Resurrection.

And this case of Mary Magdalene's is our case oftentimes. In the error of our conceit to weep, where we have no cause; to joy, where we have as little. Where we should, where we have cause to joy, we weep; and where to weep, we joy. Our *ploras* hath never a *quid.* False joys

and false sorrows, false hopes and false fears this life of ours is full of—
God help us!

Now because she erred, they ask her the cause, that she alleging it they
may take it away, and shew it to be no cause. As the elench, *a non
causâ pro causâ,* makes foul rule among us, beguiles us all our life long.

Will ye hear her answer to "Why weep you?" why? *sustulerunt,* that
was the cause, her Lord was gone, was "taken away."

And a good cause it had been, if it had been true. Any have cause to
grieve that have lost, lost a good Lord, so good and gracious a Lord as
He had been to her.

But that is not all; a worse matter, a greater grief than that. When
one dieth, we reckon him taken away; that is one kind of taking away.
But his dead body is left, so all is not taken from us; that was not her
case. For in saying, "her Lord," she means not her Lord alive—that is
not it; she means not they had slain Him, they had taken away His life
—she had wept her fill for that already. But "her Lord," that is, His
dead body. For though His life was gone, yet His body was left. And
that was all she now had left of Him that she calls her Lord, and that
"they had taken away" from her too. A poor one it was, yet some
comfort it was to her, to have even that left her to visit, to anoint, to
do other offices of love, even to that. *Etiam viso cadavere recalescit amor,*
at the sight even of that will love revive, it will fetch life of love again.
But now here is her case; that is gone and all, and nothing but an
empty grave now left to stand by. That St. Augustine saith well,
*sublatus de monumento* grieved her more than *occisus in ligno,* for
then something yet was left; now nothing at all. Right *sustulerunt,*
taken away quite and clean.

And thirdly, her *nescio ubi.* For though He be taken away, it is
some comfort yet, if we know where to fetch Him again. But here,
He is gone without all hope of recovery or getting again. For "they"
—but she knew not who, "had carried Him," she knew not whither;
"laid Him," she knew not where; there to do to Him, she knew not
what. So that now she knew not whither to go, to find any comfort.
It was *nescio ubi* with her right. Put all these together, His life taken
away, His body taken away, and carried no man knows whither; and
do they ask why she wept? or can any blame her for it?

The truth is, none had "taken away her Lord" for all this; for all
this while her Lord was well, was as she would have had Him, alive
and safe. He went away of Himself, none carried Him thence. What

of that? *Non credens suscitatum, credidit sublatum,* 'for want of belief He was risen, she believed He was carried away.' She erred in so believing; there was error in her love, but there was love in her error too.

And, give me leave to lay out three more arguments of her love, out of this verse, to make up eight, towards the making up of her *multum.*

The very title she gives Him, of *Dominum meum,* is one; "My Lord," that she gives Him that term. For it shews her love and respect was no whit abated by the scandal of His death. It was a most opprobrious, ignominious, shameful death He suffered; such, as in the eyes of the world any would have been ashamed to own Him, or say of Him, *Meum;* but any would have been afraid to honour Him with that title, to style Him *Dominum.* She was neither. *Meum,* for hers; *Dominum meum,* for her Lord she acknowledgeth Him, is neither ashamed nor afraid to continue that title still. *Amor scandalo non scandalizatus.*

Another, which I take to be far beyond this, That she having looked into the grave a little before, and seen never an Angel there, and of a sudden looking in now and seeing two, a sight able to have amazed any, any but her, it moves not her at all. The suddenness, the strangeness, the gloriousness of the sight, yea, even of Angels, move her not at all. She seems to have no sense of it, and so to be in a kind of ecstacy all the while. *Domine, propter Te est extra se,* saith Bernard. *Amor extasin patiens.*

And thirdly, as that strange sight affected her not a whit, so neither did their comfortable speech work with her at all. Comfortable I call it, for they that ask the cause why, "why weep you?" shew they would remove it if it lay in them. Neither of these did or could move her, or make her once leave her weeping—she wept on still: Christ will ask her, *quid ploras?* by and by again. If she find an Angel, if she find not her Lord, it will not serve. She had rather find His dead body, than them in all their glory. No man in earth, no Angel in Heaven can comfort her; none but He that is taken away, Christ, and none but Christ; and till she find Him again, her soul refuseth all manner of comfort, yea even from Heaven, even from the Angels themselves; these three. *Amor super amissum renuens consolari.*

Thus she, in her love, for her supposed loss or taking away. And what shall become of us in ours then? That lose Him 1. not once, but oft; 2. and not in suppose as she did, but in very deed; 3. and that by sin, the worst loss of all; 4. and that not by any other's taking away, but by our own act and wilful default; and are not grieved, nay not moved a whit, break none of our wonted sports for it, as if we reckoned Him as good lost as found. Yea, when Christ and the Holy Ghost, and the favour of God, and all is gone, how soon, how easily are we comforted again for all this! that none shall need to say, *quid ploras?* to us rather, *quid non ploras?* ask us why we weep not, having so good cause to do it as we then have? This for the Angels' part.

Ver. 14. "When she had thus said, she turned herself about, and saw Jesus standing, and knew not that it was Jesus."

Always the Angels, we see, touched the right string, and she tells them the wrong cause, but yet the right, if it had been right.

Now to this answer of hers they would have replied, and taken away her error touching her Lord's taking away; that if she knew all, she would have left her seeking, and set her down by them, and left her weeping, and been in white as well as they.

But here is a *supersedeas* to them, the Lord himself comes in place. Now come we from the seeking Him dead, to the finding Him alive. For when He saw no Angels, no sight, no speech of theirs would serve, none but her Lord could give her any comfort, her Lord comes. *Christus adest.*

*Adest Christus, nec ab eis unquam abest a quibus quæritur,* saith Augustine; 'Christ is found, found by her; and this case of hers shall be the case of all that seriously seek Him.' This woman here for one, she sought Him we see. They that went to Emmaus to-day, they but talked of Him sadly, and they both found Him. Why, He is found of them that seek Him not; but of them that seek Him, never but found. "For Thou, Lord, never failest them that seek Thee." "God is not unrighteous, to forget the work and labour of their love that seek Him."

So find Him they shall, but happily not all so fully at first, no more than she did. For first, to try her yet a little farther, He comes unknown, stands by her, and she little thought it had been He.

A case that likewise falls out full oft. Doubtless, "He is not far from every one of us," saith the Apostle to the Athenians. But He is nearer us many times than we think; even hard by us and we not aware of it, saith Job. And *O si cognovisses et tu,* O if we did know, and it standeth us in hand to pray that we may know when He is so, for that is "the time of our visitation."

St. John saith here, the Angels were sitting; St. Luke saith, they stood. They are thus reconciled. That Christ coming in presence, the Angels which before were sitting stood up. Their standing up made Mary Magdalene turn her to see who it was they rose to. And so Christ she saw, but knew Him not.

Not only not knew Him, but mis-knew Him, took Him for the gardener. Tears will dim the sight, and it was not yet scarce day, and she seeing one, and not knowing what any one should make in the ground so early but he that dressed it, she might well mistake. But it was more than so; her eyes were not holden only that she did not know Him, but over and beside He did appear ἑτέρᾳ μορφῇ, in some such shape as might resemble the gardener whom she took Him for.

Proper enough it was, it fitted well the time and place, this person. The time, it was the spring; the place, it was the garden: that place is most in request at that time, for that place and time a gardener doth well.

Of which her so taking Him, St. Gregory saith well, *profecto errando non erravit*. She did not mistake in taking Him for a gardener; though she might seem to err in some sense, yet in some other she was in the right. For in a sense, and a good sense, Christ may well be said to be a gardener, and indeed is one. For our rule is, Christ as He appears, so He is ever; no false semblant in Him.

1. A gardener He is then. The first, the fairest garden that ever was, Paradise, He was the gardener, it was of His planting. So, a gardener.

2. And ever since it is He That as God makes all our gardens green, sends us yearly the spring, and all the herbs and flowers we then gather; and neither Paul with his planting, nor Apollos with his watering, could do any good without Him. So a gardener in that sense.

3. But not in that alone; but He it is that gardens our "souls" too, and makes them, as the Prophet saith, "like a well-watered garden;" weeds out of them whatsoever is noisome or unsavory, sows and plants them with true roots and seeds of righteousness, waters them with the dew of His grace, and makes them bring forth fruit to eternal life.

But it is none of all these, but besides all these, nay over and above all these, this day if ever, most properly He was a gardener. Was one, and so after a more peculiar manner might take this likeness on Him. Christ rising was indeed a gardener, and that a strange one, Who made such an herb grow out of the ground this day as the like was never seen before, a dead body to shoot forth alive out of the grave.

I ask, was He so this day alone? No, but this profession of His, this day begun, He will follow to the end. For He it is That by virtue of this morning's act shall garden our bodies too, turn all our graves into garden plots; yea, shall one day turn land and sea and all into a great garden, and so husband them as they shall in due time bring forth live bodies, even all our bodies alive again.

Long before, did Esay see this and sing of it in his song, resembling the resurrection to a spring garden. "Awake and sing," saith he; "ye that dwell for a time are as it were sown in the dust, for His dew shall be as the dew of herbs, and the earth shall shoot forth her dead." So then, He appeared no other than He was; a gardener He was, not in show alone, but *opere et veritate,* and so came in His own likeness. This for Christ's appearing. Now to His speech, but as unknown still.

Ver. 15. "Jesus saith to her, Woman, why weepest thou? whom seekest thou?" She, supposing He had been the gardener, said to Him, "Sir, if thou have borne Him hence, tell me where thou hast laid Him, and I will take Him thence."

Still she weeps; so He begins with *Quid ploras?* asks the same question the Angels had before; only quickens it a little with *quem quæris,* "whom seek you?" So, *Quem quæris quærit a te, Quem quæris?* Whom she sought, He asks her "Whom she sought." *Si quæris, cur non cognoscis? si cognoscis, cur quæris?* saith Augustine. If she seek Him, why knows she Him not? If she know Him, why seeks she Him still? A common thing with us, this also; to seek a thing, and when we have found it, not to know we have so, but even *Christum a Christo quærere,* 'to ask Christ for Christ.' Which however it fall in other matters, in this seeking of Christ it is safe. Even when we seek Christ, to pray to Christ to help us to find Christ; we shall do it full evil without Him.

This *quid ploras?* it comes now twice. The Angels asked it, we stood not on it then. Now, seeing Christ asks it again the second time, we will think there is something in it, and stay a little at it. The rather, for that it is the very opening of His mouth, the very first words that ever came from Him, that He spake first of all, after His rising again from death. There is sure some more than ordinary matter in this *quid ploras?* if it be but even for that.

Thus say the Fathers; 1. That Mary Magdalene standing by the grave's side, and there weeping, is thus brought in to represent unto us the state of all mankind before this day, the day of Christ's rising again, weeping over the dead, as do the heathen "that have no hope;" comes Christ with His *quid ploras,* "Why do you weep?" As much to say, as *ne ploras;* "Weep not, why should you weep?" there is no cause of weeping now. Henceforth none shall need to stand by the grave to weep there any more. A question very proper for Easter-day, for the day of the Resurrection. For if there be a rising again, *quid ploras* is right, why should she, why should any weep then?

So that this *quid ploras* of Christ's wipes away tears from all eyes, and as we sing in the thirtieth Psalm, whose title is, the Psalm of the Resurrection, puts off our "sackcloth," that is our mourning weeds, girds us "with gladness," puts us all in white with the Angels.

*Ploras* then, leave that for Good-Friday, for His Passion; weep then, and spare not. But *quid ploras?* for Easter-day is in kind the feast of the Resurrection, why should there be any weeping upon it? Is not Christ risen? Shall not He raise us with Him? Is He not a gardener, to make our bodies sown to grow again? *Ploras,* leave that to the heathen that are without hope; but to the Christian man, *quid ploras?* Why should he weep? he hath hopes; the Head is already risen, the members shall in their due time follow Him.

I observe that four times this day, at four several appearings, 1. at the first, at this here, He asked her, *quid ploras?* why she wept. 2. Of them that went to Emmaus, *quid tristes estis?* "Why are ye sad?" 3. Within a verse following, the nineteenth, He saith to the Eleven, *Pax vobis,* "Peace be to them:" 4. And to the women that met Him on the way, χαίρετε, that is, "rejoice, be glad." So, no weeping, no being sad; now, nothing this day, but peace and joy; they do properly belong to this feast.

And this I note the more willingly now this year, because the last Easter we could not so well have noted it. Some wept then; all were sad, little joy there was, and there was a *quid,* a good cause for it. But blessed be God That hath now sent us a more kindly Easter, of this, by taking away the cause of our sorrow then, that we may preach of *quid ploras?* and be far from it. So much for *quid ploras?* Christ's question. Now to her answer.

She is still where she was; at *sustulerunt* before, at *sustulisti* now— *si tu sustulisti:* we shall never get that word from her.

But to Christ she seems somewhat more harsh than to the Angels. To them she complains of others; "they have taken." Christ she seems to charge, at least to suspect of the fact, as if He looked like one that had been a breaker up of graves, a carrier away of corpses out of their place of rest. Her *if* implies as much. But pardon love; as it fears where it needs not, so it suspects oft where it hath no cause. He, or any that comes in our way, hath done it, hath taken Him away, when love is at a loss. But Bernard speaks to Christ for her; *Domine, amor quem habebat in Te, et dolor quem habebat de Te, excuset eam apud Te, si forte erravit circa Te:* that 'the love she bare to Him, the sorrow she had for Him, may excuse her with Him, if she were in any error concerning Him in her saying,' *Si tu sustulisti.*

And yet see how God shall direct the tongue! In thus charging Him, *prophetat et nescit,* 'she says truer than she was aware.' For indeed, if any took Him away, it was He did it. So she was not much amiss. Her *si tu* was true, though not in her sense. For, *quod de Ipso factum est, Ipse fecit,* 'All that was done to Him, He did it Himself.' His taking away, *virtus fuit, non facinus,* 'was by His own power, not by the act of any other;' *et gloria, non injuria,* 'no other man's injury it was, but His own glory,' that she found Him not there. This was true, but this was no part of her meaning.

I cannot here pass over two more characters of her love, that so you may have the full ten I promised.

One, in *si tu sustulisti Eum,* in her *Eum,* in her "Him." Him? Which Him? Her affections seem so to transport her, as she says no man knows what. To one, a mere stranger to her, and she to him, she talks of one thrice under the term of "Him;" "if thou hast taken Him away, tell me where thou hast laid Him, and I will fetch Him;" Him, Him, and Him, and never names Him, or tells who He is. This is *solœcismus amoris,* an irregular speech, but love's own dialect. "Him" is enough with love: who knows not who that is? It supposes every body, all the world bound to take notice of him whom we look for, only by saying "Him," though we never tell his name, nor say a word more. *Amor, quem ipse cogitat, neminem putans ignorare.*

The other is in her *ego tollam:* if he would tell her where he had laid Him, she would go fetch Him, that she would. Alas, poor woman, she was not able to lift Him. There are more than one, or two either, allowed to the carrying of a corpse.

As for His, it had more than a hundred pound weight of myrrh and other odours upon it, beside the poise of a dead body. She could not do it. Well, yet she would do it though. *O mulier, non mulier,* saith Origen, for *ego tollam* seems rather the speech of a porter, or of some lusty strong fellow at least, than of a silly weak woman. But love makes women more than women, at least it makes them have νοῦν ὑπὲρ ἰσχὺν, 'the courage above the strength,' far. Never measures her own forces, no burden too heavy, no assay too hard for love, *et nihil erubescit nisi nomen difficultatis,* 'and is not ashamed of any thing but that any thing should be too hard or too heavy for it.' *Affectus sine mensurâ virium propriarum.* Both these argue *dilexit multum.* And so now, you have the full number of ten.

Ver. 16. "Jesus saith to her, Mary; she turned herself, and said to Him, Rabboni, that is to say, Master."

Now *magnes amoris amor;* 'nothing so allures, so draws love to it, as doth love itself.' In Christ specially, and in such in whom the same mind is. For when her Lord saw there was no taking away His taking away from her, all was in vain, neither men, nor Angels, nor Himself, so long as He kept Himself gardener, could get any thing of her but her Lord was gone, He was taken away, and that for the want of Jesus nothing but Jesus could yield her any comfort, He is no longer able to contain, but even discloses Himself; and discloses Himself by His voice.

For it should seem before, with His shape He had changed that also. But now He speaks to her in His known voice, in the wonted accent of it, does but name her name, Mary—no more, and that was enough. That was as much to say, *Recognosce a Quo recognosceris,* 'she would at least take notice of Him That shewed He was no stranger by calling her by her name;' for whom we call by their names, we take particular notice of. So God says to Moses, *Te autem cognovi de nomine,* "thou hast found grace in My sight, and I know thee by name." As God Moses, so Christ Mary Magdalene.

And this indeed is the right way to know Christ, to be known of Him first. The Apostle saith, now we "have known God," and then correcteth himself, "or rather have been known of God." For till He know us, we shall never know Him aright.

And now, lo Christ is found; found alive, That was sought dead. A cloud may be so thick we shall not see the sun through it. The sun must scatter that cloud, and then we may. Here is an example of it. It is strange a thick cloud of heaviness had so covered her, as see Him she could not through it; this one word, these two syllables, Mary, from His mouth, scatters it all. No sooner had His voice sounded in her ears but it drives away all the mist, dries up her tears, lightens her eyes, that she knew Him straight, and answers Him with her wonted salutation, "Rabboni." If it had lain in her power to have raised Him from the dead, she would not have failed but done it, I dare say. Now it is done to her hands.

And with this all is turned out and in; a new world now. Away with *sustulerunt;* His taking away is taken away quite. For if His taking away were her sorrow, *contrariorum contraria consequentia. Si de sublato ploravit, de suscitato exultavit,* we may be sure; 'if sad for His death, for His taking away, then glad for His rising, for His restoring again.' Surely if she would have been glad but to have found but His dead body, now she finds it and Him alive, what was her joy, how great may we think! So that by this she saw *Quid ploras* was not asked her for nought, that it was no impertinent question, as it fell out. Well now, He That was thought lost is found again, and found, not as He was sought for, not a dead body, but "a living soul;" nay, "a quickening Spirit" then. And that might Mary Magdalene well say. He shewed it, for He quickened her, and her spirits that were as good as dead. You thought you should have come to Christ's resurrection to-day, and so you do. But not to His alone, but even to Mary Magdalene's resurrection too. For in very deed a kind of resurrection it was was wrought in her; revived as it were, and raised from a dead and drooping, to a lively and cheerful estate. The gardener had done His part, made her all green on the sudden.

And all this by a word of His mouth. Such power is there in every word of His; so easily are they called, whom Christ will but speak to.

But by this we see, when He would be made known to her after His rising, He did choose to be made known by the ear rather than by the eye. By nearing rather than by appearing. Opens her ears first, and her eyes after. Her "eyes were holden" till her ears were opened; comes *aures autem aperuisti mihi,* and that opens them.

With the philosophers, hearing is the sense of wisdom. With us, in divinity, it is the sense of faith. So, most meet. Christ is the Word; hearing then, that sense, is Christ's sense; *voce quam visu,* more proper to the word. So, *sicut audivimus* goes before, and then *sic vidimus* comes after. In matters of faith the ear goes first ever, and is of more use, and to be trusted before the eye. For in many cases faith holdeth, where sight faileth.

This then is a good way to come to the knowledge of Christ, by *hodie si vocem,* to "hear His voice." Howbeit, it is not the only way. There is another way to take notice of Him by besides, and we to take notice of it. On this very day we have them both.

For twice this day came Christ; unknown first, and then known after. To Mary Magdalene here, and to them at Emmaus. To Mary Magdalene unknown, in the shape of a gardener. To those that went to Emmaus unknown, in the likeness of a traveller by the way-side. Comes to be known to her by His voice, by the word of His mouth. Not so to them. For many words He spake to them, and they felt them warm at their hearts, but knew Him not for all that. But "He was known to them in the breaking of the bread." Her eyes opened by speaking a word; their eyes opened by the breaking of bread. There is the one and the other way, and so now you have both. And now you have them, I pray you make use of them. I see I shall not be able to go farther than this verse.

It were a folly to fall to comparisons, *committere inter se,* to set them at odds together these two ways, as the fond fashion now-a-days is, whether is better, Prayer or Preaching; the Word or the Sacraments. What needs this? Seeing we have both, both are ready for us; the one now, the other by-and-by; we may end this question soon. And this is the best and surest way to end it; to esteem of them both, to thank Him for both, to make use of both; having now done with one, to make trial of the other. It may be, who knows? if the one will not work, the other may. And if by the one or by the other, by either if it be wrought, what harm have we? In case it be not, yet have we offered to God our service in both, and committed the success of both to Him. He will see they shall have success, and in His good time, as shall be expedient for us, vouchsafe every one of us as He did Mary Magdalene in the text, "to know Him and the virtue of His resurrection;" and make us partakers of both, by both the means before remembered, by His blessed word, by His holy mysteries; the means to raise our souls here, the pledges of the raising up of our bodies hereafter. Of both which He make us partakers, Who is the Author of both, "Jesus Christ the Righteous," &c.

# THE PRIVATE DEVOTIONS

*Translated and Arranged by John Henry Newman*

## COURSE OF PRAYERS FOR THE WEEK

## The Fourth Day

### Introduction

I have thought upon Thee, O Lord,
when I was waking,
for Thou hast been my helper.
Blessed art Thou, O Lord,
who madest the two Lights, Sun and Moon,
greater and lesser,
and the stars
for light, for signs, for seasons,
spring, summer, autumn, winter,
days, weeks, months, years,
to rule over day and night.

### I. Confession

Behold, Thou art angry, for we have sinned.
We are all as an unclean thing,
and all our righteousnesses
as filthy rags.
We all do fade as a leaf,
and our iniquities, like the wind,
have taken us away.
But now, O Lord, Thou art our Father,
we are clay, all Thy handiwork.
Be not wroth very sore,
nor remember iniquity for ever,
behold, see, we beseech Thee,
we are all Thy people.

O Lord, though our iniquities testify against us,
do Thou it for Thy Name's sake;
for our backslidings are many,
we have sinned against Thee.
Yet Thou, O Lord, art in the midst of us,
and we are called by Thy Name,
leave us not.
O Hope of Israel,
The Saviour thereof in time of trouble,
why shouldest Thou be as a stranger in the land,
and as a wayfaring man that turneth aside
to tarry for a night?
why shouldest Thou be as a man astonished,
as a mighty man that cannot save?
Be merciful to our unrighteousnesses,
and our iniquities remember no more.
Lord, I am carnal,
sold under sin;
there dwelleth in me, that is, in my flesh,
no good thing;
for the good that I would, I do not,
but the evil which I would not, that I do.
I consent unto the law that it is good,
I delight in it after the inner man;
But I see another law in my members,
warring against the law of my mind,
and enslaving me to the law of sin.
Wretched man that I am,
who shall deliver me from the body of this death?
I thank God through Jesus Christ,
that where sin abounded,
grace hath much more abounded.
O Lord, Thy goodness leadeth me to repentance:
O give me sometime repentance
to recover me from the snare of the devil,
who am taken captive by him
at his will.
Sufficient for me the past time of my life
to have done the will of lusts,

walking in lasciviousness, revelling, drunkenness,
and in other excess of profligacy.
O Lamb without blemish and without spot,
who hast redeemed me with Thy precious Blood,
in that very Blood pity me and save me;
in that Blood,
and in that very Name,
besides which is none other under heaven
given among men,
by which we must be saved.
O God, Thou knowest my foolishness,
and my sins are not hid from Thee.
Lord, Thou knowest all my desire,
and my groaning is not hid from Thee.
Let not them that trust in Thee,
O Lord God of hosts,
be ashamed for my cause;
let not those that seek Thee be confounded
through me,
O Lord God of Israel.
Take me out of the mire that I sink not;
O let me be delivered from them that hate me
and out of the deep waters;
Let not the water flood drown me,
neither let the deep swallow me up,
and let not the pit shut her mouth upon me.

## 2. Prayer for Grace

[Defend me from]

| | |
|---|---|
| Pride . . . . . . . | Amorite. |
| envy . . . . . . . | Hittite. |
| wrath . . . . . . . | Perizzite. |
| gluttony . . . . . . | Girgashite. |
| lechery . . . . . . . | Hivite. |
| the cares of life (*covetousness.*) . | Canaanite. |
| lukewarm indifference (*sloth.*) . | Jebusite. |

[Give me]
Humility, pitifulness, patience,
sobriety, purity, contentment, ready zeal.
One thing have I desired of the Lord
which I will require,
that I may dwell in the house of the Lord
all the days of my life,
to behold the fair beauty of the Lord,
and to visit His temple.
Two things have I required of Thee, O Lord,
deny Thou me not before I die;
remove far from me vanity and lies;
give me neither poverty nor riches,
feed me with food convenient for me;
lest I be full and deny Thee
and say, who is the Lord?
or lest I be poor and steal,
and take the Name of my God in vain.
Let me learn to abound,
let me learn to suffer need,
in whatsoever state I am,
therewith to be content.
For nothing earthly, temporal, mortal,
to long nor to wait.
Grant me a happy life
in piety, gravity, purity,
in all things good and fair,
in cheerfulness, in health, in credit,
in competency, in safety, in gentle estate, in quiet;
a happy death,
a deathless happiness.

### 3. *Profession*

I believe
in the Father, benevolent affection;
in the Almighty, saving power;
in the Creator, providence

for guarding, ruling, perfecting the universe.
In Jesus, salvation,
in Christ, anointing;
in the Only-begotten Son, sonship,
in the Lord, a master's treatment,
in His conception and birth
the cleansing of our unclean conception and birth;
in His sufferings, which we owed,
that we might not pay;
in His cross the curse of the law removed;
in His death the sting of death;
in His burial eternal destruction in the tomb;
in His descent, whither we ought,
that we might not go;
in His resurrection,
as the first fruits of them that sleep;
in His ascent, to prepare a place for us;
in His sitting, to appear and intercede;
in His return, to take unto Him His own;
in His judgment, to render to each
according to his works.
In the Holy Ghost, power from on high,
transforming unto sanctity
from without and invisibly,
yet inwardly and evidently.
In the Church, a body mystical
of the called out of the whole world,
unto intercourse in faith and holiness.
In the communion of Saints, members of this body,
a mutual participation in holy things,
for confidence of remission of sins,
for hope of resurrection, of translation,
to life everlasting.

## 4. Intercession

And I have hoped in Thy mercy
from everlasting to everlasting.
How excellent is Thy mercy, O Lord;
If I have hope, it is in Thy mercy,

O let me not be disappointed of my hope.
Moreover we beseech Thee,
remember all, Lord, for good;
have pity upon all, O Sovereign Lord,
be reconciled with us all.
Give peace to the multitudes of Thy people;
scatter offences;
abolish wars;
stop the uprisings of heresies.
Thy peace and love
vouchsafe to us, O God our Saviour,
the Hope of all the ends of the earth.
Remember to crown the year
with Thy goodness;
for the eyes of all wait upon Thee,
and Thou givest them their meat in due season.
Thou openest Thy hand,
and fillest all things living with plenteousness.
Remember Thy Holy Church,
from one end of the earth to the other;
and give her peace,
whom Thou hast redeemed with Thy precious blood;
and establish her
unto the end of the world.
Remember those who bear fruit, and act nobly,
in Thy holy Churches,
and who remember the poor and needy;
recompense to them
Thy rich and heavenly gifts;
vouchsafe to them,
for things earthly, heavenly,
for corruptible, incorruptible,
for temporal, eternal.
Remember those who are in virginity,
and purity and ascetic life;
also those who live in honourable marriage,
in Thy reverence and fear.
Remember every Christian soul
in affliction, distress, and trial,

and in need of Thy pity and succour;
also our brethren in captivity, prison, chains,
and bitter bondage;
supplying return to the wandering,
health to the sick,
deliverance to the captives.
Remember religious and faithful kings,
whom Thou hast given to rule
upon the earth;
and especially remember, Lord,
our divinely-guarded king;
strengthen his kingdom,
subdue to him all adversaries,
Speak good things to his heart,
for Thy Church, and all Thy people.
Vouchsafe to him deep and undisturbed peace,
that in his serenity
we may lead a quiet and peaceable life
with all godliness and honesty.
Remember, Lord, all power
and authority,
our brethren in the court,
those who are chief in council and judgment,
and all by land and sea
waging Thy wars for us.
Moreover, Lord, remember graciously
our holy Fathers,
the honourable Presbytery, and all the Clergy,
rightly dividing the Word of Truth,
and rightly walking in it.
Remember, Lord, our brethren around us,
and praying with us in this holy hour,
for their zeal and earnestness-sake.
Remember also those who on fair reasons are away,
and pity them and us
in the multitude of Thy pity.
Fill our garners with all manner of store,
preserve our marriages in peace and concord,
nourish our infants,

lead forward our youth,
sustain our aged,
comfort the weak-hearted,
gather together the scattered,
restore the wanderers,
and knit them to Thy Holy Catholic Apostolic
Church.
Set free the troubled
with unclean spirits,
voyage with the voyagers,
travel with the travellers,
stand forth for the widow,
shield the orphan,
rescue the captive,
heal the sick.
Those who are on trial, in mines, in exile, in galleys,
in whatever affliction, necessity, and emergence,
remember, O God;
and all who need Thy great mercy;
and those who love us,
and those who hate;
and those who have desired us unworthy
to make mention of them in our prayers;
and all Thy people remember, O Lord, our God,
and upon all pour out Thy rich pity,
to all performing their requests for salvation;
and those of whom we have not made mention,
through ignorance, forgetfulness, or number
of names,
do Thou Thyself remember, O God,
who knowest the stature and appellation of each,
who knowest every one from his mother's womb.
For Thou art, O Lord, the Succour of the succourless,
The Hope of the hopeless,
The Saviour of the tempest-tost,
the Harbour of the voyager,
the Physician of the sick,
do Thou Thyself become all things to all men.
O Thou who knowest each man and his petition,

each house, and its need,
deliver, O Lord, this city,
and all the country in which we sojourn,
from plague, famine, earthquake, flood,
fire, sword, hostile invasion,
and civil war.
End the schisms of the Churches,
quench the haughty cries of the nations,
and receive us all into Thy kingdom,
acknowledging us as sons of light;
and Thy peace and love
vouchsafe to us, O Lord, our God.
Remember O Lord, our God,
all spirits and all flesh
which we have remembered, and which we have not.
And the close of our life,
Lord, Lord, direct in peace,
Christianly, acceptably, and, should it please Thee,
painlessly,
gathering us together under the feet of Thine elect,
when Thou wilt and how Thou wilt,
only without shame and sins.
The brightness of the Lord our God be upon us,
prosper Thou the work of our hands upon us,
O prosper Thou our handiwork.
Be, Lord,
within me to strengthen me,
without me to guard me,
over me to shelter me,
beneath me to stablish me,
before me to guide me,
after me to forward me,
round about me to secure me.

### 5. Praise

Blessed art Thou, Lord, God of Israel,
our Father,
from everlasting to everlasting.

Thine, O Lord,
is the greatness and the power,
the triumph and the victory,
the praise and the strength,
for Thou rulest over all
in heaven and on earth.
At Thy face every king is troubled,
and every nation.
Thine, O Lord, is the kingdom
and the supremacy over all,
and over all rule.
With Thee is wealth, and glory is from
Thy countenance;
Thou rulest over all, O Lord,
the Ruler of all rule;
and in Thine hand is strength and power,
and in Thine hand to give to all things
greatness and strength.
And now, Lord, we confess to Thee
and we praise Thy glorious Name.

# Robert Burton
## 1577–1640

*The Anatomy of Melancholy* is a strange work, complex and often compelling. It is variously skeptical and credulous, tightly organized yet infinitely digressive, a mixture of objective observation and personal outcry.

In it Burton analyzes, or anatomizes, melancholy as a humour. He sees it as a disease stemming from an imbalance of body fluids, a disorder deeply rooted in temperament and fixed in habit, at first satisfying but ultimately compulsive and destructive. In the course of his analysis he portrays a Vanity Fair, a field of folk suffering from idleness, illusions, night-watchings, and a host of other maladies. And by contrast he offers a model society, his own Utopia.

His great Rabelaisian energy turns all this into a far-reaching compendium of useful and curious knowledge in the fields of psychology, physiology, astronomy, demonology, meteorology, geography, manners, and morals, to name only a few of the most obvious. The title page of the first edition tells the story: *The Anatomy of Melancholy, What it is. With all the Kindes, Causes, Symptomes, Prognostickes, and Several Cures of it. In Three Maine Partitions with their several Sections, Members and Subsections. Philosophically, Historically, Opened and Cut up.*

He also confesses his own predisposition to melancholy, and moves often from clinical treatise to private lament. He must, as he puts it, scratch where it itches. His book thus becomes diagnosis, complaint, and therapy. It focuses everything—all the melancholy of lovers, scholars, princes, subjects, heretics, all their symptoms and remedies, all the glum prognoses—through one aperture, the pinprick of his own melancholy.

He writes, he says, "in an extemporean style," but without apology for his carelessness. Indeed, he is contemptuous of the "affectation of big words, fustian phrases, jingling terms, tropes, strong lines, that like Acestes' arrows caught fire as they flew, strains of wit, brave heats, elogies, hyperbolical exornations, elegancies, &c., which many so much affect" (*Anatomy*, 24). His pages, though weighty, are also conversational, vigorous, and sometimes quite earthy. Occasionally he lapses into neatly Senecan, even Euphuistic, wit and contrivance: "for a pint of honey thou shalt here likely find a gallon of gall, for a dram of pleasure a pound of pain, for an inch of mirth an ell of moan" (*Anatomy*, 126). But for the most part his affinities are with a looser variant of the Senecan model: " 'tis not my study or intent to compose neatly . . . but to express myself readily & plainly as it happens" (*Anatomy*, 25). In the jumble of matter, his syntax often collapses, but however abundant, free and formless are his sentences, their meaning is always clear.

Included in the pages that follow are the passages in which he states his purpose and defines the humour of melancholy, with a sampling from his discussion of causes, symptoms, and cures. His Utopia is given in full. His description of the melancholy of students appears at length. Love melancholy is represented by his treatment of the tyranny of love, by a consideration of kissing and dancing, and by his advice on how to fall out of love. Incorporated also are the sections in which he comments on the range and variety of his style. Finally, there are the passages touching on his own anguish: "I had a heavy heart and an ugly head, a kind of impostume in my head, which I was very desirous to be unladen of" (*Anatomy*, 16).

## EDITIONS

*The Anatomy of Melancholy*, 1621; ed. by A. R. Shilleto, 1893; ed. by Floyd Dell and Paul Jordan-Smith, 1927, 1929; ed. by H. Jackson, 1932; Selections, ed. by Lawrence Babb, 1965.
*Philosophaster*, ed. by W. E. Buckley, 1862; ed. and trans. by Paul Jordan-Smith, 1931.

## HISTORICAL AND CRITICAL STUDIES

John Livingston Lowes, "The Loveres Maladye of Hereos," *MP*, XI (1914).
John Middleton Murry, "Burton's 'Anatomy,' " *Countries of the Mind*, first series, 1922.

FALCONER MADAN, ed., *Robert Burton and the Anatomy of Melancholy*, 1926.

GEORGE B. HARRISON, intro. to Nicholas Breton, *Melancholike Humours*, 1929.

LILY B. CAMPBELL, *Shakespeare's Tragic Heroes: Slaves of Passions*, 1930.

PAUL JORDAN-SMITH, *Bibliographia Burtoniana*, 1931.

HANS JORDAN GOTTLIEB, *Robert Burton's Knowledge of English Poetry*, 1937.

LLEWELYN POWYS, "Robert Burton," *Rats in the Sacristy*, 1937.

H. W. TAEUSCH, *Democritus Junior Anatomizes Melancholy*, 1937.

BERGEN EVANS, *The Psychiatry of Robert Burton*, 1944.

LAWRENCE BABB, "On the Nature of Elizabethan Psychological Literature," and Theodore Spencer, "The Elizabethan Malcontent," in *Joseph Quincy Adams Memorial Studies*, 1948.

WILLIAM R. MUELLER, "Robert Burton's Economic and Political Views," *HLQ*, XI (1948).

J. MAX PATRICK, "Robert Burton's Utopianism," *PQ*, XXVII (1948).

S. PRAWER, "Burton's 'Anatomy of Melancholy'," *Cambridge Jour.*, I (1948).

WILLIAM R. MUELLER, "Robert Burton's Frontispiece as Illustrative of the Text," *PMLA*, LXIV (1949).

ROBERT M. BROWNE, "Robert Burton and the New Cosmology," *MLQ*, XIII (1952).

WILLIAM R. MUELLER, *The Anatomy of Robert Burton's England*, 1952.

——, "Robert Burton's 'Satyricall Preface,'" *MLQ*, XV (1954).

WILLIAM J. GRACE, "Notes on Robert Burton and John Milton," *SP*, LII (1955).

JOHN L. LIEVSAY, "Robert Burton's De Consolatione," *S. Atl. Quart.*, LV (1956).

RUFUS PUTNEY, "'Our Vegetable Love': Marvell and Burton," *Studies in Honor of T. W. Baldwin*, 1958.

LAWRENCE BABB, *Sanity in Bedlam: A Study of Robert Burton's Anatomy of Melancholy*, 1959.

PAUL JORDAN-SMITH AND MARGARET MILHAUSER, *Burton's Anatomy of Melancholy and Burtoniana. A Checklist*, 1959.

FRANK P. WILSON, "Robert Burton," *Seventeenth Century Prose*, 1960.

AILEEN WARD, "Keats and Burton: A Reappraisal," *PQ*, XL (1961).

# THE ANATOMY OF MELANCHOLY

## DEMOCRITUS TO THE READER

### To Ease My Mind by Writing

If any man except against the matter or manner of treating of this my subject, & will demand a reason of it, I can allege more than one. I writ of melancholy, by being busy to avoid melancholy. There is no greater cause of melancholy than idleness, no better cure than business, as Rhasis holds: and howbeit to be busied in toys is to small purpose, yet hear that divine Seneca: Better do to no end than nothing. I writ therefore, and busied myself in this playing labour that I might avoid the torpor of laziness, with Vectius in Macrobius, and turn my leisure to purpose.

> At once to profit and to please
> And teach the reader at his ease.  (HORACE)

To this end I writ, like them, saith Lucian, that recite to trees, & declaim to pillars, for want of auditors: as Paulus Ægineta ingeniously confesseth, not that any thing was unknown or omitted, but to exercise myself, which course if some took, I think it would be good for their bodies, and much better for their souls; or peradventure as others do, for fame, to show myself: (Your knowledge is nothing unless it be proclaimed to others). I might be of Thucydides' opinion: To know a thing and not express it, is all one as if he knew it not. When I first took this task in hand, & as he saith, undertook the work, my genius impelling me, this I aimed at: to ease my mind by writing, for I had a heavy heart and an ugly head, a kind of imposthume in my head, which I was very desirous to be unladen of, & could imagine no fitter evacuation than this. Besides I might not well refrain, for one must needs scratch where it itches. . . .

### I Call a Spade a Spade

. . . Another main fault is, that I have not revised the copy, and amended the style, which now flows remissly, as it was first conceived, but my leisure would not permit. I confess it is neither as I would, nor as it should be.

> When I peruse this tract which I have writ,
> I am abash'd, and much I hold unfit.   (OVID)

And, what is most important, in the matter itself, many things I disallow at this present, which when I writ, my years are not what they were, nor yet my tastes; I would willing retract much, &c., but 'tis too late, I can only crave pardon now for what is amiss.

I might indeed (had I wisely done) have observed that precept of the poet, let them be kept quiet until the ninth year, and have taken more care: or as Alexander the Physician would have done by *Lapis Lazuli,* fifty times washed before it be used, I should have revised, corrected, and amended this tract; but I had not as (I said) that happy leisure, no amanuenses or assistants. Pancrates in Lucian, wanting a servant as he went from Memphis to Coptos in Egypt, took a door-bar, and after some superstitious words pronounced (Eucrates the relator was then present) made it stand up like a serving-man, fetch him water, turn the spit, serve in supper, and what work he would besides; and when he had done that service he desired, turn'd his man to a stick again. I have no such skill to make new men at my pleasure, or means to hire them, no whistle to call like the master of a ship, and bid them run, &c. I have no such authority, no such benefactors, as that noble Ambrosius was to Origen, allowing him six or seven amanuenses to write out his dictates; I must for that cause do my business myself, and was therefore enforced, as a bear doth her whelps, to bring forth this confused lump, I had not time to lick it into form, as she doth her young ones, but even so to publish it, as it was first written, whatever came uppermost, in an extemporean style, as I do commonly all other exercises; I put forth what my genius dictated, out of a confused company of notes, and writ with as small deliberation as I do ordinarily speak, without all affectation of big words, fustian phrases, jingling terms, tropes, strong lines, that like Acestes' arrows caught fire as they flew, strains of wit, brave heats, elogies, hyperbolical exornations, elegancies, &c., which many so much affect. I am a water-drinker, drink no wine at all, which so much improves our modern wits, a loose, plain, rude writer, & as free as loose, I call a spade a spade, I write for minds, not ears, I respect matter, not words; remembering that of Cardan, Words exist for things, not things for words; and seeking, with Seneca, rather what than how to write. For as Philo thinks, He that is conversant about matter, neglects words, and those that excel in this art of speaking, have no profound learning.

Words may sound fine, yet have no inner meaning. (PALINGENIUS)

Besides, it was the observation of that wise Seneca, When you see a fellow careful about his words, and neat in his speech, know this for a certainty, that man's mind is busied about toys, there's no solidity in him. Prettiness of style is not a manly distinction: as he said of a nightingale, A voice you are, and nothing else, &c. I am therefore in this point a professed disciple of Apollonius, a scholar of Socrates, I neglect phrases, and labour wholly to inform my reader's understanding, not to please his ear; 'tis not my study or intent to compose neatly, which an Orator requires, but to express myself readily & plainly as it happens. So that as a River runs, sometimes precipitate and swift, then dull and slow; now direct, then winding; now deep, then shallow; now muddy, then clear; now broad, then narrow; doth my style flow: now serious, then light; now comical, then satirical; now more elaborate, then remiss, as the present subject required, or as at that time I was affected. And if thou vouchsafe to read this treatise, it shall seem no otherwise to thee than the way to an ordinary Traveller, sometimes fair, sometimes foul; here champaign, there inclosed; barren in one place, better soil in another: by woods, groves, hills, dales, plain, &c. I shall lead thee over steep mountains, through treacherous valleys, dew-clad meadows and rough plowed fields, through variety of objects, that which thou shalt like and surely dislike. . . .

## Our Religious Madness

. . . 'Tis not to be denied, the world alters every day, cities fall, kingdoms are transferred; as Petrarch observes: We change language, habits, laws, customs, manners, but not vices, not diseases, not the symptoms of folly and madness,—they are still the same. And as a River, we see, keeps the like name and place, but not water, and yet ever runs, our times and persons alter, vices are the same, and ever will be. Look how nightingales sang of old, cocks crowed, kine lowed, sheep bleated, sparrows chirped, dogs barked, so they do still; we keep our madness still, play the fools still, the play's not finished yet, we are of the same humours and inclinations as our predecessors were, you shall find us all alike, much at one, we and our sons, and so shall our posterity continue to the last. But to speak of times present.

If Democritus were alive now, and should but see the superstition of our age, our religious madness, as Meteran calls it, so many professed Christians, yet so few imitators of Christ, so much talk of Religion, so much science, so little conscience, so much knowledge, so many preachers, so little practise, such variety of sects, such have and hold of all sides, banner against banner, such absurd and ridiculous traditions and ceremonies. If he should meet a Capuchin, a Franciscan, a Pharisaical Jesuit, a man-serpent, a shave-crowned Monk in his robes, a begging Friar, or see their three-crown'd Sovereign Lord the Pope, poor Peter's successor, the slave of the slaves of God, to depose Kings with his foot, to tread on Emperors' necks, make them stand bare-foot and bare-legg'd at his gates, hold his bridle and stirrup, &c., (O that Peter and Paul were alive to see this!), if he should observe a Prince creep so devoutly to kiss his toe, and those Red-cap Cardinals, poor parish priests of old, now Princes' companions, what would he say? In our folly we storm the very heavens. Had he met some of our devout pilgrims going barefoot to Jerusalem, Our Lady of Loretto, Rome, S. Iago, S. Thomas' Shrine, to creep to those counterfeit and maggot-eaten Reliques; had he been present at a Mass, and seen such kissing of Paxes, Crucifixes, cringes, duckings, their several attires and ceremonies, pictures of saints, indulgences, pardons, vigils, fastings, feasts, crossing, knocking, kneeling at Ave-Marias, bells, with many such Spectacles pleasing to the ignorant masses, praying in gibberish, and mumbling of beads. Had he heard an old woman say her prayers in Latin, their sprinkling of holy water, and going a procession,

> A thousand bands of monks go on procession;
> Why should I mention banners, crosses, idols? (NAUGER)

their breviaries, bulls, hallowed beans, exorcisms, pictures, curious crosses, fables, and baubles. Had he read the Golden Legend, the Turks' Alcoran, or Jews' Talmud, the Rabbins' Comments, what would he have thought? How dost thou think he might have been affected? Had he more particularly examined a Jesuit's life amongst the rest, he should have seen an hypocrite profess poverty, and yet possess more goods and lands than many Princes, to have infinite treasures & revenues; teach others to fast, and play the gluttons themselves; like watermen, that row one way and look another. Vow virginity, talk of holiness, and yet indeed a notorious bawd, and famous fornicator, lascivious beast, a very goat. Monks by profession, such as give over the world and the vanities of it, and yet a Machiavellian rout interested in all matters of state: holy men, peace-makers, and yet composed of envy, lust, ambition, hatred & malice, fire-brands, overgrown pests of the country, traitors, assassinates, thus do men reach the stars, and this is to supererogate, and merit heaven for themselves and others. Had he seen, on the adverse side, some of our nice and curious schismaticks in another extreme abhor all ceremonies, and rather lose their lives and livings than do or admit anything Papists have formerly used, though in things indifferent (they alone are the true Church, the salt of the earth, whereas they have the least savour of all:), formalists, out of fear and base flattery, like so many weather-cocks turn round, a rout of temporisers, ready to embrace and maintain all that is or shall be proposed in hope of preferment: another Epicurean company, lying at lurch as so many vultures, watching for a prey of Church goods, and ready to rise by the down-fall of any: as Lucian said in like case, what dost thou think Democritus would have done, had he been spectator of these things; or had he but observed the common people follow like so many sheep, one of their fellows drawn by the horns over a gap, some for zeal, some for fear, wherever the storm drives them, to credit all, examine nothing, and yet ready to die before they will abjure any of those ceremonies to which they have been accustomed; others out of hypocrisy frequent sermons, knock their breasts, turn up their eyes, pretend zeal, desire reformation, and yet professed usurers, gripers, monsters of men, harpies, devils in their lives, to express nothing less? . . .

### An Utopia of My Own

. . . I will yet, to satisfy and please myself, make an Utopia of my own, a new Atlantis, a poetical Commonwealth of mine own, in which I will freely domineer, build cities, make laws, statutes, as I list myself. And why may I not?

> Poets and painters—sure you know the plea—,
> Have always been allowed their fancy free, &c.

You know what liberty Poets ever had, and besides my predecessor Democritus was a Politician, a Recorder of Abdera, a law-maker as some say, and why may I not presume so much as he did? Howsoever

I will adventure. For the site, if you will needs urge me to it, I am not fully resolved, it may be in the Unknown Austral Land, there is room enough (for of my knowledge neither that hungry Spaniard, nor Mercurius Britannicus, have yet discovered half of it) or else one of those floating Islands in the South Sea which, like the Cyanean Isles in the Euxine Sea, alter their place, and are accessible only at set times, and to some few persons; or one of the Fortunate Isles, for who knows yet where, or which they are? There is room enough in the inner parts of America, and northern coasts of Asia. But I will choose a site, whose latitude shall be 45 degrees (I respect not minutes) in the midst of the Temperate Zone, or perhaps under the Equator, that Paradise of the world, *where the laurel is ever green, &c.,* where is a perpetual Spring: the longitude for some reasons I will conceal. Yet *be it known to all men by these presents,* that if any honest gentleman will send in so much money, as Cardan allows an Astrologer for casting a Nativity, he shall be a sharer, I will acquaint him with my project, or if any worthy man will stand for any temporal or spiritual office or dignity, (for as he said of his Archbishoprick of Utopia, tis a holy ambition, and not amiss to be sought after) it shall be freely given without all intercession, bribes, letters, &c., his own worth shall be the best spokesman; & because we shall admit of no deputies or advowsons, if he be sufficiently qualified, and as able as willing to execute the place himself, he shall have present possession. It shall be divided into 12 or 13 provinces, and those by hills, rivers, road-ways, or some more eminent limits exactly bounded. Each province shall have a *metropolis,* which shall be so placed as a centre almost in a circumference, and the rest at equal distances, some 12 Italian miles asunder, or thereabout; and in them shall be sold all things necessary for the use of man, at stated hours and days, no market towns, markets or fairs, for they do but beggar cities (no village shall stand above 6, 7, or 8 miles from a city) except those emporiums which are by the sea side, general staples, marts, as Antwerp, Venice, Bergen of old, London, &c. Cities most part shall be situate upon navigable rivers or lakes, creeks, havens, and for their form, regular, round, square, or long square, with fair, broad and straight streets, houses uniform, built of brick and stone, like Bruges, Brussels, Rhegium Lepidi, Berne in Switzerland, Milan, Mantua, Crema, Cambalu in Tartary described by Marco Polo, or that Venetian Palma. I will admit very few or no suburbs, & those of baser building, walls only to keep out man and horse, except it be in some frontier towns, or by the sea side, & those to be fortified after the latest manner of fortification, and sited upon convenient havens, or opportune places. In every so built city, I will have convenient churches, and separate-places to bury the dead in, not in church-yards; a citadel (in some, not all) to command it, prisons for offenders, opportune market-places of all sorts, for corn, meat, cattle, fuel, fish, &c. commodious courts of justice, publick halls for all societies, bourses, meeting places, armouries, in which shall be kept engines for quenching of fire, artillery gardens, publick walks, theatres, and spacious fields allotted for all gymnicks, sports, and honest recreations, hospitals of all kinds, for children, orphans, old folks, sick men, mad men, soldiers, pest-houses, &c., not built propitiatorily, or by gouty benefactors, who, when by fraud & rapine they have extorted all their lives, oppressed whole provinces, societies, &c., give something to pious uses, build a satisfactory alms-house, school, or bridge, &c., at their last end, or before perhaps, which is no otherwise than to steal a goose, and stick down a feather, rob a thousand to relieve ten: and those hospitals so built and maintained, not by collections, benevolences, donaries, for a set number (as in ours), just so many and no more at such a rate, but for all those who stand in need, be they more or less, and that at publick expense, & so still maintained; we are not born for ourselves alone, &c. I will have conduits of sweet and good water, aptly disposed in each town, common granaries, as at Dresden in Misnia [Saxony], Stettin in Pomerland, Nuremberg, &c., colleges of mathematicians, musicians, and actors, as of old at Lebedos in Ionia, alchemists, [in a footnote Burton adds: Not to make gold, but for matters of physick], physicians, artists, and philosophers; that all arts and sciences may sooner be perfected & better learned; and publick historiographers, as amongst those ancient Persians, informed and appointed by the state to register all famous acts, & not by each insufficient scribbler, partial or parasitical pedant, as in our times. I will provide publick schools of all kinds, singing, dancing, fencing, &c. especially of grammar & languages, not to be taught by those tedious precepts ordinarily used, but by use, example, conversation, as travellers learn abroad, & nurses teach their children. As I will have all such places, so will I ordain publick governors, fit officers to each place, treasurers, ædiles,[1] quæstors,[2] overseers of pupils, widows' goods, and all publick

---

[1] Commissioners of buildings.
[2] Deputies.

houses, &c. and those once a year to make strict accounts of all receipts, expenses, to avoid confusion, & so they will waste no money, (as Pliny to Trajan,) which is a shameful thing to have to mention. They shall be subordinate to those higher officers and governors of each city, which shall not be poor tradesmen, and mean artificers, but noblemen and gentlemen, which shall be tied to residence in those towns they dwell next, at such set times and seasons: for I see no reason (which Hippolytus complains of) *that it should be more dishonourable for noblemen to govern the city than the country, or unseemly to dwell there now than of old.*

I will have no bogs, fens, marshes, vast woods, deserts, heaths, commons, but all inclosed, (yet not depopulated, and therefore take heed you mistake me not), for that which is common, and every man's, is no man's; the richest countries are still inclosed,[3] as Essex, Kent, with us, &c., Spain, Italy; and where inclosures are least in quantity, they are best husbanded, as about Florence in Italy, Damascus in Syria, &c., which are liker gardens than fields. I will not have a barren acre in all my territories, not so much as the tops of mountains: where nature fails, it shall be supplied by art: lakes and rivers shall not be left desolate. All common high-ways, bridges, banks, corrivations of waters, aqueducts, channels, publick works, buildings, &c. out of a common stock curiously maintained and kept in repair; no depopulations, engrossings, alterations of wood, arable, but by the consent of some supervisors that shall be appointed for that purpose, to see what reformation ought to be had in all places, what is amiss, how to help it; and what each clime produces, and what each rejects, what ground is aptest for wood, what for corn, what for cattle, gardens, orchards, fish-ponds, &c., with a charitable division in every village, (not one domineering house greedily to swallow up all, which is too common with us), what for lords, what for tenants: and because they shall be better encouraged to improve such lands they hold, manure, plant trees, drain, fence, &c., they shall have long leases, a

---

[3] Mr. Carew, in his Survey of Cornwall, saith that before that country was inclosed, the husbandmen drank water, did eat little or no bread, their apparel was coarse, they went bare-legged, their dwelling was correspondent; but since inclosure, they live decently, and have money to spend; when their fields were common, their wool was coarse Cornish hair; but since inclosure, it is almost as good as Cotswold, and their soil much mended. Tusser, chapter 52 of his Husbandry, is of his opinion, one acre inclosed is worth three common:

> The country incloséd I praise;
> The other delighteth not me;
> For nothing of wealth it doth, raise, &c.

known rent, and known fine, to free them from those intolerable exactions of tyrannizing landlords. These supervisors shall likewise appoint what quantity of land in each manor is fit for the lord's demesnes, what for holding of tenants, how it ought to be husbanded,

> As the Magnesians famous are for horses,
> The Argonauts for rowing,  (LUCAN)

how to be manured, tilled, rectified; here you see corn crops, there grapes have kindlier growth,—other spots are green with young trees and unbidden grass; and what proportion is fit for all callings, because private possessors are many times idiots, ill husbands, oppressors, covetous, and know not how to improve their own, or else wholly respect their own, and not publick good.

Utopian parity is a kind of government to be wished for rather than effected, the Christianopolitan Republic,[4] Campanella's City of the Sun, and that New Atlantis, witty fictions, but mere Chimeras, and Plato's Community in many things is impious, absurd and ridiculous, it takes away all splendour and magnificence. I will have several orders, degrees of nobility, and those hereditary, not rejecting younger brothers in the meantime, for they shall be sufficiently provided for by pensions, or so qualified, brought up in some honest calling, they shall be able to live of themselves. I will have such a proportion of ground belonging to every barony, he that buys the land shall buy the barony, he that by riot consumes his patrimony, & ancient demesnes, shall forfeit his honours. As some dignities shall be hereditary, so some again by election, or by gift (besides free offices, pensions, annuities), like our Bishopricks, Prebends, the Bassas' palaces in Turkey, the Procurator's houses and offices in Venice, which, like the golden apple, shall be given to the worthiest & best deserving both in war and peace, as a reward of their worth and good service, as so many goals for all to aim at, (honour nourishes the arts), and encouragements to others. For I hate those severe, unnatural, harsh, German, French, and Venetian decrees, which exclude plebians from honours, be they never so wise, rich, virtuous, valiant, and well qualified, they must not be patricians, but keep their own rank; this is to war against nature,—odious to God and men, I abhor it.

My form of government shall be monarchical;

---

[4] Johann Valentin Andrea's Utopia.

If to sweet freedom you would cling
Submit unto a righteous King.  (CLAUDIAN)

few laws, but those severely kept, plainly put down, and in the mother
tongue, that every man may understand. Every city shall have a peculiar
trade or privilege, by which it shall be chiefly maintained: and parents
shall teach their children, one of three at least, bring up and instruct
them in the mysteries of their own trade. In each town these several
tradesmen shall be so aptly disposed, as they shall free the rest from
danger or offence: fire-trades, as smiths, forge-men, brewers, bakers,
metal-men, &c. shall dwell apart by themselves: dyers, tanners, fell-
mongers, and such as use water, in convenient places by themselves;
noisome or fulsome for bad smells, as butchers' slaughter-houses, chan-
dlers, curriers, in remote places, & some back lanes. Fraternities and companies I approve of, as merchants' bourses, colleges of druggers, physicians, musicians, &c., but all trades to be rated in the sale of wares, as
our clerks of the market do bakers and brewers; corn itself, what scarcity
soever shall come, not to exceed such a price. Of such wares as are transported or brought in, if they be necessary, commodious, and such as
nearly concern man's life, as corn, wood, coals, &c., and such provision
we cannot want, I will have little or no custom paid, no taxes; but for
such things as are for pleasure, delight, or ornament, as wine, spice,
tobacco, silk, velvet, cloth of gold, lace, jewels, &c. a greater impost. I will
have certain ships sent out for new discoveries every year, & some discreet men appointed to travel into all neighbour Kingdoms by land,
which shall observe what artificial inventions and good laws are in other
countries, customs, alterations, or ought else, concerning war or peace,
which may tend to the common good. Ecclesiastical discipline in the
hands of Bishops, subordinate as the other. No impropriations, no lay
patrons of church livings, or one private man, but common societies,
corporations, &c. and those Rectors of Benefices to be chosen out of the
Universities, examined and approved, as the *Literati* in China. No Parish
to contain above a thousand auditors. If it were possible, I would have
such Priests as should imitate Christ, charitable Lawyers should love
their neighbours as themselves, temperate and modest Physicians, Politicians contemn the world, Philosophers should know themselves, Noblemen live honestly, Tradesmen leave lying and cozening, Magistrates corruption, &c.; but this is impossible, I must get such as I may. I will
therefore have of lawyers, judges, advocates, physicians, chirurgeons,
&c. a set number, and every man, if it be possible, to plead his own

cause, to tell that tale to the judge, which he doth to his advocate, as at Fez in Africa, Bantam, Aleppo, Ragusa, those advocates, chirurgeons and physicians, which are allowed, to be maintained out of the common treasure, no fees to be given or taken upon pain of losing their places, or if they do, very small fees, and when the cause is fully ended. He that sues any man shall put in a pledge, which, if it be proved he hath wrongfully sued his adversary, rashly or maliciously, he shall forfeit, and lose. Or else, before any suit begin, the plaintiff shall have his complaint approved by a set delegacy to that purpose; if it be of moment, he shall be suffered as before to proceed, if otherwise, they shall determine it. All causes shall be pleaded with the parties' names concealed, if some circumstances do not otherwise require. Judges and other officers shall be aptly disposed in each Province, Villiages, Cities, as common arbitrators to hear causes, and end all controversies, and those not single, but three at least on the bench at once, to determine or give sentence, and those again to sit by turns or lots, and not to continue still in the same office. No controversy to depend above a year, but without all delays and further appeals to be speedily dispatched, and finally concluded in that time allotted. These & all other inferior Magistrates to be chosen as the *Literati*[5] in China, or by those exact suffrages of the Venetians, and such again not be eligible, or capable of magistracies, honours, offices, except they be sufficiently qualified for learning, manners, and that by the strict approbation of deputed examinators: first Scholars to take place, then Soldiers; for I am of Vegetius his opinion, a Scholar deserves better than a Soldier, because a Soldier's work lasts for an age, a Scholar's for ever. If they misbehave themselves, they shall be deposed, and accordingly punished; & whether their offices be annual or otherwise, once a year they shall be called in question, and give an account; for men are partial, and passionate, merciless, covetous, corrupt, subject to love, hate, fear, favour, &c. Every kingdom is under a greater kingdom. Like Solon's Areopagites, or those Roman Censors, some shall visit others, and be visited in turn themselves, they shall oversee that no prowling officer, under colour of authority, shall insult over his inferiors, as so many wild beasts, oppress, domineer, flea, grind, or trample on, be partial or corrupt, but that there be justice equally done, live as friends and brethren together; and, which Sesellius would have and so much desires in his Kingdom of France, *a diapason and sweet harmony*

---

[5] By competitive examinations.

*of Kings, Princes, Nobles, and Plebeians, so mutually tied and involved in love, as well as laws and authority, as that they never disagree, insult, or encroach one upon another.* If any man deserve well in his office he shall be rewarded; Who values virtue but for its reward? He that invents anything for publick good in any Art or Science, writes a Treatise, or performs any noble exploit at home or abroad, shall be accordingly enriched, honoured, and preferred. I say with Hannibal in Ennius, He who shall slay an enemy shall be to me a Carthaginian; let him be of what condition he will, in all offices, actions, he that deserves best shall have best.

Tilianus, in Philonius, out of a charitable mind no doubt, wished all his books were gold and silver, jewels and precious stones, to redeem captives, set free prisoners, and relieve all poor distressed souls that wanted means; religiously done, I deny not, but to what purpose? Suppose this were so well done, within a little after, though a man had Crœsus' wealth to bestow, there would be as many more. Wherefore I will suffer no beggars, rogues, vagabonds, or idle persons at all, that cannot give an account of their lives how they maintain themselves. If they be impotent, lame, blind, and single, they shall be sufficiently maintained in several hospitals, built for that purpose; if married and infirm, past work, or by inevitable loss, or some such like misfortune, cast behind, by distribution of corn, house-rent free, annual pensions or money, they shall be relieved, and highly rewarded for their good service they have formerly done; if able, they shall be enforced to work. *For I see no reason* (as he[6] said) *why an epicure or idle drone, a rich glutton, a usurer, should live at ease, and do nothing, live in honour, in all manner of pleasures, and oppress others, when as in the mean time a poor labourer, a smith, a carpenter, an husbandman, that hath spent his time in continual labour, as an ass to carry burdens, to do the commonwealth good, and without whom we cannot live, shall be left in his old age to beg or starve, & lead a miserable life worse than a jument!* As all conditions shall be tied to their task, so none shall be over-tired, but have their set times of recreations & holidays, to indulge their humour, feasts and merry meetings, even to the meanest artificer, or basest servant, once a week to sing or dance, (though not all at once) or do whatsoever he shall please; like that Sacred Festival amongst the Persians, those Saturnalia in Rome, as well as his master. If any be

[6] Sir Thomas More.

drunk, he shall drink no more wine or strong drink in a twelvemonth after. A bankrupt shall be publickly shamed, and he that cannot pay his debts, if by riot or negligence he have been impoverished, shall be for a twelvemonth imprisoned; if in that space his creditors be not satisfied, he shall be hanged. He that commits sacrilege shall lose his hands; he that bears false witness, or is of perjury convict, shall have his tongue cut out, except he redeem it with his head. Murder, adultery, shall be punished by death, but not theft, except it be some more grievous offence, or notorious offenders: otherwise they shall be condemned to the gallies, mines, be his slaves whom they offended, during their lives. I hate all hereditary slaves, and that hard law of the Persians, as Brisonius calls it; or as Ammianus, hard law that wife and children, friends and allies, should suffer for the father's offence!

No man shall marry untill he be 25, no woman till she be 20, unless it is otherwise arranged. If one die, the other party shall not marry till 6 months after; and because many families are compelled to live niggardly, exhaust and undone by great dowers, none shall be given at all, or very little, and that by supervisors rated; they that are foul shall have a greater portion; if fair, none at all, or very little: howsover, not to exceed such a rate as those supervisors shall think fit. And when once they come to those years, poverty shall hinder no man from marriage, or any other respect, but all shall be rather enforced than hindered, except they be dismembered, or grievously deformed, infirm, or visited with some enormous hereditary disease in body or mind; in such cases, upon a great pain or mulct, man or woman shall not marry, other order shall be taken for them to their content. If people overabound, they shall be eased by colonies.

No man shall wear weapons in any city. The same attire shall be kept, and that proper to several callings, by which they shall be distinguished. Funeral display shall be taken away, that intempestive expense moderated, and many others. Brokers, takers of pawns, biting usurers, I will not admit; yet because we converse here with men not with gods, and for the hardness of men's hearts, I will tolerate some kind of usury. If we were honest, I confess, we should have no use of it, but being as it is, we must necessarily admit it. Howsoever most Divines contradict it,

> We say No, but 'tis but a word with us,

it must be winked at by Politicians. And yet some great Doctors approve of it, Calvin, Bucer, Zanchius, P. Martyr, because by so many grand

Lawyers, decrees of Emperors, Princes' Statutes, customs of Common-wealths, Churches' approbations, it is permitted, &c. I will therefore allow it. But to no private persons, nor to every man that will, to orphans only, maids, widows, or such as by reason of their age, sex, education, ignorance of trading, know not otherwise how to employ it, and those so approved not to let it out apart, but to bring their money to a common bank which shall be allowed in every city, as in Genoa, Geneva, Nuremberg, Venice, at 5, 6, 7, not above 8 *per cent.*, as the supervisors, or managers of the treasury shall think fit. And as it shall not be lawful for each man to be an usurer that will, so shall it not be lawful for all to take up money at use, not to prodigals and spendthrifts, but to merchants, young trades-men, such as stand in need, or know honestly how to employ it, whose necessity, cause, and condition, the said supervisors shall approve of.

I will have no private monopolies, to enrich one man, and beggar a multitude, multiplicity of offices, of supplying by deputies; weights and measures the same throughout, and those rectified by the *Primum mobile,*[7] and Sun's motion, threescore miles to a degree according to observation, 1000 Geometrical paces to a mile, five foot to a pace, twelve inches to a foot, &c., & from measures known it is an easy matter to rectify weights &., to cast up all, and resolve bodies by Algebra, Stereometry. I hate wars if they be not for the welfare of the people upon urgent occasion.

We hate the hawk, because it lives by war. (OVID)

Offensive wars, except the cause be very just, I will not allow of. For I do highly magnify that saying of Hannibal to Scipio, in Livy, *It had been a blessed thing for you and us, if God had given that mind to our predecessors, that you had been content with Italy, we with Africa. For neither Sicily nor Sardinia are worth such cost and pains, so many fleets & armies, or so many famous Captains' lives.* Fair means shall first be tried. Power exercised with moderation, can effect that which violence could never accomplish. I will have them proceed with all moderation: but hear you, Fabius my General, not Minucius, for he who acts wisely hurts his enemy far more than by violence. And in such wars to abstain as much as is possible from depopulations, burning of towns, massacring of infants, &c. For defensive wars, I will have forces still ready

---

[7] Primum mobile: in the Ptolemaic system of astronomy, the tenth or outermost of the revolving spheres of the universe.

at a small warning, by land and sea, a prepared navy, soldiers, as handy, Bonifinius wishes, as a rod of iron, & money, which is the nerve of war, still in a readiness, and a sufficient revenue, a third part, as in old Rome & Egypt, reserved for the Commonwealth, to avoid those heavy taxes and impositions, as well to defray this charge of wars, as also all other publick defalcations, expenses, fees, pensions, reparations, chaste sports, feasts, donaries, rewards, and entertainments. All things in this nature especially I will have maturely done, & with great deliberation: that nothing be done rashly, or remissly and timidly. But where am I rushing to, a mere novice? To prosecute the rest would require a volume. But hands off the picture! I have been over-tedious in this subject; I could have here willingly ranged, but these straits wherein I am included will not permit. . . .

## My Purpose and Endeavour

If any man shall ask in the mean time, who I am, that so boldly censure others, have I no faults? Yes more than thou hast, whatsoever thou art. We are the merest ciphers, I confess it again, I am as foolish, as mad as any one.

> I seem to you insane, I pray you think so.    (PETRONIUS)

I do not deny it, let the mad man be removed from the people. My comfort is, I have more fellows, and those of excellent note. And though I be not so right, or so discreet as I should be, yet not so mad, so bad neither, as thou perhaps takest me to be.

To conclude, this being granted, that all the world is melancholy, or mad, dotes, and every member of it, I have ended my task, and sufficiently illustrated that which I took upon me to demonstrate at first. At this present I have no more to say. *Democritus to Sanity!* I can but wish myself and them a good Physician, and all of us a better mind.

And although, for the above-named reasons, I had a just cause to undertake this subject, to point at these particular species of dotage, that so men might acknowledge their imperfections, and seek to reform what is amiss; yet I have a more serious intent at this time; and to omit all impertinent digressions, to say no more of such as are improperly melancholy, or metaphorically mad, lightly mad, or in disposition, as stupid, angry, drunken, silly, sottish, sullen, proud, vain-glorious, ridiculous, beastly, peevish, obstinate, impudent, extravagant, dry, doting, dull, desperate, harebrain, &c., mad, frantick, foolish, heteroclites, which no new Hospital can hold, no physick help: my purpose & endeavour is, in the following discourse, to anatomize this humour of melancholy, through all his parts and species, as it is an habit, or an ordinary disease, and that philosophically, medicinally, to shew the causes, symptoms, and several cures of it, that it may be the better avoided; moved there-unto for the generality of it, and to do good, it being a disease so frequent, as Mercurialis observes, *in these our days; so often happening,* saith Laurentius, *in our miserable times,* as few there are that feel not the smart of it. . . .

## Pardon These My Witticisms

. . . The time, place, persons and all circumstances, apologize for me, and why may I not then be idle with others, speak my mind freely? If you deny me this liberty, upon these presumptions I will take it: I say again, I will take it. If there be a man who thinks that hard words are applied to him, let him reflect that this is not in attack but in self-defence. If any man take exceptions, let him turn the buckle of his girdle, I care not. I owe thee nothing (Reader), I look for no favour at thy hands, I am independent, I fear not.

No, I recant, I will not, I care, I fear, I confess my fault, acknowledge a great offence,

But 'tis well first to calm the troubled billows. (VIRGIL)

I have overshot myself, I have spoken foolishly, rashly, unadvisedly, absurdly, I have anatomized mine own folly. And now, methinks, upon a sudden I am awaked as it were out of a dream, I have had a raving fit, a phantastical fit, ranged up and down, in and out; I have insulted over most kind of men, abused some, offended others, wronged myself; and now being recovered, and perceiving mine error, cry with Orlando, Absolve me, pardon (O kind readers), that which is past, and I will make you amends in that which is to come; I promise you a more sober discourse in my following treatise.

If through weakness, folly, passion, discontent, ignorance, I have said amiss, let it be forgotten and forgiven. I acknowledge that of Tacitus to be true, a bitter jest leaves a sting behind it: and as an honourable man observes, *They fear a Satirist's wit, he their memories.* I may justly suspect the worst; and though I hope I have wronged no man, yet in Medea's words I will crave pardon,

> And in my last words this I do desire,
> That what in passion I have said, or ire,
> May be forgotten, and a better mind
> Be had of us, hereafter as you find.  (SENECA)

I earnestly request every private man, as Scaliger did Cardan, not to take offence. I will conclude in his lines: Didst know me well, thou wouldst not only pardon these my witticisms but would even consider it unmeet that so kindly a soul as I should find it necessary to avert even the slightest suspicion. If thou knewest my modesty and simplicity thou wouldst easily pardon and forgive what is here amiss, or by thee misconceived. If hereafter, anatomizing this surly humour, my hand slip, as an unskilful prentice I lance too deep, and cut through skin and all at unawares, make it smart, or cut awry, pardon a rude hand, an unskilful knife, 'tis a most difficult thing to keep an even tone, a perpetual tenor, and not sometimes to lash out; not to write satire is the difficulty, there be so many objects to divert, inward perturbations to molest, and the very best may sometimes err; if Homer, usually so good, takes a nap, it is impossible not in so much to overshoot: it is no great sin if over a long work, sleep should steal at times. But what needs all this? I hope there will no such cause of offence be given: if there be,

> Let none take these to himself, they're fables all,  (PLAUTUS)

I'll deny all (my last refuge), recant all, renounce all I have said, if any man except, and with as much facility excuse, as he can accuse; but I presume of thy good favour, and gracious acceptance (gentle reader.) Out of an assured hope and confidence thereof, I will begin.

# THE FIRST PARTITION

## Man's Excellency, Fall, Miseries, Infirmities; the Causes of Them

Man, the most excellent and noble creature of the World, *the principal and mighty work of God, wonder of Nature,* as Zoroaster calls him; *the marvel of marvels,* as Plato; *the Abridgement and Epitome of the World,* as Pliny; a Microcosm, a little world, Sovereign Lord of the Earth, Viceroy of the World, sole Commander and Governor of all the Creatures in it: to whose Empire they are subject in particular, and yield obedience; far surpassing all the rest, not in body only, but in soul;

created in God's own *Image,* to that immortal and incorporeal substance, with all the faculties and powers belonging unto it; was at first pure, divine, perfect, happy, created after God in true holiness and righteousness; Like God, free from all manner of infirmities, and put in Paradise, to know God, to praise and glorify him, to do his will: So that God might bring forth the Godlike, (as an old Poet saith) to propagate the Church.

But this most noble creature, (one exclaims) O pitiful change! is fallen from that he was, and forfeited his estate, become a wretched mannikin, a castaway, a caitiff, one of the most miserable creatures of the world, if he be considered in his own nature, an unregenerate man, and so much obscured by his fall (that some few reliques excepted) he is inferior to a beast: *man in honour that understandeth not, is like unto beasts that perish,* so David esteems him: a monster by stupend metamorphosis, a fox, a dog, a hog, what not? How much altered from that he was; before blessed and happy, now miserable and accursed! *He must eat his meat in sorrow,* subject to death & all manner of infirmities, all kinds of calamities. *Great travail is created for all men, and an heavy yoke on the sons of Adam, from the day that they go out of their mother's womb, unto that day they return to the mother of all things. Namely their thoughts, and fear of their hearts, and their imagination of things they wait for, and the day of death. From him that sitteth in the glorious throne, to him that sitteth beneath in the earth and ashes; from him that is clothed in blue silk, and weareth a Crown, to him that is clothed in simple linen. Wrath, envy, trouble, and unquietness, and fear of death, and rigour, and strife, and such things come to both man and beast, but sevenfold to the ungodly.* All this befalls him in this life, and peradventure eternal misery in the life to come.

The impulsive cause of these miseries in man, this privation or destruction of God's image, the cause of death and diseases, of all temporal and eternal punishments, was the sin of our first parent Adam, in eating of the forbidden fruit, by the devil's instigation and allurement. His disobedience, pride, ambition, intemperance, incredulity, curiosity; from whence proceeded original sin, and that general corruption of mankind, as from a fountain flowed all bad inclinations, and actual transgressions, which cause our several calamities inflicted upon us for our sins. And this belike is that which our fabulous Poets have shadowed unto us in the tale of Pandora's box, which, being opened through her curiosity, filled the world full of all manner of diseases. It is not curiosity alone, but those other crying sins of ours, which pull these several plagues and miseries upon our heads. For where there is sin, there is a storm, as Chrysostom well observes. *Fools by reason of their transgression, and because of their iniquities, are afflicted. Fear cometh like sudden desolation, and destruction like a whirlwind, affliction and anguish, because they did not fear God.* Are you shaken with wars? (as Cyprian well urgeth to Demetrius,) are you molested with dearth and famine? is your health crushed with raging diseases? is mankind generally tormented with epidemical maladies? *'tis all for your sins.* God is angry, punisheth, and threateneth, because of their obstinacy and stubbornness, they will not turn unto him. If the earth be barren then for want of rain, if, dry and squalid, it yield no fruit, if your fountains be dried up, your wine, corn, and oil blasted, if the air be corrupted & men troubled with diseases, 'tis by reason of their sins: which, like the blood of Abel, cry aloud to heaven for vengeance. *That we have sinned, therefore our hearts are heavy. We roar like bears, and mourn like doves, and want health, &c., for our sins and trespasses.* But this we cannot endure to hear, or to take notice of: *We are smitten in vain, and receive no correction;* and *Thou hast stricken them, but they have refused to receive correction, they have not returned. Pestilence he hath sent, but they have not turned to him.* Herod could not abide John Baptist, nor Domitian endure Apollonius to tell the causes of the plague at Ephesus, his injustice, incest, adultery and the like.

To punish therefore this blindness and obstinacy of ours, as a concomitant cause, and principal agent, is God's just judgement, in bringing these calamities upon us, to chastise us, I say, for our sins, and to satisfy God's wrath. For the law requires obedience or punishment, as you may read at large: *If they will not obey the Lord, and keep his commandments and ordinances, then all these curses shall come upon them. Cursed in the town and in the field, &c. Cursed in the fruit of the body, &c. The Lord shall send thee trouble and shame, because of thy wickedness.* And a little after, *The Lord shall smite thee with the botch of Egypt, and with emrods, and scab, and itch, and thou canst not be healed. With madness, blindness, and astonishing of heart.* This Paul seconds, *Tribulation and anguish on the soul of every man that doth evil.* Or else these chastisements are inflicted upon us for our humiliation, to exercise and try our patience here in this life, to bring us home, to make us to know God and ourselves, to inform & teach us wisdom. *Therefore is my people gone into captivity, because they had no knowl-*

*edge, therefore is the wrath of the Lord kindled against his people, &
he hath stretched out his hand upon them.* He is desirous of our salvation, saith Lemnius, and for that cause pulls us by the ear many times,
to put us in mind of our duties: *that they which erred might have understanding,* (as Isaiah speaks) *and so to be reformed. I am afflicted, and
at the point of death,* so David confesseth of himself, *mine eyes are
sorrowful through mine affliction:* and that made him turn unto God.
Great Alexander, in the midst of all his prosperity, by a company of
parasites deified, and now made a God, when he saw one of his wounds
bleed, remembered that he was but a man, and remitted of his pride.
As Pliny well perceived, in sickness the mind reflects upon itself, with
judgement surveys itself, and abhors its former courses; insomuch that
he concludes to his friend Maximus, that it were the period of all philosophy, if we could so continue sound, or perform but a part of that which
we promised to do, being sick. *Whoso is wise, then, will consider these
things,* as David did, and whatsoever fortune befall him, make use of
it. If he be in sorrow, need, sickness, or any other adversity, seriously
to recount with himself, why this or that malady, misery, this or that
incurable disease, is inflicted upon him; it may be for his good, truly it
is well, as Peter said of his daughter's ague. Bodily sickness is for his
soul's health, had he not been visited, he had utterly perished; for *the
Lord correcteth him whom he loveth, even as a father doth his child
in whom he delighteth.* If he be safe and sound, on the other side, and
free from all manner of infirmity,

> And that he have grace, beauty, favour, health,
> A cleanly diet, and abound in wealth;   (HORACE)

yet in the midst of his prosperity, let him remember that caveat of
Moses, *beware that he do not forget the Lord his God;* that he be not
puffed up, but acknowledge them to be his good gifts and benefits, and
the more he hath, to be more thankful, (as Agapetianus adviseth) &
use them aright.

Now the instrumental causes of these our infirmities are as divers as
the infirmities themselves. Stars, heavens, elements, &c. and all those
creatures which God hath made, are armed against sinners. They were
indeed once good in themselves, and that they are now many of them
pernicious unto us, is not in their nature, but our corruption, which hath
caused it. For, from the fall of our first parent Adam, they have been
changed, the earth accursed, the influence of stars altered, the four ele-

ments, beasts, birds, plants, are now ready to offend us. *The principal things for the use of man are water, fire, iron, salt, meal, wheat, honey, milk, oil, wine, clothing, good to the godly, to the sinners turned to evil. Fire, and hail, and famine, and dearth, all these are created for vengeance.* The heavens threaten us with their comets, stars, planets, with their great conjunctions, eclipses, oppositions, quartiles, and such unfriendly aspects; the air with his meteors, thunder and lightning, intemperate heat and cold, mighty winds, tempests, unseasonable weather; from which proceed dearth, famine, plague, and all sorts of epidemical diseases, consuming infinite myriads of men. At Cairo in Egypt, every third year, (as it is related by Boterus, and others) 300,000 die of the plague; and 200,000 in Constantinople, every fifth or seventh at the utmost. How doth the earth terrify and oppress us with terrible earthquakes, which are most frequent in China, Japan, and those Eastern Climes, swallowing up sometimes six cities at once! How doth the water rage with his inundations, irruptions, flinging down towns, cities, villages, bridges, &c. besides shipwrecks; whole Islands are sometimes suddenly overwhelmed with all their inhabitants in Zealand, Holland, and many parts of the Continent drowned, as the Lake Erne in Ireland! And we behold naught but the remains of cities in the open sea. In the fens of Friesland, 1230, by reason of tempests, the sea drowned all the country almost, men and cattle in it. How doth the fire rage, that merciless element, consuming in an instant whole cities! what town, of any antiquity or note, hath not been once, again and again, by the fury of this merciless element, defaced, ruinated, and left desolate? In a word,

> Whom fire spares, sea doth drown; whom sea,
> Pestilent air doth send to clay;
> Who war scapes, sickness takes away.   (BUCHANAN)

To descend to more particulars, how many creatures are at deadly feud with men! Lions, wolves, bears, &c. some with hoofs, horns, tusks, teeth, nails. How many noxious serpents and venomous creatures, ready to offend us with stings, breath, sight, or quite kill us! How many pernicious fishes, plants, gums, fruits, seeds, flowers, &c. could I reckon up on a sudden, which by their very smell, many of them, touch, taste, cause some grievous malady, if not death itself! Some make mention of a thousand several poisons: but these are but trifles in respect. The greatest enemy to man is man, who by the Devil's instigation is still ready to do mischief, his own executioner, a wolf, a Devil to himself and others. We are all brethren in Christ, or at least should be, members of one body, servants of one Lord, and yet no fiend can so torment, insult over, tyrannize, vex, as one man doth another. Let me not fall therefore, (saith David, when wars, plague, famine were offered) into the hands of men, merciless, and wicked men:

> Scarce are they worthy of the name of men,
> For fiercer far are they than ravening wolves.   (OVID)

We can most part foresee these epidemical diseases, and likely avoid them. Dearths, tempests, plagues, our Astrologers foretell us; earth-quakes, inundations, ruins of houses, consuming fires, come by little and little, or make some noise before-hand; but the knaveries, impostures, injuries, and villanies, of men no art can avoid. We can keep our professed enemies from our cities, by gates, walls, and towers, defend ourselves from thieves and robbers by watchfulness and weapons; but this malice of men, and their pernicious endeavours, no caution can divert, no vigilancy foresee, we have so many secret plots and devices to mischief one another.

Sometimes by the Devil's help, as Magicians, Witches: sometimes by impostures, mixtures, poisons, stratagems, single combats, wars, we hack and hew, as if we were, like Cadmus' soldiers, born to consume one another. 'Tis an ordinary thing to read of a hundred and two hundred thousand men slain in a battle; besides all manner of tortures, brazen bulls, racks, wheels, strappadoes, guns, engines, &c. We have invented more torturing instruments than there be several members in a man's body, as Cyprian well observes. To come nearer yet, our own parents by their offences, indiscretion, and intemperance, are our mortal enemies. *The fathers have eaten sour grapes, and the children's teeth are set on edge.* They cause our grief many times, and put upon us heredi-tary diseases, inevitable infirmities: they torment us, & we are ready to injure our posterity;

> Like to produce still more degenerate stock,   (HORACE)

and the latter end of the world, as Paul foretold, is still like to be worst. We are thus bad by nature, bad by kind, but far worse by art, every man the greatest enemy unto himself. We study many times to undo ourselves, abusing those good things which God hath bestowed upon us, health, wealth, strength, wit, learning, art, memory, to our own destruction; you owe to yourself your own ruin. As Judas Maccabaeus killed Apollonius with his own weapons, we arm our selves to our own overthrows; and use reason, art, judgement, all that should help us, as so many instruments to undo us. Hector gave Ajax a sword, which, so long as he fought against enemies, served for his help and defence; but after he began to hurt harmless creatures with it, turned to his own hurtless bowels. Those excellent means God hath bestowed on us, well employed, cannot but much avail us; but if otherwise perverted, they ruin and confound us: and so by reason of our indiscretion and weakness they commonly do, we have too many instances. This S. Austin acknowledgeth of himself in his humble Confessions, *promptness of wit, memory, eloquence, they were God's good gifts, but he did not use them to his glory.* If you will particularly know how, and by what means, consult Physicians, and they will tell you, that it is in offending in some of those six non-natural things, of which I shall after dilate more at large; they are the causes of our infirmities, our surfeiting, and drunkenness, our immoderate insatiable lust, and prodigious riot. It is a true saying, the board consumes more than the sword. Our intemperance it is that pulls so many several incurable diseases upon our heads, that hastens old age, perverts our temperature, and brings upon us sudden death. And last of all, that which crucifies us most, is our own folly, madness (Whom Jupiter would destroy, he first drives mad; by subtraction of his assisting grace God permits it), weakness, want of government, our facility and proneness in yielding to several lusts, in giving way to every passion and perturbation of the mind: by which means we metamorphose ourselves, and degenerate into beasts. All which that Prince of Poets observed of Agamemnon, that when he was well pleased, and could moderate his passion, he was—like Jupiter in feature, Mars in valour, Pallas in wisdom, another God; but when he became angry, he was a lion, a tiger, a dog, &c. there appeared no sign or likeness of Jupiter in him; so we, as long as we are ruled by reason, correct our inordinate appetite, and conform ourselves to God's word, are as so many living saints: but if we give reins to lust, anger, ambition, pride, and follow our own ways, we degenerate into beasts, transform ourselves, overthrow our constitutions, provoke God to anger, and heap upon us this of *Melancholy,* and all kinds of incurable diseases, as a just and deserved punishment of our sins. . . .

## A Chronick or Continuate Disease

*Melancholy,* the subject of our present discourse, is either in disposition or habit. In disposition, is that transitory *Melancholy* which goes and comes upon every small occasion of sorrow, need, sickness, trouble, fear, grief, passion, or perturbation of the mind, any manner of care, discontent, or thought, which causeth anguish, dulness, heaviness and vexation of spirit, any ways opposite to pleasure, mirth, joy, delight, causing frowardness in us, or a dislike. In which equivocal and improper sense, we call him melancholy, that is dull, sad, sour, lumpish, ill-disposed, solitary, any way moved, or displeased. And from these melancholy dispositions no man living is free, no Stoick, none so wise, none so happy, none so patient, so generous, so godly, so divine, that can vindicate himself; so well-composed, but more or less, some time or other, he feels the smart of it. Melancholy in this sense is the character of Mortality. *Man that is born of a woman, is of short continuance and full of trouble.* Zeno, Cato, Socrates himself, whom Ælian so highly commends for a moderate temper, that *nothing could disturb him; but going out, and coming in, still Socrates kept the same serenity of countenance, what misery soever befell him,* (if we may believe Plato his Disciple) was much tormented with it. Q. Metellus, in whom Valerius gives instance of all happiness, *the most fortunate man then living, born in that most flourishing city of Rome, of noble parentage, a proper man of person, well qualified, healthful, rich, honourable, a Senator, a Consul, happy in his wife, happy in his children, &c.,* yet this man was not void of Melancholy, he had his share of sorrow. Polycrates Samius, that flung his ring into the sea, because he would participate of discontent with others, and had it miraculously restored to him again shortly after by a fish taken as he angled, was not free from melancholy dispositions. No man can cure himself; the very gods had bitter pangs,[8] & frequent passions, as their own Poets put upon them. In general, *as the heaven, so is our life, sometimes fair, sometimes overcast, tempestuous and serene; as in a rose, flowers and prickles; in the year itself, a temperate summer sometimes, a hard winter, a drowth, and then again pleasant showers: so is our life intermixt with joys, hopes, fears, sorrows, calumnies.* There is a succession of pleasure and pain.

[8] Homer, *Iliad.*—Burton's note.

From the heart of this fount of joy there wells
Some bitter that, e'en mid flowers, their pleasure quells.   (SENECA)

*Even in the midst of laughing there is sorrow,* (as Solomon holds): even in the midst of all our feasting and jollity, as Austin infers in his Commentary on the 41st Psalm, there is grief and discontent. Amid our enjoyments there is always some vexation to torment us; for a pint of honey thou shalt here likely find a gallon of gall, for a dram of pleasure a pound of pain, for an inch of mirth an ell of moan; as ivy doth an oak, these miseries encompass our life; and 'tis most absurd & ridiculous for any mortal man to look for a perpetual tenor of happiness in this life. Nothing so prosperous & pleasant, but it hath some bitterness in it, some complaining, some grudging; 'tis all bitter-sweet, a mixt passion, and like a Chequer table, black & white men; families, cities, have their falls and wanes, now trines, sextiles, then quartiles and oppositions. We are not here, as those Angels, celestial powers and bodies, sun and moon, to finish our course without all offence, with such constancy, to continue for so many ages: but subject to infirmities, miseries, interrupt, tossed & tumbled up and down, carried about with every small blast, often molested & disquieted upon each slender occasion, uncertain, brittle, & so is all that we trust unto. *And he that knows not this, & is not armed to endure it, is not fit to live in this world* (as one condoles our time): *he knows not the condition of it, where with a reciprocal tie pleasure & pain are still united, and succeed one another in a ring.* Get thee gone hence, if thou canst not brook it; there is no way to avoid it, but to arm thyself with patience, with magnanimity, to oppose thyself unto it, to suffer affliction as a good soldier of Christ, as Paul adviseth, constantly to bear it. But forasmuch as so few can embrace this good counsel of his, or use it aright, but rather, as so many brute beasts, give a way to their passion, voluntarily subject & precipitate themselves into a Labyrinth of cares, woes, miseries, & suffer their souls to be overcome by them, cannot arm themselves with that patience as they ought to do, it falleth out oftentimes that these *dispositions* become *habits,* and *many affects contemned* (as Seneca notes) *makes a disease. Even as one distillation, not yet grown to custom, makes a cough, but continual and inveterate causeth a consumption of the lungs:* so do these our melancholy provocations: and, according as the humour itself is intended, or remitted in men, as their temperature of body, or rational soul, is better able to make resistance; so are they more or less affected. For that which is but a flea-biting to one, causeth insufferable torment to another; &

which one by his singular moderation and well-composed carriage can happily overcome, a second is no whit able to sustain; but upon every small occasion of misconceived abuse, injury, grief, disgrace, loss, cross, rumour, &c., (if solitary, or idle) yields so far to passion, that his complexion is altered, his digestion hindered, his sleep gone, his spirits obscured, and his heart heavy, his hypochondries misaffected; wind, crudity, on a sudden overtake him, and he himself overcome with *Melancholy*. As it is with a man imprisoned for debt, if once in the gaol, every creditor will bring his action against him, and there likely hold him: if any discontent seize upon a patient, in an instant all other perturbations (for— where a door is opened they rush) will set upon him, and, then, like a lame dog or broken-winged goose, he droops and pines away, and is brought at last to that ill habit or malady of Melancholy itself. So that as the Philosophers make eight degrees of heat and cold, we may make 88 of *Melancholy,* as the parts affected are diversely seized with it, or have been plunged more or less into this infernal gulf, or waded deeper into it. But all these *melancholy* fits, howsoever pleasing at first, or displeasing, violent & tyrannizing over those whom they seize on for the time; yet these fits I say, or men affected, are but improperly so called, because they continue not, but come and go, as by some objects they are moved. This *Melancholy* of which we are to treat, is an habit, a serious ailment, a chronick or continuate disease, a settled humour, as Aurelianus and others call it, not errant, but fixed: and as it was long increasing, so, now being (pleasant or painful) grown to an habit, it will hardly be removed.

## Digression of Anatomy

Before I proceed to define the disease of *Melancholy,* what it is, or to discourse farther of it, I hold it not impertinent to make a brief digression of the anatomy of the body and faculties of the soul, for the better understanding of that which is to follow; because many hard words will often occur, as *myrach, hypochondries, hemrods, &c., imagination, reason, humours, spirits, vital, natural, animal, nerves, veins, arteries, chylus, pituita;* which of the vulgar will not so easily be perceived, what they are, how sited, and to what end they serve. And, besides, it may peradventure give occasion to some men, to examine more accurately, search farther into this most excellent subject, and thereupon with that Royal Prophet to praise God, (for a man is fearfully and wonderfully made, and curiously wrought), that have time and leisure enough, and are sufficiently informed in all other worldly businesses, as to make a good bargain, buy and sell, to keep and make choice of a fair hawk, hound, horse, &c. But for such matters as concern the knowledge of themselves, they are wholly ignorant and careless, they know not what this body and soul are, how combined, of what parts and faculties they consist, or how a man differs from a dog. And what can be more ignominious and filthy (as Melancthon well inveighs) *than for a man not to know the structure and composition of his own body, especially since the knowledge of it tends so much to the preservation of his health, and information of his manners?* To stir them up therefore to this study, to peruse those elaborate works of Galen, Bauhinus, Plater, Vesalius, Falopius, Laurentius, Remelinus, &c., which have written copiously in Latin; or that which some of our industrious countrymen have done in our mother tongue, not long since, as that translation of Columbus, and Microcosmographia, in 13 books, I have made this brief digression. Also because Wecker, Melancthon, Fernelius, Fuchsius, and those tedious Tracts on Life (which have more compendiously handled and written of this matter) are not at all times ready to be had, to give them some small taste or notice of the rest, let this epitome suffice.

## The Four Humours

Of the parts of the Body, there be many divisions: the most approved is that of Laurentius, out of Hippocrates: which is, into parts *contained,* or *containing. Contained* are either *humours* or *spirits.*

A humour is a liquid or fluent part of the body, comprehended in it, for the preservation of it; and is either innate or born with us, or adventitious and acquisite. The radical or innate is daily supplied by nourishment, which some call *cambium,* and make those secondary humours of *ros* and *gluten* to maintain it: or acquisite, to maintain these four first primary humours, coming and proceeding from the first concoction in the liver, by which means chyle is excluded. Some divide them into profitable and excrementitious. But Crato out of Hippocrates will have all four to be juice, and not excrements, without which no living creature can be sustained: which four, though they be comprehended in the mass of *blood,* yet they have their several affections, by which they are distinguished from one another, and from those adventitious, *peccant, or diseased humours,* as Melancthon calls them.

*Blood* is a hot, sweet, temperate, red humour, prepared in the *mese-*

*raick* veins, and made of the most temperate parts of the *chylus* in the liver, whose office is to nourish the whole body, to give it strength and colour, being dispersed by the veins through every part of it. And from it *spirits* are first begotten in the heart, which afterwards by the *arteries* are communicated to the other parts.

*Pituita,* or phlegm, is a cold and moist humour, begotten of the colder parts of the *chylus* (or white juice coming out of the meat digested in the stomack) in the liver; his office is to nourish and moisten the members of the body, which, as the tongue, are moved, that they be not over dry.

*Choler* is hot and dry, bitter, begotten of the hotter parts of the *chylus,* and gathered to the gall: it helps the natural heat and senses, and serves to the expelling of excrements.

*Melancholy,* cold and dry, thick, black, and sour, begotten of the more fæculent part of nourishment, and purged from the spleen, is a bridle to the other two hot humours, *blood* and *choler,* preserving them in the blood, and nourishing the bones. These four humours have some analogy with the four elements and to the four ages in man.

To these humours you may add *serum,* which is the matter of urine, & those excrementitious humours of the third concoction, sweat & tears.

Spirit is a most subtle vapour, which is expressed from the *blood,* and the instrument of the soul, to perform all his actions; a common tie or *medium* betwixt the body and the soul, as some will have it; or, as Paracelsus, a fourth soul of itself. Melancthon holds the fountain of these spirits to be the *heart;* begotten there, and afterwards conveyed to the brain, they take another nature to them: Of these spirits there be three kinds, according to the three principal parts, *brain, heart, liver; natural, vital, animal.* The *natural* are begotten in the *liver,* and thence dispersed through the veins, to perform those natural actions. The *vital spirits* are made in the heart of the *natural,* which by the arteries are transported to all the other parts: if these *spirits* cease, then life ceaseth, as in a *syncope* or swooning. The *animal* spirits formed of the *vital,* brought up to the brain, and diffused by the nerves, to the subordinate members, give sense and motion to them all. . . .

### Definition of Melancholy, Name, Difference

Having thus briefly anatomized the body and soul of man, as a preparative to the rest, I may now freely proceed to treat of my intended object to most men's capacity, and after many ambages perspicuously define what this *Melancholy* is, shew his *name* and *differences*. The *name* is imposed from the matter, and disease denominated from the material cause, as Bruel observes, Melancholia, a sort of melaina (black) chole (choler), from black Choler. And whether it be a cause or an effect, a disease, or symptom, let Donatus Altomarus and Salvianus decide, I will not contend about it. It hath several descriptions, notations, and definitions. Fracastorius, in his second book of intellect, calls those *melancholy, whom abundance of that same depraved humour of black choler hath so misaffected, that they become mad thence, and dote in most things, or in all, belonging to election, will, or other manifest operations of the understanding.* Melanelius (out of Galen, Ruffus, Aetius) describes it to be *a bad and peevish disease, which makes men degenerate into beasts:* Galen, *a privation or infection of the middle cell of the head, &c.,* defining it from the part affected, which Hercules de Saxonia approves, calling it *a depravation of the principal function:* Fuchsius, Arnoldus, Guianerius, and others: *by reason of black choler,* Paulus adds. Halyabbas simply calls it a *commotion of the mind;* Aretæus, *a perpetual anguish of the soul, fastened on one thing, without an ague;* which definition of his Mercurialis taxeth: but Ælianus Montaltus defends for sufficient and good. The common sort define it to be *a kind of dotage without a fever, having for his ordinary companions fear and sadness, without any apparent occasion.* So doth Laurentius, Piso, Donatus Altomarus, Jacchinus (on Rhasis), Valesius, Fuchsius, &c., which common definition, howsoever approved by most, Hercules de Saxonia will not allow of, nor David Crusius; he holds it insufficient, *as rather shewing what it is not, than what it is:* as omitting the specifical difference, the phantasy and brain: but I descend to particulars. The most general class is *dotage, or anguish of the mind,* saith Aretæus, *of a principal part,* Hercules de Saxonia adds, to distinguish it from cramp and palsy, and such diseases as belong to the outward sense and motions; *depraved,* to distinguish it from folly and madness (which Montaltus makes the suffocation of the mind, to separate) in which those functions are not depraved, but rather abolished; *without an ague,* is added by all, to sever it from *phrenzy,* and that *melancholy* which is in a pestilent fever. *Fear* and *Sorrow* make it differ from *madness: without a cause* is lastly inserted, to specify it from all other ordinary passions of *Fear* and *Sorrow.* We properly call that *dotage,* as Laurentius interprets it, *when some one principal faculty of the mind, as imagination, or reason, is corrupted, as all melancholy persons have.* It is without a fever, because the humour is most part cold and dry, contrary to putrefaction. *Fear & Sorrow* are the true characters, and inseparable companions, of most melancholy, not all, as Hercules de Saxonia well excepts; for to some it is most pleasant, as to such as laugh most part; some are bold again, and free from all manner of fear and grief, as hereafter shall be declared. . . .

## Love of Learning or Over-much Study

### With a Digression of the Misery of Scholars, and Why the Muses Are Melancholy

Leonartus Fuchsius, Felix Plater, Hercules de Saxonia, speak of a peculiar *fury,* which comes by overmuch study. Fernelius puts *study, contemplation,* and continual meditation, as an especial cause of madness: and in his 86th Consultation cites the same words. Jo. Arculanus amongst other causes reckons up overmuch study: so doth Levinus Lemnius. *Many men* (saith he) *come to this malady by continual study, and night-waking, and, of all other men, scholars are most subject to it:* and such, Rhasis adds, *that have commonly the finest wits.* Marsilius Ficinus puts Melancholy amongst one of those five principal plagues of students, 'tis a common maul unto them all, and almost in some measure an inseparable companion. Varro belike for that cause calls philosophers sombre and stern: severe, sad, dry, tetrick, are common epithets to scholars: and Patritius therefore, in the Institution of Princes, would not have them to be great students. For (as Machiavel holds) study weakens their bodies, dulls their spirits, abates their strength and courage; and good scholars are never good soldiers, which a certain Goth well perceived, for when his country-men came into Greece, and would have burned all their books, he cried out against it, by all means they should [not] do it: *leave them that plague, which in time will consume all their vigour, and martial spirits.* The Turks abdicated Corcutus, the next heir, from the Empire, because he was so much given to his book: and 'tis the common tenent of the world, that learning dulls and diminisheth the spirits, and so by consequence, produceth melancholy.

Two main reasons may be given of it, why students should be more subject to this malady than others. The one is, they live a sedentary, solitary life, to themselves and letters, free from bodily exercise, and those ordinary disports which other men use: and many times, if discontent and idleness concur with it, which is too frequent, they are precipitated into this gulf on a sudden: but the common cause is overmuch study; too much learning (as Festus told Paul) hath made thee mad; 'tis that other extreme which effects it. So did Trincavellius find by his experience, in two of his patients, a young Baron, and another, that contracted this malady by too vehement study. So Forestus found in a young Divine in Louvain, that was mad, and said *he had a Bible in his head.* Marsilius Ficinus *gives many reasons why students dote more often than others.* The first is their negligence: *other men look to their tools; a painter will wash his pencils; a smith will look to his hammer, anvil, forge: an husbandman will mend his plough-irons, and grind his hatchet if it be dull; a falconer or huntsman will have an especial care of his hawks, hounds, horses, dogs, &c. a musician will string and unstring his lute,* &c., *only scholars neglect that instrument, their brain & spirits (I mean), which they daily use, and by which they range over all the world, which by much study is consumed.* See thou (saith Lucian) twist not the rope so hard, till at length it break. Ficinus in his fourth Chapter gives some other reasons; Saturn and Mercury, the Patrons of Learning, are both dry Planets: and Origanus assigns the same cause, why Mercurialists are so poor, and most part beggars; for that their President Mercury had no better fortune himself. The Destinies of old put poverty upon him as a punishment; since when Poetry and Beggary are twin-born brats, inseparable companions:

> And to this day is every scholar poor;
> Gross gold from them runs headlong to the boor.   (MARLOWE)

Mercury can help them to knowledge, but not to money. The second is contemplation, *which dries the brain and extinguisheth natural heat; for whilst the spirits are intent to meditation above in the head, the stomack and liver are left destitute, and thence come black blood and crudities by defect of concoction, and for want of exercise the superfluous vapours cannot exhale.* &c. The same reasons are repeated by Gomesius, Nymannus, Jo. Voschius: and something more they add, that hard students are commonly troubled with gouts, catarrhs, rheums, wasting, indigestion, bad eyes, stone, and colick, crudities, oppilations, *vertigo,* winds, consumptions and all such diseases as come by overmuch sitting; they are most part lean, dry, ill coloured, spend their fortunes, lose their wits, and many times their lives, and all through immoderate pains, and extraordinary studies. If you will not believe the truth of this, look upon great Tostatus and Thomas Aquinas' Works, and tell me whether those men took pains? peruse Austin, Hierome, &c., and many thousands besides.

> He that desires this wished goal to gain,
> Must sweat and freeze before he can attain,    (HORACE)

and labour hard for it. So did Seneca, by his own confession: *not a day that I spend idle, part of the night I keep mine eyes open, tired with waking, and now slumbering, to their continual task.* Hear Tully: *whilst others loitered, & took their pleasures, he was continually at his book.* So they do that will be scholars, and that to the hazard (I say) of their healths, fortunes, wits, & lives. How much did Aristotle and Ptolemy spend, they say, more than a King's ransom; how many crowns a year to perfect arts, the one about his History of Creatures, the other on his Almagest! How much time did Thebet Benchorat employ, to find out the motion of the eighth sphere! forty years and more, some write. How many poor scholars have lost their wits, or become dizzards, neglecting all worldly affairs and their own health, wealth, being & well being, to gain knowledge! for which, after all their pains, in the world's esteem they are accounted ridiculous and silly fools, idiots, asses, and (as oft they are) rejected, contemned, derided, doting, and mad! Look for examples in Hildesheim, read Trincavellius, Montanus, Garceus, Mercurialis, Prosper Calenus, in his Book On Black Bile. Go to Bedlam and ask. Or if they keep their wits, yet they are esteemed scrubs and fools by reason of their carriage: *after seven years' study*——

> In general he's more silent than a statue,
> And makes the people shake their sides with laughter.

Because they cannot ride an horse, which every clown can do; salute and court a gentlewoman, carve at table, cringe, and make congies, which every common swasher can do, &c. they are laughed to scorn, and accounted silly fools by our gallants. Yea, many times, such is their misery, they deserve it: a mere scholar, a mere ass.

> —— Who do lean awry
> Their heads, piercing the earth with a fixt eye;
> When, by themselves, they gnaw their murmuring,
> And furious silence, as 'twere balancing
> Each word upon their outstretched lip, and when
> They meditate the dreams of old sick men,

As, "Out of nothing, nothing can be brought;
And that which is, can ne'er be turn'd to nought."

(PERSIUS, translated by Mr. B. Holiday)

Thus they go commonly meditating unto themselves, thus they sit, such is their action and gesture. Fulgosus makes mention how Th. Aquinas, supping with King Lewis of France, upon a sudden knocked his fist upon the table, and cried, "The Manichees are wrong!"—his wits were a woolgathering, as they say, and his head busied about other matters; when he perceived his error, he was much abashed. Such a story there is of Archimedes in Vitruvius, that having found out the means to know how much gold was mingled with the silver in King Hiero's crown, ran naked forth of the bath and cried Eureka, I have found: *and was commonly so intent to his studies, that he never perceived what was done about him; when the city was taken, and the soldiers now ready to rifle his house, he took no notice of it.* S. Bernard rode all day long by Lake Leman, and asked at last where he was. It was Democritus' carriage alone that made the Abderites suppose him to have been mad, and send for Hippocrates to cure him: if he had been in any solemn company, he would upon all occasions fall a laughing. Theophrastus saith as much of Heraclitus, for that he continually wept, and Laertius of Menedemus, [a disciple of Colotes of] Lampsacus, because he ran like a madman, *saying, he came from hell as a spy, to tell the devils what mortal men did.* Your greatest students are commonly no better; silly, soft fellows in their outward behaviour, absurd, ridiculous to others, and no whit experienced in worldly business; they can measure the heavens, range over the world, teach others wisdom, and yet in bargains and contracts they are circumvented by every base tradesman. Are not these men fools? and how should they be otherwise, *but as so many sots in schools, when (as he well observed) they neither hear nor see such things as are commonly practised abroad?* how should they get experience, by what means? *I knew in my time many Scholars,* saith Æneas Sylvius (in an Epistle of his to Kaspar Schlick, Chancellor to the Emperor) *excellent well learned, but so rude, so silly, that they had no common civility, nor knew how to manage their domestick or publick affairs.* Paglarensis *was amazed, and said his farmer had surely cozened him, when he heard him tell that his sow had eleven pigs, and his ass had but one foal.* To say the best of this Profession, I can give no other testimony of them in general, than that of Pliny of Isæus; *he is yet a scholar, than which kind of men there is nothing so simple,* so sincere, none better; they are most part harmless, honest, *upright, innocent,* plain dealing men.

Now because they are commonly subject to such hazards, and inconveniences, as dotage, madness, simplicity, &c. Jo. Voschius would have good scholars to be highly rewarded, and had in some extraordinary respect above other men, *to have greater privileges than the rest, that adventure themselves and abbreviate their lives for the publick good.* But our Patrons of Learning are so far nowadays from respecting the *Muses,* and giving that honour to scholars, or reward, which they deserve, and are allowed by those indulgent privileges of many noble Princes, that, after all their pains taken in the *Universities,* cost and charge, expences, irksome hours, laborious tasks, wearisome days, dangers, hazards, (barred meanwhile from all pleasures which other men have, mewed up like hawks all their lives), if they chance to wade through them, they shall in the end be rejected, contemned, and, which is their greatest misery, driven to their shifts, exposed to want, poverty, and beggary. Their familiar attendants are,

> Grief, labour, care, pale sickness, miseries,
> Fear, filthy poverty, hunger that cries,
> Terrible monsters to be seen with eyes.   (VIRGIL)

If there were nothing else to trouble them, the conceit of this alone were enough to make them all melancholy. Most other Trades and Professions, after some seven years' Prenticeship, are enabled by their Craft to live of themselves. A Merchant adventures his goods at sea, and, though his hazard be great, yet, if one Ship return of four, he likely makes a saving voyage. An husbandman's gains are almost certain; which Jupiter himself cannot diminish, ('tis Cato's hyperbole, a great husband himself;) only scholars, methinks, are most uncertain, unrespected, subject to all casualties, and hazard. For first, not one of a many proves to be a scholar, all are not capable and docile, a Mercury is not to be made out of every log: we can make Mayors and Officers every year, but not Scholars: Kings can invest Knights and Barons, as Sigismund the Emperor confessed; Universities can give Degrees; and, *What you are any one i' th' world can be;* but he, nor they, nor all the world, can give Learning, make Philosophers, Artists, Orators, Poets. We can soon say, as Seneca well notes, What a good man you are! how rich!, point at a rich man, a good, an happy man, a proper man, richly clad, primped & perfumed; at what great cost of time we win such praise as,

"What a learned man you are!" but 'tis not so easily performed to find out a learned man. Learning is not so quickly got. Though they may be willing to take pains, to that end sufficiently informed, and liberally maintained by their Patrons and Parents, yet few can compass it. Or, if they be docile, yet all men's wills are not answerable to their wits, they can apprehend, but will not take pains; they are either seduced by bad companions, they come to grief with wine or women, and so spend their time to their friends' grief and their own undoings. Or, put case they be studious, industrious, of ripe wits, and perhaps good capacities, then how many diseases of body and mind must they encounter! No labour in the world like unto study! It may be, their temperature will not endure it, but, striving to be excellent, to know all, they lose health, wealth, wit, life, and all. Let him yet happily escape all these hazards, with a body of brass, and is now consummate and ripe, he hath profited in his studies, and proceeded with all applause: after many expences, he is fit for preferment: where shall he have it? he is as far to seek it (after twenty years' standing) as he was at the first day of his coming to the University. For what course shall he take, being now capable and ready? The most parable and easy, and about which many are employed, is to teach a School, turn Lecturer or Curate, and for that he shall have Falconer's wages, ten pounds a year, and his diet, or some small stipend, so long as he can please his Patron or the Parish; if they approve him not (for usually they do but a year or two) as inconstant as they that cried *Hosanna!* one day, and *Crucify him!* the other; serving-man-like, he must go and look a new Master: if they do, what is his reward?

> This too awaits: your fate may be to teach
> In some suburban school the parts of speech.    (HORACE)

Like an ass, he wears out his time for provender, and can shew a stumpe rod, saith Hædus, an old torn gown, an ensign of his infelicity, he hath his labour for his pain, a *modicum* to keep him till he be decrepit, and that is all. The scholar is not a happy man. If he be a trencher Chaplain in a Gentleman's house, as it befel Euphormio, after some seven years' service, he may perchance have a Living to the halves, or some small Rectory with the mother of the maids at length, a poor kinswoman, or a crackt chambermaid, to have and to hold during the time of his life. But if he offend his good Patron, or displease his Lady Mistress in the mean time, as Hercules did by Cacus, he shall be dragged forth of doors by the heels, away with him! If he bend his forces to some other studies, with an intent to be secretary to some Nobleman, or in such a place with an Embassador, he shall find that these persons rise like Prentices one under another, as in so many Tradesmen's shops, when the Master is dead, the Foreman of the shop commonly steps in his place. Now for Poets, Rhetoricians, Historians, Philosophers, Mathematicians, Sophisters, &c., they are like Grasshoppers, sing they must in Summer, and pine in the Winter, for there is no preferment for them. Even so they were at first, if you will believe that pleasant Tale of Socrates, which he told fair Phædrus under a Plane-tree, at the banks of the river Ilissus. About noon, when it was hot, and the Grasshoppers made a noise, he took that sweet occasion to tell him a Tale, how Grasshoppers were once Scholars, Musicians, Poets, &c., before the *Muses* were born, and lived without meat and drink, and for that cause were turned by Jupiter into Grasshoppers; and may be turned again into Tithonus' grasshoppers, or frogs of the Lycians, for any reward I see they are like to have: or else, in the mean time, I would they could live, as they did, without any viaticum, like so many *Manucodiatæ,* those Indian Birds of Paradise, as we commonly call them, those I mean that live with the Air, and Dew of Heaven, and need no other food: for, being as they are, their *Rhetorick only serves them to curse their bad fortunes,* & many of them for want of means are driven to hard shifts; from Grasshoppers they turn Humble-Bees and Wasps, plain Parasites, and make the *Muses,* Mules, to satisfy their hunger-starved paunches, and get a meal's meat. To say truth, 'tis the common fortune of most scholars to be servile and poor, to complain pitifully, and lay open their wants to their respectless Patrons, as Cardan doth, as Xylander, and many others; and, which is too common in those Dedicatory Epistles, for hope of gain, to lie, flatter, and with hyperbolical elogiums and commendations to magnify and extol an illiterate unworthy idiot for his excellent virtues, whom they should rather, as Machiavel observes, vilify and rail at downright for his most notorious villanies and vices. So they prostitute themselves, as fiddlers or mercenary tradesmen, to serve great men's turns for a small reward. They are like Indians, they have store of gold, but know not the worth of it: for I am of Synesius' opinion, *King Hiero got more by Simonides' acquaintance, than Simonides did by his:* they have their best education, good institution, sole qualification from us, and, when they have done well, their honour and immortality from us; we are the living tombs, registers, and so many trumpeters of their fames: what was Achilles without Homer? Alexander without Arrian and Curtius? who had known the Cæsars but for Suetonius and Dion?

> Many brave persons lived ere Agamemnon:
> But are all buried in night's long obscurity,
> Unwept, unknown, because they lacked a bard.    (HORACE)

They are more beholden to scholars, than scholars to them; but they under-value themselves, and so by those great men are kept down. Let them have that *Encyclopædian,* all the learning in the world; they must keep it to themselves, *live in base esteem, and starve, except they will submit,* as Budæus well hath it, *so many good parts, so many ensigns of arts, virtues, be slavishly obnoxious to some illiterate Potentate, and live under his insolent Worship, or Honour, like Parasites,* who, like mice, devour another man's bread. For, to say truth, as Guido Bonat, that great Astrologer, could foresee, they be not gainful arts these, but poor and hungry.

> The rich Physician, honour'd Lawyers ride,
> Whilst the poor Scholar foots it by their side.    (BUCHANAN)

Poverty is the *Muse's* Patrimony, and, as that Poetical divinity teacheth us, when Jupiter's daughters were each of them married to the Gods, the *Muses* alone were left solitary, Helicon forsaken of all Suitors, and I believe it was, because they had no portion.

> Why did Calliope live so long a maid?
> Because she had no dowry to be paid.    (BUCHANAN)

Ever since all their followers are poor, forsaken, and left unto themselves; in so much that, as Petronius argues, you shall likely know them by their clothes. *There came,* saith he, *by chance into my company, a fellow not very spruce to look on, that I could perceive by that note alone he was a Scholar, whom commonly rich men hate. I asked him what he was; he answered, a Poet. I demanded again why he was so ragged; he told me this kind of learning never made any man rich.*

> A merchant's gain is great, that goes to sea;
> A soldier embossed all in gold;
> A flatterer lies fox'd in brave array;
> A scholar only ragged to behold.    (PETRONIUS)

All which our ordinary Students, right well perceiving in the Universities how unprofitable these Poetical, Mathematical, and Philosophical

Studies are, how little respected, how few Patrons, apply themselves in all haste to those three commodious Professions of Law, Physick, and Divinity, sharing themselves between them, rejecting these Arts in the mean time, History, Philosophy, Philology, or lightly passing them over, as pleasant toys fitting only table talk, and to furnish them with discourse. They are not so behoveful: he that can tell his money hath Arithmetick enough: he is a true Geometrician, can measure out a good fortune to himself; a perfect Astrologer, that can cast the rise and fall of others, and mark their errant motions to his own use. The best Opticks are to reflect the beams of some great men's favour and grace to shine upon him. He is a good Engineer that alone can make an instrument to get preferment. This was the common tenent and practice of Poland, as Cromerus observed not long since in the first Book of his History; their Universities were generally base; not a Philosopher, a Mathematician, an Antiquary, &c., to be found of any note amongst them, because they had no set reward or stipend; but every man betook himself to Divinity, a good Parsonage was their aim. This was the practice of some of our near neighbors, as Lipsius inveighs; *they thrust their children to the study of Law and Divinity, before they be informed aright, or capable of such studies.* In fact the hope of gain stands before all the arts, and a load of gold is more beautiful than all that Greek and Latin dizzards have written. Such monied men come to govern the helm of State, and are present and prominent at King's councils. O my father! O my country! ——— So he complained, and so may others. For even so we find, to serve a great man, to get an Office in some Bishop's Court, to practise in some good Town, or compass a Benefice, is a mark we shoot at, as being so advantageous, the high way to preferment. . . .

Meantime learned men, endowed with the graces of a holy life, & bearing the burden and heat of the day, by some unfair destiny serve these men, perhaps contented with a very small salary, called by plain names, humble, obscure, & needy, though far more worthy, & unhonoured lead a private life, buried in some scanty country Living, or imprisoned all their lives in their Colleges, and languish in obscurity. But I will not dwell on this sad theme any longer. Hence come our tears, hence it is that the Muses are in mourning, hence it is that Religion itself, to use the words of Sesellius, is brought into ridicule & contempt, and the Priesthood is debased; and, since this is the case, I may venture to say so, and to quote the low saying of a low person about the Clergy,

—that they are a base lot, poor, ignorant, sordid, melancholy, wretched, despicable, & deserving of contempt! . . .

## From Natural and Inward Causes

To give some satisfaction to melancholy men that are troubled with these symptoms, a better means in my judgment cannot be taken than to shew them the causes whence they proceed; not from Devils, as they suppose, or that they are bewitched or forsaken of God, hear or see, &c. as many of them think, but from natural and inward causes; that so, knowing them, they may better avoid the effects, or at least endure them with more patience. The most grievous and common symptoms are fear and sorrow, and that without a cause, to the wisest and discreetest men, in this malady not to be avoided. The reason why they are so Aetius discusseth at large, in his first problem out of Galen. For Galen imputeth all to the cold that is black, and thinks that, the spirits being darkened, and the substance of the brain cloudy and dark, all the objects thereof appear terrible, and the *mind* itself, by those dark, obscure, gross fumes, ascending from black humours, is in continual darkness, fear and sorrow; divers terrible monstrous fictions in a thousand shapes & apparitions occur, with violent passions, by which the brain and phantasy are troubled and eclipsed. Fracastorius *will have cold to be the cause of fear & sorrow; for such as are cold are indisposed to mirth, dull and heavy, by nature solitary, silent; & not for any inward darkness (as Physicians think), for many melancholy men dare boldly be, continue, and walk in the dark, and delight in it:* only the cold are timid: if they be hot, they are merry, and the more hot, the more furious, and void of fear, as we see in madmen: but this reason holds not, for then no melancholy, proceeding from choler adust, should fear. Averroes scoffs at Galen for his reasons, and brings five arguments to refell them: so doth Herc. de Saxonia, assigning other causes, which are copiously censured and confuted by Ælianus Montaltus, Lod. Mercatus, Altomarus, Guianerius, Bright, Laurentius, Valesius. *Distemperature,* they conclude, *makes black juice, blackness obscures the spirits, the spirits obscured cause fear and sorrow.* Laurentius supposeth these black fumes offend especially the *diaphragma* or midriff, and so consequently, the mind, which is obscured as the Sun by a cloud. To this opinion of Galen almost all the Greeks and Arabians subscribe, the Latins new and old, as children are affrighted in the dark, so are melancholy men at all times, as having the inward cause with them, & still carrying it about. Which black vapours, whether they proceed from the black blood about the heart, as T. W. Jes.[9] thinks, in his Treatise of the passions of the mind, or stomack, spleen, midriff, or all the misaffected parts together, it boots not; they keep the mind in a perpetual dungeon, and oppress it with continual fears, anxieties, sorrows, &c. It is an ordinary thing for such as are sound to laugh at this dejected pusillanimity, and those other symptoms of melancholy, to make themselves merry with them, and to wonder at such, as toys and trifles, which may be resisted and withstood if they will themselves: but let him that so wonders consider with himself that, if a man should tell him on a sudden some of his especial friends were dead, could he choose but grieve? or set him upon a steep rock, where he should be in danger to be precipitated, could he be secure? his heart would tremble for fear, and his head be giddy. Peter Byarus gives instance (as I have said [elsewhere]): *and put case* (saith he) *in one that walks upon a plank; if it lie on the ground, he can safely do it, but if the same plank be laid over some deep water, instead of a bridge, he is vehemently moved, & 'tis nothing but his imagination,* the idea of falling being impressed upon him, *to which his other members and faculties obey.* Yea, but you infer that such men have a just cause to fear, a true object of fear; so have melancholy men an inward cause, a perpetual fume and darkness, causing fear, grief, suspicion, which they carry with them; an object which cannot be removed, but sticks as close, and is as inseparable, as a shadow to a body, and who can expel, or over-run his shadow? remove heat of the liver, a cold stomack, weak spleen: remove those adust humours and vapours arising from them, black blood from the heart, all outward perturbations; take away the cause, and then bid them not grieve nor fear, or be heavy, dull, lumpish; otherwise counsel can do little good; you may as well bid him that is sick of an ague not to be adry, or him that is wounded not to feel pain.

Suspicion follows fear and sorrow at heels, arising out of the same fountain, so thinks Fracastorius, *that fear is the cause of suspicion, and still they suspect some treachery or some secret machination to be framed against them,* still they distrust. Restlessness proceeds from the same spring, variety of fumes makes them like and dislike. Solitariness, avoiding of light, that they are weary of their lives, hate the world, arise

[9] Thomas Wright, Jesuit.

from the same causes, for their spirits and humours are opposite to light, fear makes them avoid company, and absent themselves, lest they should be misused, hissed at, or overshoot themselves, which still they suspect. They are prone to Venery by reason of wind. Angry, waspish, and fretting still, out of abundance of choler, which causeth fearful dreams, and violent perturbations to them both sleeping and waking. That they suppose they have no heads, fly, sink, they are pots, glasses, &c. is wind in their heads. Herc. de Saxonia doth ascribe this to the several motions in the animal spirits, *their dilatation, contraction, confusion, alteration, tenebrosity, hot or cold distemperature,* excluding all material humours. Fracastorius accounts it *a thing worthy of inquisition why they should entertain such false conceits, as that they have horns, great noses, that they are birds, beasts, &c.,* why they should think themselves Kings, Lords, Cardinals. For the first Fracastorius gives two reasons: *one is the disposition of the body: the other the occasion of the phantasy,* as if their eyes be purblind, their ears sing, by reason of some cold and rheum, &c. To the second Laurentius answers, the imagination, inwardly or outwardly moved, represents to the understanding, not enticements only, to favour the passion, or dislike, but a very intensive pleasure follows the passion, or displeasure, and the will and reason are captivated by delighting in it.

Why students and lovers are so often melancholy & mad, the Philosophers of Coimbra assign this reason, *because, by a vehement & continual meditation of that wherewith they are affected, they fetch up the spirits into the brain, and with the heat brought with them they incend it beyond measure: and the cells of the inward senses dissolve their temperature, which being dissolved, they cannot perform their offices as they ought.*

Why melancholy men are witty, which Aristotle hath long since maintained in his Problems, and why all learned men, famous Philosophers, and Law-givers, have still been melancholy, is a problem much controverted. Jason Pratensis will have it understood of natural melancholy, which opinion Melancthon inclines to, in his book On the Mind, and Marcilius Ficinus, but not simple, for that makes men stupid, heavy, dull, being cold and dry, fearful, fools, and solitary, but mixt with the other humours, phlegm only excepted; and they not adust, but so mixt, as that blood be half, with little or no adustion, that they be neither too hot nor too cold. Apponensis, cited by Melancthon, thinks it proceeds from melancholy adust, excluding all natural melancholy as too cold.

Laurentius condemns his *tenent,* because adustion of humours makes men mad, as lime burns when water is cast on it. It must be mixt with blood, & somewhat adust, and so that old Aphorism of Aristotle may be verified, no excellent wit without a mixture of madness. Fracastorius shall decide the controversy; *Phlegmatick are dull: Sanguine lively, pleasant, acceptable & merry, but not witty: Cholerick are too swift in motion & furious, impatient of contemplation, deceitful wits: Melancholy men have most excellent wits, but not all; this humour may be hot or cold, thick or thin; if too hot, they are furious and mad; if too cold, dull, stupid, timorous, and sad: if temperate, excellent, rather inclining to the extreme of heat than cold.* This sentence of his will agree with that of Heraclitus, a dry light makes a wise mind; temperate heat & dryness are the chief causes of a good wit; therefore, saith Ælian, an elephant is the wisest of all brute beasts, because his brain is dryest, and because of his plentiful supply of black bile: this reason Cardan approves, Jo. Baptista Silvaticus, a Physician of Milan, in his first controversy, hath copiously handled this question, Rulandus in his Problems, Cælius Rhodiginus, Valleriola, Herc. de Saxonia, Lodovicus Mercatus, Baptista Porta, and many others.

Weeping, sighing, laughing, itching, trembling, sweating, blushing, hearing and seeing strange noises, visions, wind, crudity, are motions of the body, depending upon these precedent motions of the mind. Neither are tears affections, but actions (as Scaliger holds): *the voice of such as are afraid trembles, because the heart is shaken.* Why they stut or falter in their speech, Mercurialis and Montaltus give like reasons out of Hippocrates, *dryness, which makes the nerves of the tongue torpid.* Fast speaking (which is a symptom of some few), Aetius will have caused *from abundance of wind, and swiftness of imagination: baldness comes from excess of dryness,* hirsuteness from a dry temperature. The cause of much waking is a dry brain, continual meditation, discontent, fears, & cares, that suffer not the mind to be at rest; incontinency is from wind, and an hot liver. Rumbling in the guts is caused from wind, and wind from ill concoction, weakness of natural heat, or a distempered heat and cold; palpitation of the heart from vapours; heaviness & aching from the same cause. That the belly is hard, wind is a cause, and of that leaping in many parts. Redness of the face, & itching, as if they were flea-bitten, or stung with pismires, from a sharp subtile wind: cold sweat from vapours arising from the hypochondries, which pitch upon the skin; leanness for want of good nourishment. Why their appetite is so great Aetius answers: cold in those inward parts, cold belly & hot liver causeth crudity; and intention proceeds from perturbations, our soul for want of spirits cannot attend exactly to so many intentive operations; being exhaust, & overswayed by passion, she cannot consider the reasons which may dissuade her from such affections.

Bashfulness and blushing is a passion proper to men alone, and is not only caused for some shame and ignominy, or that they are guilty unto themselves of some foul fact committed but, as Fracastorius well determines, *from fear and a conceit of our defects. The face labours and is troubled at his presence that sees our defects, & nature, willing to help, sends thither heat, heat draws the subtilest blood, & so we blush. They that are bold, arrogant, and careless, seldom or never blush, but such as are fearful.* Anthonius Lodovicus, in his book on bashfulness, will have this subtle blood to arise in the face, not so much for the reverence of our betters in presence, *but for joy and pleasure, or if anything at unawares shall pass from us, a sudden accident, occurse, or meeting,* (which Disarius in Macrobius confirms) any object heard or seen, for blind men never blush, as Dandinus observes, the night & darkness make men impudent. Or by being staid before our betters, or in company we like not, or if any thing molest and offend us, blushing turns to a continuate redness. Sometimes the extremity of the ears tingle, and are red, sometimes the whole face, even though one has done nothing wrong, as Lodovicus holds: though Aristotle is of opinion, all shame for some offence. But we find otherwise; it may as well proceed from fear, from force and inexperience, (so Dandinus holds), as vice; a hot liver, saith Duretus, *from a hot brain, from wind, the lungs heated, or after drinking of wine, strong drink, perturbations, &c.*

Laughter, what it is, saith Tully, *how caused, where, & so suddenly breaks out that, desirous to stay it, we cannot, how it comes to possess & stir our face, veins, eyes, countenance, mouth, sides, let Democritus determine.* The cause that it often affects melancholy men so much is given by Gomesius, abundance of pleasant vapours, which, in sanguine melancholy especially, break from the heart, *and tickle the midriff, because it is transverse and full of nerves: by which titillation the sense being moved, and the arteries distended, or pulled, the spirits from thence move and possess the sides, veins, countenance, eyes.* See more in Jossius, On Laughter and Weeping. Tears, as Scaliger defines, proceed from grief & pity, *or from the heating of a moist brain, for a dry cannot weep.*

That they see and hear so many phantasms, chimæras, noises, visions, &c., as Fienus hath discoursed at large in his book of imagination, & Lavater, On Spectres, their corrupt phantasy makes them see & hear that which indeed is neither heard nor seen. They that much fast, or want sleep, as melancholy or sick men commonly do, see visions, or such as are weak-sighted, very timorous by nature, mad, distracted, or earnestly seek. As the saying is, they dream of that they desire. Like Sarmiento the Spaniard, who, when he was sent to discover the Straits of Magellan, and confine places, by the Prorex[10] of Peru, standing on the top of an Hill, thought he looked down upon a most pleasant open country, magnificent buildings, numerous Hamlets, lofty Towers, splendid Temples, and brave Cities, built like ours in Europe, not, saith mine Author, that there was any such thing, but that he was very imaginative and too credulous, and would fain have had it so. Or, as Lod. Mercatus proves, by reason of inward vapours, and humours from blood, choler, &c. diversely mixt, they apprehend and see outwardly, as they suppose, divers images, which indeed are not. As they that drink wine think all runs round, when it is in their own brain, so is it with these men, the fault and cause is inward, as Galen affirms, mad men and such as are near death, have in their eyes images of what they think they see, 'tis in their brain, which seems to be before them; the brain, as a concave glass, reflects solid bodies. For the aged often have such hollow & dry brains that they fancy themselves to see that which is not, (saith Boissardus); old men are too frequently mistaken & dote in like case: or as he that looketh through a piece of red glass, judgeth every thing he sees to be red; corrupt vapours mounting from the body to the head, and distilling again from thence to the eyes, when they have mingled themselves with the watery crystal which receiveth the shadows of things to be seen, make all things appear of the same colour, which remains in the humour that overspreads our sight, as to melancholy men all is black, to phlegmatick all white, &c. Or else, as before, the organs, corrupt by a corrupt phantasy, as Lemnius well quotes, *cause a great agitation of spirits and humours, which wander to and fro in all the creeks of the brain, and cause such apparitions before their eyes.* One thinks he reads something written in the Moon, as Pythagoras is said to have done of old, another smells brimstone, hears Cerberus bark: Orestes, now mad, supposed he saw the Furies tormenting him, and his mother still ready to run upon him.

[10] Viceroy.

> O Mother! I beg you pursue me no more
> With serpentine furies that thirst for my gore.
> See! see! they attack me, they compass me sore!    (EURIPIDES)

but Electra told him, thus raving in his mad fit, he saw no such sights at all, it was but his crazed imagination.

> Rest, rest unhappy one; rest on thy bed;
> You see but the fancies of a too-fevered head.    (EURIPIDES)

So Pentheus (in Euripides' Bacchæ) saw two Suns, two Thebes, his brain alone was troubled. Sickness is an ordinary cause of such sights. Cardan saith that diseased minds, enfeebled by distress & hunger, cause themselves to see, to hear, &c. Andrew Osiander beheld strange visions, and Alexander ab Alexandro, both in their sickness, which he relates. Albategnius, that noble Arabian, on his death bed saw a ship ascending and descending, which Fracastorius records of his friend Baptista Turrianus. Weak sight, and a vain persuasion withal, may effect as much, and second causes concurring, as an oar in water makes a refraction, and seems bigger, bended double, &c. The thickness of the air may cause such effects, or any object not well discerned in the dark, fear and phantasy will suspect to be a Ghost, a Devil, &c. What the wretched overmuch desire, they easily believe; we are apt to believe and mistake in such cases. Marcellus Donatus brings in a story out of Aristotle of one Antipheron, which likely saw, wheresoever he was, his own image in the air, as in a glass. Vitellio hath such another instance of a familiar acquaintance of his, that, after the want of three or four nights' sleep, as he was riding by a river side, saw another riding with him, and using all such gestures as he did, but when more light appeared, it vanished. Eremites and Anachorites have frequently such absurd Visions, Revelations, by reason of much fasting and bad diet, many are deceived by Legerdemain, as [Reginald] Scot hath well shewed in his Book of the Discovery of Witchcraft, and Cardan. Suffites,[11] perfumes, suffumigations, mixt candles, perspective glasses, and such natural causes, make men look as if they were dead, or with horse-heads, bull's-horns, and such like brutish shapes, the room full of snakes, adders, dark, light, green, red, of all colours, as you may perceive in Baptista Porta, Alexis, Albertus, and others; glow-worms, firedrakes, meteors, *Ignis fatuus,* which Plinius calls Castor and Pollux, with many such that appear in

---

[11] Incense-burnings.

moorish grounds, about Church-yards, moist valleys, or where battles have been fought, the causes of which read in Goclenius, Velcurius, Finkius, &c. Such feats are often done to frighten children with squibs, rotten wood, &c., to make folks look as if they were dead, bigger than usual, lesser, fairer, fouler, or to appear as if standing on their heads or all on fire, or in the form of demons. Take the hairs of a black dog, &c., saith Albertus; and so 'tis ordinary to see strange uncouth sights by Catoptricks;[12] who knows not that, if in a dark room the light be admitted at one only little hole, and a paper or glass put upon it, the Sun shining will represent on the opposite wall all such objects as are illuminated by his rays? With concave and cylinder glasses we may reflect any shape of men, Devils, Anticks, (as Magicians most part do, to gull a silly spectator in a dark room), we will [see] ourselves, & that hanging in the air, when 'tis nothing but such an horrible image as Agrippa demonstrates, placed in another room. Roger Bacon of old is said to have represented his own image walking in the air by this art, though no such thing appear in his perspectives. But most part is in the brain that deceives them, although I may not deny but that oftentimes the Devil deludes them, takes his opportunity to suggest, and represent vain objects to melancholy men, and such as are ill affected. To these you may add the knavish impostures of Jugglers, Exorcists, Mass-Priests, and Mountebanks, of whom Roger Bacon speaks, &c. They can counterfeit the voices of all birds and brute beasts almost, all tones and tunes of men, and speak within their throats, as if they spoke afar off, that they make their auditors believe they hear Spirits, and are thence much astonished and affrighted with it. Besides, those artificial devices to over-hear their confessions, like that whispering place of Gloucester with us, or like the Duke's place at Mantua in Italy, where the sound is reverberated by a concave wall; a reason of which Blancanus in his Echometria gives, and mathematically demonstrates.

So that the hearing is as frequently deluded as the sight, from the same causes almost, as he that hears bells, will make them sound what he list. *As the fool thinketh, so the bell clinketh.* Theophilus, in Galen, thought he heard musick from vapours which made his ears sound, &c. Some are deceived by Echoes, some by roaring of waters, or concaves & reverberation of air in the ground, hollow places and walls. At Cadurcum, in Aquitaine, words & sentences are repeated by a strange Echo to

---

[12] Use of reflected lights, by mirrors, &c.

the full, or whatsoever you shall play upon a musical instrument, more distinctly & louder than they are spoken at first. Some Echoes repeat a thing spoken seven times, as at Olympus in Macedonia, as Pliny relates, some twelve times, as at Charenton, a village near Paris, in France. At Delphi in Greece heretofore was a miraculous Echo, and so in many other places. Cardan hath wonderful stories of such as have been deluded by these Echoes. Blancanus the Jesuit in his Echometria hath variety of examples, & gives his readers full satisfaction of all such sounds by way of demonstration. At Barry, an Isle in the Severn Mouth, they seem to hear a smith's forge: so at Lipari, & those sulphureous Isles, and many such like which Olaus speaks of in the Continent of Scandia, & those Northern Countries. Cardan mentioneth a woman, that still supposed she heard the Devil call her, & speaking to her, she was a painter's wife in Milan: & many such illusions & voices, which proceed most part from a corrupt imagination.

Whence it comes to pass that they prophesy, speak several languages, talk of Astronomy, & other unknown sciences to them, (of which they have been ever ignorant), I have in brief touched, only this I will here add, that Arculanus, Bodine, & some others, hold as a manifest token that such persons are possessed with the devil: so doth Hercules de Saxonia, and Apponensis, and fit only to be cured by a Priest. But Guianerius, Montaltus, Pomponatius of Padua, & Lemnius refer it wholly to the ill disposition of the humour, & that out of the authority of Aristotle, because such symptoms are cured by purging; & as by the striking of a flint fire is enforced, so, by the vehement motions of spirits, they do compel strange speeches to be spoken: another argument he hath from Plato's recollections, which is all out as likely as that which Marsilius Ficinus speaks of his friend Pierleonus; by a divine kind of infusion he understood the secrets of nature, & tenents of Grecian and Barbarian Philosophers, before ever he heard of, saw, or read their works: but in this I should rather hold with Avicenna and his associates, that such symptoms proceed from evil Spirits, which take all opportunities of humours decayed, or otherwise, to pervert the soul of man; and besides, the humour itself is the Devil's Bath, and, as Agrippa proves, doth entice him to seize upon them. . . .

# THE SYNOPSIS OF
# THE SECOND PARTITION

Cure of melancholy is

Sec. 1. General to all, which contains    or

**Unlawful means forbidden.**

*Mem.*

1. From the Divel, Magicians, Witches, &c. by charmes, spels, incantations, Images, &c.
  *Queſt.* 1. Whether they can cure this, or other such like diseases?
  *Queſt.* 2. Whether if they can so cure, it be lawfull to seek to them for help?
2. Immediately from God, *a Jove principiu*, by prayer, &c.
3. *Queſt.* 1. Whether Saints and their Reliques can help this infirmity?
  *Queſt.* 2. Whether it be lawfull in this case to sue to them for aide?

**Lawful means which are**      or

4. Mediately by Nature, which concerns and works by

*Subjeɛt.*

1. *Physician*, in whom is required science, confidence, honesty, &c.
2. *Patient*, in whom is required obedience, conſtancy, willingness, patience, confidence, bounty, &c. not to praɛtise on himself.
3. *Physicke*, which conſiſts of

Diæteticall ♈ .
Pharmaceuticall ♉
Chirurgicall ♊

or

Particular to the three diſtinɛt species ♋ ♌ ♍ .

♈ Sect. 2.
Diætetical,
which
consists in
reforming
those six
non-natu-
ral things
as in

Diet rec-
tified.
1. *Memb.*

Matter &
quality.
1. *Subs.*

or

Flesh { Such meats as are easie of digestion, well dressed, hot,
sod, &c. young, moist, of good nourishment, &c.
Bread of pure wheat, well baked.
Water clear from the fountain.
Wine and drink not too strong, &c.

Flesh { Mountainbirds, partridg, phesant, quails, &c.
{ Hen, capon, mutton, veale, kid, rabbit, &c.

Fish { That live in gravelly waters, as pike,
{ pearch, trowt, Sea-fish, solid, white, &c.

Hearbs { Borage, bugloss, bawm, succory, endive,
{ violets, in broth, not raw, &c.

Fruits { Raysins of the Sun, apples corrected for
& roots { wind, oranges, &c., parsnips, pota-
{ toes, &c.

2. Quan-
tity.

At seasonable and usuall times of repast, in good
order, not before the first be concocted, sparing,
not overmuch of one dish.

2. Rectification of Retention and Evacuation, as costiveness, Venery, bleeding
at nose, months stopped, baths, &c.

3. Air recti-
fied with a
Digression
of the Aire.

Naturally in the choice, and site of our contrey, dwelling-place,
to be hot and moist, light, wholsome, pleasant, &c.
Artificially, by often change of aire, avoiding winds, fogs, tempests, opening windows, perfumes, &c.

4. Exercise

Of body and minde, but moderate, as hawking, hunting, riding,
shooting, bowling, fishing, fowling, walking in fair fields, galleries, tennis, bar.
Of minde, as Chess, cards, tables, &c. to see playes, masks, &c.
serious studies, business, all honest recreations.

5. Rectification of waking and terrible dreams, &c.
6. Rectification of passions and perturbations of the minde. ♉

*Memb.* 6.
Passions
and per-
turbations
of the
minde
rectified.

From
himself

or

Subsect.
1. By using all good means of help, confessing to a friend, &c.
Avoiding all occasions of his infirmity.
Not giving way to passions, but resisting to his utmost.
2. By fair and foul means, counsell, comfort, good perswasion,
witty devices, fictions, and if it be possible to satisfie his mind.
3. Musick of all sorts aptly applyed.
4. Mirth, and merry company.

from his
friends.

Sect. 3.
A conso-
latory di-
gression,
contain-
ing reme-
dies to all
discon-
tents and
passions
of the
minde.

*Memb.*
1. Generall discontents and grievances satisfied.
2. Particular discontents, as deformity of body, sickness, baseness of birth, &c.
3. Poverty and want, such calamities and adversities.
4. Against servitude, loss of liberty, imprisonment,
banishment, &c.
5. Against vain fears, sorrows for death of friends, or
otherwise.
6. Against envy, livor, hatred, malice, emulation, ambition, and self-love, &c.
7. Against repulses, abuses, injuries, contempts, disgraces, contumelies, slanders, and scoffes, &c.
8. Against all other grievous and ordinary symptoms
of this disease of melancholy.

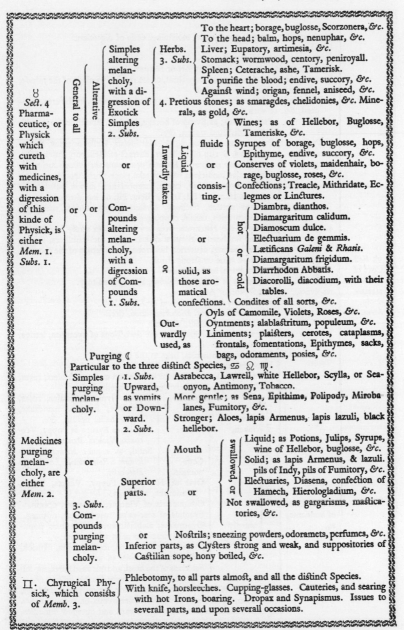

Sect. 4 Pharmaceutice, or Physick which cureth with medicines, with a digression of this kinde of Physick, is either *Mem.* 1. *Subs.* 1.

General to all

Alterative

Simples altering melancholy, with a digression of Exotick Simples 2. *Subs.*

Herbs. 3. *Subs.*

To the heart; borage, buglosse, Scorzonera, &c.
To the head; balm, hops, nenuphar, &c.
Liver; Eupatory, artimesia, &c.
Stomack; wormwood, centory, peniroyall.
Spleen; Ceterache, ashe, Tamerisk.
To purifie the blood; endive, succory, &c.
Against wind; origan, fennel, aniseed, &c.

4. Pretious stones; as smaragdes, chelidonies, &c. Minerals, as gold, &c.

Compounds altering melancholy, with a digression of Compounds 1. *Subs.*

Inwardly taken

Liquid

fluide

Wines; as of Hellebor, Buglosse, Tameriske, &c.
Syrupes of borage, buglosse, hops, Epithyme, endive, succory, &c.

or

Conserves of violets, maidenhair, borage, buglosse, roses, &c.

consisting.

Confections; Treacle, Mithridate, Eclegmes or Linctures.

or

solid, as those aromatical confections.

hot

Diambra, dianthos.
Diamargaritum calidum.
Diamoscum dulce.
Electuarium de gemmis.
Lætificans *Galeni* & *Rhasis*.

cold

Diamargaritum frigidum.
Diarrhodon Abbatis.
Diacorolli, diacodium, with their tables.
Condites of all sorts, &c.

Outwardly used, as

Oyls of Camomile, Violets, Roses, &c.
Oyntments; alablastritum, populeum, &c.
Liniments; plaisters, cerotes, cataplasms, frontals, fomentations, Epithymes, sacks, bags, odoraments, posies, &c.

Purging

Particular to the three distinct Species, ♋ ♌ ♍.

Medicines purging melancholy, are either *Mem.* 2.

Simples purging melancholy.

1. *Subs.* Upward, as vomits or Downward.

Asrabecca, Lawrell, white Hellebor, Scylla, or Seaonyon, Antimony, Tobacco.
More gentle; as Sena, Epithime, Polipody, Miroba lanes, Fumitory, &c.

2. *Subs.*

Stronger; Aloes, lapis Armenus, lapis lazuli, black hellebor.

3. *Subs.* Compounds purging melancholy.

Mouth

swallowed, or

Liquid; as Potions, Julips, Syrups, wine of Hellebor, buglosse, &c.
Solid; as lapis Armenus, & lazuli. pils of Indy, pils of Fumitory, &c.
Electuaries, Diasena, confection of Hamech, Hierologladium, &c.

Superior parts.

or

Not swallowed, as gargarisms, masticatories, &c.

or

Nostrils; sneezing powders, odoramets, perfumes, &c.
Inferior parts, as Clysters strong and weak, and suppositories of Castilian sope, hony boiled, &c.

Ⅱ. Chyrugical Physick, which consists of *Memb.* 3.

Phlebotomy, to all parts almost, and all the distinct Species.
With knife, horsleeches. Cupping-glasses. Cauteries, and searing with hot Irons, boaring. Dropax and Synapismus. Issues to severall parts, and upon severall occasions.

1. *Subsect.*
Moderate diet, meat of good juyce, moistning, easie of digestion.
Good Ayr.
Sleep more then ordinary.
Excrements daily to be avoided by Art or Nature.
Exercise of body and minde not too violent, or too remiss, passions of the minde, and perturbations to be avoided.

2. Bloud-letting if there be need, or that the blood be corrupt, in the arm, forehead, &c. or with Cupping-glasses.

3. Preparatives and purgers.
- Preparatives; as Syrup of borage, bugloss, Epithime, hops, with their distilled waters, &c.
- Purgers; as Montanus, & Matthiolus Helleborismus, Quercetanus, Syrup of Hellebor, Extract of Hellebor, Pulvis Hali, Antimony prepared, *Rulandi aqua mirabilis;* which are used, if gentler medicines will not take place, with Arnoldus, *vinum buglossatum,* Sena, cassia, mirobalanes, *aurum potabile,* or before Hamech. Pil. Indæ, Hiera. Pil. de lap. Armeno, lazuli.

4. Averters.
- Cardans nettles, frictions, clysters, suppositories, sneezings, masticatories, nasals, cupping-glasses.
- To open the Hæmrods with horsleeches, to apply horsleeches to the forehead without scarification, to the shoulders, thighs.
- Issues, boaring, cauteries, hot irons in the future of the crown.

σ̄ *Sect.* 5.
Cure of
head-
melan-
choly.
*Mem.* 1.

5. Cordials, resolvers, hinderers.
- A cup of wine or strong drink.
- Bezars stone, amber, spice.
- Conserves of Borage, Buglosse, Roses, Fumitory.
- Confection of Alchermes.
- *Electuarium lætificans Galeni & Rhasis, &c.*
- *Diamargaritum frig. Diaboraginatum, &c.*
- Odoraments of Roses, Violets.
- Irrigations of the head, with the decoctions of nymphea, lettice, mallows, &c.
- Epithemes, oyntments, bags to the heart.
- Fomentations of oyl for the Belly.
- Baths of sweet water, in which were sod mallows, violets, roses, Water-lillies, Borage flowers, rams heads, &c.

6. Correctors of accidents, as,

To procure sleep, and are

Inwardly taken,
- Simples, { Poppy, Nymphea, lettice, roses, purslane, henban, mandrake, night-shade, opium, &c.
- or { Liquid, as Syrups of Poppy, Verbasco, Violets, Roses.
- Compounds. { Solid, as *requies Nicholai, Philonium Romanum, Laudanum Paracelsi.*

or

Outwardly used as,
- Oyls of Nymphea, Poppy, Violets, Roses, Mandrake, Nutmegs.
- Odoraments of Vinegar, rosewater, opium.
- Frontals of rose-cake, rose-vinegar, nutmeg.
- Oyntments, alablastritum, unguentum populeum, simple or mixt with opium.
- Irrigations of the head, feet, spunges, Musick, murmure and noise of waters.
- Frictions of the head, and outward parts, sacculi of Henbane, wormwood at his pillow, &c.

Against terrible dreams; not to sup late, or eat pease, cabbage, venison, meats heavy of digestion, use bawm, harts-tongue, &c.
Against ruddiness and blushing, inward and outward remedies.

℞ 2. *Mem.*  Cure of melancholy over the body.

Diet, preparatives, purges, averters, cordials, correctors, as before.
Phlebotomy in this kind more necessary, and more frequent.
To correct and cleanse the blood with Fumitory, Sene, Succory, Dandelion, Endive, &c.

*Subsect.* 1.
Phlebotomy if need require.
Diet, preparatives, averters, cordials, purgers, as before, saving that they must not be so vehement.
Use of peny-royal, wormwood, centaury sod, which alone hath cured many.
To provoke urine with aniseed, daucus, asarum, &c. and stools if need be by clysters and suppositories.
To respect the spleen, stomack, liver, hypocondries.
To use Treacle now and then in winter.
To vomit after meals sometimes, if it be inveterate.

℔ Cure of Hypocondriacall, or windy melancholy, 3. *Mem.*

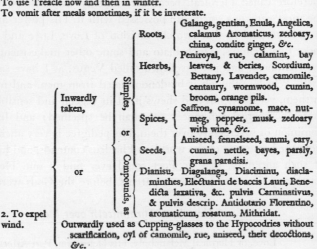

Inwardly taken, Simples, or Compounds, as

Roots, — Galanga, gentian, Enula, Angelica, calamus Aromaticus, zedoary, china, condite ginger, &c.

Hearbs, — Peniroyal, rue, calamint, bay leaves, & beries, Scordium, Bettany, Lavender, camomile, centaury, wormwood, cumin, broom, orange pils.

Spices, — Saffron, cynamome, mace, nutmeg, pepper, musk, zedoary with wine, &c.

Seeds, — Aniseed, fennelseed, ammi, cary, cumin, nettle, bayes, parsly, grana paradisi.

or — Dianisu, Diagalanga, Diaciminu, diaclaminthes, Electuariu de baccis Lauri, Benedicta laxativa, &c. pulvis Carminativus, & pulvis descrip. Antidotario Florentino, aromaticum, rosatum, Mithridat.

2. To expel wind.

Outwardly used as Cupping-glasses to the Hypocodries without scarification, oyl of camomile, rue, aniseed, their decoctions, &c.

# THE THIRD PARTITION

### Heroical Love Causing Melancholy. His Pedigree, Power, and Extent

In [a] precedent Section mention was made, amongst other pleasant objects, of the comeliness and beauty which proceeds from women, that causeth Heroical, or Love-melancholy, is more eminent above the rest, and properly called Love. The part affected in men is the liver, and therefore called Heroical, because commonly Gallants, Noblemen, and the most generous spirits are possessed with it. His power and extent is very large, and in that twofold division of Love, Love and Friendship, those two Venuses, which Plato and some other make mention of, it is most eminent, and par excellence called Venus, as I have said, or Love itself. Which, although it be denominated from men, and most evident in them, yet it extends and shews itself in vegetal and sensible creatures, those incorporeal substances (as shall be specified) and hath a large dominion of sovereignty over them. His pedigree is very ancient, derived from the beginning of the world, as Phædrus contends, and his parentage of such antiquity, that no Poet could ever find it out. Hesiod makes Earth and Chaos to be Love's parents, before the Gods were born.

### How Love Tyrannizeth over Men

Love, or Heroical Melancholy, His Definition, Part Affected

You have heard how this tyrant Love rageth with brute beasts and spirits; now let us consider what passions it causeth amongst men.

Naughty Love, to what dost thou not compel our mortal hearts? How it tickles the hearts of mortal men, I am almost afraid to relate, amazed, and ashamed, it hath wrought such stupend and prodigious effects, such foul offences. Love indeed (I may not deny) first united provinces, built Cities, and by a perpetual generation makes and preserves mankind, propagates the Church; but if it rage, it is no more Love, but burning Lust, a Disease, Phrensy, Madness, Hell. 'Tis death, 'tis an immedicable calamity, 'tis a raging madness; 'tis no virtuous habit this, but a vehement perturbation of the mind, a monster of nature, wit, and art; as Alexis in Athenæus sets it out, manfully rash, womanishly timid, furiously headlong, bitter sweet, a caressing blow, &c. It subverts kingdoms, overthrows cities, towns, families; mars, corrupts, and makes a massacre of men; thunder and lightning, wars, fires, plagues, have not done that mischief to mankind, as this burning lust, this brutish passion. Let Sodom and Gomorrah, Troy, (which Dares Phrygius, and Dictys Cretensis will make good) and I know not how many cities bear record. Helen was not the first petticoat that caused a war, &c., all succeeding ages will subscribe: Joan of Naples in Italy, Frédégunde and Brunhalt in France, all histories are full of these Basilisks. Besides those daily monomachies, murders, effusion of blood, rapes, riot, and immoderate expense, to satisfy their lust, beggary, shame, loss, torture, punishment, disgrace, loathsome diseases that proceed from thence, worse than calentures and pestilent fevers, those often Gouts, Pox, Arthritis, palsies, cramps, Sciatica, convulsions, aches, combustions, &c., which torment the body, that feral melancholy which crucifies the Soul in this life, and everlasting torments in the world to come. . . .

But this love of ours is immoderate, inordinate, and not to be comprehended in any bounds. It will not contain itself within the union of marriage, or apply to one object, but is a wandering, extravagant, a domineering, a boundless, an irrefragable, a destructive passion: sometimes this burning lust rageth after marriage, and then it is properly called Jealousy; sometimes before, and then it is called Heroical Melancholy; it extends sometimes to corrivals, &c., begets rapes, incests, murders: Marcus Antonius embraced his sister Faustina, Caracalla his stepmother Julia, Nero his mother, Caligula his sisters, Cinyras his daughter Myrrha, &c. But it is confined within no terms of blood, years, sex, or whatsoever else. Some furiously rage before they come to discretion or age. Quartilla in Petronius never remembered she was a maid: and the wife of Bath in Chaucer cracks,

> Since I was twelve years old, believe,
> Husbands at Kirk-door had I five.

Aretine's Lucretia sold her Maiden-head a thousand times before she was twenty-four years old, nor were those lacking who could make it whole again. Rahab that harlot began to be a professed quean at ten years of age, and was but fifteen when she hid the spies, as Hugh Broughton proves, to whom Serrarius the Jesuit subscribes. Generally women begin to sprout hair, as they call it, or yearn for a male, as Julius Pollux cites, out of Aristophanes, at fourteen years old, then they do offer themselves, and some plainly rage. Leo Afer saith, that in Africa a man shall scarce find a Maid at fourteen years of age, they are so forward, and many amongst us after they come into the teens, do not live without husbands, but linger [or sicken]. What pranks in this kind the middle age have played, is not to be recorded.

> Though I spoke with an hundred tongues, with an hundred mouths,
>                                                         (VIRGIL)

no tongue can sufficiently declare, every story is full of men and women's insatiable lust, Neros, Heliogabaluses, Bonoses, &c. Cœlius burned for Aufilenus, Quinctius for Aufilena, &c. They neigh after other men's wives (as Jeremiah complaineth) like fed horses, or range like Town Bulls, ravishers of virginity and widowhood, as many of our great ones do. Solomon's wisdom was extinguished in this fire of lust, Samson's strength enervated, piety in Lot's daughters quite forgot, gravity of Priesthood in Eli's sons, reverend old age in the Elders that would violate Susanna, filial duty in Absalom to his stepmothers, brotherly love in Amnon towards his sister. Human, divine laws, precepts, exhortations, fear of God and men, fair, foul means, fame, fortunes, shame, disgrace, honour, cannot oppose, stave off, or withstand the fury of it, love overcomes all, &c. No cord, nor cable, can so forcibly draw, or hold so fast, as Love can do with a twin'd thread. The scorching beams under the Æquinoctial, or extremity of cold within the circle Arctick, where the very Seas are frozen, cold or torrid zone cannot avoid, or expel this heat, fury and rage of mortal men.

> Why vainly seek to flee? Love will pursue you
> Even as far as Scythian Tanais.  (PROPERTIUS)

Of women's unnatural, unsatiable lust, what Country, what Village doth not complain? Mother and daughter sometimes dote on the same man, father and son, master and servant on one woman.

> What have desire and lust unbridled left
> Chaste and inviolate upon the earth?  (EURIPIDES)

What breach of vows and oaths, fury, dotage, madness, might I reckon up! Yet this is more tolerable in youth, and such as are still in their hot blood; but for an old fool to dote, to see an old lecher, what more odious, what can be more absurd? and yet what so common? Who so furious?

> Those who love in age,
> All the more madly rage.  (PLAUTUS)

Some dote then more than ever they did in their youth. How many decrepit, hoary, harsh, writhen, bursten-bellied, crooked, toothless, bald, blear-eyed, impotent, rotten, old men shall you see flickering still in every place! One gets him a young wife, another a courtisan, and when he can scarce lift his leg over a sill, and hath one foot already in Charon's boat, when he hath the trembling in his joints, the gout in his feet, a perpetual rheum in his head, a continuate cough, his sight fails him, thick of hearing, his breath stinks, all his moisture is dried up and gone, may not spit from him, a very child again, that cannot dress himself, or cut his own meat, yet he will be dreaming of, and honing after wenches, what can be more unseemly? Worse it is in women than in men, when she is in her declining years, an old widow, a mother so long since (in Pliny's opinion) she doth very unseemly seek to marry, yet whilst she is so old a crone, a beldam, she can neither see, nor hear, go nor stand, a mere carcass, a witch, and scarce feel; she catterwauls, and must have a stallion, a champion, she must and will marry again, and betroth herself to some young man, that hates to look on her but for her goods, abhors the sight of her, to the prejudice of her good name, her own undoing, grief of friends, and ruin of her children.

But to enlarge or illustrate this power and effects of love is to set a candle in the Sun. It rageth with all sorts and conditions of men, yet is most evident among such as are young and lusty, in the flower of their years, nobly descended, high fed, such as live idly, and at ease; and for that cause (which our Divines call burning lust) this mad and beastly passion, as I have said, is named by our Physicians Heroical Love, and a more honourable title put upon it, Noble Love, as Savanarola styles it, because Noble men and women make a common practice of it, and are so ordinarily affected with it. . . .

## Other Causes of Love-Melancholy

Many such causes may be reckoned up, but they cannot avail, except opportunity be offered of time, place, and those other beautiful objects, or artificial enticements, as kissing, conference, discourse, gestures concur, with such like lascivious provocations. Kornmannus, in his book, The Outline of Love, makes five degrees of lust, out of Lucian belike, which he handles in five Chapters: Sight, Speech, Company, Kissing, Handling. . . .

## Sight

A filthy knave, a deformed quean, a crooked carkass, a maukin, a witch, a rotten post, an hedge-stake, may be so set out, and tricked up, that it shall make as fair a shew, as much enamour as the rest: many a silly fellow is so taken. One calls it the first snare of lust; Bossus, a fatal reed; the greatest bawd, saith Matenesius, and with tears of blood to be deplored. Not that comeliness of clothes is therefore to be condemned, and those usual ornaments: there is a decency and decorum in this, as well as in other things, fit to be used, becoming several persons, and befitting their estates; he is only phantastical, that is not in fashion, and like an old Image in Arras hangings, when a manner of Attire is generally received: but when they are so new-fangled, so unstaid, so prodigious in their Attires, beyond their means and fortunes, unbefitting their age, place, quality, condition, what should we otherwise think of them? Why do they adorn themselves with so many colours of herbs, fictitious flowers, curious needleworks, quaint devices, sweet-smelling odours, with those inestimable riches of precious stones, pearls, rubies, diamonds, emeralds, &c.? Why do they crown themselves with gold and silver, use coronets, and tires of several fashions, deck themselves with pendants, bracelets, ear-rings, chains, girdles, rings, pins, spangles, embroideries, shadows, rabatoes [or turned-down collars], versicolour ribbands? Why do they make such glorious shews with their scarfs, feathers, fans, masks, furs, laces, tiffanies, ruffs, falls, cauls [or hair-nets], cuffs, damasks, velvets, tinsels, cloth of gold, silver, tissue? with colours of heavens, stars, planets? the strength of metals, stones, odours, flowers, birds, beasts, fishes, and whatsoever Africa, Asia, America, sea, land, art, and industry of man can afford? Why do they use and covet such novelty of inventions, such new-fangled tires, and spend such inestimable sums on them? To what end are those crisped, false hairs, painted faces, as the Satirist observes, such a composed gate, not a step awry? Why are they like so many Sybarites, or Nero's Poppæa, Ahasuerus' Concubines, so costly, so long a dressing as Cæsar was marshalling his army, or an hawk in pruning? They take a year to trim and comb themselves; a gardener takes not so much delight and pains in his garden, an horseman to dress his horse, scour his armour, a mariner about his ship, a merchant his shop and shop-book, as they do about their faces, and all those other parts: such setting up with corks, straightening with whalebones, why is it but, as a day-net catcheth Larks, to make young men stoop unto them? Philocharus, a gallant in Aristænetus, advised his friend Polyænus to take heed of such enticements, for it was the sweet sound and motion of his Mistress' spangles and bracelets, the smell of her ointments, that captivated him first. Saith Lucian, to what use are pins, pots, glasses, ointments, irons, combs, bodkins, setting-sticks? Why bestow they all their patrimonies and husbands' yearly revenues on such fooleries? why use they dragons, wasps, snakes, for chains, enamelled jewels on their necks, ears? They had more need some of them be tied in Bedlam with iron chains, have a whip for a fan, and haircloths next to their skins, and instead of wrought smocks, have their cheeks stigmatised with a hot iron; I say, some of our Jezebels instead of painting, if they were well served. But why is all this labour, all this cost, preparation, riding, running, far-fetched, and dear bought stuff? Because forsooth they would be fair and fine, and where nature is defective, supply it by art.

> Who blushes not by nature, doth by art,    (ovid)

and to that purpose they anoint and paint their faces, to make Helen of Hecuba—a distorted dwarf an Europa. To this intent they crush in their feet and bodies, hurt and crucify themselves, some in lax clothes, an hundred yards I think in a gown, a sleeve; and sometimes again so close, as to show their naked shape. Now long tails and trains, and then short, up, down, high, low, thick, thin, &c., now little or no bands, then as big as cart wheels; now loose bodies, then great fardingales and close girt, &c. Why is all this, but with the whore in the Proverbs, to intoxicate some or other? A snare for the eyes, one therefore calls it, and the trap of lust, and sure token, as an Ivy-bush is to a Tavern.

> O Glycere, in that you paint so much,
> Your hair is so bedeckt in order such,
> With rings on fingers, bracelets in your ear,
> Although no prophet, tell I can, I fear.

To be admired, to be gazed on, to circumvent some novice, as many times they do, that instead of a Lady he loves a cap and a feather, instead of a maid that should have true color, a solid body, and plenty of juice, (as Chærea describes his mistress in the Poet), a painted face, a ruff-band, fair and fine linen, a coronet, a flower.

> He thinks that nature which is due to art,    (stroza, filius)

a wrought waistcoat he dotes on, or a pied petticoat, a pure dye instead of a proper woman. For generally, as with rich furred Conies, their cases are far better than their bodies, and like the bark of a Cinnamon tree which is dearer than the whole bulk, their outward accoutrements are far more precious than their inward endowments. 'Tis too commonly so. . . .

### Dalliance and Kisses

To kiss and to be kissed, which amongst other lascivious provocations, is as a burden in a song, and a most forcible battery, as infectious, Xenophon thinks, as the poison of a spider; a great allurement, a fire itself, the prologue of burning lust (as Apuleius adds), lust itself.

> It hath the very quintessence of Venus's nectar.    (HORACE)

A strong assault, that conquers Captains, and those all-commanding forces,

> You conquer with swords, but are conquered with a kiss.    (HEINSIUS)

Aretine's Lucretia, when she would in kindness overcome a suitor of hers, and have her desire of him, took him about the neck, and kissed him again and again, and to that, which she could not otherwise effect, she made him so speedily and willingly condescend. And 'tis a continual assault,

> Beginning ever, ending never,    (PETRONIUS)

always fresh, and ready to begin as at first, a kiss that hath no close, yet is ever new, and hath a fiery touch with it.

> The least touch of her body,
> And you're all ablaze already.    (PETRONIUS)

Especially when they shall be lasciviously given, as he feelingly said, when Fotis gave him a hard kiss, laced in her arms, with lips twisted cunningly.

> So sharply sweet her kiss,
> 'Tis less a kiss than a wound;
> And at my lips, my soul
> Lies in a breathless swound.    (In AULUS GELLIUS)

The soul and all is moved; with the shock of many kisses, saith Petronius, the lips ache, and breaths are mixt breathlessly, and in the stress of mutual embraces the soul is at its last gasp:

———— Hotly cleaving each to each,
And by each other's eager lips transpierced,
Your souls will stray: such lovers may ye be.   (PETRONIUS)

They breathe out their souls and spirits together with their kisses, saith Balthasar Castilio, change hearts and spirits, and mingle affections, as they do kisses, and it is rather a connexion of the mind than of the body. And although these kisses be delightsome and pleasant, Ambrosial kisses, such as Ganymede gave Jupiter, sweeter than Nectar, Balsom, Honey, Love-dropping kisses; for

The Gilliflower, the Rose is not so sweet,
As sugared kisses be when Lovers meet,

yet they leave an irksome impression, like that of Aloes or Gall,

At first ambrose itself was not sweeter,
At last black hellebore was not so bitter.   (CATULLUS)

They are deceitful kisses,

Why dost within thine arms me lap,
And with false kisses me entrap?   (BUCHANAN)

They are destructive, and the more the worse:

A thousand kisses, that were my utter ruin.   (OVID)

They are the bane of these miserable Lovers. There be honest kisses I deny not, the respectful kiss, friendly kisses, modest kisses, Vestal-Virgin kisses, officious and ceremonial kisses, &c. Kissing and embracing are proper gifts of nature to a man: but these are too lascivious kisses,

With arms about my neck enfolded tight,   (OVID)

too continuate, and too violent; they cling like Ivy, close as an Oyster, bill as Doves, meretricious [or courtesan's] kisses, biting of lips, with other tricks, mouth-suckings (saith Lucian), such as the lips can scarce be withdrawn from, with bitings between, and with open mouth caressing the paps, &c., such kisses as she gave to Giton, in Petronius, innumerable kisses not unpleasing to the lad, assaulting the neck, &c. More than kisses, or too homely kisses: as those that he [Apuleius] spake of, having had from her the seven sweet kinds of love, with such other obscenities that vain Lovers use, which are abominable and pernicious. If, as Peter de Ledesmo holds, *every kiss a man gives his wife after marriage be a mortal sin,* or that of Hierome, *whoever is hotly in love with his own wife is an adulterer,* or that of Thomas Secundus, *handling and kissing is a mortal sin,* or that of Durandus, *married folks should abstain from caresses during the entire time when the nuptial deed is interdicted,* what shall become of all such immodest kisses, and obscene actions, the forerunners of brutish lust, if not lust itself? What shall become of them, that often abuse their own wives? But what have I to do with this?

That which I aim at, is to shew you the progress of this burning lust: to epitomize therefore all this which I have hitherto said, with a familiar example out of that elegant Musæus; observe but with me those amorous proceedings of Leander and Hero. They began first to look one on the other with a lascivious look,

> With becks and nods he first began
>   To try the wench's mind,
> With becks and nods and smiles again
>   An answer he did find.
> And in the dark he took her by the hand,
> And wrung it hard, and sighed grievously,
> And kiss'd her too, and woo'd her as he might,
> With Pity me, sweetheart, or else I die,
> And with such words and gestures as there past,
> He won his Mistress' favour at the last.

## Dancing

. . . Yet were it so, that these of which I have hitherto spoken, and such like enticing baits be not sufficient, there be many others, which will of themselves intend this passion of burning lust, amongst which, dancing is none of the least; and it is an engine of such force, I may not omit it. Petrarch calls it the spur of lust, a circle of which the Devil himself is the centre. Many women that use it have come dishonest home, most indifferent, none better. Another terms it, the companion of all filthy delights and enticements, and 'tis not easily told what inconveniences come by it, what scurrile talk, obscene actions, and many times such monstrous gestures, such lascivious motions, such wanton tunes, meretricious kisses, homely embracings,—

> Comes now some Gaditanian with his troop
> Of naughty singers, and the wanton pranks
> Of much applauded dancing girls that stoop
> And rouse desire with undulating flanks—    (JUVENAL)

that it will make the spectators mad. When that Epitomizer of Trogus had to the full described and set out King Ptolemy's riot, as a chief engine and instrument of his overthrow, he adds fiddling and dancing; the King was not a spectator only, but a principal actor himself. A thing nevertheless frequently used, and part of a Gentlewoman's bringing up, to sing, dance, and play on the Lute, or some such instrument, before she can say her Pater Noster, or ten Commandments. 'Tis the next way their Parents think to get them husbands, they are compelled to learn, and by that means, from earliest years their thoughts run to wantonness. 'Tis a great allurement as it is often used, and many are undone by it. Thais, in Lucian, inveigled Lamprias in a dance. Herodias so far pleased Herod, that she made him swear to give her what she would ask, John Baptist's head in a platter. Robert, Duke of Normandy, riding by Falais, spied Arletta a fair maid, as she danced on a green, and was so much enamoured with the object, that he must needs lie with her that night, (of whom he begat William the Conqueror; by the same token she tore her smock down, saying, &c.). Owen Tudor won Queen Katherine's affection in a dance, falling by chance with his head in her lap. Who cannot parallel these stories out of his experience? Speucippus, a noble gallant in that Greek Aristænetus, seeing Panareta a fair young Gentlewoman dancing by accident, was so far in love with her, that for a long time after he could think of nothing but Panareta; he came raving home full of Panareta. Who would not admire her, who would not love her, that should but see her dance as I did? O admirable, O divine Panareta! I have seen old and new Rome, many fair Cities, many proper women, but never any like to Panareta, they are dross, dowdies all to Panareta! O how she danced, how she tript, how she turn'd, with what a grace! happy is that man that shall enjoy her! O most incomparable, only Panareta!— When Xenophon in the Symposium or Banquet, had discoursed of love, and used all the engines that might be devised, to move Socrates amongst the rest, to stir him the more, he shuts up all with a pleasant interlude or dance of Dionysus and Ariadne: First Ariadne dressed like a bride came in and took her place; by and by Dionysus entered, dancing to the Musick. The spectators did all admire the young man's carriage; and Ariadne herself was so much affected with the sight, that she could scarce sit. After a while Dionysus beholding Ariadne, and incensed with love, bowing to her knees, embraced her first, and kissed her with a grace; she embraced him again, and kissed him with like affection, &c., as the dance required: but they that stood by and saw this, did much applaud and commend them both for it. And when Dionysus rose up, he raised her up with him, and many pretty gestures, embraces, kisses, and love compliments passed between them; which when they saw fair Bacchus and beautiful Ariadne so sweetly and so unfeignedly kissing each other, so really embracing, they swore they loved indeed, and were so inflamed with the object, that they began to rouse up themselves, as if they would have flown. At the last when they saw them still so willing embracing, and now ready to go to the Bride-chamber, they were so ravished with it, that they that were unmarried swore they would forthwith marry, and those that were married, called instantly for their horses, and galloped home to their wives. . . .

## Remedies of Love

Let her be such a one throughout, as Lucian deciphers in his Images; as Euphranor of old painted Venus, Aristænetus describes Lais, another Helen, Chariclea, Leucippe, Lucretia, Pandora; let her have a box of beauty to repair herself still, such a one as Venus gave Phaon, when he carried her over the Ford; let her use all helps Art and Nature can yield; be like her, and her, and whom thou wilt, or all these in one; a little sickness, a fever, small pox, wound, scar, loss of an eye, or limb, a violent passion, a distemperature of heat or cold, mars all in an instant, disfigures all; child-bearing, old age, that Tyrant Time, will turn Venus to Erinnys; raging Time, care, rivels her upon a sudden; after she hath been married a small while, and the black ox hath trodden on her toe, she will be so much altered, and wax out of favour, thou wilt not know her. One grows too fat, another too lean, &c., modest Matilda, pretty pleasing Peg, sweet singing Susan, mincing merry Moll, daintly dancing Doll, neat Nancy, jolly Joan, nimble Nell, kissing Kate, bouncing Bess with black eyes, fair Phyllis with fine white hands, fiddling Frances, tall Tib, slender Sib, &c., will quickly lose their grace, grow fulsome, stale, sad, heavy, dull, sour, and all at last out of fashion. Where now the speaking look, the pleasing pleasantries, the blandishing smiles? &c. Those fair sparkling eyes will look dull, her soft coral lips, will be pale, dry, cold, rough, and blue, her skin rugged, that soft and tender surface will be hard and harsh, her whole complexion change in a moment, and as Matilda writ to King John,

> I am not now as when thou saw'st me last,
> That favour soon is vanishèd and past:
> That rosy blush lapt in a lilly vale,
> Now is with morphew overgrown and pale. (DRAYTON)

'Tis so in the rest, their beauty fades as a tree in winter, which Deianira hath elegantly expressed in the Poet:

> And as a tree that in the green wood grows,
> With fruit and leaves, and in the Summer blows,
> In Winter like a stock deformèd shows:
> Our beauty takes his race and journey goes,
> And doth decrease, and lose, and come to nought,
> Admir'd of old, to this by child-birth brought:
> And mother hath bereft me of my grace,
> And crooked old age coming on apace. (SENECA)

To conclude with Chrysostom, When thou seest a fair and beautiful person, (a brave Bonaroba, or well-dress'd woman, a beautiful Donna who'd make your mouth water, a merry girl and one not hard to love)[13] a comely woman, having bright eyes, a merry countenance, a shining lustre in her look, a pleasant grace, wringing thy soul, and increasing thy concupiscence; bethink with thyself that it is but earth thou lovest, a mere excrement, which so vexeth thee, which thou so admirest, and thy ranging soul will be at rest. Take her skin from her face, and thou shalt see [saith Chrysostom] all loathsomeness under it, that beauty is a superficial skin and bones, nerves, sinews: suppose her sick, now rivel'd, hoary headed, hollow cheeked, old: within she is full of filthy fleam, stinking, putrid, excremental stuff: snot and snivel in her nostrils, spittle in her mouth, water in her eyes, what filth in her brains, &c.——— Or take her at her best, and look narrowly upon her in the light, stand nearer her, nearer yet, thou shalt perceive almost as much, and love less; as Cardan well writes, they love less who see sharply, though Scaliger deride him for it: if he see her near, or look exactly at such a posture, whosoever he is, according to the true rules of symmetry and proportion, those I mean of Albert Durer, Lomatius, and Taisnier, examine him of her. If he be a good judge of fine faces, he shall find many faults in Physiognomy, and ill colour, ill form, one side of the face likely bigger than the other, or crooked nose, bad eyes, prominent veins, concavities about the eyes, wrinkles, pimples, red streaks,

---

[13] The words in parentheses are Burton's interjection into the celebrated passage on woman's beauty by the great Christian divine.

freckons [or freckles], hairs, warts, neves [or moles], inequalities, roughness, scabredity, paleness, yellowness, and as many colours as are in a Turkey-cock's neck, many indecorums in their other parts; what you wish is to lop something off, one leers, another frowns, a third gapes, squints, &c. And 'tis true that he [Cardan] saith, seldom shall you find an absolute face without fault, as I have often observed; not in the face alone is this defect or disproportion to be found, but in all the other parts, of body and mind; she is fair indeed, but foolish; pretty, comely, and decent, of a majestical presence, but peradventure imperious, unhonest, self-will'd: she is rich, but deformed; hath a sweet face, but bad carriage, no bringing up, a rude and wanton flirt; a neat body she hath, but it is a nasty quean otherwise, a very slut, of a bad kind. As flowers in a garden have colour some, but no smell, others have a fragrant smell, but are unseemly to the eye; one is unsavoury to the taste as rue, as bitter as wormwood, and yet a most medicinal cordial flower, most acceptable to the stomack; so are men and women, one is well qualified, but of ill proportion, poor and base: a good eye she hath, but a bad hand and foot, a fine leg, bad teeth, a vast body, &c. Examine all parts of body and mind, I advise thee to enquire of all. See her angry, merry, laugh, weep, hot, cold, sick, sullen, dressed, undressed, in all attires, sites, gestures, passions, eat her meals, &c., and in some of these you will surely dislike. . . .

## A Corollary and Conclusion

Last of all: if the party affected shall certainly know this malady to have proceeded from too much fasting, meditation, precise life, contemplation of God's judgments (for the Devil deceives many by such means) in that other extreme he circumvents Melancholy itself, reading some Books, Treatises, hearing rigid Preachers, &c. If he shall perceive that it hath begun first from some great loss, grievous accident, disaster, seeing others in like case, or any such terrible object, let him speedily remove the cause, which to the cure of this disease Navarrus so much commends, turn away his thoughts from the painful subject, by all opposite means, art, and industry, let him ease the soul by all honest recreations, refresh and recreate his distressed soul; let him direct his thoughts, by himself and other of his friends. Let him read no more such tracts or subjects, hear no more such fearful tones, avoid such companies, and by all means open himself, submit himself to the advice of good Physicians, and Divines, which is a relief in uneasiness, as he calls it, hear them speak to whom the Lord hath given the tongue of the learned, to be able to minister a word to him that is weary, whose words are as flagons of wine. Let him not be obstinate, head-strong, peevish, wilful, self-conceited (as in this malady they are) but give ear to good advice, be ruled and persuaded; and no doubt but such good counsel may prove as prosperous to his soul, as the Angel was to Peter, that opened the Iron-gates, loosed his bands, brought him out of prison, and delivered him from bodily thraldom; they may ease his afflicted mind, relieve his wounded soul, and take him out of the jaws of Hell itself. I can say no more, or give better advice to such as are any way distressed in this kind, than what I have given and said. Only take this for a corollary and conclusion, as thou tenderest thine own welfare in this, and all other melancholy, thy good health of body and mind, observe this short Precept, give not way to solitariness and idleness. Be not solitary, be not idle.

HOPE, YE MISERABLE,

YE HAPPY, TAKE HEED

Dost thou wish to be free from doubt? dost desire to escape uncertainty? be penitent, then, while still sound, of wholesome mind; being so, thou art safe, I tell thee, because thou hast been penitent whilst thou mightest have been sinning: so saith Austin.

## Finis

# John Donne
## 1572–1631

John Donne's father, John Donne the Elder, was a merchant, moderately well off, a warden of the Company of Ironmongers. His mother was the daughter of John Heywood, the dramatist. In 1584 Donne was sent to Hart Hall (now Hertford College), Oxford, where he remained until 1587. According to Walton, he then spent three years at Cambridge.

It was during the decade of the 1590s that he wrote most of his Songs and Sonnets, Satires, Elegies, and the *Paradoxes and Problems*. He was admitted as a law student at Thavies Inn in 1591, and then moved to Lincoln's Inn in 1592, though he reported, in a letter to Sir Henry Goodyer, that he was diverted from the study of law "by the worst voluptuousness, which is an Hydroptique immoderate desire of human learning and languages." It was during this period also that he began, and finished, a promising secular career. In 1595 and 1596 he took part in the expeditions to Cadiz and the Azores under Essex and Raleigh, and in 1597 he became secretary to Sir Thomas Egerton, Lord Keeper of the Seal. In 1601 he married Ann, daughter of Sir George More, who promptly saw to it that Donne was dismissed from his post and barred from further political preferment.

Though intensified by his reverses and his burdens (before her death in 1617 Ann bore him twelve children, of whom seven survived), his serious interest in religious matters dated from his earliest years. We know nothing of the religion of his father, but his mother was a devoted Roman Catholic throughout her life. Growing up in a time and in a setting of religious unrest, he was always conscious of this Catholic heritage: he "derived from such a stocke and race," he wrote in the *Pseudo-Martyr*, (sig. ¶ 1) "as, I beleeve no family, (which is not of farre larger extent, and greater branches,) hath endured and suffered more in their persons and fortunes, for obeying the Teachers of Romane Doctrine, then it hath done." Walton tells us that while Donne was still in his twenties he began "seriously to survey and consider the body of Divinity, as it was then controverted betwixt the Reformed and the Roman Church," and that in 1607, when the Dean of Gloucester in-vited him to take orders, Donne declined on the ground that "some irregularities of my life have been so visible" as to bring dishonor to the sacred calling, even though he had made his peace with God "by penitentiall resolutions."

In *Biathanatos* (1608 or earlier) he examined a question that had both theological and personal importance for him—suicide. In *Pseudo-Martyr* (1610) he argued that Catholics in England, by refusing to take the Oath of Allegiance imposed on them after the Gunpowder Plot, were courting only a pseudomartyrdom. *Ignatius His Conclave* (1611) was a bitter and witty satire against the Jesuits. To this period belong also the two *Anniversaries* and most of the devotional poems, with their record of spiritual struggle. The *Essays in Divinity* (1614), combining scrip-tural analysis and fervent prayer, marked the last stage of his prepara-tion and purification. He was now ready to undertake the responsibilities of holy orders, and was ordained in 1615. At Lincoln's Inn he preached before many who must have known him from his student days; at St. Dunstan's one of his parishioners was Isaac Walton; in 1621 he was named Dean of St. Paul's, and had no rival (certainly after the death of Lancelot Andrewes in 1626) as the foremost preacher in England.

The *Devotions upon Emergent Occasions* (1624) trace, with a fever-ish sharpness of detail, the course of what he thought was a fatal illness. His concern spreads outward from his own crisis, as in the famous passage on the tolling of the bells, and as in his wry and occasionally sardonic comments about the world he was leaving, but the work re-mains intensely personal while he gropes for humility and consolation amidst the absurdities of life.

He was not a theologian, not even primarily pastor of his flock, but he proved to be a great preacher. "I have always been more sorry, when I could not preach," he once wrote, "then any could be, that they could not hear me." And Walton described him as "a preacher in earnest, weeping sometimes for his Auditory, sometimes with them: always preaching to himself, like an angel from a cloud, but in none; . . . and all this with a most peculiar grace & an unexpressible addition of comeliness." Donne preached sermons as he offered communion or recited a ceremony of marriage—as though they were sacramental in themselves. Therefore he could insist that sermons must be comely and harmonious because they signify the symmetry of divine order, that the preacher offers a love song when he preaches love of God, that preaching should be grave but never sullen, sordid, barbarous, or negligent, that the preacher, like John the Baptist, is a forerunner of Christ himself.

All the laws and commandments, he preached, may be abridged into two: love God, and love thy neighbor, that is, faith and works. Though grace is not produced by nature, still it can take root only in nature, and we must do good in this world. But Donne permitted himself and his congregation no comforting equivocation: not only must we choose between the two objects of love, this world and the next; not only must we know that this world is all vanity, that the honey of this world must be vomited up, we must know also that "not in any morall integrity, not in keeping the conscience of an honest man, in generall, but in using well the meanes ordain'd by Christ in the Christian Church, am I justified."

Similarly, faith and reason have a common center, teach the same truth, are both autonomous; yet faith is needed to fulfill reason, whereas reason is not to be trusted except in a man regenerate with faith. "The light of nature gives a glimmering before, and it gives a reflexion after faith, but the meridianall noone is in faith." The light of faith may not be tested by the light of reason, lest faith vanish, and extinguish reason too. And Donne would dwell on the mysteries and paradoxes of faith: the mystery of mysteries is God and man in one person; all the mysteries of all the religions in the world are but milk in respect of this bone, but alphabets in respect of this hard style.

Preaching on the twin themes of love and sin, he laments the distance between God and man, and yearns for a union that eludes him. He looks ahead to the time when he will be married to the Lamb, with Christ a husband to his soul. The love of God transcends and supersedes all other love, and human love as an end in itself is a stooping under the burden; yet love is a noble and sovereign affection, love of the creature is an image and a promise of divine love, and he who loves not at all is truly accursed.

In preaching of sin, as he does frequently, Donne is stern yet compassionate. He would startle us out of our lethargy, yet he understands well our doubts, our guilt, our betrayals of ourselves and of others, our poverty of love. He feels the burden both of his own sin and of the sin and suffering of others, and points to the common heritage of our frailty: the original sin that is at the root of sin and is never grubbed up. We must come to know our illness and be purged ("O Lord, be angry with me, . . . if I taste no bitternesse, I have no Physick"); then a radical joy will arise out of the bosom and womb and bowels of the tribulation itself. The heaviest weight to bear is the separation from God, the possibility that God should let my soul fall out of His hand, should let this soul go away as a smoke, a vapor, a bubble. In the end God's mercy is not measured by man's merit; there are many gates to heaven, and every man has a key, and oil to anoint the key. (See, for example, *Sermons,* I, 184–185, 241–242, 295; II, 51, 121, 132, 164–172, 215–216, 261, 324, 362; III, 48–49, 225–238, 293–297, 343, 357–361, 365–368; V, 266–267; X, 103, 112, 116; also *Letters* [1651], 51, 210.)

His style ranges as widely as his mood, his subject, and the occasion, though always beneath the intricate dialectic and the textual analysis the subject is his own inner life. His metaphors are rarely as central to his argument as they are in his poetry, but if anything they are even more varied in source and in tone. Sometimes, as when he probes through nerve and sinew in search of contrition, his language is exalted, his cadences those of Hebrew poetry or the English Bible, his formal rhetoric sweeping, balancing, and controlling his clauses to a resonant climax. Sometimes the effect is quite the opposite, the idiom blunt and homely, conversational. At other times, especially in dealing with the paradoxes of faith or the ironies of our lives, it is his wit which prevails—in sentences that can be either disjointed or tightly knit, in passages terse, knotty, marked by unresolved contradictions. Whatever the style, the sermons are moving because they are also confessional. Haunting them is a sense of man's aloneness. For Donne, especially after his wife's death, this can be repaired only in Christ's arms. Where he is severe, it is because he would burn away his own rusts and deformities. He is himself the sinner, the doubter, the sufferer, and the saved.

## EDITIONS

*Pseudo-Martyr,* 1610.
*Ignatius His Conclave,* 1611; in J. Hayward, *Complete Poetry and Selected Prose,* 1929; facsimile, C. M. Coffin, 1941.

Sermons: Six were published separately, 1622–1627; *Deaths Duell,* 1632; *Six Sermons,* 1634; *LXXX Sermons,* 1640; *Fifty Sermons,* 1649; *XXVI Sermons,* 1660; *The Sermons of John Donne,* ed. by G. R. Potter and E. M. Simpson, 1953–1962; *Sermons on the Psalms and Gospels,* ed. by E. M. Simpson, 1963.

*Devotions Upon Emergent Occasions,* 1624; ed. by John Sparrow, 1923; ed. by William H. Draper, 1925, 1959.

*Poems,* 1633; ed. by H. J. C. Grierson, 1912; ed. by R. E. Bennett, 1942, 1958; *The Divine Poems,* ed. by H. Gardner, 1952.

*Juvenilia: or Certaine Paradoxes and Problems,* 1633; ed. by G. L. Keynes, 1923; facsimile, R. E. Bennett, 1936.

*Biathanatos,* 1646–1647; facsimile, J. W. Hebel, 1930.

*Essayes in Divinity,* 1651; ed. by A. Jessopp, 1855; ed. by E. M. Simpson, 1952.

*Letters to Severall Persons of Honour,* 1651; ed. by C. E. Merrill, 1910. *A Collection of Letters, Made by Sir Tobie Mathews,* 1660. E. Gosse, *The Life and Letters of John Donne,* 1899. E. M. Simpson, *A Study of the Prose Works,* 1924, 1948.

*The Courtier's Library,* ed. by E. M. Simpson, 1930.

*The Works of John Donne,* ed. by Henry Alford, 1839. *Complete Poetry and Selected Prose,* ed. by John Hayward, 1929; ed. by Charles M. Coffin, 1952.

## HISTORICAL AND CRITICAL STUDIES

Izaak Walton, "The Life and Death of Dr. Donne" (with *LXXX Sermons*), 1640; *The Life of John Donne,* "corrected and enlarged," 1658; *Walton's Lives,* ed. by S. B. Carter, 1951.

Samuel Johnson, "The Life of Cowley," *The Lives of the Most Eminent English Poets,* 1779.

Edmund Gosse, *The Life and Letters of John Donne,* 1899.

Mary Paton Ramsey, *Les Doctrines médiévales chez Donne,* 1917; 2d ed., 1924.

Louis I. Bredvold, "The Naturalism of Donne in Relation to Some Renaissance Traditions," *JEGP,* XXII (1923).

Hugh Fausset, *John Donne, A Study in Discord,* 1924.

Louis Bredvold, "The Religious Thought of Donne in Relation to Medieval and Later Traditions," *University of Michigan Studies in Shakespeare, Milton and Donne,* 1925.

John Sparrow, "John Donne and Contemporary Preachers," *Essays and Studies . . . Eng. Assoc.,* XVI (1931).

———, "Donne's Religious Development," *Theology,* XII (1931).

Evelyn M. Simpson, "Donne's 'Paradoxes and Problems,'" John Hayward, "A Note on Donne the Preacher," and Mary Paton Ramsey, "Donne's Relation to Philosophy," in *A Garland for John Donne,* ed. by Theodore Spencer, 1931.

G. C. Haddow, "Donne's Prose," *Queen's Quart.,* XL (1933).

Merritt Y. Hughes, "Kidnapping Donne," and George Potter, "John Donne's

Discovery of Himself," in *University of California Essays in Criticism,* second series, IV (1934).

ADOLPH M. WASILIFSKY, *John Donne the Rhetor: A Study of the Tropes and Figures of the St. Paul Sermons,* 1935.

HERBERT H. UMBACH, "The Rhetoric of Donne's Sermons," *PMLA,* LII (1937).

CHARLES MONROE COFFIN, *John Donne and the New Philosophy,* 1937, 1958.

ITRAT HUSAIN, *The Dogmatic and Mystical Theology of John Donne,* 1938.

DON CAMERON ALLEN, "Donne's Suicides," *MLN,* LVI (1941).

R. E. BENNETT, "Donne's *Letters to Severall Persons of Honour,*" *PMLA,* LVI (1941).

R. W. BATTENHOUSE, "The Grounds of Religious Toleration in the Thought of John Donne," *Church History,* XI (1942).

EVELYN HARDY, *Donne: A Spirit in Conflict,* 1942.

WILLIAM WHITE, *John Donne Since 1900: A Bibliography of Periodical Articles,* 1942.

DON CAMERON ALLEN, "Dean Donne Sets His Text," *ELH,* X (1943).

MICHAEL F. MOLONEY, *John Donne: His Flight from Mediaevalism,* 1944 (*Illinois Studies in Language and Literature,* XXIX).

H. H. UMBACH, "The Merit of Metaphysical Style in Donne's Easter Sermons," *ELH,* XII (1945).

D. R. ROBERTS, "The Death Wish of John Donne," *PMLA,* LXII (1947).

EVELYN M. SIMPSON, *A Study of the Prose Works of John Donne,* 1924; rev., 1948.

H. J. C. GRIERSON, "John Donne and the 'Via Media'" (*MLR,* 1948), *Criticism and Creation,* 1949.

P. N. SIEGEL, "Donne's 'Paradoxes and Problems,'" *PQ,* XXVIII (1949).

J. C. MAXWELL, "Donne and the 'New Philosophy,'" *Durham University Jour.,* XII (1951).

EVELYN M. SIMPSON, "The Biographical Value of Donne's Sermons," *RES,* n. s., II (1951).

HERBERT H. UMBACH, ed., *The Prayers of John Donne . . . with an Essay on Donne's Idea of Prayer,* 1951.

HELEN WHITE, "John Donne and the Psychology of Spiritual Effort," in R. F. Jones, *et al., The Seventeenth Century,* 1951.

GEORGE POTTER, "John Donne: Poet to Priest," *Five Gayley Lectures,* 1954.

CHARLES MONROE COFFIN, "Donne's Divinity," *Kenyon Rev.,* XVI (1954).

AUSTIN WARREN, "The Very Reverend Dr. Donne," *Kenyon Rev.,* XVI (1954).

K. W. GRANSDEN, *John Donne,* 1954.

ROBERTA BRINKLEY, *Coleridge on the Seventeenth Century,* 1955.

ROBERT L. HICKEY, "Donne's Art of Preaching," *Tenn. Studies in Lit,* I (1956).

ROBERT ORNSTEIN, "Donne, Montaigne, and Natural Law," *JEGP,* LV (1956).

LUCILLE STOCK COBB, "John Donne and the Common Law," Dissertation, Washington University, 1956; *Dissertation Abstr.* XVII (1957).

FRANK KERMODE, *John Donne,* 1957.

A. E. MALLOCH, "The Definition of Sin in Donne's *Biathanatos,*" *MLN,* LXXII (1957).

ROBERT L. HICKEY, "Donne's Art of Memory," *Tenn. Studies in Lit.*, III (1958).

GEOFFREY L. KEYNES, *A Bibliography of Dr. John Donne*, 3d ed., 1958.

DENNIS QUINN, "Donne's Christian Eloquence," *ELH*, XXVII (1960). See also "John Donne's Sermons of the Psalms and the Traditions of Biblical Exegesis," Dissertation, University of Wisconsin, 1958; *Dissertation Abstr.*, XVIII (1958).

IAN SOWTON, "Religious Opinion in the Prose Letters of John Donne," *Canadian J. Theol.*, VI (1960).

GEORGE WILLIAMSON, "The Libertine Donne" (*PQ*, 1934), *Seventeenth Century Contexts*, 1960.

IRVING LOWE, "John Donne: The Middle Way. The Reason-Faith Equation in Donne's Sermons," *JHI, XXII* (1961). See also "Both Centers One: The Reason-Faith Equation in Donne's Sermons," Dissertation, Stanford University, 1957; *Dissertation Abstr.*, XVIII (1958).

BETTIE ANNE YOUNG DOEBLER, "Death in the Sermons of John Donne," Dissertation, University of Wisconsin, 1961; *Dissertation Abstr.*, XXI (1961).

SAMUEL E. SPROTT, *The English Debate on Suicide: From Donne to Hume*, 1961.

GEORGE HOWARD BRUCE, "John Donne and the Anglican Faith," Dissertation, University of Rochester, 1962; *Dissertation Abst.*, XXIII (1963).

VICTOR HARRIS, "John Donne and the Theatre," *PQ*, XLI (1962).

DIETRICH A. HILL, "The *Modus Praedicandi* of John Donne: A Rhetorical Analysis of Selected Sermons of John Donne with regard specifically to the Theory of Preaching Which He Put into Practice," Dissertation, University of Illinois, 1962; *Dissertation Abst.*, XXIII (1963).

FRANK KERMODE, ed., *Discussions of John Donne*, 1962.

WILLIAM MUELLER, *John Donne, Preacher*, 1962.

DENNIS B. QUINN, "John Donne's Principles of Biblical Exegesis," *JEGP*, LXI (1962).

WILLIAM J. J. ROONEY, "John Donne's 'Second Prebend Sermon'— A Stylistic Analysis," *Texas Studies in Lit. and Lang.*, IV (1962).

EVELYN M. SIMPSON, "The Literary Value of Donne's Sermons," *The Sermons*, Vol. I (1953); reprinted in Helen Gardner, ed., *John Donne: A Collection of Critical Essays*, 1962.

JOAN WEBBER, "The Prose Styles of John Donne's *Devotions Upon Emergent Occasions*," *Anglia*, LXXIX (1962).

TOSHIHIKO KAWASAKI, "From Southwell to Donne," *Studies in Eng. Lit.* (Tokyo), XXXIX (1963).

THOMAS F. VAN LAAN, "John Donne's *Devotions* and the Jesuit Spiritual Exercises," *SP*, LX (1963).

JOAN WEBBER, *Contrary Music: The Prose Style of John Donne*, 1963. See also "Contrary Music: A Study of the Prose Styles of John Donne," Dissertation, University of Wisconsin, 1960; *Dissertation Abstr.*, XX (1960).

R. C. BALD, "Historical Doubts Respecting Walton's Life of Donne," *Essays in English Literature . . . Presented to A. S. P. Woodhouse,* ed. by F. W. Watt, 1964.

———, "A Latin Version of Donne's Problems," *MP,* LXI (1964).

ROBERT L. HICKEY, "Donne's Delivery," *Tenn. Studies in Lit.,* IX (1964).

ROBERT KRUEGER, "The Publication of John Donne's Sermons, *Rev. of English Studies,* XV (1964).

DAVID NOVARR, "The Two Hands of John Donne," *MP,* LXII (1964).

N. J. C. ANDREASEN, "Donne's *Devotions* and the Psychology of Assent," *MP,* LXII (1965).

SISTER M. GERALDINE, "John Donne and the Mindes Indeavours," *Studies in Eng. Lit., 1500–1900,* V (1965).

EDWARD LE COMTE, *Grace to a Witty Sinner: A Life of Donne,* 1965.

# JUVENILIA: OR CERTAINE PARADOXES AND PROBLEMS

## PARADOXES

I. A Defence of Womens Inconstancy.
II. That Women Ought to Paint.
III. That by Discord Things Increase.
IV. That Good Is More Common than Evill.
V. That All Things Kill Themselves.
VI. That It Is Possible to Find Some Vertue in Some Women.
VII. That Old Men Are More Fantastike than Young.
VIII. That Nature Is Our Worst Guide.
IX. That Only Cowards Dare Dye.
X. That a Wise Man Is Known by Much Laughing.
XI. That the Gifts of the Body Are Better than Those of the Minde.

## I. A Defence of Womens Inconstancy.

That Women are *Inconstant,* I with any man confesse, but that *Inconstancy* is a bad quality, I against any man will maintaine: For every thing as it is one better than another, so is it fuller of *change;* The *Heavens* themselves continually turne, the *Starres* move, the *Moone* changeth; *Fire* whirleth, *Aire* flyeth, *Water* ebbs and flowes, the face of the *Earth* altereth her lookes, *time* staies not; the Colour that is most light will take most dyes: soe in Men, they that have the most reason are the most intolerable in their designes and the darkest or most ignorant, doe seldomest change; therefore Women changing more than Men, have also more *Reason.* . . . *Philosophers* write against them for spite, not desert, that having attained to some knowledge in all other things, in them onely they know nothing, but are meerely ignorant: *Activ* and *Experienced* men raile against them, because they love in their livelesse & decrepit age, when all goodnesse leaves them. These envious *Libellers* ballad against them, because having nothing in themselves able to deserve their love, they maliciously discommend all they cannot obtaine, thinking to make men beleeve they know much, because they are able to dispraise much, and rage against *Inconstancy,* when they were never admitted into so much favour as to bee forsaken. In mine Opinion such Men are happy that Women are *Inconstant,* for so may they chance to be beloved of some excellent Women (when it comes to their turne) out of their *Inconstancy* and mutability though not out of their owne desert. And what reason is there to clog any Woman with one Man, be he never so singular? Women had rather, and it is farre better and more Judiciall to enjoy all the vertues in severall Men, than but some of them in one, for otherwise they lose their taste, like diverse sorts of meate minced together in one dish: and to have all excellencies in one Man (if it were possible) is *Confusion* and *Diversity.* Now who can deny, but such as are obstinately bent to undervalue their worth, are those that have not soule enough to comprehend their excellency, Women being the most excellentest Creatures, in that Man is able to subject all things else, & to grow wise in every thing, but still persists a foole in Woman? The greatest *Scholler* if he once take a wife, is found so unlearned, that he must begin his *Hornebooke,* and all is by *Inconstancy.* To conclude therefore; this name of *Inconstancy,* which hath so much beene poisoned with slaunders, ought to be changed into *variety,* for the which the world is so delightfull, and a Woman for that the most delightfull thing in this world.

## II. That Women Ought to Paint.

*Foulenesse* is *Lothsome:* can that be so which helpes it? who forbids his beloved to gird in her wast? to mend by shooing, her uneven lamenesse? to burnish her teeth? Or to perfume her breath? yet that the *Face* be more precisely regarded, it concernes more: For as open confessing sinners are alwayes punished, but the wary and concealing offendors without witnesse doe it also without punishment; so the secret parts needs the lesse respect; but of the *Face,* discovered to all Examinations and survayes, there is not too nice a Jealousie. Nor doth it onely draw the busy eyes, but it is subject to the divinest touch of all, to *kissing,* the strange and mysticall union of soules. If she should prostitute her selfe to a more unworthy Man than thy selfe, how earnestly and justly wouldst thou exclaime? that for want of this easier and ready way of repairing, to betray her body to ruine & deformity (the tyrannous *Ravishers,* and sodaine *deflourers* of all Women) what a heynous Adultery is it? What thou lovest in her *face* is *colour,* and *painting* gives that, but thou hatest it, not because it is, but because thou knowest it.

Foole, whom Ignorance makes happy, the Starres, the Sunne, the Skye whom thou admirest, alas, have no *colour,* but are faire because they seeme to be coloured: if this seeming will not satisfye thee in her, thou hast good assurance of her *colour,* when thou seest her *lay* it on. If her *face* be *painted* on a Boord or Wall, thou wilt love it, and the Boord, and the Wall: Canst thou loath it then when it speakes, smiles, and kisses, because it is *painted?* Are wee not more delighted with seeing Birds, Fruites, and Beasts *painted* than wee are with naturalls? And doe wee not with pleasure behold the *painted* shape of monsters and Divells, whom true, wee durst not regard? Wee repaire the ruines of our houses, but first cold tempests warnes us of it, and bytes us through it; wee mend the wracke and staines of our Apparell, but first our eyes, and other bodies are offended; but by this providence of Women, this is prevented. If in *kissing* or *breathing* upon her, the *painting* fall off, thou art angry, wilt thou bee so, if it sticke on? Thou didst love her, if thou beginnest to hate her, then 'tis because shee is not *painted.* If thou wilt say now, thou didst hate her before; thou didst hate her and love her together, be constant in something, and love her who shewes her great *love* to thee, in taking this paines to seeme *lovely* to thee.

### III. That by Discord Things Increase.

*Nullos esse Deos inane Cœlum*
*Affirmat Cœlius, probatq; quod se*
*Factum vidit, dum negat hæc, beatum.*

So I assevere this the more boldly, because while I maintaine it, and feele the *Contrary repugnancies* and *adverse fightings* of the *Elements* in my Body, my Body increaseth; and whilst I differ from common opinions by this *Discord,* the number of my *Paradoxes* increaseth. All the rich benefits we can frame to our selves in Concord, is but an *Even* conservation of things, in which *Evennesse* wee can expect no *change,* no *motion;* therefore no *increase* or *augmentation,* which is a *member of Motion. And if this unitie* and *peace* can give *increase* to things, how mightily is *discord* and *warre* to that purpose, which are indeed the onely ordinary *Parents* of *Peace. Discord* is never so barren that it affords no fruit; for the *fall* of one *estate* is at the *worst* the *increaser* of another, because it is as impossible to find a *discommodity* without *advantage,* as to find *Corruption* without *Generation:* But it is the *Nature* and

*Office* of *Concord* to *preserve* onely, which property when it leaves, it differs from it selfe, which is the greatest *discord* of all. All *victories* & *Emperies* gayned by *warre,* and all *Judicial* decidings of doubts in *peace,* I doe claime children of Discord. And who can deny but *Controversies* in *Religion* are growne greater by *discord,* and not the *Controversie,* but *Religion* it selfe: For in a *troubled misery* Men are alwaies more *Religious* than in a *secure peace.* The number of *good* men, the onely charitable nourishers of *Concord,* wee see is thinne, and daily melts and waines; but of *bad discording* it is infinite, & growes hourely. Wee are ascertained of all *Disputable* doubts onely by *arguing* and differing in *Opinion,* and if formall *disputation* (which is but a painted, counterfeit, and dissembled *discord*) can worke us this benefit, what shall not a full and maine *discord* accomplish? Truly me thinkes I owe a *devotion,* yea a *sacrifice* to *discord,* forecasting that *Ball* upon *Ida,* and for all that businesse of *Troy,* whom ruin'd I admire more than *Babylon, Rome,* or *Quinzay,* removed *Corners,* not only fulfilled with her *fame,* but with *Cities* and *Thrones* planted by her *Fugitives.* Lastly, betweene *Cowardice* and *despaire, Valour* is gendred; and so the *Discord* of *Extreames* begets all vertues, but of the *like things* there is no issue without a miracle:

> *Uxor pessima, pessimus maritus*
> *Miror tam malè convenire.*

He wonders that betweene two so *like,* there could bee any *discord,* yet perchance for all this *Discord* there was nere the lesse *Increase.*

## IV. That Good Is More Common than Evill.

I have not beene so pittifully tired with any *vanity,* as with silly *old Mens* exclaiming against these times, and extolling their owne: Alas! they betray themselves, for if the *times* bee *changed,* their manners have changed them. But their senses are to *pleasures,* as *sicke Mens* tastes are to *Liquors;* for indeed no *new thing* is done in the *world;* all things are what, and as they were, and *Good* is as ever it was, more plenteous, and must of necessity bee *more common than Evill,* because it hath this for *nature* and *perfection* to bee *common.* It makes *Love* to all *Natures,* all, all affect it. So that in the *Worlds* early *Infancy,* there was a time when nothing was Evill, but if this *World* shall suffer *dotage* in the extreamest *Crookednesse* thereof, there shall be no time when nothing shall bee *good.* It dares appeare and spread, and glister in the *World,* but *Evill* buries it selfe in night and darkenesse, and is chastised and suppressed when *Good* is cherished and rewarded. And as *Imbroderers, Lapidaries,* and other *Artisans,* can by all things adorne their workes; for by adding better things, the better they shew in *Lush* and in *Eminency;* so *Good* doth not onely prostrate her *Amiablenesse* to all, but refuses no end, no not of her utter contrary *Evill,* that she may bee the more *common* to us. For *Evill manners* are *Parents* of good *Lawes;* and in every *Evill* there is an *excellency,* which (in common speech) we call *good.* For the fashions of *habits,* for our moving in *gestures,* for phrases in our *speech,* wee say they were *good* as long as they were used, that is, as long as they were *common;* and wee eate, wee walke, onely when it is, or seemes *good* to doe so. All *faire,* all *profitable,* all *vertuous,* is *good,* and these three things I thinke embrace all things, but their utter *contraries;* of which also *faire* may be *rich* and *vertuous; poore,* may be *vertuous* and *faire; vitious,* may be *faire* and *rich;* so that *Good* hath this good meanes to be *common,* that some subjects she can possesse entirely; and in subjects poysoned with *Evill,* she can humbly stoope to accompany the *Evill.* And of *Indifferent* things many things are become perfectly good by being *Common,* as *Customes* by use are made binding *Lawes.* But I remember nothing that is therefore *ill,* because it is *Common,* but *Women,* of whom also; *They that are most Common, are the best of that Occupation they professe.*

## V. That All Things Kill Themselves.

To affect, yea to effect their owne *death,* all *living* things are importun'd, not by *Nature* onely which perfects them, but by *Art* and *Education,* which perfects her. *Plants* quickened and inhabited by the most unworthy *soule,* which therefore neither *will* nor *worke,* affect an *end,* a *perfection,* a *death;* this they spend their *spirits* to attaine, this attained, they languish & wither. And by how much more they are by mans *Industry* warm'd, and cherished, and pampered; so much the more early they climbe to this *perfection,* this *death.* And if amongst *Men* not to *defend* be to *kill,* what a haynous *selfe-murther* is it, not to *defend* it selfe. This *defence* because *Beasts* neglect, they kill themselves, because they exceed us in *number, strength,* and a *lawlesse liberty:* yea, of *Horses* and other beasts, they that inherit *most courage* by being bred of *gallantest parents,* and by *Artificiall nursing* are bettered, will runne to their owne *deaths,* neither sollicited by *spurres* which they need not, nor by *honour* which they apprehend not. If then the *valiant* kill himselfe, who can excuse the *coward?* Or how shall *Man* bee free from this, since the *first Man* taught us this, except we cannot kill our selves, because he kill'd us all. Yet lest something should repaire this *Common ruine,* wee daily kill our *bodies* with *surfets,* and our *minds* with *Anguishes.* Of our *powers, remembring* kills our *memory;* Of *Affections, Lusting* our *lust;* Of *vertues, Giving* kills *Liberality.* And if these things kill themselves, they doe it in their best and supreme *perfection:* for after *perfection* immediately followes *excesse,* which changeth the natures & the names, and makes them not the same things. If then the best things kill themselves soonest (for no *Affection* endures, and all things labour to this *perfection*), all travell to their owne *death,* yea the frame of the whole *World,* if it were possible for *God* to be *idle,* yet because it *began,* must *dye.* Then in this *idlenesse* imagined in *God,* what could kill the *World* but it selfe, since *out of it, nothing is?*

## VI. That It Is Possible To Find Some Vertue in Some Women.

I am not of that fear'd *Impudence* that I dare defend *Women,* or pronounce them good; yet wee see *Physitians* allow some *vertue* in every *poyson.* Alas! why should we except *Women?* Since certainly, they are good for *Physicke* at least, so as some *wine* is good for a *feaver.* And though they be the *Occasioners* of many sinnes, they are also the *Punishers* and *Revengers* of the same sinnes: For I have seldome seene one which consumes his *substance* and *body* upon them, escape *diseases,* or *beggery;* and this is their *justice.* And if *suum cuiq; dare,* bee the fulfilling of all *Civill Justice,* they are *most just,* for they deny that which is theirs to no man.

*Tanquam non liceat nulla puella negat.*

And who may doubt of great wisdome, in them, that doth but observe with how much labour and cunning our *Justicers* and other *dispensers* of the *Lawes* study to imbrace them: and how zealously our *Preachers* dehort men from them, only by urging their *subtilties,* and *policies,* and *wisdome,* which are in them? Or who can deny them a good measure of *Fortitude,* if he consider how *valiant men* they have overthrowne, & being themselves overthrown how much, and how patiently they *beare?* And though they be most *intemperate* I care not, for I undertooke to furnish them with *some vertue,* not with all. *Necessity,* which makes even bad things good, prevailes also for them, for wee must say of them, as of some sharpe pinching *Lawes;* If men were free from *infirmities,* they were needlesse. These or none must serve for *reasons,* and it is my great happinesse that *Examples* prove not *rules,* for to confirme this *Opinion,* the World yeelds not *one Example.*

## VII. That Old Men Are More Fantastique than Young.

Who reades this *Paradoxe* but thinks me more *Fantastike* now, than I was yesterday, when I did not thinke thus: And if one day make this sensible change in men, what will the burthen of many yeares? To bee *fantastique* in *young men* is *conceiptfull distemperature,* and a *witty madnesse;* but in *old men,* whose senses are withered, it becomes *naturall,* therefore more full and perfect. For as when we *sleepe* our *fancy* is most strong; so it is in *Age,* which is a *slumber* of the *deepe sleepe of death.* They taxe us of *Inconstancy,* which in themselves *young* they allowed; so that reproving that which they did approove, their *Inconstancy* exceedeth ours, because they have changed *once more* than wee. Yea, they are more idly busied in *conceited Apparell* than wee; for we, when we are *Melancholy,* wee are *blacke;* when *lusty, Greene;* when *forsaken, Tawney;* pleasing our owne *inward* affections, leaving them to others indifferent; but they prescribe *lawes,* and constraine the *Noble,* the *Scholler,* the *Merchant,* and all *Estates* to a certaine *habit.* The *Old men* of our time have changed with patience their owne *bodies,* much of their *lawes,* much of their *languages;* yea their *Religion,* yet they accuse us. To be *amorous* is proper and *naturall* in a *Young man,* but in an *old man* most *fantastike.* And that *ridling humour* of *Jealousie,* which seekes and would not find, which requires and repents his knowledge, is in them most common, yet most *fantastike.* Yea, that which falls never in *young men,* is in them most *fantastike* and *naturall,* that is, *Covetousnesse;* even at their *journeyes end* to make great provision. Is any *habit* of *young men so fantastike,* as in the hottest seasons to be *double-gowned* or *hooded* like our *Elders?* Or seemes it so *ridiculous* to weare *long* haire, as to weare *none.* Truly, as among the *Philosophers,* the *Skeptike,* which *doubts all,* was more contentious, than either the *Dogmatike* which *affirmes,* or *Academike* which *denyes* all; so are these uncertaine *Elders,* which both calls them *fantastike* which follow others *inventions,* and them also which are led by their owne humorous suggestion, more *fantastike* than other.

## VIII. That Nature Is Our Worst Guide.

Shall she be *guide* to all *Creatures*, which is herselfe one? Or if she also have a *guide*, shall any *Creature* have a better guide than wee? The affections of *lust* and *anger*, yea even to *erre* is *Naturall;* shall we follow these? Can she be a good *guide* to us, which hath *corrupted* not us only but herselfe? Was not the *first man* by the desire of *knowledge* corrupted even in the *whitest integrity* of Nature? And did not *Nature* (if *Nature* did anything) infuse into him this desire of *knowledge*, & so this *Corruption* in him, into us? If by *Nature* we shall understand our *essence*, our *definition*, or *reason*, *noblenesse*, then this being alike common to all (the *Idiot* and the *wizard* being equally *reasonable*) why should not all men having equally all one *nature*, follow one course? Or if wee shall understand our *inclinations;* alas! how unable a guide is that which followes the *temperature* of our slimie *bodies?* for we cannot say that we derive our *inclinations*, our *mindes*, or *soules* from our *Parents* by any way: to say that it is *all, from all,* is *errour* in *reason*, for then with the first nothing remaines; or is a *part from all,* is *errour* in *experience*, for then this *part* equally imparted to many children, would like *Gavell-kind lands,* in few generations become nothing; or to say it by *communication*, is *errour* in *Divinity*, for to communicate the *ability* of communicating *whole essence* with any but God, is utterly *blasphemy*. And if thou hit thy *Fathers nature* and *inclination*, hee also had his *Fathers*, and so climbing up, all comes of one man, all have one *nature*, all shall imbrace one course; but that cannot be, therefore our *Complexions* and whole *Bodies*, we inherit from *parents;* our *inclinations* and mindes follow that: For our *mind* is heavy in our *bodies afflictions*, and rejoyceth in our *bodies pleasure:* how then shall this *nature* governe us, that is governed by the worst part of us? *Nature though oft chased away, it will returne;* 'tis true, but those *good motions* and *inspirations* which bee our guides must be *wooed, Courted,* and *welcomed*, or else they abandon us. And that old *Axiome, nihil inuita, &c.* must not be said thou *shalt*, but thou *wilt* doe nothing against *Nature;* so *unwilling* he notes us to curbe our *naturall appetites*. Wee call our *bastards* alwayes our *natural issue*, and wee define a Foole by nothing so ordinary, as by the name of *Naturall*. And that poore knowledge whereby we conceive what *raine* is, what *wind*, what *Thunder*, we call *Metaphysicke, supernaturall;* such *small* things, such *no* things doe we allow to our pliant *Natures* apprehension. Lastly, by following her, wee lose the pleasant, and lawfull *Commodities* of this *life,* for we shall drinke water and eate rootes, and those not sweet and delicate, as now by Mans *art* and *industry* they are made: wee shall lose all the necessities of *societies, lawes, arts,* and *sciences,* which are all the *workemanship* of *Man:* yea, we shall lacke the last *best refuge* of misery *Death;* because *no death is naturall:* for if yee wil not dare to call all *death violent* (though I see not why *sicknesses* be not *violences*) yet *causes* of all *deaths* proceed of the *defect* of that which *nature* made perfect, and would preserve, and therefore all against *nature.*

## IX. That Only Cowards Dare Dye.

*Extreames* are equally remooved from the *meane;* so that headlong *desperatenesse* as much offends true *valour,* as backward *Cowardice:* of which sort I reckon justly all *un-inforced deaths.* When will your *valiant* man dye of necessity? so *Cowards* suffer what cannot be avoided: and to runne into *death unimportun'd,* is to runne into the first condemned desperatenesse. Will he dye when hee is *rich* and *happy?* then by living hee may doe more good: and in *Afflictions* and *miseries, death* is the chosen refuge of *Cowards.*

*Fortiter ille facit, qui misser esse potest.*

But it is taught and practiced among our *Gallants,* that rather than our reputations suffer any *maime,* or wee any *misery,* wee shall offer our *brests* to the *Cannons* mouth, yea to our *swords* points: And this seemes a very *brave* and a very *climbing* (which is a *Cowardly,* earthly, and indeed a very *groveling*) *spirit.* Why doe they *chaine* these slaves to the *Gallyes,* but that they thrust their *deaths,* & would at every loose leape into the *sea?* Why doe they take weapons from *condemned* men, but to barre them of that ease which *Cowards* affect, *a speedy death.* Truly this *life* is a *Tempest* and a *warfare,* and he which *dares dye,* to escape the *Anguish* of it, seemes to me, but so *valiant,* as he which dares *hang* himselfe, left he bee *prest* to the *wars.* I have seene one in that extremity of *Melancholy,* which was then become *Madnesse,* to make his owne *breath* an *Instrument* to stay his breath, and labour to choake himselfe; but alas, hee was *mad.* And we knew another that languished under the *oppression* of a poore *disgrace* so much, that he tooke more *paines to* dye, than would have served to have nourished *life* and *spirit* enough to have out-lived his *disgrace.* What *Foole* will call this *Cowardlinesse,*

*Valour?* Or this *Basenesse, Humility?* And lastly, of these men which dye the *Allegoricall death* of entring into *Religion,* how few are found fit for any shew of *valiancy?* but only a *soft* and *supple metall,* made onely for *Cowardly* solitarinesse.

## X. That a Wise Man Is Knowne by Much Laughing.

*Ride, si sapis, ô puella ride;* If thou beest *wise, laugh:* for since the *powers* of *discourse* and *Reason,* and *laughter* bee equally *proper* unto Man onely, why shall not he be onely most *wise,* which hath most use of *laughing,* as well as he which hath most of *reasoning* and *discoursing?* I alwayes did, and shall understand that *Adage;*

*Per risum multum possis cognoscere stultum,* that by much *laughing* thou maist know there is a *Foole,* not, that the *laughers* are *Fooles,* but that among them there is some *Foole* at whom *wisemen* laugh: which moved *Erasmus* to put this as his first *Argument* in the mouth of his *Folly,* that *she made Beholders laugh:* for *Fooles* are the most laughed at, and laugh the least themselves of any. And *Nature* saw this *faculty* to be so necessary in Man, that she hath beene content that by *more causes* we should be importuned to *laugh,* than to the *exercise* of any other *power;* for things in themselves utterly *contrary,* beget this effect; for we laugh both at *witty* and *absurd* things: At both which sorts I have seene Men *laugh so long* and *so earnestly,* that at last they have *wept* that they could laugh no more. And therefore the *Poët* having described the *quietnesse* of a *wise retired man,* faith in one, what we have said before in many lines; *Quid facit Canius tuus? ridet.* We have received that even the *Extremity* of *laughing,* yea of *weeping* also, hath beene accounted *wisedome:* And that *Democritus* and *Heraclitus,* the *lovers* of these *Extreames,* have beene called *lovers of wisedome.* Now among our *wisemen* I doubt not, but many would bee found who would laugh at *Heraclitus* weeping, none which weepe at *Democritus* laughing. At the hearing of *Comedies* or other *witty* reports, I have noted some, which not understanding *jests,* &c. have yet chosen this as the best meanes to seeme *wise* and *understanding,* to *laugh* when their *Companions laugh;* and I have presumed them *ignorant,* whom I have seene *unmoved.* A *Foole* if he come into a *Princes Court,* and see a *Gay* man leaning at the wall, so *glistering,* and so *painted* in many *colours,* that he is hardly discerned, from one of the *pictures* in the *Arras,* hanging his *body* like an *Iron-bound-chest,* girt in and thicke ribb'd with *broad gold laces,* may (and commonly doth) envy him. But alas; shall a *wiseman,* which may not onely not *envy,* but not *pitty* this *monster,* doe nothing? Yes, let him *laugh.* And if one of these *hot, cholerike firebrands,* which nourish themselves by *quarrelling,* and kindling others, spit upon a *foole* one *sparke* of *disgrace;* Hee, like a *thatcht house* quickly burning, may be *angry;* but the *wise man,* as *cold* as the *Salamander,* may not onely not bee *angry* with him, but not be *sorry* for him; therefore let him *laugh:* so he shall bee knowne a *Man,* because hee can *laugh;* a *wise Man* that hee knowes at *what* to laugh, and a *valiant Man* that he *dares* laugh: for hee that *laughs* is justly reputed more *wise,* than at whom it is *laughed.* And hence I thinke proceeds that which in these later *formall* times I have much noted; that now when our *superstitious Civility* of *manners* is become a mutuall *tickling flattery* of one another, almost every man affecteth an *humour* of *jesting,* and is content to be *deject,* and to *deforme* himselfe, yea become *foole* to no other *end* that I can spye, but to give his *wise Companion* occasion to *laugh;* and to shew themselves in *promptnesse* of *laughing* is so great in *wisemen,* that I thinke all *wisemen,* if any *wisemen* doe read this *Paradox,* will *laugh* both at it and me.

### XI. That the Gifts of the Body Are Better than Those of the Minde.

I say againe, that the *body* makes the *mind,* not that it created it a *minde,* but *formes* it a *good* or a *bad mind;* and this *mind* may be confounded with *soule* without any violence or injustice to *Reason* or *Philosophy:* then the *soule* it seemes is enabled by our *body,* not this by it. My *Body* licenseth my *soule* to *see* the Worlds *beauties* through mine *eyes;* to *heare* pleasant things thorough mine *eares;* and affords it apt *Organs* for the conveiance of all perceiveable *delight.* But alas! my *soule* cannot make any *part,* that is not of it selfe disposed, to *see* or *heare,* though without doubt she be as able & as willing to see *behind* as *before.* Now if my *soule* would say, that shee enables any part to tast these *pleasures,* but is her selfe onely delighted with those rich *sweetnesses* which her *inward eyes* and *senses* apprehend, shee should dissemble; for I see her often solaced with *beauties,* which shee sees through mine *eyes,* and with *musicke* which through mine eares she heares. This *perfection* then my *body* hath, that it can impart to my *mind* all his *pleasures;* and my *mind* hath still many, that shee can neither teach my *indisposed* parts her *faculties,* nor to the best *espoused* parts shew it *beauty* of *Angells, of Musicke,* of *Sphæres,* whereof she boasts the *Contemplation.* Are *Chastity, Temperance,* and *Fortitude* gifts of the *mind?* I appeale to *Physitians* whether the *cause* of these be not in the *body; health* is the gift of the *body,* and *patience* in sicknesse the gift of the *mind:* then who will say that *patience* is as good a happinesse, as *health,* when we must be extreamely *miserable* to purchase this *happinesse.* And for nourishing of *Civill Societies* and *mutuall love* amongst Men, which is our *chiefe end* while wee are men; I say, this *beauty, presence,* and *proportion* of the *body,* hath a more *masculine* force in begetting this *love,* than the *vertues* of the *mind:* for it strikes us *suddenly,* and possesseth us *immoderately;* when to know those *vertues* requires some *Judgment* in him which shall discerne, a *long time* and *conversation* betweene them. And even at *last* how much of our *faith* and *beleefe* shall wee bee driven to bestow, to assure our selves that these *vertues* are not *counterfeited:* for it is the same to *be,* and *seeme vertuous,* because that he that hath *no vertue,* can *dissemble* none, but hee which hath a *little,* may *gild* and *enamell,* yea and transforme much *vice* into *vertue:* For allow a man to be *discreet* and *flexible* to *complaints,* which are great *vertuous gifts* of the *mind,* this *discretion* will be to him the *soule* and *Elixir* of all *vertues,* so that touched with this, even *pride* shall be made *Humility;* and *Cowardice,* honorable and wise *valour.* But in things *seene* there is not this *danger,* for the *body* which thou lovest and esteemest *faire,* is *faire;* certenly if it be not *faire* in *perfection,* yet it is *faire* in the same *degree* that thy *judgment* is good. And in a *faire body,* I doe seldome suspect a *disproportioned mind,* and as seldome hope for a *good,* in a *deformed.* When I see a *goodly house* I assure my selfe of a *worthy possessour,* from a *ruinous weather-beaten building* I turne away, because it seemes either stuff'd with *varlets* as a *prison,* or handled by an *unworthy* and *negligent Tenant,* that so suffers the *waste* thereof. And truly the *gifts* of *Fortune,* which are *riches,* are onely *handmaides,* yea *Pandars* of the *bodies pleasure;* with their service wee nourish *health,* and preserve *dainty,* and wee buy *delights;* so that *vertue* which must bee loved for *it selfe,* and respects no further *end,* is indeed *nothing:* And *riches,* whose *end is* the *good* of the *body,* cannot bee so *perfectly good,* as the *end* whereto it levells.

# THE PROBLEMES

I. Why Have Bastards Best Fortunes?
II. Why Puritans Make Long Sermons?
III. Why Did the Divell Reserve Jesuites till the Latter Dayes?
IV. Why Is There More Variety of Greene, than of Any Other Colour?
V. Why Doe Young Lay-men So Much Study Divinity?
VI. Why Hath the Common Opinion Afforded Women Soules?
VII. Why Are the Fairest Falsest?
VIII. Why *Venus* Starre Only Doth Cast a Shadow?
IX. Why Is *Venus* Starre Multinominous, Called Both *Hesperus* and *Vesper?*
X. Why Are New Officers Least Oppressing?

## I. Why Have Bastards Best Fortune?

As *Nature* (which is *lawes patterne*) having denied women *Constancy* to *one*, hath provided them with *cunning* to allure *many*, and so *Bastards de jure* should have better *wits* and *experience*. But besides that by *experience* wee see many *fooles* amongst them; we should take from them one of their chiefest helpes to *preferment*, and we should deny them to be *fooles;* and (that which is onely left) that *Women* chuse *worthier* men than their *husbands* is false *de facto*, either then it must be that the *Church* having removed them from all place in the *publike service* of *God*, they have better meanes than others to bee *wicked*, and so *fortunate;* Or else because the two *greatest powers* in this *world*, the *Divell* and *Princes* concurre to their *greatnesse;* the one giving *bastardye*, the other *legitimation*: As *nature* frames and conserves great *bodies* of *Contraries*. Or the cause is, because they abound most at *Court*, which is the *forge* where *fortunes* are made; or at least the *shop* where they be *sold*.

## II. Why Puritanes Make Long Sermons?

It needs not for *perspicuousnesse*, for God knowes they are plaine enough: nor doe all of them use *Sem-briefe-Accents* for some of them have *Crotchets* enough. It may be they intend not to rise like *glorious Tapers* and *Torches*, but like *thinne-wretched-sicke-watching-Candles* which *languish* and are in a divine *Consumption* from the first minute, yea in their *snuffe*, and *stinke* when others are in their more profitable *glory*. I have thought sometimes that out of *Conscience*, they allow *long measure* to *course Ware.* And sometimes that *usurping* in that place a *liberty* to *speake freely* of *Kings,* they would *raigne* as long as they could. But now I thinke they doe it out of a *zealous Imagination,* that, *It is their duty to preach on till their Auditory wake.*

### III. Why Did the Divell Reserve Jesuites till These Latter Dayes?

Did hee know that our *Age* would deny the *Divels possessing,* and therefore provided by these to *possesse* Men and kingdomes? Or to end the *disputation* of *Schoolemen,* why the *Divell* could not make *lice* in *Ægypt;* and whether those things he *presented,* there might be *true,* hath he sent us a *true* and *reall plague,* worse than those *ten?* Or in *ostentation* of the *greatnesse* of his *Kingdome,* which even *division* cannot *shake,* doth he send us these which *disagree* with all the rest? Or knowing that our *times* should discover the *Indies,* and abolish their *Idolatry,* doth he send these to give them *another* for it? Or peradventure they have beene in the *Roman Church* these *thousand yeares* though wee have called them by *other names.*

### IV. Why Is There More Variety of Greene, than of Other Colours?

It is because it is the figure of *Youth,* wherein *Nature* would provide as many *Greene,* as *Youth* hath *Affections;* and so present a *Sea-greene* for *profuse wafters* in *voyages;* a *Grasse-greene* for sudden *new men enobled* from *Grasiers;* and a *Goose-greene* for such *Polititians* as pretend to preserve the *Capitoll.* Or else *Prophetically* foreseeing an *Age* wherein they shall all *hunt.* And for such as *misse-demeane* themselves a *willow-greene;* For *Magistrates* must aswell have *Fasces* borne before them to *chastize* the *small* offences, as *Secures* to *cut off* the *great.*

### V. Why Doe Young Lay-men So Much Studie Divinity?

Is it because others tending busily *Churches preferment* neglect *studie?* Or had the *Church* of *Rome* shut up all our wayes, till the *Lutherans* broke downe their *uttermost stubborne dores,* and the *Calvinists* picked their *inwardest* and *subtlest lockes?* Surely the *Divell* cannot bee such a *Foole* to hope that hee shall make this study *contemptible,* by making it *common.* Nor that as the *Dwellers* by the river *Origus* are said (by drawing infinite *ditches* to sprinkle their *barren Countrey*) to have exhausted and intercepted their *maine channell,* and so lost their more profitable course to the *Sea;* so wee, by providing every *ones selfe, divinity* enough for his *owne use,* should neglect our *Teachers* and *Fathers*. Hee cannot hope for better *heresies* than he hath had, nor was his *Kingdome* ever so much advanced by *debating Religion* (though with some *aspersions of Error*) as by a *Dull* and *stupid security,* in which many *grosse things* are swallowed. Possible out of such an *Ambition* as we have now, to speake *plainely* and *fellow-like* with *Lords* and *Kings,* wee thinke also to acquaint our selves with *Gods secrets:* Or perchance when wee study it by *mingling humane* respects, *It is not Divinity*.

## VI. Why Hath the Common Opinion Afforded Women Soules?

It is agreed that wee have not so much from them as any *part* of either our *mortall soules* of *sense,* or *growth;* and wee deny *soules* to others equall to them in all but in *speech* for which they are beholding to their *bodily instruments:* For perchance an *Oxes* heart, or a *Goates,* or a *Foxes,* or a *Serpents* would speake just so, if it were in the *breast,* and could move that *tongue and jawes*. Have they so many *advantages* and *meanes* to hurt us (for, ever their *loving* destroyed us) that we dare not *displease* them, but give them what they will? And so when some call them *Angells,* some *Goddesses,* and the *Palpulian Heretikes* make them *Bishops,* wee descend so much with the streame, to allow them *soules?* Or doe we somewhat (in this dignifying of them) flatter *Princes* and *great personages* that are so much *governed* by them? Or doe wee in that *easinesse,* and *prodigality,* wherein wee daily lose our owne *soules* to wee care not whom, so labour to perswade our selves, that sith a *woman* hath a *soule,* a *soule* is no *great matter?* Or doe we lend them *soules* but for *use,* since they for our *sakes,* give their *soules* againe, and their *bodies* to boote? Or perchance because the *Divell* (who is all *soule*) doth most *mischiefe,* and for *convenience* and *proportion,* because they would come *neerer* him, wee allow them some *soules,* and so as the *Romans* naturalized some *Provinces* in revenge, and made them *Romans,* onely for the *burthen* of the *Commonwealth;* so wee have given *women* soules only to make them capable of *Damnation?*

## VII. Why Are the Fairest, Falsest?

I meane not of false *Alchimy Beauty,* for then the *question* should be inverted, *why are the Falsest, Fairest?* It is not only because they are *much solicited* and *sought* for, so is *gold*, yet it is not so *common;* and this *suite* to them, should teach them their *value*, and make them more *reserved*. Nor is it because the *delicatest blood* hath the *best spirits*, for what is that to the flesh? perchance such *Constitutions* have the *best wits*, and there is no *proportionable subject*, for *Womens wit*, but *deceipt?* doth the *mind* so follow the *temperature* of the *body*, that because those *Complexions* are aptest to change, the *mind* is therefore so? Or as *Bells* of the *purest metall* retaine their *tinckling* and *sound* longest; so the *memory* of the last *pleasure* lasts longer in these, and disposeth them to the next. But sure it is not in the *Complexion*, for those that doe but *thinke* themselves *faire*, are presently inclined to this *multiplicity* of *loves*, which being but *faire in conceipt* are *false in deed:* and so perchance when they are *borne to this beauty*, or have *made* it, or have *dream'd* it, they easily beleeve all *Addresses* and *Applications* of every *Man*, out of a *sense* of their owne *worthinesse* to bee directed to them, which others *lesse worthy* in their owne throughts apprehend not, or discredit. But I thinke the *true reason* is, that being like *Gold* in many properties (as that *all snatch* at them, but the *worst* possesse them, that they care not how *deepe* we dig for them, and that by the *Law* of *Nature*, *Occupandi conceditur*) they would be like also in this, that as *Gold* to make it selfe of use admits, *Allay*, so they, that they may be *tractable*, *mutable*, and *currant*, have to their allay *Falshood*.

## VIII. Why Venus-Starre Onely Doth Cast a Shadow?

Is it because it is *neerer* the *earth?* But they whose *profession* it is to see that nothing be done in *heaven* without their *consent* (as Re- saies in himselfe of *Astrologers*) have bid *Mercury* to bee *neerer*. Is it because the *workes* of *Venus* want *shadowing*, *covering*, and *disguising?* But those of *Mercury* needs it more; for *Eloquence*, his *Occupation*, is all *shadow* and *colours;* let our *life* be a *sea*, and then our *reason* and *Even passions* are *wind* enough to carry us whether we should go, but *Eloquence* is a *storme* and *tempest* that miscarries: and who doubts that *Eloquence* which must perswade *people* to take a *yoke* of *soveraignty* (and then beg and make *lawes* to tye them *faster*, and then give money to the *Invention*, repair and strengthen it) needs more *shadowes* and *colouring*, than to perswade any Man or Woman to that which is *naturall*. And *Venus markets* are so *naturall*, that when we solicite the best way (which is by *marriage*) our perswasions worke not so much to *draw* a woman *to us,* as against her *Nature* to draw her *from all other* besides. And so when we goe against *Nature,* and from *Venus-worke* (for *marriage* is *chastity*) we need *shadowes* and *colours,* but not else. In *Seneca's* time it was a course, an *un-romane* and a *contemptible* thing even in a *Matrone,* not to have had a *love* beside her *husband,* which though the *Law* required not at their hands, yet they did it *zealously* out of the counsell of *Custome* and *fashion,* which was *venery* of *Supererogation:*

*Et te spectator plusquam delectat Adulter,* saith *Martial:* And *Horace,* because many *lights* would not shew him enough, created many *images* of the same *Object* by *wainscoting* his *chamber* with *looking-glasses:* so that *Venus* flyes not light, so much as *Mercury,* who creeping into our *understanding,* our *darkenesse* would bee defeated, if hee were perceived. Then either this *shaddow* confesseth that same darke *Melancholy Repentance,* which accompanies; or that so *violent fires,* needes some *shadowy refreshing,* and *Intermission.* Or else *light* signifying both *day* and *youth,* and *shadow* both *night* and *Age,* shee pronounceth by this that shee professeth both all *persons* and *times.*

### IX. Why Is Venus-Starre Multi-nominous, Called Both Hesperus and Vesper?

The *Moone* hath as many *names,* but not as she is a *starre,* but as she hath divers *governments;* but *Venus* is *multinominous* to give example to her *prostitute disciples,* who so often, either to *renew* or *refresh* themselves towards *lovers, or to disguise* themselves from *Magistrates,* are to take *new names.* It may be she takes *new names* after her many *functions,* for as she is *Supreme Monarch* of all *Sunnes* at large (which is *lust*) so is she joyned in commission with all *Mythologicks,* with *Juno, Diana,* and all others for *Marriage.* It may bee because of the divers *names* to her selfe, for her *Affections* have more *names* than any *vice: scilicet; Pollution, Fornication, Adultery, Lay-Incest, Church-Incest, Rape, Sodomy, Mastupration, Masturbation* and a thousand others. Perchance her divers *names* shewed her appliablenesse to divers men, for *Neptune* distilled and wet her in *Love,* the *Sunne* warmes and melts her, *Mercury* perswaded and swore her, *Jupiters* authority secur'd, and *Vulcan* hammer'd her. As *Hesperus* she presents you with her *bosum utile,* because it is *wholesomest* in the *morning:* As *Vesper* with her *bonum delectabile,* because it is *pleasantest* in the *Evening.* And because *industri-*

58    *John Donne*

*ous* men rise and indure with the *Sunne* in their *civill* businesses, this *starre* calls them up a little before, and remembers them againe a little after for her businesse; for certainely;

*Venit Hesperus, ite capellæ:*

was spoken to *lovers* in the persons of *Goates*.

## X. Why Are New Officers Least Oppressing?

Must the old Proverbe, that *Old dogges bite sorest,* bee true in all kind of *dogges?* Me thinkes the fresh *memory* they have of the *mony* they parted with for the *place,* should hasten them for the *re-imbursing:* And perchance they do but seeme easier to their *suitors;* who (as all other *Patients*) do account all change of paine, easie. But if it bee so, it is either because the sodaine *sense* and *contentment* of the *honour* of the *place,* retards and remits the *rage* of their *profits,* and so having stayed their stomackes, they can forbeare the second *course* a while: Or having overcome the *steepest* part of the *bill,* and clambered above *Competitions* and *Oppositions* they dare loyter, and take breath: Perchance being come from *places,* where they tasted *no gaine,* a *little* seemes *much* to them at first, for it is *long before a Christian conscience overtakes, or strayes into an Officers heart.* It may be that out of the *generall disease* of all men not to love the *memory* of a *predecessor,* they seeke to disgrace them by such *easinesse,* and make good *first Impressions,* that so having drawne much *water* to their *Mill,* they may afterwards *grind* at ease: For if from the rules of good *Horse-manship,* they thought it wholesome to *jet* out in a moderate *pace,* they should also take up towards their *journey's* end; not to mend their *pace* continually, and *gallop* to their *Innesdoore,* the *Grave;* except perchance their *conscience* at that time so touch them; that they thinke it an *Injury* and *damage* both to him that must *sell,* and to him that must *buy* the *Office* after their *death;* and a kind of *dilapidation* if they by continuing *honest* should discredit the *place,* and bring it to a *lower-rent,* or *under-value.*

**Finis**

# IGNATIUS HIS CONCLAVE

. . . In the twinckling of an eye, I saw all the roomes in Hell open to my sight. And by the benefit of certain spectacles, I know not of what making, but, I thinke, of the same, by which *Gregory* the great, and *Beda* did discerne so distinctly the soules of their friends, when they were discharged from their bodies, and sometimes the soules of such men as they knew not by sight, and of some that were never in the world, and yet they could distinguish them flying into Heaven, or conversing with living men, I saw all the channels in the bowels of the Earth; and all the inhabitants of all nations, and of all ages were suddenly made familiar to me. I thinke truely, *Robert Aquinas* when he tooke *Christs* long Oration, as he hung upon the Crosse, did use some such instrument as this, but applied to the eare: And so I thinke did he, which dedicated to *Adrian 6,* that Sermon which *Christ* made in prayse of his father *Joseph:* for else how did they heare that, which none but they ever heard? As for the *Suburbs* of Hel (I meane both *Limbo* and *Purgatory*) I must confesse I passed them over so negligently, that I saw them not: and I was hungerly caried, to find new places, never discovered before. For *Purgatory* did not seeme worthy to me of much diligence, because it may seeme already to have beene beleeved by some persons, in some corners of the *Romane Church,* for about 50 yeares; that is, ever since the Councell of *Trent* had a minde to fulfill the prophecies of *Homer, Virgil,* and the other *Patriarkes* of the *Papists;* and beeing not satisfied with making one *Transubstantiation,* purposed to bring in another: which is, to change *fables* into *Articles* of faith. Proceeding therefore to more inward places, I saw a secret place, where there were not many, beside *Lucifer* himselfe; to which, onely they had title, which had so attempted any innovation in this life, that they gave an affront to all antiquitie, and induced doubts, and anxieties, and scruples, and after, a libertie of beleeving what they would; at length established opinions, directly contrary to all established before. Of which place in *Hell, Lucifer* affoarded us heretofore some little knowledge, when more than 200 yeares since, in an *Epistle* written to the *Cardinall S. Sexti,* hee promised him a roome *in his palace, in the remotest part of his eternall Chaos,* which I take to bee this place. And here Pope *Boniface 3,* and *Mahomet,* seemed to contend about the highest roome. Hee gloried of having expelled an old Religion, and *Mahomet* of having brought in a new: each of them a great deluge to the world. But it is to be feared, that *Mahomet* will faile therein, both because hee attributed something to the old *Testament,* and because he used *Sergius* as his fellow-bishop, in making the *Alcoran;* whereas it was evident to the supreme Judge *Lucifer,* (for how could he be ignorant of that, which himselfe had put into the Popes mind?) that *Boniface* had not onely neglected, but destroyed the policy of the State of *Israel,* established in the old *Testament,* when he prepared *Popes* a way, to tread upon the neckes of *Princes,* but that he also abstained from all Example and Coadjutor, when he took upon him that newe Name, which *Gregorie* himselfe (a Pope neither very foolish, nor over-modest) ever abhord. Besides that, every day affoords new Advocates to *Boniface* his side. For since the *Franciscans* were almost worne out (of whome their General, *Francis,* had seene 6000 souldiers in one army, that is, in one chapter) which, because they were then but fresh souldiers, he saw assisted with 1800 Divels, the *Jesuits* have much recompenced those decayes and damages, who sometimes have maintained in their Tents 200000 schollers. For though the Order of *Benedict* have ever bene so fruitfull, that they say of it, *That all the new Orders, which in later times have broken out, are but little springs, or drops, and that Order the Ocean, which hath sent out 52 Popes,* 200 *Cardinals,* 1600 *Archbishops,* 4000 *Bishops, and* 50000 *Saints approved by the Church,* and therefore it cannot be denied, but that *Boniface* his part is much releeved by that Order; yet if they be compared to the *Jesuits,* or to the weake and unperfect Types of them, the *Franciscans,* it is no great matter that they have done. Though therefore they esteeme *Mahomet* worthy of the name of an *Innovator,* & therein, perchance not much inferiour to *Boniface,* yet since his time, to ours, almost all which have followed his sect, have lived barren in an unanimity, and idle concord, and cannot boast that they have produced any new matter: whereas *Boniface* his successors, awakened by him, have ever beene fruitfull in bringing forth new sinnes, and new pardons, and idolatries, and King-killings. Though therefore it may religiously, and piously be beleeved, that *Turkes,* as well as *Papists,* come daily in troupes to the ordinary and common places of *Hell;* yet certainly to this more honourable roome, reserved for especiall *Innovators,* the *Papists* have more frequent accesse; and therefore *Mahomet* is out of hope to prevaile, and must imitate the *Christian Emperours,* and be content to sit (as yet hee doth) at the Popes feet. Now to this place, not onely such endeavour to come, as have innovated in matters, directly concerning the soule, but they also which have done so, either in the Arts, or in conversation, or in any thing which exerciseth the faculties of the soule, and may so provoke to quarrel-some and brawling controversies: For so the truth be lost, it is no matter how. But the gates are seldome opened, nor scarce oftener then once in an Age. But my destiny favoured mee so much, that I was present then, and saw all the pretenders, and all that affected an entrance, and *Lucifer* himselfe, who then came out into the outward chamber, to heare them pleade their owne Causes. As soone as the doore creekt, I spied a cer-taine *Mathematitian,* which till then had bene busied to finde, to deride, to detrude *Ptolomey;* and now with an erect countenance, and setled pace, came to the gates, and with hands and feet (scarce respecting *Lucifer* himselfe) beat the dores, and cried; "Are these shut against me, to whom all the Heavens were ever open, who was a Soule to the Earth, and gave it motion?"

By this I knew it was *Copernicus.* For though I had never heard ill of his life, and therefore might wonder to find him there; yet when I remembered, that the *Papists* have extended the name, & the punish-ment of Heresie, almost to every thing, and that as yet I used *Gregories* and *Bedes* spectacles, by which one saw *Origen, who* deserved so well of the *Christian Church, burning in Hell,* I doubted no longer, but assured my selfe that it was *Copernicus* which I saw. To whome *Lucifer* sayd; "Who are you? For though even by this boldnesse you seeme worthy to enter, and have attempted a new faction even in *Hell,* yet you must first satisfie those which stand about you, and which expect the same fortune as you do." "Except, *O Lucifer,"* answered *Copernicus,* "I thought thee of the race of the starre *Lucifer,* with which I am so well acquainted, I should not vouchsafe thee this discourse. I am he, which pitying thee who wert thrust into the Center of the world, raysed both thee, and thy prison, the Earth, up into the Heavens; so as by my meanes *God* doth not enjoy his revenge upon thee. The Sunne, which was an officious spy, and a betrayer of faults, and so thine enemy, I have appointed to go into the lowest part of the world. Shall these gates be open to such as have innovated in small matters? and shall they be shut against me, who have turned the whole frame of the world, and am thereby almost a new Creator?" More then this he spoke not. *Lucifer* stuck in a medi-tation. For what should he do? It seemed unjust to deny entry to him which had deserved so well, and dangerous to graunt it, to one of so great ambitions, and undertakings: nor did he thinke that himselfe had attempted greater matters before his fall. Something he had which he might have conveniently opposed, but he was loath to utter it, least he should confesse his feare. But *Ignatius Layola* which was got neere his chaire, a subtile fellow, and so indued with the Divell, that he was able to tempt, and not onely that, but (as they say) even to possesse the Divell, apprehended this perplexity in *Lucifer*. And making himselfe sure of his owne entrance, and knowing well, that many thousands of his family aspired to that place, he opposed himselfe against all others. He was content they should bee damned, but not that they should governe. And though when hee died he was utterly ignorant in all great learning, and knew not so much as *Ptolomeys,* or *Copernicus* name, but might have beene perswaded, that the words *Almagest, Zenith,* and *Nadir,* were Saints names, and fit to bee put into the *Litanie,* and *Ora pro nobis* joyned to them; yet after hee had spent some time in hell, he had learnt somewhat of his *Jesuites,* which daily came thither. And whilst he staied at the threshold of *Hell;* that is, from the time when he delivered himselfe over to the Popes will, hee tooke a little taste of learning. Thus furnished, thus hee undertakes *Copernicus.* "Do you thinke to winne our *Lucifer* to your part, by allowing him the honour of being of the race of that starre? who was not onely made before all the starres, but being glutted with the glory of shining there, trans- ferred his dwelling and Colonies unto this Monarchy, and thereby gave our Order a noble example, to spy, to invade, and to possesse forraine kingdomes. Can our *Lucifer,* or his followers have any honour from that starre *Lucifer,* which is but *Venus?* whose face how much wee scorne, appeares by this, that, for the most part we use her aversly and preposterously. Rather let our Lucifer glory in *Lucifer* the *Calaritan Bishop;* not therefore because he is placed amongst Heretiques, onely for affirming the propagation of the soule; but especially for this, that he was the first that opposed the dignity of Princes, and imprinted the names of *Antichrist, Judas,* and other stigmatique markes upon the *Emperour;* But for you, what new thing have you invented, by which our *Lucifer* gets anything? What cares hee whether the earth travell, or stand still? Hath your raising up of the earth into heaven, brought men to that confidence, that they build new towers or threaten God againe? Or do they out of this motion of the earth conclude, that there is no hell, or deny the punishment of sin? Do not men beleeve? do they not live just, as they did before? Besides, this detracts from the dignity of your learning, and derogates from your right and title of comming to this place, that those opinions of yours may very well be true. If therfore any man have honour or title to this place in this matter, it belongs wholly to our *Clavius,* who opposed himselfe opportunely against you, and the truth, which at that time was creeping into every mans minde. Hee onely can be called the Author of all contentions, and schoole-combats in this cause; and no greater profit can bee hoped for heerein, but that for such brabbles, more necessarie matters bee neglected. And yet not onely for this is our *Clavius* to bee *honoured,* but for the great paines also which hee tooke in the *Gregorian Calender,* by which both the peace of the Church, & Civill businesses have beene egregiously troubled: nor hath heaven it selfe escaped his violence, but hath ever since obeied his apointments: so that *S. Stephen, John Baptist,* & all the rest, which have bin commanded to worke miracles at certain appointed daies, where their Reliques are preserved, do not now attend till the day come, as they were accustomed, but are awaked ten daies sooner, and constrained by him to come downe from heaven to do that businesse; But your inventions can scarce bee called yours, since long before you, *Heraclides, Ecphantus,* & *Aristarchus* thrust them into the world: who notwithstanding content themselves with lower roomes amongst the other Philosophers, & aspire not to this place, reserved onely for *Antichristian Heroes:* neither do you agree so wel amongst your-selves, as that you can be said to have made a *Sect,* since, as you have perverted and changed the order and *Scheme* of others: so *Tycho Brachy* hath done by yours, and others by his. Let therefore this little *Mathe-matitian* (dread Emperour) withdraw himselfe to his owne company. And if heereafter the fathers of our Order can draw a *Cathedrall Decree* from the Pope, by which it may be defined as a matter of faith: *That the earth doth not move;* & an *Anathema* inflicted upon all which hold the contrary: then perchance both the Pope which shall decree that, and *Copernicus* his followers, (if they be Papists) may have the dignity of this place." *Lucifer* signified his assent; and *Copernicus,* without mutter-ing a word, was as quiet, as he thinks the sunne, when he which stood next him, entred into his place. . . .

    . . . I came backe againe, to spie (if the gates were stil open) with what affection *Ignatius,* and they who were in auncient possession of that place, behaved themselves towardes one an other. And I found him yet in the porch, and there beginning a new contention: for having presently cast his eyes to the principall place, next to *Lucifers* owne *Throne,* and finding it possest, he stopt *Lucifer,* and asked him, who it was that sate there. It was answered, that it was *Pope Boniface;* to whom, as a principall Innovator, for having first chalenged the name of *Universall Bishop,* that honour was affoorded. Is he an Innovator thundred *Ignatius?* shall I suffer this, when all my Disciples have laboured all this while to prove to the world, that all the *Popes* before his time did use that name? And that *Gregory* did not reprehend the *Patriarch John* for taking to himselfe an Antichristian name, but for usurping a name which was due to none but the *Pope.* And could it be fit for you, *Lucifer,* (who in this were either unmindfull of the *Romane Church,* or else too weake and incapable of her secrets and mysteries) to give way to any sentence in *Hell,* which (though it were according to truth,) yet differed from the Jesuites *Oracles?* With this *Ignatius* flyes upwardes, and rushes upon *Boniface,* and throwes him out of his Seate: And *Lucifer* went up with him as fast, and gave him assistance, least, if hee should forsake him, his owne seate might bee endangered. And I returned to my body; which

> As a flower wet with last nights dew, and then
> Warm'd with the new Sunne, doth shake of agen
> All drowsinesse, and raise his trembling Crowne,
> Which crookedly did languish, and stoope downe
> To kisse the earth, and panted now to finde
> Those beames return'd, which had not long time shin'd,

was with this returne of my soule sufficiently refreshed. And when I had seene all this, and considered how fitly and proportionally *Rome* & *Hell* answered one another, after I had seene a Jesuit turne the *Pope* out of his *Chaire* in *Hell,* I suspected that that *Order* would attempt as much at *Rome.*

# ESSAYES IN DIVINITY

. . . Only to paraphrase the History of this Delivery, without amplifying, were furniture and food enough for a meditation of the best perseverence, and appetite, and digestion; yea, the least word in the History would serve a long rumination. If this be in the bark, what is in the tree? If in the superficiall grass, the letter; what treasure is there in the hearty and inward Mine, the Mistick and retired sense? Dig a little deeper, O my poor lazy soul, and thou shalt see that thou, and all mankind are delivered from an Egypt; and more miraculously then these. For, Almightiness is so naturall to God, that nothing done by his power, is very properly miracles, which is above all Nature. But God delivered us, by that which is most contrary to him; by being *impotent;* by being *sin;* by being *Dead.* That great *Pharoah,* whose Egypt all the world is by usurpation, (for *Pharoah* is but *exemptus* and *privilegiatus;* and that Name, (I hope not the Nature) is strai'd into our word *Baro*) whom God hath made *Prince of the air,* and *Prince of Darkness;* that is, of all light and aiery illusions, and of all sad and earnest wickedness, of Vanity, and of sin; had made us fetch our own straw, that is, painfully seek out light and blasing Vanities; and then burn his brick, which is, the clay of our own bodies with concupiscences and ambitions, to build up with our selves his Kingdome; He made us travell more for hell, then would have purchased Heaven; He enfeebled us from begetting or conceiving Male children, which are our good thoughts, and those few which we had, he strangled in the birth: And then, camest thou, O Christ, thine own *Moses,* and deliveredst us; not by doing, but suffering; not by killing, but dying. Go one step lower, that is higher, and nearer to God, O my soul, in this Meditation, and thou shalt see, that even in this moment, when he affords thee these thoughts, he delivers thee from an Egypt of dulness and stupiditie. As often as he moves thee to pray to be delivered from the Egypt of sin, he delivers thee. And as often as thou promisest him not to return thither, he delivers thee. Thou hast delivered me, O God, from the Egypt of confidence and presumption, by interrupting my fortunes, and intercepting my hopes; And from the Egypt of despair by contemplation of thine abundant treasures, and my portion therein; from the Egypt of lust, by confining my affections; and from the monstrous and unnaturall Egypt of painfull and wearisome idleness, by the necessities of domestick and familiar cares and duties. Yet as an Eagle, though she enjoy her wing and beak, is wholly prisoner, if she be held by but one talon; so are we, though we could be delivered of all habit of sin, in bondage still, if Vanity hold us but by a silken thred. But, O God, as mine inward corruptions have made me mine own *Pharoah,* and mine own *Egypt;* so thou, by the inhabitation of thy Spirit, and application of thy merit, hast made me mine own Christ; and contenting thy self with being my Medicine, allowest me to be my Physician. . . .

## PRAYER

O Eternall God, as thou didst admit thy faithful servant *Abraham,* to make the granting of one petition an incouragement and rise to another, and gavest him leave to gather upon thee from fifty to ten; so I beseech thee, that since by thy grace, I have thus long meditated upon thee, and spoken of thee, I may now speak to thee. As thou hast enlightned and enlarged me to contemplate thy greatness, so, O God, descend thou and stoop down to see my infirmities and the Egypt in which I live; and (If thy good pleasure be such) hasten mine *Exodus* and deliverance, for I desire to be dissolved, and be with thee. O Lord, I most humbly acknowledg and confess thine infinite Mercy, that when thou hadst almost broke the staff of bread, and called a famine of thy word almost upon all the world, then thou broughtest me into this Egypt, where thou hadst appointed thy stewards to husband thy blessings, and to feed thy flock. Here also, O God, thou hast multiplied thy children in me, by begetting and cherishing in me reverent devotions, and pious affections towards thee, but that mine own corruption, mine own *Pharoah* hath ever smothered and strangled them. And thou hast put me in my way towards thy land of promise, thy Heavenly *Canaan,* by removing me from the Egypt of frequented and populous, glorious places, to a more solitary and desart retiredness, where I may more safely feed upon both thy Mannaes, thy self in thy Sacrament, and that other, which is true Angells food, contemplation of thee. O Lord, I most humbly acknowledg and confess, that I feel in me so many strong effects of thy Power, as only for the Ordinariness and frequency thereof, they are not Miracles. For hourly thou rectifiest my lameness, hourly thou restorest my sight, and hourly not only deliverest me from the Egypt, but raisest me from the death of sin. My sin, O God, hath not onely caused thy descent hither, and passion here; but by it I am become that hell into which thou descendedst after thy Passion; yea, after thy glorification: for hourly thou in thy Spirit descendest into my heart, to overthrow there Legions of Spirits of Disobedience, and Incredulity, and Murmuring. O Lord, I most humbly acknowledg and confesse, that by thy Mercy I have a sense of thy Justice; for not onely those afflictions with which it pleaseth thee to exercise mee, awaken me to consider how terrible thy severe justice is; but even the rest and security which thou affordest mee, puts me often into fear, that thou reservest and sparest me for a greater measure of punishment. O Lord, I most humbly acknowledge and confesse, that I have understood sin, by understanding thy laws and judgments; but have done against thy known and revealed will. Thou hast set up many candlesticks, and kindled many lamps in mee; but I have either blown them out, or carried them to guide me in by and forbidden ways. Thou hast given mee a desire of knowledg, and some meanes to it, and some possession of it; and I have arm'd my self with thy weapons against thee: Yet, O God, have mercy upon me, for thine own sake have mercy upon me. Let not sin and me be able to exceed thee, nor to defraud thee, nor to frustrate thy purposes: But let me, in despite of Me, be of so much use to thy glory, that by thy mercy to my sin, other sinners may see how much sin thou canst pardon. Thus show mercy to many in one: And shew thy power and al-mightinesse upon thy self, by casting manacles upon thine own hands, and calling back those Thunder-bolts which thou hadst thrown against mee. Show thy Justice upon the common Seducer and Devourer of us all: and show to us so much of thy Judgments, as may instruct, not condemn us. Hear us, O God, hear us, for this contrition which thou hast put into us, who come to thee with that watchword, by which thy Son hath assured us of access. *Our Father which art in Heaven,* etc.

# DEVOTIONS UPON EMERGENT OCCASIONS

## DEVOTION NO. 9

*Upon their Consultation, they [the doctors] prescribe.*

### Meditation

They have seene me, and heard mee, arraign'd mee in these fetters, and receiv'd the *evidence;* I have cut up mine *Anatomy,* dissected my selfe, and they are gon to *read* upon me. O how manifold, and perplexed a thing, nay, how wanton and various a thing is *ruine* and *destruction? God* presented to *David* three kinds, *War, Famine,* and *Pestilence; Satan* left out these, and brought in, *fires from heaven,* and *windes from the wilderness.* As if there were no *ruine* but *sicknes,* wee

see, the Masters of that *Art,* can scarce *number,* nor *name* all sicknesses; every thing that *disorders* a faculty, and the function of that
is a sicknesse: The names wil not serve them which are given from
the *place affected,* the *Plurisie* is so; nor from the *effect* which it works,
the *falling sicknes* is so; they cannot have names ynow, from *what it
does,* nor *where it is,* but they must extort names from what *it is like,*
what it *resembles,* and but in some one thing, or els they would lack
names; for the *Wolf,* and the *Canker,* and the *Polypus* are so; and that
question, *whether there be more names or things,* is as perplexd in
sicknesses, as in any thing else; except it be easily resolvd upon that
side, that there are more *sicknesses* then *names.* If *ruine* were reduc'd
to that one way, that Man could perish noway but by *sicknes,* yet his
danger were infinit; and if *sicknes* were reduc'd to that one way, that
there were no *sicknes* but a *fever,* yet the way were infinite still; for it
would overlode, and oppress any naturall, disorder and discompose any
artificiall *Memory,* to deliver the *names* of severall *fevers;* how intricate
a worke then have they, who are gone to *consult,* which of these *sicknesses* mine is, and then which of these *fevers,* and then what it would
do, and then how it may be countermind. But even in *ill,* it is a degree of
*good,* when the *evil* wil admit *consultation.* In many *diseases,* that which
is but an *accident,* but a *symptom* of the main *disease,* is so violent, that
the *Phisician* must attend the cure of that, though hee pretermit (so
far as to intermit) the cure of the *disease* itself. Is it not so in *States* too?
sometimes the insolency of those that are *great,* puts the people into
*commotions;* the great disease, and the greatest danger to the *Head,*
is the *insolency of the great ones;* and yet, they execute *Martial law,*
they come to present executions upon the *people,* whose commotion
was indeed but a *simptom,* but an *accident* of the maine *disease;* but
this *symptom,* grown so violent, wold allow no time for a *consultation.*
Is it not so in the accidents of the *diseases* of our *mind* too? Is it not
evidently so in our *affections,* in our *passions?* If a *cholerick* man be
ready to strike, must I goe about to purge his *choler,* or to breake the
blow? But where there is room for *consultation,* things are not desperate.
They *consult;* so there is nothing *rashly, inconsideratly* done; and then
they prescribe, they *write,* so there is nothing *covertly, disguisedly, un-
avowedly* done. In *bodily diseases* it is not alwaies so; sometimes, assoon
as the *Phisicians* foote is in the *chamber,* his *knife* is in the patients *arme;*
the disease would not allow a *minutes* forbearing of *blood,* nor *prescribing* of other remedies. In States and matter of government it is so too;

they are sometimes surprizd with such *accidents,* as that the *Magistrat* asks not what may be done by *law,* but does that, which must necessarily be don in that case. But it is a degree of *good,* in *evill,* a degree that carries hope and comfort in it, when we may have recourse to that which is *written,* and that the proceedings may be apert, and ingenuous, and candid, and avowable, for that gives satisfaction, and acquiescence. They who have received my *Anatomy* of my selfe, *consult,* and end their *consultation* in *prescribing,* and in prescribing *Phisick;* proper and convenient remedy: for if they shold come in again, and chide mee, for some disorder, that had occasion'd, and induced, or that had hastned and exalted this *sicknes,* or if they should begin to write now rules for my *dyet,* and *exercise* when I were well, this were to *antidate,* or to *postdate* their *Consultation,* not to give *Phisicke.* It were rather a vexation, then a reliefe, to tell a condemnd prisoner, you might have liv'd if you had done this; and if you can get pardon, you shal do wel, to take this, or this course hereafter. I am glad they know (I have hid nothing from them) glad they consult, (they hide nothing from one another) glad they write (they hide nothing from the world) glad that they write and prescribe *Phisick,* that there are *remedies* for the present case.

## Expostulation

My *God,* my *God,* allow me a just indignation, a holy detestation of the insolency of that man, who because he was of that high ranke, of whom thou hast said, *They are gods,* thought himselfe more then equall to thee; that *King* of *Aragon Alfonsus,* so perfit in the motions of the heavenly bodies, as that hee adventured to say, That *if he had bin of councell with thee, in the making of the heavens, the heavens should have bene disposed in a better order, then they are.* The *King Amasiah* would not indure thy *Prophet* to reprehend him, but asked him in anger, *Art thou made of the kings councell?* When thy Prophet *Esaias* askes that question, *who hath directed the spirit of the Lord, or being his councellor hath taught him?* It is after hee had setled and determined that office, upon thy *Son,* and him *onely,* when he joyns with those great *Titles, The mighty God,* and the *prince of peace,* this also, *the Councellor;* and after he had setled upon him, *the spirit of might, and of councell.* So that then, thou O *God,* thogh thou have no *councell* from Man, yet doest nothing upon man, without *councell;* In the making of

Man there was a *consultation; Let us make man*. In the preserving of
Man, *O Thou great preserver of men*, thou proceedest by *councell;* for
all thy *externall* workes, are the workes of the whole *Trinity*, and their
hand is to every action. How much more must I apprehend, that al you
blessed, and glorious persons of the *Trinitie* are in *consultation* now,
what you wil do with this infirm *body*, with this leprous *Soule*, that
attends, guiltily, but yet comfortably, your determination upon it. I offer
not to counsell them, who meet in *consultation* for my *body* now, but I
open my infirmities, I anatomise my *body* to them. So I do my *soule*
to thee, O my *God*, in an humble confession, That there is no *veine* in
mee, that is not full of the bloud of thy *Son*, whom I have crucified, and
Crucified againe, by multiplying many, and often repeating the same
sinnes: that there is no *Artery* in me, that hath not the *spirit of error,
the spirit of lust, the spirit of giddiness* in it; no *bone* in me that is not
hardned with the custome of sin, and nourished, and soupled with
the *marrow of sinn;* no *sinews*, no *ligaments*, that do not tie, and chain
sin and sin together. Yet, *O blessed and glorious Trinity, O holy, and
whole Colledge*, and yet but one *Phisician*, if you take this confession
into a *consultation*, my case is not desperate, my destruction is not *decreed;* If your *consultation* determine in *writing*, if you refer mee to
that which is *written*, you intend my recovery: for al the way, *O my God*,
(ever constant to thine owne wayes) thou hast proceeded *openly, intel-
ligibly, manifestly, by the book*. From thy first *book*, the book of *life*,
never shut to thee, but never throughly open to us; from thy second
*book*, the *booke* of *Nature*, wher though subobscurely, and in shadowes,
thou hast expressed thine own *Image;* from thy third *booke*, the Scriptures, where thou hadst written all in the *Old*, and then lightedst us a
candle to read it by, in the *New Testament;* To these thou hast added
the *booke* of just, and usefull *Lawes*, established by them, to whom thou
hast committed thy people; To those, the *Manualls*, the *pocket*, the
*bosome books* of our owne *Consciences;* To those thy particular *books*
of all our particular sins; and to those, the *Booke* with *seven seals*,
which only *the Lamb which was slaine, was found worthy to open;*
which, I hope, it shall not disagree with the meaning of thy blessed
*Spirit*, to interprete, the *promulgation of their pardon, and righteousnes,
who are washed in the blood of that Lambe;* And if thou refer me to
these *bookes*, to a new reading, a new triall by these *bookes*, this fever
may be but a burning in the hand, and I may be saved, thogh not by
my book, mine own *conscience*, nor by thy other *books*, yet by thy *first*,

the book of *life*, thy *decree for my election*, and by thy *last*, the booke of the *Lamb*, and the shedding of his blood upon me; If I be stil under *consultation*, I am not condemned yet; if I be sent to these books I shall not be condemn'd at all: for, though there be something written in some of those *books* (particularly in the *Scriptures*) which some men turne to *poyson*, yet upon these *consultations* (these *confessions*, these *takings* of our particular cases, into thy consideration) thou intendest all for *phisick*, and even from those *Sentences*, from which a too-late *Repenter* will sucke *desperation*, he that seeks thee early, shall receive thy *morning dew*, thy seasonable *mercy*, thy forward *consolation*.

## Prayer

O Eternall and most gracious *God*, who art of so pure eyes, as that thou canst not look upon *sinn*, and we of so unpure constitutions, as that wee can present no object but *sin*, and therefore might justly feare, that thou wouldst turn thine *eyes* for ever from us, as, though we cannot indure *afflictions* in our selves, yet in *thee* we can; so thogh thou canst not indure *sinne* in us, yet in thy *Sonn* thou canst, and he hath taken upon him selfe, and presented to thee, al those *sins*, which might displease thee in us. There is an *Eye* in *Nature*, that kills, as soon as it sees, the eye of a *Serpent;* no eye in *Nature*, that *nourishes* us by looking upon us; But thine *Eye, O Lord*, does so. Looke therefore upon me, *O Lord*, in this distresse, and that will recall mee from the borders of this bodily death; Look upon me, and that wil raise me again from that *spirituall death*, in which my parents buried me, when they begot mee in *sinne*, and in which I have pierced even to the jawes of *hell*, by multiplying such heaps of actuall sins, upon that foundation, that root of *originall sinn*. Yet take me again, into your *Consultation, O blessed* and *glorious Trinitie;* and thogh the *Father* know, that I have defaced his *Image* received in my *Creation;* though the *Son* know, I have neglected mine interest in the *Redemption*, yet, *O blessed spirit*, as thou art to my *Conscience*, so be to them a witnes, that at this *minute*, I accept that which I have so often, so often, so rebelliously refused, they blessed inspirations; be thou my witnes to them, that at more poores then this slacke body sweates teares, this sad soule weeps blood; and more for the *displeasure* of my *God*, then for the stripes of his displeasure. Take me then, *O blessed*, and *glorious Trinitie*, into a *Reconsultation*, and prescribe me any *phisick;* If it bee a long, and painful holding of this *soule* in *sicknes,* it is *phisick,* if I may discern thy hand to give it, and it is *phisick,* if it be a speedy departing of this *Soule,* if I may discerne thy hand to receive it.

# DEVOTION NO. 10

*They find the Disease to steale on insensibly, and endeavour to meet with it so.*

## Meditation

This is *Natures nest of Boxes;* The Heavens containe the *Earth,* the *Earth, Cities, Cities, Men.* And all these are *Concentrique;* the common *center* to them all, is *decay, ruine;* only that is *Eccentrique,* which was never made; only that place, or garment rather, which we can *imagine,* but not *demonstrate,* That light, which is the very emanation of the light of *God,* in which the *Saints* shall dwell, with which the *Saints* shall be appareld, only that bends not to this *Center,* to *Ruine;* that which was not made of *Nothing,* is not threatned with this annihilation. All other things are; even *Angels,* even our *soules;* they move upon the same *poles,* they bend to the same *Center;* and if they were not made immortall by *preservation,* their *Nature* could not keep them from sinking to this *center, Annihilation.* In all these (the *frame of the heavens,* the *States upon earth,* and *Men in them,* comprehend all) those are the greatest mischifs, which are least discerned; the most insensible in their *wayes* come to bee the most sensible in their *ends.* The *Heavens* have had their *Dropsie,* they drownd the world, and they shall have their *Fever,* and burn the world. Of the *dropsie,* the flood, the world had a foreknowledge 120 yeares before it came; and so some made provision against it, and were saved; the *fever* shall break out in an instant, and consume all; The *dropsie* did no harm to the *heavens,* from whence it fell, it did not put out those *lights,* it did not quench those *heates;* but the *fever,* the fire shall burne the *furnace* it selfe, annihilate those *heavens,* that breath it out; Though the *Dog-Starre* have a pestilent breath, an infectious exhalation, yet because we know when it wil rise, we clothe our selves, and wee diet our selves, and we shadow our selves to a sufficient prevention; but *Comets* and *blazing starres,* whose effects, or significations no man can interpret or frustrat, no man foresaw: no *Almanack* tells us, when a *blazing starre* will break out, the matter is carried up in secret; no *Astrologer* tels us when the effects will be accomplished, for thats a secret of a higher spheare, then the other; and that which is most *secret,* is most *dangerous.* It is so also here in the *societies* of men, in *States,* and *Commonwealths.* Twentie *rebellious drums* make not so dangerous a noise, as a few *whisperers,* and secret plotters in corners. The *Canon* doth not so much hurt against a wal, as a *Myne* under the wall; nor a thousand enemies that threaten, so much as a few that take an *oath* to say *nothing. God* knew many heavy sins of the people, in the wildernes and after, but still he charges them with that one, with *Murmuring, murmuring* in their *hearts,* secret disobediences, secret repugnances against his declar'd wil; and these are the most deadly, the most pernicious. And it is so to, with the *diseases* of the *body;* and that is my case. The *pulse,* the *urine,* the *sweat,* all have sworn to say nothing, to give no *Indication,* of any dangerous *sicknesse.* My forces are not enfeebled, I find no decay in my strength; my provisions are not cut off, I find no abhorring in mine appetite; my counsels are not corrupted or infatuated, I find no false apprehensions, to work upon mine understanding; and yet they see, that invisibly, and I feele, that insensibly the *disease* prevailes. The *disease* hath established a *Kingdome,* an *Empire* in mee, and will have certaine *Arcana Imperii, secrets of State,* by which it will proceed, and not be bound to *declare* them. But yet against those secret conspiracies in the State, the *Magistrate* hath the *rack;* and against the insensible diseases, *Phisicians* have their *examiners;* and those these employ now.

## DEVOTION NO. 17

*Now, this Bell tolling softly for another, saies to me, Thou must die.*

### Meditation

Perchance hee for whom this *Bell* tolls, may be so ill, as that he knowes not it tolls for him; And perchance I may thinke my selfe so much better than I am, as that they who are about mee, and see my state, may have caused it to toll for mee, and I know not that. The *Church* is *Catholike, universall,* so are all her *Actions; All* that she does, belongs to *all.* When she *baptizes a child,* that action concernes mee; for that child is thereby connected to that *Head* which is my *Head* too, and engraffed into that *body,* whereof I am a *member.* And when she *buries a Man,* that actions concerns me: All *mankinde* is of one *Author,* and is one *volume;* when one Man dies, one *Chapter* is not *torne* out of the *booke,* but *translated* into a better *language;* and every *Chapter* must be so *translated;* God emploies several *translators;* some peeces are translated by *age,* some by *sicknesse,* some by *warre,* some by *justice;* but *Gods* hand is in every *translation;* and his hand shall binde up all our scattered leaves againe, for that *Librarie* where every *booke* shall lie open to one another: As therefore the *Bell* that rings to a *Sermon,* calls not upon the *Preacher* onely, but upon the *Congregation* to come; so this *Bell* calls us all: but how much more mee, who am brought so neere the *doore* by this *sicknesse.* There was a *contention* as farre as a *suite,* (in which both *pietie* and *dignitie, religion,* and *estimation,* were mingled) which of the religious *Orders* should ring to *praiers* first in the *Morning;* and it was *determined,* that *they should ring first that rose earliest.* If we understand aright the *dignitie* of this *Bell* that tolls for our *evening prayer,* wee would bee glad to make it ours, by rising early, in that *application,* that it might bee ours, as wel as his, whose indeed it is. The *Bell* doth toll for him that *thinkes* it doth; and though it *intermit* againe, yet from that *minute,* that that occasion wrought upon him, hee is united to *God.* Who casts not up his *Eie* to the *Sunne* when it rises? but who takes off his *Eie* from a *Comet* when that breakes out? Who bends not his *eare* to any *bell,* which upon any occasion rings? but who can remove it from that *bell,* which is passing a *peece of himselfe* out of this *world?* No man is an *Iland,* intire of it selfe; every man is a *peece* of the *Continent,* a part of the *maine;* if a *Clod* bee washed away by the *Sea, Europe* is the lesse, as well as if a *Promontorie* were, as well as if a *Mannor* of thy *friends* or of *thine owne were;* any mans *death* diminishes *me,* because I am involved in *Mankinde;* And therefore never send to know for whom the *bell* tolls; It tolls for *thee.* Neither can we call this a *begging* of *Miserie* or a *borrowing* of *Miserie,* as though we were not miserable enough of our selves, but must fetch in more from the next house, in taking upon us the *Miserie* of our *Neighbours.* Truly it were an excusable *covetousnesse* if wee did; for *affliction* is a *treasure,* and scarce any man hath *enough* of it. No man hath *affliction* enough that is not matured, and ripened by it, and made fit for *God* by that *affliction.* If a man carry *treasure* in *bullion,* or in a *wedge* of *gold,* and have none coined into *currant Monies,* his *treasure* will not defray him as he travells. *Tribulation* is *Treasure* in the *nature* of it, but it is not *currant money* in the *use* of it, except wee get nearer and nearer our *home,* *Heaven,* by it. Another man may be *sicke* too, and sick to *death,* and this *affliction* may lie in his *bowels,* as *gold* in a *Mine,* and be of no use to him; but this *bell,* that tells me of his *affliction,* digs out, and applies that *gold* to *mee:* if by this consideration of anothers danger, I take mine owne into contemplation, and so secure my selfe, by making my recourse to my *God,* who is our onely securitie.

# LETTERS

## TO MY HONOURED FRIEND S^r T. LUCEY

*Sir,*

I make account that this writing of letters, when it is with any serious-ness, is a kind of extasie, and a departure and secession and suspension of the soul, w^ch doth then communicate it self to two bodies: And as I would every day provide for my souls last convoy, though I know not when I shall die, and perchance I shall never die; so for these extasies in letters, I oftentimes deliver my self over in writing when I know not when those letters shall be sent to you, and many times they never are, for I have a little satisfaction in seeing a letter written to you upon my table, though I meet no opportunity of sending it. Especially this sum-mer, when either by my early retiring home, or your irresolutions of your own purposes, or some other possessions of yours you did lesse reveale to me your progresses, and stations, and where I might crosse you by letters, then heretofore: I make shift to lay little fault upon you, because my pardon might be easier, if I transgress into a longer and busier letter then your Countrey sports admit; but you may read it in winter: And by that time I may more clearly express my self for those things which have entred into me, concerning your soul: for as the greatest advantage which mans soul is thought to have beyond others, is that which they call *Actum reflexum,* and *iteratum,* (for Beasts do the same things as we do, but they do not consider nor remember the cir-cumstances and inducements; and by what power, and faculty, it is that they do them) so of those which they call *Actum reflexum* the noblest is that which reflects upon the soul it self, and considers and meditates it,

Into which consideration when I walke after my slow and unperfect pace, I begin to think that as litigious men tyred with suits, admit any arbitrement; and Princes travailed with long and wastfull war, descend to such conditions of peace, as they are soon after ashamed to have embraced: so Philosophers, and so all sects of Christians, after long disputations and controversies, have allowed many things for positive and dogmaticall truths which are not worthy of that dignity; And so many doctrines have grown to be the ordinary diet and food of our spirits, and have place in the pap of Catechismes, which were admitted but as Physick in that present distemper, or accepted in a lazie wearinesse, when men, so they might have something to relie upon, and to excuse themselves from more painfull inquisition, never examined what that was. To which indisposition of ours, the Casuists are so indulgent, as that they allow a conscience to adhere to any probable opinion against a more probable, and do never binde him to seek out which is the more probable, but give him leave to dissemble it and to depart from it, if by mischance he come to know it. This, as it appears in all sciences, so most manifestly in Physick, which for a long time considering nothing, but plain curing and that but by example and precedent, the world at last longed for some certain Canons and Rules, how these cures might be accomplished; And when men are inflamed with this desire, and that such a fire breaks out that rages and consumes infinitly by heat of argument, except some of authority interpose. This produced *Hippocrates* his Aphorismes; and the world slumbred or took breath, in his resolution divers hundreds of years: And then in *Galens* time, which was not satisfied with the effect of curing, nor with the knowledge how to cure, broke out another desire of finding out the causes why those simples wrought those effects. Then *Galen* rather to stay their stomachs then that he gave them enough, taught them the qualities of the four Elements, and arrested them upon this, that all differences of qualities proceeded from them. And after, (not much before our time) men perceiving that all effects in Physick could not be derived from these beggerly and impotent properties of the Elements, and that therefore they were driven often to that miserable refuge of specifique form, and of antipathy and sympathy, we see the world hath turned upon new principles which are attributed to *Paracelsus,* but (indeed) too much to his honour. Certainly it is also so in the Physick of our soul Divinity, for in the Primitive Church, when amongst the Fathers there were so divers opinions of the state of the soul, presently after this life, they easily inclined to be content to do as much for them dead as when they were alive, and so concurred in a charitable disposition to pray for them; which manner of prayer then in use, no Christian Church at this day having received better light, will allow of. So also when in the beginning of *S. Augustines* time, Grace had been so much advanced that mans Nature was scarce admitted to be so much as any means or instrument (not onely no kinde of cause) of his own good works: And soon after in S. *Augustines* time also mans free will (by fierce opposition and arguing against the former error) was too much overvalued, and admitted into too near degrees of fellowship with Grace; those times admitted a doctrine and form of reconciliation, which though for reverence to the time, both the Dominicans and Jesuits at this day in their great quarrell about Grace and Free will would yet seem to maintaine, yet indifferent and dispassioned men of that Church see there is no possibility in it, and therefore accuse it of absurdity and almost of heresie. I think it falls out thus also in the matter of the soul: for Christian Religion presuming a soul, and intending principally her happiness in the life to come, hath been content to accept any way which hath been obtruded; how this soul is begun in us. Hence it is that whole Christian Churches arest themselves upon propagation from parents; and other whole Christian Churches allow onely infusion from God. In both which opinions there appear such infirmities as it is time to look for a better: for whosoever will adhere to the way of propagation; can never evict necessarily and certainly a naturall immortality in the soul, if the soul result out of matter, nor shall he ever prove that all mankind hath any more then one soul: as certainly of all beasts, if they receive such souls as they have from their parents, every species can have but one soul. And they which follow the opinion of infusion from God, and of a new creation (which is now the more common opinion) as they can very hardly defend the doctrin of original sin (the soul is forced to take this infection, and comes not into the body of her own disposition) so shall they never be able to prove that all those whom we see in the shape of men have an immortall and reasonable soul, because our parents are as able as any other species is to give us a soul of growth and of sense, and to perform all vitall and animall functions. And so without infusion of such a soul may produce a creature as wise and well disposed as any horse or Elephant, of which degree many whom we see come far short; nor hath God bound or declared himself that he will always create a soul for every embryon, there is yet therefore no opinion in Philosophy, nor Divinity, so well established as constrains us to beleeve, both that the soul is immortall, and that every particular man hath such a soul: which since out of the great mercy of our God we do constantly beleeve, I am ashamed that we do not also know it by searching farther: But as sometimes we had rather beleeve a Travellers lie then go to disprove him; so men rather cleave to these ways then seek new: yet because I have meditated therein, I will shortly aquaint you with what I think; for I would not be in danger of that law of *Moses,* That if a man dig a pit, and cover it not, he must recompense those which are damnified by it: which is often interpreted of such as shake old opinions, and do not establish new as certain, but leave consciences in a worse danger then they found them in. I beleeve that law of *Moses* hath in it some mysterie and appliablenesse; for by that law men are onely then bound to that indemnity and compensation, if an Oxe or an Asse (that is, such as are of a strong constitution and accustomed to labour) fall therein; but it is not said so, if a Sheep or a Goat fall: no more are we, if men in a sillinesse or wantonnesse will stumble or take a scandall, bound to rectifie them at all times. And therefore because I justly presume you strong and watchfull enough, I make account that I am not obnoxious to that law, since my meditations are neither too wide nor too deep for you, except onely that my way of expressing them may be extended beyond your patience and pardon, which I will therefore tempt no longer at this time.

From *Micham,* my                          *Your very affectionate friend*
close prison ever                              *and servant and lover*
since I saw you,
9 Octob.                                                                    J. Donne

## TO THE RIGHT HONOURABLE THE COUNTESS
## OF MONTGOMERY

*Madam,*

Of my ability to doe your Ladiship service, any thing may be an embleme good enough; for as a word vanisheth, so doth any power in me to serve you; things that are written are fitter testimonies, because they remain and are permanent: in writing this Sermon which your Ladiship was pleased to hear before, I confesse I satisfie an ambition of mine own, but it is the ambition of obeying your commandment, not onely an ambition of leaving my name in the memory, or in the Cabinet: and yet, since I am going out of the Kingdom, and perchance out of the world, (when God shall have given my soul a place in heaven) it shall the lesse diminish your Ladiship, if my poor name be found about you. I know what dead carkasses things written are, in respect of things spoken. But in things of this kinde, that soul that inanimates them, receives debts from them: The Spirit of God that dictates them in the speaker or writer, and is present in his tongue or hand, meets himself again (as we meet our selves in a glass) in the eies and hearts of the hearers and readers: and that Spirit, which is ever the same to an equall devotion, makes a writing and a speaking equall means to edification. In one circumstance, my preaching and my writing this Sermon is too equall: that that your Ladiship heard in a hoarse voyce then, you read in a course hand now: but in thankfulnesse I shall lift up my hands as clean as my infirmities can keep them, and a voyce as clear as his spirit shall be pleased to tune in my prayers in all places of the world, which shall either sustain or bury.

*Your Ladiships humble servant*
*in Christ Jesus*
J. D.

## TO SIR H. R.

If a whole year be but *Annus ab Annulo,* because it returnes into it self, what *Annululus* shall be diminutive enough, to express our weekly revolutions? In chaines the least linkes have most curiosity, but that can be no emblem of us: but they have also the most strength, and that may. The first sphere onely which is resisted by nothing, absolves his course every day; and so doth true friendship well placed, often iterate in act or purpose, the same offices. But as the lower spheres, subject to the violence of that, and yet naturally encouraged to a reluctation against it, have therefore many distractions, and eccentricities, and some trepidations, and so return but lamely, and lately to the same place, and office: so that friendship which is not moved primarily by the proper intelligence, discretion, and about the naturall center, vertue, doth perchance sometimes, some things, somewhat like true friendship; but hath many deviations, which are strayings into new loves, (not of other men; for that is proper to true wise friendship, which is not a marring; but of other things) and hath such trepidations as keep it from shewing it self, where great persons do not love; and it returns to the true first station and place of friendship planetarily, which is uncertainly and seldome. I have ever seen in *London* and our Court, as some colours, and habits, and continuances, and motions, and phrases, and accents, and songs, so friends in fashion and in season: and I have seen them as sodainly abandoned altogether, though I see no change in them, nor know more why they were left, then why they were chosen. To do things by example, and upon confidence of anothers judgment may be some kinde of a second wisdome; but it is but writing by a copy: or indeed it is the hardest of all, and the issue of the first wisdome, for I cannot know that this example should be followed, except I knew that it is good, and so I judge my Judge. Our assent therefore, and arrest, must be upon things, not persons. And when we are sure we are in the right way, for great persons, we may be glad of their company, if they go our way; we may for them change our place, but not our end, nor our way, if there be but one, us in Religion. In persevering in it, it concerns as much what our companions be, but very much what our friends. In which I know I speak not dangerously nor mis-appliably to you, as though I averted you from any of those friends, who are of other impressions then you or I in some great circumstances of Religion. You know I never fettered nor imprisoned the word Religion; not straightning it Frierly, *ad Religiones factitias,* (as the *Romans* call well their orders of Religion) nor immuring it in a *Rome,* or a *Wittemberg,* or a *Geneva;* they are all virtuall beams of one Sun, and wheresoever they finde clay hearts, they harden them, and moulder them into dust; and they entender and mollifie waxen. They are not so contrary as the North and South Poles; and that they are connaturall pieces of one circle. Religion is Christianity, which being too spirituall to be seen by us, doth therefore take an apparent body of good life and works, so salvation requires an honest Christian. These are the two Elements, and he which elemented from these, hath the complexion of a good man, and a fit friend. The diseases are, too much intention into indiscreet zeal, and too much remisnesse and negligence by giving scandall: for our condition and state in this, is as infirm as in our bodies; where physitians consider only two degrees; sicknesse, and neutrality; for there is no health in us. This, Sir, I use to say to you, rather to have so good a witnesse and corrector of my meditations, then to advise; and yet to do that too, since it is pardonable in a friend: Not to slack you towards those friends which are religious in other clothes then we; (for *Amici vitia si feras facis tua,* is true of such faults) but to keep you awake against such as the place where you must live will often obtrude, which are not onely naked, without any fashion of such garments, but have neither the body of Religion, which is morall honesty, and sociable faithfulness, nor the soul, Christianity. I know not how this paper scaped last week which I send now; I was so sure that I enwrapped it then, that I should be so still, but that I had but one copy; forgive it as you use to do. From *Micham* in as much haste, and with as ill Pen and Inke, as the letter can accuse me of; but with the last and the next weeks heart and affection.

*Yours very truely and affectionately*
J. Donne

## TO SIR H. G.

*Sir,*

This letter hath more merit, then one of more diligence, for I wrote it in my bed, and with much pain. I have occasion to sit late some nights in my study, (which your books make a prety library) and now I finde that that room hath a wholesome emblematique use: for having under it a vault, I make that promise me, that I shall die reading, since my book and a grave are so near. But it hath another unwholesomenesse, that by raw vapors rising from thence, (for I can impute it to nothing else) I have contracted a sicknesse which I cannot name nor describe. For it hath so much of a continuall Cramp, that it wrests the sinews, so much of a Tetane, that it withdraws and puls the mouth, and so much of the Gout, (which they whose counsell use, say it is) that it is not like to be cured, though I am too hasty in three days to pronounce it. If it be the Gout, I am miserable; for that affects dangerous parts, as my neck and brest, and (I think fearfully) my stomach, but it will not kill me yet; I shall be in this world, like a porter in a great house, ever nearest the door, but seldomest abroad: I shall have many things to make me weary, and yet not get leave to be gone. If I go, I will provide by my best means that you suffer not for me, in your bonds. The estate which I should leave behinde me of any estimation, is my poor fame, in the memory of my friends, and therefore I would be curious of it, and provide that they repent not to have loved me. Since my imprisonment in my bed, I have made a meditation in verse, which I call a Litany; the word you know imports no other then supplication, but all Churches have one forme of supplication, by that name. Amongst ancient annals I mean some 800 years, I have met two Letanies in Latin verse, which gave me not the reason of my meditations, for in good faith I thought not upon them then, but they give me a defence, if any man; to a Lay man, and a private, impute it as a fault, to take such divine and publique names, to his own little thoughts. The first of these was made by *Ratpertus* a Monk of *Suevia;* and the other by *S. Notker,* of whom I will give you this note by the way, that he is a private Saint, for a few Parishes; they were both but Monks, and the Letanies poor and barbarous enough; yet Pope *Nicolas* the 5, valued their devotion so much, that he canonized both their Poems, and commanded them for publike service in their Churches: mine is for lesser Chappels, which are my friends, and though a copy of it were due to you, now, yet I am so unable to serve my self with writing it for you at this time, (being some 30 staves of 9 lines) that I must intreat you to take a promise that you shall have the first, for a testimony of that duty which I owe to your love, and to my self, who am bound to cherish it by my best offices. That by which it will deserve best acceptation, is, That neither the Roman Church need call it defective, because it abhors not the particular mention of the blessed Triumphers in heaven; nor the Reformed can discreetly accuse it, of attributing more then a rectified devotion ought to doe. The day before I lay down, I was at *London,* where I delivered your Letter for Sʳ *Ed. Conway,* and received another for you, with the copy of my Book, of which it is impossible for me to give you a copy so soon, for it is not of much lesse then 300 pages. If I die, it shall come to you in that fashion that your Letter desires it. If I warm again, (as I have often seen such beggers as my indisposition is, end themselves soon, and the patient as soon) you and I shal speak together of that, before it be too late to serve you in that commandment. At this time I onely assure you, that I have not appointed it upon any person, nor ever purposed to print it: which later perchance you thought, and grounded your request thereupon. A Gent. that visited me yesterday told me that our Church hath lost Mʳ *Hugh Broughton,* who is gone to the Roman side. I have known before, that *Serarius* the Jesuit was an instrument from Cardinall *Baronius* to draw him to *Rome,* to accept a stipend, onely to serve the Christian Churches in controversies with the Jews, without indangering himself to change of his perswasion in particular deductions between these Christian Churches, or being enquired of, or tempted thereunto. And I hope he is no otherwise departed from us. If he be, we shall not escape scandall in it; because, though he be a man of many distempers, yet when he shall come to eat assured bread, and to be removed from partialities, to which want drove him, to make himself a reputation, and raise up favourers; you shall see in that course of opposing the Jews, he will produce worthy things: and our Church will perchance blush to have lost a Souldier fit for that great battell; and to cherish onely those single Duellisms, between *Rome* and *England,* or that more single, and almost self-homicide, between the unconformed Ministers, and Bishops. I writ to you last week that the plague increased; by which you may see that my Letters —————— [*sic*] opinion of the song, not that I make such trifles for praise; but because as long as you speak comparatively of it with mine own, and not absolutely, so long I am of your opinion even at this time; when I humbly thank God, I ask & have, his comfort of sadder meditations; I doe not condemn in my self, that I have given my wit such evaporations, as those, if they be free from prophaneness, or obscene provocations. S^r you would pity me if you saw me write, and therefore will pardon me if I write no more: my pain hath drawn my head so much awry, and holds it so, that mine eie cannot follow mine hand: I receive you therefore into my prayers, with mine own weary soul, and commend my self to yours. I doubt not but next week I shall be good news to you, for I have mending or dying on my side, which is two to one. If I continue thus, I shall have comfort in this, that my B. Saviour exercising his Justice upon my two worldly parts, my fortune, and body, reserves all his mercy for that which best tasts it, and most needs it, my soul. I professe to you truly, that my lothnesse to give over now, seems to my self an ill sign, that I shall write no more.

*Your poor friend, and Gods poor patient.*
Jo. Donne

## TO SIR G. F.

*Sir,*

I writ to you once this week before; yet I write again, both because it seems a kinde of resisting of grace, to omit any commodity of sending into *England,* and because any Pacquet from me into *England* should go, not only without just fraight, but without ballast, if it had not a letter to you. In Letters that I received from Sir *H. Wotton* yesterday from *Amyens,* I had one of the 8 of *March* from you, and with it one from M^rs. *Danterey,* of the 28 of *January:* which is a strange disproportion. But Sir, if our Letters come not in due order, and so make not a certain and concurrent chain, yet if they come as Atomes, and so meet at last, by any crooked, and casuall application, they make up, and they nourish bodies of friendship; and in that fashion, I mean one way or other, first or last, I hope all the Letters which have been addressed to us by one another, are safely arrived, except perchance that pacquet by the Cook be not, of which before this time you are cleare; for I received (as I told you) a Letter by M. *Nat. Rich,* and if you sent none by him, then it was that Letter, which the Cook tells you he delivered to M. *Rich;* which, with all my criticismes, I cannot reconcile; because in your last Letter, I find mention of things formerly written, which I have not found. However, I am yet in the same perplexity, which I mentioned before, which is, that I have received no syllable, neither from her self, nor by any other, how my wife hath passed her danger, nor do I know whether I be increased by a childe, or diminished by the losse of a wife. I hear from *England* of many censures of my book, of M^ris. *Drury;* if any of those censures do but pardon me my descent in Printing any thing in verse, (which if they do, they are more charitable then my self; for I do not pardon my self, but confesse that I did it against my conscience, that is, against my own opinion, that I should not have done so) I doubt not but they will soon give over that other part of that indictment, which is that I have said so much; for no body can imagine, that I who never saw her, could have any other purpose in that, then that when I had received so very good testimony of her worthinesse, and was gone down to print verses, it became me to say, not what I was sure was just truth, but the best that I could conceive; for that had been a new weaknesse in me, to have praised any body in printed verses, that had not been capable of the best praise that I could give. Presently after Easter we shall (I think) go to *Frankford* to be there at the election, where we shall meet Sir *H. Wotton* and Sir *Ro. Rich,* and after that we are determined to passe some time, in the Palatinate. I go thither with a great deale of devotion; for me thinkes it is a new kinde of piety, that as Pilgrims went heretofore to places which had been holy and happy, so I go to a place now, which shall be so, and more, by the presence of the worthiest Princess of the world, if that marriage proceed. I have no greater errand to the place then that at my return into *England,* I may be the fitter to stand in her presence, and that after I have seen a rich and abundant Countrey, in his best seasons, I may see that Sun which shall always keep it in that height. Howsoever we stray, if you have leasure to write at any time, adventure by no other way, then M. *Bruer,* at the Queens Armes, a Mercer, in *Cheapside.* I shall omit no opportunity, of which I doubt not to finde more then one before we go from *Paris.* Therefore give me leave to end this, in which if you did not finde the remembrance of my humblest services to my Lady *Bedford,* your love and faith ought to try all the experiments of pouders, and dryings, and waterings to discover some lines which appeared not; because it is impossible that a Letter should come from me, with such an ungratefull silence.

> *Your very true poor friend and*
> *servant and lover*
> J. Donne

## TO THE BEST KNIGHT SIR H. WOOTTON

*Sir,*

When I saw your good Countesse last, she let me think that her message by her foot-man would hasten you up. And it furthered that opinion in me, when I knew how near M. *Mathews* day of departing this kingdome was. To counterpoyse both these, I have a little Letter from you brought to me to *Micham* yesterday, but left at my lodging two days sooner: and because that speaks nothing of your return, I am content to be perplexed in it: and as in all other, so in this perplexity to do that which is safest. To me it is safest to write, because it performes a duty, and leaves my conscience well: and though it seem not safest for the Letter, which may perish, yet I remember, that in the Crociate for the warres in the *Holy Land,* and so in all Pilgrimages enterprised in devotion, he which dies in the way, enjoyes all the benefit and indulgences which the end did afford. Howsoever, all that can encrease the danger of your Letter, encrease my merit; for, as where they immolate men, it is a scanter devotion, to sacrifice one of many slaves or of many children, or an onely child, then to beget and bring up one purposely to sacrifice it, so if I ordain this Letter purposely for destruction, it is the largest expressing of that kinde of piety, and I am easie to beleeve (because I wish it) your hast hither: Not that I can fear any slacknesse in that business which drew you down, because your fortune and honour are a paire of good spurs to it; but here also you have both true businesse and many *Quasi negotia,* which go two and two to a businesse; which are visitations, and such, as though they be not full businesses, yet are so near them that they serve as for excuses, in omissions of the other. As when abjurations was in use in this land, the State and law was satisfied if the abjuror came to the sea side, and waded into the sea, when windes and tydes resisted, so we think our selves justly excusable to our friends and our selves, if when we should do businesse, we come to the place of businesse, as Courts and the houses of great Princes and officers. I do not so much intimate your infirmity in this, as frankly confesse mine own. The master of Latine language says, *Oculi & aures aliorum te speculantur & custodiunt.* So those two words are synonimous, & only the observation of others upon me, is my preservation from extream idlenesse, else I professe, that I hate businesse so much, as I am sometimes glad to remember, that the *Roman Church* reads that verse *A negotio perambulante in tenebris,* which we reade from the pestilence walking by night, so equall to me do the plague and businesse deserve avoiding, but you will neither beleeve that I abhor businesse, if I inlarge this Letter, nor that I would afford you that ease which I affect, Therefore returne to your pleasures.

*Your unprofitablest friend*

March 14, 1607                                                            Jo. Donne

## TO HIS MOTHER: COMFORTING HER AFTER THE DEATH OF HER DAUGHTER

*My most dear mother,*

When I consider so much of your life, as can fall within my memorie and observation, I find it to have been a Sea, under a continuall Tempest, where one wave hath ever overtaken another. Our most wise and blessed Saviour chuseth what way it pleaseth him, to conduct those which he loves, to his Haven, and eternall Rest. The way which he hath chosen for you, is strait, stormie, obscure, and full of sad apparitions of death, and wants, and sundry discomforts; and it hath pleased him, that one discomfort should still succeed, and touch another, that he might leave you no leasure, by anie pleasure or abundance, to stay or step out of that way, or almost to take breath in that way, by which he hath determined to bring you home, which is his glorious Kingdom. One of the most certain marks and assurances, that all these are his works, and to that good end, is your inward feeling and apprehension of them, and patience in them. As long as the Spirit of God distills and dews his cheerfulnesse upon your heart; as long as he instructs your understanding, to interpret his mercies and his judgments aright; so long your comfort must needs be as much greater than others, as your afflictions are greater than theirs. The happinesse which God afforded to your first young time, which was the love and care of my most dear and provident Father, whose soul, I hope, hath long since enjoyed the sight of our blessed Saviour, and had compassion of all our miseries in this world, God removed from you quickly. And hath since taken from you all the comfort, that that Marriage produced. All those children (for whose maintenance his industrie provided, and for whose education you were so carefullie and so chargeablie diligent) he hath now taken from you. All that worth which he left, God hath suffered to be gone from us all. So that God hath seemed to repent, that he allowed any part of your life and earthly happinesse, that he might keep your Soul in continuall exercise, and longing, and assurance, of comming immediately to him. I hope therefore, my most dear Mother, that your experience of the calamities of this life, your continuall acquaintance with the visitations of the holy Ghost, which gives better inward comforts, than the world can outward discomforts, your wisdom, to distinguish the value of this world from the next, and your religious fear of offending our mercifull God, by repining at any thing which he doth, will preserve you from any inordinate and dangerous sorrow, for this losse of my most beloved Sister. For my part, which am onely left now, to do the office of a child; though the poornesse of my fortune, and the greatnesse of my charge, hath not suffered me to expresse my duty towards you, as became me; yet, I protest to you before Almighty God, and his Angells and Saints in Heaven, that I do, and ever shall, esteem my selfe, to be as stronglie bound to look to you, and provide for your relief, as for my own poor wife and children. For, whatsoever I shall be able to do, I acknowledge to be a debt to you, from whom I had that education, which must make my fortune. This I speak not, as though I feared my father *Rainsford's* care of you, or his means to provide for you; for he hath been with me, and, as I perceive in him, a loving and industrious care to give you contentment; so, I see in his businesse, a happie and considerable forwardnesse.

In the mean time, good Mother, take heed, that no sorrow nor dejection in your heart, interrupt or disappoint God's purpose in you; his purpose is, to remove out of your heart, all such love of this world's happinesse, as might put Him out of possession of it. He will have you entirelie. And, as God is comfort enough, so Hee is inheritance enough. Joyne with God, and make his visitations and afflictions, as he intended them, mercies and comforts. And, for God's sake, pardon those negligences, which I have heretofore used towards you; and assist me, with your blessing to me, and all mine; and with your prayers to our blessed Saviour, that thereby both my mind and fortune may be apt to do all my duties, especially those that belong to you.

God, whose omnipotent strength can change the nature of any thing, by his raising-Spirit of comfort, make your Povertie Riches, your Afflictions Pleasure, and all the Gall and Wormwood of your life, Hony and Manna to your taste, which he hath wrought, whensoever you are willing to have it so. Which, because I cannot doubt in you, I will forbear more lines at this time, and most humblie deliver my self over to your devotions, and good opinion of me, which I desire no longer to live, than I may have.

## TO SIR ROBERT CARRE NOW EARLE OF ANKERUM, WITH MY BOOK *BIATHANATOS* AT MY GOING INTO GERMANY

*Sir,*                                                                    [April 1619]

I had need do somewhat towards you above my promises; How weak are my performances, when even my promises are defective! I cannot promise, no not in mine own hopes, equally to your merit towards me. But besides the Poems, of which you took a promise, I send you another Book to which there belongs this History. It was written by me many years since; and because it is upon a misinterpretable subject, I have always gone so near suppressing it, as that it is onely not burnt: no hand hath passed upon it to copy it, nor many eyes to read it: onely to some particular friends in both Universities, then when I writ it, I did communicate it: And I remember, I had this answer, That certainly, there was a false thread in it, but not easily found: Keep it, I pray, with the same jealousie; let any that your discretion admits to the sight of it, know the date of it; and that it is a Book written by *Jack Donne,* and not by D. *Donne:* Reserve it for me, if I live, and if I die, I only forbid it the Presse, and the Fire: publish it not, but yet burn it not; and between those, do what you will with it. Love me still, thus farre, for your owne sake, that when you withdraw your love from me, you will finde so many unworthinesses in me, as you grow ashamed of having had so long, and so much, such a thing as

*Your poor servant in Christ Jesus*
J. Donne.

# SERMON PREACHED AT THE FUNERALS OF SIR WILLIAM COKAYNE KNIGHT, ALDERMAN OF LONDON, DECEMBER 12. 1626.

Joh. 11.21. Lord, If Thou Hadst Been Here, My Brother Had Not Died

God made the first Marriage, and man made the first Divorce; God married the Body and Soule in the Creation, and man divorced the Body and Soule by death through sinne, in his fall. God doth not admit, not justifie, not authorize such Super-inductions upon such Divorces, as some have imagined; That the soule departing from one body, should become the soule of another body, in a perpetuall revolution and trans-migration of soules through bodies, which hath been the giddinesse of some Philosophers to think; Or that the body of the dead should become the body of an evill spirit, that that spirit might at his will, and to his purposes informe, and inanimate that dead body; God allowes no such Super-inductions, no such second Marriages upon such divorces by death, no such disposition of soule or body, after their dissolution by death. But because God hath made the band of Marriage indissoluble but by death, farther then man can die, this divorce cannot fall upon man; As farre as man is immortall, man is a married man still, still in possession of a soule, and a body too; And man is for ever immortall in both; Immortall in his soule by Preservation, and immortall in his body by Reparation in the Resurrection. For, though they be separated *à Thoro & Mensa,* from Bed and Board, they are not divorced; Though the soule be at the *Table of the Lambe,* in Glory, and the body but at the table of *the Serpent, in dust;* Though the soule be *in lecto florido,* in that bed which is alwayes green, in an everlasting spring, in *Abrahams bosome;* And the body but in that green-bed, whose covering is but a yard and a halfe of Turfe, and a Rugge of grasse, and the sheet but a winding sheet, yet they are not divorced; they shall returne to one another againe, in an inseparable re-union in the Resurrection. To establish this assurance of a Resurrection in us, God does sometimes in this life, that which he hath promised for the next; that is, he gives a Resurrection to life, after a bodily death here. God hath made two Testaments, two Wills; And in both, he hath declared his Power, and his Will, to give this new life after death, in this world. To the Widows sonne of *Zarephtha,* he bequeaths new life; and to the Shunamites sonne, he gives the same legacy, in the Old Testament. In the New Testament, to the widow of *Naims* sonne, he bequeaths new life; And to *Jairus* daughter he gives the same legacy: And out of the surplusage of his inexhaustible estate, out of the overflowing of his Power, he enables his Executors to doe as he did; for *Peter* gives *Dorcas* this Resurrection too. Divers examples hath he given us, of the Resurrection of every particular man, in particular Resurrections; such as we have named; And one of the generall Resurrection, in the Resurrection of Christ himselfe; for, in him, we all rose; for, he was All in All; *Con-vivificavit,* sayes the Apostle; and *Considere nos fecit, God hath quickned us,* (all us; not onely S. *Paul,* and his Ephesians, but all) and *God hath raised us,* and *oth hath made us sit together in heavenly places, in Christ Jesus.* They that are not faln yet by any actuall sinne, (children newly baptized) are risen already in him; And they that are not dead yet, nay, not alive yet, not yet borne, have a Resurrection in him, who was not onely the Lambe *slaine* from the beginning, but from before all beginnings was *risen* too; and all that shall ever have part in the second Resurrection, are risen with him from that time. Now, next to that great Propheticall action, that type of the generall Resurrection, in the Resurrection of Christ, the most illustrious Evidence, of the Resurrection of particular men, is this Resuscitation of *Lazarus;* whose sister *Martha,* directed by faith, and yet transported by passion, seeks to entender and mollifie, and supple him to impressions of mercy and compassion, who was himselfe the Mold, in which all mercy was cast, nay, the substance, of which all mercy does consist, Christ Jesus, with this imperfect piece of Devotion, which hath a tincture of Faith, but is deeper dyed in Passion, *Lord, if thou hadst been here, my brother had not dyed.*

This Text which you Heare, *Martha's* single words, complicated with this Text which you See, The dead body of this our Brother, makes up between them this body of Instruction for the soule; first, That there is nothing in this world perfect; And then, That such as it is, there is nothing constant, nothing permanent. We consider the first, That there is nothing perfect, in the best things, in spirituall things; Even *Martha's* devotion and faith hath imperfections in it; And we consider the other, That nothing is permanent in temporall things; Riches prosperously multiplied, Children honorably bestowed, Additions of Honor and Titles, fairly acquired, Places of Command and Government, justly received, and duly executed; All testimonies, all evidences of worldly happinesse, have a Dissolution, a Determination in the death of this, and of every such Man: There is nothing, no spirituall thing, perfect in this world; Nothing, no temporall thing, permanent and durable; And these two Considerations shall be our two parts; And then, these the branches from these two roots; First, in the first, we shall see in generall, The weaknesse of Mans best actions; And secondly, more particularly, The weaknesses in *Martha's* Action; And yet, in a third place, the easinesse, the propensnesse, the largenesse of Gods goodnesse towards us, in the acceptation of our imperfect Sacrifices; for, Christ does not refuse, nor discourage *Martha,* though her action have these imperfections; And in this largenesse of his Mercy, which is the end of all, we shall end this part. And in our second, That as in spirituall things nothing is perfect, so in temporall things nothing is permanent, we shall, by the same three steps, as in the former, looke first upon the generall consideration, the fluidnesse, the transitorinesse of all such temporall things; And then, consider it more particularly, in Gods Master-piece, amongst mortall things, the body of man, That even that flowes into putrefaction; And then lastly, returne to that, in which we determined the former part, The largenesse of Gods goodnesse to us, in affording even to mans body, so dissolved into putrefaction, an incorruptible and a glorious state. So have you the frame set up, and the roomes divided; The two parts, and the three branches of each; And to the furnishing of them, with meditations fit for this Occasion, we passe now.

In entring upon the first branch of our first part, That in spirituall things nothing is perfect, we may well afford a kinde of spirituall nature to knowledge; And how imperfect is all our knowledge? What one thing doe we know perfectly? Whether wee consider Arts, or Sciences, the servant knows but according to the proportion of his Masters knowledge in that Art, and the Scholar knows but according to the proportion of his Masters knowledge in that Science; Young men mend not their sight by using old mens Spectacles; and yet we looke upon Nature, but with *Aristotles* Spectacles, and upon the body of man, but *Galens,* and upon the frame of the world, but with *Ptolomies Spectacles.* Almost all knowledge is rather like a child that is embalmed to make Mummy, then that is nursed to make a Man; rather conserved in the stature of the first age, then growne to be greater; And if there be any addition to knowledge, it is rather a new knowledge, then a greater knowledge; rather a singularity in a desire of proposing something that was not knowne at all before, then an emproving, an advancing, a multiplying of former inceptions; and by that meanes, no knowledge comes to be perfect. One Philosopher thinks he is dived to the bottome, when he sayes, he knows nothing but this, That he knows nothing; and yet another thinks, that he hath expressed more knowledge then he, in saying, That he knows not so much as that, That he knows nothing. S. *Paul* found that to be all knowledge, To know Christ; And Mahomet thinks himselfe wise therefore, because he knows not, acknowledges not Christ, as S. *Paul* does. Though a man knew not, that every sin casts another shovell of Brimstone upon him in Hell, yet if he knew that every riotous feast cuts off a year, and every wanton night seaven years of his seventy in this world, it were some degree towards perfection in knowledge. He that purchases a Mannor, will thinke to have an exact Survey of the Land: But who thinks of taking so exact a survey of his Conscience, how that money was got, that purchased that Mannor? We call that a mans meanes, which he hath; But that is truly his meanes, what way he came by it. And yet how few are there, (when a state comes to any great proportion) that know that; that know what they have, what they are worth? We have seen great Wills, dilated into glorious uses, and into pious uses, and then too narrow an estate to reach to it; And we have seen Wills, where the Testator thinks he hath bequeathed all, and he hath not knowne halfe his own worth. When thou knowest a wife, a sonne, a servant, a friend no better, but that that wife betrayes thy bed, and that sonne thine estate, and that servant thy credit, and that friend thy secret, what canst thou say thou knowest? But we must not insist upon this Consideration of knowledge; for, though knowledge be of a spirituall nature, yet it is but as a terrestriall Spirit, conversant upon Earth; Spirituall things, of a more rarified nature then knowledge, even faith it selfe, and all that grows from that in us, falls within this Rule, which we have in hand, That even in spirituall things, nothing is perfect.

We consider this therefore *in Credendis,* In things that we are bound to Beleeve, there works our faith; And then, *in Petendis,* In things that we are bound to pray for, there works our hope; And lastly, *in Agendis,* In things that we are bound to doe, and there works our charity; And there is nothing in any of these three perfect. When you remember who they were, that made that prayer, *Domine adauge,* That the Apostles themselves prayed, that their faith might receive an encrease, *Lord increase our faith,* you must necessarily second that consideration with a confession, That no mans faith is perfect. When you heare Christ so often upbraid, sometimes whole Congregations, with that, *Modicæ fidei, O yee of little faith;* And sometimes his Disciples alone, with the same reproach, *Modicæ fidei, O yee of little faith;* when you may be perplexed with the variety of opinions amongst the ancient Interpreters, whether Christ spoke but to the incredulous Jewes, or to his own Disciples, when he said, *O faithlesse and perverse generation, how long shall I be with you? how long shall I suffer you?* (for many Interpreters goe one way, and many the other) And when you may be cleared without any colour of perplexity, that to whom soever Christ spoke in that place, he spoke plainly to his owne Disciples, when he said, *Because of your unbeliefe you cannot doe this;* In which Disciples of his, he denies also, that there is such a proportion of faith, as a graine of Mustard-seed, can ye place a perfectnesse of faith in any? When the Apostle takes knowledge of the good estate and condition of the Thessalonians, and gave God thanks for their *Workes of faith,* for *their labours of love,* for their *patience of hope, in our Lord Jesus Christ:* does he conclude them to be perfect? No; for after this he sayes, *Night and day we pray exceedingly, that we may perfect that which is lacking in your faith.* And after this, he sees the fruit of those prayers, *We are bound to thanke God alwayes, because your faith groweth exceedingly;* still, at the best, it is but a growing faith, and it may be better. There are men that are said to be *Rich in faith;* men that are come from the *weake and beggarly elements of Nature, or of the Law,* to the knowledge of the precious and glorious *Gospell,* and so are *Rich in faith,* enriched, emproved by faith. There are men that *Abound in faith;* that is, in comparison of the emptiness of other men, or of their owne emptinesse before they embraced the Gospell, they abound now; But still it is, *As God hath given the measure of faith to every man;* Not as of his Manna, a certaine measure, and an equall measure, and a full measure to every man; no man hath such a measure of faith, as that he needs no more, or that he may not lose at least some of that. When Christ speakes so doubtfully, *When the Son of man commeth, shall he finde faith upon earth?* Any faith in any man? If the Holy Ghost be come into this presence, into this Congregation, does he find faith in any? A perfect faith he does not.

Deceive not your selves then, with that new charme and flattery of the soule, That if once you can say to your selves you have faith, you need no more, or that you shall alwaies keepe that alive; The Apostle sayes, *All boasting,* that is, all confidence, *is excluded; By what Law?* sayes he, *by the Law of faith,* Not by faith, but by the Law of faith; There is a Law of faith; a rule that ordinates, and regulates our faith; by which law and rule, the Apostle cals upon us, To examine our selves whether we be in the faith, or no; not onely by the internall motions, and private inspirations of his blessed Spirit, but by the Law and the Rule, which he hath delivered to us in the Gospell. The Kings pardon flowes from his meere grace, and from his brest; but we must have the writing and the Seale, that we may plead it: So does faith from God; But we must see it our selves, and shew it to others, or else we doe not observe the Law of faith. *Abraham received the Seale of the righteousnesse of faith,* sayes the Apostle; Hee had an outward testimony to proceed by; And then, *Abraham* became an outward testimony and Rule to the faithfull, *Walke in the steps of the faith of Abraham,* sayes that Apostle in that place; Not a faith conceived onely, but a faith which you saw, The faith of *Abraham;* for, so the Apostle proposing to us the example of other men says, *Their faith follow you,* Not faith in generall, but their faith. So that it is not enough to say, I feele the inspiration of the Spirit of God, He infuses faith, and faith infused cannot be withdrawne; but, as there is a Law of faith, and a practise of faith, a Rule of faith, and an example of faith, apply thy selfe to both; Regulate thy faith by the Rule, that is, the Word, and by Example, that is, Beleeve those things which the Saints of God have constantly and unanimely beleeved to be necessary to salvation: The Word is the Law, and the Rule, The Church is the Practise, and the Precedent that regulates thy faith; And if thou make imaginary revelations, and inspirations thy Law, or the practise of Sectaries thy Precedent, thou doest but call Fancie and

Imagination, by the name of Reason and Understanding, and Opinion by the name of Faith, and Singularity, and Schisme, by the name of Communion of Saints. The Law of thy faith is, That that that thou beleevest, be Universall, Catholique, beleeved by all; And then, that the Application be particular, To beleeve, that as Christ dyed sufficiently for all, so he dyed effectually for thee. And of this effectuall dying for thee, there arises an evidence from thy selfe, in thy conformity to him; Thy conformity consists in this, That thou art willing to live according to his Gospell, and ready to dye for him, that dyed for thee. For, till a man have resisted unto blood, he cannot know experimentally what degrees towards perfection his faith hath: And though he may conceive in himselfe a holy purpose to dye for Christ, yet till he have dyed for Christ, or dyed in Christ, that is, as long as we are in this valley of tentations, there is nothing, no not in spirituall things, not in faith it selfe, perfect.

It is not *In credendis,* in our embracing the object of faith; we doe not that perfectly; It is not *In petendis,* in our directing our prayers faithfully neither; we doe not that; our faith is not perfect, nor our hope is not perfect; for, so argues the Apostle, *Ye aske, and receive not, because ye aske amisse;* you cannot hope constantly, because you doe not pray aright: And to make a Prayer a right Prayer, there go so many essentiall circumstances, as that the best man may justly suspect his best Prayer: for, since Prayer must bee of faith, Prayer can be but so perfect, as the faith is perfect; and the imperfections of the best faith we have seene. Christ hath given us but a short Prayer; and yet we are weary of that. Some of the old Heretiques of the Primitive Church abridged that Prayer, and some of our later Schismatiques have annihilated, evacuated that Prayer: The Cathari then, left out that one Petition, *Dimitte nobis, Forgive us our trespasses,* for they thought themselves so pure, as that they needed no forgivenesse, and our new men leave out the whole Prayer, because the same Spirit that spake in Christ, speakes in their extemporall prayers, and they can pray, as well as Christ could teach them. And (to leave those, whom we are bound to leave, those old Heretiques, those new Schismatiques) which of us ever, ever sayes over that short Prayer, with a deliberate understanding of every Petition as we passe, or without deviations, and extravagancies of our thoughts, in that halfe-minute of our Devotion? We have not leasure to speake of the abuse of prayer in the Roman Church; where they wil antidate and postdate their prayers; Say to morrows prayers to day, and to dayes prayers to morrow, if they have other uses and employments of the due time betweene; where they will trade, and make merchandise of prayers by way of exchange, My man shall fast for me, and I will pray for my man; or my Atturney, and Proxy shall pray for us both, at my charge; nay, where they will play for prayers, and the loser must pray for both; To this there belongs but a holy scorne; and I would faine passe it over quickly. But when we consider with a religious seriousnesse the manifold weaknesses of the strongest devotions in time of Prayer, it is a sad consideration. I throw my selfe downe in my Chamber, and I call in, and invite God, and his Angels thither, and when they are there, I neglect God and his Angels, for the noise of a Flie, for the ratling of a Coach, for the whining of a doore; I talke on, in the same posture of praying; Eyes lifted up; knees bowed downe; as though I prayed to God; and, if God, or his Angels should aske me, when I thought last of God in that prayer, I cannot tell: Sometimes I finde that I had forgot what I was about, but when I began to forget it, I cannot tell. A memory of yesterdays pleasures, a feare of to morrows dangers, a straw under my knee, a noise in mine eare, a light in mine eye, an any thing, a nothing, a fancy, a Chimera in my braine, troubles me in my prayer. So certainely is there nothing, nothing in spirituall things, perfect in this world.

Not *In credendis,* In things that belong to Faith; not *In petendis,* In things that belong to Hope; nor *In agendis,* In things that belong to Action, to Workes, to Charity, there is nothing perfect there neither. I would be loath to say, That every good is a sin; That were to say, That every deformed, or disordered man were a beast, or that every corrupt meat were poyson; It is not utterly so; not so altogether; But it is so much towards it, as that there is no worke of ours so good, as that wee can looke for thanks at Gods hand for that worke; no worke, that hath not so much ill mingled with it, as that wee need not cry God mercy for that worke. There was so much corruption in the getting, or so much vaine glory in the bestowing, as that no man builds an Hospitall, but his soule lies, though not dead, yet lame in that Hospitall; no man mends a high-way, but he is, though not drowned, yet mired in that way; no man relieves the poore, but he needs reliefe for that reliefe. In all those workes of Charity, the world that hath benefit by them, is bound to confesse and acknowledge a goodnesse, and to call them good workes; but the man that does them, and knows the weaknesses of them, knows they are not good works. It is possible to Art, to purge a peccant humour out of a sick bodie; but not possible to raise a dead bodie to life. God, out of my Confession of the impuritie of my best actions, shall vouchsafe to take off his eyes from that impurity, as though there were none; but no spirituall thing in us, not Faith, not Hope, not Charitie, have any puritie, any perfection in themselves; which is the generall Doctrine wee proposed at first; And our next Consideration is, how this weakenesse appeares in the Action, and in the Words of *Martha* in our Text, *Lord, if thou hadst beene here, my brother had not dyed.*

Now lest we should attribute this weakenesse, onely to weake persons, upon whom we had a prejudice, to *Martha* alone, we note to you first, that her sister *Mary,* to whom in the whole Story very much is ascribed, when she comes to Christ, comes also in the same voice of infirmity, *Lord, if thou hadst beene here, my brother had not died.* No person so perfect, that hath not of these imperfections; Both these holy Sisters, howsoever there might be differences of degrees in their holinesse, have imperfections in all three, in the consideration of their Faith, and their Hope, and their Charity; though in all three they had also, and had both, good degrees towards perfection. Looke first upon their Faith; they both say, *Lord, if thou hadst beene here, our brother had not died.* We cannot say so to any Consultation, to any Colledge of Physitians; not to a *Chiron,* to an *Esculapius,* to a God of Physicke, could any man say, If you had beene here, my friend had not died? though surely there be much assistance to be received from them, whom God had endowed with knowledge to that purpose. And yet there was a weakenesse in these Sisters, in that they said but so, and no more to Christ. They thought Christ to be the best amongst good men; but yet they were not come to the knowledge that he was God. *Martha* saies, *I know, that even now, whatsoever thou askest of God, God will give it thee;* but she does not know him to be God himselfe. I doe not here institute a confutation, but here, and every where I lament the growth, and insinuation of that pestilent Heresie of Socinianisme; That Christ was a holy, a thrice-holy man, an unreproachable, an irreprehensible, an admirable, an incomparable man; A man, to whom, he that should equall any other man, were worse than a Devill; A man worthy to bee called God, in a farre higher sense then any Magistrate, any King, any Prophet; But yet hee was no God, say they, no Son of God; A Redeemer, by way of good example; but no Redeemer, by way of equivalent satisfaction, say those Heretiques. S. *Paul* sayes, *He is an Atheist, that is without Christ;* And he is as much an Atheist still, that pretends to receive Christ, and not as God; For if the receiving of Christ must redeeme him from being an Atheist, there can no other way be imagined, but by receiving him as God, for that onely, and no other good opinion of Christ, overcomes, and removes his Atheisme. After the last day, whatsoever is not Heaven, is Hell; Hee that then shall be where the Sunne is now, (if he be not then in heaven) shall be as farre from heaven, as if hee were where the Center of the earth is now! Hee that confesses not all Christ, confesses no Christ. *Horribile dictu, dicam tamen,* sayes S. *Augustine* in another case; There belongs a holy trembling to the saying of it, yet I must say it, *If Christ were not God, hee was a devill that durst say he was God.* This then was one weaknesse in these Sisters faith, that it carried them not up to the consideration of Christ as God; And then another rose out of that, That they insisted so much, relied so much, upon his corporall, and personall presence, and promised themselves more from that, then hee had ever given them ground for; which was that which Christ diverted *Mary* from, when after his Resurrection manifesting himselfe to her, and shee flying unto him with that impatient zeale, and that impetuous devotion, *Rabboni, Master, My Master,* Christ said to her, *Touch mee not, for I am not ascended to my Father;* that is, Dwell not upon this passionate consideration of my bodily, and personall presence, but send thy thoughts, and thy reverence, and thy devotion, and thy holy amorousnesse up, whither I am going, to the right hand of my Father, and consider me, contemplate mee there. S. *Peter* had another holy distemper of another kinde, upon the personall presence of Christ; He was so astonished at his presence in the power of a Miracle, that he fell downe at his feet, and said, *Depart from me, for I am a sinfull man, O Lord.* These Sisters longed for him, and S. *Peter* longed as much to be delivered of him; both out of weaknesse and error. So is it an error, and a weaknesse to attribute too much, or too little to Christs presence in his Sacraments, or other Ordinances. To imprison Christ *in Opere operato,* to conclude him so, as that where that action is done, Christ must necessarily bee, and necessarily work, this is to say weakly with these Sisters, *Lord, if thou hadst beene here, our brother had not died.* As long as we are present at thine Ordinance, thou art present with us. But to banish Christ from those holy actions, and to say, That he is no otherwise present, or works no otherwise in those actions, then in other times, and places, this is to say with *Peter,* in his astonishment, *Exi à me Domine, O Lord depart from me;* It is enough that thy Sacrament be a signe; I do not look that it should be a Seal, or a Conduit of Grace; This is the danger, this is the distemper, to ascribe too much, or too little to Gods visible Ordinances, and Institutions, either to say with those holy Sisters, *Lord, if thou hadst been here, our brother had not died,* If we have a Sacrament, if we have a Sermon all is well, we have enough; or else with *Peter, Exi à me,* Leave me to my selfe, to my private motions, to my bosome inspirations, and I need no Churchwork, no Sermons, no Sacraments, no such assistances.

So there was weaknesse in their Faith, there was so too in their Hope, in their confidence in Christ, and in their manner of expressing it. For, they did not goe to him, when their brother was sick, but sent. *Nicodemus* came in person for his sick soule; And the *Centurion* in person, for his sick servant; And *Jairus* in person, for his sick daughter; And the woman with the bloody Issue in person, for her sick selfe. These sisters did but send, but piously, and reverendly; Their Messenger was to say to Christ, not *Lazarus,* not *Our Brother,* but *He whom thou lovest, is sick;* And they left this intimation to work upon Christ; But that was not enough, we must bring Christ and our necessities neerer together then so. There is good instruction in the severall expressings of Christs curings of *Peters* mother in the Evangelists. S. *Marke* sayes, *They told him of her;* And S. *Luke* sayes, *They brought him up to her;* And S. *Matthew* sayes, *He saw her, and tooke her by the hand.* I must not wrap up all my necessities in generall termes in my prayers, but descend to particulars; For this places my devotion upon particular considerations of God, to consider him in every Attribute, what God hath done for me in Power, what in Wisedome, what in Mercy; which is a great assistance, and establishing, and propagation of devotion. As it is a degree of unthankfulnesse, to thank God too generally, and not to delight to insist upon the waight, and measure, and proportion, and the goodnesse of every particular mercy: so is it an irreverent, and inconsiderate thing, not to take my particular wants into my thoughts, and into my prayers, that so I may take a holy knowledge, that I have nothing, nothing but from God, and by prayer. And as God is an accessible God, as he is his owne *Master of Requests,* and is ever open to receive thy Petitions, in how small a matter soever: so is he an inexhaustible God, he can give infinitely, and an indefatigable God, he cannot be pressed too much. Therefore hath Christ given us a Parable of getting *Bread at midnight* by *Importunity,* and not otherwise; And another of a *Judge* that heard the widows cause by *Importunity,* and not otherwise; And, not a Parable, but a History, and a History of his own, of a woman of *Canaan,* that overcame him in the behalfe of her daughter, by *Importunity;* when, but by importunity, she could not get so much as an answer, as a deniall at his hands. Pray personally, rely not upon dead nor living Saints; Thy Mother the Church prayes for thee, but pray for thy selfe too; Shee can open her bosome, and put the breast to thy mouth, but thou must draw, and suck for they selfe. Pray personally, and pray frequently; *David* had many stationary times of the day, and night too, to pray in. Pray frequently, and pray fervently; God took it not ill, at *Davids* hands, to be *awaked,* and to be called up, as though hee were asleepe at our prayers, and to be called upon, *to pull his hand out of his bosome,* as though he were slack in relieving our necessities. This was a weaknesse in those Sisters, that they solicited not Christ in person; still get as neare God as you can; And that they declared not their case particularly; It is not enough to pray, nor to confesse in generall terms; And, that they pursued not their prayer earnestly, thorowly; It is not enough to have prayed once; Christ does not onely excuse, but enjoine Importunity.

And then a weaknesse there was in their Charity too, even towards their dead brother. To lament a dead friend is naturall, and civill; and he is the deader of the two, the verier carcasse, that does not so. But inordinate lamentation implies a suspition of a worse state in him that is gone; And if I doe beleeve him to be in heaven, deliberately, advisedly to wish him here, that is in heaven, is an uncharitable desire. For, for me to say, He is preferred by being where he is, but I were better, if he were againe where I am, were such an indisposition, as if the Princes servant should be loath to see his Master King, because he should not hold the same place with him, being King, as he did when he was Prince. Not to hope well of him that is gone, is uncharitablenesse; and at the same time, when I beleeve him to be better, to wish him worse, is uncharitablenesse too. And such weaknesses were in those holy and devout Sisters of *Lazarus;* which establishes our Conclusion, There is nothing in this world, no not in spirituall things, not in knowledge, not in faith, not in hope, not in charity perfect. But yet, for all these imperfections, Christ doth not refuse, nor chide, but cherish their piety, which is also another circumstance in that Part.

There is no forme of Building stronger then an Arch, and yet an Arch hath declinations, which even a flat-roofe hath not; The flat-roofe lies equall in all parts; the Arch declines downwards in all parts, and yet the Arch is a firme supporter. Our Devotions doe not the lesse beare us upright, in the sight of God, because they have some declinations towards natural affections: God doth easilier pardon some neglectings of his grace, when it proceeds out of a tendernesse, or may be excused out of good nature, then any presuming upon his grace. If a man doe depart in some actions, from an exact obedience of Gods will, upon infirmity, or humane affections, and not a contempt, God passes it over oftentimes. For, when our Saviour Christ says, *Be pure as your Father in heaven is pure,* that is a rule for our purity, but not a measure of our purity; It is that we should be pure so, not that we should be so pure as our Father in heaven. When we consider that weaknesse, that went through the Apostles, even to Christs Ascension, that they looked for a temporall Kingdome, and for preferment in that; when we consider the weaknesse in the chiefe of them, S. *Peter,* at the *Transfiguration,* when, as the Text sayes, *He knew not what to say;* when we consider the weaknesse of his action, that for feare of death, he renounced the Lord of Life, and denied his Master; when in this very story, when Christ said that *Lazarus* was *asleepe,* and that *he would goe to awake him,* they could understand it so impertinently, as that Christ should goe such a journey, to come to the waking of a man, asleep at that time when he spoke; All these infirmities of theirs, multiply this consolation upon us, That though God look upon the Inscription, he looks upon the metall too, Though he look that his Image should be preserved in us, he looks in what earthen vessels this Image is put, and put by his own hand; and though he hate us in our rebellions, yet he pities us in our grievances; though he would have us better, he forsakes us not for every degree of illnesse. There are three great dangers in this consideration of perfectnesse, and purity; First to distrust of Gods mercy, if thou finde not this purity in thy selfe, and this perfectnesse; And then to presume upon God, nay upon thine own right, in an overvaluing of thine own purity, and perfectnesse; And againe, to condemne others, whom thou wilt needs thinke lesse pure, or perfect then thy selfe. Against this diffidence in God, to thinke our selves so desperately impure, as that God will not look upon us; And this presumption in God, to thinke our selves so pure, as that God is bound to look upon us; And this uncharitablenesse towards others, to think none pure at all, that are not pure our way; Christ armes us by his Example, He receives these sisters of *Lazarus,* and accomplishes as much as they desired, though there were weaknesses in their Faith, in their Hope, in their Charity, expressed in that unperfect speech, *Lord, if thou hadst been here, my brother had not dyed:* for, there is nothing, not in spirituall things perfect. This we have seen out of the Text we have Heard; And now out of the Text, which we See, we shall see the rest, That as in spirituall things, there is nothing Perfect, so in temporall, there is nothing Permanent.

I need not call in new Philosophy, that denies a settlednesse, an acquiescence in the very body of the Earth, but makes the Earth to move in that place, where we thought the Sunne had moved; I need not that helpe, that the Earth it selfe is in Motion, to prove this, That nothing upon Earth is permanent; The Assertion will stand of it selfe, till some man assigne me some instance, something that a man may relie upon, and find permanent. Consider the greatest Bodies upon Earth, The Monarchies; Objects, which one would thinke, Destiny might stand and stare at, but not shake; Consider the smallest bodies upon Earth, The haires of our head, Objects, which one would thinke, Destiny would not observe, or could not discerne; And yet Destiny, (to speak to a naturall man) And God, (to speake to a Christian) is no more troubled to make a Monarchy ruinous, then to make a haire gray. Nay, nothing needs be done to either, by God, or Destiny; A Monarchy will ruine, as a haire will grow gray, of it selfe. In the Elements themselves, of which all sub-elementary things are composed, there is no acquiescence, but a vicissitudinary transmutation into one another; Ayre condensed becomes water, a more solid body, And Ayre rarified becomes fire, a body more disputable, and in-apparant. It is so in the Conditions of men too; A Merchant condensed, kneaded and packed up in a great estate, becomes a Lord; And a Merchant rarified, blown up by a perfidious Factor, or by a riotous Sonne, evaporates into ayre, into nothing, and is not seen. And if there were any thing permanent and durable in this world, yet we got nothing by it, because howsoever that might last in it selfe, yet we could not last to enjoy it; If our goods were not amongst Movables, yet we our selves are; if they could stay with us, yet we cannot stay with them; which is another Consideration in this part.

The world is a great Volume, and man the Index of that Booke; Even in the body of man, you may turne to the whole world; This body is an Illustration of all Nature; Gods recapitulation of all that he had said before, in his *Fiat lux,* and *Fiat firmamentum,* and in all the rest, said or done, in all the six dayes. Propose this body to thy consideration in the highest exaltation thereof; as it is the *Temple of the Holy Ghost:* Nay, not in a Metaphor, or comparison of a Temple, or any other similitudinary thing, but as it was really and truly the very body of God, in the person of Christ, and yet this body must wither, must decay, must languish, must perish. When *Goliah* had armed and fortified this body, And *Jezabel* had painted and perfumed this body, And *Dives* had pampered and larded this body, As God said to *Ezekiel,* when he brought him to the *dry bones, Fili hominis, Sonne of Man, doest thou thinke these bones can live?* They said in their hearts to all the world, Can these bodies die? And they are dead. *Jezabels* dust is not Ambar, nor *Goliahs* dust *Terra sigillata,* Medicinall; nor does the Serpent, whose meat they are both, finde any better relish in *Dives* dust, then in *Lazarus.* But as in our former part, where our foundation was, That in nothing, no spirituall thing, there was any perfectnesse which we illustrated in the weaknesses of Knowledge, and Faith, and Hope, and Charity, yet we concluded, that for all those defects, God accepted those their religious services; So in this part, where our foundation is, That nothing in temporall things is permanent, as we have illustrated that, by the decay of that which is Gods noblest piece in Nature, The body of man; so we shall also conclude that, with this goodnesse of God, that for all this dissolution, and putrefaction, he affords this Body a Resurrection.

The Gentils, and their Poets, describe the sad state of Death so, *Nox una obeunda,* That it is one everlasting Night; To them, a Night; But to a Christian, it is *Dies Mortis,* and *Dies Resurrectionis,* The day of Death, and The day of Resurrection; We die in the light, in the sight of God's presence, and we rise in the light, in the sight of his very Essence. Nay, Gods corrections, and judgements upon us in this life, are still expressed so, *Dies visitationis,* still it is a Day, though a *Day of visitation;* and still we may discerne God to be in the action. The *Lord of Life* was the first that named *Death; Morte morieris,* sayes God, Thou shalt die the Death. I doe the lesse feare, or abhorre Death, because I finde it in his mouth; Even a malediction hath a sweetnesse in his mouth; for there is a blessing wrapped up in it; a mercy in every correction, a Resurrection upon every Death. When *Jezabels* beauty, exalted to that height which it had by art, or higher then that, to that height which it had in her own opinion, shall be infinitely multiplied upon every Body; And as God shall know no man from his own Sonne, so as not to see the very righteousnesse of his own Sonne upon that man; So the Angels shall know no man from Christ, so as not to desire to looke upon that mans face, because the most deformed wretch that is there, shall have the very beauty of Christ himselfe; So shall *Goliahs* armour, and *Dives* fulnesse, be doubled, and redoubled upon us. And every thing that we can call good, shall first be infinitely exalted in the goodnesse, and then infinitely multiplied in the proportion, and againe infinitely extended in the duration. And since we are in an action of preparing this dead Brother of ours to that state, (for the Funerall is the Easter-eve, The Buriall is the depositing of that man for the Resurrection) As we have held you, with Doctrine of Mortification, by extending the Text, from *Martha* to this occasion; so shall we dismisse you with Consolation, by a like occasionall inverting the Text, from passion in *Martha's* mouth, *Lord, if thou hadst been here, my Brother had not dyed,* to joy in ours, *Lord, because thou wast here, our Brother is not dead.*

The Lord was with him in all these steps; with him in his life; with him in his death; He is with him in his funerals, and he shall be with him in his Resurrection; and therefore, because the Lord was with him, our Brother is not dead. He was with him in the beginning of his life, in this manifestation, That though he were of Parents of a good, of a great Estate, yet his possibility and his expectation from them, did not slacken his own industry; which is a Canker that eats into, nay that hath eat up many a family in this City, that relying wholly upon what the Father hath done, the Sonne does nothing for himselfe. And truly, it falls out too often, that he that labours not for more, does not keepe his own. God imprinted in him an industrious disposition, though such hopes from such parents might have excused some slacknesse, and God prospered his industry so, as that when his Fathers estate came to a distribution by death, he needed it not. God was with him, as with *David* in a Dilatation, and then in a Repletion; God enlarged him, and then he filled him; He gave him a large and a comprehensive understanding, and with it, A publique heart; And such as perchance in his way of education, and in our narrow and contracted times, in which every man determines himselfe in himselfe, and scarce looks farther, it would be hard to finde many Examples of such largenesse. You have, I thinke, a phrase of Driving a Trade; And you have, I know, a practise of Driving away Trade, by other use of money; And you have lost a man, that drove a great Trade, the right way in making the best use of our home-commodity. To fetch in Wine, and Spice, and Silke, is but a drawing of Trade; The right driving of trade, is, to vent our owne outward; And yet, for the drawing in of that, which might justly seeme most behoofefull, that is, of Arts, and Manufacturers, to be imployed upon our owne Commodity within the Kingdome, he did his part, diligently, at least, if not vehemently, if not passionately. This City is a great Theater, and he Acted great and various parts in it; And all well; And when he went higher, (as he was often heard in Parliaments, at Councell tables, and in more private accesses to the late King of ever blessed memory) as, for that comprehension of those businesses, which he pretended to understand, no man doubts, for no man lacks arguments and evidences of his ability therein, So for his manner of expressing his intentions, and digesting and uttering his purposes, I have sometimes heard the greatest Master of Language and Judgment, which these times, or any other did, or doe, or shall give, (that good and great King of ours) say of him, That he never heard any man of his breeding, handle businesses more rationally, more pertinently, more elegantly, more perswasively; And when his purpose was, to do a grace to a Preacher, of very good abilities, and good note in his owne Chappell, I have heard him say, that his language, and accent, and manner of delivering himselfe, was like this man. This man hath God accompanied all his life; and by performance thereof seems to have made that Covenant with him, which he made to *Abraham, Multiplicabo te vehementer, I will multiply thee exceedingly.* He multiplied his estate so, as was fit to endow many and great Children; and he multiplied his Children so, both in their number, and in their quality, as they were fit to receive a great Estate. God was with him all the way, In *a Pillar of Fire,* in the brightnesse of prosperity, and in the *Pillar of Clouds* too, in many darke, and sad, and heavy crosses: So great a Ship, required a great Ballast, So many blessings, many crosses; And he had them, and sailed on his course the steadier for them; The *Cloud* as well as the *Fire*, was a *Pillar* to him; His crosses, as well as his blessings established his assurance in God; And so, in all the course of his life, *The Lord was here,* and therefore *our Brother is not dead;* not dead in the evidences and testimonies of life; for he, whom the world hath just cause to celebrate, for things done, when he was alive, is alive still in their celebration.

The Lord was here, that is, with him at his death too. He was served with the Processe here in the City, but his cause was heard in the Country; Here he sickned, There he languished, and dyed there. In his sicknesse there, those that assisted him, are witnesses, of his many expressings, of a religious and a constant heart towards God, and of his pious joyning with them, even in the holy declaration of kneeling, then, when they, in favour of his weakenesse, would disswade him from kneeling. I must not defraud him of this testimony from my selfe, that into this place where we are now met, I have observed him to enter with much reverence, and compose himselfe in this place with much declaration of devotion. And truly it is that reverence, which those persons who are of the same ranke that he was in the City, that reverence that they use in this place, when they come hither, is that that makes us, who have now the administration of this Quire, glad, that our Predecessors, but a very few yeares before our time, (and not before all our times neither) admitted these Honourable and worshipfull Persons of this City, to sit in this Quire, so, as they do upon Sundayes: The Church receives an honour in it; But the honour is more in their reverence, then in their presence; though in that too: And they receive an honour, and an ease in it; and therefore they do piously towards God, and prudently for themselves, and gratefully towards us, in giving us, by their reverent comportment here, so just occasion of continuing that honour, and that ease to them here, which to lesse reverend, and unrespective persons, we should be lesse willing to doe. To returne to him in his sicknesse; He had but one dayes labour, and all the rest were Sabbaths, one day in his sicknesse he converted to businesse; Thus; He called his family, and friends together; Thankfully he acknowledged Gods manifold blessings, and his owne sins as penitently: And then, to those who were to have the disposing of his estate, joyntly with his Children, he recommended his servants, and the poore, and the Hospitals, and the Prisons, which, according to his purpose, have beene all taken into consideration; And after this (which was his Valediction to the world) he seemed alwaies loath to returne to any worldly businesse, His last Commandement to Wife and Children was Christs last commandement to his Spouse the Church, in the Apostles, *To love one another*. He blest them, and the Estate devolved upon them, unto them: And by Gods grace shall prove as true a Prophet to them in that blessing, as he was to himselfe, when in entring his last bed, two dayes before his Death, he said, *Help me off with my earthly habit, and let me go to my last bed*. Where, in the second night after, he said, *Little know ye what paine I feele this night, yet I know, I shall have joy in the morning;* And in that morning he dyed. The forme in which he implored his Saviour, was evermore, towards his end, this, *Christ Jesus, which dyed on the Crosse, forgive me my sins; He have mercy upon me:* And his last and dying words were the repetition of the name of Jesus; And when he had not strength to utter that name distinctly and perfectly, they might heare it from within him, as from a man a far off; even then, when his hollow and remote naming of Jesus, was rather a certifying of them, that he was with his Jesus, then a prayer that he might come to him. And so *The Lord was here,* here with him in his Death; and because *the Lord was here, our Brother is not dead;* not dead in the eyes and eares of God; for as the blood of *Abel* speaks yet, so doth the zeale of Gods Saints; and their last prayers (though we heare them not) God continues still; and they pray in Heaven, as the Martyrs under the Altar, even till the Resurrection.

He is with him now too; Here in his Funerals. Buriall, and Christian Buriall, and Solemne Buriall are all evidences, and testimonies of Gods presence. God forbid we should conclude, or argue an absence of God, from the want of Solemne Buriall, or Christian Buriall, or any Buriall; But neither must we deny it, to be an evidence of his favour and presence, where he is pleased to afford these. So God makes that the seale of all his blessings to *Abraham, That he should be buried in a good age;* God established *Jacob* with that promise, *That his Son Joseph should have care of his Funerals:* And *Joseph* does cause his servants, *The Physitians, to embalme him, when he was dead.* Of Christ it was Prophecied, *That he should have a glorious Buriall;* And therefore Christ interprets well that profuse, and prodigall piety of the Woman that poured out the Oyntment upon him, *That she did it to Bury him;* And so shall *Joseph* of Arimathea be ever celebrated, for his care in celebrating Christs Funerals. If we were to send a Son, or a friend, to take possession of any place in Court, or forraine parts, we would send him out in the best equipage: Let us not grudge to set downe our friends, in the Antichamber of Heaven, the Grave, in as good manner, as without vaine-gloriousnesse, and wastfulnesse we may; And, in inclining them, to whom that care belongs, to expresse that care as they doe this day, *The Lord is with him,* even in this Funerall; And because *The Lord is here, our brother is not dead;* Not dead in the memories and estimation of men.

And lastly, that we may have God present in all his Manifestations, *Hee that was, and is, and is to come,* was with him, in his life and death, and is with him in this holy Solemnity, and shall bee with him againe in the Resurrection. God sayes to *Jacob, I will goe downe with thee into Egypt, and I will also surely bring thee up againe.* God goes downe with a good man into the Grave, and will surely bring him up againe. When? The Angel promised to returne to *Abraham* and *Sarah,* for the assurance of the birth of *Isaac, according to the time of life;* that is, in such time, as by nature a woman may have a childe. God will returne to us in the Grave, *according to the time of life;* that is, in such time, as he, by his gracious Decree, hath fixed for the Resurrection. And in the meane time, no more then the God-head departed from the dead body of our Saviour, in the grave, doth his power, and his presence depart from our dead bodies in that darknesse; But that which *Moses* said to the whole Congregation, I say to you all, both to you that heare me, and to him that does not, *All ye that did cleave unto the Lord your God, are alive, every one of you, this day;* Even hee, whom we call dead, is alive this day. In the presence of God, we lay him downe; In the power of God, he shall rise; In the person of Christ, he is risen already. And so into the same hands that have received his soule, we commend his body; beseeching his blessed Spirit, that as our charity enclines us to hope confidently of his good estate, our faith may assure us of the same happinesse, in our owne behalfe; And that for all our sakes, but especially for his own glory, he will be pleased to hasten the consummation of all, in that kingdome which that Son of God hath purchased for us, with the inestimable price of his incorruptible blood. *Amen.*

# Ben Jonson
## 1572–1637

Ben Jonson was poet, playwright, critic, writer of masques—an all-round man of letters, the greatest in England in his time. The Tribe of Ben, held together by his wit and will, was a unique convergence of intellectuals, professional literary men, and distinguished patrons of literature and learning. Shakespeare, and Shakespeare alone, was his peer on the Elizabethan and Jacobean stage.

Jonson is a deliberate master of his art, a craftsman who thinks and writes a good deal about his craft. His *Art of Poetry* was unfortunately lost in the fire that cost him his library as well, but many of his critical statements remain—some scattered throughout his plays (largely in prologues and epilogues), some reported by William Drummond after Jonson's visit to Scotland in the winter of 1618–1619, and others collected in the commonplace book *Timber, or Discoveries,* which contains pieces ranging from a few sentences to several pages in length, on a variety of literary and ethical subjects.

Much of this material has its origin in earlier writings, mostly Roman, though many moderns are also represented. Still, he clearly sets his own stamp upon his borrowings, and what emerges is the portrayal of a man as independent as he is vigorous in his judgments. Authority and antiquity must be given their due, he insists, but no more. His criteria are classical, their application sturdily and realistically his own.

In writing about poetry he writes also about manners and the good life, and about virtues and vices; for he holds that no man can be a better poet than he is a man, and "he which can faine a *Common-wealth* (which is the *Poet*) can governe it with *Counsels,* strengthen it with *Lawes,* correct it with *Judgements,* informe it with *Religion,* and

*Morals*." In Jonson the critic we find again Jonson the moralist of the mordant comedies:

> What a deale of cold busines doth a man mis-spend the better part of life in! in scattering *complements*, tendring *visits*, gathering and venting *newes*, following *Feasts* and *Playes*, making a little winter-love in a darke corner.

His own style and his comments on style have the virtues of the man. Style should be pure, neat, and plain, he says, not wanton with far-fetched descriptions, or marred by ingenious wresting of the language, but not daintily smooth either. What he stresses always is the congruent and harmonious fitting of parts in the whole, both in verse and in prose, both the well-joining of words in a sentence and the composition of an entire poem or play. "Our style," he writes, "should be like a skeine of silke, to be carried, and found by the right thred, not ravel'd and perplex'd," not all in "a knot, a heape."

This edition reprints most of *Timber* and the *Conversations with Drummond*. Included are Jonson's remarks on metaphor, decorum, critics, wit, imitation, comedy, style, the fable, and the relation of poetry to painting, rhetoric and philosophy, as well as his estimates of Shakespeare, Spenser, and Donne.

## EDITIONS

*The Workes of Benjamin Jonson*, 1616, 1640 (includes the first publication of *Timber, or Discoveries*); ed. by C. H. Herford and P. Simpson, 1925–1952.

*Timber, or Discoveries*, 1640 (in *The Workes*); ed. by M. Castelain, 1906; ed. by G. B. Harrison, 1923; in Herford and Simpson, Vol. VIII, 1947 (introduction in Vol. II, 1925); ed. by Ralph Walker, 1953.

*The Works of William Drummond, of Hawthornden*, 1711. Includes the first publication of the conversations held when Jonson visited Scotland; ed. by G. B. Harrison, 1923; ed. by R. F. Patterson, 1923; in Herford and Simpson, Vol. I, 1925.

## HISTORICAL AND CRITICAL STUDIES

Algernon Swinburne, *A Study of Ben Jonson*, 1889.
Maurice Castelain, *Ben Jonson: L'Homme et L'Oeuvre*, 1907.

PERCY SIMPSON, "'Tanquam Explorator': Jonson's Method in the 'Discoveries,'" *MLR*, II (1907).

G. GREGORY SMITH, *Ben Jonson*, 1919.

SAMUEL A. TANNENBAUM, *Ben Jonson: A Concise Bibliography*, 1938; supplement, 1947.

ALEXANDER H. SACKTON, *Rhetoric as a Dramatic Language in Ben Jonson*, 1948.

C. J. SISSON, "Ben Jonson of Gresham College," *TLS*, Sept. 21, 1951.

JOSEPH ALLEN BRYANT, JR., "The Significance of Ben Jonson's First Requirement for Tragedy: 'Truth of Argument,'" *SP*, XLIX (1952).

RALPH S. WALKER, "Ben Jonson's *Discoveries*: A New Analysis," *Essays and Studies*, V (1952).

MARCHETTE CHUTE, *Ben Jonson of Westminster*, 1953.

JOHN B. BAMBOROUGH, *Ben Jonson*, 1959.

JONAS A. BARISH, *Ben Jonson and the Language of Prose Comedy*, 1960.

FRANK R. FIELER, "The Impact of Bacon and the New Science upon Jonson's Critical Thought in *Timber*," *Renaissance Papers*, ed. by George W. Williams, 1961.

WESLEY TRIMPI, "Jonson and the Neo-Latin Authorities for the Plain Style," *PMLA*, LXXVII (1962).

JONAS A. BARISH, ed., *Ben Jonson: a collection of Critical Essays*, 1963.

ARNOLD STEIN, "Plain Style, Plain Criticism, Plain Dealing, and Ben Jonson," *ELH*, XXX (1963).

# BEN JONSON'S CONVERSATIONS WITH WILLIAM DRUMMOND OF HAWTHORNDEN

## INFORMATIONS BE BEN JOHNSTON TO W. D. WHEN HE CAME TO SCOTLAND UPON FOOT

### 1619

### *Certain Informations and Maners of Ben Johnsons to W. Drumond*

1. That he had ane intention to perfect ane Epick Poeme intitled Heroologia of the Worthies of his Country, rowsed by fame, and was to dedicate it to his Country, it is all in Couplets, for he detesteth all other Rimes, said he had written a discourse of Poesie both against Campion & Daniel especially this Last, wher he proves couplets to be the bravest sort of Verses, especially when they are broken, like Hexameters and that crosse Rimes and Stanzaes (becaus the purpose would lead him beyond 8 lines to conclude) were all forced.

2. He recommended to my reading Quintilian {who (he said) would tell me the faults of my Verses as if he had Lived with me} and Horace, Plinius dus Epistles, Tacitus, Juvenall, Martiall, whose Epigrame Vitam quæ faciunt Beatiorem etc: he heth translated

3. *Censure of Sidney:* His Censure of the English Poets was this, that Sidney did not keep a Decorum in making every one speak as well as himself.

*Spencer:* Spencers stanzaes pleased him not, nor his matter, the meaning of which Allegorie he had delivered in Papers to Sⁱʳ Walter Raughlie.

*Samuel Daniel:* Samuel Daniel was a good honest Man, had no children, bot no poet.

That Michael Draytons Polya⟨l⟩bion {if ⟨he⟩ had performed what he

312

promised to writte the deads of all ye) Worthies} had been excellent his Long Verses pleased him not.

*Silvester:* That Silvesters translation of Du Bartas was not well done, and that he wrote his Verses befor it err he understood to conferr.

Nor that of Fairfax his.

*Of ye translation of Homer and Virgill:* That the translations of Homer and Virgill in Long Alexandrines were but Prose.

That John Haringtones Ariosto, under all translations was the worst.

*Harington:* That when Sir John Harrington desyred him to tell the Truth of his Epigrames, he answered him that he loved not the Truth, for they were Narrations and not Epigrames.

*Warner:* That Warner since the Kings comming to England ⟨ha⟩d marrd all his Albions England.

*Donne:* That Dones Anniversarie was profane and full of Blasphemies

That he told Mr Donne, if it had been written of ye Virgin Marie it had been something, to which he answered that he described the Idea of a Woman and not as she was. that Done for not keeping of accent deserved hanging.

*Of Shakspear:* That Shaksperr wanted Arte

*Of Sharpham, Day and Dicker:* That Sharpham, Day, Dicker were all Rogues and

*Minshew:* That Minshew was one.

*Abram Francis:* That Abram Francis in his English Hexameters was a Foole

*Of Fletcher and Chapman:* That next himself only Fletcher and Chapman could make a Mask.

4. His judgement of Stranger Poets was

*Of Bartas:* That he thought not Bartas a Poet but a Verser, because he wrote not Fiction.

*Of Petrarch:* He cursed Petrarch for redacting Verses to Sonnets, which he said were like that Tirrants bed, wher some who were too short were racked, others too long cut short.

*Of Guarini:* That Guarini in his Pastor Fido kept not decorum in making shepherds speek as well as himself could.

*Of Lucan:* That Lucan taken in parts was Good divided, read alltogidder merited not the name of a Poet

*Of Bonefonius:* That Bonefonius Vigilium Veneris was excellent

*Of Cardinal Perron:* That he told Cardinal deperron at his being in France anno 1613 who shew him in his translations of Virgill that they were naught.

*Of Ronsard:* That the best pieces of Ronsard were his Odes.

all this was to no purpose, for he neither doeth understand French nor Italianne/

5. *Of Horace:* He read his translation of that ode of Horace

*Beatūs ille qui procul Negotiis etc:*

& admired it.

*Of Petronius:* Of ane Epigrame of Petronius

*fœda et brevis est veneris voluptas*

Concluding it was better to lie still and Kisse then pante.

To me he read the Preface of his arte of Poesie, upon Horace Arte of poesie, wher he heth ane apologie of a Play of his St Bartholomees faire, by Criticus is understood Done. ther is ane Epigrame of Sir Edward Herberts befor it, the ⟨translation⟩ he said he had done in my Lord Aubanies House 10 yeers since anno 1604.

The most common place of his repetition was a dialogue Pastoral be-teen a shepherd & shipherdesse about singing

An other Parabostes Pariane with his Letter,

That Epigrame of Gout, my Lady Bedfoords Bucke

His verses of Drinking, drinke to me bot with thyne Eyes,

Swell me a Bowle etc, his verses of a Kisse

bot Kisse me once and Faith I will begone
and I will touch as Harmelesse as the Bee
that doeth bot taste the flower and flee away.

that is but half a one,

what should be done but once, should be done long.

He read a Satyre of a Lady come from the Bath.

Verses on the Pucelle of the Court Mistriss Boulstred, whose Epitaph Donne made.

A Satyre telling there was no abuses to writte a Satyre of and ⟨in⟩ which he repeateth all the abuses in England and the world.

He insisted in that of Martia

*vitam quæ faciūnt Beatiorem*

6. *Censur of Hawthor⟨n⟩de⟨ns⟩ verses:* His censure of my verses was that they were all good, especiallie my Epitaph of the Prince save that they smelled too much of yᵉ schooles and were not after the Fancie of ye tyme. for a child sayes he may writte after the fashion of yᵉ Greeks & latine verses in running. yett that he wished to please the King, that piece of Forth-Feasting had been his ownc.

7. He esteemeth John Done the first poet in the World in some things his verses of the Lost Chaine, he heth by Heart & that passage of the calme, that dust and feathers doe not stirr, all was so quiet. affirmeth Done to have written all his best pieces err he was 25 years old.

Sir Edward Wottons verses of a happie lyfe he hath by Heart, and a peice of Chapmans translation of ye 13 of the Iliads, which he thinketh well done.

That Donne said to him he wrott that Epitaph on Prince Henry

Look to me Fath

to match Sir Ed: Herbert in obscurenesse.

He hath by Heart some verses of Spensers Calender about wyne between Coline & percye.

8. The Conceit of Donnes transformation or μετεμψυχοσις was that he sought the soule of that Aple which Eva pulled, and therafter made it the soule of a Bitch, then of a sheewolf & so of a woman. his generall purpose was to have brought in all the bodies of the Hereticks from ye soule of Cain & at last left it in ye body of Calvin. of this he never wrote but one sheet, & now since he was made Doctor repenteth highlie & seeketh to destroy all his poems.

9. That Petronius, Plinius Secundus, Tacitus speke best Latine, that Quintilianes 6. 7. 8. bookes, were not only to be read but altogither digested. Juvenal, Perse, Horace, Martiall for delight & so was Pindar. for Health Hippocrates.

Of their Nation Hookers Ecclesiasticall historie (whose children are now beggars) for church matters. Seldens titles of honour for Antiquities here & ane book of the Gods of ye Gentiles whose Names are in the scripture of Seldens.

Tacitus he said wrott the secrets of the Councill and Senate, as Sue-
toniũs did those of the Cabinet and Courte.

10. For a Heroik poeme he said ther was no such Ground as King
Arthurs fiction & yt S. P. Sidney had ane intention to have transform'd
all his Arcadia to ye stories of King Arthure.

11. His acquaintance & Behaviour with Poets Living with him.
Daniel was at Jealousies with him.
Drayton feared him, and he esteemed not of him,
That Francis Beamont loved too much himself & his own verses
Yt S^r John Roe loved him & when they two were ushered by my Lord
Suffolk from a Mask, Roe wrott a moral epistle to him, which began that
next to plays the Court and the State were the best. God threateneth
Kings, Kings Lords & Lords do us
He beate Marston and took his pistoll from him.
Sir W. Alexander was not half Kinde unto him & neglected him
because a friend to Drayton.
That Sir R. Aiton loved him dearly,
Nid field was his Schollar & he had read to him the Satyres of Horace
& some Epigrames of Martiall.
That Markham (who added his English Arcadia) was not of the
number of the Faithfull .j. Poets and but a base fellow
That such were Day and Midleton.
That Chapman and Fletcher were loved of him,
Overbury was first his friend. then turn'd his mortall enimie.

12. Particulars of the actions of other Poets and apothegmes.
That the Irish having Robd Spensers goods & burnt his house & a
litle child new born, he and his wyfe escaped, & after he died for lake
of bread in King street and refused 20 pieces sent to him by my Lord of
Essex & said he was sorrie he had no time to spend them.
That in yt paper S. W Raughly had of ye Allegories of his Fayrie
Queen by ye Blating beast the Puritans were understood by y^e false
Duessa the Q of Scots.
That Southwell was hanged yett so he had written that piece of his
ye burning babe he would have been content to destroy many of his.
Franc: Beaumont died err he was 30 years of age,
S^r John Roe was ane infinit Spender & used to Say when he had no

more to spende he could die. he died in his armes of the pest & he furnished his charges 20 lb, which was given him back.

That Drayton was chalenged for intitling one book Mortimuriados

That S. J. Davies played in ane Epigrame on Drayton, who in a Sonnet concluded his Mistriss might been the ninth worthy & said he used a phrase like Dametas in Arcadia, who said for wit his mistresse might be a Gyant.

Dones Grandfather on the mother side was Heywood the Epigrammatist.

That Done himself for not being understood would perish.

That S$^r$ W. Raughlye esteemed more of fame than conscience/

The best wits of England were Employed for making of his historie.

Ben himself had written a peice to him of ye punick warre which he altered and set in his booke.

S. W. heth written the lyfe of Queen Elizabeth, of which ther is copies extant

Sir P. Sidney had translated some of the Psalmes, which went abroad under the name of ye Countesse of Pembrock.

Marston wrott his Father in Lawes preachings & his Father in Law his Commedies.

Sheakspear in a play brought in a number of men saying they had suffered Shipwrack in Bohemia, wher y$^r$ is no Sea neer by some 100 Miles.

Daniel wrott civill warres & yett hath not one batle in all his Book.

The countess of Rutland was nothing inferior to her Father S. P. Sidney in Poesie. Sir Th: Overburie was in love with her, and caused Ben to read his wyffe to her, which he with ane excellent grace did & praised the Author. that the Morne Thereafter he discorded with Overburie, who would have him to intend a sute yt was unlawfull. the lines my Lady Keepd in remembrance he comes to near, who comes to be denied.

Beamont wrot that Elegie on the death of the Countess of Rutland, and in effect her husband wanted the half of his in his travells.

Owen is a pure Pedantique Schoolmaster sweeping his living from the Posteriors of litle children, and hath no thinge good in him, his Epigrames being bare narrations.

Chapman hath translated Musæus in his verses like his Homer Flesher and Beaumont ten yeers since hath written the Fathfull Shipheardesses a Tragicomedie well done.

Dyer died unmaried.

S. P. Sidney was no pleasant man in countenance, his face being spoilled with Pimples & of high blood & Long, that My Lord lisle earle of Worster his eldest son resembleth him.

### 13.  Of his owne lyfe, education, birth, actions

His Grandfather came from Carlisle & he thought from Anandale to it, he served King Henry 8 & was a Gentleman his father Losed all his estate under Queen Marie, having been cast in prisson and forfaitted, at last turn'd Minister So he was a Ministers son, he himself was Posthumous born a moneth after his fathers decease, brought up poorly, putt to school by a friend (his master Cambden) after taken from it, and put to ane other Craft (I thinke was to be a Wright or Bricklayer) which he could not endure, then went he to ye low Countries but returning soone he betook himself to his wonted studies. In his servuce in the Low Countries, he had in the face of both the Campes Killed ane Enimie & taken opima spolia from him, and since his comming to England being appealed to the fields he had Killed his adversarie, which had hurt him in the arme & whose sword was 10 Inches Longer than his, for the which he was Emprissoned and almost at the Gallowes. then took he his Religion by trust of a priest who Visited him in Prison. thereafter he was 12 yeares a Papist

He was Master of Arts in both ye Universities by y$^r$ favour not his studie.

He maried a wyfe who was a shrew yet honest, 5 yeers he had not bedded w$^t$ her but remained w$^t$ my Lord Aulbanie.

In the tyme of his close Imprissonment under Queen Elisabeth his judges could gett nothing of him to all y$^r$ demands bot I and No, they placed two damn'd Villans to catch advantage of him, w$^t$ him, but he was advertised by his Keeper, of the Spies he hath ane Epigrame.

When the King came in England, at that tyme the Pest was in London, he being in the Country at S$^r$ Robert Cottons house with old Cambden, he saw in a vision his eldest sone (y$^n$ a child and at London) appear unto him w$^t$ ye Marke of a bloodie crosse on his forehead as if it had been cutted w$^t$ a suord, at which amazed he prayed unto God, and in ye morning he came to M$^r$. Cambdens chamber to tell him, who persuaded him it was but ane appreehension of his fantasie at which he sould not be disjected⟨.⟩ in ye mean tyme comes yr letters from his wife of ye death of yt Boy in ye plague. he appeared to him he said of a

Manlie shape & of yt Grouth that he thinks he shall be at the resurrection.

He was delated by S$^r$ James Murray to the King for writting something against the Scots in a play Eastward hoe & voluntarly Imprissonned himself w$^t$ Chapman and Marston, who had written it amongst y$^m$. the report was that they should then had their ears cutt & noses. after y$^r$ delivery he banqueted all his friends, y$^r$ was Camden Selden and others. at the midst of the Feast his old Mother Dranke to him & shew him a paper which she had (if the Sentence had taken execution) to have mixed in y$^e$ Prisson among his drinke, which was full of Lustie strong poison & that she was no churle she told she minded first to have Drunk of it herself.

He had many quarrells with Marston beat him & took his Pistol from him, wrote his Poetaster on him the beginning of y$^m$ were that Marston represented him in the stage

In his youth given to Venerie. he thought the use of a maide, nothing in comparison to ye wantoness of a wyfe & would never have ane other Mistress. he said two accidents strange befell him, one that a man made his own wyfe to Court him, whom he enjoyed two yeares erre he knew of it, & one day finding them by chance Was passingly delighted with it, one other lay diverse tymes with a woman, who shew him all that he wished except the last act, which she would neuer agree unto.

S. W. Raulighe sent him Governour w$^t$ his son anno 1613 to France. this Youth being knavishly inclyned, among other pastimes (as the setting of the favour of Damosells on a Cod piece) caused him to be Drunken & dead drunk, so that he knew not wher he was, thereafter laid him on a Carr which he made to be Drawen by Pioners through the streets, at every corner showing his Governour streetched out & telling them that was a more Lively image of ye Crucifix then any they had, at which Sporte young Raughlies mother delyghted much (saying his father young was so inclyned) though the father abhorred it.

He can set Horoscopes, but trusts not in y$^m$, he with ye consent of a friend Cousened a lady, with whom he had made ane apointment to meet ane old Astrologer in the suburbs, which she Keeped & it was himself disguysed in a Longe Gowne & a whyte beard at the light of ⟨a⟩ Dimm burning Candle up in a litle Cabinet reached unto by a Ledder.

Every first day of the new year he had 20 lb sent him from the Earl of Pembrok to buy bookes.

After he was reconciled with the Church & left of to be a recusant at his first communion in token of true Reconciliation, he drank out all the full cup of wyne.

Being at ye end of my Lord Salisburie's table with Inigo Jones & demanded by my Lord, why he was not glad My Lord said he yow promised I should dine with yow, bot I doe not, for he had none of his meate, he esteamed only yt his meate which was of his owne dish.

He heth consumed a whole night in lying looking to his great toe, about which he hath seen tartars & turks Romans and Carthaginions feight in his imagination.

Northampton was his mortall enimie for brauling on a S$^t$ Georges day one of his attenders, he was called befor ye Councell for his Sejanus & accused both of popperie and treason by him.

Sundry tymes he heth devoured his bookes .j. sold y$^m$ all for Necessity.

He heth a minde to be a churchman, & so he might have favour to make one Sermon to the King, he careth not what y$^r$after sould befall him, for he would not flatter though he saw Death. at his hither comming S$^r$ Francis Bacon said to him, he loved not to sie poesy goe on other feet y$^n$ poetical dactil & spondæ.

14. His Narrations of great ones

He never esteemed of a man for the name of a Lord.

Queen Elizabeth never saw her self after she became old in a true Glass. they painted her & sometymes would vermilion her nose, she had allwayes about Christmass evens set dice, that threw sixes or five, & she knew not they were other, to make her win & esteame her self fortunate. that she had a Membrana on her which made her uncapable of man, though for her delight she tryed many, at the comming over of Monsieur, ther was a French Chirurgion who took in hand to cut it, yett fear stayed her & his death. King Philip had intention by dispensation of ye Pope to have maried her.

S$^r$ P. Sidneyes mother Licesters sister after she had ye litle pox never shew her self in Court y$^r$after bot Masked:

The Earl of Licester Gave a botle of liquor to his Lady which he willed her to use in any faintness which she after his returne from court not knowing it was Poison gave him and so he died Salisbury never cared for any man longer nor he could make use of him.

My Lord Lisles daughter my Lady wroth is unworthily maried on a Jealous husband.

Ben one day being at table with my Lady Rutland, her husband comming in, accused her that she keept table to poets, of which she wrott a letter to him which he answered My Lord intercepted the letter, but never chalenged him.

My Lord Chancelor of England wringeth his speeches from the strings of his band & other Councellours from ye pyking of y$^r$ teeth.

Pembrok and his Lady discoursing the Earl said the Woemen were mens shadowes, and she maintained y$^m$, both appealing to Johnson, he affirmed it true, for which my Lady gave a pennance to prove it in Verse, hence his Epigrame

Essex wrotte that Epistle or preface before the translation of y$^e$ last part of Tacitus which is A B. the last book ye Gentlemen durst not translate for ye evill it containes of ye Jewes.

The King said Sir P. Sidney was no poet neither did he see ever any verses in England to ye Scullors

It were good that the half of the Preachers of England were Plain ignorants for that either in ther sermons they flatter, or strive to show their owne Eloquence.

## 15. His opinion of Verses

That he wrott all his first in prose, for so his master Cambden had Learned him.

That Verses stood by sense without either Colour's or accent, which yett other tymes he denied.

A Great many Epigrams were ill, because they expressed in the end, who sould have been understood, by what was said
that of S. John Davies.

Some loved running Verses plus mihi com⟨m⟩a placet

He imitated the description of a night from Bonifonius his Vigilium Veneris

He scorned such verses as could be transponed

> wher is the man yt never yett did hear
> of faire Penelope Ulisses Queene—
> of faire Penelope Ulisses Queen
> wher is the man yt never yett did hear

## 16. Of his workes.

That the half of his comedies were not in Print, he heth a Pastorall intitled the May Lord, his own name is Alkin Ethra the Countess of

Bedfoords Mogibell overberry, the old Countesse of Suffolk ane inchanteress other names are given to somersets Lady, Pemb⟨r⟩ook the Countess of Rutland, Lady Wroth.

In his first storie Alkin commeth in mending his broken pipe. contrary to all other pastoralls, he bringeth the Clownes making Mirth and foolish Sports

He heth intention to writt a fisher or Pastorall play & sett the stage of it in the Lowmond Lake.

That Epithalamium that wants a name in his Printed Workes was made at the Earl of Essex Mariage.

He is to writt his foot pilgrimage hither & to call it a discoverie in a poem he calleth Edinborough the hart of Scotland Britaines other eye.

A play of his upon which he was accused the Divell is ane ass, according to Comedia Vetus, in England the divell was brought in either w$^t$ one Vice or other, the Play done the divel caried away the Vice, he brings in ye divel so overcome w$^t$ ye wickednes of this age that ⟨he⟩ thought himself ane ass⟨.⟩ παρεργως is discoursed of the Duke of Drown land. the King desyred him to conceal it.

He heth commented & translated Horace Art of Poesie, it is in Dialogue wayes by Criticus he understandeth D$^r$. Done.

The old book yt goes about (the art of English Poesie) was done 20 yeers since & Keept Long in wrytte as a secret.

He had ane intention to have made a play like Plaut Amphitrio but left it of, for that he could never find two so like others that he could persuade the spectators they were one

17. Of his Jeasts and Apothegms

At what tyme Henry the 4t turn'd Catholick, pasquill had in his hand a booke & was asked by Morphorius what it was, he told him it was Gramer, Why doe ye studie Gramer being so old asked Morphorius, because answered he I have found a Positive that heth no superlative, and a superlative that wants a positive, the King of Spain is Rex Catholicus & is not Catholicissimus & the French King Christianissimus yett is not Christianus.

When they drank on him he cited yt of plinie that they had call'd him ad prandium non ad pœnam et notam.

& said of that Panagyrist who wrott Panagyriques in acrostics, Windowes crosses, that he was homo Miserrimæ patientiæ, he scorned Anagrams & had ever in his mouth

*turpe est, difficiles amare Nugas.*
*et stultus labor est ineptiarum*

A Cook who was of ane Evill lyfe, when a minister told him he would to hell, askt what torment was y^r, being answered fyre, fire (said he) that is my Play fellow.

A Lord playing at Tenis & having asked those in the Gallerie whither a strock was chase or Losse, a Brother of my Lord Northumberlands answered it was loss. the Lord demanded if he did say it. I say it said he, what are yow. I have played your worth said ye Lord, ye know not the Worth of a Gentleman replyed the other. & it proved so for err he died, he was greater then the other. ane other English Lord lossed all his Game, if he had seen a face that liked him not he stroke his Balls at y^t Gallerie.

Ane English man who had maintained democritus opinion of atomes, being old wrott a book to his son (who was not then Six years of age) in which he left him arguments to maintain and answer objections, for all that was in his book, only if they objected obscuritie against his book he bid him answer that his father above all names in the world hated most the name of Lucifer, and all open writters were Luciferi.

Butlar excommunicat from his table all reporters of Long Poems, wilfull disputers, tedious discoursers, the best banquets were those, wher they mistered no Musitians to chase tym

The greatest sport he saw in france, was the picture of our saviour with ye apostles eating ye Pascall Lamb yt was all Larded.

At a supper wher a Gentlewoman had Given him unsavory wild-foul & yrafter to wash sweet water, he commendet her that shee gave him sueet water, because her flesh stinked.

He said to Prince Charles of Inigo Jones, that when he wanted words to express the greatest Villaine in ye world he would call him ane Inigo.

Jones having accused him for naming him behind his back a foole he denied it but sayes he. I said he was ane arrant knave & I avouch it.

One who fired a Tobacco pipe with a ballet the next day having a sore head, swoare he had a great singing in his heade & he thought it was the ballet. a Poet should detest a Ballet maker. He saw a picture painted by a bad painter of Easter, Haman & Assuerus, Haman courting Esther in a Bed after the fashion of ours, was only seen by one Leg, assuerus back was turned with this Verse over him & wilt thou Haman he so malitious as to lye wt myne own wyfe in myne house

He himself being once so taken the Good man said, I would not believe yee would abuse my house so

In a Profound Contemplation a student of Oxeford ran over a Man in the fields & walked 12 Miles ere he knew what he was doing

One who wore side hair, being asked of ane other who was Bald, why he suffered his haire to grow so long, answered it was to sie if his haire would grow to seed, yt he might sow of it on Bald Pates.

A painter who could paint nothing but a Rose, when ane Innkeeper had advised wt him about ane Ensing, said that a horse was a good one. so was a Hare, but a Rose was above y$^m$ all a litle man drinking prince Henries Health, between two tall Fellowes said he made up the H.

Sir Henry Wotton, befor his Majesties going to England, being Disguised at Lieth, on sunday when all the rest were at Church being interupted of his Occupation, by ane other Wenche who came in at the Door, cryed out Pox on the, for thou hast hindered the procreation of a Chyld & betrayed himself.

A Justice of peace would have comanded a Captaine to sit first, at a table because sayes he, I ame a Justice of Peace, the other drawing his suord comanded him for sayeth he I ame a Justice of War.

What is that, that the more yow cut of it, groweth still y$^e$ longer? a ditch.

He used to say that they who delight to fill men extraordinarie full in their own houses, loved to have their meate againe.

A Certain puritain Minister, would not give the Comunion save unto 13 at once (imitating as he thought our master) now when they were sett & one bethinking himself that some of y$^m$ must represent Judas, that it sould not be he returned & so did all y$^e$ rest understanding his thought.

A Gentlewoman fell in such a Phantasie or Phrensie w$^t$ one M$^r$ Dod a Puritan preacher yt she requeested her husband that for the procreation of ane Angel or Saint he might lye wt her, which having obtained it was bot ane ordinarie birth.

Scaliger writtes ane Epistle to Casawbone wher he scorns the Englishe speak of Latine for He thought he had speken English to him.

A Gentleman reading a Poem yt began with

> Wher is that man that never yet did hear
> of fair Penelope, Ulisses Queene.

calling his Cook asked if he had ever hard of her, who ansuering no, demonstrate to him

> Lo ther the man that never yet did hear
> of fair Penelope Ulisses Queene

A waiting woman having cockered w^t Muskadel and eggs her Misteresse page, for a shee meeting in the dark, his mistress invaded of whom she would of such boldness have a reason. faith Lady said hee I have no reason. save that such was the good Pleasure of Muscadel and eggs.

A Judge comming a long a Hall, and being stopped by a throng cried Dominum cognoscite vestrum, one of y^m y^r said they would if he durst say the beginning of yt verse (for he had a fair wyfe).

> *Actæon ego sum*

cryed he, and went on

A Packet of letters which had fallen over Boord was devored of a Fish, that was tane at flushing, and the letters were safely delivered to him to whom they were written at London

He scorned that simplicitie of Cardan, about the peeble stone of Dover, which he thought had y^t vertue keeped, betweene ones teeth as to save him from being sick.

A schollar expert in Latine and Greke but Nothing in the English said of Hott broath, that he would make the danger of it. for it could not be ill English yt was good Latine facere periculum

A translatour of the Emperours lyves, translated Antonius Pius, Antonie Pye.

The word Harlott was taken from Arlotte, who was the mother of William the Conquerour, a Rogue from the Latine erro, by putting a G to it.

S^r Geslaine Piercy asked the Major of Plimmouth, whither it was his own Beard or the Towns Beard that he came to wellcome my Lord with, for he thought it was so long, that he thought every one of the Town had eked some part to it.

That he stroke at S^r Hierosme Bowes Breast, and asked him, if he was within.

An epitaph was made upon one who had a Long Beard.

> here Lyes a Man at a Beards end etc.

He said to the King his master M. G. Buchanan, had corrupted his eare when young & learned him to sing Verses, when he sould have read them.

S$^r$ Francis Walsingham said of our King when he was Ambassadour in Scotland, hic nunquam regnabit super nos

Of all his Playes he never Gained 2 hundreth pounds.

He had oft this Verse, though he scorned it

> so long as we may, let us enjoy this breath
> for nought doth kill a man so soon, as death.

One Master Gryse told the King of a man who being consumed occupied his wife with a Dildoe, and she never knew of it till on day he all slepperie had ther left his.

Heywood the Epigrammatist being apparelled in Velvet by Queen Mary with his Cap on in the presence, in spight of all the Gentlemen, till the Queen her self asked him what he meaned, and then he asked her if he was Heywood, for she had made him so brave that he almost had misknowen himself.

His Impresa was a Compass with one foot in Center, the other Broken, the word. Deest quod duceret orbem.

Essex after his brothers death M$^r$ D'Evreux in France at Tilt had a black shield void, the word Par nulla figura dolori. ane other tyme, when the Queen was offended at him. a Diamond with its own ashes with which it is Cutt, about it the word Dum Formas Minuis.

He gave the Prince Fax gloria mentis honestæ.

He said to me that I was too good and simple, and that oft a mans modestie, made a fool of his witt.

His armes were three spindles or Rhombi, his own word about y$^m$ percunctabor or perscrutator.

His Epitaph by a companion written is

> here Lyes Benjamin Johnson dead
> and hath no more with than ⟨a⟩ goose in his head,
> that as he was wont, so doth he still
> live by his wit, and evermore will.

ane other

> here lyes honest Ben
> that had not a beard on his chen.

18. Miscellanies

John Stow had monstrous observations in his Chronicle and was of his craft a Tailour. he and I walking alone he asked two Criples what they would have to take him to their order.

In his Sejanus he hath translated a whole oration of Tacitus.

The first four bookes of Tacit ignorantly done in Englishe.

J. Selden liveth on his owne, is the Law book of ye Judges of England, the bravest man in all Languages, his booke titles of honour, written to his chamber fellow Heyward.

Tailor was sent along here to scorn him.

Cambden wrot that book remaines of Bretagne.

Joseph Hall the Herbenger to Dones Anniversarie

The Epigrame of Martial Vin Verpum he Vantes to expone.

Lucan, Sidney, Guarini make every man speak as well as themselves, forgetting decorum, for Dametas sometymes speaks Grave sentences, Lucan taken in parts excellent; altogidder naught.

He dissuaded me from Poetrie, for that she had beggered him, when he might have been a rich lawyer, Physitian or Marchant.

Questioned about English, them, they, those. they is still the Nominative, those accusative, them Newter, collective, not them men them trees, but them by it self referrd to Many.

Which, who, be relatives, not that.

Flouds, Hilles, he would have Masculines.

He was better Versed & knew more in Greek and Latin, than all the Poets in England and quintessence⟨th⟩ their braines.

He made Much of that Epistle of Plinius, wher ad prandium non ad notam is & yt other of Marcellinus who plinie made to be removed from the table, & of the Grosse Turbat.

One wrote ane Epigrame to his father & vanted he had slain ten. the quantity of decem being false, an other answered the Epigrame telling that decem was false. S. J. Davies Epigrame of the Whoores C. compared to a Coule.

Of all stiles he loved most to be named honest, and hath of that ane hundreth letters so naming him

He had this oft

> thy flattering Picture Phrenee is lyke the
> only in this that ye both painted be.

In his merry humor, he was wont to name himself the Poet

He went from Lieth homeward the 25 of January 1619 in a pair of shoes, which he told lasted him since he came from Darnton, which he minded to take back that farr againe they were appearing like Coriats, the first two dayes he was all excoriate.

If he died by the Way, he promised to send me his papers of this Country, Hewen as they were.

I have to send him descriptions of Edinbrough Borrow lawes, of the Lowmond.

That piece of the Pucelle of the Court, was stollen out of his pocket by a Gentleman who drank him drousie & given Mistress Boulstraid, which brought him great displeasur.

19. He sent to me this Madrigal

> on a lovers dust, made sand for ane Hourse Glasse
> Doe but consider this small dust here running in yᵉ Glasse
>    by atomes moved
> could thou believe that this the bodie ever was
>    of one that loved?
> and, in his Mistresse flaming Playing like the Flye,
>    turn'd to Cinders by her eye?
>     Yes, and in death, as lyfe unblest
>      to have it exprest
>       Even ashes of lovers find no rest.

and this which is (as he said) a picture of himselfe.

> I doubt that love is rather deafe than blinde
>   for else it could not bee
>     that shee,
> whom I adore so much should so slight mee,
> and cast my sute behinde.
>   I' am sure my Language to her is as sweet
>   and all my closes meet
>   in numbers of as subtile feete,
>     as makes the youngest hee
>     that fits in shadow of Apollos tree.

> O, but my conscious feares
>   that flye my thoughts betweene,
> prompt mee, that shee hath seene
>   my hundred of Gray haires,
>   told Six and forty yeares,
> read so much Waste as she cannot embrace
> my Mountaine belly and my rockye face.
> and all these through her eies, have stop'd her eares.

January 19, 1619.

He is a great lover and praiser of himself, a contemner and Scorner of others, given rather to losse a friend, than a Jest, jealous of every word and action of those about him (especiallie after drink, which is one of the Elements in which he liveth) a dissembler of ill parts which raigne in him, a bragger of some good that he wanteth, thinketh nothing well bot what either he himself, or some of his friends and Countrymen hath said or done. he is passionately kynde and angry, carelesse either to gaine or keep, Vindicative, but if he be well answered, at himself.

For any religion as being versed in both.

Interpreteth best sayings and deeds often to the worst:

Oppressed with fantasie, which hath ever mastered his reason, a generall disease in many poets. his inventions are smooth and easie, but above all he excelleth in a translation.

When his Play of a Silent woman was first acted, ther was found Verses after on the stage against him, concluding that, that play was well named the Silent Woman. ther was never one man to say plaudite to it

**Finis**

# TIMBER, OR DISCOVERIES

### Winter-Love in a Dark Corner

What a deale of cold busines doth a man mis-spend the better part of life in! in scattering *complements,* tendring *visits,* gathering and venting *newes,* following *Feasts* and *Playes,* making a little winter love in a darke corner. . . .

### Ancients and Moderns

I cannot thinke *Nature* is so spent, and decay'd, that she can bring forth nothing worth her former yeares. She is alwayes the same, like her selfe: And when she collects her strength, is abler still. Men are decay'd, and *studies:* Shee is not.

I know *Nothing* can conduce more to letters, then to examine the writings of the *Ancients,* and not to rest in their sole Authority, or take all upon trust from them; provided the plagues of *Judging,* and *Pronouncing* against them, be away; such as are *envy, bitternesse, precipitation, impudence,* and *scurrile scoffing.* For to all the observations of the *Ancients,* wee have our owne experience: which, if wee will use, and apply, wee have better meanes to pronounce. It is true they open'd the gates, and made the way, that went before us; but as Guides, not Commanders: *Non Domini nostri, sed Duces fuêre.* Truth lyes open to all; it is no mans *severall. Patet omnibus veritas; nondum est occupata. Multum ex illâ, etiam futuris relictum est.*

If in some things I dissent from others, whose *Wit, Industry, Diligence,* and *Judgement* I looke up at, and admire: let me not therefore heare presently of Ingratitude, and Rashnesse. For I thanke those, that have taught me, and will ever: but yet dare not thinke the *scope* of their labour, and enquiry, was to envy their posterity, what they also could adde, and find out. . . .

### The Trimming of a Scholar

What a sight it is, to see *Writers* committed together by the eares, for *Ceremonies, Syllables, Points, Colons, Comma's, Hyphens,* and the like? fighting, as for their fires, and their Altars; and angry that none are frighted at their noyses, and loud brayings under their asses skins?

There is hope of getting a fortune without digging in these quarries. *Sed meliore* (*in omne*) *ingenio, animoque quàm fortunâ, sum usus.*

*Pingue solum lassat: sed juvat ipse labor.*

Wits made out their severall expeditions then, for the discovery of *Truth,* to find out great and profitable *Knowledges;* had their severall instruments for the disquisition of Arts. Now, there are certaine *Scioli,* or *smatterers,* that are busie in the skirts, and out-sides of Learning, and have scarce any thing of solide literature to commend them. They may have some edging, or trimming of a Scholler, a welt, or so: but it is no more.

*Imposture* is a specious thing; yet never worse, then when it faines to be best, and to none discover'd sooner, then the simplest. For *Truth* and *Goodnesse* are plaine, and open: but *Imposture* is ever asham'd of the light.

*A Puppet-play* must be shadow'd, and seene in the darke: For draw the Curtaine, *Et sordet gesticulatio.* . . .

## Artificers as Liars

*Envy* is no new thing, nor was it borne onely in our times. The Ages past have brought it forth, and the comming Ages will. So long as there are men fit for it, *quorum odium virtute relictâ placet,* it will never be wanting. It is a barbarous envy, to take from those mens vertues, which because thou canst not arrive at, thou impotently despaires⟨t⟩ to imitate. Is it a crime in me that I know that, which others had not yet knowne, but from me? or that I am the Author of many things, which never would have come in thy thought, but that I taught them? It is a new, but a foolish way you have found out, that whom you cannot equall, or come neere in doing, you would destroy, or ruine with evill speaking: As if you had bound both your wits, and natures prentises to slander, and then came forth the best Artificers, when you could forme the foulest calumnies.

*Indeed,* nothing is of more credit, or request now, then a petulant paper, or scoffing verses; and it is but convenient to the times and manners wee live with, to have then the worst writings, and studies flourish, when the best begin to be despis'd. *Ill Arts* begin, where good end.

The time was, when men would learne, and study good things; not envie those that had them. Then men were had in price for learning: now, letters onely make men vile. Hee is upbraydingly call'd a *Poet,* as if it were a most contemptible *Nick-name.* But the *Professors* (indeed) have made the learning cheape. Rayling, and tinckling *Rimers,* whose Writings the vulgar more greedily reade; as being taken with the scurrility, and petulancie of such wits. Hee shall not have a Reader now, unlesse hee jeere and lye. It is the food of mens natures: the diet of the times! *Gallants* cannot sleepe else. The Writer must lye, and the gentle Reader rests happy, to heare the worthiest workes misinterpreted; the clearest actions obscured; the innocent'st life traduc'd; And in such a licence of lying, a field so fruitfull of slanders, how can there be matter wanting to his laughter? Hence comes the *Epidemicall* Infection. For how can they escape the contagion of the Writings, whom the virulency of the calumnies hath not stav'd off from reading?

*Nothing* doth more invite a greedy Reader, then an unlook'd-for *subject.* And what more unlook'd-for, then to see a person of an un-

blam'd life, made ridiculous, or odious, by the Artifice of lying? But
it is the disease of the Age: and no wonder if the world, growing old,
begin to be infirme: Old age it selfe is a disease. It is long since the
sick world began to doate, and talke idly: Would she had but doated
still; but her dotage is now broke forth into a madnesse, and become
a meere phrency. . . .

## Eloquence

*Eloquence* is a great, and diverse thing: Nor did she yet ever favour
any man so much, as to become wholly his. Hee is happy, that can
arrive to any degree of her grace. Yet there are, who prove themselves
Masters of her, and absolute Lords: but I beleeve, they may mistake their
evidence: For it is one thing to be *eloquent* in the *Schooles,* or in the
*Hall;* another at the *Barre,* or in the *Pulpit.* There is a difference betweene *Mooting,* and *Pleading;* between *Fencing,* and *Fighting.* To
make Arguments in my Study, and confute them, is easie; where I
answer my selfe, not an Adversary. So, I can see whole *volumes* dispatch'd by the *umbraticall* Doctors on all sides: But draw these forth
into the just lists; let them appeare *sub dio,* and they are chang'd with
the place, like bodies bred i' the *shade;* they cannot suffer the *Sunne,*
or a *Showre;* nor beare the open Ayre: they scarce can find themselves,
they that were wont to domineere so among their Auditors: but indeed
I would no more chuse a *Rhetorician,* for reigning in a *Schoole;* then
I would a *Pilot,* for rowing in a Pond. . . .

## Wits, Poets, and Playrights

I doe heare them say often: Some men are not witty; because they
are not every where witty; then which nothing is more foolish. If an
eye or a nose bee an excellent part in the face, therefore be all eye or
nose? I thinke the eye-brow, the fore-head, the cheeke, chyn, lip, or any
part else, are as necessary, and naturall in the place. But now nothing
is good that is naturall: Right and naturall language seeme⟨s⟩ to have
least of the wit in it; that which is writh'd and tortur'd, is counted the
more exquisite. Cloath of Bodkin, or Tissue, must be imbrodered; as if
no face were faire, that were not pouldred, or painted? No beauty to be
had, but in wresting, and writhing our owne tongue? Nothing is fash-
ionable, till it bee deform'd; and this is to write like a *Gentleman.* All

must bee as affected, and preposterous as our Gallants cloathes, sweet bags, and night-dressings: in which you would thinke our men lay in, like *Ladies:* it is so curious.

*Nothing* in our Age, I have observ'd, is more preposterous, then the *running Judgements* upon *Poetry,* and *Poets* when wee shall heare those things commended, and cry'd up for the best writings, which a man would scarce vouchsafe, to wrap any wholsome drug in; hee would never light his *Tobacco* with them. And those men almost nam'd for *Miracles,* who yet are so vile, that if a man should goe about, to examine, and correct them, hee must make all they have done, but one blot. Their good is so intangled with their bad, as forcibly one must draw on the others death with it. A Sponge dipt in Inke will doe all:

> ———*Comitetur punica librum*
> *Spongia.*———

Et paulò post,

> *Non possunt . . . multæ, una litura potest.*

Yet their vices have not hurt them: Nay, a great many they have profited; for they have beene lov'd for nothing else. And this false opinion growes strong against the best men: if once it take root with the *Ignorant. Cestius,* in his time, was preferr'd to *Cicero;* so farre, as the Ignorant durst: They learn'd him without booke, and had him often in their mouthes. But a man cannot imagine that thing so foolish, or rude, but will find, and enjoy an Admirer; at least, a Reader, or *Spectator.* The Puppets are seene now in despight of the Players: *Heath's Epigrams,* and the *Skullers Poems* have their applause. There are never wanting, that dare preferre the worst *Preachers,* the worst *Pleaders,* the worst *Poets:* not that the better have left to write, or speake better, but that they that heare them judge worse; *Non illi pejus dicunt, sed hi corruptiùs judicant.* Nay, if it were put to the question of the Water-rimers workes, against *Spencers;* I doubt not, but they would find more *Suffrages;* because the most favour common vices, out of a Prerogative the vulgar have, to lose their judgements, and like that which is naught.

*Poetry,* in this latter Age, hath prov'd but a meane *Mistresse,* to such as have wholly addicted themselves to her, or given their names up to her family. They who have but saluted her on the by, and now and then tendred their visits, shee hath done much for, and advanced in the way of their owne professions (both the *Law,* and the *Gospel*) beyond all they could have hoped, or done for themselves, without her favour. Wherein she doth emulate the judicious, but preposterous bounty of the times *Grandes:* who accumulate all they can upon the *Parasite,* or *Fresh-man* in their friendship; but thinke an old Client, or honest servant, bound by his place to write, and starve.

*Indeed,* the multitude commend Writers, as they doe Fencers, or Wrastlers; who if they come in robustiously, and put for it, with a deale of violence, are received for the *braver-fellowes:* when many times their owne rudenesse is a cause of their disgrace; and a slight touch of their Adversary, gives all that boisterous force the foyle. But in these things, the unskilfull are naturally deceiv'd, and judging wholly by the bulke, thinke rude things greater then polish'd; and scatter'd more numerous, then compos'd: Nor thinke this only to be true in the sordid multitude, but the neater sort of our *Gallants:* for all are the multitude; only they differ in cloaths, not in judgement or understanding.

*I remember,* the Players have often mentioned it as an honour to *Shakespeare,* that in his writing, (whatsoever he penn'd) hee never blotted out line. My answer hath beene, Would he had blotted a thousand. Which they thought a malevolent speech. I had not told posterity **this,** but for their ignorance, who choose that circumstance to commend their friend by, wherein he most faulted. And to justifie mine owne candor, (for I lov'd the man, and doe honour his memory (on this side Idolatry) as much as any.) Hee was (indeed) honest, and of an open, and free nature: had an excellent *Phantsie;* brave notions, and gentle expressions: wherein hee flow'd with that facility, that sometime it was necessary he should be stop'd: *Sufflaminandus erat;* as *Augustus* said of *Haterius.* His wit was in his owne power; would the rule of it had beene so too. Many times hee fell into those things, could not escape laughter: As when hee said in the person of *Cæsar,* one speaking to him; *Cæsar, thou dost me wrong.* Hee replyed: *Cæsar did never wrong, but with just cause:* and such like; which were ridiculous. But hee redeemed his vices, with his vertues. There was ever more in him to be praysed, then to be pardoned.

*In the difference of wits,* I have observ'd; there are many notes: And it is a little *Maistry* to know them: to discerne, what every nature, every disposition will beare: For, before wee sow our land, we should plough it. There are no fewer formes of minds, then of bodies amongst us. The variety is incredible; and therefore wee must search. Some are fit to make *Divines,* some *Poets,* some *Lawyers,* some *Physicians;* some to be sent to the plough, and trades.

There is no doctrine will doe good, where nature is wanting. Some wits are swelling, and high; others low and still: Some hot and fiery; others cold and dull: One must have a bridle, the other a spurre.

*There* be some that are forward, and bold; and these will doe every little thing easily: I meane, that is hard by, and next them; which they will utter, unretarded, without any shamefastnesse. These never performe much, but quickly. They are, what they are on the sudden; they shew presently, like *Graine,* that, scatter'd on the top of the ground, shoots up, but takes no root; has a yellow blade, but the eare empty. They are wits of good promise at first, but there is an *Ingeni-stitium\*:* They stand still at sixteene, they get no higher.

You have others, that labour onely to ostentation; and are ever more busie about the colours, and surface of a worke, then in the matter, and foundation: For that is hid, the other is seene.

*Others,* that in composition are nothing, but what is rough, and broken: *Quæ per salebras, altaque saxa cadunt.* And if it would come gently, they trouble it of purpose. They would not have it run without rubs, as if that stile were more strong and manly, that stroke the eare with a kin dof uneven⟨n⟩esse. These men erre not by chance, but knowingly, and willingly; they are like men that affect a fashion by themselves, have some singularity in a Ruffe, Cloake, or Hat-band; or their beards, specially cut to provoke beholders, and set a marke upon themselves. They would be reprehended, while they are look'd on. And this vice, one that is in authority with the rest, loving, delivers over to them to bee imitated: so that oft-times the faults which he fell into, the others seeke for: This is the danger, when vice becomes a *Precedent.*

Others there are, that have no composition at all; but a kind of tuneing, and riming fall, in what they write. It runs and slides, and onely makes a sound. Womens-*Poets* they are call'd: as you have womens-*Taylors.*

> They write a verse, as smooth, as soft, as creame;
> In which there is no torrent, nor scarce streame.

\* A witstand.

You may sound these wits, and find the depth of them, with your middle finger. They are *Creame-bowle,* or but puddle deepe.

*Some,* that turne over all bookes, and are equally searching in all papers, that write out of what they presently find or meet, without choice; by which meanes it happens, that what they have discredited, and impugned in one worke, they have before, or after, extolled the same in another. Such are all the *Essayists,* even their Master *Mountaigne.* These, in all they write, confesse still what bookes they have read last; and therein their owne folly, so much, that they bring it to the *Stake* raw, and undigested: not that the place did need it neither; but that they thought themselves furnished, and would vent it.

*Some* againe, who (after they have got authority, or, which is lesse, opinion, by their writings, to have read much) dare presently to faine whole bookes, and Authors, and lye safely. For what never was, will not easily be found; not by the most *curious.*

*And some,* by a cunning protestation against all reading, and false vendition of their owne *naturals,* thinke to divert the *sagacity* of their Readers from themselves, and coole the sent of their owne *fox-like* thefts; when yet they are so ranke, as a man may find whole pages together usurp'd from one Author, their necessities compelling them to read for present use, which could not be in many books; and so come forth more ridiculously, and palpably guilty, then those, who, because they cannot trace, they yet would slander their industry.

*But* the Wretcheder are the obstinate contemners of all helpes, and Arts: such as presuming on their owne *Naturals* (which perhaps are excellent) dare deride all diligence, and seeme to mock at the terms, when they understand not the things; thinking that way to get off wittily, with their Ignorance. These are imitated often by such, as are their Peeres in negligence, though they cannot be in nature: And they utter all they can thinke, with a kind of violence, and *indisposition;* unexamin'd, without relation, either to person, place, or any fitnesse else; and the more wilfull, and stubborne, they are in it, the more learned they are esteem'd of the *multitude,* through their excellent vice of Judgement: who thinke those things the stronger, that have no Art: as if to breake, were better then to open; or to rent asunder, gentler then to loose.

*It cannot* but come to passe, that these men, who commonly seeke to doe more than enough, may sometimes happen on some thing that is good, and great; but very seldome: And when it comes, it doth not recompence the rest of their ill. For their jests, and their sentences (which they onely, and ambitiously seeke for) sticke out, and are more eminent; because all is sordid, and vile about them; as lights are more discern'd in a thick darkenesse, then a faint shadow. Now because they speake all they can (how ever unfitly) they are thought to have the greater copy; Where the learned use ever election, and a meane; they looke back to what they intended at first, and make all an even, and proportion'd body. The true Artificer will not run away from nature, as hee were afraid of her; or depart from life, and the likenesse of Truth; but speake to the capacity of his hearers. And though his language differ from the vulgar somewhat; it shall not fly from all humanity, with the *Tamerlanes,* and *Tamer-Chams* of the late Age, which had nothing in them but the *scenicall* strutting, and furious vociferation, to warrant them to the ignorant gapers. Hee knowes it is his onely Art, so to carry it, as none but Artificers perceive it. In the meane time perhaps hee is call'd barren, dull, leane, a poore Writer (or by what contumelious word can come in their cheeks) by these men, who without labour, judgement, knowledge, or almost sense, are received, or preferr'd before him. He gratulates them, and their fortune. An other Age, or juster men, will acknowledge the vertues of his studies: his wisdome, in dividing: his subtilty, in arguing: with what strength hee doth inspire his Readers; with what sweetnesse hee strokes them: in inveighing, what sharpenesse; in Jest, what urbanity hee uses. How he doth raigne in mens affections; how invade, and breake in upon them; and makes their minds like the thing he writes. Then in his Elocution to behold, what word is proper: which hath ornament: which height: what is beautifully translated: where figures are fit: which gentle, which strong to shew the composition *Manly.* And how hee hath avoyded faint, obscure, obscene, sordid, humble, improper, or effeminate *Phrase;* which is not only prais'd of the most, but commended, (which is worse) especially for that it is naught. . . .

## Masters of Wit and Language

*Cicero* is said to bee the only wit, that the people of *Rome* had equall'd to their *Empire. Ingenium par imperio.* We have had many, and in their severall Ages, (to take in but the former *Seculum.*) *Sir Thomas Moore,* the elder *Wiat; Henry,* Earle of *Surrey; Chaloner, Smith, Eliot,* B. *Gardiner,* were for their times admirable: and the more, because they began Eloquence with us. Sir *Nico: Bacon,* was singular, and almost alone, in the beginning of Queene *Elizabeths* times. Sir *Philip Sidney,* and Mr. *Hooker* (in different matter) grew great Masters of wit, and language; and in whom all vigour of Invention, and strength of judgement met. The Earle of *Essex,* noble and high; and Sir *Walter Rawleigh,* not to be contemn'd, either for judgement, or stile. Sir *Henry Savile* grave, and truly letter'd; Sir *Edwin Sandes,* excellent in both: Lo: *Egerton,* the Chancellor, a grave, and great Orator; and best, when hee was provok'd. But his learned, and able (though unfortunate) *Successor* is he, who hath fill'd up all numbers; and perform'd that in our tongue, which may be compar'd, or preferr'd, either to insolent *Greece,* or haughty *Rome.* In short, within his view, and about his times, were all the wits borne, that could honour a language, or helpe study. Now things daily fall: wits grow downe-ward, and *Eloquence* growes back-ward: So that hee may be nam'd, and stand as the *marke,* and ἀκμὴ of our language.

### Francis Bacon

*I have* ever observ'd it, to have beene the office of a wise Patriot, among the greatest affaires of the *State,* to take care of the *Commonwealth* of Learning. For Schooles, they are the *Seminaries* of State: and nothing is worthier the study of a States-man, then that part of the *Republicke,* which wee call the *advancement* of Letters. Witnesse the care of *Julius Cæsar;* who, in the heat of the civill warre, writ his bookes of *Analogie,* and dedicated them to *Tully.* This made the late Lord S. *Albane* entitle his worke, *nouum Organum.* Which though by the most of superficiall men, who cannot get beyond the Title of *Nominals,* it is not penetrated, nor understood: it really openeth all defects of Learning, whatsoever; and is a Booke,

> *Qui longum noto scriptori porriget ævum.*

My conceit of his Person was never increased toward him, by his place, or honours. But I have, and doe reverence him for the greatnesse, that was onely proper to himselfe, in that hee seem'd to mee ever, by his worke, one of the greatest men, and most worthy of admiration, that had beene in many Ages. In his adversity I ever prayed, that *God* would give him strength: for *Greatnesse* hee could not want. Neither could I condole in a word, or syllable for him; as knowing no Accident could doe harme to vertue; but rather helpe to make it manifest. . . .

## Poets and the Good Life

*There* be some men are borne only to sucke out the poyson of bookes: *Habent venenum pro victu: imò, pro deliciis.* And such are they that only rellish the obscene, and foule things in *Poets:* Which makes the profession taxed. But by whom? men, that watch for it, and (had they not had this hint) are so unjust valuers of Letters; as they thinke no Learning good, but what brings in gaine. It shewes, they themselves would never have beene of the professions they are; but for the profits and fees. But, if an other Learning, well used, can instruct to good life, informe manners; no lesse perswade, and leade men, then they threaten, and compell; and have no reward: is it therefore the worse study? I could never thinke the study of *Wisdome* confin'd only to the Philosopher: or of *Piety* to the *Divine:* or of *State* to the *Politicke.* But that he which can faine a *Common-wealth* (which is the *Poet*) can governe it with *Counsels,* strengthen it with *Lawes,* correct it with *Judgements,* informe it with *Religion,* and *Morals;* is all these. Wee doe not require in him meere *Elocution;* or an excellent faculty in verse; but the exact knowledge of all vertues, and their Contraries; with ability to render the one lov'd, the other hated, by his proper embattaling them. The Philosophers did insolently, to challenge only to themselves that which the greatest *Generals,* and gravest *Counsellors* never durst. For such had rather doe, then promise the best things. . . .

## I Durst Not Leave Myself Undefended

*A good man* will avoide the spot of any sinne. The very aspersion is grievous: which makes him choose his way in his life, as hee would in his journey. The *Ill-man* rides through all confidently; hee is coated, and booted for it. The oftner hee offends, the more openly; and the fowler, the fitter in fashion. His modesty, like a riding Coat, the more it is worne, is the lesse car'd for. It is good enough for the durt still; and the wayes he travels in. *An Innocent* man needs no *Eloquence:* his *Innocence* is in stead of it: else I had never come off so many times from these *Precipices,* whether mens malice hath pursued me. It is true,

I have beene accus'd to the Lords, to the *King;* and by great ones: but it hap'ned my accusers had not thought of the Accusation with themselves; and so were driven, for want of crimes, to use invention, which was found slander: or too late, (being entred so farre) to seeke starting-holes for their rashnesse, which were not given them. And then they may thinke, what accusation that was like to prove, when they, that were the Ingineers, fear'd to be the Authors. Nor were they content, to faine things against mee, but to urge things, fain'd by the Ignorant, against my profession: which though from their hired, and mercenary impudence, I might have past by, as granted to a Nation of Barkers, that let out their tongues to lick others sores; yet I durst not leave my selfe undefended, having a paire of eares unskilfull to heare lyes; or have those things said of me, which I could truly prove of them. They objected, making of verses to me, when I could object to most of them, their not being able to reade them, but as worthy of scorne. Nay, they would offer to urge mine owne Writings against me; but by pieces, (which was an excellent way of malice) as if any mans Context, might not seeme dangerous, and offensive, if that which was knit, to what went before, were defrauded of his beginning; or that things, by themselves utter'd, might not seeme subject to Calumnie, which read entire, would appeare most free. At last they upbraided my poverty; I confesse, shee is my Domestick; sober of diet, simple of habit; frugall, painefull; a good Counsellor to me; that keepes me from Cruelty, Pride, or other more delicate impertinences, which are the Nurse-children of Riches. But let them looke over all the great, and monstruous wickednesses, they shall never find those in poore families. They are the issue of the wealthy *Giants,* and the mighty *Hunters:* Whereas no great worke, or worthy of praise, or memory, but came out of poore cradles. It was the ancient poverty, that founded Common-weales; built Cities, invented Arts, made wholesome Lawes; armed men against vices; rewarded them with their owne vertues; and preserv'd the honour, and state of Nations, till they betray'd themselves to Riches. . . .

## Poetry and Picture

*Poetry,* and *Picture,* are Arts of a like nature; and both are busie about imitation. It was excellently said of *Plutarch, Poetry* was a speaking Picture, and *Picture* a mute Poesie. For they both invent, faine, and devise many things, and accommodate all they invent to the use, and service of nature. Yet of the two, the Pen is more noble, then the Pencill. For that can speake to the Understanding; the other, but to the Sense. They both behold pleasure, and profit, as their common Object; but should abstaine from all base pleasures, lest they should erre from their end; and while they seeke to better mens minds, destroy their manners. They both are borne *Artificers,* not made. Nature is more powerful in them then study.

*Whosoever* loves not *Picture,* is injurious to Truth: and all the wisdome of *Poetry.* Picture is the invention of Heaven: the most ancient, and most a kinne to Nature. It is it selfe a silent worke: and alwayes of one and the same habit: Yet it doth so enter, and penetrate the inmost affection (being done by an excellent Artificer) as sometimes it orecomes the power of speech, and oratory. There are diverse graces in it; so are there in the Artificers. One excels in care, another in reason, a third in easinesse, a fourth in nature and grace. Some have diligence, and comelinesse: but they want Majesty. They can expresse a humane forme in all the graces, sweetnesse, and elegancy; but they misse the Authority. They can hit nothing but smooth cheeks; they cannot expresse roughnesse, or gravity. Others aspire to Truth so much, as they are rather Lovers of likenesse, then beauty. *Zeuxis,* and *Parrhasius,* are said to be contemporaries: The first, found out the reason of lights, and shadowes in Picture: the other, more subtily examined the lines.

*In Picture,* light is requir'd no lesse then shadow: so in stile, height, as well as humblenesse. But beware they be not too humble; as *Pliny* pronounc'd of *Regulus* writings: You would thinke them written, not on a child, but by a child. Many, out of their owne obscene Apprehensions, refuse proper and fit words; as *occupie, nature,* and the like: So the curious industry in some of having all alike good, hath come neerer a vice, then a vertue.

*Picture* tooke her faining from *Poetry:* from *Geometry* her rule, compasse, lines, proportion, and the whole *Symmetry. Parrhasius* was the first wan reputation, by adding *Symmetry* to Picture: hee added subtility to the countenance, elegancy to the haire, lovelines to the face; and, by the publike voice of all Artificers, deserved honour in the outer lines. *Eupompus* gave it splendor by numbers, and other elegancies. From the *Opticks* it drew reasons; by which it considered, how things plac'd at distance, and a farre off, should appeare lesse: how above, or beneath the head, should deceive the eye, &c. So from thence it tooke shadowes, recessor, light, and heightnings. From morall *Philosophy* it tooke the soule, the expression of Senses, Perturbations, Manners, when they would paint an angry person, a proud, an inconstant, an ambitious, a brave, a magnanimous, a just, a mercifull, a compassionate, an humble, a dejected, a base, and the like. They made all heightnings bright, all shadowes darke, all swellings from a plane; all solids from breaking. See where he complaines of their painting *Chimæra's,* by the vulgar unaptly called *Grottesque:* Saying, that men who were borne truly to study, and emulate nature, did nothing but make monsters against nature; which *Horace* so laught at. The Art *Plasticke* was moulding in clay, or potters earth anciently. This is the Parent of *Statuary: Sculpture, Graving* and *Picture,* cutting in brasse, and marble, all serve under her. *Socrates* taught *Parrhasius,* and *Clito* (two noble Statuaries) first to expresse manners by their looks in Imagery. *Polygnotus,* and *Aglaophon* were ancienter. After them *Zeuxis,* who was the Law-giver to all Painters, after *Parrhasius.* They were contemporaries, and liv'd both about *Philips* time, the Father of *Alexander* the Great.

There liv'd in this latter Age six famous Painters in *Italy:* who were excellent, and emulous of the Ancients: *Raphael de Urbino, Michel Angelo Buonarota, Titian, Antonie of Correggio, Sebastian of Venice, Julio Romano,* and *Andrea Sartorio.*

### Flatterers and Gossips

*There* are Flatterers for their bread, that praise all my oraculous Lord do's or sayes, be it true or false: invent tales that shall please: make baites for his Lordships eares: and if they be not receiv'd in what they offer at, they shift a point of the Compasse, and turne their tale, presently tacke about; deny what they confest, and confesse what they denied; fit their discourse to the persons, and occasions. What they snatch up, and devoure at one table, utter at another: and grow suspected of the Master, hated of the servants, while they inquire, and reprehend, and compound, and delate busines of the house they have nothing to doe with: They praise my *Lords* wine, and the sauce he likes; observe the Cooke, and Bottle-man, while they stand in my Lords favour, speake for a pension for them: but pound them to dust upon my Lords least distaste, or change of his palate.

*How* much better is it, to bee silent; or at least, to speake sparingly! For it is not enough to speake good, but timely things. If a man be asked a question, to answer, but to repeat the Question, before hee answer, is well, that hee be sure to understand it, to avoid absurdity. For it is lesse dishonour, to heare imperfectly, then to speake imperfectly. The eares are excus'd, the understanding is not. And in things unknown to a man, not to give his opinion, lest by affectation of knowing too much, hee lose the credit hee hath by speaking, or knowing the wrong way, what hee utters. Nor seeke to get his Patrons favour, by imbarking himselfe in the Factions of the Family: to inquire after domesticke simulties, their sports, or affections. They are an odious, and vile kind of creatures, that fly about the house all day; and picking up the filth of the house, like Pies or Swallowes, carry it to their nest (the Lords eares) and oftentimes report the lyes they have fain'd, for what they have seene and heard.

*These* are call'd instruments of grace, and power, with great persons; but they are indeed the Organs of their impotencie, and markes of weaknesse. For sufficient Lords are able to make these Discoveries themselves. Neither will an honourable person inquire, who eats, and drinks together, what that man playes, whom this man loves; with whom such a one walkes; what discourse they held; who sleepes with whom. They are base, and servile natures, that busie themselves about these disquisitions. How often have I seene, (and worthily) these Censors of the family, undertaken by some honest *Rustick,* and cudgel'd thriftily? These are commonly the off-scowring, and dregs of men, that doe these things, or calumniate others: Yet I know not truly which is worse; hee that malignes all, or that praises all. There is as great a vice in praising, and as frequent, as in detracting. . . .

## Think, Excogitate, Repeat, Imitate

*For* a man to write well, there are required three Necessaries. To reade the best Authors, observe the best Speakers: and much exercise of his owne style. In style to consider, what ought to be written; and after what manner; Hee must first thinke, and excogitate his matter; then choose his words, and examine the weight of either. Then take care in placing, and ranking both matter, and words, that the composition be comely; and to doe this with diligence, and often. No matter how slow the style be at first, so it be labour'd, and accurate: seeke the best, and be not glad of the forward conceipts, or first words, that offer themselves to us, but judge of what wee invent; and order what wee approve. Repeat often, what wee have formerly written; which beside, that it helpes the consequence, and makes the juncture better, it quickens the heate of imagination, that often cooles in the time of setting downe, and gives it new strength, as if it grew lustier, by the going back. As wee see in the contention of leaping, they jumpe farthest, that fetch their race largest: or, as in throwing a Dart, or Javelin, wee force back our armes, to make our loose the stronger. Yet, if we have a faire gale of wind, I forbid not the steering out of our sayle, so the favour of the gale deceive us not. For all that wee invent doth please us in the conception, or birth; else we would never set it downe. But the safest is to returne to our Judgement, and handle over againe those things, the easinesse of which might make them justly suspected. So did the best Writers in their beginnings; they impos'd upon themselves care, and industry. They did nothing rashly. They obtain'd first to write well, and then custome made it easie, and a habit. By little and little, their matter shew'd it selfe to 'hem more plentifully; their words answer'd, their composition followed; and all, as in a well-order'd family, presented it selfe in the place. So that the summe of all is: Ready writing makes not good writing; but good writing brings on ready writing: Yet when wee thinke wee have got the faculty, it is even then good to resist it: as to give a Horse a check sometimes with ⟨a⟩ bit, which doth not so much stop his course, as stirre his mettle. Againe, whether a mans *Genius* is best able to reach, thither it should more and more contend, lift and dilate it selfe, as men of low stature, raise themselves on their toes; and so oft-times get even, if not eminent. Besides, as it is fit for grown and able Writers to stand of themselves, and worke with their owne strength, to trust and endeavour by their owne faculties: so it is fit for the beginner, and learner, to study others, and the best. For the mind, and memory are more sharpely exercis'd in comprehending an other mans things, then our owne; and such as accustome themselves, and are familiar with the best Authors, shall ever and anon find somewhat of them in themselves, and in the expression of their minds, even when they feele it not, be able to utter something like theirs, which hath an Authority above their owne. Nay, sometimes it is the reward of a mans study, the praise of quoting an other man fitly: And though a man be more prone, and able for one kind of writing, then another, yet hee must exercise all. For as in an Instrument, so in style, there must be a Harmonie, and concent of parts.

## Sidney Before Donne

I take this labour in teaching others, that they should not be alwayes to bee taught; and I would bring my Precepts into practise. For rules are ever of lesse force, and valew, then experiments. Yet with this purpose, rather to shew the right way to those that come after, then to detect any that have slipt before by errour, and I hope it will bee more profitable. For men doe more willingly listen, and with more favour, to precept, then reprehension. Among diverse opinions of an Art, and most of them contrary in themselves, it is hard to make election; and therefore, though a man cannot invent new things after so many, he may doe a welcome worke yet to helpe posterity to judge rightly of the old. But Arts and Precepts availe nothing, except nature be beneficiall, and ayding. And therefore these things are no more written to a dull disposition, then rules of husbandry to a barren Soyle. No precepts will profit a Foole; no more then beauty will the blind, or musicke the deafe. As wee should take care, that our style in writing, be neither dry, nor empty: wee should looke againe it be not winding, or wanton with far-fetcht descriptions; Either is a vice. But that is worse which proceeds out of want, then that which riots out of plenty. The remedy of fruitfulnesse is easie, but no labour will helpe the contrary: I will like, and praise some things in a young Writer; which yet if hee continue in, I cannot but justly hate him for the same. There is a time to bee given all things for maturity; and that even your Countrey-husband-man can teach; who to a young plant will not put the proyning knife, because it seemes to feare the iron, as not able to admit the scarre. No more would I tell a greene Writer all his faults, lest I should make him grieve and faint, and at last despaire. For nothing doth more hurt, then to make him so afraid of all things, as hee can endeavour nothing. Therefore youth ought to be instructed betimes, and in the best things: for we hold those longest, wee take soonest. As the first sent of a Vessell lasts: and that tinct the wooll first receives. Therefore a Master should temper his owne powers, and descend to the others infirmity. If you powre a glut of water upon a Bottle, it receives little of it; but with a Funnell, and by degrees, you shall fill many of them, and spill little of your owne; to their capacity they will all receive, and be full. And as it is fit to reade the best Authors to youth first, so let them be of the openest, and clearest. As *Livy* before *Salust, Sydney* before *Donne:* and beware of letting them taste *Gower,* or *Chaucer* at first, lest falling too much in love with

Antiquity, and not apprehending the weight, they grow rough and barren in language onely. When their judgements are firme, and out of danger, let them reade both, the old and the new: but no lesse take heed, that their new flowers, and sweetnesse doe not as much corrupt, as the others drinesse, and squallor, if they choose not carefully. *Spencer*, in affecting the Ancients, writ no Language: Yet I would have him read for his matter; but as *Virgil* read *Ennius*. The reading of *Homer* and *Virgil* is counsell'd by *Quintilian*, as the best way of informing youth, and confirming man. For besides, that the mind is rais'd with the height, and sublimity of such a verse, it takes spirit from the greatnesse of the matter, and is tincted with the best things. *Tragicke*, and *Liricke* Poetry is good too: and *Comicke* with the best, if the manners of the Reader be once in safety. In the *Greeke* Poets, as also in *Plautus*, wee shall see the Oeconomy, and disposition of *Poems*, better observed then in *Terence*, and the later: who thought the sole grace, and vertue of their Fable, the sticking in of sentences, as ours doe the forcing in of jests. . . .

## Pure and Neat Language

*It* is not the passing through these Learnings that hurts us, but the dwelling and sticking about them. To descend to those extreame anxieties, and foolish cavils of *Grammarians*, is able to breake a wit in pieces; being a worke of manifold misery, and vainenesse, to bee *Elementarii senes*. Yet even Letters are, as it were, the Banke of words, and restore themselves to an Author, as the pawnes of Language. But talking and Eloquence are not the same: to speake, and to speake well, are two things. A foole may talke, but a wise man speakes, and out of the observation, knowledge, and use of things. Many Writers perplexe their Readers, and Hearers with meere *Non-sense*. Their writings need sunshine. Pure and neat Language I love, yet plaine and customary. A barbarous Phrase hath often made mee out of love with a good sense; and doubtfull writing hath wrackt mee beyond my patience. The reason why a *Poet* is said, that hee ought to have all knowledges, is that hee should not be ignorant of the most, especially of those hee will handle. And indeed, when the attaining of them is possible, it were a sluggish, and base thing to despaire. For frequent imitation of any thing, becomes a habit quickly. If a man should prosecute as much, as could be said of every thing; his worke would find no end.

*Speech* is the only benefit man hath to expresse his excellencie of mind above other creatures. It is the Instrument of *Society*. Therefore *Mercury,* who is the President of Language, is called *Deorum hominumque interpres.* In all speech, words and sense, are as the body, and the soule. The sense is as the life and soule of Language, without which all words are dead. Sense is wrought out of experience, the knowledge of humane life, and actions, or of the liberall Arts, which the *Greeks* call'd E'γκυκλοπαιδείαν. Words are the Peoples; yet there is a choise of them to be made. For *Verborum delectus, origo est eloquentiæ.* They are to be chose according to the persons wee make speake, or the things wee speake of. Some are of the Campe, some of the Councellboard, some of the Shop, some of the Sheepe-coat, some of the Pulpit, some of the Barre, &c. And herein is seene their Elegance, and Propriety, when wee use them fitly, and draw them forth to their just strength and nature, by way of Translation, or *Metaphore.* But in this Translation wee must only serve necessity (*Nam temerè nihil transfertur à prudenti*) or commodity, which is a kind of necessity; that is, when wee either absolutely want a word to expresse by, and that is necessity; or when wee have not so fit a word, and that is commodity. As when wee avoid losse by it, and escape obscenenesse, and gaine in the grace and property, which helpes significance. *Metaphors* farfet hinder to be understood, and affected, lose their grace. Or when the person fetcheth his translations from a wrong place. As if a Privie-Counsellor should at the Table take his *Metaphore* from a Dicing-house, or Ordinary, or a Vintners Vault; or a Justice of Peace draw his similitudes from the *Mathematicks;* or a *Divine* from a Bawdy-house, or Tavernes; or a Gentleman of *Northampton-shire, Warwick-shire,* or the *Mid-land,* should fetch all his Illustrations to his country neighbours from shipping, and tell them of the maine *sheat,* and the *Boulin. Metaphors* are thus many times deform'd, as in him that said, *Castratam morte Aphricani Rempublicam.* And an other, *stercus curiæ Glauciam.* And *Canâ nive conspuit Alpes.* All attempts that are new in this kind, are dangerous, and somewhat hard, before they be softned with us. A man coynes not a new word without some perill, and lesse fruit; for if it happen to be received, the praise is but moderate; if refus'd, the scorne is assur'd. Yet wee must adventure, for things, at first hard and rough, are by use made tender and gentle. It is an honest errour that is committed, following great *Chiefes.*

*Custome* is the most certaine Mistresse of Language, as the publicke stampe makes the current money. But wee must not be too frequent with the mint, every day coyning. Nor fetch words from the extreme and utmost ages; since the chiefe vertue of a style is perspicuitie, and nothing so vitious in it, as to need an Interpreter. Words borrow'd of Antiquity, doe lend a kind of Majesty to style, and are not without their delight sometimes. For they have the Authority of yeares, and out of their intermission doe win to themselves a kind of grace like newnesse. But the eldest of the present, and newest of the past Language is the best. For what was the ancient Language, which some men so doate upon, but the ancient Custome? Yet when I name Custome, I understand not the vulgar Custome: For that were a precept no lesse dangerous to Language, then life, if wee should speake or live after the manners of the vulgar: But that I call Custome of speech, which is the consent of the Learned; as Custome of life, which is the consent of the good. *Virgill* was most loving of Antiquity; yet how rarely doth hee insert *aquai,* and *pictai! Lucretius* is scabrous and rough in these; hee seekes 'hem: As some doe *Chaucerismes* with us, which were better expung'd and banish'd. Some words are to be cull'd out for ornament and colour, as wee gather flowers to straw houses, or make Garlands; but they are better when they grow to our style; as in a Meadow, where though the meere grasse and greennesse delights, yet the variety of flowers doth heighten and beautifie. Marry, we must not play, or riot too much with them, as in *Paranomasies:* Nor use too swelling, or ill-sounding words; *Quæ per salebras, altaque saxa cadunt.* It is true, there is no sound but shall find some Lovers, as the bitter'st confections are gratefull to some palats. Our composition must bee more accurate in the beginning and end, then in the midst; and in the end more, then in the beginning; for through the midst the streame beares us. And this is attain'd by Custome more then care, or diligence. Wee must expresse readily, and fully, not profusely. There is difference betweene a liberall, and a prodigall hand. As it is a great point of Art, when our matter requires it, to enlarge, and veere out all sayle; so to take it in, and contract it, is of no lesse praise when the Argument doth aske it. Either of them hath their fitnesse in the place. A good man alwayes profits by his endeavour, by his helpe; yea, when he is absent; nay, when he is dead, by his example and memory. So good Authors in their style: A strict and succinct style is that, where you can take away nothing without losse, and that losse to be manifest. The briefe style is that which expresseth much in little. The concise style, which expresseth not enough, but leaves somewhat to bee understood. The abrupt style, which hath many breaches, and doth not seeme to end, but fall. The congruent, and harmonious fitting of parts in a sentence, hath almost the fastning, and force of knitting, and connexion: As in stones well squar'd, which will rise strong a great way without mortar.

Periods are beautifull when they are not too long; for so they have their strength too, as in a Pike or Javelin. As wee must take the care that our words and sense bee cleare; so, if the obscurity happen through the Hearers, or Readers want of understanding, I am not to answer for them; no more then for their not listning or marking; I must neither find them eares, nor mind. But a man cannot put a word so in sense, but some thing about it will illustrate it, if the Writer understand himselfe. For Order helpes much to Perspicuity, as Confusion hurts. *Rectitudo lucem adfert; obliquitas et circumductio offuscat.* We should therefore speake what wee can, the neerest way, so as wee keepe our gate, not leape; for too short may as well be not let into the memory, as too long not kept in. Whatsoever looseth the grace, and clearenesse, converts into a Riddle; the obscurity is mark'd, but not the valew. That perisheth, and is past by, like the Pearle in the Fable. Our style should be like a skeine of silke, to be carried, and found by the right thred, not ravel'd, and perplex'd; then all is a knot, a heape. There are words, that doe as much raise a style, as others can depresse it. Superlation, and overmuchnesse amplifies. It may be above faith, but never above a meane. It was ridiculous in *Cestius,* when hee said of *Alexander: Fremit Oceanus, quasi indignetur, quòd terras relinquas;* But propitiously from *Virgil:*—

> *Credas innare reuulsas*
> *Cycladas.*

Hee doth not say it was so, but seem'd to be so. Although it be somewhat incredible, that is excus'd before it be spoken. But there are *Hyperboles,* which will become one Language, that will by no meanes admit another. As *Eos esse* P. R. *exercitus, que cœlum possint perrumpere:* who would say this with us, but a mad man? Therefore wee must consider in every tongue what is us'd, what receiv'd. *Quintilian* warnes us, that in no kind of Translation, or *Metaphore,* or *Allegory,* wee make a turne from what wee began; As if wee fetch the originall of our *Metaphore* from sea, and billowes; wee end not in flames and ashes; It is a most fowle inconsequence. Neither must wee draw out our *Allegory* too long, lest either wee make our selves obscure, or fall into affectation, which is childish. But why doe men depart at all from the right, and naturall wayes of speaking? Sometimes for necessity, when wee are driven, or thinke it fitter to speake that in obscure words, or by circumstance, which utter'd plainely would offend the hearers. Or to avoid obscenenesse, or sometimes for pleasure, and variety; as Travailers turne out of the high way, drawne, either by the commodity of a footpath, or the delicacy, or freshnesse of the fields. And all this is call'd ἐσχηματισμένη, or figur'd Language.

## Language Plain and Juicy

*Language* most shewes a man: speake that I may see thee. It springs out of the most retired, and inmost parts of us, and is the Image of the Parent of it, the mind. No glasse renders a mans forme, or likenesse, so true as his speech. Nay, it is likened to a man; and as we consider feature, and composition in a man; so words in Language: in the greatnesse, aptnesse, sound, structure, and harmony of it. Some men are tall, and bigge, so some Language is high and great. Then the words are chosen, their sound ample, the composition full, the absolution plenteous, and powr'd out, all grave, sinnewye and strong. Some are little, and Dwarfes: so of speech it is humble, and low, the words poore and flat; the members and *Periods,* thinne and weake, without knitting, or number. The middle are of a just stature. There the Language is plaine, and pleasing: even without stopping, round without swelling; all welltorn'd, compos'd, elegant, and accurate. The vitious Language is vast, and gaping, swelling, and irregular; when it contends to be high, full of Rocke, Mountaine, and pointednesse: as it affects to be low, it is abject, and creeps, full of bogs, and holes. And according to their Subject, these stiles vary, and lose their names: For that which is high and lofty, declaring excellent matter, becomes vast and tumorous, speaking of petty and inferiour things: so that which was even, and apt in a meane and plaine subject, will appeare most poore and humble in a high Argument. Would you not laugh, to meet a great Counsellor of state in a flat cap, with his trunck hose, and a hobby-horse Cloake, his Gloves under his girdle, and yond Haberdasher in a velvet Gowne, furr'd with sables? There is a certaine latitude in these things, by which wee find the degrees. The next thing to the stature, is the figure and feature in Language: that is, whether it be round, and streight, which consists of short and succinct *Periods,* numerous, and polish'd; or square and firme, which is to have equall and strong parts, every where answerable, and weighed. The third is the skinne, and coat, which rests in the well-joyning, cementing, and coagmentation of words; when as it is smooth, gentle, and sweet; like a Table, upon which you may runne your finger without rubs, and your nayle cannot find a joynt; not horrid, rough, wrinckled, gaping, or chapt. After these the flesh, blood, and bones come in question. Wee say it is a fleshy style, when there is much *Periphrasis,* and circuit of words; and when with more then enough, it growes fat and corpulent; *Arvina orationis,* full of suet and tallow. It hath blood, and juyce, when the words are proper and apt, their sound sweet, and the *Phrase* neat and pick'd. *Oratio uncta, & benè pasta.* But where there is Redundancy, both the blood and juyce are faulty, and vitious. *Redundat sanguine, quæ multò plus dicit, quàm necesse est.* Juyce in Language is somewhat lesse then blood; for if the words be but becomming, and signifying, and the sense gentle, there is Juyce: but where that wanteth, the Language is thinne, flagging, poore, starv'd, scarce covering the bone; and shewes like stones in a sack. Some men, to avoid Redundancy, runne into that; and while they strive to have no ill blood, or Juyce, they loose their good. There be some styles, againe, that have not lesse blood, but lesse flesh, and corpulence. These are bony, and sinnewy: *Ossa habent, et nervos.*

## Awake Antiquity

It was well noted by the late L. St. *Alban,* that the study of words is the first distemper of Learning: Vaine matter the second: And a third distemper is deceit, or the likenesse of truth; Imposture held up by credulity. All these are the Cobwebs of Learning, and to let them grow in us, is either sluttish or foolish. Nothing is more ridiculous, then to make an Author a *Dictator,* as the schooles have done *Aristotle.* The dammage is infinite, knowledge receives by it. For to many things a man should owe but a temporary beliefe, and a suspension of his owne Judgement, not an absolute resignation of himselfe, or a perpetuall captivity. Let *Aristotle,* and others have their dues; but if wee can make farther Discoveries of truth and fitnesse then they, why are we envied? Let us beware, while wee strive to adde, wee doe not diminish, or deface; wee may improve, but not augment. By discrediting falshood, Truth growes in request. Wee must not goe about like men anguish'd. and perplex'd, for vitious affectation of praise: but calmely study the separation of opinions, find the errours have intervened, awake Antiquity, call former times into question; but make no parties with the present, nor follow any fierce undertakers, mingle no matter of doubtfull credit, with the simplicity of truth, but gently stirre the mould about the root of the Question, and avoid all digladiations, facility of credit, or superstitious simplicity; seeke the consonancy, and concatenation of Truth; stoope only to point of necessity, and what leads to convenience. Then make exact animadversion where style hath degenerated, where flourish'd and thriv'd in choisenesse of Phrase, round and cleane composition of sentence, sweet falling of the clause, varying an illustration by tropes and figures, weight of Matter, worth of Subject, soundnesse of Argument, life of Invention, and depth of Judgement. This is *Monte potiri,* to get the hill. For no perfect Discovery can bee made upon a flat or a levell.

## The Writing of Letters

*Now,* that I have informed you in the knowing these things; let mee leade you by the hand a little farther, in the direction of the use; and make you an able Writer by practice. The conceits of the mind are Pictures of things, and the tongue is the Interpreter of those Pictures. The order of Gods creatures in themselves, is not only admirable, and glorious, but eloquent; Then he who could apprehend the consequence of things in their truth, and utter his apprehensions as truly, were the best Writer, or Speaker. Therefore *Cicero* said much, when hee said, *Dicere rectè nemo potest, nisi qui prudenter intelligit.* The shame of speaking unskilfully were small, if the tongue onely thereby were disgrac'd: But as the Image of a *King,* in his Seale ill-represented, is not so much a blemish to the waxe, or the Signet that seal'd it, as to the Prince it representeth; so disordered speech is not so much injury to the lips that give it forth, as to the disproportion, and incoherence of things in themselves, so negligently expressed. Neither can his mind be thought to be in tune, whose words doe jarre; nor his reason in frame, whose sentence is preposterous; nor his Elocution cleare and perfect, whose utterance breakes it selfe into fragments and uncertainties: Were it not a dishonour to a mighty Prince, to have the Majesty of his embassage spoyled by a carelesse Ambassadour? and is it not as great an Indignity, that an excellent conceit and capacity, by the indiligence of an idle tongue, should be disgrac'd? Negligent speech doth not onely discredit the person of the Speaker, but it discrediteth the opinion of his reason and judgement; it discrediteth the force and uniformity of the matter, and substance. If it be so then in words, which fly and escape censure, and where one good *Phrase* begs pardon for many incongruities, and faults; how shall he then be thought wise, whose penning is thin and shallow? How shall you looke for wit from him, whose leasure and head, assisted with the examination of his eyes, yeeld you no life, or sharpenesse in his writing?

*In writing* ⟨of letters⟩ there is to be regarded the Invention, and the Fashion. For the *Invention,* that ariseth upon your busines; whereof there can bee no rules of more certainty, or precepts of better direction given, then conjecture can lay downe, from the severall occasions of mens particular lives, and vocations: But sometimes men make businesse of kindnesse: As (*I could not satisfie my selfe, till I had discharged my remembrance, and charged my Letter with commendations to you.*) Or, (*My busines is no other, then to testifie my love to you, and to put you in mind of my willingnesse to doe you all kind offices.*) Or, (*Sir, have you leasure to descend to the remembring of that assurance you have long possest in your servant; and upon your next opportunity, make him happy with some commands from you?*) Or, the like; that goe a begging for some meaning, and labour to be deliver'd of the great burthen of nothing. When you have invented, and that your busines bee matter, and not bare forme, or meere Ceremony, but some earnest: then are you to proceed to the ordering of it, and digesting the parts, which is had out of two circumstances. One is the understanding of the Persons, to whom you are to write; the other is the coherence of your Sentence. For mens capacity, ⟨you are⟩ to weigh, what will be apprehended with greatest attention, or leisure; what next regarded, and long'd for especially; and what last will leave ⟨most⟩ satisfaction, and (as it were) the sweetest memoriall, and briefe of all that is past in his understanding, whom you write to. For the consequence of Sentences, you must bee sure, that every clause doe give the Q. one to the other, and be bespoken ere it come. So much for *Invention* and *order*.

Now for fashion, it consists in foure things, which are Qualities of your style. The first is *Brevity*. For they must not be Treatises, or Discourses (your Letters) except it be to learned men. And even among them, there is a kind of thrift, and saving of words. Therefore you are to examine the clearest passages of your understanding, and through them to convey the sweetest, and most significant words you can devise; that you may the easier teach them the readiest way to an other mans apprehension, and open their meaning fully, roundly, and distinctly. So as the Reader may not thinke a second view cast away upon your letter. And though respect bee a part following this; yet now here, and still I must remember it. If you write to a man, whose estate and [cense as] senses you are familiar with, you may the bolder (to set a taske to his braine) venter on a knot. But if to your Superior, you are bound to measure him in three farther points: First, your interest in him: Secondly, his capacity in your Letters: Thirdly, his leasure to peruse them. For your interest, or favour with him, you are to bee the shorter, or longer, more familiar, or submisse, as hee will afford you time. For his capacity, you are to be quicker, and fuller of those reaches, and glances of wit, or learning, as hee is able to entertaine them. For his leasure, you are commanded to the greater briefnesse, as his place is of greater discharges, and cares. But, with your betters, you are not to put Riddles of wit, by being too scarse of words: nor to cause the trouble of making *Breviates,* by writing too riotous, and wastingly. *Brevity* is attained in matter, by avoiding idle Complements, Prefaces, Protestations, Parentheses, superfluous circuit of figures, and digressions: In the composition, by omitting Conjunctions, (*Not onely; But Also*) (*Both the one, and the other*) (*Whereby it commeth to passe*) and such like idle Particles, that have no great busines in a serious Letter, but breaking of sentences; as often times a short journey is made long, by unnecessary baits.

But, as *Quintilian* saith, there is a briefnesse of the parts sometimes, that makes the whole long, as, *I came to the staires, I tooke a paire of oares, they launch'd out, rowed a pace, I landed at the Court-gate, I paid my fayre, went up to the Presence, ask'd for my Lord, I was admitted.* All this is but, *I went to the Court, and spake with my Lord.* This is the fault of some Latine Writers, within these last hundred years, of my reading, and perhaps *Seneca* may be appeacht of it; I accuse him not.

The next property of *Epistolarie* style is *Perspicuity,* and is often-times ⟨indangered by the former qualitie (brevity), often-times⟩ by affectation of some wit ill angled for, or ostentation of some hidden termes of Art. Few words they darken speech, and so doe too many: as well too much light hurteth the eyes, as too little; and a long Bill of *Chancery* confounds the understanding, as much as the shortest note. Therefore, let not your Letters be penn'd like English Statutes, and this is obtain'd. These vices are eschewed by pondering your busines well, and distinctly conceiving your selfe, which is much furthered by uttering your thoughts, and letting them as well come forth to the light, and Judgement of your owne outward senses, as to the censure of other mens eares: For that is the reason, why many good Schollers speake but fumblingly; like a rich man, that, for want of particular note and difference, can bring you no certaine ware readily out of his shop. Hence it is, that talkative shallow men doe often content the Hearers, more then the wise. But this may find a speedier redresse in writing; where all comes under the last examination of the eyes. First mind it well, then pen it, then examine it, then amend it; and you may bee in the better hope of doing reasonably well. Under this vertue may come Plainenesse, which is not to be curious in the order, as to answer a letter, as if you were to answer to Intergatories: As to the first, first; and to the second, secondly, &c. But both in method ⟨and wordes⟩ to use (as Ladies doe in their attyre) a diligent kind of negligence, and their sportive freedome; though with some men you are not to jest, or practise tricks: yet the delivery of the most important things, may be carried with such a grace, as that it may yeeld a pleasure to the conceit of the Reader. There must bee store, though no excesse of termes; as if you are to name *Store,* sometimes you may call it choyse, sometimes plenty; sometimes copiousnesse, or variety: but ever so, that the word which comes in lieu, have not such difference of meaning, as that it may put the sense of the first in hazard to be mistaken. You are not to cast a Ring for the perfumed termes of the time, as *Accommodation, Complement, Spirit, &c.* But use them properly in their place, as others.

There followeth *Life,* and *Quicknesse,* which is the strength and sinnewes (as it were) of your penning by pithy Sayings, Similitudes, and Conceits, Allusions ⟨to⟩ some knowne History, or other common place, such as are in the *Courtier,* and the second booke of *Cicero de oratore.*

The last is; Respect to discerne, what fits your selfe; him to whom you write; and that which you handle, which is a quality fit to conclude the rest, because it doth include all. And that must proceed from ripenesse of judgement, which, as one truly saith, is gotten by foure meanes, *God, Nature, Diligence, and Conversation.* Serve the first well, and the rest will serve you.

## Of Poets and Poetry

*We have* spoken sufficiently of Oratory; let us now make a diversion to *Poetry*. *Poetry,* in the Primogeniture, had many peccant humours, and is made to have more now, through the Levity, and inconstancie of mens Judgements. Whereas, indeed, it is the most prevailing Eloquence, and of the most exalted *Charact.* Now the discredits and disgraces are many it hath receiv'd, through mens study of Depravation or Calumny: their practise being to give it diminution of Credit, by lessening the Professors estimation, and making the Age afraid of their Liberty: And the Age is growne so tender of her fame, as she cals all writings *Aspersions.* That is the State-word, the Phrase of Court, (*Placentia Colledge*) which some call *Parasites Place,* the Inne of *Ignorance.*

*Whilst* I name no persons, but deride follies; why should any man confesse, or betray himselfe? why doth not that of *S. Hierome* come into their minde; *Ubi generalis est de vitiis disputatio, ibi nullius esse personæ injuriam?* Is it such an inexpiable crime in *Poets,* to taxe vices generally; and no offence in them who, by their exception, confesse they have committed them particularly? Are wee fal'ne into those times that wee must not

*Auriculas teneras mordaci rodere vero?*

*Remedii votum semper verius erat, quàm spes.* If men may by no meanes write freely, or speake truth, but when it offends not; why doe *Physicians* cure with sharpe medicines, or corrosives? Is not the same equally lawfull in the cure of the minde, that is in the cure of the body? Some vices, (you will say) are soe foule, that it is better they should bee done, then spoken. But they that take offence where no Name, Character, or Signature doth blazon them, seeme to mee like affected as woemen; who, if they heare any thing ill spoken of the ill of their Sexe, are presently mov'd, as if the contumely respected their particular: and, on the contrary, when they heare good of good woemen, conclude, that it belongs to them all. If I see any thing that toucheth mee, shall I come forth a betraier of my selfe, presently? No; if I be wise, I'le dissemble it; if honest, I'le avoid it: lest I publish that on my owne forehead, which I saw there noted without a title. A man, that is on the mending hand, will either ingeniously confesse, or wisely dissemble his disease. And, the wise, and vertuous, will never thinke any thing belongs to themselves that is written, but rejoyce that the good are warn'd not to bee such; and the ill to leave to bee such. The Person offended hath no reason to bee offended with the writer, but with himselfe; and so to declare that properly to belong to him, which was so spoken of all men, as it could bee no mans severall, but his that would willfully and desperately clayme it. It sufficeth I know, what kinde of persons I displease, men bred in the declining, and decay of vertue, betroth'd to their owne vices; that have abandoned, or prostituted their good names; hungry and ambitious of infamy, invested in all deformity, enthrall'd to ignorance and malice, of a hidden and conceal'd malignitie, and that hold a concomitancy with all evill.

## What Is a Poet?

*A Poet* is that, which by the *Greeks* is call'd κατ᾽ ἐξοχὴν, ὁ Ποιητὴς, a Maker, or a fainer: His Art, an Art of imitation, or faining; expressing the life of man in fit measure, numbers, and harmony, according to *Aristotle:* From the word ποιεῖν, which signifies to make, or fayne. Hence, hee is call'd a *Poet,* not hee which writeth in measure only; but that fayneth and formeth a fable, and writes things like the Truth. For, the Fable and Fiction is (as it were) the forme and Soule of any Poeticall worke, or *Poeme.*

## What Meane You by a Poeme?

*A Poeme* is not alone any worke, or composition of the Poets in many, or few verses; but even one alone verse sometimes makes a perfect *Poeme.* As, when *Aeneas* hangs up, and consecrates the Armes of *Abas,* with this Inscription;

*Aeneas hæc de Danais victoribus arma.*

And calls it a *Poeme,* or *Carmen.* Such are those in *Martiall.*

*Omnia, Castor, emis: sic fiet, ut omnia vendas.*

And,

*Pauper videri Cinna vult, & est pauper.*

So were *Horace* his *Odes* call'd, *Carmina;* his *Lyrik* Songs. And *Lucretius* designes a whole booke, in his sixt:

*Quod in primo quoque carmine claret.*

And anciently, all the Oracles were call'd *Carmina;* or, what ever Sentence was express'd were it much, or little, it was call'd, an *Epick*, *Dramatick, Lyrike, Elegiake,* or *Epigrammatike Poeme.*

### But, How Differs a Poeme from What Wee Call Poesy?

*A Poeme,* as I have told you, is the worke of the Poet; the end, and fruit of his labour, and studye. *Poesy* is his skill, or Crafte of making: the very Fiction it selfe, the reason, or forme of the worke. And these three voices differ, as the thing done, the doing, and the doer; the thing fain'd, the faining, and the fainer: so the *Poeme,* the *Poesy,* and the *Poet.* Now, the *Poesy* is the habit, or the Art: nay, rather the Queene of Arts: which had her Originall from heaven, received thence from the *'Ebrewes,* and had in prime estimation with the *Greeks,* transmitted to the *Latines,* and all Nations, that profess'd Civility. The Study of it (if wee will trust *Aristotle*) offers to mankinde a certaine rule, and Patterne of living well, and happily; disposing us to all Civill offices of Society. If wee will beleive *Tully,* it nourisheth, and instructeth our Youth; delights our Age; adornes our prosperity; comforts our Adversity; entertaines us at home; keepes us company abroad, travailes with us; watches; divides the times of our earnest, and sports; shares in our Country recesses, and recreations; insomuch as the wisest and best learned have thought her the absolute Mistresse of manners, and neerest of kin to Vertue. And, wheras they entitle *Philosophy* to bee a rigid, and austere *Poesie:* they have (on the contrary) stiled *Poesy,* a dulcet, and gentle *Philosophy,* which leades on, and guides us by the hand to Action, with a ravishing delight, and incredible Sweetnes. But, before wee handle the kindes of *Poems,* with their speciall differences; or make court to the Art it selfe, as a Mistresse, I would leade you to the knowledge of our *Poet,* by a perfect Information, what he is, or should bee by nature, by exercise, by imitation, by Studie; and so bring him downe through the disciplines of *Grammar, Logicke, Rhetoricke,* and the *Ethicks,* adding somewhat, out of all, peculiar to himselfe, and worthy of your Admittance, or reception.

*First,* wee require our *Poet,* or maker, (for that Title our Language affordes him, elegantly, with the *Greeke*) a goodnes of naturall wit. For, wheras all other Arts consist of Doctrine, and Precepts: the *Poet* must bee able by nature, and instinct, to powre out the Treasure of his minde; and, as *Seneca* saith, *Aliquando secundum Anacreontem insanire, jucundum esse:* by which hee understands, the *Poeticall Rapture.* And according to that of *Plato; Frustrà Poeticas fores sui compos pulsavit:* And of *Aristotle; Nullum magnum ingenium sine mixturâ dementiæ fuit. Nec potest grande aliquid, & supra cæteros loqui, nisi mota mens.* Then it riseth higher, as by a divine Instinct, when it contemnes common, and knowne conceptions. It utters somewhat above a mortall mouth. Then it gets a loft, and flies away with his Ryder, whether, before, it was doubtfull to ascend. This the *Poets* understood by their *Helicon, Pegasus,* or *Parnassus;* and this made *Ovid* to boast:

> *Est, Deus in nobis; agitante calescimus illo:*
> *Sedibus æthereis spiritus ille venit.*

And *Lipsius,* to affirme; *Scio, Poetam neminem præstantem fuisse, sine parte quâdam uberiore divinæ auræ.* And, hence it is, that the comming up of good Poets, (for I minde not *mediocres,* or *imos*) is so thinne and rare among us; Every beggerly Corporation affoords the State a *Major,* or two *Bailiffs,* yearly: but, *solus Rex, aut Poeta, non quotannis nascitur.* To this perfection of Nature in our *Poet,* wee require Exercise of those parts, and frequent. If his wit will not arrive soddainly at the dignitie of the Ancients, let him not yet fall out with it, quarrell, or be over-hastily Angry: offer, to turne it away from Study, in a humor; but come to it againe upon better cogitation; try an other time, with labour. If then it succeed not, cast not away the Quills, yet: nor scratch the Wainescott, beate not the poore Deske; but bring all to the forge, and file, againe; tourne it a newe. There is no Statute *Law* of the Kingdome bidds you bee a Poet, against your will; or the first Quarter. If it come, in a yeare, or two, it is well. The common Rymers powre forth Verses, such as they are, (*ex tempore*) but there never come(s) from them one Sense, worth the life of a Day. A Rymer, and a *Poet,* are two things. It is said of the incomparable *Virgil,* that he brought forth his verses like a Beare, and after form'd them with licking. *Scaliger,* the Father, writes it of him, that he made a quantitie of verses in the morning, which afore night hee reduced to a lesse number. But, that which *Valerius Maximus* hath left recorded of *Euripides,* the *tragicke Poet,* his answer to *Alcestis,* an other *Poet,* is as memorable, as modest: who, when it was told to *Alcestis,* that *Euripides* had in three daies brought forth but three verses, and those with some difficultie, and throwes; *Alcestis,* glorying hee could with ease have sent forth a hundred in the space; *Euripides* roundly repl⟨i⟩'d, Like enough. But, here is the difference; Thy verses will not last those three daies; mine will to all time. Which was, as to tell him, he could not write a verse. I have met many of these Rattles, that made a noyse, and buz'de. They had their humme; and, no more. Indeed, things, wrote with labour, deserve to be so read, and will last their Age. The third requisite in our *Poet,* or Maker, is *Imitation,* to bee able to convert the substance, or Riches of an other *Poet,* to his owne use. To make choise of one excellent man above the rest, and so to follow him, till he grow very *Hee:* or, so like him, as the Copie may be mistaken for the Principall. Not, as a Creature, that swallowes, what it takes in, crude, raw, or indigested; but, that feedes with an Appetite, and hath a Stomacke to concoct, divide, and turne all into nourishment. Not, to imitate servilely, as *Horace* saith, and catch at vices, for vertue: but, to draw forth out of the best, and choisest flowers, with the Bee, and turne all into Honey, worke it into one relish, and savour: make our *Imitation* sweet: observe, how the best writers have imitated, and follow them. How *Virgil,* and *Statius* have imitated *Homer;* how *Horace, Archilochus;* how *Alcæus,* and the other *Lyricks:* and so of the rest. But, that, which wee especially require in him is an exactnesse of Studie, and multiplicity of reading, which maketh a full man, not alone enabling him to know the *History,* or Argument of a *Poeme,* and to report it: but so to master the matter, and Stile, as to shew, hee knowes, how to handle, place, or dispose of either, with *elegancie,* when need shall bee. And not thinke, hee can leape forth suddainely a *Poet,* by dreaming hee hath been in *Parnassus,* or, having washt his lipps (as they say) in *Helicon.* There goes more to his making, then so. For to Nature, Exercise, Imitation, and Studie, *Art* must bee added, to make all these perfect. And, though these challenge to themselves much, in the making up of our Maker, it is Art only can lead him to perfection, and leave him there in possession, as planted by her hand. It is the assertion of *Tully,* If to an excellent nature, there happen an accession, or conformation of Learning, and Discipline, there will then remaine somewhat noble, and singular. For, as *Simylus* saith in *Stobæus;*

Οὔτε φύσις ἱκανὴ γίνεται τέχνης ἄτερ,
οὔτε πᾶν τέχνη μὴ φύσιν κεκτημένη·

without Art, Nature can ne're bee perfect; &, without Nature, Art can clayme no being. But, our Poet must beware, that his Studie bee not only to learne of himself; for, hee that shall affect to doe that, confesseth his ever having a Foole to his master. Hee must read many; but, ever the best, and choisest: those, that can teach him any thing, hee must ever account his masters, and reverence: among whom *Horace,* and (hee that taught him) *Aristotle,* deserve to bee the first in estimation.

## Poets and Critics

*Aristotle* was the first accurate *Criticke,* and truest Judge; nay, the greatest *Philosopher,* the world ever had: for, hee noted the vices of all knowledges, in all creatures, and out of many mens perfections in a Science, hee formed still one Art. So hee taught us two Offices together, how we ought to judge rightly of others, and what wee ought to imitate specially in our selves. But all this in vaine, without a naturall wit, and a Poeticall nature in chiefe. For, no man, so soone as hee knowes this, or reades it, shall be able to write the better; but as he is adapted to it by Nature, he shall grow the perfecter Writer. Hee must have *Civil prudence,* and *Eloquence,* & that whole; not taken up by snatches, or peeces, in Sentences, or remnants, when he will handle businesse, or carry Counsells, as if he came then out of the Declamors Gallerie, or Shadowe, but furnish'd out of the body of the State, which commonly is the Schoole of men. The *Poet* is the neerest Borderer upon the Orator, and expresseth all his vertues, though he be tyed more to numbers; is his equall in ornament, and above him in his strengths. And, (of the kind) the *Comicke* comes neerest: Because, in moving the minds of men, and stirring of affections (in which Oratory shewes, and especially approves her eminence) hee chiefly excells. What figure of a Body was *Lysippus* ever able to forme with his Graver, or *Apelles* to paint with his Pencill, as the Comedy to life expresseth so many, and various affections of the minde? There shall the Spectator see some, insulting with Joy; others, fretting with Melancholy; raging with Anger; mad with Love; boiling with Avarice; undone with Riot; tortur'd with expectation; consum'd with feare: no perturbation in common life, but the Orator findes an example of it in the Scene. And then, for the Elegancy of Language, read but this Inscription on the *Grave* of a *Comicke Poet:*

*Immortales mortales, si fas esset, flere,*
*Flerent divæ Camœnæ Nævium Poetam;*
*Itaque postquam est Orcino traditus thesauro,*
*Obliti sunt Romæ, linguâ loqui Latinâ.*

Or, that modester Testimonie given by *Lucius Aelius Stilo* upon *Plautus;* who affirmed, *Musas, si latinè loqui voluissent, Plautino sermone fuisse loquuturas.* And that illustrious judgement by the most learned *M. Varro* of him; who pronounced him the *Prince* of *Letters,* and *Elegancie,* in the *Roman* Language.

I am not of that opinion to conclude a *Poets* liberty within the narrowe limits of lawes, which either the *Grammarians,* or *Philosophers* prescribe. For, before they found out those Lawes, there were many excellent Poets, that fulfill'd them. Amongst whome none more perfect then *Sophocles,* who liv'd a little before *Aristotle.* Which of the *Greekelings* durst ever give precepts to *Demosthenes?* or to *Pericles,* (whom the Age surnam'd *heavenly*) because he seem'd to thunder, and lighten, with his Language? or to *Alcibiades,* who had rather Nature for his guide, then Art for his master?

But, whatsoever Nature at any time dictated to the most happie, or long exercise to the most laborious; that the wisdome, and Learning of *Aristotle,* hath brought into an Art: because, he understood the Causes of things: and what other men did by chance or custome, he doth by reason; and not only found out the way not to erre, but the short way we should take, not to erre.

Many things in *Euripides* hath *Aristophanes* wittily reprehended; not out of Art, but out of Truth. For, *Euripides* is sometimes peccant, as he is most times perfect. But, Judgement when it is greatest, if reason doth not accompany it, is not ever absolute.

To judge of Poets is only the facultie of Poets; and not of all Poets, but the best. *Nemo infæliciùs de Poetis judicavit, quàm qui de Poetis scripsit.* But, some will say, *Criticks* are a kind of Tinkers; that make more faults, then they mend ordinarily. See their diseases, and those of *Grammarians.* It is true, many bodies are the worse for the medling with: And the multitude of *Physicians* hath destroyed many sound patients, with their wrong practise. But the office of a true *Critick,* or *Censor,* is, not to throw by a letter any where, or damne an innocent Syllabe, but lay the words together, and amend them; judge sincerely of the Author, and his matter, which is the signe of solid, and perfect learning in a man. Such was *Horace,* an Author of much Civilitie; and (if any one among the heathen can be) the best master, both of vertue, and wisdome; an excellent, and true judge upon cause, and reason; not because he thought so; but because he knew so, out of use and experience.

*Cato,* the *Grammarian,* a defender of *Lucilius.*

> *Cato Grammaticus, Latina Syren,*
> *Qui solus legit, & facit Poetas.*

*Quintilian* of the same heresie, but rejected.

*Horace* his judgement of *Chærilus,* defended against *Joseph Scaliger.* And, of *Laberius,* against *Julius.*

But chiefly his opinion of *Plautus,* vindicated against many, that are offended, and say, it is a hard Censure upon the parent of all conceipt, and sharpnesse. And, they wish it had not fallen from so great a master, and Censor in the Art: whose bondmen knew better how to judge of *Plautus,* then any that dare patronize the family of learning in this age; who could not bee ignorant of the judgement of the times, in which hee liv'd, when *Poetrie,* and the *Latin* Language were at the height: especially, being a man so conversant, and inwardly familiar with the censures of great men, that did discourse of these things daily amongst themselves. Againe, a man so gratious, and in high favour with the Emperour, as *Augustus* often called him his wittie *Manling,* (for the littlenes of his stature;) and (if wee may trust Antiquity) had design'd him for a Secretary of Estate; and invited him to the P(a)lace, which he modestly praid off, and refus'd.

## Comedy

*Horace* did so highly esteeme *Terence* his Comedies, as he ascribes the Art in Comedie to him alone, among the *Latines,* and joynes him with *Menander.*

Now, let us see what may be said for either, to defend *Horace* his judgement to posterity; and not wholly to condemne *Plautus.*

The parts of a Comedie are the same with a *Tragedie,* and the end is partly the same. For, they both delight, and teach: the *Comicks* are call'd διδάσκαλοι, of the Greekes; no lesse then the *Tragicks.*

Nor, is the moving of laughter alwaies the end of *Comedy,* that is rather a fowling for the peoples delight, or their fooling. For, as *Aristotle* saies rightly, the moving of laughter is a fault in Comedie, a kind of turpitude, that depraves some part of a mans nature without a disease. As a wry face without paine moves laughter, or a deformed vizard, or a rude Clowne, drest in a Ladies habit, and using her actions, wee dislike, and scorne such representations; which made the ancient Philosophers ever thinke laughter unfitting in a wise man. And this induc'd *Plato* to esteeme of *Homer,* as a sacrilegious Person; because he presented the *Gods* sometimes laughing. As, also, it is divinely said of *Aristotle,* that to seeme ridiculous is a part of dishonesty, and foolish.

So that, what either in the words, or Sense of an Author, or in the language, or Actions of men, is a wry, or depraved, doth strangely stirre meane affections, and provoke for the most part to laughter. And therfore it was cleare that all insolent, and obscene speaches; jest⟨s⟩ upon the best men; injuries to particular persons; perverse, and sinister Sayings (and the rather unexpected) in the old Comedy, did move laughter; especially, where it did imitate any dishonesty; and scurrility came forth in the place of wit: which who understands the nature and *Genius* of laughter, cannot but perfectly know.

Of which *Aristophanes* affords an ample harvest, having not only outgone *Plautus,* or any other in that kinde; but express'd all the moods, and figures, of what is ridiculous, oddly. In short, as Vinegar is not accounted good, untill the wine be corrupted: so jests that are true and naturall, seldome raise laughter, with the beast, the multitude. They love nothing, that is right, and proper. The farther it runs from reason, or possibility with them, the better it is. What could have made them laugh, like to see *Socrates* presented, that Example of all good life, honesty, and vertue, to have him hoisted up with a Pullie, and there play the Philosopher, in a basquet? Measure, how many foote a Flea could skip *Geometrically,* by a just Scale, and edifie the people from the ingine? This was *Theatricall* wit, right Stage-jesting, and relishing a Play-house, invented for scorne, and laughter; whereas, if it had savour'd of equity, truth, perspicuity, and Candor, to have tasten a wise, or a learned Palate, spit it out presently; this is bitter and profitable, this instructs, and would informe us: what neede wee know any thing, that are nobly borne, more than a Horse-race, or a hunting-match, our day to breake with Citizens, and such innate mysteries? This is truly leaping from the Stage to the Tumbrell againe, reducing all witt to the originall Dungcart.

## Of the Magnitude, and Compasse of Any Fable, Epicke, or Dramatick

To the resolving of this *Question,* wee must first agree in the definition of the Fable. The Fable is call'd the *Imitation* of one intire, and
perfect Action; whose parts are so joyned, and knitt together, as nothing in the structure can be chang'd, or taken away, without impairing,
or troubling the whole; of which there is a proportionable magnitude
in the members. As for example; if a man would build a house, he
would first appoint a place to build it in, which he would define
within certaine bounds: So in the Constitution of a *Poeme,* the Action
is aym'd at by the *Poet,* which answers Place in a building; and that
Action hath his largenesse, compasse, and proportion. But, as a Court,
or Kings Palace, requires other dimensions then a private house: So the
*Epick* askes a magnitude, from other Poëms. Since, what is Place in the
one, is Action in the other, the difference is in space. So that by this
definition wee conclude the fable, to be the *imitation* of one perfect,
and intire Action; as one perfect, and intire place is requir'd to a
building. By perfect, wee understand that, to which nothing is wanting;
as Place to the building, that is rais'd, and Action to the fable, that is
form'd. It is perfect, perhaps, not for a Court, or Kings Palace, which
requires a greater ground; but for the structure wee would raise. So
the space of the Action, may not prove large enough for the *Epick
Fable,* yet bee perfect for the *Dramatick,* and whole.

*Whole,* wee call that, and perfect, which hath a *beginning,* a *mid'st,*
and an *end.* So the place of any building may be whole, and intire,
for that worke; though too little for a palace. As, to a *Tragedy* or a
*Comedy,* the Action may be convenient, and perfect, that would not fit
an *Epicke Poeme* in Magnitude. So a Lion is a perfect creature in
himselfe, though it bee lesse, then ⟨an Elephant. The head of a Lion
is a whole, though it be lesse, then⟩ that of a *Buffalo,* or a *Rhinocerote.*
They differ; but *in specie:* either in the kinde is absolute. Both have
their parts, and either the whole. Therefore, as in every body; so in
every Action, which is the subject of a just worke, there is requir'd a
certaine proportionable greatnesse, neither too vast, nor too minute.
For that which happens to the Eyes, when wee behold a body, the same
happens to the Memorie, when wee contemplate an action. I looke
upon a monstrous Giant, as *Tityus,* whose body cover'd nine Acres of
Land, and mine eye stickes upon every part; the whole that consists of
those parts, will never be taken in at one intire view. So in a *Fable,*

if the Action be too great, wee can never comprehend the whole together in our Imagination. Againe, if it be too little, there ariseth no pleasure out of the object, it affords the view no stay: it is beheld and vanisheth at once. As if wee should looke upon an Ant or Pismyre, the parts fly the sight, and the whole considered is almost nothing. The same happens in Action, which is the object of Memory, as the body is of sight. Too vast oppresseth the Eyes, and exceeds the Memory: too little scarce admits either.

Now, in every Action it behooves the *Poet* to know which is his utmost bound, how farre with fitnesse, and a necessary proportion, he may produce, and determine it. That is, till either good fortune change into the worse, or the worse into the better. For, as a body without proportion cannot be goodly, no more can the Action, either in *Comedy,* or *Tragedy,* without his fit bounds. And every bound, for the nature of the Subject, is esteem'd the best that is largest, till it can increase no more: so it behooves the Action in *Tragedy,* or *Comedy,* to be let grow, till the necessity aske a Conclusion: wherein two things are to be considered; First, that it exceed not the compasse of one Day: Next, that there be place left for digression, and Art. For the *Episodes,* and digressions in a Fable, are the same that household stuffe, and other furniture are in a house. And so farre for the measure, and extent of a *Fable Dramaticke.*

*Now,* that it should be one, and intire. One is considerable two waies: either, as it is only separate, and by it self: or as being compos'd of many parts, it beginnes to be one, as those parts grow, or are wrought together. That it should be one the first way alone, and by it self, no man that hath tasted letters ever would say, especially having required before a just Magnitude, and equall Proportion of the parts in themselves. Neither of which can possibly bee, if the Action be single and separate, not compos'd of parts, which laid together in themselves, with an equall and fitting proportion, tend to the same end; which thing out of Antiquitie it selfe, hath deceiv'd many; and more this Day it doth deceive.

So many there be of old, that have thought the Action of one man to be one: As of *Hercules, Theseus, Achilles, Ulysses,* and other *Heroes;* which is both foolish and false; since by one and the same person many things may be severally done, which cannot fitly be referred, or joyned to the same end: which not only the excellent *Tragick-Poets,* but the best Masters of the *Epick,* *Homer,* and *Virgil* saw. For, though the Argument of an *Epick-Poeme* be farre more *diffus'd,* & powr'd out, then that of *Tragedy;* yet *Virgil,* writing of *Aeneas,* hath pretermitted many things. He neither tells how he was borne, how brought up; how he fought with *Achilles;* how he was snatch'd out of the battaile by *Venus;* but that one thing, how *he came into Italie,* he prosecutes in twelve bookes. The rest of his journey, his error by Sea, the Sacke of *Troy,* are put not as the Argument of the worke, but *Episodes* of the Argument. So *Homer* lai'd by many things of *Ulysses* and handled no more, then he saw tended to one and the same end.

*Contrarie* to which and foolishly those *Poets* did, whom the *Philosopher* taxeth; Of whom one gather'd all the Actions of *Theseus;* another put all the Labours of *Hercules* in one worke. So did he, whom *Juvenal* mentions in the beginning, *hoarse Codrus,* that recited a volume compil'd, which he call'd his *Theseide,* not yet finish'd, to the great trouble both of his hearers and himself: Amongst which there were many parts had no coherence, nor kindred one with other, so farre they were from being one Action, one *Fable.* For as a house, consisting of diverse materialls, becomes one structure, and one dwelling; so an Action, compos'd of diverse parts, may become one *Fable Epicke,* or *Dramaticke.* For *example,* in a *Tragedy,* looke upon *Sophocles* his *Ajax: Ajax* depriv'd of *Achilles's* Armour, which he hop'd from the suffrage of the *Greekes,* disdaines; and, growing impatient of the Injurie, rageth, and turnes mad. In that humour he doth many senselesse things; and at last falls upon the *Grecian* flocke, and kills a great Ramme for *Ulysses:* Returning to his Sense, he growes asham'd of the scorne, and kills himself; and is by the *Chiefes* of the *Greekes* forbidden buriall. These things agree, and hang together, not as they were done; but as seeming to be done; which made the Action whole, intire, and absolute.

*For* the *whole,* as it consisteth of parts; so without all the parts it is not the whole; and to make it absolute, is requir'd, not only the parts, but such parts as are true. For a part of the whole was true; which if you take away, you either change the whole, or it is not the whole. For, if it be such a part, as being present or absent, nothing concernes the whole, it cannot be call'd a part of the whole: and such are the *Episodes,* of which hereafter. For the present, here is one example; The single Combat of *Ajax* with *Hector,* as it is at large describ'd in *Homer,* nothing belongs to this *Ajax* of *Sophocles.*

You admire no *Poems,* but such as run like a Brewers-cart upon the stones, hobling,

> *Et, quæ per salebras, altaque saxa cadunt.*
> *Actius, & quidquid Pacuviusque vomunt.*
> *Attonitusque legis terrai, frugiferai.*

## Finis

# Thomas Hobbes

## 1588–1679

Hobbes was born on Good Friday, 1588, to a father who was an ignorant country parson and a mother who "fell in labour with him upon the fright of the Invasion of the Spaniards." Precocious in school, he was sent to Magdalen Hall, Oxford, in 1603, and took his degree in 1608. Then followed a long career as tutor, secretary, and companion in the household of the Earls of Devonshire. For a time during the Interregnum he served as tutor to the Prince of Wales, later Charles II. He moved in intellectual and literary circles that included Galileo, Harvey, Dryden, Herbert of Cherbury, Mersenne, Gassendi, and Cowley; Aubrey reports that Ben Jonson was "his loving and familiar Friend," and that Bacon "loved to converse with him."

But he also made enemies. He fled to France in 1640 when his militant Royalism began to seem dangerous in England, and then back to England in 1651 when publication of the *Leviathan* aroused hostility among his fellow exiles. With Charles' favor renewed at the Restoration, he nevertheless continued to be looked on with suspicion, and his right to publish in England was severely restricted. He also engaged in extended controversies on philosophical and scientific issues with Descartes, Boyle, and others. Here he was sometimes badly overmatched, as when he took on Wallis in an attempt to prove that he had squared the circle.

But in political philosophy he was formidable indeed. The only basis for society is enlightened self-love, he argued, since men are moved not by reason but by their appetites and aversions, in the light of which they rationalize their principles of good and evil. Thus he offered a science of natural justice, a clear anticipation of Hume's empirical ethics, and a wholesale and often contemptuous rejection of Christian humanism. To oppose thus openly the prevailing belief in a natural and moral law that had its sanctions both in Christianity and in reason took a good deal of courage, particularly from a man who described himself as timid and no trouble-maker. Waller is said to have remarked that Hobbes, "being but *one,* and a private Person," nevertheless "pulled-downe all their Churches, dispelled the mists of Ignorance, and layd-open their Priest-craft." In addition, Hobbes' skeptical, nominalist, materialist package included the rejection of free will, of an immortal soul, and of final causes. From pulpits and pamphlets, from Cambridge Platonists and vestigial Aristotelians, from Deists and theists, from the pious and the prudent, came the shocked protests at this unflattering and unpalatable doctrine; today there are those who still report "a queer sense of lost bearings" (Basil Willey) as they wander about Hobbes' spiny, Swiftian landscape.

Hobbes was freely labelled atheist, but he was no atheist. For all his attacks on the clergy and on scholasticism, and on "Fancies, Ghosts, and every empty Shade," he was no atheist or even Deist, but a practicing, conforming adherent of the Church of England. That the tenets of the Church might be inconsistent with his philosophy did not matter, since he saw religion as a question of will and law and not of belief or truth. Law is the product of authority, religious law of religious authority. Only this authority can distinguish between religion and superstition, both derived equally from a fear of the unknown. Thus Hobbes, in the absence of any universal religious authority he could accept, held the Erastian view that in each state the civil magistrate is also head of the church, else there is a dangerous division of authority, and ultimately civil war.

Occasioned by what Hobbes called the present disorders, the *Leviathan* is a defense of a central authority strong enough to keep the peace. Stability and order are best achieved when the authority is vested in a single monarch with unlimited power. Once men have consented to relinquish their natural right to destroy each other, and have contracted to replace the state of nature with the state of law, they have no residual rights as subjects. There is no room for factions or for private judgments.

Though he was principally philosopher and moralist (he would have said mathematician instead), his literary activities were diverse also, and included translations of Thucydides and of the *Iliad* and the *Odyssey,* an autobiography in Latin verse, two attempts to set standards for the epic ("Answer to Davenant," and "The Virtues of an Heroic Poem," which prefaced his translation of Homer), and—even amidst the political issues central to the *Leviathan*—some sophisticated remarks on poetry and the imagination. In addition, Aubrey reports that Hobbes spent two years (and then regretted them) reading romances and plays, and that he always kept books of prick-song lying on the table, and would sing them at night when the doors had been made fast. In his old age he could still turn a compliment in the form of a courtly ditty:

> Tho' I am now past ninety, and too old
> T'expect preferment in the Court of Cupid,
> And many Winters made mee ev'n so cold
> I am become almost all over stupid.
>
> Yet I can love and have a Mistresse too,
> As far as can be and as wise as fair;
> And yet not proud, nor anything will doe
> To make me of her favour to despair.
>
> To tell you who she is were very bold;
> But if i'th'Character your Selfe you find
> Thinke not the man a Fool tho he be old
> Who loves in Body fair, a fairer mind.

His analysis of the imagination presented poetry in a freshly psychological context. The imagination, he wrote, has wondrous power, recalling, combining, and constantly recombining our perceptions. He showed how fancy and judgment come into play in the writing of a poem, and thus he shifted the center of critical attention from formal, moral, or ontological considerations to the working of the mind in the poetic process. Fancy provides the matter and words, the ideas and images, as well as the ornaments, of the poem; it delights in discovering likenesses; it brings sublimity and poetical fury on the one hand, and celerity of thought on the other. It is knowing much, as judgment is knowing well. Judgment discerns differences; it leads to propriety, and prevents levity; it provides the strength and structure of the poem. "And both *Fancie* and *Judgement* are commonly comprehended under the name of *Wit*."

He found the ambiguity of language a mixed bag. Certainly in philosophy or science he would have his words unequivocal, clear, and exact, signifying real, knowable things; "The Light of humane minds is Perspicuous Words, but by exact definitions first snuffed, and purged free from ambiguity." Else a man could be entangled in words as a bird in limetwigs. Even in poetry a metaphor or conceit can be an indecency, especially if inappropriate to the use made of it, or so far-fetched that the similitude disappears entirely. But Hobbes recognized also that fictions and figurative language are everywhere, and have their uses, that the poet needs amplitude and variety both in expression and in content, and that metaphors, if not sharp and extraordinary, enrich the poem. Metaphors, he admitted, are derived by observing things that have "similitude and proportion one to another. And the more unlike, and unproportionable the things be otherwise, the more *grace* hath the *Metaphor*." The *Leviathan* is itself of course a sustained metaphor: the state, created by the art and will of man, is the great Leviathan or "Artificiall Man," the sovereign is its soul, the magistrate its joints, rewards and punishments its nerves, and so on.

Hobbes' own prose style is Senecan, sometimes curt, sometimes loose, usually plain, after the Baconian model admired by members of the Royal Society. Sprat called it a round, close style, sparing of similes, though ever extraordinarily decent in them. But it is not a transparent, scientific style. Though perspicuous it is also animated, witty, often charged with malice. It reflects his great energy and his occasional irascibility, his comprehensive if not always consistent intelligence, his stubborn determination to clean out the rubbish of centuries of sloppy thinking.

Towards the close of the *Leviathan,* for example, he likens the Kingdom of Darkness (Roman Church) to the Kingdom of Fairies. The Pope becomes Oberon. Both have their enchanted castles and cathedrals. Both skim the cream from the milk. Both show their displeasure by pinching.

> The *Fairies* are not to be seized on; and brought to answer for the hurt they do. So also the *Ecclesiastiques* vanish away from the Tribunals of Civill Justice. . . .
>
> The *Fairies* marry not; but there be amongst them *Incubi,* that have copulation with flesh and bloud. The *Priests* also marry not. . . .
>
> The *Ecclesiastiques* take from young men, the use of Reason, by certain Charms compounded of Metaphysiques, and Miracles, and Traditions, and Abused Scripture, whereby they are good for nothing else, but to execute what they command them. The *Fairies* likewise are said to take young Children out of their Cradles, and to change them into Naturall Fools, which Common people do therefore call *Elves,* and are apt to mischief. . . .

Both Church and fairies draw their power from the fears and fancies of ignorant people.

> It was not therefore a very difficult matter, for Henry 8. by his Exorcisme; nor for Qu. Elizabeth by hers, to cast them out. But who knows that this Spirit of Rome, now gone out, and walking by Missions through the dry places of China, Japan, and the Indies, that yeeld him little fruit, may not return, or rather an Assembly of Spirits worse than he, enter, and inhabite this clean swept house, and make the End thereof worse than the Beginning? For it is not the Romane Clergy onely, that pretends the Kingdome of God to be of this World, and thereby to have a Power therein, distinct from that of the Civill State. And this is all I had a designe to say, concerning the Doctrine of the POLITIQUES. . . .

## EDITIONS

*De Cive*, 1642; *De Cive: Or, the Citizen*, ed. by Sterling Lamprecht, 1949.

*A Discourse upon Gondibert, An Heroick Poem Written by Sr. William D'Avenant. With an Answer to It by Mr. Hobbs*, 1650. In J. E. Spingarn, *Critical Essays of the Seventeenth Century*, 1908.

*Humane Nature*, 1650; *De Corpore Politico, Or the Elements of Law*, 1650; both ed. by Ferdinand Tönnies, 1889, as *The Elements of Law*.

*Leviathan*, 1651; ed. by A. R. Waller, 1904; ed. by Michael Oakeshott, 1946; ed. by John Plamenatz, 1962.

*The Travels of Ulysses*, 1673. *Homer's Odysses . . . With a Large Preface Concerning the Vertues of an Heroique Poem*, 1675.

*Behemoth*, 1679 (as *The History of the Civil Wars of England*), 1680, 1682 (in *Tracts*); ed. by Ferdinand Tönnies, 1889.

*Opera Philosophica*, 1668.

*The English Works of Thomas Hobbes*, ed. by W. Molesworth, 1839–1845; reprinted 1962.

## HISTORICAL AND CRITICAL STUDIES

SIR LESLIE STEPHEN, *Hobbes*, 1904.

FRITHIOF BRANDT, *Thomas Hobbes' Mechanical Conception of Nature*, 1928.

JOHN LAIRD, *Hobbes*, 1934.

LEO STRAUSS, *The Political Philosophy of Hobbes: Its Basis and Its Genesis*, trans. by Elsa Sinclair, 1936; 1952.

A. E. TAYLOR, "An Apology for Mr. Hobbes," *Seventeenth Century Studies Presented to Sir Herbert Grierson*, 1938.

A. E. TAYLOR, "The Ethical Doctrine of Hobbes," *Philosophy*, XIII (1938).

CLARENCE THORPE, *The Aesthetic Theory of Thomas Hobbes*, 1940, 1964.

MARTIN KALLICH, "The Association of Ideas and Critical Theory: Hobbes, Locke, and Addison," *ELH,* XII (1945).

HANNAH ARENDT, "Expansion and the Philosophy of Power," *Sewanee Rev.,* LIV (1946).

GEORGE L. MOSSE, "Thomas Hobbes: Jurisprudence at the Crossroads," *University of Toronto Quar.,* XV (1946).

DAVID G. JAMES, *The Life of Reason: Hobbes, Locke, Bolingbroke,* 1949.

H. L. STEWART, "Hobbes and His England," *Queen's Quar.,* LVII (1950).

WALTER J. ONG, "Hobbes and Talon's Ramist Rhetoric," *Trans. Cambridge Bibl. Soc.,* I (1951).

JOHN BOWLE, *Hobbes and His Critics: A Study in Seventeenth Century Constitutionalism,* 1951.

NATHANIEL H. HENRY, "Milton and Hobbes: Mortalism and the Intermediate State," *SP,* XLVIII (1951).

HUGH AND MARY MACDONALD, *Thomas Hobbes, a Bibliography,* 1952.

GEORGES DAVY, *Thomas Hobbes et J. J. Rousseau,* 1953.

MARTIN KALLICH, "The Argument Against the Association of Ideas in Eighteenth-Century Aesthetics," *MLQ,* XV (1954).

AARON LEVY, "Economic Views of Thomas Hobbes," *JHI,* XV (1954).

GEORGE WATSON, "Hobbes, and the Metaphysical Conceit," *JHI,* XVI (1955).

THEODORE M. GANG, "Hobbes and the Metaphysical Conceit—A Reply," *JHI,* XVII (1956).

DOROTHEA KROOK, "Thomas Hobbes's Doctrine of Meaning and Truth," *Philosophy,* XXXI (1956).

RICHARD PETERS, *Hobbes,* 1956.

DAVID OGG, "Thomas Hobbes: An Attempted Re-Assessment," *Renaissance Papers,* ed. by Allan H. Gilbert, 1957.

R. S. PETERS AND H. TAJFEL, "Hobbes and Hull—Metaphysicians of Behaviour," *British Journal for the Philosophy of Science,* VIII (1957).

V. DE S. PINTO, "Was Hobbes an Ogre?" *Essays in Criticism,* VII (1957).

HOWARD WARRENDER, *The Political Philosophy of Hobbes,* 1957.

J. B. STEWART, "Hobbes Among the Critics" *Political Science Quar.,* LXXIII (1958).

STUART M. BROWN, JR., "Hobbes: The Taylor Thesis," *Phil. Rev.,* LXVIII (1959).

HOWARD WARRENDER, "The Place of God in Hobbes's Philosophy," *Political Studies,* VIII (1960).

LOUIS FRANCIS MAY, JR., "A Literary Analysis of Thomas Hobbes' *Leviathan,*" Dissertation, St. Louis Univ., 1959; *Dissertation Abstr.,* XX (1960).

THOMAS E. JESSOP, *Thomas Hobbes,* 1960.

J. ROLAND PENNOCK, "Hobbes's Confusing 'Clarity'—The Case of 'Liberty,' " *Am. Political Science Rev.,* LIV (1960).

JOHN D. SEELYE, "Hobbes' *Leviathan* and the Giantism Complex in the First Book of *Gulliver's Travels,*" *JEGP,* LX (1960).

MORRIS ENGEL, "Hobbes's 'Table of Absurdity,' " *Phil. Rev.,* LXX (1961).

BERNARD GERT, "The Moral Philosophy of Thomas Hobbes," Dissertation, Cornell University, 1962; *Dissertation Abstr.,* XXIII (1963).

MORRIS ENGEL, "Analogy and Equivocation in Hobbes," *Philos.*, XXXVII (1962).

CRAWFORD B. MACPHERSON, *The Political Theory of Possessive Individualism: Hobbes to Locke,* 1962.

SAMUEL I. MINTZ, *The Hunting of Leviathan: Seventeenth-Century Reactions to the Materialism and Moral Philosophy of Thomas Hobbes,* 1962.

EUGENE J. ROESCH, *The Totalitarian Threat: The Fruition of Modern Individualism, as Seen in Hobbes and Rousseau,* 1963.

I. BERLIN, "Hobbes, Locke and Professor Macpherson," *Political Q.,* XXXV (1964).

R. L. BRETT, "Thomas Hobbes," in *The English Mind,* ed. by Hugh Sykes Davies and George Watson, 1964.

FRANCIS CAMPBELL HOOD, *The Divine Politics of Thomas Hobbes: An Interpretation of Leviathan,* 1964.

LEONARD KRIEGER, "The Distortions of Political Theory: The XVIIth-Century Case," *JHT,* XXV (1964).

# THE ANSWER TO THE PREFACE
# TO GONDIBERT

*Sir,*

If to commend your poem, I should only say, in general terms, that in the choice of your argument, the disposition of the parts, the maintenance of the characters of your persons, the dignity and vigour of your expression, you have performed all the parts of various experience, ready memory, clear judgment, swift and well-governed fancy: though it were enough for the truth, it were too little for the weight and credit of my testimony. For I lie open to two exceptions, one of an incompetent, the other of a corrupted witness. Incompetent, because I am not a poet; and corrupted with the honour done me by your preface. The former obliges me to say something, by the way, of the nature and differences of poesy.

As philosophers have divided the universe, their subject, into three regions, *celestial, aerial,* and *terrestrial;* so the poets, whose work it is, by imitating human life, in delightful and measured lines, to avert men from vice, and incline them to virtuous and honourable actions, have lodged themselves in the three regions of mankind, *court, city,* and *country,* correspondent, in some proportion, to those three regions of the world. For there is in princes, and men of conspicuous power, anciently called *heroes,* a lustre and influence upon the rest of men, resembling that of the heavens; and an insincereness, inconstancy, and troublesome humour in those that dwell in populous cities, like the mobility, blustering, and impurity of the air; and a plainness, and, though dull, yet a nutritive faculty in rural people, that endures a comparison with the earth they labour.

From hence have proceeded three sorts of poesy, *heroic, scommatic,* and *pastoral.* Every one of these is distinguished again in the manner of *representation;* which sometimes is *narrative,* wherein the poet himself relateth; and sometimes *dramatic,* as when the persons are every one adorned and brought upon the theatre, to speak and act their own parts. There is therefore neither more nor less than six sorts of poesy. For the heroic poem narrative, such as is yours, is called an *epic* poem; the heroic poem dramatic, is *tragedy.* The scommatic narrative is *satire;* dramatic is *comedy.* The pastoral narrative, is called simply *pastoral,* anciently *bucolic;* the same dramatic, *pastoral comedy.* The figure therefore of an epic poem, and of a tragedy, ought to be the same: for they differ no more but in that they are pronounced by one, or many persons; which I insert to justify the figure of yours, consisting of five books divided into songs, or cantos; as five acts divided into scenes, has ever been the approved figure of a tragedy.

They that take for poesy whatsoever is writ in verse, will think this division imperfect, and call in sonnets, epigrams, eclogues, and the like pieces, which are but essays, and parts of an entire poem; and reckon Empedocles and Lucretius, natural philosophers, for poets; and the moral precepts of Phocylides Theognis, and the quatrains of Pybrach, and the history of Lucan, and others of that kind, amongst poems: bestowing on such writers, for honour, the name of poets, rather than of historians or philosophers. But the subject of a poem is the manners of men, not natural causes; manners presented, not dictated; and manners feigned, as the name of poesy imports, not found in men. They that give entrance to fictions writ in prose, err not so much; but they err; for prose requireth delightfulness, not only of fiction, but of style; in which if prose contend with verse, it is with disadvantage and, as it were, on foot against the strength and wings of Pegasus. . . .

Time and education beget experience; experience begets memory; memory begets judgment and fancy; judgment begets the strength and structure, and fancy begets the ornaments of a poem. The ancients therefore fabled not absurdly, in making Memory the mother of the Muses. For memory is the world, though not really, yet so as in a looking-glass, in which the judgment, the severer sister, busieth herself in a grave and rigid examination of all the parts of nature, and in registering by letters their order, causes, uses, differences, and resemblances; whereby the fancy, when any work of art is to be performed, finds her materials at hand and prepared for use, and needs no more than a swift motion over them, that what she wants, and is there to be had, may not lie too long unespied. So that when she seemeth to fly from one Indies to the other, and from heaven to earth, and to penetrate into the hardest matter and obscurest places, into the future, and into herself, and all this in a point of time, the voyage is not very great, herself being all she seeks. And her wonderful celerity, consisteth not so much in motion, as in copious imagery discreetly ordered, and perfectly registered in the memory; which most men under the name of philosophy have a glimpse of, and is pretended to by many, that grossly mistaking her, embrace contention in her place. But so far forth as the fancy of man has traced the ways of true philosophy, so far it hath produced very marvellous effects to the benefit of mankind. All that is beautiful or defensible in building; or marvellous in engines and instruments of motion; whatsoever commodity men receive from the observations of the heavens, from the description of the earth, from the account of time, from walking on the seas; and whatsoever distinguisheth the civility of Europe, from the barbarity of the American savages; is the workmanship of fancy, but guided by the precepts of true philosophy. But where these precepts fail, as they have hitherto failed in the doctrine of moral virtue, there the architect Fancy must take the philosopher's part upon herself. He, therefore, who undertakes an heroic poem, which is to exhibit a venerable and amiable image of heroic virtue, must not only be the poet, to place and connect, but also the philosopher, to furnish and square his matter; that is, to make both body and soul, colour and shadow of his poem out of his own store; which, how well you have performed I am now considering. . . .

There are some that are not pleased with fiction, unless it be bold; not only to exceed the *work,* but also the *possibility* of nature; they would have impenetrable armours, enchanted castles, invulnerable bodies, iron men, flying horses, and a thousand other such things, which are easily feigned by them that dare. Against such I defend you, without assenting to those that condemn either Homer or Virgil; by dissenting only from those that think the beauty of a poem consisteth in the exorbitancy of the fiction. For as truth is the bound of historical, so the resemblance of truth is the utmost limit of poetical liberty. In old time amongst the heathen, such strange fictions and metamorphoses were not so remote from the articles of their faith, as they are now from ours, and therefore were not so unpleasant. Beyond the actual works of nature a poet may now go; but beyond the conceived possibility of nature, never. I can allow a geographer to make in the sea, a fish or a ship, which by the scale of his map would be two or three hundred miles long, and think it done for ornament, because it is done without the precincts of his undertaking: but when he paints an elephant so, I presently apprehend it as ignorance, and a plain confession of *terra incognita*.

As the description of great men and great actions is the constant design of a poet; so the descriptions of worthy circumstances are necessary accessions to a poem, and being well performed, are the jewels and most precious ornaments of poesy. Such in Virgil are the funeral games of Anchises, the duel of Æneas and Turnus, &c. And such in yours, are *the Hunting, the Battle, the City Mourning, the Funeral, the House of Astragon, the Library and the Temple;* equal to his, or those of Homer whom he imitated.

There remains now no more to be considered but the expression, in which consisteth the countenance and colour of a beautiful Muse; and is given her by the poet out of his own provision, or is borrowed from others. That which he hath of his own, is nothing but experience and knowledge of nature, and specially human nature; and is the true and natural colour. But that which is taken out of books, the ordinary boxes of counterfeit complexion, shows well or ill, as it hath more or less resemblance with the natural; and are not to be used without examination unadvisedly. For in him that professes the imitation of nature, as all poets do, what greater fault can there be, than to betray an ignorance of nature in his poem; especially, having a liberty allowed him, if he meet with any thing he cannot master, to leave it out?

That which giveth a poem the true and natural colour, consisteth in two things; which are, *to know well,* that is, to have images of nature in the memory distinct and clear; and *to know much.* A sign of the first is perspicuity, propriety, and decency; which delight all sorts of men, either by instructing the ignorant, or soothing the learned in their knowledge. A sign of the latter is novelty of expression, and pleaseth by excitation of the mind; for novelty causeth admiration, and admiration curiosity, which is a delightful appetite of knowledge.

There be so many words in use at this day in the English tongue, that, though of magnific sound, yet like the windy blisters of troubled waters, have no sense at all, and so many others that lose their meaning by being ill coupled; that it is a hard matter to avoid them. For having been obtruded upon youth in the schools, by such as make it, I think, their business there, as it is expressed by the best poet

> With terms to charm the weak and pose the wise,
>                          [GONDIBERT, Book ii. Canto 5, verse 44.]

they grow up with them, and gaining reputation with the ignorant, are not easily shaken off.

To this palpable darkness, I may also add the ambitious obscurity of expressing more than is perfectly conceived; or perfect conception in fewer words than it requires. Which expressions, though they have had the honour to be called strong lines, are indeed no better than riddles, and not only to the reader, but also after a little time to the writer himself, dark and troublesome.

To the propriety of expression I refer that clearness of memory, by which a poet when he hath once introduced any person whatsoever, speaking in his poem, maintaineth in him to the end the same character he gave him in the beginning. The variation whereof, is a change of pace, that argues the poet tired.

Of the indecencies of an heroic poem, the most remarkable are those that show disproportion either between the persons and their actions, or between the manners of the poet and the poem. Of the first kind, is the uncomeliness of representing in great persons the inhuman vice of cruelty, or the sordid vices of lust and drunkenness. To such parts, as those the ancient approved poets thought it fit to suborn, not the persons of men, but of monsters and beastly giants, such as Polyphemus, Cacus, and the Centaurs. For it is supposed a Muse, when she is invoked to sing a song of that nature, should maidenly advise the poet to set such persons to sing their own vices upon the stage; for it is not so unseemly in a *tragedy*. Of the same kind it is to represent scurrility, or any action or language that moveth much laughter. The delight of an *epic* poem consisteth not in mirth, but admiration. Mirth and laughter are proper to *comedy* and *satire*. Great persons, that have their minds employed on great designs, have not leisure enough to laugh, and are pleased with the contemplation of their own power and virtues, so as they need not the infirmities and vices of other men to recommend themselves to their own favour by comparison, as all men do when they laugh. Of the second kind, where the disproportion is between the poet and the persons of his poem, one is in the dialect of the inferior sort of people, which is always different from the language of the court. Another is, to derive the illustration of any thing from such metaphors or comparisons as cannot come into men's thoughts, but by mean conversation, and experience of humble or evil arts, which the person of an epic poem cannot be thought acquainted with.

From *knowing much,* proceedeth the admirable variety and novelty of metaphors and similitudes, which are not possible to be lighted on in the compass of a narrow knowledge. And the want whereof compelleth a writer to expressions that are either defaced by time, or sullied with vulgar or long use. For the phrases of poesy, as the airs of music, with often hearing become insipid; the reader having no more sense of their force, than our flesh is sensible of the bones that sustain it. As the sense we have of bodies, consisteth in change of variety of impression, so also does the sense of language in the variety and changeable use of words. I mean not in the affectation of words newly brought home from travel, but in new, and withal significant, translation to our purposes, of those that be already received; and in far-fetched, but withal, apt, instructive, and comely similitudes. . . .

# LEVIATHAN

## THE INTRODUCTION

NATURE, the art whereby God hath made and governs the world, is by the *art* of man, as in many other things, so in this also imitated, that it can make an artificial animal. For seeing life is but a motion of limbs, the beginning whereof is in some principal part within; why may we not say, that all *automata* (engines that move themselves by springs and wheels as doth a watch) have an artificial life? For what is the *heart*, but a *spring;* and the *nerves,* but so many *strings;* and the *joints,* but so many *wheels,* giving motion to the whole body, such as was intended by the artificer? *Art* goes yet further, imitating that rational and most excellent work of nature, *man.* For by art is created that great LEVIATHAN called a COMMONWEALTH, or STATE, in Latin CIVITAS, which is but an artificial man; though of greater stature and strength than the natural, for whose protection and defence it was intended; and in which the *sovereignty* is an artificial *soul,* as giving life and motion to the whole body; the *magistrates,* and other *officers* of judicature and execution, artificial *joints; reward* and *punishment,* by which fastened to the seat of the sovereignty every joint and member is moved to perform his duty, are the *nerves,* that do the same in the body natural; the *wealth* and *riches* of all the particular members, are the *strength; salus populi,* the *people's safety,* its *business; counsellors,* by whom all things needful for it to know are suggested unto it, are the *memory; equity,* and *laws,* an artificial *reason* and *will; concord, health; sedition, sickness;* and *civil war, death.* Lastly, the *pacts* and *covenants,* by which the parts of this body politic were at first made, set together, and united, resemble that *fiat,* or the *let us make man,* pronounced by God in the creation.

To describe the nature of this artificial man, I will consider

First, the *matter* thereof, and the *artificer;* both which is *man.*

Secondly, *how,* and by what *covenants* it is made; what are the *rights* and just *power* or *authority* of a *sovereign;* and what it is that *preserveth* and *dissolveth* it.

Thirdly, what is a *Christian commonwealth.*

Lastly, what is the *kingdom of darkness.*

Concerning the first, there is a saying much usurped of late, that *wisdom* is acquired, not by reading of *books,* but of *men.* Consequently whereunto, those persons, that for the most part can give no other proof of being wise, take great delight to show what they think they have read in men, by uncharitable censures of one another behind their backs. But there is another saying not of late understood, by which they might learn truly to read one another, if they would take the pains; that is, *nosce teipsum, read thyself:* which was not meant, as it is now used, to countenance, either the barbarous state of men in power, towards their inferiors; or to encourage men of low degree, to a saucy behaviour towards their betters; but to teach us, that for the similitude of the thoughts and passions of one man, to the thoughts and passions of another, whosoever looketh into himself, and considereth what he doth, when he does *think, opine, reason, hope, fear,* &c. and upon what grounds; he shall thereby read and know, what are the thoughts and passions of all other men upon the like occasions. I say the similitude of *passions,* which are the same in all men, *desire, fear, hope,* &c.; not the similitude of the *objects* of the passions, which are the things *desired, feared, hoped,* &c.: for these the constitution individual, and particular education, do so vary, and they are so easy to be kept from our knowledge, that the characters of man's heart, blotted and confounded as they are with dissembling, lying, counterfeiting, and erroneous doctrines, are legible only to him that searcheth hearts. And though by men's actions we do discover their design sometimes; yet to do it without comparing them with our own, and distinguishing all circumstances, by which the case may come to be altered, is to decipher without a key, and be for the most part deceived, by too much trust, or by too much diffidence; as he that reads, is himself a good or evil man.

But let one man read another by his actions never so perfectly, it serves him only with his acquaintance, which are but few. He that is to govern a whole nation, must read in himself, not this or that particular man; but mankind: which though it be hard to do, harder than to learn any language or science; yet when I shall have set down my own reading orderly, and perspicuously, the pains left another, will be only to consider, if he also find not the same in himself. For this kind of doctrine admitteth no other demonstration.

# THE FIRST PART: OF MAN

## *Chapter II, of Imagination*

. . . When a body is once in motion, it moveth, unless something else hinder it, eternally; and whatsoever hindreth it, cannot in an instant, but in time, and by degrees, quite extinguish it; and as we see in the water, though the wind cease, the waves give not over rolling for a long time after: so also it happeneth in that motion, which is made in the internal parts of a man, then, when he sees, dreams, &c. For after the object is removed, or the eye shut, we still retain an image of the thing seen, though more obscure than when we see it. And this is it, the Latins call *imagination,* from the image made in seeing; and apply the same, though improperly, to all the other senses. But the Greeks call it *fancy;* which signifies *appearance,* and is as proper to one sense, as to another. IMAGINATION therefore is nothing but *decaying sense;* and is found in men, and many other living creatures, as well sleeping, as waking.

The decay of sense in men waking, is not the decay of the motion made in sense; but an obscuring of it, in such manner as the light of the sun obscureth the light of the stars; which stars do no less exercise their virtue, by which they are visible, in the day than in the night. But because amongst many strokes, which our eyes, ears, and other organs receive from external bodies, the predominant only is sensible; therefore, the light of the sun being predominant, we are not affected with the action of the stars. And any object being removed from our eyes, though the impression it made in us remain, yet other objects more present succeeding, and working on us, the imagination of the past is obscured, and made weak, as the voice of a man is in the noise of the day. From whence it followeth, that the longer the time is, after the sight or sense of any object, the weaker is the imagination. For the continual change of man's body destroys in time the parts which in sense were moved: so that distance of time, and of place, hath one and the same effect in us. For as at a great distance of place, that which we look at appears dim, and without distinction of the smaller parts; and as voices grow weak, and inarticulate; so also, after great distance of time, our imagination of the past is weak; and we lose, for example, of cities we have seen, many particular streets, and of actions, many particular circumstances. This *decaying sense,* when we would express the thing itself, I mean *fancy* itself, we call *imagination,* as I said before: but when we would express the decay, and signify that the sense is fading, old, and past, it is called *memory.* So that imagination and memory are but one thing, which for divers considerations hath divers names.

MEMORY. Much memory, or memory of many things, is called *experience.* Again, imagination being only of those things which have been formerly perceived by sense, either all at once, or by parts at several times; the former, which is the imagining the whole object as it was presented to the sense, is *simple* imagination, as when one imagineth a man, or horse, which he hath seen before. The other is *compounded;* as when, from the sight of a man at one time, and of a horse at another, we conceive in our mind a Centaur. So when a man compoundeth the image of his own person with the image of the actions of another man, as when a man imagines himself a Hercules or an Alexander, which happeneth often to them that are much taken with reading of romances, it is a compound imagination, and properly but a fiction of the mind. There be also other imaginations that rise in men, though waking, from the great impression made in sense: as from gazing upon the sun, the impression leaves an image of the sun before our eyes a long time after; and from being long and vehemently attent upon geometrical figures, a man shall in the dark, though awake, have the images of lines and angles before his eyes; which kind of fancy hath no particular name, as being a thing that doth not commonly fall into men's discourse. . . .

## Chapter VIII, of the Virtues Commonly Called Intellectual; and Their Contrary Defects

INTELLECTUAL VIRTUE DEFINED. VIRTUE generally, in all sorts of subjects, is somewhat that is valued for eminence; and consisteth in comparison. For if all things were equal in all men, nothing would be prized. And by *virtues intellectual,* are always understood such abilities of the mind, as men praise, value, and desire should be in themselves; and go commonly under the name of a *good wit;* though the same word *wit,* be used also, to distinguish one certain ability from the rest.

WIT, NATURAL, OR ACQUIRED.   These *virtues* are of two sorts; *natural,* and *acquired.* By natural, I mean not, that which a man hath from his birth: for that is nothing else but sense; wherein men differ so little one from another, and from brute beasts, as it is not to be reckoned amongst virtues. But I mean, that *wit,* which is gotten by use only, and experience; without method, culture, or instruction. This NATURAL WIT, consisteth principally in two things; *celerity of imagining,* that is, swift succession of one thought to another; and *steady direction* to some approved end. On the contrary a slow imagination, maketh that defect, or fault of the mind, which is commonly called DULLNESS, *stupidity,* and sometimes by other names that signify slowness of motion, or difficulty to be moved.

GOOD WIT, OR FANCY.   And this difference of quickness, is caused by the difference of men's passions; that love and dislike, some one thing, some another: and therefore some men's thoughts run one way, some another; and are held to, and observe differently the things that pass through their imagination. And whereas in this succession of men's thoughts, there is nothing to observe in the things they think on, but either in what they be *like one another,* or in what they be *unlike, or what they serve for,* or *how they serve to such a purpose;* those that observe their similitudes, in case they be such as are but rarely observed by others, are said to have a *good wit;* by which, in this occasion, is meant a *good fancy.*

GOOD JUDGMENT AND DISCRETION.   But they that observe their differences, and dissimilitudes; which is called *distinguishing,* and *discerning,* and *judging* between thing and thing; in case, such discerning be not easy, are said to have a *good judgment:* and particularly in matter of conversation and business; wherein, times, places, and persons are to be discerned, this virtue is called DISCRETION. The former, that is, fancy, without the help of judgment, is not commended as a virtue: but the latter which is judgment, and discretion, is commended for itself, without the help of fancy. Besides the discretion of times, places, and persons, necessary to a good fancy, there is required also an often application of his thoughts to their end; that is to say, to some use to be made of them. This done; he that hath this virtue, will be easily fitted with similitudes, that will please, not only by illustrations of his discourse, and adorning it with new and apt metaphors; but also, by the rarity of their invention. But without steadiness, and direction to some end, a great fancy is one kind of madness; such as they have, that entering into any discourse, are snatched from their purpose, by every thing that comes in their thought, into so many, and so long digressions, and parentheses, that they utterly lose themselves: which kind of folly, I know no particular name for: but the cause of it is, sometimes want of experience; whereby that seemeth to a man new and rare, which doth not so to others: sometimes pusillanimity; by which that seems great to him, which other men think a trifle: and whatsoever is new, or great, and therefore thought fit to be told, withdraws a man by degrees from the intended way of his discourse.

In a good poem, whether it be *epic,* or *dramatic;* as also in *sonnets, epigrams,* and other pieces, both judgment and fancy are required: but the fancy must be more eminent; because they please for the extravagancy; but ought not to displease by indiscretion.

In a good history, the judgment must be eminent; because the goodness consisteth, in the method, in the truth, and in the choice of the actions that are most profitable to be known. Fancy has no place, but only in adorning the style.

In orations of praise, and in invectives, the fancy is predominant; because the design is not truth, but to honour or dishonour; which is done by noble, or by vile comparisons. The judgment does but suggest what circumstances make an action laudable, or culpable.

In hortatives, and pleadings, as truth, or disguise serveth best to the design in hand; so is the judgment, or the fancy most required.

In demonstration, in counsel, and all rigorous search of truth, judgment does all, except sometimes the understanding have need to be opened by some apt similitude; and then there is so much use of fancy. But for metaphors, they are in this case utterly excluded. For seeing they openly profess deceit; to admit them into counsel, or reasoning, were manifest folly.

And in any discourse whatsoever, if the defect of discretion be apparent, how extravagant soever the fancy be, the whole discourse will be taken for a sign of want of wit; and so will it never when the discretion is manifest, though the fancy be never so ordinary.

The secret thoughts of a man run over all things, holy, profane, clean, obscene, grave, and light, without shame, or blame; which verbal discourse cannot do, farther than the judgment shall approve of the time, place, and persons. An anatomist, or a physician may speak, or write his judgment of unclean things; because it is not to please, but profit: but for another man to write his extravagant, and pleasant fancies of the same, is as if a man, from being tumbled into the dirt, should come and present himself before good company. And it is the want of discretion that makes the difference. Again, in professed remissness of mind, and familiar company, a man may play with the sounds and equivocal significations of words; and that many times with encounters of extraordinary fancy: but in a sermon, or in public, or before persons unknown, or whom we ought to reverence; there is no jingling of words that will not be accounted folly: and the difference is only in the want of discretion. So that where wit is wanting, it is not fancy that is wanting, but discretion. Judgment therefore without fancy is wit, but fancy without judgment, not. . . .

## Chapter XII, of Religion

RELIGION IN MAN ONLY. SEEING there are no signs, nor fruit of *religion,* but in man only; there is no cause to doubt, but that the seed of *religion,* is also only in man; and consisteth in some peculiar quality, or at least in some eminent degree thereof, not to be found in any other living creatures.

FIRST, FROM HIS DESIRE OF KNOWING CAUSES. And first, it is peculiar to the nature of man, to be inquisitive into the causes of the events they see, some more, some less; but all men so much, as to be curious in the search of the causes of their own good and evil fortune.

FROM THE CONSIDERATION OF THE BEGINNING OF THINGS. Secondly, upon the sight of any thing that hath a beginning, to think also it had a cause, which determined the same to begin, then when it did, rather than sooner or later.

FROM HIS OBSERVATION OF THE SEQUEL OF THINGS. Thirdly, whereas there is no other felicity of beasts, but the enjoying of their quotidian food, ease, and lusts; as having little or no foresight of the time to come, for want of observation, and memory of the order, consequence, and dependence of the things they see; man observeth how one event hath been produced by another; and remembereth in them antecedence and consequence; and when he cannot assure himself of the true causes of things, (for the causes of good and evil fortune for the most part are invisible,) he supposes causes of them, either such as his own fancy suggesteth; or trusteth the authority of other men, such as he thinks to be his friends, and wiser than himself.

THE NATURAL CAUSE OF RELIGION, THE ANXIETY OF THE TIME TO COME. The two first, make anxiety. For being assured that there be causes of all things that have arrived hitherto, or shall arrive hereafter; it is impossible for a man, who continually endeavoureth to secure himself against the evil he fears, and procure the good he desireth, not to be in a perpetual solicitude of the time to come; so that every man, especially those that are over provident, are in a state like to that of Prometheus. For as Prometheus, which interpreted, is, *the prudent man,* was bound to the hill Caucasus, a place of large prospect, where, an eagle feeding on his liver, devoured in the day, as much as was repaired in the night: so that man, which looks too far before him, in the care of future time, hath his heart all the day long, gnawed on by fear of death, poverty, or other calamity; and has no repose, nor pause of his anxiety, but in sleep.

WHICH MAKES THEM FEAR THE POWER OF INVISIBLE THINGS. This perpetual fear, always accompanying mankind in the ignorance of causes, as it were in the dark, must needs have for object something. And therefore when there is nothing to be seen, there is nothing to accuse, either of their good, or evil fortune, but some *power,* or agent *invisible:* in which sense perhaps it was, that some of the old poets said, that the gods were at first created by human fear: which spoken of the gods, that is to say, of the many gods of the Gentiles, is very true. But the acknowledging of one God, eternal, infinite, and omnipotent, may more easily be derived, from the desire men have to know the causes of natural bodies, and their several virtues, and operations; than from the fear of what was to befall them in time to come. For he that from any effect he seeth come to pass, should reason to the next and immediate cause thereof, and from thence to the cause of that cause, and plunge himself profoundly in the pursuit of causes; shall at last come to this, that there must be, as even the heathen philosophers confessed, one first mover; that is, a first, and an eternal cause of all things; which is that which men mean by the name of God: and all this without thought of their fortune; the solicitude whereof, both inclines to fear, and hinders them from the search of the causes of other things; and thereby gives occasion of feigning of as many gods, as there be men that feign them.

AND SUPPOSE THEM INCORPOREAL. And for the matter, or substance of the invisible agents, so fancied; they could not by natural cogitation, fall upon any other conceit, but that it was the same with that of the soul of man; and that the soul of man, was of the same substance, with that which appeareth in a dream, to one that sleepeth; or in a looking-glass, to one that is awake; which, men not knowing that such apparitions are nothing else but creatures of the fancy, think to be real, and external substances; and therefore call them ghosts; as the Latins called them *imagines,* and *umbræ;* and thought them spirits, that is, thin aërial bodies; and those invisible agents, which they feared, to be like them; save that they appear, and vanish when they please. But the opinion that such spirits were incorporeal, or immaterial, could never enter into the mind of any man by nature; because, though men may put together words of contradictory signification, as *spirit,* and *incorporeal;* yet they can never have the imagination of any thing answering to them: and therefore, men that by their own meditation, arrive to the acknowledgment of one infinite, omnipotent, and eternal God, chose rather to confess he is incomprehensible, and above their understanding, than to define his nature by *spirit incorporeal,* and then confess their definition to be unintelligible: or if they give him such a title, it is not *dogmatically,* with intention to make the divine nature understood; but *piously,* to honour him with attributes, of significations, as remote as they can from the grossness of bodies visible.

BUT KNOW NOT THE WAY HOW THEY EFFECT ANY THING. Then, for the way by which they think these invisible agents wrought their effects; that is to say, what immediate causes they used, in bringing things to pass, men that know not what it is that we call *causing,* that is, almost all men, have no other rule to guess by, but by observing, and remembering what they have seen to precede the like effect at some other time, or times before, without seeing between the antecedent and subsequent event, any dependence or connexion at all: and therefore from the like things past, they expect the like things to come; and hope for good or evil luck, superstitiously, from things that have no part at all in the causing of it: as the Athenians did for their war at Lepanto, demand another Phormio; the Pompeian faction for their war in Africa, another Scipio; and others have done in divers other occasions since. In like manner they attribute their fortune to a stander by, to a lucky or unlucky place, to words spoken, especially if the name of God be amongst them; as charming and conjuring, the liturgy of witches; insomuch as to believe, they have power to turn a stone into bread, bread into a man, or any thing into any thing.

BUT HONOUR THEM AS THEY HONOUR MEN. Thirdly, for the worship which naturally men exhibit to powers invisible, it can be no other, but such expressions of their reverence, as they would use towards men; gifts, petitions, thanks, submission of body, considerate addresses, sober behaviour, premeditated words, swearing, that is, assuring one another of their promises, by invoking them. Beyond that reason suggesteth nothing; but leaves them either to rest there; or for further ceremonies, to rely on those they believe to be wiser than themselves.

AND ATTRIBUTE TO THEM ALL EXTRAORDINARY EVENTS. Lastly, concerning how these invisible powers declare to men the things which shall hereafter come to pass, especially concerning their good or evil fortune in general, or good or ill success in any particular undertaking, men are naturally at a stand; save that using to conjecture of the time to come, by the time past, they are very apt, not only to take casual things, after one or two encounters, for prognostics of the like encounter ever after, but also to believe the like prognostics from other men, of whom they have once conceived a good opinion.

FOUR THINGS, NATURAL SEEDS OF RELIGION. And in these four things, opinion of ghosts, ignorance of second causes, devotion towards what men fear, and taking of things casual for prognostics, consisteth the natural seed of *religion;* which by reason of the different fancies, judgments, and passions of several men, hath grown up into ceremonies so different, that those which are used by one man, are for the most part ridiculous to another. . . .

## Chapter XIII, of the Natural Condition of Mankind as Concerning Their Felicity, and Misery

MEN BY NATURE EQUAL. NATURE hath made men so equal, in the faculties of the body, and mind; as that though there be found one man sometimes manifestly stronger in body, or of quicker mind than another; yet when all is reckoned together, the difference between man, and man, is not so considerable, as that one man can thereupon claim to himself any benefit, to which another may not pretend, as well as he. For as to the strength of body, the weakest has strength enough to kill the strongest, either by secret machination, or by confederacy with others, that are in the same danger with himself.

And as to the faculties of the mind, setting aside the arts grounded upon words, and especially that skill of proceeding upon general, and infallible rules, called science; which very few have, and but in few things; as being not a native faculty, born with us; nor attained, as prudence, while we look after somewhat else, I find yet a greater equality amongst men, than that of strength. For prudence, is but experience; which equal time, equally bestows on all men, in those things they equally apply themselves unto. That which may perhaps make such equality incredible, is but a vain conceit of one's own wisdom, which almost all men think they have in a greater degree, than the vulgar; that is, than all men but themselves, and a few others, whom by fame, or for concurring with themselves, they approve. For such is the nature of men, that howsoever they may acknowledge many others to be more witty, or more eloquent, or more learned; yet they will hardly believe there be many so wise as themselves; for they see their own wit at hand, and other men's at a distance. But this proveth rather that men are in that point equal, than unequal. For there is not ordinarily a greater sign of the equal distribution of any thing, than that every man is contented with his share.

FROM EQUALITY PROCEEDS DIFFIDENCE. From this equality of ability, ariseth equality of hope in the attaining of our ends. And therefore if any two men desire the same thing, which nevertheless they cannot both enjoy, they become enemies; and in the way to their end, which is principally their own conservation, and sometimes their delectation only, endeavour to destroy, or subdue one another. And from hence it comes to pass, that where an invader hath no more to fear, than another man's single power; if one plant, sow, build, or possess a convenient seat, others may probably be expected to come prepared with forces united, to dispossess, and deprive him, not only of the fruit of his labour, but also of his life, or liberty. And the invader again is in the like danger of another.

FROM DIFFIDENCE WAR.   And from this diffidence of one another, there is no way for any man to secure himself, so reasonable, as anticipation; that is, by force, or wiles, to master the persons of all men he can, so long, till he see no other power great enough to endanger him: and this is no more than his own conservation requireth, and is generally allowed. Also because there be some, that taking pleasure in contemplating their own power in the acts of conquest, which they pursue farther than their security requires; if others, that otherwise would be glad to be at ease within modest bounds, should not by invasion increase their power, they would not be able, long time, by standing only on their defence, to subsist. And by consequence, such augmentation of dominion over men being necessary to a man's conservation, it ought to be allowed him.

Again, men have no pleasure, but on the contrary a great deal of grief, in keeping company, where there is no power able to over-awe them all. For every man looketh that his companion should value him, at the same rate he sets upon himself: and upon all signs of contempt, or undervaluing, naturally endeavours, as far as he dares, (which amongst them that have no common power to keep them in quiet, is far enough to make them destroy each other), to extort a greater value from his contemners, by damage; and from others, by the example.

So that in the nature of man, we find three principal causes of quarrel. First, competition; secondly, diffidence; thirdly, glory.

The first, maketh men invade for gain; the second, for safety; and the third, for reputation. The first use violence, to make themselves masters of other men's persons, wives, children, and cattle; the second, to defend them; the third, for trifles, as a word, a smile, a different opinion, and any other sign of undervalue, either direct in their persons, or by reflection in their kindred, their friends, their nation, their profession, or their name.

OUT OF CIVIL STATES, THERE IS ALWAYS WAR OF EVERY ONE AGAINST EVERY ONE.   Hereby it is manifest, that during the time men live without a common power to keep them all in awe, they are in that condition which is called war; and such a war, as is of every man, against every man. For WAR, consisteth not in battle only, or the act of fighting; but in a tract of time, wherein the will to contend by battle is sufficiently known: and therefore the notion of *time,* is to be considered in the nature of war; as it is in the nature of weather. For as the nature of foul weather, lieth not in a shower or two of rain; but in an inclination thereto of many days together: so the nature of war, consisteth not in actual fighting; but in the known disposition thereto, during all the time there is no assurance to the contrary. All other time is PEACE.

THE INCOMMODITIES OF SUCH A WAR. Whatsoever therefore is consequent to a time of war, where every man is enemy to every man; the same is consequent to the time, wherein men live without other security, than what their own strength, and their own invention shall furnish them withal. In such condition, there is no place for industry; because the fruit thereof is uncertain: and consequently no culture of the earth; no navigation, nor use of the commodities that may be imported by sea; no commodious building; no instruments of moving, and removing, such things as require much force; no knowledge of the face of the earth; no account of time; no arts; no letters; no society; and which is worst of all, continual fear, and danger of violent death; and the life of man, solitary, poor, nasty, brutish, and short.

It may seem strange to some man, that has not well weighed these things; that nature should thus dissociate, and render men apt to invade, and destroy one another: and he may therefore, not trusting to this inference, made from the passions, desire perhaps to have the same confirmed by experience. Let him therefore consider with himself, when taking a journey, he arms himself, and seeks to go well accompanied; when going to sleep, he locks his doors; when even in his house he locks his chests; and this when he knows there be laws, and public officers, armed, to revenge all injuries shall be done him; what opinion he has of his fellow-subjects, when he rides armed; of his fellow citizens, when he locks his doors; and of his children, and servants, when he locks his chests. Does he not there as much accuse mankind by his actions, as I do by my words? But neither of us accuse man's nature in it. The desires, and other passions of man, are in themselves no sin. No more are the actions, that proceed from those passions, till they know a law that forbids them: which till laws be made they cannot know: nor can any law be made, till they have agreed upon the person that shall make it.

It may peradventure be thought, there was never such a time, nor condition of war as this; and I believe it was never generally so, over all the world: but there are many places, where they live so now. For the savage people in many places of America, except the government of small families, the concord whereof dependeth on natural lust, have no government at all; and live at this day in that brutish manner, as I said before. Howsoever, it may be perceived what manner of life there would be, where there were no common power to fear, by the manner of life, which men that have formerly lived under a peaceful government, use to degenerate into, in a civil war.

But though there had never been any time, wherein particular men were in a condition of war one against another; yet in all times, kings, and persons of sovereign authority, because of their independency, are in continual jealousies, and in the state and posture of gladiators; having their weapons pointing, and their eyes fixed on one another; that is, their forts, garrisons, and guns upon the frontiers of their kingdoms; and continual spies upon their neighbours; which is a posture of war. But because they uphold thereby, the industry of their subjects; there does not follow from it, that misery, which accompanies the liberty of particular men.

IN SUCH A WAR NOTHING IS UNJUST. To this war of every man, against every man, this also is consequent; that nothing can be unjust. The notions of right and wrong, justice and injustice have there no place. Where there is no common power, there is no law: where no law, no injustice. Force, and fraud, are in war the two cardinal virtues. Justice, and injustice are none of the faculties neither of the body, nor mind. If they were, they might be in a man that were alone in the world, as well as his senses, and passions. They are qualities, that relate to men in society, not in solitude. It is consequent also to the same condition, that there be no propriety, no dominion, no *mine* and *thine* distinct; but only that to be every man's, that he can get: and for so long, as he can keep it. And thus much for the ill condition, which man by mere nature is actually placed in; though with a possibility to come out of it, consisting partly in the passions, partly in his reason.

THE PASSIONS THAT INCLINE MEN TO PEACE. The passions that incline men to peace, are fear of death; desire of such things as are necessary to commodious living; and a hope by their industry to obtain them. And reason suggesteth convenient articles of peace, upon which men may be drawn to agreement. These articles, are they, which otherwise are called the Laws of Nature: whereof I shall speak more particularly, in the two following chapters.

## Chapter XIV, of the First and Second Natural Laws, and of Contracts

RIGHT OF NATURE WHAT. THE RIGHT OF NATURE, which writers commonly call *jus naturale,* is the liberty each man hath, to use his own power, as he will himself, for the preservation of his own nature; that is to say, of his own life; and consequently, of doing any thing, which in his own judgment, and reason, he shall conceive to be the aptest means thereunto.

LIBERTY WHAT. By LIBERTY, is understood, according to the proper signification of the word, the absence of external impediments: which impediments, may oft take away part of a man's power to do what he would; but cannot hinder him from using the power left him, according as his judgment, and reason shall dictate to him.

A LAW OF NATURE WHAT. A LAW OF NATURE, *lex naturalis,* is a precept or general rule, found out by reason, by which a man is forbidden to do that, which is destructive of his life, or taketh away the means of preserving the same; and to omit that, by which he thinketh it may be best preserved. For though they that speak of this subject, use to confound *jus,* and *lex, right* and *law:* yet they ought to be distinguished; because RIGHT, consisteth in liberty to do, or to forbear: whereas LAW, determineth, and bindeth to one of them: so that law, and right, differ as much, as obligation, and liberty; which in one and the same matter are inconsistent.

THE FUNDAMENTAL LAW OF NATURE. And because the condition of man, as hath been declared in the precedent chapter, is a condition of war of every one against every one; in which case every one is governed by his own reason; and there is nothing he can make use of, that may not be a help unto him, in preserving his life against his enemies; it followeth, that in such a condition, every man has a right to every thing; even to one another's body. And therefore, as long as this natural right of every man to every thing endureth, there can be no security to any man, how strong or wise soever he be, of living out the time, which nature ordinarily alloweth men to live. And consequently it is a precept, or general rule of reason, *that every man, ought to endeavour peace, as far as he has hope of obtaining it; and when he cannot obtain it, that he may seek, and use, all helps, and advantages of war.* The first branch of which rule, containeth the first, and fundamental law of nature; which is, *to seek peace, and follow it.* The second, the sum of the right of nature; which is, *by all means we can, to defend ourselves.*

THE SECOND LAW OF NATURE.    From this fundamental law of nature, by which men are commanded to endeavour peace, is derived this second law; *that a man be willing, when others are so too, as far-forth, as for peace, and defence of himself he shall think it necessary, to lay down this right to all things; and be contented with so much liberty against other men, as he would allow other men against himself.* For as long as every man holdeth this right, of doing any thing he liketh; so long are all men in the condition of war. But if other men will not lay down their right, as well as he; then there is no reason for any one, to divest himself of his: for that were to expose himself to prey, which no man is bound to, rather than to dispose himself to peace. This is that law of the Gospel; *whatsoever you require that others should do to you, that do ye to them.* And that law of all men, *quod tibi fieri non vis, alteri ne feceris.*

WHAT IT IS TO LAY DOWN A RIGHT.    To *lay down* a man's *right* to any thing, is to *divest* himself of the *liberty,* of hindering another of the benefit of his own right to the same. For he that renounceth, or passeth away his right, giveth not to any other man a right which he had not before; because there is nothing to which every man had not right by nature: but only standeth out of his way, that he may enjoy his own original right, without hindrance from him; not without hindrance from another. So that the effect which redoundeth to one man, by another man's defect of right, is but so much diminution of impediments to the use of his own right original.

RENOUNCING A RIGHT, WHAT IT IS. Right is laid aside, either by simply renouncing it; or by transferring it to another. By *simply* RENOUNCING; when he cares not to whom the benefit thereof redoundeth.

TRANSFERRING RIGHT WHAT. OBLIGATION. DUTY. INJUSTICE. By TRANS-FERRING; when he intendeth the benefit thereof to some certain person, or persons. And when a man hath in either manner abandoned, or granted away his right; then he is said to be OBLIGED, or BOUND, not to hinder those, to whom such right is granted, or abandoned, from the benefit of it: and that he *ought,* and it is his DUTY, not to make void that voluntary act of his own: and that such hindrance is INJUSTICE, and INJURY, as being *sine jure;* the right being before renounced, or transferred. So that *injury,* or *injustice,* in the controversies of the world, is somewhat like to that, which in the disputations of scholars is called *absurdity.* For as it is there called an absurdity, to contradict what one maintained in the beginning: so in the world, it is called injustice, and injury, voluntarily to undo that, which from the beginning he had voluntarily done. The way by which a man either simply renounceth, or transferreth his right, is a declaration, or signification, by some voluntary and sufficient sign, or signs, that he doth so renounce, or transfer; or hath so renounced, or transferred the same, to him that accepteth it. And these signs are either words only, or actions only; or, as it happeneth most often, both words, and actions. And the same are the BONDS, by which men are bound, and obliged: bonds, that have their strength, not from their own nature, for nothing is more easily broken than a man's word, but from fear of some evil consequence upon the rupture.

NOT ALL RIGHTS ARE ALIENABLE. Whensoever a man transferreth his right, or renounceth it; it is either in consideration of some right recip-rocally transferred to himself; or for some other good he hopeth for thereby. For it is a voluntary act: and of the voluntary acts of every man, the object is some *good to himself.* And therefore there be some rights, which no man can be understood by any words, or other signs, to have abandoned, or transferred. As first a man cannot lay down the right of resisting them, that assault him by force, to take away his life; because he cannot be understood to aim thereby, at any good to himself. The same may be said of wounds, and chains, and imprison-ment; both because there is no benefit consequent to such patience;

as there is to the patience of suffering another to be wounded, or imprisoned: as also because a man cannot tell, when he seeth men proceed against him by violence, whether they intend his death or not. And lastly the motive, and end for which this renouncing, and transferring of right is introduced, is nothing else but the security of a man's person, in his life, and in the means of so preserving life, as not to be weary of it. And therefore if a man by words, or other signs, seem to despoil himself of the end, for which those signs were intended; he is not to be understood as if he meant it, or that it was his will; but that he was ignorant of how such words and actions were to be interpreted.

CONTRACT WHAT.    The mutual transferring of right, is that which men all call CONTRACT. . . .

# THE SECOND PART: OF COMMONWEALTH

## Chapter XVII, of the Causes, Generation, and Definition of a Commonwealth

THE END OF COMMONWEALTH, PARTICULAR SECURITY.    The final cause, end, or design of men, who naturally love liberty, and dominion over others, in the introduction of that restraint upon themselves, in which we see them live in commonwealths, is the foresight of their own preservation, and of a more contented life thereby; that is to say, of getting themselves out from that miserable condition of war, which is necessarily consequent, as hath been shown (chapter XIII), to the natural passions of men, when there is no visible power to keep them in awe, and tie them by fear of punishment to the performance of their covenants, and observation of those laws of nature set down in the fourteenth and fifteenth chapters.

WHICH IS NOT TO BE HAD FROM THE LAW OF NATURE.    For the laws of nature, as *justice, equity, modesty, mercy,* and, in sum, *doing to others, as we would be done to,* of themselves, without the terror of some power, to cause them to be observed, are contrary to our natural passions, that carry us to partiality, pride, revenge, and the like. And covenants, without the sword, are but words, and of no strength to secure a man at all. Therefore notwithstanding the laws of nature (which every one hath then kept, when he has the will to keep them, when he can do it safely) if there be no power erected, or not great enough for our security; every man will, and may lawfully rely on his own strength and art, for caution against all other men. And in all places, where men have lived by small families, to rob and spoil one another, has been a trade, and so far from being reputed against the law of nature, that the greater spoils they gained, the greater was their honour; and men observed no other laws therein, but the laws of honour; that is, to abstain from cruelty, leaving to men their lives, and instruments of husbandry. And as small families did then; so now do cities and kingdoms which are but greater families, for their own security, enlarge their dominions, upon all pretences of danger, and fear of invasion, or assistance that may be given to invaders, and endeavour as much as they can, to subdue, or weaken their neighbours, by open force, and secret arts, for want of other caution, justly; and are remembered for it in after ages with honour.

NOR FROM THE CONJUNCTION OF A FEW MEN OR FAMILIES. Nor is it the joining together of a small number of men, that gives them this security; because in small numbers, small additions on the one side or the other, make the advantage of strength so great, as is sufficient to carry the victory; and therefore gives encouragement to an invasion. The multitude sufficient to confide in for our security, is not determined by any certain number, but by comparison with the enemy we fear; and is then sufficient, when the odds of the enemy is not of so visible and conspicuous moment, to determine the event of war, as to move him to attempt.

NOR FROM A GREAT MULTITUDE, UNLESS DIRECTED BY ONE JUDGMENT. And be there never so great a multitude; yet if their actions be directed according to their particular judgments, and particular appetites, they can expect thereby no defence, nor protection, neither against a common enemy, nor against the injuries of one another. For being distracted in opinions concerning the best use and application of their strength, they do not help but hinder one another; and reduce their strength by mutual opposition to nothing: whereby they are easily, not only subdued by a very few that agree together; but also when there is no common enemy, they make war upon each other, for their particular interests.

For if we could suppose a great multitude of men to consent in the observation of justice, and other laws of nature, without a common power to keep them all in awe; we might as well suppose all mankind to do the same; and then there neither would be, nor need to be any civil government, or commonwealth at all; because there would be peace without subjection.

AND THAT CONTINUALLY. Nor is it enough for the security, which men desire should last all the time of their life, that they be governed, and directed by one judgment, for a limited time; as in one battle, or one war. For though they obtain a victory by their unanimous endeavour against a foreign enemy; yet afterwards, when either they have no common enemy, or he that by one part is held for an enemy, is by another part held for a friend, they must needs by the difference of their interests dissolve, and fall again into a war amongst themselves.

WHY CERTAIN CREATURES WITHOUT REASON, OR SPEECH, DO NEVERTHELESS LIVE IN SOCIETY, WITHOUT ANY COERCIVE POWER. It is true, that certain living creatures, as bees, and ants, live sociably one with another, which are therefore by Aristotle numbered amongst political creatures; and yet have no other direction, than their particular judgments and appetites; nor speech, whereby one of them can signify to another, what he thinks expedient for the common benefit: and therefore some man may perhaps desire to know, why mankind cannot do the same. To which I answer,

First, that men are continually in competition for honour and dignity, which these creatures are not; and consequently amongst men there ariseth on that ground, envy and hatred, and finally war; but amongst these not so.

Secondly, that amongst these creatures, the common good differeth not from the private; and being by nature inclined to their private, they procure thereby the common benefit. But man, whose joy consisteth in comparing himself with other men, can relish nothing but what is eminent.

Thirdly, that these creatures, having not, as man, the use of reason, do not see, nor think they see any fault, in the administration of their common business; whereas amongst men, there are very many, that think themselves wiser, and abler to govern the public, better than the rest; and these strive to reform and innovate, one this way, another that way; and thereby bring it into distraction and civil war.

Fourthly, that these creatures, though they have some use of voice, in making known to one another their desires, and other affections; yet they want that art of words, by which some men can represent to others, that which is good, in the likeness of evil; and evil, in the likeness of good; and augment, or diminish the apparent greatness of good and evil; discontenting men, and troubling their peace at their pleasure.

Fifthly, irrational creatures cannot distinguish between *injury,* and *damage;* and therefore as long as they be at ease, they are not offended with their fellows: whereas man is then most troublesome, when he is most at ease: for then it is that he loves to shew his wisdom, and control the actions of them that govern the commonwealth.

Lastly, the agreement of these creatures is natural; that of men, is by covenant only, which is artificial: and therefore it is no wonder if there be somewhat else required, besides covenant, to make their agreement constant and lasting; which is a common power, to keep them in awe, and to direct their actions to the common benefit.

THE GENERATION OF A COMMONWEALTH. The only way to erect such a common power, as may be able to defend them from the invasion of foreigners, and the injuries of one another, and thereby to secure them in such sort, as that by their own industry, and by the fruits of the earth, they may nourish themselves and live contentedly, is, to confer all their power and strength upon one man, or upon one assembly of men, that may reduce all their wills, by plurality of voices, unto one will: which is as much as to say, to appoint one man, or assembly of men, to bear their person; and every one to own, and acknowledge himself to be author of whatsoever he that so beareth their person, shall act, or cause to be acted, in those things which concern the common peace and safety; and therein to submit their wills, every one to his will, and their judgments, to his judgment. This is more than consent, or concord; it is a real unity of them all, in one and the same person, made by covenant of every man with every man, in such manner, as if every man should say to every man, *I authorize and give up my right of governing myself, to this man, or to this assembly of men, on this condition, that thou give up thy right to him, and authorize all his actions in like manner.* This done, the multitude so united in one person, is called a COMMONWEALTH, in Latin CIVITAS. This is the generation of that great LEVIATHAN, or rather, to speak more reverently, of that *mortal god,* to which we owe under the *immortal God,* our peace and defence. For by this authority, given him by every particular man in the commonwealth, he hath the use of so much power and strength conferred on him, that by terror thereof, he is enabled to form the wills of them all, to peace at home, and mutual aid against their enemies abroad. And in him consisteth the essence of the commonwealth; which, to define it, is *one person, of whose acts a great multitude, by mutual covenants one with another, have made themselves every one the author, to the end he may use the strength and means of them all, as he shall think expedient, for their peace and common defence.*

SOVEREIGN, AND SUBJECT, WHAT. And he that carrieth this person, is called SOVEREIGN, and said to have *sovereign power;* and every one besides, his SUBJECT.

The attaining to this sovereign power, is by two ways. One, by natural force; as when a man maketh his children, to submit themselves, and their children to his government, as being able to destroy them if they refuse; or by war subdueth his enemies to his will, giving them their lives on that condition. The other, is when men agree amongst themselves, to submit to some man, or assembly of men, voluntarily, on confidence to be protected by him against all others. This latter, may be called a political commonwealth, or commonwealth by *institution;* and the former, a commonwealth by *acquisition.* And first, I shall speak of a commonwealth by institution.

# THE FOURTH PART: OF THE KINGDOM OF DARKNESS

## Chapter XLVI, of Darkness from Vain Philosophy, and Fabulous Traditions

WHAT PHILOSOPHY IS. By PHILOSOPHY is understood *the knowledge acquired by reasoning, from the manner of the generation of any thing, to the properties: or from the properties, to some possible way of generation of the same; to the end to be able to produce, as far as matter, and human force permit, such effects, as human life requireth.* So the geometrician, from the construction of figures, findeth out many properties thereof; and from the properties, new ways of their construction, by reasoning; to the end to be able to measure land, and water; and for infinite other uses. So the astronomer, from the rising, setting, and moving of the sun, and stars, in divers parts of the heavens, findeth out the causes of day, and night, and of the different seasons of the year; whereby he keepeth an account of time; and the like of other sciences.

PRUDENCE NO PART OF PHILOSOPHY. By which definition it is evident, that we are not to account as any part thereof, that original knowledge called experience, in which consisteth prudence: because it is not attained by reasoning, but found as well in brute beasts, as in man; and is but a memory of successions of events in times past, wherein the omission of every little circumstance altering the effect, frustrateth the expectation of the most prudent: whereas nothing is produced by reasoning aright, but general, eternal, and immutable truth.

NO FALSE DOCTRINE IS PART OF PHILOSOPHY. Nor are we therefore to give that name to any false conclusions: for he that reasoneth aright in words he understandeth, can never conclude an error:

NO MORE IS REVELATION SUPERNATURAL. Nor to that which any man knows by supernatural revelation; because it is not acquired by reasoning:

NOR LEARNING TAKEN UPON CREDIT OF AUTHORS. Nor that which is gotten by reasoning from the authority of books; because it is not by reasoning from the cause to the effect, nor from the effect to the cause; and is not knowledge but faith.

OF THE BEGINNINGS AND PROGRESS OF PHILOSOPHY. The faculty of reasoning being consequent to the use of speech, it was not possible, but that there should have been some general truths found out by reasoning, as ancient almost as language itself. The savages of America, are not without some good moral sentences; also they have a little arithmetic, to add, and divide in numbers not too great: but they are not, therefore, philosophers. For as there were plants of corn and wine in small quantity dispersed in the fields and woods, before men knew their virtue, or made use of them for their nourishment, or planted them apart in fields and vineyards; in which time they fed on acorns, and drank water: so also there have been divers true, general, and profitable speculations from the beginning; as being the natural plants of human reason. But they were at first but few in number; men lived upon gross experience; there was no method; that is to say, no sowing, nor planting of knowledge by itself, apart from the weeds, and common plants of error and conjecture. And the cause of it being the want of leisure from procuring the necessities of life, and defending themselves against their neighbours, it was impossible, till the erecting of great commonwealths, it should be otherwise. *Leisure* is the mother of *philosophy;* and *Commonwealth,* the mother of *peace* and *leisure.* Where first were great and flourishing *cities,* there was first the study of *philosophy.* The *Gymnosophists* of India, the *Magi* of Persia, and the *Priests* of Chaldea and Egypt, are counted the most ancient philosophers; and those countries were the most ancient of kingdoms. *Philosophy* was not risen to the Grecians, and other people of the west, whose *commonwealths,* no greater perhaps than Lucca or Geneva, had never *peace,* but when their fears of one another were equal; nor the *leisure* to observe anything but one another. At length, when war had united many of these Grecian lesser cities, into fewer, and greater; then began *seven men,* of several parts of Greece, to get the reputation of being *wise;* some of them for *moral* and *politic* sentences; and others for the learning of the Chaldeans and Egyptians, which was *astronomy,* and *geometry.* But we hear not yet of any *schools of philosophy.*

OF THE SCHOOLS OF PHILOSOPHY AMONGST THE ATHENIANS. After the Athenians, by the overthrow of the Persian armies, had gotten the dominion of the sea; and thereby, of all the islands, and maritime cities of the Archipelago, as well of Asia as Europe; and were grown wealthy; they that had no employment, neither at home nor abroad, had little else to employ themselves in, but either (as St. Luke says, *Acts* xvii. 21), *in telling and hearing news,* or in discoursing of *philosophy* publicly to the youth of the city. Every master took some place for that purpose. Plato, in certain public walks called *Academia,* from one *Academus:* Aristotle in the walk of the temple of Pan, called *Lyceum:* others in the *Stoa,* or covered walk, wherein the merchants' goods were brought to land: others in other places; where they spent the time of their leisure, in teaching or in disputing of their opinions: and some in any place, where they could get the youth of the city together to hear them talk. And this was it which Carneades also did at Rome, when he was ambassador: which caused Cato to advise the senate to dispatch him quickly, for fear of corrupting the manners of the young men, that delighted to hear him speak, as they thought, fine things.

From this it was, that the place where any of them taught, and disputed, was called *schola,* which in their tongue signifieth *leisure;* and their disputations, *diatribæ,* that is to say, *passing of the time.* Also the philosophers themselves had the name of their sects, some of them from these their Schools: for they that followed Plato's doctrine, were called *Academics;* the followers of Aristotle *Peripatetics,* from the walk he taught in; and those that Zeno taught *Stoics,* from the *Stoa;* as if we should denominate men from *Moor-fields,* from *Paul's Church,* and from the *Exchange,* because they meet there often, to prate and loiter.

Nevertheless, men were so much taken with this custom, that in time it spread itself over all Europe, and the best part of Africa; so as there were schools publicly erected and maintained, for lectures and disputations, almost in every commonwealth.

OF THE SCHOOLS OF THE JEWS.    There were also schools, anciently, both before and after the time of our Saviour, amongst the Jews; but they were schools of their law. For though they were called *synagogues,* that is to say, congregations of the people; yet, inasmuch as the law was every sabbath-day read, expounded, and disputed in them, they differed not in nature, but in name only, from public schools; and were not only in Jerusalem, but in every city of the Gentiles, where the Jews inhabited. There was such a school at Damascus, whereinto Paul entered, to persecute. There were others at Antioch, Iconium, and Thessalonica, whereinto he entered to dispute: and such was the synagogue of the *Libertines, Cyrenians, Alexandrians, Cilicians,* and those of Asia; that is to say, the school of *Libertines,* and of *Jews* that were strangers in Jerusalem; and of this school they were that disputed (*Acts* vi. 9) with St. Stephen.

THE SCHOOLS OF THE GRECIANS UNPROFITABLE.    But what has been the utility of those schools? What science is there at this day acquired by their readings and disputings? That we have of geometry, which is the mother of all natural science, we are not indebted for it to the schools. Plato, that was the best philosopher of the Greeks, forbade entrance into his school to all that were not already in some measure geometricians. There were many that studied that science to the great advantage of mankind: but there is no mention of their schools; nor was there any sect of geometricians; nor did they then pass under the name of philosophers. The natural philosophy of those schools was rather a dream than science, and set forth in senseless and insignificant language; which cannot be avoided by those that will teach philosophy, without having first attained great knowledge in geometry. For nature worketh by motion; the ways and degrees whereof cannot be known, without the knowledge of the proportions and properties of lines and figures. Their moral philosophy is but a description of their own passions. For the rule of manners, without civil government, is the law of nature; and in it, the law civil, that determineth what is *honest* and *dishonest,* what is *just* and *unjust,* and generally what is *good* and *evil.* Whereas they make the rules of *good* and *bad,* by their own *liking* and *disliking:* by which means, in so great diversity of taste, there is nothing generally agreed on; but every one doth, as far as he dares, whatsoever seemeth good in his own eyes, to the subversion of commonwealth. Their *logic,* which should be the method of reasoning, is nothing else but captions of words, and inventions how to puzzle such as should go about to pose them. To conclude, there is nothing so absurd, that the old philosophers, as Cicero saith, (who was one of them,) have not some of them maintained. And I believe that scarce anything can be more absurdly said in natural philosophy, than that which now is called *Aristotle's Metaphysics;* nor more repugnant to government, than much of that he hath said in his *Politics;* nor more ignorantly, than a great part of his *Ethics.*

THE SCHOOLS OF THE JEWS UNPROFITABLE. The school of the Jews was originally a school of the law of Moses; who commanded (*Deut.* xxxi. 10) that at the end of every seventh year, at the Feast of the Tabernacles, it should be read to all the people, that they might hear and learn it. Therefore the reading of the law, which was in use after the captivity, every Sabbath day, ought to have had no other end, but the acquainting of the people with the Commandments which they were to obey, and to expound unto them the writings of the prophets. But it is manifest, by the many reprehensions of them by our Saviour, that they corrupted the text of the law with their false commentaries, and vain traditions; and so little understood the prophets, that they did neither acknowledge Christ, nor the works he did, of which the prophets prophesied. So that by their lectures and disputations in their synagogues, they turned the doctrine of their law into a fantastical kind of philosophy, concerning the incomprehensible nature of God, and of spirits; which they compounded of the vain philosophy and theology of the Grecians, mingled with their own fancies, drawn from the obscurer places of the Scripture, and which might most easily be wrested to their purpose; and from the fabulous traditions of their ancestors.

UNIVERSITY, WHAT IT IS. That which is now called an *University,* is a joining together, and an incorporation under one government, of many public schools, in one and the same town or city. In which, the principal schools were ordained for the three professions, that is to say, of the Roman religion, of the Roman law, and of the art of medicine. And for the study of philosophy, it hath no otherwise place, than as a handmaid to the Roman religion: and since the authority of Aristotle is only current there, that study is not properly philosophy, (the nature whereof dependeth not on authors,) but *Aristotelity.* And for geometry, till of very late times it had no place at all; as being subservient to nothing but rigid truth. And if any man by the ingenuity of his own nature, had attained to any degree of perfection therein, he was commonly thought a magician, and his art diabolical.

ERRORS BROUGHT INTO RELIGION FROM ARISTOTLE'S METAPHYSICS. Now to descend to the particular tenets of vain philosophy, derived to the Universities, and thence into the Church, partly from Aristotle, partly from blindness of understanding; I shall first consider their principles. There is a certain *philosophia prima,* on which all other philosophy ought to depend; and consisteth principally, in right limiting of the significations of such appellations, or names, as are of all others the most universal; which limitations serve to avoid ambiguity and equivocation in reasoning; and are commonly called definitions: such as are the definitions of body, time, place, matter, form, essence, subject, substance, accident, power, act, finite, infinite, quantity, quality, motion, action, passion, and divers others, necessary to the explaining of a man's conceptions concerning the nature and generation of bodies. The explication, that is, the settling of the meaning, of which, and the like terms, is commonly in the Schools called *metaphysics;* as being a part of the philosophy of Aristotle, which hath that for title. But it is in another sense; for there it signifieth as much as *books written or placed after his natural philosophy:* but the Schools take them for *books of supernatural philosophy:* for the word *metaphysics* will bear both these senses. And indeed that which is there written, is for the most part so far from the possibility of being understood, and so repugnant to natural reason, that whosoever thinketh there is anything to be understood by it, must needs think it supernatural. . . .

AND THAT ALL GOVERNMENT BUT POPULAR IS TYRANNY. From Aristotle's civil philosophy they have learned, to call all manner of commonwealths but the popular, (such as was at that time the state of Athens), *tyranny.* All kings they called tyrants; and the aristocracy of the thirty governors set up there by the Lacedemonians that subdued them, the thirty tyrants. As also to call the condition of the people under the democracy, *liberty. A tyrant* originally signified no more simply, but a *monarch.* But when afterwards in most parts of Greece that kind of government was abolished, the name began to signify, not only the thing it did before, but with it, the hatred which the popular states bare towards it. As also the name of king became odious after the deposing of the kings in Rome, as being a thing natural to all men, to conceive some great fault to be signified in any attribute, that is given in despite, and to a great enemy. And when the same men shall be displeased with those that have the administration of the democracy, or aristocracy, they are not to seek for disgraceful names to express their anger in; but call readily the one *anarchy,* and the other *oligarchy,* or the *tyranny of a few.* And that which offendeth the people, is no other thing, but that they are governed, not as every one of them would himself, but as the public representant, be it one man, or an assembly of men, thinks fit; that is, by an arbitrary government: for which they give evil names to their superiors; never knowing, till perhaps a little after a civil war, that without such arbitrary government, such war must be perpetual; and that it is men, and arms, not words and promises, that make the force and power of the laws.

THAT NOT MEN, BUT LAW GOVERNS. And therefore this is another error of Aristotle's politics, that in a well-ordered commonwealth, not men should govern, but the laws. What man, that has his natural senses, though he can neither write nor read, does not find himself governed by them he fears, and believes can kill or hurt him when he obeyeth not? Or that believes the law can hurt him; that is, words and paper, without the hands and swords of men? And this is of the number of pernicious errors: for they induce men, as oft as they like not their governors, to adhere to those that call them tyrants, and to think it lawful to raise war against them: and yet they are many times cherished from the pulpit, by the clergy.

LAWS OVER THE CONSCIENCE. There is another error in their civil philosophy, which they never learned of Aristotle, nor Cicero, nor any other of the heathen, to extend the power of the law, which is the rule of actions only, to the very thoughts and consciences of men, by examination, and *inquisition* of what they hold, notwithstanding the conformity of their speech and actions. By which, men are either punished for answering the truth of their thoughts, or constrained to answer an untruth for fear of punishment. It is true, that the civil magistrate, intending to employ a minister in the charge of teaching, may enquire of him, if he be content to preach such and such doctrines; and in case of refusal, may deny him the employment. But to force him to accuse himself of opinions, when his actions are not by law forbidden, is against the law of nature; and especially in them, who teach, that a man shall be damned to eternal and extreme torments, if he die in a false opinion concerning an article of the Christian faith. For who is there, that knowing there is so great danger in an error, whom the natural care of himself, compelleth not to hazard his soul upon his own judgment, rather than that of any other man that is unconcerned in his damnation?

PRIVATE INTERPRETATION OF LAW. For a private man, without the authority of the commonwealth, that is to say, without permission from the representant thereof, to interpret the law by his own spirit, is another error in the politics: but not drawn from Aristotle, nor from any other of the heathen philosophers. For none of them deny, but that in the power of making laws, is comprehended also the power of explaining them when there is need. And are not the Scriptures, in all places where they are law, made law by the authority of the commonwealth, and consequently, a part of the civil law?

Of the same kind it is also, when any but the sovereign restraineth in any man that power which the commonwealth hath not restrained; as they do, that impropriate the preaching of the gospel to one certain order of men, where the laws have left it free. If the state give me leave to preach, or teach; that is, if it forbid me not, no man can forbid me. If I find myself amongst the idolaters of America, shall I that am a Christian, though not in orders, think it a sin to preach Jesus Christ, till I have received orders from Rome? Or when I have preached, shall not I answer their doubts, and expound the Scriptures to them; that is, shall I not teach? But for this may some say, as also for administering to them the sacraments, the necessity shall be esteemed for a sufficient mission; which is true: but this is true also, that for whatsoever, a dispensation is due for the necessity, for the same there needs no dispensation, when there is no law that forbids it. Therefore to deny these functions to those, to whom the civil sovereign hath not denied them, is a taking away of a lawful liberty, which is contrary to the doctrine of civil government.

LANGUAGE OF SCHOOL DIVINES. More examples of vain philosophy, brought into religion by the doctors of School divinity, might be produced; but other men may if they please observe them of themselves. I shall only add this, that the writings of School divines, are nothing else for the most part, but insignificant trains of strange and barbarous words, or words otherwise used, than in the common use of the Latin tongue; such as would pose Cicero, and Varro, and all the grammarians of ancient Rome. Which if any man would see proved, let him, as I have said once before, see whether he can translate any School divine into any of the modern tongues, as French, English, or any other copious language: for that which cannot in most of these be made intelligible, is not intelligible in the Latin. Which insignificancy of language, though I cannot note it for false philosophy; yet it hath a quality, not only to hide the truth, but also to make men think they have it, and desist from further search.

ERRORS FROM TRADITION. Lastly, for the errors brought in from false, or uncertain history, what is all the legend of fictitious miracles, in the lives of the saints; and all the histories of apparitions, and ghosts, alleged by the doctors of the Roman Church, to make good their doctrines of hell, and purgatory, the power of exorcism, and other doctrines which have no warrant, neither in reason nor Scripture; as also all those traditions which they call the unwritten word of God: but old wives' fables? Whereof, though they find dispersed somewhat in the writings of the ancient fathers; yet those fathers were men, that might too easily believe false reports; and the producing of their opinions for testimony of the truth of what they believed, hath no other force with them that, according to the counsel of St. John (1 *John* iv. 1), examine spirits, than in all things that concern the power of the Roman Church, (the abuse whereof either they suspected not, or had benefit by it), to discredit their testimony, in respect of too rash belief of reports; which the most sincere men, without great knowledge of natural causes, such as the fathers were, are commonly the most subject to. For naturally, the best men are the least suspicious of fraudulent purposes. Gregory the Pope, and St. Bernard have somewhat of apparitions of ghosts, that said they were in purgatory; and so has our Bede: but nowhere, I believe, but by report from others. But if they, or any other, relate any such stories of their own knowledge, they shall not thereby confirm the more such vain reports; but discover their own infirmity, or fraud.

SUPPRESSION OF REASON. With the introduction of false, we may join also the suppression of true philosophy, by such men, as neither by lawful authority, nor sufficient study, are competent judges of the truth. Our own navigations make manifest, and all men learned in human sciences, now acknowledge there are antipodes: and every day it appeareth more and more, that years and days are determined by motions of the earth. Nevertheless, men that have in their writings but supposed such doctrine, as an occasion to lay open the reasons for, and against it, have been punished for it by authority ecclesiastical. But what reason is there for it? Is it because such opinions are contrary to true religion? That cannot be, if they be true. Let therefore the truth be first examined by competent judges, or confuted by them that pretend to know the contrary. Is it because they be contrary to the religion established? Let them be silenced by the laws of those, to whom the teachers of them are subject; that is, by the laws civil. For disobedience may lawfully be punished in them, that against the laws teach even true philosophy. Is it because they tend to disorder in government, as countenancing rebellion, or sedition? Then let them be silenced, and the teachers punished by virtue of his power to whom the care of the public quiet is committed; which is the authority civil. For whatsoever power ecclesiastics take upon themselves, (in any place where they are subject to the state), in their own right, though they call it God's right, is but usurpation.

# A REVIEW, AND CONCLUSION

. . . And thus I have brought to an end my Discourse of Civil and Ecclesiastical Government, occasioned by the disorders of the present time, without partiality, without application, and without other design than to set before men's eyes the mutual relation between protection and obedience; of which the condition of human nature, and the laws divine, both natural and positive, require an inviolable observation. And though in the revolution of states, there can be no very good constellation for truths of this nature to be born under, (as having an angry aspect from the dissolvers of an old government, and seeing but the backs of them that erect a new), yet I cannot think it will be condemned at this time, either by the public judge of doctrine, or by any that desires the continuance of public peace. And in this hope I return to my interrupted speculation of bodies natural; wherein, if God give me health to finish it, I hope the novelty will as much please, as in the doctrine of this artificial body it useth to offend. For such truth, as opposeth no man's profit, nor pleasure, is to all men welcome.

# Sir Thomas Browne

## 1605-1682

Browne was born in London, received his education at Winchester and at Oxford, and then continued his medical studies at Montpellier, Padua, and Leyden, where he took his medical degree. In 1637 he settled in Norwich, where he was to remain until his death, a busy and prosperous country doctor, something of a character, the town's principal luminary. Anglican and Royalist, he had little to say (at least in print) about the political and ecclesiastical revolutions of his time. Instead he sat out the Civil War, dealing with life and death at first hand in his daily work, and at very long remove in his speculations about the great mutations of the world, about oblivion, and about the foolish dream of diurturnity.

He wrote some of the most eloquent passages in the language on the vanity of human wishes and on the absurdity of clutching at duration. Yet what he wrote had none of Donne's terror, pity, and distaste, none of Burton's more homely intimacy with despair. Browne's detachment was complete, even in the privacy of the *Religio Medici*. That the world is not an inn to live in but a hospital to die in was no cry of anguish but an objective if compassionate observation. Our grip on life is chancy, our grasping at it absurd (six of Browne's children died young). In Browne's foreshortened view, only a small particle of futurity remains for any man, or for the world itself. It is the long habit of living that indisposes us for dying. We may be ashamed of the way we die, but hardly afraid of death unless Hell and damnation await us. And Browne leaves us with a hope, even a reassurance, that this too is absurd.

His theology was conventional, if urbane and tolerant. He believed in spirits, including witches, else there would be a gap in the scale of creatures. He opposed religious persecution, was permissive toward others' creeds and modes of worship, and suggested that even the heathen if virtuous might have a chance at salvation. He took pleasure in the rituals and traditional forms of the church, in the civilities of knee, hat, and hand. Respectful to the claims of reason, he was himself most at home among the irrationalities and impossibilities of faith, and loved to lose himself in a mystery. Where Scriptures were silent, the church was his text; where neither spoke, he was willing to turn to reason. Whatever his subject, he always came around to exploring the inner life (primarily his own, of course) and man's unstable mixture of body and spirit.

Though it is better to inquire into first causes than into second causes, he said, the world was nevertheless made to be studied by men: God's wisdom receives small honor from those vulgar heads that rudely stare about, and with a gross rusticity admire His works. He endorsed Bacon's inductive method and borrowed from his analysis of idols or errors, and he saw himself as a worker in Bacon's vineyard. He praised the discoveries of Gilbert and Harvey, and expressed a skeptical interest in Copernicus and Galileo. In *Urn Burial,* before moving to his peroration on the pathos and irony of our attempts to outwit mortality, he offered a factual discourse on burial customs, noting with equal detachment that Christians preferred depositure to absumption, and that Romans declined the visible degeneration into worms. In *Pseudodoxia Epidemica* he explored in "the America and untravelled parts of truth," sifting out fact from folklore, correcting where he could our vulgar errors in natural philosophy. In *Christian Morals* he praised his century for prevailing "against the tenacity of Prejudice and Prescription." It was in his attitude toward new learning, and not in any addition to scientific knowledge, that Browne (like Bacon) spoke in the modern idiom:

> The mortallest enemy unto knowledge, and that which hath done the greatest execution upon truth, hath been a peremptory adhesion unto Authority, and more especially the establishing of our beliefe upon the dictates of Antiquities.

In the end it is clear that Browne lived in what were for him two compatible worlds. Though these worlds, of spirit and body, must remain divided and distinguished, man the microcosm was "that middle form that links those two together." For Browne the figures that symbolized this unity in division have their grounding (as all true symbols must) in literal truth. Man as microcosm is no mere pleasant trope of rhetoric, he insisted; man, "that amphibious piece between a corporal and spiritual Essence," carries within him the wonders he seeks outside, and moves literally through all the levels of existence—matter, plant, animal, man, and spirit. The circle which relates us to the whole universe is also the physical circle of the womb and the circles of celestial forms and motions, as well as the circle of God's enveloping providence. Music of the spheres is no fanciful metaphor, for music is "an hieroglyphical and shadowed lesson of the whole world . . . a sensible fit of that harmony which intellectually sounds in the ears of God."

Browne's accommodation to his divided worlds shows up in other features of his style also. He is, indeed, something of a virtuoso at ringing out the great harmonies while also pointing up with crisp wit and epigram the ironies, gaps, and contradictions of our existence. In the former vein his affinities lie with the old-fashioned Ciceronians—voluminous, formal, eloquent—though his prose is more intricately cadenced and more deliberately poetic:

> What Song the *Syrens* sang, or what name *Achilles* assumed when he hid himself among women, though puzling Questions, are not beyond all conjecture. What time the persons of these Ossuaries entred the famous Nations of the dead, and slept with Princes and Counsellours, might admit a wide solution. But who were the proprietaries of these bones, or what bodies these ashes made up, were a question above Antiquarism.

Or:

> Since our longest sunne sets at right descensions, and makes but winter arches, and therefore it cannot be long before we lie down in darknesse, and have our light in ashes. Since the brother of death daily haunts us with dying *memento's,* and time that grows old in it self, bids us hope no long duration: Diuturnity is a dream and folly of expectation.

But Browne's sentences are not oratorical. They are not heavily loaded with subordinate elements. With all their elegance they have also a direct and colloquial immediacy, a dry, restrained clarity closer to Seneca or Ovid than to Cicero, and frequently a terse turn of wit:

> Time hath spared the epitaph of Adrian's horse, confounded that of himself.

That she [Eve] was edified out of the Rib of Adam I believe, yet raise no question who shall arise with that Rib at the Resurrection.

[We are cannibals and self-devourers], for all this mass of flesh which we behold, came in at our mouths; this frame we look upon, hath been upon our trenchers.

The way to be immortal is to dye daily.

Some bones make best Skeletons, some bodies quick and speediest ashes. Who would expect a quick flame from Hydropticall *Heraclitus?*

## EDITIONS

*Religio Medici,* 1642 (two editions unauthorized), 1643; facsimile, 1883; ed. by W. Murison, 1922; ed. by G. L. Keynes, 1939, 1940; ed. by Jean-Jacques Denonain, 1953, 1955; ed. by Vittoria Sanna, 1958; ed. by James Winny, 1963.
*Pseudodoxia Epidemica,* 1646.
*Hydriotaphia, Urne-Buriall* (with *The Garden of Cyrus*), 1658; ed. by W. Murison, 1922; facsimile, 1927; ed. by J. Carter, 1932, 1958.
*Christian Morals,* ed. by J. Jeffery, 1716; ed. by S. C. Roberts, 1927; ed. by J. Carter, 1958.
*The Works,* 1686; ed. by S. Wilkin, 1835–1836; ed. by G. L. Keynes, 1928–1931, 1963; *Religio Medici and Other Works,* ed. by L. C. Martin, 1964.

## HISTORICAL AND CRITICAL STUDIES

Sir Kenelm Digby, *Observations Upon Religio Medici,* 1643, 1909.
Alexander Ross, *Medicus Medicatus,* 1645.
Samuel Johnson, *Christian Morals: by Sir Thomas Browne . . . with a Life of the Author, by Samuel Johnson,* 1756.
E. Dowden, *Puritan and Anglican,* 1900.
Edmund Gosse, *Sir Thomas Browne,* 1905.
Geoffrey L. Keynes, *A Bibliography of Sir Thomas Browne,* 1924.
William Dunn, *Sir Thomas Browne: A Study in Religious Philosophy,* 1926; 3d ed., 1958.
Oliver Leroy, *Le Chevalier Thomas Browne,* 1931.
J. Needham, *The Great Amphibium,* 1931.
Alwin Thaler, "Sir Thomas Browne and the Elizabethans," *SP,* XXVIII (1931).
Gordon Chalmers, "Sir Thomas Browne, True Scientist," *Osiris,* II (1936).
J. M. Cline, *"Hydriotaphia," Five Studies in Literature,* ed. by B. H. Bronson, 1940.

Dewey K. Ziegler, *In Divided and Distinguished Worlds*, 1943.

A. C. Howell, "Sir Thomas Browne as Wit and Humorist," *SP*, XLII (1945).

Charles E. Raven, *English Naturalists from Neckham to Ray*, 1947.

Egon S. Merton, "Sir Thomas Browne's Scientific Quest," *J. of the Hist. of Med.*, III (1948).

M. L. Wiley, "Sir Thomas Browne and the Genesis of Paradox," *JHI*, IX (1948).

Egon S. Merton, *Science and Imagination in Sir Thomas Browne*, 1949.

———, "Sir Thomas Browne's Interpretation of Dreams," *PQ*, XXVIII (1949).

Gordon K. Chalmers, " 'That Universal and Publick Manuscript,' " *Virginia Quar. Rev.*, XXVI (1950).

Jeremiah Finch, *Sir Thomas Browne: A Doctor's Life of Science & Faith*, 1950.

M. A. Heideman, "*Hydriotaphia* and *The Garden of Cyrus:* A Paradox and a Cosmic Vision," *University of Toronto Quar.*, XIX (1950).

Austin Warren, "The Style of Sir Thomas Browne," *Kenyon Rev.*, XIII (1951).

Frank L. Huntley, "Sir Thomas Browne and the Metaphor of the Circle," *JHI*, XIV (1953).

———, "The Publication and Immediate Reception of *Religio Medici*," *Libr. Quar.*, XXV (1955).

Joan Bennett, "A Note on *Religio Medici* and Some of Its Critics," *Studies in the Renaissance*, III (1956).

Frank L. Huntley, "Sir Thomas Browne: The Relationship of *Urn Burial* and *The Garden of Cyrus*," *SP*, LIII (1956).

Margaret Bottrall, *Every Man a Phoenix*, 1958.

Leonard Goldstein, "Science and Literary Style in Robert Burton's 'Cento out of Divers Writers,' " *J. of the Rutgers University Library*, XXI (1958).

Jean-Jacques Denonain, "La Personnalité de Sir Thomas Browne," *Publications de la Faculté des Lettres et Sciences humaines d'Alger*, XXXIII (1959).

Peter Green, *Sir Thomas Browne*, 1959.

Michael F. Moloney, "Metre and *Cursus* in Sir Thomas Browne's Prose," *JEGP*, LVIII (1959).

Frank P. Wilson, "Sir Thomas Browne," *Seventeenth Century Prose*, 1960.

Joan Bennett, *Sir Thomas Browne*, 1962.

Frank L. Huntley, *Sir Thomas Browne: A Biographical and Critical Study*, 1962.

Mother Elizabeth Stuyvesant White, "A Study of Symmetrical and Asymmetrical Tendencies in the Sentence Structure of Sir Thomas Browne's *Urne Buriall*," Dissertation, Catholic University, 1962; *Dissertation Abstr.*, XXIV (1963).

N. J. Endicott, "Some Aspects of Self-Revelation and Self-Portraiture in *Religio Medici*," *Essays . . . Presented to A. S. P. Woodhouse*, ed. by F. W. Watt, 1964.

George Williamson, "The Purple of *Urn Burial*," *MP*, LXII (1964).

# RELIGIO MEDICI

## PART I

SECT. 1.  For my Religion, though there be severall circumstances that might perswade the world I have none at all, as the generall scandall of my profession, the naturall course of my studies, the indifferency of my behaviour, and discourse in matters of Religion, neither violently defending one, nor with that common ardour and contention opposing another; yet in despight hereof I dare, without usurpation, assume the honorable stile of a Christian: not that I meerely owe this title to the Font, my education, or Clime wherein I was borne, as being bred up either to confirme those principles my Parents instilled into my unwary understanding; or by a generall consent proceed in the Religion of my Countrey: But that having, in my riper yeares, and confirmed judgement, seene and examined all, I finde my selfe obliged by the principles of Grace, and the law of mine owne reason, to embrace no other name but this; neither doth herein my zeale so farre make me forget the generall charitie I owe unto humanity, as rather to hate then pity Turkes, Infidels, and (what is worse) the Jewes, rather contenting my selfe to enjoy that happy stile, then maligning those who refuse so glorious a title.

SECT. 2.  But because the name of a Christian is become too generall to expresse our faith, there being a Geography of Religions as well as Lands, and every Clime distinguished not onely by their lawes and limits, but circumscribed by their doctrines and rules of Faith; To be particular, I am of that reformed new-cast Religion, wherein I mislike nothing but the name, of the same beliefe our Saviour taught, the Apostles disseminated, the Fathers authorised, and the Martyrs confirmed; but by the sinister ends of Princes, the ambition and avarice of Prelates, and the fatall corruption of times, so decaied, impaired, and fallen from its native beauty, that it required the carefull and charitable hands of these times to restore it to its primitive integrity: Now the accidentall occasion whereon, the slender meanes whereby, the low and abject condition of the person by whom so good a worke was set on foot, which in our adversaries beget contempt and scorn, fills me with wonder, and is the very same objection the insolent Pagans first cast at Christ and his Disciples.

SECT. 3. Yet have I not so shaken hands with those desperate Resolutions, who had rather venture at large their decaied bottome, then bring her in to be new trim'd in the dock; who had rather promiscuously retaine all, then abridge any, and obstinately be what they are, then what they have beene, as to stand in diameter and swords point with them: we have reformed from them, not against them; for omitting those improperations and termes of scurrility betwixt us, which onely difference our affections, and not our cause, there is between us one common name and appellation, one faith, and necessary body of principles common to us both; and therefore I am not scrupulous to converse and live with them, to enter their Churches in defect of ours, and either pray with them, or for them: I could never perceive any rationall consequence from those many texts which prohibite the children of Israel to pollute themselves with the Temples of the Heathens; we being all Christians, and not divided by such detested impieties as might prophane our prayers, or the place wherein we make them; or that a resolved conscience may not adore her Maker any where, especially in places devoted to his service; where if their devotions offend him, mine may please him, if theirs prophane it, mine may hallow it; Holy water and Crucifix (dangerous to the common people) deceive not my judgement, nor abuse my devotion at all: I am, I confesse, naturally inclined to that, which misguided zeale termes superstition; my common conversation I do acknowledge austere, my behaviour full of rigour, sometimes not without morosity; yet at my devotion I love to use the civility of my knee, my hat, and hand, with all those outward and sensible motions, which may expresse, or promote my invisible devotion. I should violate my owne arme rather then a Church, nor willingly deface the memory of Saint or Martyr. At the sight of a Crosse or Crucifix, I can dispence with my hat, but scarce with the thought and memory of my Saviour; I cannot laugh at but rather pity the fruitlesse journeys of Pilgrims, or contemne the miserable condition of Friers; for though misplaced in circumstance, there is somewhat in it of devotion: I could never heare the *Ave Marie* Bell [1] without an elevation, or thinke it a

---

[1] A Church Bell that tolls every day at 6 and 12 of the Clocke, at the hearing whereof every one in what place soever either of house or street betakes him to his prayer, which is commonly directed to the *Virgin*.

sufficient warrant, because they erred in one circumstance, for me to
erre in all, that is in silence and dumbe contempt; whilst therefore they
directed their devotions to her, I offered mine to God, and rectified the
errours of their prayers by rightly ordering mine owne; At a solemne
Procession I have wept abundantly, while my consorts, blinde with
opposition and prejudice, have fallen into an excesse of scorne and laughter: There are questionlesse both in Greek, Roman, and African
Churches, solemnities, and ceremonies, whereof the wiser zeales doe
make a Christian use, and stand condemned by us, not as evill in themselves, but as allurements and baits of superstition to those vulgar heads
that looke asquint on the face of truth, and those unstable Judgements
that cannot consist in the narrow point and centre of vertue without a
reele or stagger to the circumference.

SECT. 4.  As there were many Reformers, so likewise many reforma-
tions; every Countrey proceeding in a peculiar Method, according as
their nationall interest together with their constitution and clime inclined them, some angrily and with extremitie, others calmely, and with
mediocrity, not rending, but easily dividing the community, and leaving
an honest possibility of a reconciliation, which though peaceable Spirits
doe desire, and may conceive that revolution of time, and the mercies
of God may effect, yet that judgement that shall consider the present
antipathies between the two extreames, their contrarieties in condition,
affection and opinion, may with the same hopes expect an union in the
poles of Heaven.

SECT. 5.  But to difference my self neerer, and draw into a lesser circle:
There is no Church wherein every point so squares unto my conscience,
whose articles, constitutions, and customes seeme so consonant unto
reason, and as it were framed to my particular devotion, as this whereof
I hold my beliefe, the Church of *England,* to whose faith I am a sworne
subject, and therefore in a double obligation, subscribe unto her Articles, and endeavour to observe her Constitutions. No man shall reach my
faith unto another Article, or command my obedience to a Canon more:
whatsoever is beyond, as points indifferent, I observe according to the
rules of my private reason, or the humor and fashion of my devotion,
neither believing this, because *Luther* affirmed it, or disapproving that, because *Calvin* hath disavouched it. I condemne not all things in the Councell of *Trent* nor approve all in the Synod of *Dort.* In briefe, where the

Scripture is silent, the Church is my Text; where that speakes, 'tis but my Comment; where there is a joynt silence of both, I borrow not the rules of my Religion from *Rome* or *Geneva,* but the dictates of my owne reason. It is an unjust scandall of our adversaries, and a grosse error in our selves, to compute the Nativity of our Religion from *Henry* the eighth, who though he rejected the Pope, refus'd not the faith of *Rome,* and effected no more but what his owne Predecessors desired and assayed in ages past, and was conceived the State of *Venice* would have attempted in our dayes. It is as uncharitable a point in us to fall upon those popular scurrilities and opprobrious scoffes of the Bishop of *Rome,* whom as a temporall Prince, we owe the duty of good language: I confesse there is cause of passion betweene us; by his sentence I stand excommunicate and my posterity, Heretick is the best language he affords me; yet can no eare witnesse I ever returned to him the name of Antichrist, Man of Sin, or whore of *Babylon;* It is the method of charity to suffer without reaction; those usuall Satyrs, and invectives of the Pulpit may by chance produce a good effect on the vulgar, whose eares are opener to Rhetorick then Logick, yet doe they in no wise confirme the faith of wiser beleevers, who know that a good cause needs not to be patron'd by a passion, but can sustaine it selfe upon a temperate dispute.

SECT. 6. I could never divide my selfe from any man upon the difference of an opinion, or be angry with his judgement for not agreeing with mee in that, from which perhaps within a few dayes I should dissent my selfe. I have no Genius to disputes in Religion, and have often thought it wisedome to decline them, especially upon a disadvantage, or when the cause of truth might suffer in the weaknesse of my patronage: where we desire to be informed, 'tis good to contest with men above our selves; but to confirme and establish our opinions, 'tis best to argue with judgements below our own, that the frequent spoyles and victories over their reasons may settle in our selves an esteeme, and confirmed opinion of our owne. Every man is not a proper Champion for Truth, nor fit to take up the Gantlet in the cause of Veritie: Many, from the ignorance of these Maximes, and an inconsiderate zeale unto Truth, have too rashly charged the troopes of error, and remaine as Trophees unto the enemies of Truth: A man may be in as just possession of Truth as of a City, and yet bee forced to surrender; 'tis therefore farre better to enjoy her with peace, then to hazzard her on a battell: If, therefore, there rise any doubts in my way, I doe forget them, or at least defer them till my better setled judgement and more manly reason be able to resolve them; for I perceive every mans owne reason is his best *Oedipus,* and will, upon a reasonable truce, find a way to loose those bonds, wherewith the subtilties of errour have enchained our more flexible and tender judgements. In Philosophy where truth seemes double-faced, there is no man more paradoxicall then my self: but in Divinity I love to keepe the road, and, though not in an implicite, yet an humble faith, follow the great wheele of the Church, by which I move, not reserving any proper poles or motion from the epicycle of my own braine; by this meanes I leave no gap for Heresies, Schismes, or Errors, of which at present I hope I shall not injure Truth to say, I have no taint or tincture. I must confesse my greener studies have beene polluted with two or three, not any begotten in the latter Centuries, but old and obsolete, such as could never have been revived, but by such extravagant and irregular heads as mine; for indeed Heresies perish not with their Authors, but, like the river *Arethusa,* though they lose their currents in one place, they rise up againe in another: one generall Councell is not able to extirpate one singular Heresie, it may be canceld for the present, but revolution of time, and the like aspects from Heaven, will restore it, when it will flourish till it be condemned againe; for as though there were a *Metempsuchosis,* and the soule of one man passed into another, opinions doe find, after certain revolutions, men and mindes like those that first begat them. To see our selves againe, we need not looke for *Platoes*[2] yeare; every man is not onely himselfe; there have been many *Diogenes,* and as many *Timons,* though but few of that name: men are lived over againe, the world is now as it was in ages past; there was none then, but there hath been some one since that parallels him, and is, as it were, his revived selfe.

SECT. 7.   Now the first of mine was that of the *Arabians,* That the soules of men perished with their bodies, but should yet bee raised againe at the last day; not that I did absolutely conceive a mortality of the soule; but if that were, which faith, not Philosophy hath yet throughly disproved, and that both entred the grave together, yet I held the same conceit thereof that wee all doe of the body, that it should rise

---

[2] A revolution of certain thousand yeares when all things should returne unto their former estate, and he be teaching againe in his schoole as when he delivered this opinion.

againe. Surely it is but the merits of our unworthy natures, if wee sleepe
in darkenesse, untill the last alarum: A serious reflex upon my own
unworthiness did make me backward from challenging this prerogative
of my soule; so I might enjoy my Saviour at last, I could with patience
be nothing almost unto eternity. The second was that of *Origen,* that
God would not persist in his vengeance for ever, but after a definite time
of his wrath hee would release the damned soules from torture; Which
error I fell into upon a serious contemplation of the great attribute of
God, his mercy; and did a little cherish it in my selfe, because I found
therein no malice, and a ready weight to sway me from that other
extream of despaire, whereunto melancholy and contemplative natures
are too easily disposed. A third there is which I did never positively
maintaine or practise, but have often wished it had been consonant to
Truth, and not offensive to my Religion, and that is the prayer for the
dead; whereunto I was inclined from some charitable inducements,
whereby I could scarce containe my prayers for a friend at the ringing
out of a Bell, or behold his corpse without an oraison for his soule:
'Twas a good way me thought to be remembered by Posterity, and farre
more noble then an History. These opinions I never maintained with
pertinacity, or endeavoured to enveagle any mans beliefe unto mine, nor
so much as ever revealed or disputed them with my dearest friends; by
which meanes I neither propagated them in others, nor confirmed them
in my selfe, but suffering them to flame upon their owne substance,
without addition of new fuell, they went out insensibly of themselves;
therefore these opinions, though condemned by lawful Councels, were
not Heresies in me, but bare Errors, and single Lapses of my understanding, without a joynt depravity of my will: Those have not only
depraved understandings but diseased affections, which cannot enjoy a
singularity without a Heresie, or be the author of an opinion without
they be of a Sect also; this was the villany of the first Schisme of
*Lucifer,* who was not content to erre alone, but drew into his faction
many Legions of Spirits; and upon this experience hee tempted only
*Eve,* as well understanding the communicable nature of sin, and that to
deceive but one, was tacitely and upon consequence to delude them both.

SECT 8. That Heresies should arise, we have the prophecy of Christ,
but that old ones should be abolished wee hold no prediction. That
there must be heresies, is true, not onely in our Church, but also in any
other: even in Doctrines hereticall, there will be super-heresies; and

Arians not onely divided from their Church, but also among themselves: for heads that are disposed unto Schisme and complexionally propense to innovation, are naturally indisposed for a community, nor will ever be confined unto the order or oeconomy of one body; and therefore, when they separate from others, they knit but loosely among themselves; nor contented with a generall breach or dichotomie with their Church, do subdivide and mince themselves almost into Atomes. 'Tis true, that men of singular parts and humors have not beene free from singular opinions and conceits in all ages; retaining something, not onely beside the opinion of his own Church or any other, but also any particular Author; which notwithstanding, a sober judgement may doe without offence or heresie; for there is yet, after all the decrees of counsells and the niceties of the Schooles, many things untouch'd, unimagin'd, wherein the libertie of an honest reason may play and expatiate with security, and farre without the circle of an heresie.

SECT. 9.  As for those wingy mysteries in Divinity, and ayery subtilties of Religion, which have unhing'd the braines of better heads, they never stretch the *Pia Mater* of mine; me thinkes there be not impossibilities enough in Religion for an active faith; the deepest mysteries ours containes have not only been illustrated, but maintained, by syllogisme, and the rule of reason: I love to lose my selfe in a mystery, to pursue my Reason to an *oh altitudo*. 'Tis my solitary recreation to pose my apprehension with those involved aenigma's and riddles of the Trinity, with Incarnation, and Resurrection. I can answer all the objections of Satan, and my rebellious reason with that odde resolution I learned of *Tertullian, Certum est, quia impossibile est*. I desire to exercise my faith in the difficultest points, for to credit ordinary and visible objects is not faith but perswasion. Some beleeve the better for seeing Christ his Sepulchre, and, when they have seene the Red Sea, doubt not of the miracle. Now contrary, I blesse my selfe and am thankeful that I lived not in the dayes of miracles, that I never saw Christ nor his Disciples; I would not have beene one of the Israelites that passed the Red Sea, nor one of Christs Patients on whom he wrought his wonders; then had my faith beene thrust upon me, nor should I enjoy that greater blessing pronounced to all that believe and saw not. 'Tis an easie and necessary beliefe, to credit what our eye and sense hath examined: I believe he was dead, buried, and rose againe; and desire to see him in his glory, rather than to contemplate him in his Cenotaphe or Sepulchre. Nor is this much to beleeve; as we have reason, we owe this faith unto History: they only had the advantage of a bold and noble Faith, who lived before his comming, who upon obscure prophesies and mysticall Types could raise a beliefe, and expect apparent impossibilities.

SECT. 10. 'Tis true, there is an edge in all firme beliefe, and with an easie Metaphor wee may say the sword of faith; but in these obscurities I rather use it in the adjunct the Apostle gives it, a Buckler; under which I perceive a wary combatant may lie invulnerable. Since I was of understanding to know we know nothing, my reason hath beene more pliable to the will of faith; I am now content to understand a mystery without a rigid definition, in an easie and Platonick description. That allegorical description of *Hermes*[3] pleaseth mee beyond all the Metaphysicall definitions of Divines; where I cannot satisfie my reason, I love to humour my fancy: I had as leive you tell me that *anima est angelus hominis, est Corpus Dei*, as *Entelechia; Lux est umbra Dei*, as *actus perspicui*: where there is an obscurity too deepe for our reason, 'tis good to sit downe with a description, periphrasis, or adumbration; for by acquainting our reason how unable it is to display the visible and obvious effects of nature, it becomes more humble and submissive unto the subtilties of faith; and thus I teach my haggard and unreclaimed reason to stoope unto the lure of faith. I doe believe there was already a tree whose fruit our unhappy parents tasted, though, in the same Chapter, where God forbids it, 'tis positively said, the plants of the field were not yet growne, for God had not caused it to raine upon the earth. I beleeve that the Serpent (if we shall literally understand it,) from his proper forme and figure, made his motion on his belly before the curse. I find the triall of the Pucellage and Virginity of women, which God ordained the Jewes, is very fallible. Experience, and History informes me, that not onely many particular women, but likewise whole Nations, have escaped that curse of childbed, which God seemes to pronounce upon the whole Sex; yet do I beleeve that all this is true, which indeed my reason would perswade me to be false; and this I think is no vulgar part of faith, to believe a thing not only above, but contrary to reason, and against the arguments of our proper senses.

[3] *Sphaera cujus centrum ubique, circumferentia nullibi.*

SECT. 11.   In my solitary and retired imagination (*Neque enim cum porticus aut me lectulus accipit, desum mihi*) I remember I am not alone, and therefore forget not to contemplate him and his attributes who is ever with mee, especially those two mighty ones, his wisedome and eternitie; with the one I recreate, with the other I confound my understanding; for who can speake of eternitie without a soloecisme, or thinke thereof without an extasie? Time we may comprehend; 'tis but five dayes elder then our selves, and hath the same Horoscope with the world; but to retire so farre backe as to apprehend a beginning, to give such an infinite start forward as to conceive an end in an essence that wee affirme hath neither the one nor the other; it puts my Reason to Saint *Pauls* Sanctuary *O! Altitudo!;* my Philosophy dares not say the Angells can doe it; God hath not made a creature that can comprehend him, 'tis the priviledge of his owne nature; *I am that I am,* was his owne definition unto *Moses;* and 'twas a short one, to confound mortalitie, that durst question God, or aske him what hee was. Indeed he onely is, all others have beene and shall be, but in eternity there is no distinction of Tenses; and therefore that terrible terme *Predestination,* which hath troubled so many weake heads to conceive, and the wisest to explaine, is in respect of God no previous determination of our estates to come, but a definitive blast of his will already fulfilled, and at the instant that he first decreed it; for to his eternitie which is indivisible and altogether, the last Trumpe is already sounded, the reprobates in the flame, and the blessed in *Abrahams* bosome. Saint *Peter* spake modestly when hee said, a thousand yeares to God are but as one day; for, to speake like a Philosopher, those continued instants of time which flow into a thousand yeares, make not to him one moment; what to us is to come, to his Eternitie is present, his whole duration being but one permanent point, without succession, parts, flux, or division.

SECT. 12.   There is no Attribute that adds more difficulty to the mystery of the Trinity, where though in a relative way of Father and Son, we must deny a priority. I wonder how *Aristotle* should conceive the world eternall, or how hee could make good two Eternities: his similitude of a Triangle comprehended in a square, doth somewhat illustrate the Trinitie of our soules, and that the Triple Unity of God; for there is in us not three, but a Trinity of soules, because there is within us, if not three distinct soules, yet different faculties, that can, and doe subsist apart in different subjects, and yet in us are so united as to make but one soule

and substance; if one soule were so perfect as to informe three distinct
bodies, that were a petty Trinity: conceive the distinct number of three,
not divided nor separated by the intellect, but actually comprehended in
its Unity, and that is a perfect Trinity. I have often admired the mysticall way of *Pythagoras,* and the secret Magicke of numbers; Beware of
Philosophy, is a precept not to be received in too large a sense; for in this
masse of nature there is a set of things which carry in their front,
though not in capitall letters, yet in stenography, and short Characters,
something of Divinitie, which to wiser reasons serve as Luminaries in
the abysse of knowledge, and to judicious beliefes as scales and roundles
to mount the pinnacles and highest pieces of Divinity. The severe
Schooles shall never laugh me out of the Philosophy of *Hermes,* that this
visible World is but a picture of the invisible, wherein, as in a pourtract,
things are not truely, but in equivocall shapes, and as they counterfeit
some more reall substance in that invisible fabrick. . . .

SECT. 21. I confesse I have perused them all, and can discover nothing
that may startle a discreet beliefe: yet are there heads carried off with
the wind and breath of such motives. I remember a Doctor in Physick
of Italy, who could not perfectly believe the immortality of the soule,
because *Galen* seemed to make a doubt thereof. With another I was
familiarly acquainted in France, a Divine, and a man of singular parts,
that on the same point was so plunged and gravelled with three lines of
*Seneca,* that all our Antidotes, drawne from both Scripture and Philosophy, could not expel the poyson of his errour. There are a set of
heads, that can credit the relations of Mariners, yet question the testimony of Saint *Paul;* and peremptorily maintaine the traditions of *Ælian*
or *Pliny,* yet in Histories of Scripture raise Quere's and objections, beleeving no more than they can parallel in humane Authors. I confesse
there are in Scripture stories that doe exceed the fables of Poets, and to
a captious Reader sound like *Garagantua* or *Bevis:* Search all the
Legends of times past, and the fabulous conceits of these present, and
'twill be hard to find one that deserves to carry the buckler unto *Sampson,* yet is all this of an easie possibility, if we conceive a divine concourse or an influence but from the little finger of the Almighty. It is
impossible that either in the discourse of man, or in the infallible voyce
of God, to the weaknesse of our apprehension, there should not appeare
irregularities, contradictions, and antinomies: my selfe could shew a
catalogue of doubts, never yet imagined nor questioned by any, as I

know, which are not resolved at the first hearing, not queries fantastick or objections of ayre: For I cannot heare of Atoms in Divinity. I can read the story of the Pigeon that was sent out of the Ark, and returned no more, yet not question how shee found out her mate that was left behind: That *Lazarus* was raised from the dead, yet not demand where in the interim his soule awaited; or raise a Law-case, whether his heire might lawfully detaine his inheritance, bequeathed unto him by his death; and he, though restored to life, have no Plea or title unto his former possessions. Whether *Eve* was framed out of the left side of *Adam,* I dispute not; because I stand not yet assured which is the right side of a man, or whether there be any such distinction in Nature: that she was edified out of the ribbe of *Adam* I believe, yet raise no question who shall arise with that ribbe at the Resurrection. Whether *Adam* was an Hermaphrodite, as the Rabbines contend upon the Letter of the Text; because it is contrary to all reason that there should bee an Hermaphrodite before there was a woman, or a composition of two natures before there was a second composed. Likewise, whether the world was created in Autumne, Summer, or Spring, because it was created in them all; for whatsoever Signe the Sun possesseth, those foure seasons are actually existent: It is the nature of this Luminary to distinguish the severall seasons of the yeare, all which it makes at one time in the whole earth, and successively in any part thereof. There are a bundle of curiosities, not onely in Philosophy but in Divinity, proposed and discussed by men of the most supposed abilities, which indeed are not worthy our vacant hours, much lesse our more serious studies; Pieces onely fit to be placed in *Pantagruels* Library, or bound up with *Tartaretus De modo Cacandi.* . . .

sect. 34.  These are certainly the Magisteriall and master pieces of the Creator, the Flower, or (as we may say,) the best part of nothing; actually existing, what we are but in hopes, and probabilitie; we are onely that amphibious piece betweene a corporall and spirituall essence, that middle frame that linkes those two together, and makes good the method of God and nature, that jumps not from extreames, but unites the incompatible distances by some middle and participating natures; that wee are the breath and similitude of God, it is indisputable, and upon record of holy Scripture, but to call our selves a Microcosme, or little world, I thought it onely a pleasant trope of Rhetorick, till my nearer judgement and second thoughts told me there was a reall truth therein: for first wee are a rude masse, and in the ranke of creatures which only are, and have a dull kinde of being not yet priviledged with life, or preferred to sense or reason; next we live the life of plants, the life of animals, the life of men, and at last the life of spirits, running on in one mysterious nature those five kinds of existences, which comprehend the creatures not of the world onely, but of the Universe; thus is man that great and true *Amphibium,* whose nature is disposed to live not onely like other creatures in divers elements, but in divided and distinguished worlds; for though there bee but one world to sense, there are two to reason, the one visible, the other invisible; whereof *Moses* seemes to have left description, and of the other so obscurely, that some parts thereof are yet in controversie; and truely for the first chapters of *Genesis,* I must confesse a great deale of obscurity; though Divines have to the power of humane reason endeavoured to make all goe in a literall meaning, yet those allegoricall interpretations are also probable, and perhaps the mysticall method of *Moses* bred up in the Hieroglyphicall Schooles of the *Egyptians.* . . .

# PART II

SECT. 8. I thanke God, amongst those millions of vices I doe inherit, and hold from *Adam,* I have escaped one, and that a mortall enemy to Charity, the first and father sin, not onely of man, but of the devil, Pride, a vice whose name is comprehended in a Monosyllable, but in its nature not circumscribed with a world. I have escaped it in a condition that can hardly avoid it: those petty acquisitions and reputed perfections that advance and elevate the conceits of other men, adde no feathers unto mine; I have seene a Grammarian toure and plume himselfe over a single line in *Horace,* and shew more pride in the construction of one Ode, than the Author in the composure of the whole book. For my owne part, besides the *Jargon* and *Patois* of severall Provinces, I understand no lesse than six Languages, yet I protest I have no higher conceit of my selfe, than had our Fathers before the confusion of *Babel,* when there was in the world but one Language, and none to boast himselfe either Linguist or Criticke. I have not onely seene severall Countries, beheld the nature of their climes, the Chorography of their Provinces, Topography of their Cities, but understand their severall Lawes, Customes and Policies; yet cannot all this perswade the dulnesse of my

spirit unto such an opinion of my self, as I behold in nimbler and conceited heads, that never looked a degree beyond their nests. I know the
names, and somewhat more, of all the constellations in my Horizon, yet
I have seene a prating Mariner, that could onely name the Poynters and
the North Starre, out-talke mee, and conceit himselfe a whole Spheare
above mee. I know most of the Plants of my Countrey, and of those
about mee; yet methinkes I do not know so many as when I did but
know an hundred, and had scarcely ever Simpled further than Cheapside: for indeed, heads of capacity, and such are not full with a handfull,
or easie measure of knowledg, thinke they know nothing till they know
all; which being impossible, they fall upon the opinion of *Socrates,* and
onely know they know not any thing. I cannot think that *Homer* pin'd
away upon the riddle of the Fisherman, or that *Aristotle,* who understood the uncertainty of knowledge, and confessed so often the reason
of man too weake for the workes of nature, did ever drowne himselfe
upon the flux and reflux of *Euripus:* wee doe but learne to-day what our
better advanced judgements will unteach us to-morrow: and *Aristotle*
doth but instruct us, as *Plato* did him; that is, to confute himselfe. I
have runne through all sects, yet finde no rest in any: though our first
studies and junior endeavors may stile us Peripateticks, Stoicks, or Aca-
demicks, yet I perceive the wisest heads prove, at last, almost all Scep-
ticks, and stand like *Janus* in the field of knowledge. I have therefore
one common and authentick Philosophy I learned in the Schooles,
whereby I discourse and satisfie the reason of other men, another more
reserved, and drawne from experience, whereby I content mine owne.
*Solomon,* that complained of ignorance in the height of knowledge, hath
not onely humbled my conceits, but discouraged my endeavours. There
is yet another conceit that hath sometimes made me shut my bookes;
which tels mee it is a vanity to waste our dayes in the blind pursuit of
knowledge, it is but attending a little longer, and wee shall enjoy that
by instinct and infusion which we endeavour at here by labour and
inquisition. It is better to sit downe in a modest ignorance, and rest
contented with the naturall blessing of our owne reasons, then buy the
uncertaine knowledge of this life with sweat and vexation, which death
gives every foole gratis, and is an accessory of our glorification.

SECT. 9. I was never yet once, and commend their resolutions who never
marry twice; not that I disallow of second marriage; as neither in all
cases of Polygamy, which, considering some times, and the unequall

number of both sexes, may bee also necessary. The whole woman was
made for man, but the twelfth part of man for woman: man is the
whole world, and the breath of God; woman the rib and crooked piece
of man. I could be content that we might procreate like trees, without
conjunction, or that there were any way to perpetuate the world without
this triviall and vulgar way of coition; It is the foolishest act a wise
man commits in all his life; nor is there any thing that will more deject
his coold imagination, when hee shall consider what an odde and unworthy piece of folly hee hath committed; I speake not in prejudice, nor
am I averse from that sweet sexe, but naturally amorous of all that is
beautifull; I can looke a whole day with delight upon a handsome Picture, though it be but of an Horse. It is my temper, and I like it the
better, to affect all harmony, and sure there is a musicke even in the
beauty, and the silent note which *Cupid* strikes, farre sweeter than the
sound of an instrument. For there is a musicke where-ever there is a
harmony, order, or proportion; and thus farre we may maintain
the musick of the spheares; for those well-ordered motions, and regular
paces, though they give no sound unto the eare, yet to the understanding
they strike a note most full of harmony. Whosoever is harmonically
composed delights in harmony; which makes me much mistrust the
symmetry of those heads which declaime against all Church musicke.
For my selfe, not only from my obedience, but my particular genius, I
doe imbrace it: for even that vulgar and Taverne Musicke, which makes
one man merry, another mad, strikes mee into a deepe fit of devotion,
and a profound contemplation of the first Composer; there is something
in it of Divinity more than the eare discovers. It is a Hieroglyphicall
and shadowed lesson of the whole world, and the Creatures of God,
such a melody to the eare, as the whole world well understood, would
afford the understanding. In briefe, it is a sensible fit of that Harmony,
which intellectually sounds in the eares of God. It unties the ligaments
of my frame, takes me to pieces, dilates me out of my self, and by degrees, me thinkes, resolves me into Heaven. I will not say, with *Plato,*
the Soule is an Harmony, but harmonicall, and hath its neerest sympathy unto musicke: thus, some whose temper of body agrees, and
humours the constitution of their soules, are borne Poets, though indeed
all are naturally inclined unto Rhythme. [4]This made *Tacitus,* in the very
first line of his Story, fall upon a verse; and *Cicero,* the worst of Poets,

[4] *Urbem Romam in principio Reges habuere.*

but [5]declayming for a Poet, fall in the very first sentence upon a perfect [6]Hexameter. I feele not in me those sordid, and unchristian desires of my profession; I doe not secretly implore and wish for Plagues, rejoyce at Famines, revolve Ephemerides, and Almanacks in expectation of malignant Aspects, fatall conjunctions, and Eclipses. I rejoyce not at unwholsome Springs, nor unseasonable Winters: my Prayers go with the Husbandsmans; I desire every thing in its proper season, that neither men nor the times bee out of temper. Let mee bee sicke my selfe, if sometimes the malady of my patient be not a disease unto me; I desire rather to cure his infirmities than my owne necessities. Where I do no good me thinkes it is scarce honest gaine, though I confesse 'tis but the worthy salary of our well-intended endeavours: I am not onely ashamed, but heartily sorry, that besides death, there are diseases incurable, yet not for my own sake, or that they be beyond my art, but for the generall cause and sake of humanity whose common cause I apprehend as mine own: And to speak more generally, those three Noble Professions which all civil Common wealths doe honour, are raised upon the fall of *Adam,* and are not any way exempt from their infirmities; there are not onely diseases incurable in Physicke, but cases indissoluble in Lawes, Vices incorrigible in Divinity: if general Councells may erre, I doe not see why particular Courts should be infallible; their perfectest rules are raised upon the erroneous reason of Man, and the Lawes of one doe but con- demn the rules of another; as *Aristotle* oft-times the opinions of his predecessours, because, though agreeable to reason, yet were not con- sonant to his owne rules, and the Logicke of his proper principles. Againe, to speake nothing of the sinne against the Holy Ghost, whose cure not onely, but whose nature is unknowne, I can cure the gout or stone in some, sooner than Divinity, Pride, or Avarice in others. Further I can clure vices by Physicke, when they remaine incurable by Divinity, and they shall obey my pils, when they contemne their precepts. I boast nothing, but plainely say, we all labour against our owne cure, for death is the cure of all diseases. There is no Catholicon or universall remedy I know but this; which, though nauseous to queasier stomachs, yet to prepared appetites is Nectar, and a pleasant potion of immortality. . . .

sect. 11.  Now for my life, it is a miracle of thirty yeares, which to relate, were not an History, but a peece of Poetry, and would sound to

---

[5] *Pro Archia Poeta.*
[6] *In qua me non inficior mediocriter esse.*

common eares like a fable; for the world, I count it not an Inne, but an Hospitall, and a place, not to live, but to die in. That world which I regard is my selfe; it is the Microcosme of mine owne frame that I cast mine eye on; for the other, I use it but like my Globe, and turne it round sometimes for my recreation. Men that look upon my outside, perusing onely my condition, and fortunes, do erre in my altitude; for I am above *Atlas* his shoulders, and, though I seeme on earth to stand, on tiptoe in heaven. The earth is a point not onely in respect of the heavens above us, but of that heavenly and celestiall part within us: that masse of flesh that circumscribes me, limits not my mind: that surface that tells the heavens it hath an end, cannot perswade me I have any; I take my circle to be above three hundred and sixty; though the number of the Arke do measure my body, it comprehendeth not my minde; whilst I study to finde how I am a Microcosme, or little world, I finde my selfe something more than the great. There is surely a peece of Divinity in us, something that was before the Elements, and owes no homage unto the Sun. Nature tels me I am the Image of God as well as Scripture; he that understands not thus much, hath not his introduction or first lesson, and is yet to begin the Alphabet of man. Let me not injure the felicity of others, if I say I am as happy as any. I have that in me that can convert poverty into riches, transforme adversity into prosperity: I am more invulnerable than *Achilles;* Fortune hath not one place to hit me. *Ruat coelum, Fiat voluntas tua,* salveth all; so that whatsoever happens, it is but what our daily prayers desire. In briefe, I am content, and what should providence adde more? Surely this is it wee call Happinesse, and this doe I enjoy; with this I am happy in a dreame, and as content to enjoy a happinesse in a fancie, as others in a more apparent truth and reality. There is surely a neerer apprehension of any thing that delights us in our dreames, than in our awaked senses; with this I can be a King without a Crowne, rich without a royalty, in heaven though on earth, enjoy my friend and embrace him at a distance; without which I cannot behold him; without this I were unhappy; for my awaked judgement discontents me, ever whispering unto me, that I am from my friend; but my friendly dreames in the night requite me, and make me thinke I am within his armes. I thanke God for my happy dreames, as I doe for my good rest; for there is a satisfaction in them unto reasonable desires, and such as can be content with a fit of happinesse; and surely it is not a melancholy conceite to thinke we are all asleepe in this world, and that the conceits of this life are as neere

dreames to those of the next, as the Phantasmes of the night, to the conceits of the day. There is an equall delusion in both, and the one doth
but seeme to bee the embleme and picture of the other; we are somewhat more than our selves in our sleepes, and the slumber of the body
seems to be but the waking of the soule. It is the ligation of sense, but
the liberty of reason; our waking conceptions doe not match the fancies
of our sleepes. At my Nativity, my ascendant was the watery signe of
*Scorpius;* I was borne in the Planetary hour of *Saturne,* and I think I
have a peece of that Leaden Planet in me. I am no way facetious, nor
disposed for the mirth and galliardize of company, yet in one dreame I
can compose a whole comedy, behold the action, apprehend the jests,
and laugh my selfe awake at the conceits thereof; were my memory as
faithfull as my reason is then fruitfull, I would never study but in my
dreames; and this time also would I chuse for my devotions, but our
grosser memories have then so little hold of our abstracted understandings, that they forget the story, and can only relate to our awaked soules,
a confused and broken tale of what hath passed. *Aristotle,* who hath
written a singular tract of sleepe, hath not me thinkes throughly defined
it, nor yet Galen, though hee seeme to have corrected it; for those
*Noctambuloes* and night-walkers, though in their sleepe, doe yet enjoy
the action of their senses: we must therefore say that there is something
in us that is not in the jurisdiction of *Morpheus;* and that these abstracted and ecstaticke soules doe walke about in their owne corps, as
spirits with the bodies they assume, wherein they seeme to heare, see,
and feele, though indeed the organs are destitute of sense, and their
natures of those faculties that should informe them. Thus it is observed
that men sometimes, upon the houre of their departure, doe speake and
reason above themselves; For then the soule, beginning to bee freed
from the ligaments of the body, begins to reason like her selfe, and to
discourse in a straine above mortality. . . .

# PSEUDODOXIA EPIDEMICA

## Of the Causes of Common Errors

The First and Father-cause of common Error, is, The common infirmity of Human Nature; of whose deceptible condition, although perhaps there should not need any other eviction, than the frequent Errors we shall our selves commit, even in the express declarement hereof: yet shall we illustrate the same from more infallible constitutions, and persons presumed as far from us in condition, as time, that is, our first and ingenerated forefathers. From whom as we derive our Being, and the several wounds of constitution, so may we in some manner excuse our infirmities in the depravity of those parts, whose Traductions were pure in them, and their Originals but once removed from God. Who notwithstanding (if posterity may take leave to judg of the fact, as they are assured to suffer in the punishment) were grosly deceived, in their perfection; and so weakly deluded in the clarity of their understanding, that it hath left no small obscurity in ours, How error should gain upon them.

## Of the Second Cause of Popular Errors, the Erroneous
## Disposition of the People

Having thus declared the fallible nature of Man even from his first production, we have beheld the general cause of Error. But as for popular Errors, they are more neerly founded upon an erroneous inclination of the people; as being the most deceptable part of Mankind and ready with open armes to receive the encroachments of Error. Which condition of theirs although deducible from many Grounds, yet shall we evidence it but from a few, and such as most neerly and undeniably declare their natures.

How unequal discerners of truth they are, and openly exposed unto Error, will first appear from their unqualified intellectuals, unable to umpire the difficulty of its dissentions. For Error, to speak largely, is a false judgment of things, or, an essent unto falsity. Now whether the object whereunto they deliver up their assent be true or false, they are incompetent judges.

For the assured truth of things is derived from the principles of knowledg, and causes which determine their verities. Whereof their uncultivated understandings, scarce holding any theory, they are but bad discerners of verity; and in the numerous track of Error, but casually do hit the point and unity of truth.

### Arguments of Sensitive Quality Most Prevailing upon Vulgar Capacities

Their understanding is so feeble in the discernment of falsities, and averting the Errors of reason, that it submitteth unto the fallacies of sense, and is unable to rectifie the Error of its sensations. Thus the greater part of Mankind having but one eye of Sense and Reason, conceive the Earth far bigger than the Sun, the fixed Stars lesser than the Moon, their figures plain, and their spaces from Earth equidistant. For thus their Sense informeth them, and herein their reason cannot Rectifie them; and therefore hopelessly continuing in mistakes, they live and die in their absurdities; passing their days in perverted apprehensions, and conceptions of the World, derogatory unto God, and the wisdom of the Creation.

Again, being so illiterate in the point of intellect, and their sense so incorrected, they are farther indisposed ever to attain unto truth; as commonly proceeding in those wayes, which have most reference unto sense, and wherein there lyeth most notable and popular delusion.

## Of Credulity and Supinity

A third cause of common Errors is the Credulity of men, that is, an easie assent to what is obtruded, or a believing at first ear, what is delivered by others. This is a weakness in the understanding, without examination assenting unto things, which from their Natures and Causes do carry no perswasion; whereby men often swallow falsities for truths, dubiosities for certainties, feasibilities for possibilities, and things impossible as possibilities themselves. Which, though the weakness of the Intellect, and most discoverable in vulgar heads; yet hath it sometime fallen upon wiser brains, and great advancers of Truth. Thus many wise Athenians so far forgot their Philosophy, and the nature of humane production, that they descended unto belief, that the original of their Nation was from the Earth, and had no other beginning then the seminality and womb of their great Mother. Thus is it not without wonder, how those learned Arabicks so tamely delivered up their belief unto the absurdities of the Alcoran. How the noble Geber, Avicenna, and Almanzor, should rest satisfied in the nature and causes of Earthquakes, delivered from the doctrine of their Prophet; that is, from the motion of a great Bull, upon whose horns all the earth is poised. How their faiths could decline so low, as to concede their generations in Heaven to be made by the smell of a Citron, or that the felicity of their Paradise should consist in a Jubile of copulation, that is, a coition of one act prolonged unto fifty years. Thus is it almost beyond wonder, how the belief of reasonable creatures, should ever submit unto Idolatry: and the credulity of those men scarce credible (without presumption of a second Fall) who could believe a Deity in the work of their own hands. For although in that ancient and diffused adorations of Idols, unto the Priests and subtiler heads, the worship perhaps might be symbolical, and as those Images some way related unto their Deities; yet was the Idolatry direct and down-right in the people; whose credulity is illimitable, who may be made believe that any thing is God; and may be made believe there is no God at all.

### Obstinate and Irrational Scepticism, Justly Censured

And as credulity is the cause of Error, so Incredulity oftentimes of not enjoying truth: and that not only an obstinate incredulity, whereby we will not acknowledge assent unto what is reasonably inferred, but any Academical reservation in matters of easie truth, or rather sceptical infidelity against the evidence of reason and sense. For these are conceptions befalling wise men, as absurd as the apprehensions of fools, and the credulity of the people which promiscuously swallow any thing. For this is not only derogatory unto the wisdom of God, who hath proposed the World unto our knowledge, and thereby the notion of Himself; but also detractory unto the intellect, and sense of man expressedly disposed for that inquisition. And therefore, *hoc tantum scio, quod nihil scio,* is not to be received in an absolute sense, but is comparatively expressed unto the number of things whereof our knowledg is ignorant. Nor will it acquit the insatisfaction of those which quarrel with all things, or dispute of matters, concerning whose verities we have conviction from reason, or decision form the inerrable and requisite conditions of sense. And therefore if any affirm, the earth doth move, and will not believe with us, it standeth still; because he hath probable reasons for it, and I no infallible sense, nor reason against it, I will not quarrel with his assertion. But if, like Zeno, he shall walk about, and yet deny there is any motion in Nature, surely that man was constituted for Anticera, and were a fit companion for those, who having a conceit they are dead, cannot be convicted into the society of the living. . . .

## Of Adherence unto Antiquity

### Immoderate Respect unto Antiquity, a General Cause of Error

But the mortallest enemy unto Knowledge, and that which hath done the greatest execution upon truth, hath been a peremptory adhesion unto Authority, and more especially, the establishing of our belief upon the dictates of Antiquity. For (as every capacity may observe) most men of Ages present, so superstitiously do look on Ages past, that the Authorities of the one exceed the reasons of the other: Whose persons indeed being far removed from our times, their works, which seldom with us pass uncontrouled, either by contemporaries, or immediate successors, are now become out of the distance of Envies: and the farther removed from present times, are conceived to approach the nearer unto truth it self. Now hereby methinks we manifestly delude our selves, and widely walk out of the track of Truth. . . .

## Of Sex in Hares

The double sex of single Hares, or that every Hare is both male and female, beside the vulgar opinion, was the affirmative of Archelaus, of Plutarch, Philostratus, and many more. Of the same belief have been the Jewish Rabbins: the same is likewise confirmed from the Hebrew word; which, as though there were no single males of that kind, hath only obtained a name of the feminine gender. As also from the symbolical foundation of its prohibition in the law, and what vices therein are figured; that is, not only pusillanimity and timidity from its temper, feneration or usury from its fœcundity and superfetation; but from this mixture of sexes, unnatural venery and degenerous effemination. Nor are there hardly any who either treat of mutation or mixtion of sexes, who have not left some mention of this point; some speaking positively, others dubiously, and most resigning it unto the enquiry of the Reader. Now hereof to speak distinctly, they must be male and female by mutation and succession of sexes; or else by composition, mixture or union thereof.

### Transmutation of Sexes, viz. of Women into Men, Granted

As for the mutation of sexes, or transition into one another, we cannot deny it in Hares, it being observable in Man. For hereof beside Empedocles or Tiresias, there are not a few examples: and though very few, or rather none which have emasculated or turned women, yet very many who from an esteem or reality of being Women have infallibly proved Men. Some at the first point of their menstruous eruptions, some in the day of their marriage, others many years after: which occasioned disputes at Law, and contestations concerning a restore of the dowry. And that not only mankind, but many other Animals may suffer this transexion, we will not deny, or hold it at all impossible: although I confess by reason of the postick and backward position of the feminine parts in quadrupedes, they can hardly admit the substitution of a protrusion, effectual unto masculine generation; except it be in Retromingents, and such as couple backward.

Nor shall we only concede the succession of sexes in some, but shall not dispute the transition of reputed species in others; that is, a transmutation, or (as Paracelsians term it) Transplantation of one into another. Hereof in perfect Animals of a congenerous seed, or near affinity of natures, examples are not unfrequent, as in Horses, Asses, Dogs, Foxes, Pheasants, Cocks, &c. but in imperfect kinds, and such where the discrimination of sexes is obscure, these transformations are more common: and in some within themselves without commixtion, as particularly, in Caterpillars or Silkworms, wherein there is a visible and triple transfiguration. But in Plants, wherein there is no distinction of sex, these transplantations are conceived more obvious then any; as that of Bailey into Oats, of Wheat into Darnel; and those grains which generally arise among Corn, as Cockle, *Aracus, Ægilops,* and other degenerations; which come up in unexpected shapes, when they want the support and maintenance of the primary and master-forms. And the same do some affirm concerning other Plants in less analogy of figures; as the mutation of Mint into Cresses, Basil into Serpoile, and Turneps into Radishes. In all which, as Severinus conceiveth, there may be equivocal seeds and Hermaphroditical principles, which contain the radicality and power of different forms; thus in the seed of Wheat there lieth obscurely the seminality of Darnel, although in a secondary or inferiour way, and at some distance of production; which nevertheless if it meet with convenient promotion, or a conflux and conspiration of causes more powerful then the other; it then beginneth to edifie in chief, and contemning the superintendent form, produceth the signatures of its self.

Now therefore although we deny not these several mutations, and do allow that Hares may exchange their sex, yet this we conceive doth come to pass but sometimes, and not in that vicissitude or annual alteration as is presumed. That is, from imperfection to perfection, from perfection to imperfection; from female unto male, from male to female again, and so in a circle to both without a permansion in either. For beside the inconceivable mutation of temper, which should yearly alternate the sex; this is injurious unto the order of nature, whose operations do rest in the perfection of their intents; which having once attained, they maintain their accomplished ends, and relapse not again into their progressional imperfections. So if in the minority of natural vigor, the parts of feminality take place; when upon the encrease or growth thereof the masculine appear, the first design of nature is atchieved, and those parts are after maintained.

But surely it much impeacheth this iterated transexion of Hares, if that be true which Cardan and other Physicians affirm, that Transmutation of sex is only so in opinion; and that these transfeminated persons were really men at first; although succeeding years produced the manifesto or evidence of their virilities. Which although intended and formed, was not at first excluded: and that the examples hereof have undergone no real or new transexion, but were Androgynally born, and under some kind of Hermaphrodites. For though Galen do favour the opinion, that the distinctive parts of sexes are only different in Position, that is, inversion or protrusion; yet will this hardly be made out from the Anatomy of those parts. The testicles being so seated in the female, that they admit not of protrusion; and the neck of the matrix wanting those parts which are discoverable in the organ of virility.

The second and most received acception, is, that Hares are male and female by conjunction of both sexes; and such as are found in mankind, Poetically called Hermaphrodites; supposed to be formed from the equality, or *non victorie* of either seed; carrying about them the parts of Man and Woman; although with great variety in perfection, site and ability; not only as Aristotle conceived, with a constant impotency in one; but as later observers affirm, sometimes with ability of either venery. And therefore the providence of some Laws have thought good, that at the years of maturity they should elect one sex, and the errors in the other should suffer a severer punishment. Whereby endeavouring to prevent incontinency, they unawares enjoyned perpetual chastity; for being executive in both parts, and confined unto one, they restrained a natural power, and ordained a partial virginity. Plato and some of the Rabbins proceeded higher; who conceived the first Man an Hermaphrodite; and Marcus Leo the learned Jew, in some sense hath allowed it; affirming that Adam in one *suppositum* without division, contained both Male and Female. And therefore whereas it is said in the text, That *God created man in his own Image, in the Image of God created he him, male and female created he them:* applying the singular and plural unto Adam, it might denote, that in one substance, and in himself he included both sexes, which was after divided, and the female called Woman. The opinion of Aristotle extendeth farther, from whose assertion all men should be Hermaphrodites; for affirming that Women do not spermatize, and confer a place or receptacle rather then essential principles of generation, he deductively includes both sexes in mankind; for from the father proceed not only males and females, but from him also must Hermaphroditical and masculo-feminine generations be derived, and a commixtion of both sexes arise from the seed of one. But the Schoolmen have dealt with that sex more hardly then any other; who though they have not much disputed their generation, yet have they controverted their Resurrection, and raised a querie, whether any at the last day should arise in the sex of Women; as may be observed in the supplement of Aquinas.

### Consisting of Man and Woman

Now as we must acknowledge this Androgynal condition in Man, so can we not deny the like doth happen in beasts. Thus do we read in Pliny, that Neroe's Chariot was drawn by four Hermaphroditical Mares, and Cardan affirms he also beheld one at Antwerp. And thus may we also concede, that Hares have been of both sexes, and some have ocularly confirmed it; but that the whole species or kind should be bisexous or double-sexed, we cannot affirm, who have found the parts of male and female respectively distinct and single in any wherein we have enquired: And the like success had Bacchinus in such as he dissected. And whereas it is conceived, that being an harmless Animal and delectable food unto man, nature hath made them with double sexes, that actively and passively performing they might more numerously increase; we forget an higher providence of nature whereby she especially promotes the multiplication of Hares, which is by superfetation; that is, a conception upon a conception, or an improvement of a second fruit before the first be excluded; preventing hereby the usual intermission and vacant time of generation; which is very common and frequently observable in Hares, mentioned long ago by Aristotle, Herodotus, and Pliny; and we have often observed, that after the first cast, there remain successive conceptions, and other younglings very immature, and far from their term of exclusion.

### Superfetation Possible in Women, and that unto a Perfect Birth

Nor need any man to question this in Hares, for the same we observe doth sometime happen in Women; for although it be true, that upon conception the inward orifice of the matrix exactly closeth, so that it commonly admitteth nothing after; yet falleth it out sometime, that in the act of coition, the avidity of that part dilateth it self, and receiveth a second burden; which if it happen to be near in time unto the first, they do commonly both proceed unto perfection, and have legitimate exclusions, periodically succeeding each other. But if the superfetation be made with considerable intermission, the latter most commonly proves abortive; for the first being confirmed, engrosseth the aliment from the other. How ever therefore the project of Julia, seem very plausible, and that way infallible, when she received not her passengers, before she had taken in her lading, yet was there a fallibility therein: nor indeed any absolute security in the policy of adultery after conception. For the Matrix (which some have called another Animal within us, and which is not subjected unto the law of our will) after reception of its proper Tenant, may yet receive a strange and spurious inmate. As is confirmable by many examples in Pliny; by Larissæa in Hippocrates and that merry one in Plautus urged also by Aristotle: that is, of Iphicles and Hercules, the one begat by Jupiter, the other by Amphitryon upon Alcmæna; as also in those super-conceptions, where one child was like the father, the other like the adulterer, the one favoured the servant, the other resembled the master.

Now the grounds that begat, or much promoted the opinion of a double sex in Hares, might be some little bags or tumours, at first glance representing stones or Testicles, to be found in both sexes about the parts of generation; which men observing in either sex, were induced to believe a masculine sex in both. But to speak properly, these are no Testicles or parts official unto generation, but glandulous substances that seem to hold the nature of Emunctories. For herein may be perceived slender perforations, at which may be expressed a black and fœculent matter. If therefore from these we shall conceive a mixtion of sexes in Hares, with fairer reason we may conclude it in Bevers; whereof both sexes contain a double bag or Tumour in the groin, commonly called the Cod of Castor, as we have delivered before.

Another ground were certain holes or cavities observable about the siedge; which being perceived in Males, made some conceive there might be also a fœmenine nature in them. And upon this very ground, the same opinion hath passed upon the Hyæna, and is declared by Aristotle, and thus translated by Scaliger; *Quod autem aiunt utriusque sexus habere genitalia, falsum est, quod videtur esse fœmineum sub cauda est simile figura fœminino, verum pervium non est;* and thus is it also in Hares, in whom these holes, although they seem to make a deep cavity, yet do they not perforate the skin, nor hold a community with any part of generation: but were (as Pliny delivereth) esteemed the marks of their age, the number of those deciding their number of years. In which opinion what truth there is we shall not contend; for if in other Animals there be authentick notations, if the characters of years be found in the horns of Cows, or in the Antlers of Deer; if we conjecture the age of Horses from joints in their docks, and undeniably presume it from their teeth; we cannot affirm, there is in this conceit, any affront unto nature; although who ever enquireth shall find no assurance therein.

The last foundation was Retromingency or pissing backward; for men observing both sexes to urine backward, or aversly between their legs, they might conceive there was a fœminine part in both; wherein they are deceived by the ignorance of the just and proper site of the Pizzel, or part designed unto the Excretion of urine; which in the Hare holds not the common position, but is aversly seated, and in its distention enclines unto the Coccix or Scut. Now from the nature of this position, there ensueth a necessity of Retrocopulation, which also promoteth the conceit: for some observing them to couple without ascension, have not been able to judge of male or female, or to determine the proper sex in either. And to speak generally, this way of copulation is not appropriate unto Hares, nor is there one, but many ways of coition: according to divers shapes and different conformations. For some couple laterally or sidewise, as Worms: some circularly or by complication, as Serpents: some pronely, that is, by contaction of the ventral parts in both, as Apes, Porcupines, Hedgehogs, and such as are termed *Mollia,* as the Cuttle-fish and the Purple; some mixtly, that is, the male ascending the female, or by application of the ventral parts of the one, unto the postick parts of the other, as most Quadrupeds: Some aversly, as all Crustaceous Animals, Lobsters, Shrimps, and Crevises, and also Retromingents, as Panthers, Tygers, and Hares. This is the constant Law of their Coition, this they observe and transgress not: onely the vitiosity of man hath acted the varieties hereof; nor content with a digression from sex or species, hath in his own kind run thorow the Anomalies of venery; and been so bold, not only to act, but represent to view, the irregular ways of Lust. . . .

## Concerning Weight

That Men weigh heavier dead then alive, if experiment hath not failed us, we cannot reasonably grant. For though the trial hereof cannot so well be made on the body of Man, nor will the difference be sensible in the abate of scruples or dragms, yet can we not confirm the same in lesser Animals, from whence the inference is good; and the affirmative of Pliny saith, that it is true in all. For exactly weighing and strangling a Chicken in the Scales, upon an immediate ponderation, we could discover no sensible difference in weight; but suffering it to lie eight or ten hours, untill it grew perfectly cold, it weighed most sensibly lighter; the like we attempted, and verified in Mice, and performed their trials in Scales, that would turn upon the eighth or tenth part of a grain.

Now whereas some alledge that spirits are lighter substances, and naturally ascending, do elevate and waft the body upward, whereof dead bodies being destitute, contract a greater gravity; although we concede that spirits are light, comparatively unto the body, yet that they are absolutely so, or have no weight at all, we cannot readily allow. For since Philosophy affirmeth, that spirits are middle substances between the soul and body, they must admit of some corpority, which supposeth weight or gravity. Beside, in carcasses warm, and bodies newly disanimated, while transpiration remaineth, there do exhale and breath out vaporous and fluid parts, which carry away some power of gravitation. Which though we allow, we do not make answerable unto living expiration; and therefore the Chicken or Mice were not so light being dead, as they would have been after ten hours kept alive; for in that space a man abateth many ounces. Nor if it had slept, for in that space of sleep, a Man will sometimes abate fourty ounces; nor if it had been in the middle of summer, for then a Man weigheth some pounds less, then in the height of winter; according to experience, and the statick Aphorisms of Sanctorius.

Again, Whereas Men affirm they perceive an addition of ponderosity in dead bodies, comparing them usually unto blocks and stones, whensoever they lift or carry them; this accessional preponderancy is rather in appearance then reality. For being destitute of any motion, they confer no relief unto the Agents, or Elevators; which makes us meet with the same complaints of gravity in animated and living bodies, where the Nerves subside, and the faculty locomotive seems abolished; as may be observed in the lifting or supporting of persons inebriated, Apoplectical, or in Lipothymies and swoundings.

Many are also of opinion, and some learned Men maintain, that Men are lighter after meals then before, and that by a supply and addition of spirits obscuring the gross ponderosity of the aliment ingested; but the contrary hereof we have found in the trial of sundry persons in different sex and ages. And we conceive Men may mistake if they distinguish not the sense of levity unto themselves, and in regard of the scale or decision of trutination. For after a draught of wine, a Man may seem lighter in himself from sudden refection, although he be heavier in the balance, from a corporal and ponderous addition; but a Man in the morning is lighter in the scale, because in sleep some pounds have perspired; and is also lighter unto himself, because he is refected.

And to speak strictly, a Man that holds his breath is weightier while his lungs are full, then upon expiration. For a bladder blown is weightier then one empty, and if it contain a quart, expressed and emptied it will abate about a quarter of a grain. And therefore we somewhat mistrust the experiment of a pumice stone taken up by Montanus, in his Comment upon Avicenna, where declaring how the rarity of parts, and numerosity of pores, occasioneth a lightness in bodies, he affirms that a pumice-stone powdered, is lighter then one entire; which is an experiment beyond our satisfaction; for beside that abatement can hardly be avoided in the Trituration; if a bladder of good capacity will scarce include a grain of air, pumice of three or four dragms, cannot be presumed to contain the hundred part thereof; which will not be sensible upon the exactest beams we use. Nor is it to be taken strictly which is delivered by the learned Lord Verulam, and referred unto further experiment: That a dissolution of Iron in *aqua fortis,* will bear as good weight as their bodies did before, notwithstanding a great deal of wast by a thick vapour that issueth during the working; for we cannot find it to hold neither in Iron nor Copper, which is dissolved with less ebullition; and hereof we made trial in Scales of good exactness: wherein if there be a defect, or such as will not turn upon quarter grains, there may be frequent mistakes in experiments of this nature. That also may be considered which is delivered by Hamerus Poppius, that Antimony calcin'd or reduced to ashes by a burning glass, although it emit a gross and ponderous exhalation, doth rather exceed then abate its former gravity. Nevertheless, strange it is, how very little and almost insensible abatement there will be sometimes in such operations, or rather some encrease, as in the refining of metals, in the test of bone ashes, according to experience: and in a burnt brick, as Monsieur de Clave affirmeth. Mistake may be made in this way of trial, when the Antimony is not weighed immediately upon the calcination; but permitted the air, it imbibeth the humidity thereof, and so repaireth its gravity. . . .

## Of the Picture of Adam and Eve with Navels

Another mistake there may be in the Picture of our first Parents, who after the manner of their posterity are both delineated with a Navel. And this is observable not only in ordinary and stained pieces, but in the Authentick draughts of Urbin, Angelo and others. Which notwithstanding cannot be allowed, except we impute that unto the first cause, which we impose not on the second; or what we deny unto nature, we impute unto Naturity it self; that is, that in the first and most accomplished piece, the Creator affected superfluities, or ordained parts without use or office.

### What the Navel Is, and for What Use

For the use of the Navel is to continue the Infant unto the Mother, and by the vessels thereof to convey its aliment and sustentation. The vessels whereof it consisteth, are the umbilical vein, which is a branch of the Porta, and implanted in the Liver of the Infant; two Arteries likewise arising from the Iliacal branches, by which the Infant receiveth the purer portion of blood and spirits from the mother; and lastly, the Urachos or ligamental passage derived from the bottom of the bladder, whereby it dischargeth the waterish and urinary part of its aliment. Now upon the birth, when the Infant forsaketh the womb, although it dilacerate, and break the involving membranes, yet do these vessels hold, and by the mediation thereof the Infant is connected unto the womb, not only before, but a while also after the birth. These therefore the midwife cutteth off, contriving them into a knot close unto the body of the Infant; from whence ensueth that tortuosity or complicated nodosity we usually call the Navel; occasioned by the colligation of vessels before mentioned. Now the Navel being a part, not precedent, but subsequent unto generation, nativity or parturition, it cannot be well imagined at the creation or extraordinary formation of Adam, who immediately issued from the Artifice of God; nor also that of Eve; who was not solemnly begotten, but suddenly framed, and anomalously proceeded from Adam.

## That Adam and Eve Had Not Navels

And if we be led into conclusions that Adam had also this part, because we behold the same in our selves, the inference is not reasonable; for if we conceive the way of his formation, or of the first animals, did carry in all points a strict conformity unto succeeding productions, we might fall into imaginations that Adam was made without Teeth; or that he ran through those notable alterations in the vessels of the heart, which the Infant suffereth after birth: we need not dispute whether the egg or bird were first; and might conceive that Dogs were created blind, because we observe they are littered so with us. Which to affirm, is to confound, at least to regulate creation unto generation, the first Acts of God, unto the second of Nature; which were determined in that general indulgence, Encrease and Multiply, produce or propagate each other; that is, not answerably in all points, but in a prolonged method according to seminal progression. For the formation of things at first was different from their generation after; and although it had nothing to precede it, was aptly contrived for that which should succeed it. And therefore though Adam were framed without this part, as having no other womb than that of his proper principles, yet was not his posterity without the same: for the seminality of his fabrick contained the power thereof; and was endued with the science of those parts whose predestinations upon succession it did accomplish.

All the Navel therefore and conjunctive part we can suppose in Adam, was his dependency on his Maker, and the connexion he must needs have unto heaven, who was the Son of God. For holding no dependence on any preceding efficient but God; in the act of his production there may be conceived some connexion, and Adam to have been in a momental Navel with his Maker. And although from his carnality and corporal existence, the conjunction seemeth no nearer than of causality and effect; yet in his immortal and diviner part he seemed to hold a nearer coherence, and an umbilicality even with God himself. And so indeed although the propriety of this part be found but in some animals, and many species there are which have no Navel at all; yet is there one link and common connexion, one general ligament, and necessary obligation of all what ever unto God. Whereby although they act themselves at distance, and seem to be at loose; yet do they hold a continuity with their Maker. Which catenation or conserving union when ever his pleasure shall divide, let go, or separate; they shall fall from their existence, essence, and operations: in brief, they must retire unto their primitive nothing, and shrink into their Chaos again. . . .

# HYDRIOTAPHIA, URNE-BURIALL

## CHAPTER III

Playstered and whited Sepulchres, were anciently affected in cadaverous, and corruptive Burials; And the rigid Jews were wont to garnish the Sepulchres of the righteous; Ulysses in Hecuba cared not how meanly he lived, so he might finde a noble Tomb after death. Great Persons affected great Monuments, and the fair and larger Urnes contained no vulgar ashes, which makes that disparity in those which time discovereth among us. The present Urnes were not of one capacity, the largest containing above a gallon, Some not much above half that measure; nor all of one figure, wherein there is no strict conformity, in the same or different Countreys; Observable from those represented by Casalius, Bosio, and others, though all found in Italy: While many have handles, ears, and long necks, but most imitate a circular figure, in a spherical and round composure; whether from any mystery, best duration or capacity, were but a conjecture. But the common form with necks was a proper figure, making our last bed like our first; nor much unlike the Urnes of our Nativity, while we lay in the nether part of the earth, and inward vault of our Microcosme. Many Urnes are red, these but of a black colour, somewhat smooth, and dully sounding, which begat some doubt, whether they were burnt, or onely baked in Oven or Sun: According to the ancient way, in many Bricks, Tiles, Pots, and testaceous works; and as the word *testa* is properly to be taken, when occurring without addition. And chiefly intended by Pliny, when he commendeth Bricks and Tiles of two years old, and to make them in the spring. Nor onely these concealed peeces, but the open magnificence of Antiquity, ran much in the Artifice of Clay. Hereof the house of Mausolus was built, thus old Jupiter stood in the Capitol, and the *Statua* of Hercules made in the Reign of Tarquinius Priscus, was extant in Plinie's dayes. And such as declined burning or Funeral Urnes, affected Coffins of Clay, according to the mode of Pythagoras, and way preferred by Varro. But the spirit of great ones was above these circumscriptions, affecting Copper, Silver, Gold, and Porphyrie Urnes, wherein Severus lay, after a serious view and sentence on that which should contain him. Some of these Urnes were thought to have been silvered over, from sparklings in several pots, with small Tinsel parcels; uncertain whether from the earth, or the first mixture in them.

Among these Urnes we could obtain no good account of their coverings; onely one seemed arched over with some kinde of brickwork. Of those found at Buxton some were covered with flints, some in other parts with Tiles, those at Yarmouth Caster, were closed with Romane bricks. And some have proper earthen covers adapted and fitted to them. But in the Homerical Urne of Patroclus, whatever was the solid Tegument, we finde the immediate covering to be a purple peece of silk: And such as had no covers might have the earth closely pressed into them, after which disposure were probably some of these, wherein we found the bones and ashes half mortered unto the sand and sides of the Urne; and some long roots of Quich, or Dogs-grass wreathed about the bones.

No Lamps, included Liquors, Lachrymatories, or Tear-Bottles attended these rural Urnes, either as sacred unto the *Manes,* or passionate expressions of their surviving friends. While with rich flames, and hired tears they solemnized their Obsequies, and in the most lamented Monuments made one part of their Inscriptions. Some finde sepulchral Vessels containing liquors, which time hath incrassated into gellies. For beside these Lachrymatories, notable Lamps, with Vessels of Oyles and Aromatical Liquors attended noble Ossuaries. And some yet retaining a Vinosity and spirit in them, which if any have tasted they have far exceeded the Palats of Antiquity. Liquors not to be computed by years of annual Magistrates, but by great conjunctions and the fatal periods of Kingdoms. The draughts of Consulary date, were but crude unto these, and Opimian Wine but in the muste unto them.

In sundry graves and Sepulchres, we meet with Rings, Coynes, and Chalices; Ancient frugality was so severe, that they allowed no gold to attend the Corps, but onely that which served to fasten their teeth. Whether the Opaline stone in this Urne were burnt upon the finger of the dead, or cast into the fire by some affectionate friend, it will consist with either custome. But other incinerable substances were found so fresh, that they could feel no sindge from fire. These upon view were judged to be wood, but sinking in water and tried by the fire, we found them to be bone or Ivory. In their hardnesse and yellow colour they most resembled Box, which in old expressions found the Epithete of Eternal, and perhaps in such conservatories might have passed uncorrupted.

That Bay-leaves were found green in the Tomb of S. Humbert, after an hundred and fifty yeers, was looked upon as miraculous. Remarkable it was unto old Spectators, that the Cypresse of the Temple of Diana, lasted so many hundred years: The wood of the Ark and Olive Rod of Aaron were older at the Captivity. But the Cypresse of the Ark of Noah, was the greatest vegetable Antiquity, if Josephus were not deceived, by some fragments of it in his dayes. To omit the Moore-logs, and Firre-trees found under-ground in many parts of England; the undated ruines of winds, flouds or earthquakes; and which in Flanders still shew from what quarter they fell, as generally lying in the North-East position.

But though we found not these peeces to be wood, according to first apprehension, yet we missed not altogether of some woody substance; for the bones were not so clearly pickt, but some coals were found amongst them; A way to make wood perpetual, and a fit associat for metal, whereon was laid the foundation of the great Ephesian Temple, and which were made the lasting tests of old boundaries, and Land-marks; Whilest we look on these we admire not observations of Coals found fresh, after four hundred years. In a long deserted habitation, even Egge-shels have been found fresh, not tending to corruption.

In the Monument of King Childerick, the iron Reliques were found all rusty and crumbling into peeces. But our little iron pins which fas-tened the ivory works, held well together, and lost not their Magneticall quality, though wanting a tenacious moisture for the firmer union of parts; although it be hardly drawn into fusion, yet that metal soon submitteth unto rust and dissolution. In the brazen peeces we admired not the duration, but the freedom from rust, and ill savour upon the hardest attrition; but now exposed unto the piercing Atomes of aire, in the space of a few moneths, they begin to spot and betray their green entrals. We conceive not these Urns to have descended thus naked as they appear, or to have entred their graves without the old habit of flowers. The Urne of Philopœmen was so laden with flowers and ribbons, that it afforded no sight of it self. The rigid Lycurgus allowed Olive and Myrtle. The Athenians might fairely except against the practise of Democritus to be buried up in honey; as fearing to embezzle a great commodity of their Country, and the best of that kinde in Europe. But Plato seemed too frugally politick, who allowed no larger monument then would contain four Heroick verses, and de-signed the most barren ground for sepulture: Though we cannot com-mend the goodnesse of that sepulchral ground, which was set at no higher rate then the mean salary of Judas. Though the earth had con-founded the ashes of these Ossuaries, yet the bones were so smartly burnt, that some thin plates of brasse were found half melted among them: whereby we apprehended they were not of the meanest carcasses, perfunctorily fired as sometimes in military, and commonly in pestilence, burnings; or after the manner of abject corps, huddled forth and care-lesly burnt, without the Esquiline Port at Rome; which was an affront contrived upon Tiberius, while they but half burnt his body, and in the Amphitheater, according to the custome in notable Malefactors; whereas Nero seemed not so much to fear his death, as that his head should be cut off and his body not burnt entire.

Some finding many fragments of sculs in these Urnes, suspected a mixture of bones; In none we searched was there cause of such con-jecture, though sometimes they declined not that practise; The ashes of Domitian were mingled with those of Julia, of Achilles with those of Patroclus: All Urnes contained not single ashes; Without confused burnings they affectionately compounded their bones; passionately endeavouring to continue their living Unions. And when distance of death denied such conjunctions, unsatisfied affections conceived some satisfaction to be neighbours in the grave, to lye Urne by Urne, and touch but in their names. And many were so curious to continue their living relations, that they contrived large, and family Urnes, wherein the Ashes of their nearest friends and kindred might successively be received, at least some parcels thereof, while their collateral memorials lay in minor vessels about them.

Antiquity held too light thoughts from Objects of mortality, while some drew provocatives of mirth from Anatomies, and Juglers shewed tricks with Skeletons. When Fidlers made not so pleasant mirth as Fencers, and men could sit with quiet stomacks while hanging was plaid before them.[1] Old considerations made few *memento's* by sculs and bones upon their monuments. In the Ægyptian Obelisks and Hieroglyphical figures, it is not easie to meet with bones. The sepulchral Lamps speak nothing lesse then sepulture; and in their literal draughts prove often obscene and antick peeces: where we finde *D.M.* it is obvious to meet with sacrificing *patera's,* and vessels of libation, upon old sepulchral monuments. In the Jewish *Hypogæum* and subterranean Cell at Rome, was little observable beside the variety of Lamps, and frequent draughts of the holy Candlestick. In authentick draughts of Anthony and Jerome, we meet with thigh-bones and death's-heads; but the cemiterial Cels of ancient Christians and Martyrs, were filled with draughts of Scripture Stories; not declining the flourishes of Cypresse, Palms and Olive; and the mystical Figures of Peacocks, Doves and Cocks. But iterately affecting the pourtraits of Enoch, Lazarus, Jonas, and the vision of Ezechiel, as hopeful draughts, and hinting imagery of the Resurrection; which is the life of the grave, and sweetens our habitations in the Land of Moles and Pismires.

Gentile inscriptions precisely delivered the extent of men's lives, seldome the manner of their deaths, which history itself so often leaves obscure in the records of memorable persons. There is scarce any Phi-

---

[1] Ἀγχώνην παίζειν, a barbarous pastime at Feasts, when men stood upon a rolling Globe, with their necks in a Rope fastned to a beame, and a knife in their hands, ready to cut it when the stone was rolled away, wherein if they failed, they lost their lives to the laughter of their spectators. Athenæus.

losopher but dies twice or thrice in Laertius; Nor almost any life without two or three deaths in Plutarch; which makes the tragical ends of noble persons more favourably resented by compassionate Readers, who finde some relief in the Election of such differences.

The certainty of death is attended with uncertainties, in time, manner, places. The variety of Monuments hath often obscured true graves: and Cœnotaphs confounded Sepulchres. For beside their real Tombs, many have found honorary and empty sepulchres, The variety of Homer's Monuments made him of various Countreys. Euripides had his Tomb in Africa, but his sepulture in Macedonia. And Severus found his real Sepulchre in Rome, but his empty grave in Gallia.

He that lay in a golden Urne eminently above the earth, was not like to finde the quiet of these bones. Many of these Urnes were broke by a vulgar discoverer in hope of inclosed treasure. The ashes of Marcellus were lost above ground, upon the like account. Where profit hath prompted, no age hath wanted such miners. For which the most barbarous Expilators found the most civil Rhetorick. Gold once out of the earth is no more due unto it; What was unreasonably committed to the ground is reasonably resumed from it: Let Monuments and rich Fabricks, not Riches adorn men's ashes, the commerce of the living is not to be transferred unto the dead: It is not injustice to take that which none complaines to lose, and no man is wronged where no man is possessor.

What virtue yet sleeps in this *terra damnata* and aged cinders, were petty magick to experiment; These crumbling reliques and long fired particles superannuate such expectations: Bones, hairs, nails, and teeth of the dead, were the treasures of old Sorcerers. In vain we revive such practices; Present superstition too visibly perpetuates the folly of our forefathers, wherein unto old Observation this Island was so compleat, that it might have instructed Persia.

Plato's historian of the other world, lies twelve dayes incorrupted, while his soul was viewing the large stations of the dead. How to keep the corps seven dayes from corruption by anointing and washing, without exenteration, were an hazardable peece of art, in our choisest practise. How they made distinct separation of bones and ashes from fiery admixture, hath found no historical solution. Though they seemed to make a distinct collection, and overlooked not Pyrrhus his toe.[2] Some

[2] Which could not be burnt.

provision they might take by fictile Vessels, Coverings, Tiles, or flat stones, upon and about the body. And in the same Field, not far from these Urnes, many stones were found under ground, as also by careful separation of extraneous matter, composing and raking up the burnt bones with forks, observable in that notable lamp of Galvanus. Marlianus, who had the sight of the *Vas Ustrinum,* or vessel wherein they burnt the dead, found in the Esquiline Field at Rome, might have afforded clearer solution. But their insatisfaction herein begat that remarkable invention in the Funeral Pyres of some Princes, by incombustible sheets made with a texture of Asbestos, incremable flax, or Salamanders' wool, which preserved their bones and ashes incommixed.

How the bulk of a man should sink into so few pounds of bones and ashes, may seem strange unto any who considers not its constitution, and how slender a mass will remain upon an open and urging fire of the carnal composition. Even bones themselves reduced into ashes, do abate a notable proportion. And consisting much of a volatile salt, when that is fired out, make a light kind of cinders. Although their bulk be disproportionable to their weight, when the heavy principle of Salt is fired out, and the Earth almost onely remaineth; Observable in sallow, which makes more Ashes then Oake; and discovers the common fraud of selling Ashes by measure, and not by ponderation.

Some bones make best Skeletons,[3] some bodies quick and speediest ashes: Who would expect a quick flame from Hydropical Heraclitus? The poisoned Souldier when his Belly brake, put out two pyres in Plutarch. But in the plague of Athens, one private pyre served two or three Intruders; and the Saracens burnt in large heaps, by the King of Castile, shewed how little Fuel sufficeth. Though the Funeral pyre of Patroclus took up an hundred foot, a peece of an old boat burnt Pompey; And if the burthen of Isaac were sufficient for an holocaust, a man may carry his own pyre.

From animals are drawn good burning lights, and good medicines against burning; Though the seminal humor seems of a contrary nature to fire, yet the body compleated proves a combustible lump, wherein fire findes flame even from bones, and some fuel almost from all parts. Though the Metropolis[4] of humidity seems least disposed unto it, which

---

[3] Old bones according to Lyserus. Those of young persons not tall nor fat according to Columbus.
[4] The brain: Hippocrates.

might render the sculls of these Urnes less burned then other bones. But all flies and sinks before fire almost in all bodies. When the common ligament is dissolved, the attenuable parts ascend, the rest subside in coal, calx or ashes.

To burn the bones of the King of Edom for Lyme, seems no irrational ferity; But to drink of the ashes of dead relations, a passionate prodigality. He that hath the ashes of his friend, hath an everlasting treasure: where fire taketh leave, corruption slowly enters; In bones well burnt, fire makes a wall against it self, experimented in copels, and tests of metals, which consist of such ingredients. What the Sun compoundeth, fire analyseth, not transmuteth. That devouring agent leaves almost alwayes a morsel for the Earth, whereof all things are but a colony; and which, if time permits, the mother Element will have in their primitive mass again.

He that looks for Urnes and old sepulchral reliques, must not seek them in the ruines of Temples: where no Religion anciently placed them. These were found in a Field, according to ancient custome, in noble or private burial; the old practise of the Canaanites, the Family of Abraham, and the burying place of Josua, in the borders of his possessions; and also agreeable unto Romane practice to bury by highwayes, whereby their Monuments were under eye: Memorials of themselves, and *memento's* of mortality unto living passengers; whom the Epitaphs of great ones were fain to beg to stay and look upon them, a language though sometimes used, not so proper in Church-Inscriptions. The sensible Rhetorick of the dead, to exemplarity of good life, first admitted the bones of pious men, and Martyrs within Church-wals; which in succeeding ages crept into promiscuous practise. While Constantine was peculiarly favoured to be admitted unto the Church Porch; and the first thus buried in England was in the dayes of Cuthred.

Christians dispute how their bodies should lye in the grave. In urnal enterrment they clearly escaped this Controversie: Though we decline the Religious consideration, yet in cemeterial and narrow burying places, to avoid confusion and cross position, a certain posture were to be admitted; which even Pagan civility observed. The Persians lay North and South, The Megarians and Phœnicians placed their heads to the East: The Athenians, some think, towards the West, which Christians still retain. And Beda will have it to be the posture of our Saviour. That he was crucified with his face towards the West, we will not contend with tradition and probable account; But we applaud not the hand of the Painter, in exalting his Cross so high above those on either side; since hereof we finde no authentick account in history and even the crosses found by Helena pretend no such distinction from longitude or dimension.

To be gnaw'd out of our graves, to have our sculs made drinking bowls, and our bones turned into Pipes, to delight and sport our Enemies, are Tragical abominations, escaped in burning Burials.

Urnal enterrments, and burnt Reliques lye not in fear of worms, or to be an heritage for Serpents; In carnal sepulture, corruptions seem peculiar unto parts, and some speak of snakes out of the spinal marrow. But while we suppose common wormes in graves, 'tis not easie to finde any there; few in Church-yards above a foot deep, fewer or none in Churches, though in fresh decayed bodies. Teeth, bones, and hair, give the most lasting defiance to corruption. In an Hydropical body ten years buried in a Church yard, we met with a fat concretion, where the nitre of the Earth, and the salt and lixivious liquor of the body, had coagulated large lumps of fat, into the consistence of the hardest Castle-soap; whereof part remaineth with us. After a battle with the Persians, the Romane Corps decayed in a few dayes, while the Persian bodies remained dry and uncorrupted. Bodies in the same ground do not uniformly dissolve, nor bones equally moulder; whereof in the opprobrious disease we expect no long duration. The body of the Marquess of Dorset seemed sound and handsomely cereclothed, that after seventy-eight years was found uncorrupted.[5] Common Tombs preserve not beyond powder: A firmer consistence and compage of parts might be expected from Arefaction, deep burial or Charcoal. The greatest Antiquities of mortal bodies may remain in petrified bones, whereof, though we take not in the pillar of Lot's wife, or Metamorphosis of Ortelius, some may be older then Pyramids, in the petrified Reliques of the general inundation.[6] When Alexander opened the Tomb of Cyrus, the remaining bones discovered his proportion, whereof urnal fragments afford but a bad conjecture, and have this disadvantage of grave enterrments, that they leave us ignorant of most personal discoveries. For since bones afford

---

[5] Of Thomas Marquesse of Dorset, whose body being buried 1530, was 1608 upon the cutting open of the Cerecloth found perfect and nothing corrupted, the flesh not hardened, but in colour, proportion, and softnesse like an ordinary corps newly to be interred. Burton's *descript. of Leicestershire*.

[6] Wherein great numbers of men, oxen, and sheep were petrified.

not only rectitude and stability, but figure unto the body; It is no impossible Physiognomy to conjecture at fleshly appendencies; and after what shape the muscles & carnous parts might hang in their full consistences. A full spread *Cariola*[7] shews a well-shaped horse behinde, handsome formed sculls, give some analogy of flesh resemblance. A critical view of bones makes a good distinction of sexes. Even colour is not beyond conjecture, since it is hard to be deceived in the distinction of Negro's sculls.[8] Dante's[9] Characters are to be found in sculls as well as faces. Hercules is not onely known by his foot. Other parts make out their comproportions, and inferences upon whole, or parts. And since the dimensions of the head measure the whole body, and the figure thereof gives conjecture of the principal faculties; Physiognomy outlives our selves, and ends not in our graves.

Severe contemplators observing these lasting reliques, may think them good monuments of persons past, little advantage to future beings. And considering that power which subdueth all things unto it self, that can resume the scattered Atomes, or identifie out of any thing, conceive it superfluous to expect a resurrection out of Reliques. But the soul subsisting, other matter clothed with due accidents, may salve the individuality: Yet the Saints we observe arose from graves and monuments, about the holy City. Some think the ancient Patriarchs so earnestly desired to lay their bones in Canaan, as hoping to make a part of that Resurrection, and though thirty miles from Mount Calvary, at least to lie in that Region, which should produce the first-fruits of the dead. And if according to learned conjecture, the bodies of men shall rise where their greatest Reliques remain, many are not like to erre in the Topography of their Resurrection, though their bones or bodies be after translated by Angels into the field of Ezechiel's vision, or as some will order it, into the Valley of Judgement, or Jehosaphat.

[7] That part in the Skeleton of an Horse, which is made by the haunch-bones.
[8] For their extraordinary thicknesse.
[9] The Poet Dante in his view of Purgatory, found gluttons so meagre, and extenuated, that he conceited them to have been in the Siege of Jerusalem, and that it was easie to have discovered *Homo* or *Omo* in their faces: M being made by the two lines of their cheeks, arching over the Eyebrows to the nose, and their sunk eyes making O O which makes up *Omo*.

*Parean l'occhiaie anella sanza gemme:*
*Chi nel viso degli huomini legge huomo,*
*Ben havria quivi conosciuto l'emme.*

## CHAPTER IV

Christians have handsomely glossed the deformity of death, by careful consideration of the body, and civil rites which take off brutal terminations. And though they conceived all reparable by a resurrection, cast not off all care of enterrment. For since the ashes of Sacrifices burnt upon the Altar of God, were carefully carried out by the Priests, and deposed in a clean field; since they acknowledged their bodies to be the lodging of Christ, and temples of the holy Ghost, they devolved not all upon the sufficiency of soul existence; and therefore with long services and full solemnities concluded their last Exequies, wherein to all distinctions the Greek devotion seems most pathetically ceremonious.

Christian invention hath chiefly driven at Rites, which speak hopes of another life, and hints of a Resurrection. And if the ancient Gentiles held not the immortality of their better part, and some subsistence after death; in several rites, customes, actions and expressions, they contradicted their own opinions: wherein Democritus went high, even to the thought of a resurrection, as scoffingly recorded by Pliny. What can be more express than the expression of Phocyllides? Or who would expect from Lucretius a sentence of Ecclesiastes? Before Plato could speak, the soul had wings in Homer, which fell not, but flew out of the body into the mansions of the dead; who also observed that handsome distinction of *Demas* and *Soma,* for the body conjoyned to the soul, and body separated from it. Lucian spoke much truth in jest, when he said, that part of Hercules which proceeded from Alchmena perished, that from Jupiter remained immortal. Thus Socrates[1] was content that his friends should bury his body, so they would not think they buried Socrates, and regarding onely his immortal part, was indifferent to be burnt or buried. From such Considerations Diogenes might contemn Sepulture. And being satisfied that the soul could not perish, grow careless of corporal enterrment. The Stoicks who thought the souls of wise men had their habitation about the Moon, might make slight account of subterraneous deposition; whereas the Pythagorians and transcorporating Philosophers, who were to be often buried, held great care of their enterrment. And the Platonicks rejected not a due care of the grave, though

[1] Plato in *Phæd.*

they put their ashes to unreasonable expectations, in their tedious term of return and long set revolution.

Men have lost their reason in nothing so much as their Religion, wherein stones and clouts make Martyrs; and since the Religion of one seems madness unto another, to afford an account or rational of old Rites, requires no rigid Reader; That they kindled the pyre aversly, or turning their face from it, was an handsome Symbole of unwilling ministration; That they washed their bones with wine and milk, that the mother wrapt them in Linnen, and dryed them in her bosome, the first fostering part, and place of her nourishment; That they opened their eyes towards heaven before they kindled the fire, as the place of their hopes or original, were no improper Ceremonies. Their last valediction[2] thrice uttered by the attendants was also very solemn and somewhat answered by Christians, who thought it too little, if they threw not the earth thrice upon the enterred body. That in strewing their Tombs the Romanes affected the Rose, the Greeks *Amaranthus* and myrtle; that the Funeral pyre consisted of sweet fuel, Cypress, Firre, *Larix,* Yewe, and Trees perpetually verdant, lay silent expressions of their surviving hopes: Wherein Christians which deck their Coffins with Bays have found a more elegant Embleme. For that tree seeming dead, will restore it self from the root, and its dry and exuccous leaves resume their verdure again; which if we mistake not, we have also observed in Furze. Whether the planting of Yewe in Churchyards, hold not its original from ancient Funeral Rites, or as an Embleme of Resurrection from its perpetual verdure, may also admit conjecture.

They made use of Musick to excite or quiet the affections of their friends, according to different harmonies. But the secret and symbolical hint was the harmonical nature of the soul; which delivered from the body went again to enjoy the primitive harmony of heaven, from whence it first descended; which according to its progresse traced by antiquity, came down by *Cancer,* and ascended by *Capricornus.*

They burnt not children before their teeth appeared, as apprehending their bodies too tender a morsel for fire, and that their gristly bones would scarce leave separable relicks after the pyral combustion. That they kindled not fire in their houses for some dayes after, was a strict memorial of the late afflicting fire. And mourning without hope, they

[2] *Vale, vale, vale, nos te ordine quo natura permittet sequamur.*

had an happy fraud against excessive lamentation, by a common opinion that deep sorrows disturbed their ghosts.

That they buried their dead on their backs, or in a supine position, seems agreeable unto profound sleep, and common posture of dying; contrary to the most natural way of birth; Nor like our pendulous posture, in the doubtful state of the womb. Diogenes was singular, who preferred a prone situation in the grave, and some Christians like neither, who declined the figure of rest, and make choice of an erect posture.

That they carried them out of the world with their feet forward, not inconsonant unto reason: As contrary unto the native posture of man, and his production first into it. And also agreeable unto their opinions, while they bid adieu unto the world, not to look again upon it; whereas Mahometans who think to return to a delightful life again, are carried forth with their heads forward, and looking towards their houses.

They closed their eyes as parts which first die or first discover the sad effects of death. But their iterated clamations to excitate their dying or dead friends, or revoke them unto life again, was a vanity of affection; as not presumably ignorant of the critical tests of death, by apposition of feathers, glasses, and reflexion of figures, which dead eyes represent not, which however not strictly verifiable in fresh and warm cadavers, could hardly elude the test, in corps of four or five dayes.[3]

That they sucked in the last breath of their expiring friends, was surely a practice of no medical institution, but a loose opinion that the soul passed out that way, and a fondnesse of affection from some Pythagorical foundation, that the spirit of one body passed into another; which they wished might be their own.

That they powred oyle upon the pyre, was a tolerable practise, while the intention rested in facilitating the accension; But to place good Omens in the quick and speedy burning, to sacrifice unto the winds for a dispatch in this office, was a low form of superstition.

The Archimime or Jester attending the Funeral train, and imitating the speeches, gesture, and manners of the deceased, was too light for such solemnities, contradicting their funeral Orations, and doleful rites of the grave.

That they buried a peece of money with them as a Fee of the Elysian

---

[3] At least by some difference from living eyes.

Ferriman, was a practise full of folly. But the ancient custome of placing coynes in considerable Urnes, and the present practise of burying medals in the Noble Foundations of Europe, are laudable wayes of historical discoveries, in actions, persons, Chronologies; and posterity will applaud them.

We examine not the old Laws of Sepulture, exempting certain persons from burial or burning. But hereby we apprehend that these were not the bones of persons Planet-struck or burnt with fire from Heaven: No Relicks of Traitors to their countrey, Self-killers, or Sacrilegious Malefactors; Persons in old apprehension unworthy of the earth; condemned unto the Tartarus of Hell, and bottomlesse pit of Pluto, from whence there was no redemption.

Nor were onely many customes questionable in order to their Obsequies, but also sundry practises, fictions, and conceptions, discordant or obscure, of their state and future beings; whether unto eight or ten bodies of men to adde one of a woman, as being more inflammable, and unctuously constituted for the better pyrall combustion, were any rational practise; Or whether the compliant of Periander's Wife be tolerable, that wanting her funeral burning she suffered intolerable cold in Hell, according to the constitution of the infernal house of Pluto, wherein cold makes a great part of their tortures; it cannot passe without some question.

Why the Female Ghosts appear unto Ulysses, before the Heroes and masculine spirits? Why the *Psyche* or soul of Tiresias is of the masculine gender; who being blinde on earth sees more then all the rest in hell; Why the Funeral Suppers consisted of Egges, Beans, Smallage, and Lettuce, since the dead are made to eat Asphodels about the Elyzian medows? Why since there is no Sacrifice acceptable, nor any propitiation for the Covenant of the grave; men set up the Deity of *Morta,* and fruitlesly adored Divinities without ears? it cannot escape some doubt.

The dead seem all alive in the humane Hades of Homer, yet cannot well speak, prophesie, or know the living, except they drink blood, wherein is the life of man. And therefore the soules of Penelope's Paramours conducted by Mercury chiriped like bats, and those which followed Hercules made a noise but like a flock of birds.

The departed spirits know things past and to come, yet are ignorant of things present. Agamemnon fortels what should happen unto Ulysses, yet ignorantly enquires what is become of his own Son. The ghosts are afraid of swords in Homer, yet Sybilla tells Æneas in Virgil, the thin habit of spirits was beyond the force of weapons. The spirits put off their malice with their bodies, and Cæsar and Pompey accord in Latine Hell, yet Ajax in Homer endures not a conference with Ulysses: And Deiphobus appears all mangled in Vergil's Ghosts, yet we meet with perfect shadows among the wounded ghosts of Homer.

Since Charon in Lucian applauds his condition among the dead, whether it be handsomely said of Achilles, that living contemner of death, that he had rather be a plowman's servant then Emperour of the dead? How Hercules his soul is in hell, and yet in heaven, and Julius his soul in a Star, yet seen by Æneas in hell, except the Ghosts were but images and shadows of the soul, received in higher mansions, according to the ancient division of body, soul, and image or *simulachrum* of them both. The particulars of future beings must needs be dark unto ancient Theories, which Christian Philosophy yet determines but in a Cloud of Opinions. A Dialogue between two Infants in the womb concerning the state of this world, might handsomly illustrate our ignorance of the next, whereof methinks we yet discourse in Plato's den, and are but Embryon Philosophers.

Pythagoras escapes in the fabulous hell of Dante, among that swarm of Philosophers, wherein whilest we meet with Plato and Socrates, Cato is to be found in no lower place then purgatory. Among all the set, Epicurus is most considerable, whom men make honest without an Elyzium, who contemned life without encouragement of immortality, and making nothing after death, yet made nothing of the King of terrours.

Were the happinesse of the next world as closely apprehended as the felicities of this, it were a martyrdome to live; and unto such as consider none hereafter, it must be more then death to die, which makes us amazed at those audacities, that durst be nothing, and return into their Chaos again. Certainly such spirits as could contemn death, when they expected no better being after, would have scorned to live had they known any. And therefore we applaud not the judgement of Machiavel, that Christianity makes men cowards, or that with the confidence of but half dying, the despised vertues of patience & humility, have abased the spirits of men, which Pagan principles exalted, but rather regulated the wildnesse of audacities, in the attempts, grounds, and eternal sequels of death, wherein men of the boldest spirits are often prodigiously temerarious. Nor can we extenuate valour of ancient Martyrs, who contemned death in the uncomfortable scene of their lives, and in their decrepit Martyrdomes did probably lose not many moneths of their dayes, or parted with life when it was scarce worth the living. For (beside that long time past holds no consideration unto a slender time to come) they had no small disadvantage from the constitution of old age, which naturally makes men fearful; complexionally superannuated from the bold and couragious thoughts of youth and fervent years. But the contempt of death from corporal animosity, promoteth not our felicity. They may set in the Orchestra, and noblest Seats of Heaven, who have held up shaking hands in the fire, and humanely contended for glory.

Mean while Epicurus lies deep in Dante's hell, wherein we meet with Tombs enclosing souls which denied their immortalities. But whether the virtuous heathen, who lived better than he spake, or erring in the principle of himself, yet lived above Philosophers of more specious Maximes, lie so deep as he is placed; at least so low as not to rise against Christians, who beleeving or knowing that truth, have lastingly denied it in their practise and conversation, were a quæry too sad to insist on.

But all or most apprehensions rested in Opinions of some future being, which ignorantly or coldly beleeved, beget those perverted conceptions, Ceremonies, Sayings, which Christians pity or laugh at. Happy are they, which live not in that disadvantage of time, when men could say little for futurity, but from reason. Whereby the noblest mindes fell often upon doubtful deaths, and melancholly Dissolutions; With these hopes Socrates warmed his doubtful spirits, against that cold potion, and Cato before he durst give the fatal stroak, spent part of the night in reading the immortality of Plato, thereby confirming his wavering hand unto the animosity of that attempt.

It is the heaviest stone that melancholy can throw at a man, to tell him he is at the end of his nature; or that there is no further state to come, unto which this seemes progressional, and otherwise made in vain; Without this accomplishment the natural expectation and desire of such a state, were but a fallacy in nature. Unsatisfied Considerators would quarrel the justice of their constitutions, and rest content that Adam had fallen lower, whereby by knowing no other Original, and deeper ignorance of themselves, they might have enjoyed the happinesse of inferiour Creatures who in tranquility possess their constitutions, as having not the apprehension to deplore their own natures. And being framed below the circumference of these hopes, or cognition of better being, the wisdom of God hath necessitated their contentment: But the superiour ingredient and obscured part of our selves, whereunto all present felicities afford no resting contentment, will be able at last to tell us we are more then our present selves; and evacuate such hopes in the fruition of their own accomplishments.

## CHAPTER V

Now since these dead bones have already out-lasted the living ones of Methuselah, and in a yard under ground, and thin walls of clay, out-worn all the strong and specious buildings above it; and quietly rested under the drums and tramplings of three conquests; What Prince can promise such diuturnity unto his Reliques, or might not gladly say,

*Sic ego componi versus in ossa velim.* (TIBULLUS)

Time which antiquates Antiquities, and hath an art to make dust of all things, hath yet spared these minor monuments. In vain we hope to be known by open and visible conservatories, when to be unknown was the means of their continuation, and obscurity their protection: If they dyed by violent hands, and were thrust into their Urnes, these bones become considerable, and some old Philosophers would honour them, whose soules they conceived most pure, which were thus snatched from their bodies; and to retain a stronger propension unto them: whereas they weariedly left a languishing corps, and with faint desires of re-union. If they fell by long and aged decay, yet wrapt up in the bundle of time, they fall into indistinction, and make but one blot with infants. If we begin to die when we live, and long life be but a pro- longation of death; our life is a sad composition; we live with death, and die not in a moment. How many pulses made up the life of Methu- selah, were work for Archimedes: Common Counters sum up the life of Moses his name.[1] Our dayes become considerable like petty sums

---

[1] In the Psalme of Moses.

by minute accumulations; where numerous fractions make up but small round numbers; and our dayes of a span long make not one little finger.[2]

If the nearnesse of our last necessity, brought a nearer conformity unto it, there were a happinesse in hoary hairs, and no calamity in half senses. But the long habit of living indisposeth us for dying; When Avarice makes us the sport of death; When even David grew politickly cruel; and Solomon could hardly be said to be the wisest of men. But many are too early old, and before the date of age. Adversity stretcheth our dayes, misery makes Alcmena's nights,[3] and time hath no wings unto it. But the most tedious being is that which can unwish it self, content to be nothing, or never to have been, which was beyond the *male*-content of Job, who cursed not the day of his life, but his nativity: Content to have so far been, as to have a title to future being; Although he had lived here but in an hidden state of life, and as it were an abortion.

What Song the Syrens sang, or what name Achilles assumed when he hid himself among women, though puzling questions are not beyond all conjecture. What time the persons of these Ossuaries entred the famous Nations of the dead, and slept with Princes and Counsellors, might admit a wide solution. But who were the proprietaries of these bones, or what bodies these ashes made up, were a question above Antiquarism; not to be resolved by man, nor easily perhaps by spirits, except we consult the Provincial Guardians, or tutelary observators. Had they made as good provision for their names, as they have done for their Reliques, they had not so grosly erred in the art of perpetuation. But to subsist in bones, and be but Pyramidally extant, is a fallacy in duration. Vain ashes, which in the oblivion of names, persons, times and sexes, have found unto themselves, a fruitlesse continuation, and onely arise unto late posterity, as Emblemes of mortal vanities; Antidotes against pride, vainglory, and madding vices. Pagan vainglories which thought the world might last for ever, had encouragement for ambition, and finding an *Atropos* unto the immortality of their names, were never dampt with the necessity of oblivion. Even old ambitions had the

---

[2] According to the ancient Arithmetick of the hand wherein the little finger of the right hand contracted, signified an hundred. Pierius in *Hieroglyph*.

[3] One night as long as three.

advantage of ours, in the attempts of their vainglories, who acting early, and before the probable Meridian of time, have by this time found great accomplishment of their designes, whereby the ancient Heroes have already outlasted their Monuments, and Mechanical preservations. But in this latter Scene of time we cannot expect such Mummies unto our memories, when ambition may fear the Prophecy of Elias,[4] and Charles the fift can never hope to live within two Methusela's of Hector.[5]

And therefore restlesse inquietude for the diuturnity of our memories unto present considerations, seemes a vanity almost out of date, and superannuated peece of folly. We cannot hope to live so long in our names, as some have done in their persons, one face of Janus holds no proportion to the other. 'Tis too late to be ambitious. The great muta-tions of the world are acted, or time may be too short for our designes. To extend our memories by Monuments, whose death we dayly pray for, and whose duration we cannot hope, without injury to our expecta-tions, in the advent of the last day, were a contradiction to our beliefs. We whose generations are ordained in this setting part of time, are providentially taken off from such imaginations. And being necessitated to eye the remaining particle of futurity, are naturally constituted unto thoughts of the next world, and cannot excusably decline the considera-tion of that duration, which maketh Pyramids pillars of snow, and all that's past a moment.

Circles and right lines limit and close all bodies, and the mortal right-lined-circle[6] must conclude and shut up all. There is no antidote against the Opium of time, which temporally considereth all things; Our fathers finde their graves in our short memories, and sadly tell us how we may be buried in our Survivors. Grave-stones tell truth scarce fourty yeers[7] : Generations passe while some trees stand, and old Families last not three Oakes. To be read by bare inscriptions like many in Gruter,[8] to hope for Eternity by Ænigmatical Epithetes, or first letters of our names, to be studied by Antiquaries, who we were, and have new

---

[4] That the world may last but six thousand years.
[5] Hector's fame lasting above two lives of Methuselah, before that famous Prince was extant.
[6] Θ The Character of death.
[7] Old ones being taken up, and other bodies laid under them.
[8] *Gruteri Inscriptiones Antiquæ.*

Names given us like many of the Mummies,[9] are cold consolations unto the Students of perpetuity, even by everlasting Languages.

To be content that times to come should onely know there was such a man, not caring whether they knew more of him, was a frigid ambition in Cardan: disparaging his horoscopal inclination and judgement of himself, who cares to subsist like Hippocrates' Patients, or Achilles' horses in Homer, under naked nominations, without deserts and noble acts, which are the balsame of our memories, the Entelechia and soul of our subsistences. To be namelesse in worthy deeds exceeds an infamous history. The Canaanitish woman lives more happily without a name, then Herodias with one. And who had not rather have been the good theef, then Pilate?

But the iniquity of oblivion blindly scattereth her poppy, and deals with the memory of men without distinction to merit of perpetuity. Who can but pity the founder of the Pyramids? Herostratus lives that burnt the Temple of Diana, he is almost lost that built it. Time hath spared the Epitaph of Adrian's horse, confounded that of himself. In vain we compute our felicities by the advantage of our good names, since bad have equal durations; and Thersites is like to live as long as Agamemnon. Who knows whether the best of men be known? or whether there be not more remarkable persons forgot, then any that stand remembred in the known account of time? Without the favour of the everlasting register the first man had been as unknown as the last, and Methusclah's long life had been his only Chronicle.

Oblivion is not to be hired: The greater part must be content to be as though they had not been, to be found in the register of God, not in the record of man. Twenty seven names make up the first story,[10] and the recorded names ever since contain not one living Century. The number of the dead long exceedeth all that shall live. The night of time far surpasseth the day, and who knows when was the Æquinox? Every houre addes unto that current Arithmetique, which scarce stands one moment. And since death must be the Lucina of life, and even Pagans could doubt whether thus to live, were to die; Since our longest Sun sets at right descensions, and makes but winter arches, and there-

[9] Which men show in several Countries, giving them what names they please; and unto some the names of the old Ægyptian Kings out of Herodotus.
[10] Before the flood.

fore it cannot be long before we lie down in darknesse, and have our light in ashes,[11] Since the brother of death daily haunts us with dying *memento's,* and time that grows old it self, bids us hope no long duration: Diuturnity is a dream and folly of expectation.

Darknesse and light divide the course of time, and oblivion shares with memory, a great part even of our living beings; we slightly remember our felicities, and the smartest stroaks of affliction leave but short smart upon us. Sense endureth no extremities, and sorrows destroy us or themselves. To weep into stones are fables. Afflictions induce calosities; miseries are slippery, or fall like snow upon us, which notwithstanding is no unhappy stupidity. To be ignorant of evils to come, and forgetful of evils past, is merciful provision in nature, whereby we digest the mixture of our few and evil dayes, and, our delivered senses not relapsing into cutting remembrances, our sorrows are not kept raw by the edge of repetitions. A great part of Antiquity contented their hopes of subsistency with a transmigration of their souls: a good way to continue their memories, while having the advantage of plural successions, they could not but act something remarkable in such variety of beings, and enjoying the fame of their passed selves, make accumulation of glory unto their last durations. Others rather then be lost in the uncomfortable night of nothing, were content to recede into the common being, and made one particle of the publick soul of all things, which was no more then to return into their unknown and divine Original again. Ægyptian ingenuity was more unsatisfied, contriving their bodies in sweet consistences, to attend the return of their souls. But all was vanity, feeding the winde, and folly. The Ægyptian Mummies, which Cambyses or time hath spared, avarice now comsumeth. Mummie is become Merchandise, Mizraim cures wounds, and Pharoah is sold for balsams.

In vain do individuals hope for immortality, or any patent from oblivion, in preservations below the Moon: Men have been deceived even in their flatteries above the Sun, and studied conceits to perpetuate their names in heaven. The various Cosmography of that part hath already varied the names of contrived constellations; Nimrod is lost in Orion, and Osyris in the Dogge-star. While we look for incorruption in the heavens, we finde they are but like the Earth; Durable in their

---

[11] According to the custome of the Jewes, who place a lighted wax-candle in a pot of ashes by the corps. Leo [of Modena].

main bodies, alterable in their parts: whereof beside Comets and new Stars, perspectives begin to tell tales. And the spots that wander about the Sun, with Phæton's favour, would make clear conviction.

There is nothing strictly immortal, but immortality; whatever hath no beginning may be confident of no end (all others have a dependent being, and within the reach of destruction); which is the peculiar of that necessary essence that cannot destroy it self; And the highest strain of omnipotency to be so powerfully constituted, as not to suffer even from the power of it self. But the sufficiency of Christian Immortality frustrates all earthly glory, and the quality of either state after death makes a folly of posthumous memory. God who can onely destroy our souls, and hath assured our resurrection, either of our bodies or names hath directly promised no duration. Wherein there is so much of chance that the boldest expectants have found unhappy frustration; and to hold long subsistence, seems but a scape in oblivion. But man is a noble Animal, splendid in ashes, and pompous in the grave, solemnizing Nativities and Deaths with equal lustre, nor omitting Ceremonies of bravery, in the infamy of his nature.

Life is a pure flame, and we live by an invisible Sun within us. A small fire sufficeth for life, great flames seemed too little after death, while men vainly affected precious pyres, and to burn like Sardanapalus; but the wisdom of funeral Laws found the folly of prodigal blazes, and reduced undoing fires unto the rule of sober obsequies, wherein few could be so mean as not to provide wood, pitch, a mourner, and an Urne.

Five Languages secured not the Epitaph of Gordianus.[12] The man of God lives longer without a Tomb then any by one, invisibly interred by Angels, and adjudged to obscurity, though not without some marks directing humane discovery. Enoch and Elias without either tomb or burial, in an anomalous state of being, are the great examples of perpetuity, in their long and living memory, in strict account being still on this side death, and having a late part yet to act upon this stage of earth. If in the decretory term of the world we shall not all die but be changed, according to received translation; the last day will make but few graves; at least quick Resurrections will anticipate lasting Sepultures; Some graves will be opened before they be quite closed, and

---

[12] The epitaph of Gordianus in Greek, Latine, Hebrew, Ægyptian, Arabick, defaced by Licinius the Emperour.

Lazarus be no wonder. When many that feared to die shall groan that they can die but once, the dismal state is the second and living death, when life puts despair on the damned; when men shall wish the coverings of Mountains, not of Monuments, and annihilation shall be counted.

While some have studied Monuments, others have studiously declined them: and some have been so vainly boisterous, that they durst not acknowledge their Graves; wherein Alaricus seems most subtle, who had a River turned to hide his bones at the bottome. Even Sylla that thought himself safe in his Urne, could not prevent revenging tongues, and stones thrown at his Monument. Happy are they whom privacy makes innocent, who deal so with men in this world, that they are not afraid to meet them in the next, who when they die, make no commotion among the dead, and are not toucht with that poeticall taunt of Isaiah.[13]

Pyramids, Arches, Obelisks, were but the irregularities of vain-glory, and wilde enormities of ancient magnanimity. But the most magnanimous resolution rests in the Christian Religion, which trampleth upon pride, and sets on the neck of ambition, humbly pursuing that infallible perpetuity, unto which all others must diminish their diameters and be poorly seen in Angles of contingency.[14]

Pious spirits who passed their dayes in raptures of futurity, made little more of this world, then the world that was before it, while they lay obscure in the Chaos of preordination, and night of their fore-beings. And if any have been so happy as truely to understand Christian annihilation, extasis, exolution, liquefaction, transformation, the kisse of the Spouse, gustation of God, and ingression into the divine shadow, they have already had an handsome anticipation of heaven; the glory of the world is surely over, and the earth in ashes unto them.

To subsist in lasting Monuments, to live in their productions, to exist in their names, and prædicament of Chymera's, was large satisfaction unto old expectations and made one part of their Elyziums. But all this is nothing in the Metaphysicks of true belief. To live indeed is to be again our selves, which being not onely an hope but an evidence in noble beleevers, 'tis all one to lie in St. Innocent's[15] Church-yard, as in

[13] Isa. 14.
[14] *Angulus contingentiæ,* the least of Angles.
[15] In Paris where bodies soon consume.

the Sands of Ægypt: Ready to be anything, in the extasie of being ever, and as content with six foot as the Moles of Adrianus.[16]

Lucan
—*Tabesne cadavera solvat*
*An rogus haud refert.*—

**Finis**

[16] A stately Mausoleum or sepulchral pyle built by Adrianus in Rome, where now standeth the Castle of St. Angelo.

# Jeremy Taylor

## 1613–1667

"Jeremy Taylor tumbled out of his mother's womb into the laps of the Muses at Cambridge," and quickly fulfilled the bright promise of his youth, wrote Anthony à Wood:

> . . . his excellent discourses, which are enough of themselves to furnish a library . . . will be famous to all succeeding generations for the exactness of wit, profoundness of judgment, richness of fancy, clearness of expression, copiousness of invention, and general usefulness to all the purposes of a Christian. By which he soon after got a great reputation among all persons of judgment and indifference and his name grew greater still, as the world grew better and wiser.

This was Wood's cheerful estimate, both of Taylor and of the world, not long after Taylor's death. Since Wood's time, except for those Romantics who knew his work and ranked it next to Shakespeare's, Taylor has been more respected than read. He remains one of the master craftsmen of the language, however, and his guidebooks to living and dying still offer much wit and humanity.

The son of a Cambridge barber, Taylor studied at the Perse School and then at Gonville and Caius College, Cambridge. Because he attracted the attention of Archbishop Laud, he was named Fellow of All Souls' College at Oxford, and then Laud's own chaplain. Later he was appointed chaplain to the King, rector of Uppingham, and in 1642 chaplain to the Royalist Army. He was imprisoned by the Parliamentarians in 1645, but after a short time was permitted to retire to Wales as chaplain to the Earl of Carbery. After the Restoration he was named Bishop of Down and Conner, administrator of Dromore, and vice-chancellor of the University of Dublin.

His many works included *The Liberty of Prophesying,* a plea for religious toleration; *Holy Living* and *Holy Dying,* a pair of devotional manuals; and *Ductor Dubitantium,* a massive casebook designed to prove that conscience can be an adequate guide to moral actions. In the manuals particularly, but scattered everywhere in his work, there were threnodies, warnings, a refrain of *contemptus mundi.* But there was also a recurrent lyrical note of delight in the world's varied beauty. Usually his position was latitudinarian, liberal, individualistic. His God was far more often amiable than irate. He defended free will and the "private liberty of persuasion," rejected doctrines of predestination and original sin. He was a Christian humanist, though of the seventeenth and not of the sixteenth century: a dedicated Anglican, committed to the forms and substance of the Church, he was nevertheless willing to accept the Apostles' Creed as the only necessary guide to religious belief, and in the end he met the challenge of skeptics and scientists by sacrificing Hooker's Anglo-Catholic traditions of reason and natural law to the claims of faith, will, and obedience.

His style is distinguished by its copious elegance on the one hand, and by a fresh, forceful directness on the other. His periods tend to be long, his language stately, sensuous, and luxuriant. His cadences are sustained and sinuous. He is richly inventive also in his figures, which range widely in source and play vividly upon his argument. Our sorrows, he writes, are "like ponderous weights, which by the greatness of their burden make a swifter motion, and descend into the grave to rest and ease our wearied limbs." Or man spins in the roulette of fortune:

> . . . a wise man is placed in the variety of chances like the Nave or Centre of a wheel, in the midst of all the circumvolutions and changes of posture, without violence or change, save that it turns gently in complyance with its changed parts, and is indifferent which part is up and which is down. . . .

His sentences are clear, and often terse and crisp: "As our life is very short, so it is very miserable; and therefore it is well it is short." Illustrations and anecdotes are drawn from the most familiar circumstances:

> . . . why art thou troubled at the losse of thy money? what should a damned man do with money . . . ? Did ever any man upon the rack, afflict himself because he had received a crosse answer from his Misstresse? or call for the particulars of a purchase upon the gallows?

If thou doest really believe thou shalt be damned, I do not say it will *cure* the sadnesse of thy poverty, but it will *swallow* it up.

The grace, fullness, and simplicity of Taylor's prose, his love for a world he has learned to value little, the mixture of magnificent formality and wistful charm, may all be seen in the opening paragraphs of *Holy Dying:*

> A man is a bubble . . . men rise up in their several generations, like bubbles descending . . . and some of these instantly sink into the deluge of their first parent, and are hidden in a sheet of water . . . others float up and down two or three turns, and suddenly disappear . . . and they that live longest upon the face of the waters, are in perpetual motion, restless and uneasy; and, being crushed . . . sink into a flatness and a froth. . . .
>
> So is every man . . . he comes into the world like morning mushrooms, soon thrusting up their heads into the air . . . and as soon they turn into dust and forgetfulness . . . others ride longer in the storm . . . and then peradventure the sun shines hot upon their heads, and they fall. . . .
>
> But if the bubble . . . outlives the chances of a child, of a careless nurse, of drowning in a pail of water, of being overlaid by a sleepy servant, or such like accidents, then the young man dances like a bubble, empty and gay, and shines like a dove's neck, or the image of a rainbow . . . and so he dances out the gaiety of his youth . . . and endures only because he is not knocked on the head by a drop of bigger rain, or crushed by the pressure of a load of indigested meat, or quenched by the disorder of an ill-placed humour. . . .
>
> The sum of all is this: that thou art a man, than whom there is not in the world any greater instance of heights and declensions, of lights and shadows, of misery and folly, of laughter and tears, of groans and death.

## EDITIONS

*A Discourse of the Liberty of Prophesying,* 1647; ed. by R. Cattermole, 1834.
*The Great Exemplar of Sanctity and Holy Life,* 1649; 1849.
*The Rule and Exercises of Holy Living,* 1650; Bohn's Standard Library, 1850; ed. by A. R. Waller, 1900; ed. by T. S. Kepler, 1956. *The Rule and Exercises of Holy Dying,* 1651; Bohn's Standard Library, 1850; ed. by T. S. Kepler, 1952.
*XXVIII Sermons Preached at Golden Grove,* 1651; *XXV Sermons,* 1653.
*The Golden Grove, Or a Manuall of Daily Prayers and Letanies,* 1655; 1868.
*A Discourse of the Nature, Offices and Measures of Friendship,* 1657; issued as *Opuscula,* 1675.

*Ductor Dubitantium, Or the Rule of Conscience,* 1660.
*The Whole Works,* ed. by Reginald Heber, 1822; rev. by C. P. Eden, 1847–1854.
*The Poems and Verse-translations of Jeremy Taylor,* ed. by A. B. Grosart, 1870.
*The Golden Grove: Selected Passages from the Sermons and Writings of Jeremy Taylor,* ed. by Logan P. Smith, 1930.
*The House of Understanding: Selections from the Writings of Jeremy Taylor,* ed. (with intr.) by Margaret Gest, 1954.

## HISTORICAL AND CRITICAL STUDIES

EDMUND GOSSE, *Jeremy Taylor,* 1903.
GEORGE WORLEY, *Jeremy Taylor: A Sketch of His Life and Times,* 1904.
FRANK J. POWICKE, "Jeremy Taylor and His Doctrine of Toleration," *Constructive Quar.,* September, 1915.
H. GLICKSMAN, "Figurative Quality in Jeremy Taylor's *Holy Dying,*" *Sewanee Rev.,* XXX (1922).
WILLIAM J. BROWN, *Jeremy Taylor,* 1925.
NEWPORT J. D. WHITE, *Four Good Men,* 1927.
MARJORIE H. NICOLSON, "New Material on Jeremy Taylor," *PQ,* VIII (1929).
W. F. MITCHELL, *English Pulpit Oratory from Andrewes to Tillotson,* 1932.
T. G. STEFFAN, "Jeremy Taylor's Criticism of Abstract Speculation," *Studies in English,* 1940.
SALOME ANTOINE, *The Rhetoric of Jeremy Taylor's Prose,* 1946.
G. B. BENTLEY, "Jeremy Taylor's *Ductor dubitantium,*" *Theology,* L (1947).
ROBERTA F. BRINKLEY, "Coleridge's Criticism of Jeremy Taylor," *HLQ,* XIII (1950).
ROBERT HOOPES, "Voluntarism in Jeremy Taylor and the Platonic Tradition," *HLQ,* XIII (1950).
JAMES T. ADDISON, "Jeremy Taylor, Preacher and Pastor," *Hist. Mag. of the Protestant Episcopal Church,* XXI (1952).
C. J. STRANKS, *The Life and Writings of Jeremy Taylor,* 1952. See also *Church Quar. Rev.,* CXXXI (1940).
MARGARET L. WILEY, "Jeremy Taylor, the Sceptic as Churchman," *The Subtle Knot,* 1952.
HUGH ROSS WILLIAMSON, *Jeremy Taylor,* 1952.
THOMAS WOOD, *English Casuistical Divinity during the Seventeenth Century, with Special Reference to Jeremy Taylor,* 1952.
PAUL ELMEN, "Jeremy Taylor and the Fall of Man," *MLQ,* XIV (1953).
F. R. BOLTON, *The Caroline Tradition of the Church of Ireland, with Particular Reference to Bishop Jeremy Taylor,* 1958.
HENRY T. HUGHES, *The Piety of Jeremy Taylor,* 1960.

# THE RULE AND EXERCISES OF HOLY LIVING

## Sect. I. The First General Instrument of Holy Living, Care of Our Time

He that is choice of his time will also be choice of his company, and choice of his actions; lest the first engage him in vanity and loss; and the latter, by being criminal, be a throwing his time and himself away, and a going back in the accounts of eternity.

God hath given to man a short time here upon earth, and yet upon this short time eternity depends; but so, that for every hour of our life (after we are persons capable of laws, and know good from evil) we must give account to the great Judge of men and angels. And this is it which our blessed Saviour told us, that we must account for every idle word; not meaning, that every word which is not designed to edification, or is less prudent, shall be reckoned for a sin; but that the time which we spend in our idle talking and unprofitable discoursings, that time which might and ought to have been employed to spiritual and useful purposes, that is to be accounted for.

For we must remember, that we have a great work to do, many enemies to conquer, many evils to prevent, much danger to run through, many difficulties to be mastered, many necessities to serve, and much good to do; many children to provide for, or many friends to support, or many poor to relieve, or many diseases to cure; besides the needs of nature and of relation, our private and our public cares, and duties of the world, which necessity and the providence of God have adopted into the family of Religion.

And that we need not fear this instrument to be a snare to us, or that the duty must end in scruple, vexation, and eternal fears, we must remember, that the life of every man may be so ordered (and indeed must) that it may be a perpetual serving of God: the greatest trouble and most busy trade and worldly encumbrances, when they are necessary, or charitable, or profitable in order to any of those ends which we are bound to serve, whether public or private, being a doing God's work. For God provides the good things of the world to serve the needs of nature, by the labours of the ploughman, the skill and pains of the artisan, and the dangers and traffic of the merchant: these men are, in their calling, the ministers of the Divine Providence, and the stewards of the creation, and servants of a great family of God, the world, in the employment of procuring necessaries for food and clothing, ornament, and physic. In their proportions, also, a king, and a priest, and a prophet, a judge, and an advocate, doing the works of their employment accord· ing to their proper rules, are doing the work of God; because they serve those necessities which God hath made, and yet made no provisions for them but by their ministry. So that no man can complain that his calling takes him off from religion; his calling itself, and his very worldly employment in honest trades and offices, is a serving of God; and, if it be moderately pursued, and according to the rules of Christian prudence, will leave void spaces enough for prayers and retirements of a more spiritual religion.

God hath given every man work enough to do, that there shall be no room for idleness; and yet hath so ordered the world, that there shall be space for devotion. He that hath the fewest businesses of the world is called upon to spend more time in the dressing of his soul; and he that hath the most affairs may so order them that they shall be a service of God; whilst at certain periods, they are blessed with prayers and actions of religion, and all day long are hallowed by a holy intention.

However, so long as idleness is quite shut out from our lives, all the sins of wantonness, softness, and effeminacy are prevented, and there is but little room left for temptation; and, therefore, to a busy man temptation is fain to climb up together with his businesses, and sins creep upon him only by accidents and occasions; whereas to an idle person they come in a full body, and with open violence, and the impudence of a restless importunity.

Idleness is called "the sin of Sodom and her daughters," and indeed is "the burial of a living man;" an idle person being so useless to any purposes of God and man, that he is like one that is dead, unconcerned in the changes and necessities of the world; and he only lives to spend his time, and eat the fruits of the earth: like a vermin or a wolf, when their time comes they die and perish, and in the mean time do no good; they neither plough nor carry burdens; all that they do either is unprofitable or mischievous.

Idleness is the greatest prodigality in the world; it throws away that which is invaluable in respect of its present use, and irreparable when it is past, being to be recovered by no power of art or nature. But the way to secure and improve our time we may practise in the following Rules.

## Rules for Employing Our Time

1. In the morning, when you awake, accustom yourself to think first upon God, or something in order to his service; and at night also, let him close thine eyes: and let your sleep be necessary and healthful, not idle and expensive of time, beyond the needs and conveniences of nature; and sometimes be curious to see the preparation which the sun makes, when he is coming forth from his chambers of the east.

2. Let every man that hath a calling be diligent in pursuance of its employment, so as not lightly or without reasonable occasion to neglect it in any of those times which are usually, and by the custom of prudent persons and good husbands employed in it.

3. Let all the intervals or void space of time be employed in prayers, reading, meditating, works of nature, recreation, charity, friendliness and neighbourhood, and means of spiritual and corporal health; ever remembering so to work in our calling, as not to neglect the work of our high calling; but to begin and end the day with God, with such forms of devotion as shall be proper to our necessities.

4. The resting days of Christians, and festivals of the church, must, in no sense, be days of idleness; for it is better to plough upon holy days, than to do nothing or to do viciously: but let them be spent in the works of the day, that is, of religion and charity, according to the rules appointed.

5. Avoid the company of drunkards and busy-bodies, and all such as are apt to talk much to little purpose; for no man can be provident of his time that is not prudent in the choice of his company; and if one of the speakers be vain, tedious, and trifling, he that hears, and he that answers, in the discourse, are equal losers of their time.

6. Never walk with any man, or undertake any trifling employment, merely to pass the time away; for every day well spent may become a "day of salvation," and time rightly employed is an "acceptable time." And remember, that the time thou triflest away was given thee to repent in, to pray for pardon of sins, to work out thy salvation, to do the work of grace, to lay up against the day of judgment a treasure of good works, that thy time may be crowned with eternity.

7. In the midst of the works of thy calling, often retire to God in short prayers and ejaculations; and those may make up the want of those larger portions of time, which, it may be, thou desirest for devotion, and in which thou thinkest other persons have advantage of thee; for so thou reconcilest the outward work and thy inward calling, the church and the commonwealth, the employment of the body and the interest of thy soul: for be sure that God is present at thy breathings and hearty sighings of prayer, as soon as at the longer offices of less busied persons; and thy time is as truly sanctified by a trade, and devout though shorter prayers, as by the longer offices of those whose time is not filled up with labour and useful business.

8. Let your employment be such as may become a reasonable person; and not be a business fit for children or distracted people, but fit for your age and understanding. For a man may be very idly busy, and take great pains to so little purpose, that, in his labours and expense of time, he shall serve no end but of folly and vanity. There are some trades that wholly serve the ends of idle persons and fools, and such as are fit to be seized upon by the severity of laws and banished from under the sun; and there are some people who are busy, but it is, as Domitian was, in catching flies.

9. Let your employment be fitted to your person and calling. Some there are that employ their time in affairs infinitely below the dignity of their person; and, being called by God or by the republic to help to bear great burdens, and to judge a people, do enfeeble their understandings and disable their persons by sordid and brutish business. Thus Nero went up and down Greece, and challenged the fiddlers at their trade. Aeropus, a Macedonian king, made lanterns. Harcatius, the king of Parthia, was a mole-catcher: and Biantes, the Lydian, filed needles. He that is appointed to minister in holy things must not suffer secular affairs and sordid arts to eat up great portions of his employment: a clergyman must not keep a tavern, nor a judge be an innkeeper: and it was a great idleness in Theophylact, the patriarch of C. P., to spend his time in his stable of horses, when he should have been in his study, or the pulpit, or saying his holy offices. Such employments are the diseases of labour, and the rust of time, which it contracts, not by lying still, but by dirty employment.

10. Let our employment be such as becomes a Christian; that is, in no sense mingled with sin: for he that takes pains to serve the ends of covetousness, or ministers to another's lust, or keeps a shop of impurities

or intemperance, is idle in the worst sense: for every hour so spent runs him backward, and must be spent again in the remaining and shorter part of his life, and spent better.

11. Persons of great quality, and of no trade, are to be most prudent and curious in their employment and traffic of time. They are miserable, if their education hath been so loose and undisciplined as to leave them unfurnished of skill to spend their time: but most miserable are they, if such misgovernment and unskilfulness make them fall into vicious and baser company, and drive on their time by the sad minutes and periods of sin and death. They that are learned know the worth of time, and the manner how well to improve a day; and they are to prepare themselves for such purposes, in which they may be most useful in order to arts or arms, to counsel in public, or government in their country; but for others of them, that are unlearned, let them choose good company, such as may not tempt them to a vice, or join with them in any; but that may supply their defects by counsel and discourse, by way of conduct and conversation. Let them learn easy and useful things, read history and the laws of the land, learn the customs of their country, the condition of their own estate, profitable and charitable contrivances of it: let them study prudently to govern their families, learn the burdens of their tenants, the necessities of their neighbours, and in their proportion supply them, and reconcile their enmities, and prevent their lawsuits, or quickly end them; and in this glut of leisure and disemployment, let them set apart greater portions of their time for religion and the necessities of their souls.

12. Let the women of noble birth and great fortunes do the same things in their proportions and capacities; nurse their children, look to the affairs of the house, visit poor cottages, and relieve their necessities; be courteous to the neighbourhood, learn in silence of their husbands or their spiritual guides, read good books, pray often and speak little, and "learn to do good works for necessary uses;" for by that phrase St. Paul expresses the obligation of Christian women to good housewifery, and charitable provisions for their family and neighbourhood.

13. Let all persons of all conditions avoid all delicacy and niceness in their clothing or diet, because such softness engages them upon great misspendings of their time, while they dress and comb out all their opportunities of their morning devotion, and half the day's severity, and sleep out the care and provision for their souls.

14. Let every one of every condition avoid curiosity, and all inquiry

into things that concern them not. For all business in things that concern us not, is an employing our time to no good of ours, and therefore
not in order to a happy eternity. In this account our neighbours' necessities are not to be reckoned; for they concern us, as one member is concerned in the grief of another: but going from house to house, tattlers
and busy-bodies, which are the canker and rust of idleness, as idleness is
the rust of time, are reproved by the apostle in severe language, and forbidden in order to this exercise.

15. As much as may be, cut off all impertinent and useless employments of your life, unnecessary and fantastic visits, long waitings upon
great personages, where neither duty, nor necessity, nor charity obliges
us; all vain meetings, all laborious trifles, and whatsoever spends much
time to no real, civil, religious, or charitable purpose.

16. Let not your recreations be lavish spenders of your time; but
choose such which are healthful, short, transient, recreative, and apt to
refresh you; but at no hand dwell upon them, or make them your great
employment; for he that spends his time in sports, and calls it recreation,
is like him whose garment is all made of fringes, and his meat nothing
but sauces; they are healthless, chargeable, and useless. And therefore
avoid such games which require much time or long attendance, or
which are apt to steal thy affections from more severe employments. For
to whatsoever thou hast given thy affections, thou wilt not grudge to
give thy time. Natural necessity, and the example of St. John, who re-
created himself with sporting with a tame partridge, teach us that it is
lawful to relax and unbend our bow, but not to suffer it to be unready
or unstrung.

17. Set apart some portions of every day for more solemn devotion
and religious employment, which be severe in observing: and if variety
of employment, or prudent affairs, or civil society, press upon you, yet
so order thy rule, that the necessary parts of it be not omitted; and
though just occasions may make our prayers shorter, yet let nothing but
a violent, sudden, and impatient necessity make thee, upon any one day,
wholly to omit thy morning and evening devotions; which, if you be
forced to make very short, you may supply and lengthen with ejaculations and short retirements in the day-time, in the midst of your employment or of your company.

18. Do not the "work of God negligently" and idly: let not thy heart
be upon the world when thy hand is lifted up in prayer; and be sure

to prefer an action of religion, in its place and proper season, before all worldly pleasure, letting secular things, that may be dispensed with in themselves, in these circumstances wait upon the other: not like the patriarch, who ran from the altar in St. Sophia to his stable, in all his pontificals, and in the midst of his office, to see a colt newly fallen from his beloved and much-valued mare Phorbante. More prudent and severe was that of Sir Thomas More, who, being sent for by the king when he was at his prayers in public, returned answer he would attend him when he had first performed his service to the King of kings. And it did honour to Rusticus, that, when letters from Cæsar were given to him, he refused to open them till the philosopher had done his lecture. In honouring God and doing his work, put forth all thy strength; for of that time only thou mayest be most confident that it is gained, which is prudently and zealously spent in God's service.

19. When the clock strikes, or however else you shall measure the day, it is good to say a short ejaculation every hour, that the parts and returns of devotion may be the measure of your time: and do so also in all the breaches of thy sleep; that those spaces which have in them no direct business of the world, may be filled with religion.

20. If, by thus doing, you have not secured your time by an early and fore-handed care, yet be sure by a timely diligence to redeem the time; that is, to be pious and religious in such instances in which formerly you have sinned, and to bestow your time especially upon such graces, the contrary whereof you have formerly practised, doing actions of chastity and temperance with as great a zeal and earnestness as you did once act your uncleanness; and then, by all arts, to watch against your present and future dangers, from day to day securing your standing: this is properly to redeem your time, that is, to buy your security of it at the rate of any labour and honest arts.

21. Let him that is most busied set apart some "solemn time every year," in which, for the time, quitting all worldly business, he may attend wholly to fasting and prayer, and the dressing of his soul by confessions, meditations, and attendances upon God; that he may make up his accounts, renew his vows, make amends for his carelessness, and retire back again, from whence levity and the vanities of the world, or the opportunity of temptations, or the distraction of secular affairs, have carried him.

22. In this we shall be much assisted, and we shall find the work

more easy, if, before we sleep, every night, we examine the actions of the past day with a particular scrutiny, if there have been any accident extraordinary; as long discourse, a feast, much business, variety of company. If nothing but common hath happened, the less examination will suffice; only let us take care that we sleep not without such a recollection of the actions of the day, as may represent any thing that is remarkable and great, either to be the matter of sorrow or thanksgiving: for other things a general care is proportionable.

23. Let all these things be done prudently and moderately, not with scruple and vexation. For these are good advantages, but the particulars are not Divine commandments; and, therefore, are to be used as shall be found expedient to every one's condition. For, provided that our duty be secured, for the degrees and for the instruments every man is permitted to himself, and the conduct of such who shall be appointed to him. He is happy that can secure every hour to a sober or a pious employment: but the duty consists not scrupulously in minutes and half-hours, but in greater portions of time; provided that no minute be employed in sin, and the greater portions of our time be spent in sober employment, and all the appointed days, and some portions of every day, be allowed for religion. In all the lesser parts of time, we are left to our own elections and prudent management, and to the consideration of the great degrees and differences of glory that are laid up in heaven for us, according to the degrees of our care, and piety, and diligence.

## The Benefits of This Exercise

This exercise, besides that it hath influence upon our whole lives, it hath a special efficacy for the preventing of, 1. beggarly sins: that is, those sins which idleness and beggary usually betray men to; such as are lying, flattery, stealing, and dissimulation. 2. It is a proper antidote against carnal sins, and such as proceed from fulness of bread and emptiness of employment. 3. It is a great instrument of preventing the smallest sins and irregularities of our life, which usually creep upon idle, disemployed, and curious persons. 4. It not only teaches us to avoid evil, but engages us upon doing good, as the proper business of all our days. 5. It prepares us so against sudden changes, that we shall not easily be surprised at the sudden coming of the day of the Lord: for he that is curious of his time will not easily be unready and unfurnished.

## Sect. II. The General Instrument of Holy Living, Purity of Intention

That we should intend and design God's glory in every action we do, whether it be natural or chosen, is expressed by St. Paul, "Whether ye eat or drink, do all to the glory of God." Which rule when we observe, every action of nature becomes religious, and every meal is an act of worship, and shall have its reward in its proportion, as well as an act of prayer. Blessed be that goodness and grace of God, which, out of infinite desire to glorify and save mankind, would make the very works of nature capable of becoming acts of virtue, that all our lifetime we may do him service.

This grace is so excellent that it sanctifies the most common action of our life; and yet so necessary that, without it, the very best actions of our devotion are imperfect and vicious. For he that prays out of custom, or gives alms for praise, or fasts to be accounted religious, is but a Pharisee in his devotion, and a beggar in his alms, and a hypocrite in his fast. But a holy end sanctifies all these and all other actions which can be made holy, and gives distinction to them, and procures acceptance.

For as to know the end distinguishes a man from a beast, so to choose a good end distinguishes him from an evil man. Hezekiah repeated his good deeds upon his sick-bed, and obtained favour of God, but the Pharisee was accounted insolent for doing the same thing: because this man did it to upbraid his brother, the other to obtain a mercy of God. Zacharias questioned with the angel about his message, and was made speechless for his incredulity; but the blessed Virgin Mary questioned too, and was blameless; for she did it to inquire after the manner of the thing, but he did not believe the thing itself: he doubted of God's power, or the truth of the messenger; but she, only of her own incapacity. This was it which distinguished the mourning of David from the exclamation of Saul; the confession of Pharaoh from that of Manasses; the tears of Peter from the repentance of Judas: "for the praise is not in the deed done, but in the manner of its doing. If a man visits his sick friend, and watches at his pillow for charity's sake, and because of his old affection, we approve it; but if he does it in hope of legacy, he is a vulture, and only watches for the carcass. The same things are honest and dishonest: the manner of doing them, and the end of the design, makes the separation." [1]

[1] Seneca.

Holy intention is to the actions of a man that which the soul is to the body, or form to its matter, or the root to the tree, or the sun to the world, or the fountain to a river, or the base to a pillar: for without these the body is a dead trunk, the matter is sluggish, the tree is a block, the world is darkness, the river is quickly dry, the pillar rushes into flatness and a ruin; and the action is sinful, or unprofitable and vain. The poor farmer that gave a dish of cold water to Artaxerxes was rewarded with a golden goblet; and he that gives the same to a disciple in the name of a disciple, shall have a crown: but if he gives water in despite, when the disciple needs wine or a cordial, his reward shall be to want that water to cool his tongue.

But this duty must be reduced to rules:—

### Rules for Our Intentions

1. In every action reflect upon the end; and in your undertaking it, consider why you do it, and what you propound to yourself for a reward, and to your action as its end.

2. Begin every action in the name of the Father, of the Son, and of the Holy Ghost; the meaning of which is, 1. that we be careful that we do not the action without the permission or warrant of God: 2. that we design it to the glory of God, if not in the direct action, yet at least in its consequence; if not in the particular, yet at least in the whole order of things and accidents: 3. that it may be so blessed, that what you intend for innocent and holy purposes may not by any chance, or abuse or misunderstanding of men, be turned into evil, or made the occasion of sin.

3. Let every action of concernment be begun with prayer, that God would not only bless the action, but sanctify your purpose; and make an oblation of the action to God: holy and well-intended actions being the best oblations and presents we can make to God; and, when God is entitled to them, he will the rather keep the fire upon the altar bright and shining.

4. In the prosecution of the action, renew and re-enkindle your purpose by short ejaculations to these purposes: "Not unto us, O Lord, not unto us, but unto thy name let all praise be given:" and consider, "Now I am working the work of God; I am his servant, I am in a happy employment, I am doing my Master's business, I am not at my own dispose, I am using his talents, and all the gain must be his:" for then be

sure, as the glory is his, so the reward shall be thine. If thou bringest his goods home with increase, he will make thee ruler over cities.

5. Have a care that, while the altar thus sends up a holy fume, thou dost not suffer the birds to come and carry away the sacrifice: that is, let not that which began well, and was intended for God's glory, decline and end in thy own praise, or temporal satisfaction, or a sin. A story told to represent the vileness of unchastity, is well begun; but if thy female auditor be pleased with thy language, and begins rather to like thy person for thy story than to dislike the crime, be watchful lest this goodly head of gold descend in silver and brass, and end in iron and clay, like Nebuchadnezzar's image; for from the end it shall have its name and reward.

6. If any accidental event, which was not first intended by thee, can come to pass, let it not be taken into thy purposes, nor at all be made use of; as if, by telling a true story, you can do an ill turn to your enemy, by no means do it; but when the temptation is found out, turn all thy enmity upon that.

7. In every more solemn action of religion join together many good ends, that the consideration of them may entertain all your affections; and that, when any one ceases, the purity of your intention may be supported by another supply. He that fasts only to tame a rebellious body, when he is provided of a remedy either in grace or nature, may be tempted to leave off fasting. But he that in his fast intends the mortification of every unruly appetite, and accustoming himself to bear the yoke of the Lord, a contempt of the pleasures of meat and drink, humiliation of all wilder thoughts, obedience and humility, austerity and charity, and the convenience and assistance to devotion, and to do an act of repentance; whatever happens, will have reason enough to make him to continue his purpose, and to sanctify it. And certain it is, the more good ends are designed in an action, the more degrees of excellency the man obtains.

8. If any temptation to spoil your purpose happens in a religious duty, do not presently omit the action, but rather strive to rectify your intention, and to mortify the temptation. St. Bernard taught us this rule: for when the devil, observing him to preach excellently and to do much benefit to his hearers, tempted him to vain-glory, hoping that the good man, to avoid that, would cease preaching, he gave this answer only, "I neither began for thee, neither for thee will I make an end."

9. In all actions which are of long continuance, deliberation, and

abode, let your holy and pious intention be actual; that is, that it be, by a special prayer or action, by a peculiar act of resignation or oblation, given to God: but in smaller actions, and little things and indifferent, fail not to secure a pious habitual intention; that is, that it be included within your general care, that no action have an ill end; and that it be comprehended in your general prayers, whereby you offer yourself and all you do to God's glory.

10. Call not every temporal end a defiling of thy intention, but only, 1. when it contradicts any of the ends of God; or, 2. when it is principally intended in an action of religion. For sometimes a temporal end is part of our duty; and such are all the actions of our calling, whether our employment be religious or civil. We are commanded to provide for our family: but if the minister of divine offices shall take upon him that holy calling for covetous or ambitious ends, or shall not design the glory of God principally and especially, he hath polluted his hands and his heart; and the fire of the altar is quenched, or it sends forth nothing but the smoke of mushrooms or unpleasant gums. And it is a great unworthiness to prefer the interest of a creature before the ends of God the Almighty Creator.

But because many cases may happen in which a man's heart may deceive him, and he may not well know what is in his own spirit; therefore by these following signs we shall best make a judgment whether our intentions be pure and our purposes holy. . . .

# THE RULE AND EXERCISES OF HOLY DYING

### Sect. I. Consideration of the Vanity and Shortness of Man's Life

A man is a bubble, (said the Greek proverb,) which Lucian represents with advantages and its proper circumstances, to this purpose; saying, that all the world is a storm, and men rise up in their several generations, like bubbles descending *à Jove pluvio,* from God and the dew of heaven, from a tear and a drop of rain, from nature and Providence; and some of these instantly sink into the deluge of their first parent, and are hidden in a sheet of water, having had no other business in the world but to be born, that they might be able to die; others float up and down two or three turns, and suddenly disappear, and give their place to others: and they that live longest upon the face of the waters, are in perpetual motion, restless and uneasy; and, being crushed with the great drop of a cloud, sink into flatness and a froth; the change not being great, it being hardly possible it should be more a nothing than it was before. So is every man: he is born in vanity and sin; he comes into the world like morning mushrooms, soon thrusting up their heads into the air, and conversing with their kindred of the same production, and as soon they turn into dust and forgetfulness—some of them without any other interest in the affairs of the world, but that they made their parents a little glad and very sorrowful: others ride longer in the storm; it may be until seven years of vanity be expired, and then peradventure the sun shines hot upon their heads, and they fall into the shades below, into the cover of death and darkness of the grave to hide them. But if the bubble stands the shock of a bigger drop, and outlives the chances of a child, of a careless nurse, of drowning in a pail of water, of being overlaid by a sleepy servant, or such little accidents, then the young man dances like a bubble, empty and gay, and shines like a dove's neck, or the image of a rainbow, which hath no substance, and whose very imagery and colours are fantastical; and so he dances out the gaiety of his youth, and is all the while in a storm, and endures only because he is not knocked on the head by a drop of bigger rain, or crushed by the pressure of a load of indigested meat, or quenched by the disorder of an ill-placed humour: and to preserve a man alive in the midst of so many chances and hostilities, is as great a miracle as to create him; to preserve him from rushing into nothing, and at first to draw him up from nothing, were equally the issues of an almighty power. And therefore the wise men of the world have contended who shall best fit man's condition with words signifying his vanity and short abode. Homer calls a man, "a leaf," the smallest, the weakest piece of a short-lived, unsteady plant. Pindar calls him, "the dream of a shadow:" another "the dream of the shadow of smoke." But St. James spake by a more excellent Spirit, saying, "Our life is but a vapour," viz. drawn from the earth by a celestial influence; made of smoke, or the lighter parts of water, tossed with every wind, moved by the motion of a superior body, without virtue in itself, lifted up on high, or left below, according as it pleases the sun, its foster-father. But it is lighter yet. It is but "appearing;" a fantastic vapour, an apparition, nothing real; it is not so much as a mist, not the matter of a shower, nor substantial enough to make a cloud; but it is like Cassiopeia's chair, or Pelops' shoulder, or the circles of heaven, φαινόμενα, than which you cannot have a word that can signify a verier nothing. And yet the expression is one degree more made diminutive: a *vapour,* and *fantastical,* or a *mere appearance,* and this but for a little while neither; the very dream, the phantasm, disappears in a small time, "like the shadow that departed; or, like a tale that is told; or as a dream when one awaketh." A man is so vain, so unfixed, so perishing a creature, that he cannot long last in the scene of fancy; a man goes off, and is forgotten, like the dream of a distracted person. The sum of all is this: that thou art a man, than whom there is not in the world any greater instance of heights and declensions, of lights and shadows, of misery and folly, of laughter and tears, of groans and death.

And because this consideration is of great usefulness and great necessity to many purposes of wisdom and the spirit, all the succession of time, all the changes in nature, all the varieties of light and darkness, the thousand thousands of accidents in the world, and every contingency to every man, and to every creature, doth preach our funeral sermon, and calls us to look and see how the old sexton, Time, throws up the earth, and digs a grave, where we must lay our sins or our sorrows, and sow our bodies, till they rise again in a fair or an intolerable eternity. Every revolution which the sun makes about the world divides between life and death; and death possesses both those portions by the next morrow; and we are dead to all those months which we have already lived, and we shall never live them over again: and still God makes little periods of our age. First we change our world, when we come from the womb to feel the warmth of the sun. Then we sleep and enter into the image of death, in which state we are unconcerned in all the changes of the world: and if our mothers or our nurses die, or a wild boar destroy our vineyards, or our king be sick, we regard it not, but, during that state, are as disinterested as if our eyes were closed with the clay that weeps in the bowels of the earth. At the end of seven years our teeth fall and die before us, representing a formal prologue to the tragedy; and still, every seven years it is odds but we shall finish the last scene: and when nature, or chance, or vice, takes our body in pieces, weakening some parts and loosing others, we taste the grave and the solemnities of our own funerals, first, in those parts that ministered to vice; and, next, in them that served for ornament; and in a short time, even they that served for necessity become useless and entangled like the wheels of a broken clock. Baldness is but a dressing to our funerals, the proper ornament of mourning, and of a person entered very far into the regions and possession of death: and we have many more of the same significa-tion—gray hairs, rotten teeth, dim eyes, trembling joints, short breath, stiff limbs, wrinkled skin, short memory, decayed appetite. Every day's necessity calls for a reparation of that portion which death fed on all night, when we lay in his lap, and slept in his outer chambers. The very spirits of a man prey upon the daily portion of bread and flesh, and every meal is a rescue from one death, and lays up for another; and while we think a thought, we die; and the clock strikes, and reckons on our portion of eternity: we form our words with the breath of our nostrils—we have the less to live upon for every word we speak.

Thus nature calls us to meditate of death by those things which are the instruments of acting it; and God, by all the variety of his provi-dence, makes us see death every where, in all variety of circumstances, and dressed up for all the fancies, and the expectation of every single person. Nature hath given us one harvest every year, but death hath two: and the spring and the autumn send throngs of men and women to charnel-houses; and all the summer long men are recovering from their evils of the spring, till the dog-days come, and then the Sirian star makes the summer deadly; and the fruits of autumn are laid up for all the year's provision, and the man that gathers them eats and surfeits, and dies and needs them not, and himself is laid up for eternity; and he that escapes till winter only stays for another opportunity, which the dis-tempers of that quarter minister to him with great variety. Thus, death reigns in all the portions of our time. The autumn with its fruits pro-vides disorders for us, and the winter's cold turns them into sharp dis-eases, and the spring brings flowers to strew our hearse, and the summer gives green turf and brambles to bind upon our graves. Calentures and surfeit, cold and agues, are the four quarters of the year, and all minis-ter to death; and you can go no whither, but you tread upon a dead man's bones.

The wild fellow, in Petronius, that escaped upon a broken table from the furies of a shipwreck, as he was sunning himself upon the rocky shore, espied a man, rolled upon his floating bed of waves, ballasted with sand in the folds of his garment, and carried by his civil enemy, the sea, towards the shore to find a grave: and it cast him into some sad thoughts; that, peradventure, this man's wife, in some part of the con-tinent, safe and warm, looks next month for the good man's return; or, it may be, his son knows nothing of the tempest; or his father thinks of that affectionate kiss, which still is warm upon the good old man's cheek, ever since he took a kind farewell; and he weeps with joy to think how blessed he shall be when his beloved boy returns into the circle of his father's arms. These are the thoughts of mortals, this is the end and sum of all their designs; a dark night and an ill guide, a boisterous sea and a broken cable, a hard rock and a rough wind, dashed to pieces the fortune of a whole family; and they that shall weep loudest for the accident are not yet entered into the storm, and yet have suffered shipwreck. Then, looking upon the carcass, he knew it, and found it to be the master of the ship, who, the day before, cast up the accounts of his patrimony and his trade, and named the day when he thought to be at home: see how the man swims who was so angry two days since; his passions are becalmed with the storm, his accounts cast up, his cares at an end, his voyage done, and his gains are the strange events of death, which, whether they be good or evil, the men that are alive seldom trouble themselves concerning the interest of the dead.

But seas alone do not break our vessel in pieces: every where we may be shipwrecked. A valiant general, when he is to reap the harvest of his crowns and triumphs, fights unprosperously, or falls into a fever with joy and wine, and changes his laurel into cypress, his triumphal chariot to a hearse; dying the night before he was appointed to perish in the drunkenness of his festival joys. It was a sad arrest of the loose-nesses and wilder feasts of the French court, when their king (Henry II.) was killed really by the sportive image of a fight. And many brides have died under the hands of paranymphs and maidens, dressing them for uneasy joy, the new and undiscerned chains of marriage, according to the saying of Bensirah, the wise Jew, "The bride went into her chamber, and knew not what should befall her there." Some have been paying their vows, and giving thanks for a prosperous return to their own house, and the roof hath descended upon their heads, and turned their loud religion into the deeper silence of a grave. And how many teeming mothers have rejoiced over their swelling wombs, and pleased themselves in becoming the channels of blessing to a family; and the midwife hath quickly bound their heads and feet, and carried them forth to burial! Or else the birth-day of an heir hath seen the coffin of the father brought into the house, and the divided mother hath been forced to travail twice, with a painful birth and a sadder death.

There is no state, no accident, no circumstance of our life, but it hath been soured by some sad instance of a dying friend: a friendly meeting often ends in some sad mischance, and makes an eternal parting; and when the poet Æschylus was sitting under the walls of his house, an eagle, hovering over his bald head, mistook it for a stone, and let fall his oyster, hoping there to break the shell, but pierced the poor man's skull.

Death meets us every where, and is procured by every instrument, and in all chances, and enters in at many doors; by violence and secret influence, by the aspect of a star and the stink of a mist, by the emissions of a cloud and the meeting of a vapour, by the fall of a chariot and the stumbling at a stone, by a full meal or an empty stomach, by watching at the wine or by watching at prayers, by the sun or the moon, by a heat or a cold, by sleepless nights or sleeping days, by water frozen into the hardness and sharpness of a dagger, or water thawed into the floods of a river, by a hair or a raisin, by violent motion or sitting still, by severity or dissolution, by God's mercy or God's anger; by every thing in providence and every thing in manners, by every thing in nature and every thing in chance. *Eripitur persona, manet res;* we take pains to heap up things useful to our life, and get our death in the purchase; and the person is snatched away, and the goods remain. And all this is the law and constitution of nature; it is a punishment to our sins, the unalterable event of Providence, and the decree of Heaven. The chains that confine us to this condition are strong as destiny, and immutable as the eternal laws of God.

I have conversed with some men who rejoiced in the death or calamity of others, and accounted it as a judgment upon them for being on the other side, and against them in the contention: but within the revolution of a few months, the same man met with a more uneasy and unhandsome death; which, when I saw, I wept, and was afraid; for I knew that it must be so with all men; for we also die, and end our quarrels and contentions by passing to a final sentence.

### Sect. II. The Consideration Reduced to Practice

It will be very material to our best and noblest purposes, if we represent this scene of change and sorrow a little more dressed up in circumstances; for so we shall be more apt to practise those rules, the doctrine of which is consequent to this consideration. It is a mighty change that is made by the death of every person, and it is visible to us who are alive. Reckon but from the sprightfulness of youth and the fair cheeks and full eyes of childhood, from the vigorousness and strong flexure of the joints of five-and-twenty, to the hollowness and dead paleness, to the loathsomeness and horror of a three days' burial, and we shall perceive the distance to be very great and very strange. But so have I seen a rose newly springing from the clefts of its hood, and, at first, it was fair as the morning, and full with the dew of heaven, as a lamb's fleece; but when a ruder breath had forced open its virgin modesty, and dismantled its too youthful and unripe retirements, it began to put on darkness, and to decline to softness and the symptoms of a sickly age: it bowed the head and broke its stalk; and, at night, having lost some of its leaves and all its beauty, it fell into the portion of weeds and outworn faces. The same is the portion of every man and every woman: the heritage of worms and serpents, rottenness and cold dishonour, and our beauty so changed that our acquaintance quickly knew us not; and that change mingled with so much horror, or else meets so with our fears and weak discoursings, that they who, six hours ago, tended upon us, either with charitable or ambitious services, cannot, without some regret, stay in the room alone where the body lies stripped of its life and honour. I have read of a fair young German gentleman, who, living, often refused to be pictured, but put off the importunity of his friends' desire by giving way, that, after a few days' burial, they might send a painter to his vault, and, if they saw cause for it, draw the image of his death unto the life. They did so, and found his face half eaten, and his midriff and backbone full of serpents; and so he stands pictured among his armed ancestors. So does the fairest beauty change, and it will be as bad for you and me; and then what servants shall we have to wait upon us in the grave? what friends to visit us? what officious people to cleanse away the moist and unwholesome cloud reflected upon our faces from the sides of the weeping vaults, which are the longest weepers for our funeral?

This discourse will be useful, if we consider and practise by the following rules and considerations respectively.

1. All the rich and all the covetous men in the world will perceive, and all the world will perceive for them, that it is but an ill recompence for all their cares, that, by this time, all that shall be left will be

this, that the neighbours shall say, "He died a rich man;" and yet his wealth will not profit him in the grave, but hugely swell the sad accounts of doomsday. And he that kills the Lord's people with unjust or ambitious wars, for an unrewarding interest, shall have this character, that he threw away all the days of his life, that one year might be reckoned with his name, and computed by his reign or consulship: and many men, by great labours and affronts, many indignities and crimes, labour only for a pompous epitaph, and a loud title upon their marble; whilst those, into whose possessions their heirs or kindred are entered, are forgotten, and lie unregarded as their ashes, and without concernment or relation, as the turf upon the face of their grave. A man may read a sermon, the best and most passionate that ever man preached, if he shall but enter into the sepulchres of kings. In the same Escurial where the Spanish princes live in greatness and power, and decree war or peace, they have wisely placed a cemetery, where their ashes and their glory shall sleep till time shall be no more; and where our kings have been crowned their ancestors lie interred, and they must walk over their grandsire's head to take his crown. There is an acre sown with royal seed, the copy of the greatest change, from rich to naked, from ceiled roofs to arched coffins, from living like gods to die like men. There is enough to cool the flames of lust, to abate the heights of pride, to appease the itch of covetous desires, to sully and dash out the dissembling colours of a lustful, artificial, and imaginary beauty. There the warlike and the peaceful, the fortunate and the miserable, the beloved and the despised princes mingle their dust, and pay down their symbol of mortality, and tell all the world that, when we die, our ashes shall be equal to kings', and our accounts easier, and our pains or our crowns shall be less. To my apprehension, it is a sad record which is left by Athenæus concerning Ninus, the great Assyrian monarch, whose life and death are summed up in these words: "Ninus, the Assyrian, had an ocean of gold, and other riches, more than the sand in the Caspian Sea; he never saw the stars, and perhaps he never desired it; he never stirred up the holy fire among the Magi, nor touched his god with the sacred rod according to the laws; he never offered sacrifice, nor worshipped the deity, nor administered justice, nor spake to his people, nor numbered them; but he was most valiant to eat and drink, and having mingled his wines, he threw the rest upon the stones. This man is dead; behold his sepulchre; and now hear where Ninus is. Sometimes I was Ninus, and drew the breath of a living man; but now am nothing but clay. I have nothing but what I did eat, and what I served to myself in lust; that was and is all my portion. The wealth with which I was esteemed blessed, my enemies, meeting together, shall bear away, as the mad Thyades carry a raw goat. I am gone to hell; and when I went thither I neither carried gold, nor horse, nor silver chariot. I that wore a mitre am now a little heap of dust." I know not any thing that can better represent the evil condition of a wicked man, or a changing greatness. From the greatest secular dignity to dust and ashes his nature bears him; and from thence to hell his sins carry him, and there he shall be for ever under the dominion of chains and devils, wrath and an intolerable calamity. This is the reward of an unsanctified condition, and a greatness ill-gotten or ill-administered.

2. Let no man extend his thoughts, or let his hopes wander towards future and far-distant events and accidental contingencies. This day is mine and yours, but ye know not what shall be on the morrow; and every morning creeps out of a dark cloud, leaving behind it an ignorance and silence deep as midnight and undiscerned as are the phantasms that make a chrisom-child to smile; so that we cannot discern what comes hereafter, unless we had a light from heaven brighter than the vision of an angel, even the spirit of prophecy. Without revelation we cannot tell whether we shall eat to-morrow, or whether a squinancy shall choke us: and it is written in the unrevealed folds of Divine pre-destination, that many who are this day alive shall to-morrow be laid upon the cold earth, and the women shall weep over their shroud, and dress them for their funeral. St. James, in his Epistle, notes the folly of some men, his contemporaries, who were so impatient of the event of to-morrow, or the accidents of next year, or the good, or evils of old age, that they would consult astrologers and witches, oracles and devils, what should befall them the next calends—what should be the event of such a voyage—what God had written in his book concerning the success of battles, the election of emperors, the heirs of families, the price of merchandise, the return of the Tyrian fleet, the rate of Sidonian carpets: and as they were taught by the crafty and lying demons, so they would expect the issue: and oftentimes, by disposing their affairs in order towards such events, really did produce some little accidents according to their expectation; and that made them trust the oracles in greater things, and in all. Against this he opposes his counsel, that we should not search after forbidden records, much less by uncertain sig-nifications; for whatsoever is disposed to happen by the order of natural

causes or civil counsels, may be rescinded by a peculiar decree of Providence, or be prevented by the death of the interested persons; who, while their hopes are full, and their causes conjoined, and the work brought forward, and the sickle put into the harvest, and the first-fruits offered and ready to be eaten, even then, if they put forth their hand to an event that stands but at the door, at that door their body may be carried forth to burial before the expectation shall enter into fruition. When Richilda, the widow of Albert, earl of Ebersberg, had feasted the emperor Henry III., and petitioned in behalf of her nephew, Welpho, for some lands formerly possessed by the earl her husband, just as the emperor held out his hand to signify his consent, the chamber-floor suddenly fell under them, and Richilda falling upon the edge of a bathing-vessel, was bruised to death, and stayed not to see her nephew sleep in those lands which the emperor was reaching forth to her, and placed at the door of restitution.

3. As our hopes must be confined, so must our designs: let us not project long designs, crafty plots, and diggings so deep that the intrigues of a design shall never be unfolded till our grandchildren have forgotten our virtues or our vices. The work of our soul is cut short, facile, sweet, and plain, and fitted to the small portions of our shorter life: and as we must not trouble our inquiry, so neither must we intricate our labour and purposes with what we shall never enjoy. This rule does not forbid us to plant orchards, which shall feed our nephews with their fruit; for by such provisions they do something towards an imaginary immortality, and do charity to their relatives; but such projects are reproved which discompose our present duty by long and future designs; such which, by casting our labours to events at distance, make us less to remember our death standing at the door. It is fit for a man to work for his day's wages, or to contrive for the hire of a week, or to lay a train to make provisions for such a time as is within our eye, and in our duty, and within the usual periods of man's life; for whatsoever is made necessary is also made prudent: but while we plot and busy ourselves in the toils of an ambitious war, or the levies of a great estate, night enters in upon us, and tells all the world how like fools we lived, and how deceived and miserably we died. Seneca tells of Senecio Cornelius, a man crafty in getting, and tenacious in holding, a great estate, and one who was as diligent in the care of his body as of his money, curious of his health as of his possessions, that he all day long attended upon his sick and dying friend; but when he went away, was quickly comforted, supped

merrily, went to bed cheerfully, and on a sudden being surprised by a squinancy, scarce drew his breath until the morning, but by that time died, being snatched from the torrent of his fortune, and the swelling tide of wealth, and a likely hope bigger than the necessities of ten men. This accident was much noted then in Rome, because it happened in so great a fortune, and in the midst of wealthy designs; and presently it made wise men to consider how imprudent a person he is who disposes of ten years to come, when he is not lord of to-morrow.

4. Though we must not look so far off, and pry abroad, yet we must be busy near at hand; we must, with all arts of the spirit, seize upon the present, because it passes from us while we speak, and because in it all our certainty does consist. We must take our waters as out of a torrent and sudden shower, which will quickly cease dropping from above and quickly cease running in our channels here below: this instant will never return again, and yet, it may be, this instant will declare or secure the fortune of a whole eternity. The old Greeks and Romans taught us the prudence of this rule: but Christianity teaches us the religion of it. They so seized upon the present, that they would lose nothing of the day's pleasure. "Let us eat and drink, for to-morrow we shall die:" that was their philosophy; and at their solemn feasts they would talk of death to heighten the present drinking, and that they might warm their veins with a fuller chalice, as knowing the drink that was poured upon their graves would be cold and without relish. "Break the beds, drink your wine, crown your head with roses, and besmear your curled locks with nard; for God bids you to remember death:" so the epigrammatist speaks the sense of their drunken principles. Something towards this signification is that of Solomon, "There is nothing better for a man than that he should eat and drink, and that he should make his soul enjoy good in his labour; for that is his portion; for who shall bring him to see that which shall be after him?" But, although he concludes all this to be vanity, yet because it was the best thing that was then commonly known, that they should seize upon the present with a temperate use of permitted pleasures, I had reason to say that Christianity taught us to turn this into religion. For he that by a present and constant holiness secures the present, and makes it useful to his noblest purposes, he turns his condition into his best advantage, by making his unavoidable fate become his necessary religion.

To the purpose of this rule is that collect of Tuscan hieroglyphics which we have from Gabriel Simeon: "Our life is very short, beauty is a cozenage, money is false and fugitive; empire is odious, and hated by them that have it not, and uneasy to them that have; victory is always uncertain, and peace, most commonly, is but a fraudulent bargain; old age is miserable, death is the period, and is a happy one, if it be not sorrowed by the sins of our life: but nothing continues but the effects of that wisdom which employs the present time in the acts of a holy religion and a peaceable conscience." For they make us to live even beyond our funerals, embalmed in the spices and odours of a good name, and entombed in the grave of the holy Jesus, where we shall be dressed for a blessed resurrection to the state of angels and beatified spirits.

5. Since we stay not here, being people but of a day's abode, and our age is like that of a fly and contemporary with a gourd, we must look some where else for an abiding city, a place in another country to fix our house in, whose walls and foundation is God, where we must find rest, or else be restless for ever. For whatsoever case we can have or fancy here, is shortly to be changed into sadness or tediousness; it goes away too soon, like the periods of our life, or stays too long, like the sorrows of a sinner; its own weariness, or a contrary disturbance, is its load; or it is eased by its revolution into vanity and forgetfulness: and where either there is sorrow, or an end of joy, there can be no true felicity; which, because it must be had by some instrument, and in some period of our duration, we must carry up our affections to the mansions prepared for us above, where eternity is the measure, felicity is the state, angels are the company, the Lamb is the light, and God is the portion and inheritance.

### Sect. III. Rules and Spiritual Arts of Lengthening our Days, and To Take Off the Objection of a Short Life

In the accounts of a man's life, we do not reckon that portion of days in which we are shut up in the prison of the womb; we tell our years from the day of our birth; and the same reason that makes our reckoning to stay so long, says also, that then it begins too soon. For then we are beholden to others to make the account for us; for we know not of a long time whether we be alive or no, having but some little approaches and symptoms of a life. To feed, and sleep, and move a little, and imperfectly, is the state of an unborn child; and when he is born he does no more for a good while; and what is it that shall make him to be esteemed to live the life of a man? and when shall that account begin? For we should be loth to have the accounts of our age taken by the measures of a beast; and fools and distracted persons are reckoned as civilly dead; they are no parts of the commonwealth, not subject to laws, but secured by them in charity, and kept from violence as a man keeps his ox: and a third part of our life is spent before we enter into a higher order, into the state of a man.

2. Neither must we think that the life of a man begins when he can feed himself, or walk alone, when he can fight, or beget his like; for so he is contemporary with a camel or a cow; but he is first a man when he comes to a certain steady use of reason, according to his proportion: and when that is, all the world of men cannot tell precisely. Some are called at age at fourteen; some at one-and-twenty; some never; but all men late enough; for the life of a man comes upon him slowly and insensibly. But as, when the sun approaches towards the gates of the morning, he first opens a little eye of heaven, and sends away the spirits of darkness, and gives light to a cock, and calls up the lark to matins, and by and by gilds the fringes of a cloud, and peeps over the eastern hills, thrusting out his golden horns, like those which decked the brows of Moses when he was forced to wear a veil because himself had seen the face of God; and still, while a man tells the story, the sun gets up higher, till he shows a fair face and a full light, and then he shines one whole day, under a cloud often, and sometimes weeping great and little showers, and sets quickly; so is a man's reason and his life. He first begins to perceive himself to see or taste, making little reflections upon his actions of sense, and can discourse of flies and dogs, shells and play, horses and liberty; but when he is strong enough to enter into arts and little institutions, he is at first entertained with trifles and impertinent things, not because he needs them, but because his understanding is no bigger, and little images of things are laid before him, like a cock-boat to a whale, only to play withal; but before a man comes to be wise, he is half dead with gouts and consumptions, with catarrhs and aches, with sore eyes and a worn-out body. So that, if we must not reckon the life of a man but by the accounts of his reason, he is long before his soul be dressed; and he is not to be called a man without a wise and an adorned soul, a soul at least furnished with what is necessary towards his well-being: but by that time his soul is thus furnished his body is decayed; and then you can hardly reckon

him to be alive, when his body is possessed by so many degrees of death.

3. But there is yet another arrest. At first he wants strength of body, and then he wants the use of reason; and when that is come, it is ten to one but he stops by the impediments of vice, and wants the strength of the spirit; and we know that body, and soul, and spirit, are the constituent parts of every Christian man. And now let us consider what that thing is which we call years of discretion. The young man is past his tutors, and arrived at the bondage of a caitiff spirit; he is run from discipline, and is let loose to passion; the man by this time hath wit enough to choose his vice, to act his lust, to court his mistress, to talk confidently, and ignorantly, and perpetually, to despise his betters, to deny nothing to his appetite, to do things that, when he is indeed a man, he must for ever be ashamed of; for this is all the discretion that most men show in the first stage of their manhood; they can discern good from evil; and they prove their skill by leaving all that is good, and wallowing in the evils of folly and an unbridled appetite. And, by this time, the young man hath contracted vicious habits, and is a beast in manners, and therefore it will not be fitting to reckon the beginning of his life; he is a fool in his understanding, and that is a sad death; and he is dead in trespasses and sins, and that is sadder; so that he hath no life but a natural, the life of a beast or a tree; in all other capacities he is dead; he neither hath the intellectual nor the spiritual life, neither the life of a man nor of a Christian; and this sad truth lasts too long. For old age seizes upon most men while they still retain the minds of boys and vicious youth, doing actions from principles of great folly, and a mighty ignorance, admiring things useless and hurtful, and filling up all the dimensions of their abode with businesses of empty affairs, being at leisure to attend no virtue: they cannot pray because they are busy, and because they are passionate; they cannot communicate because they have quarrels and intrigues of perplexed causes, complicated hostilities, and things of the world, and therefore they cannot attend to the things of God; little considering that they must find a time to die in; when death comes they must be at leisure for that. Such men are like sailors loosing from a port, and tossed immediately with a perpetual tempest lasting till their cordage crack, and either they sink or return back again to the same place; they did not make a voyage, though they were long at sea. The business and impertinent affairs of most men steal all their time, and they are restless in a

foolish motion: but this is not the progress of a man; he is no further advanced in the course of a life, though he reckon many years; for still his soul is childish and trifling like an untaught boy.

If the parts of this sad complaint find their remedy, we have by the same instruments also cured the evils and the vanity of a short life. Therefore,

1. Be infinitely curious you do not set back your life in the accounts of God by the intermingling of criminal actions, or the contracting vicious habits. There are some vices which carry a sword in their hand, and cut a man off before his time. There is a sword of the Lord, and there is a sword of a man, and there is a sword of the devil. Every vice of our own managing in the matter of carnality, of lust or rage, ambition or revenge, is a sword of Satan put into the hands of a man: these are the destroying angels; sin is the Apollyon, the destroyer that is gone out, not from the Lord, but from the tempter: and we hug the poison, and twist willingly with the vipers, till they bring us into the regions of an irrecoverable sorrow. We use to reckon persons as good as dead if they have lost their limbs and their teeth, and are confined to a hospital, and converse with none but surgeons and physicians, mourners and divines, those *pollinctores,* the dressers of bodies and souls to funeral; but it is worse when the soul, the principle of life, is employed wholly in the offices of death: and that man was worse than dead of whom Seneca tells, that, being a rich fool, when he was lifted up from the baths and set into a soft couch, asked his slaves, *An ego jam sedeo?* Do I now sit? The beast was so drowned in sensuality and the death of his soul, that whether he did sit or no, he was to believe another. Idleness and every vice are as much of death as a long disease is, or the expense of ten years; and "she that lives in pleasure is dead while she liveth" (saith the apostle); and it is the style of the Spirit concerning wicked persons, "they are dead in trespasses and sins." For, as every sensual pleasure and every day of idleness and useless living lops off a little branch from our short life; so every deadly sin and every habitual vice does quite destroy us: but innocence leaves us in our natural portions and perfect period; we lose nothing of our life if we lose nothing of our soul's health; and, therefore, he that would live a full age must avoid a sin as he would decline the regions of death and the dishonours of the grave.

2. If we would have our life lengthened, let us begin betimes to live in the accounts of reason and sober counsels, of religion and the spirit,

and then we shall have no reason to complain that our abode on earth is so short; many men find it long enough, and indeed it is so to all senses. But when we spend in waste what God hath given us in plenty, when we sacrifice our youth to folly, our manhood to lust and rage, our old age to covetousness and irreligion, not beginning to live till we are to die, designing that time to virtue which indeed is infirm to every thing and profitable to nothing; then we make our lives short, and lust runs away with all the vigorous and healthful part of it, and pride and animosity steal the manly portion, and craftiness and interest possess old age: *velut ex pleno et abundanti perdimus,* we spend as if we had too much time, and knew not what to do with it: we fear every thing, like weak and silly mortals, and desire strangely and greedily, as if we were immortal: we complain our life is short, and yet we throw away much of it, and are weary of many of its parts: we complain the day is long, and the night is long, and we want company, and seek out arts to drive the time away, and then weep because it is gone too soon. But so the treasure of the capitol is but a small estate when Cæsar comes to finger it, and to pay with it all his legions; and the revenue of all Egypt and the eastern provinces was but a little sum when they were to support the luxury of Mark Antony, and feed the riot of Cleopatra; but a thousand crowns is a vast proportion to be spent in the cottage of a frugal person, or to feed a hermit. Just so is our life: it is too short to serve the ambition of a haughty prince, or a usurping rebel; too little time to purchase great wealth, to satisfy the pride of a vain-glorious fool, to trample upon all the enemies of our just or unjust interest: but for the obtaining virtue, for the purchase of sobriety and modesty, for the actions of religion, God gave us time sufficient, if we make the "outgoings of the morning and evening," that is, our infancy and old age, to be taken into the computations of a man. Which we may see in the following particulars.

(1) If our childhood, being first consecrated by a forward baptism, it be seconded by a holy education and a complying obedience; if our youth be chaste and temperate, modest and industrious, proceeding through a prudent and sober manhood to a religious old age; then we have lived our whole duration, and shall never die, but be changed, in a just time, to the preparations of a better and an immortal life.

(2) If, besides the ordinary returns of our prayers and periodical and festival solemnities, and our seldom communions, we would allow to religion and the studies of wisdom those great shares that are trifled

away upon vain sorrow, foolish mirth, troublesome ambition, busy covetousness, watchful lust, and impertinent amours, and balls, and revellings, and banquets,—all that which was spent viciously, and all that time that lay fallow and without employment,—our life would quickly amount to a great sum. Tostatus Abulensis was a very painful person, and a great clerk, and in the days of his manhood he wrote so many books, and they not ill ones, that the world computed a sheet for every day of his life; I suppose they meant after he came to the use of reason and the state of a man: and John Scotus died about the two-and-thirtieth year of his age; and yet, besides his public disputations, his daily lectures of divinity in public and private, the books that he wrote, being lately collected and printed at Lyons, do equal the number of volumes of any two the most voluminous fathers of the Latin church. Every man is not enabled to such employments, but every man is called and enabled to the works of a sober and a religious life; and there are many saints of God that can reckon as many volumes of religion and mountains of piety as those others did of good books. St. Ambrose (and I think, from his example, St. Augustine) divided every day into three *tertias* of employment: eight hours he spent in the necessities of nature and recreation; eight hours in charity and doing assistance to others, despatching their businesses, reconciling their enmities, reproving their vices, correcting their errors, instructing their ignorances, transacting the affairs of his diocese; and the other eight hours he spent in study and prayer. If we were thus minute and curious in the spending our time, it is impossible but our life would seem very long. For so have I seen an amorous person tell the minutes of his absence from his fancied joy, and while he told the sands of his hour-glass, or the throbs and little beatings of his watch, by dividing an hour into so many members, he spun out its length by number, and so translated a day into the tedious-ness of a month. And if we tell our days by canonical hours of prayer, our weeks by a constant revolution of fasting-days or days of special devotion, and over all these draw a black cypress, a veil of penitential sorrow and severe mortification, we shall soon answer the calumny and objection of a short life. He that governs the day and divides the hours hastens from the eyes and observation of a merry sinner; but loves to stand still, and behold, and tell the sighs, and number the groans and sadly delicious accents, of a grieved penitent. It is a vast work that any man may do if he never be idle: and it is a huge way that a man may go in virtue if he never goes out of his way by a vicious habit or a great crime: and he that perpetually reads good books, if his parts be answerable, will have a huge stock of knowledge. It is so in all things else. Strive not to forget your time, and suffer none of it to pass undiscerned; and then measure your life, and tell me how you find the measure of its abode. However, the time we live is worth the money we pay for it; and therefore it is not to be thrown away.

(3) When vicious men are dying, and scared with the affrighting truths of an evil conscience, they would give all the world for a year, for a month: nay, we read of some that called out with amazement, *inducias usque ad mane,* truce but till the morning; and if that year or some few months were given, those men think they could do miracles in it. And let us awhile suppose what Dives would have done if he had been loosed from the pains of hell, and permitted to live on earth one year. Would all the pleasures of the world have kept him one hour from the temple? would he not perpetually have been under the hands of priests, or at the feet of the doctors, or by Moses' chair, or attending as near the altar as he could get, or relieving poor Lazarus, or praying to God, and crucifying all his sin? I have read of a melancholy person, who saw hell but in a dream or vision, and the amazement was such, that he would have chosen ten times to die rather than feel again so much of that horror: and such a person cannot be fancied but that he would spend a year in such holiness that the religion of a few months would equal the devotion of many years, even of a good man. Let us but compute the proportions. If we should spent all our years of reason so as such a person would spend that one, can it be thought that life would be short and trifling in which he had performed such a religion, served God with so much holiness, mortified sin with so great a labour, purchased virtue at such a rate and so rare an industry? It must needs be that such a man must die when he ought to die, and be like ripe and pleasant fruit falling from a fair tree, and gathered into baskets for the planter's use. He that hath done all his business, and is begotten to a glorious hope by the seed of an immortal Spirit, can never die too soon, nor live too long.

Xerxes wept sadly when he saw his army of 2,300,000 men, because he considered that within a hundred years all the youth of that army should be dust and ashes: and yet, as Seneca well observes of him, he was the man that should bring them to their graves; and he consumed all that army in two years for whom he feared and wept the death after a hundred. Just so we do all. We complain that within thirty or forty years, a little more or a great deal less, we shall descend again into the bowels of our mother, and that our life is too short for any great employment; and yet we throw away five-and-thirty years of our forty, and the remaining five we divide between art and nature, civility and customs, necessity and convenience, prudent counsels and religion: but the portion of the last is little and contemptible, and yet that little is all that we can prudently account of our lives. We bring that fate and that death near us of whose approach we are so sadly apprehensive.

(4) In taking the accounts of your life, do not reckon by great distances, and by the periods of pleasure, or the satisfaction of your hopes, or the sating your desires; but let every intermedial day and hour pass with observation. He that reckons he hath lived but so many harvests, thinks they come not often enough, and that they go away too soon: some lose the day by longing for the night, and the night in waiting for the day. Hope and fantastic expectations spend much of our lives; and while with passion we look for a coronation, or the death of an enemy, or a day of joy, passing from fancy to possession without any intermedial notices, we throw away a precious year, and use it but as the burden of our time, fit to be pared off and thrown away, that we may come at those little pleasures which first steal our hearts, and then steal our life.

(5) A strict course of piety is the way to prolong our lives in the natural sense, and to add good portions to the number of our years; and sin is sometimes by natural causality, very often by the anger of God and the Divine judgment, a cause of sudden and untimely death. Concerning which I shall add nothing, (to what I have some where else said of this article,) but only the observation of Epiphanius; that for three thousand three hundred and thirty-two years, even to the twentieth age, there was not one example of a son that died before his father; but the course of nature was kept, that he who was first born in the descending line did first die, (I speak of natural death, and therefore Abel cannot be opposed to this observation,) till that Terah, the father of Abraham, taught the people a new religion, to make images of clay and worship them; and concerning him it was first remarked, that "Haran died before his father Terah in the land of his nativity:" God, by an unheard-of judgment and a rare accident, punishing his newly-invented crime by the untimely death of his son.

(6) But if I shall describe a living man, a man that hath that life that distinguishes him from a fool or a bird, that which gives him a capacity

next to angels, we shall find that even a good man lives not long, because it is long before he is born to this life, and longer yet before he hath a man's growth. "He that can look upon death, and see its face with the same countenance with which he hears its story; that can endure all the labours of his life with his soul supporting his body; that can equally despise riches when he hath them and when he hath them not; that is not sadder if they lie in his neighbour's trunks, nor more brag if they shine round about his own walls: he that is neither moved with good fortune coming to him nor going from him; that can look upon another man's lands evenly and pleasedly, as if they were his own, and yet look upon his own, and use them too, just as if they were another man's; that neither spends his goods prodigally and like a fool, nor yet keeps them avariciously and like a wretch; that weighs not benefits by weight and number, but by the mind and circumstances of him that gives them; that never thinks his charity expensive if a worthy person be the receiver; he that does nothing for opinion sake, but every thing for conscience, being as curious of his thoughts as of his actings in markets and theatres, and is as much in awe of himself as of a whole assembly; he that knows God looks on, and contrives his secret affairs as in the presence of God and his holy angels; that eats and drinks because he needs it, not that he may serve a lust or load his belly; he that is bountiful and cheerful to his friends, and charitable and apt to forgive his enemies; that loves his country, and obeys his prince, and desires and endeavours nothing more than that he may do honour to God:"—this person may reckon his life to be the life of a man, and compute his months, not by the course of the sun, but the zodiac and circle of his virtues; because these are such things which fools and children, and birds and beasts, cannot have; these are, therefore, the actions of life, because they are the seeds of immortality. That day in which we have done some excellent thing we may as truly reckon to be added to our life as were the fifteen years to the days of Hezekiah.

### Sect. IV. Consideration of the Miseries of Man's Life

As our life is very short, so it is very miserable; and therefore it is well it is short. God, in pity to mankind, lest his burden should be insupportable, and his nature an intolerable load, hath reduced our state of misery to an abbreviature; and the greater our misery is, the less while it is like to last: the sorrows of a man's spirit being like ponderous weights, which, by the greatness of their burden, make a swifter motion, and descend into the grave to rest and ease our wearied limbs; for then only we shall sleep quietly when those fetters are knocked off, which not only bound our souls in prison, but also ate the flesh, till the very bones opened the secret garments of their cartilages, discovering their nakedness and sorrow.

1. Here is no place to sit down in, but you must rise as soon as you are set, for we have gnats in our chambers, and worms in our gardens, and spiders and flies in the palaces of the greatest kings. How few men in the world are prosperous! What an infinite number of slaves and beggars, of persecuted and oppressed people, fill all corners of the earth with groans, and heaven itself with weeping, prayers, and sad remembrances! How many provinces and kingdoms are afflicted by a violent war, or made desolate by popular diseases! Some whole countries are remarked with fatal evils or periodical sicknesses. Grand Cairo in Egypt feels the plague every three years returning like a quartan ague, and destroying many thousands of persons. All the inhabitants of Arabia the desert are in a continual fear of being buried in huge heaps of sand, and therefore dwell in tents, and ambulatory houses, or retire to unfruitful mountains, to prolong an uneasy and wilder life. And all the countries round about the Adriatic Sea feel such violent convulsions by tempests and intolerable earthquakes, that sometimes whole cities find a tomb, and every man sinks with his own house made ready to become his monument, and his bed is crushed into the disorders of a grave. Was not all the world drowned at one deluge and breach of the Divine anger? And shall not all the world again be destroyed by fire? Are there not many thousands that die every night, and that groan and weep sadly every day? But what shall we think of that great evil which for the sins of men God hath suffered to possess the greatest part of mankind? Most of the men that are now alive, or that have been living for many ages, are Jews, heathens, or Turks: and God was pleased to suffer a base epileptic person, a villain and a vicious, to set up a religion which hath filled all the nearer parts of Asia, and much of Africa, and some part of Europe; so that the greatest number of men and women born in so many kingdoms and provinces are infallibly made Mahometans, strangers and enemies to Christ, by whom alone we can be saved. This consideration is extremely sad, when we remember how universal and how great an evil it is; that so many millions of sons and daughters are

born to enter into the possession of devils to eternal ages. These evils are the miseries of great parts of mankind, and we cannot easily consider more particularly the evils which happen to us, being the inseparable affections or incidents to the whole nature of man.

2. We find that all the women in the world are either born for barrenness or the pains of childbirth, and yet this is one of our greatest blessings; but such, indeed, are the blessings of this world, we cannot be well with nor without many things. Perfumes make our heads ache, roses prick our fingers, and in our very blood, where our life dwells, is the scene under which nature acts many sharp fevers and heavy sicknesses. It were too sad if I should tell how many persons are afflicted with evil spirits, with spectres and illusions of the night; and that huge multitudes of men and women live upon man's flesh, nay, worse yet, upon the sins of men, upon the sins of their sons and of their daughters, and they pay their souls down for the bread they eat, buying this day's meal with the price of the last night's sin.

3. Or if you please in charity to visit a hospital, which is indeed a map of the whole world, there you shall see the effects of Adam's sin, and the ruins of human nature; bodies laid up in heaps like the bones of a destroyed town, *homines precarii spiritus et male hærentis,* men whose souls seem to be borrowed, and are kept there by art and the force of medicine, whose miseries are so great, that few people have charity or humanity enough to visit them, fewer have the heart to dress them, and we pity them in civility or with a transient prayer, but we do not feel their sorrows by the mercies of a religious pity: and therefore, as we leave their sorrows in many degrees unrelieved and uneased, so we contract by our unmercifulness a guilt by which ourselves become liable to the same calamities. Those many that need pity, and those infinities of people that refuse to pity, are miserable upon a several charge, but yet they almost make up all mankind.

4. All wicked men are in love with that which entangles them in huge varieties of troubles; they are slaves to the worst of masters, to sin and to the devil, to a passion and to an imperious woman. Good men are for ever persecuted, and God chastises every son whom he receives; and whatsoever is easy is trifling and worth nothing; and whatsoever is excellent is not to be obtained without labour and sorrow; and the conditions and states of men that are free from great cares, are such as have in them nothing rich and orderly, and those that have, are stuck full of thorns and trouble. Kings are full of care: and learned men in

all ages have been observed to be very poor, *honestas miserias accusant,* they complain of their honest miseries.

5. But these evils are notorious and confessed; even they also whose felicity men stare at and admire, besides their splendour and the sharpness of their light, will with their appendant sorrows wring a tear from the most resolved eye: for not only the winter quarter is full of storms and cold and darkness, but the beauteous spring hath blasts and sharp frosts; the fruitful teeming summer is melted with heat, and burnt with the kisses of the sun her friend, and choked with dust; and the rich autumn is full of sickness; and we are weary of that which we enjoy, because sorrow is its biggest portion: and when we remember, that upon the fairest face is placed one of the worst sinks of the body, the nose, we may use it not only as a mortification to the pride of beauty, but as an allay to the fairest outside of condition which any of the sons and daughters of Adam do possess. For look upon kings and conquerors; I will not tell that many of them fall into the condition of servants, and their subjects rule over them, and stand upon the ruins of their families, and that to such persons the sorrow is bigger than usually happens in smaller fortunes: but let us suppose them still conquerors, and see what a goodly purchase they get by all their pains, and amazing fears, and continual dangers. They carry their arms beyond Ister, and pass the Euphrates, and bind the Germans with the bounds of the river Rhine: I speak in the style of the Roman greatness: for now-a-days the biggest fortune swells not beyond the limits of a petty province or two, and a hill confines the progress of their prosperity, or a river checks it; but whatsoever tempts the pride and vanity of ambitious persons is not so big as the smallest star which we see scattered in disorder and unregarded upon the pavement and floor of heaven. And if we would suppose the pismires had but our understandings, they also would have the method of a man's greatness, and divide their little molehills into provinces and exarchates: and if they also grew as vicious and as miserable, one of their princes would lead an army out, and kill his neighbour ants, that he might reign over the next handful of a turf. But then, if we consider at what price and with what felicity all this is purchased, the sting of the painted snake will quickly appear, and the fairest of their fortunes will properly enter into this account of human infelicities.

We may guess at it by the constitution of Augustus's fortune, who struggled for his power, first, with the Roman citizens, then with Brutus and Cassius, and all the fortune of the republic; then with his colleague,

Mark Antony; then with his kindred and nearest relatives; and after he was wearied with slaughter of the Romans, before he could sit down and rest in his imperial chair, he was forced to carry armies into Macedonia, Galatia, beyond Euphrates, Rhine, and Danubius: and when he dwelt at home in greatness and within the circles of a mighty power, he hardly escaped the sword of the Egnatii, of Lepidus, Cæpio, and Muræna: and after he had entirely reduced the felicity and grandeur into his own family, his daughter, his only child, conspired with many of the young nobility, and, being joined with adulterous complications, as with an impious sacrament, they affrighted and destroyed the fortune of the old man, and wrought him more sorrow than all the troubles that were hatched in the baths and beds of Egypt between Antony and Cleopatra. This was the greatest fortune that the world had then or ever since, and therefore we cannot expect it to be better in a less prosperity.

6. The prosperity of this world is so infinitely soured with the overflowing of evils, that he is counted the most happy who hath the fewest; all conditions being evil and miserable, they are only distinguished by the number of calamities. The collector of the Roman and foreign examples, when he had reckoned two-and-twenty instances of great fortunes, every one of which had been allayed with great variety of evils; in all his reading or experience, he could tell but of two who had been famed for an entire prosperity—Quintus Metellus, and Gyges the king of Lydia: and yet concerning the one of them he tells, that his felicity was so inconsiderable (and yet it was the bigger of the two) that the oracle said, that Aglaus Sophidius, the poor Arcadian shepherd, was more happy than he, that is, he had fewer troubles; for so, indeed, we are to reckon the pleasures of this life; the limit of our joy is the absence of some degree of sorrow, and he that hath the least of this is the most prosperous person. But then we must look for prosperity, not in palaces or courts of princes, not in the tents of conquerors, or in the gaieties of fortunate and prevailing sinners; but something rather in the cottages of honest, innocent, and contented persons, whose mind is no bigger than their fortune, nor their virtue less than their security. As for others, whose fortune looks bigger, and allures fools to follow it, like the wandering fires of the night, till they run into rivers, or are broken upon rocks with staring and running after them, they are all in the condition of Marius, than whose condition nothing was more constant, and nothing more mutable: if we reckon them amongst the happy, they are the most happy men; if we reckon them amongst the miserable,

they are the most miserable. For just as is a man's condition, great or little, so is the state of his misery; all have their share; but kings and princes, great generals and consuls, rich men and mighty, as they have the biggest business and the biggest charge, and are answerable to God for the greatest accounts, so they have the biggest trouble; that the uneasiness of their appendage may divide the good and evil of the world, making the poor man's fortune as eligible as the greatest; and also restraining the vanity of man's spirit, which a great fortune is apt to swell from a vapour to a bubble; but God in mercy hath mingled wormwood with their wine, and so restrained the drunkenness and follies of prosperity.

7. Man never hath one day to himself of entire peace from the things of the world, but either something troubles him, or nothing satisfies him, or his very fulness swells him, and makes him breathe short upon his bed. Men's joys are troublesome; and, besides that the fear of losing them takes away the present pleasure, (and a man hath need of another felicity to preserve this,) they are also wavering and full of trepidation, not only from their inconstant nature, but from their weak foundation: they arise from vanity, and they dwell upon ice, and they converse with the wind, and they have the wings of a bird, and are serious but as the resolutions of a child, commenced by chance, and managed by folly, and proceed by inadvertency, and end in vanity and forgetfulness. So that, as Livius Drusus said of himself, he never had any play-days or days of quiet when he was a boy; for he was troublesome and busy, a restless and unquiet man; the same may every man observe to be true of himself; he is always restless and uneasy, he dwells upon the waters, and leans upon thorns, and lays his head upon a sharp stone. . . .

## The Wealth of My Hope

. . . I consider that the ground of my trouble is my sin; and if it were not for that, I should not need to be troubled; but the help that all the world looks for is such as supposes a man to be a sinner. Indeed, if from myself I were to derive my title to heaven, then my sins were a just argument of despair; but now that they bring me to Christ, that they drive me to an appeal to God's mercies and to take sanctuary in the cross, they ought not, they cannot, infer a just cause of despair. I am sure it is a stranger thing that God should take upon him hands and feet, and those hands and feet should be nailed upon a cross, than that a man should be partaker of the felicities of pardon and life eternal; and it were stranger yet that God should do so much for man, and that a man that desires it, that labours for it, that is in life and possibilities of working his salvation, should inevitably miss that end for which that God suffered so much. For what is the meaning, and what is the extent, and what are the significations, of the Divine mercy in pardoning sinners? If it be thought a great matter that I am charged with original sin, I confess I feel the weight of it in loads of temporal infelicities and proclivities to sin; but I fear not the guilt of it, since I am baptized, and it cannot do honour to the reputation of God's mercy that it should be all spent in remissions of what I never chose, never acted, never knew of, could not help, concerning which I received no commandment, no prohibition. But, blessed be God, it is ordered in just measures that that original evil which I contracted without my will should be taken away without my knowledge; and what I suffered before I had a being was cleansed before I had a useful understanding. But I am taught to believe God's mercies to be infinite, not only in himself but to us; for mercy is a relative term, and we are its correspondent: of all the creatures which God made, we only, in a proper sense, are the subjects of mercy and remission. Angels have more of God's bounty than we have, but not so much of his mercy; and beasts have little rays of his kindness, and effects of his wisdom and graciousness in petty donatives, but nothing of mercy; for they have no laws, and therefore no sins, and need no mercy, nor are capable of any. Since therefore man alone is the correlative or proper object and vessel of reception of an infinite mercy, and that mercy is in giving and forgiving, I have reason to hope that he will so forgive me that my sins shall not hinder me of heaven; or because it is a gift, I may also, upon the stock of the same infinite mercy, hope he will give heaven to me; and if I have it either upon the title of giving or forgiving, it is alike to me, and will alike magnify the glories of the Divine mercy. And because eternal life is the gift of God, I have less reason to despair; for if my sins were fewer, and my disproportions towards such a glory were less, and my evenness more, yet it is still a gift, and I could not receive it but as a free and a gracious donative, and so I may still: God can still give it me; and it is not an impossible expectation to wait and look for such a gift at the hands of the God of mercy; the best men deserve it not, and I who am the worst may have it given me. And I consider that God hath set no measures of his mercy, but that we be within the covenant, that is, repenting persons endeavouring to serve him with an honest, single heart; and that within this covenant, there is a very great latitude, and variety of persons, and degrees, and capacities; and therefore that it cannot stand with the proportions of so infinite a mercy, that obedience be exacted to such a point, which he never expressed, unless it should be the least, and that to which all capacities, though otherwise unequal, are fitted and sufficiently enabled. But, however, I find that the Spirit of God taught the writers of the New Testament to apply to us all in general, and to every single person in particular, some gracious words which God in the Old Testament spake to one man upon a special occasion in a single and temporal instance. Such are the words which God spake to Joshua; "I will never fail thee, nor forsake thee:" and upon the stock of that promise St. Paul forbids covetousness and persuades contentedness, because those words were spoken by God to Joshua in another case. If the gracious words of God have so great extension of parts, and intention of kind purposes, then how many comforts have we upon the stock of all the excellent words which are spoken in the prophets and in the Psalms! and I will never more question whether they be spoken concerning me, having such an authentic precedent so to expound the excellent words of God; all the treasures of God which are in the Psalms are my own riches, and the wealth of my hope; there will I look, and whatsoever I can need, that I will depend upon. For certainly, if we could understand it, that which is infinite (as God is) must needs be some such kind of thing: it must go whither it was never sent, and signify what was not first intended, and it must warm with its light, and shine with its heat, and refresh when it strikes, and heal when it wounds, and ascertain where it makes afraid, and intend all when it warns one, and mean a great deal in a small word. And as the sun, passing to its southern tropic, looks with an open eye upon his sunburnt Ethiopians, but at the same time sends light from its posterns, and collateral influences from the back side of his beams, and sees the corners of the east when his face tends towards the west, because he is a round body of fire, and hath some little images and resemblances of the Infinite; so is God's mercy: when it looked upon Moses, it relieved St. Paul, and it pardoned David, and gave hope to Manasses, and might have restored Judas if he would have had hope, and used himself accordingly. . . .